Catering and Hospitality
NVQ/SVQ 2

on

Tony Groves, Bob Kenyon, David Klaasen, Pam Rabone, Danny Stevenson, Harry Tallon, Malcolm Ware

First published in 1993 by:
Stanley Thornes (Publishers) Ltd
Second edition 1996

Reprinted in 2001 by:
Nelson Thornes Ltd
Delta Place
27 Bath Road
CHELTENHAM
GL53 7TH
United Kingdom

02 03 04 05 06 / 15 14 13 12 11 10 9 8 7 6

A catalogue record for this book is available from the British Library

ISBN 0 7487 2566 0

Illustrations by Linda Herd
Page make-up by Columns Design Ltd

Printed in Great Britain by Scotprint

Contents

CONTENTS

Acknowledgements

The authors and publishers would like to thank Ian Bligh, Graham Chester, Tony Groves, Jim Mair, Lawrie Mills, Bill Moorcroft, Joachim Schafheitle, Regency Fish Bar, Weymouth and Weymouth College for their help and advice. They would also like to thank the following for permission to reproduce photographs: Rowland Foote (Preparing and cooking dough products; Preparing, cooking and decorating cakes and biscuits; Preparing and cooking fresh pasta). Danny Stevenson (p. 87). Rank Holidays & Hotels Limited (pp. 152, 154, 156). Burton District Hospital (p. 327) and Regethermic UK Ltd (pp. 319, 328, 330).

Planning your time

INTRODUCTION

While working in the kitchen, you need to use your time and energy in the most effective manner. In order to achieve this, you will need to plan every activity in advance, making the most of the limited time available to you. Once you have gained experience in food preparation you will be able to plan effectively automatically, but while training you will need to adopt a more strategic approach towards time planning.

THE PROCESS

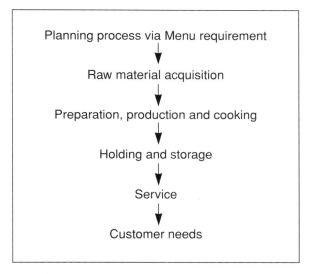

A simple analysis of the task or menu should provide you with the information you need to work out what is required from you, although you may need to consult your supervisor or *chef de partie* if you have any queries.

Before undertaking any task, ask yourself the following questions:
● What is to be done?
● Why is it to be done?
● Where is it to be done?
● When is it to be done?
● How is it to be done?

In order to use your time effectively, you will need information about the tasks you are to perform. Some of this information will be obtained directly from your immediate supervisor, but some may have to be confirmed through checking the recipe or reading your study books.

Basic information may be categorised under the following headings:
● name or menu description of foodstuffs

- preparation prior to cooking
- size of the portion and amounts required
- weight and measure of ingredients
- cooking methods and processes
- oven temperatures and cooking times
- holding times of foodstuffs
- style of service
- time required.

You are aiming to improve your performance in the kitchen and maximise use of energy. When considering time planning, you will also need to consider the following factors:
- arrange items requiring preparation so that the sequence of work requires the least movement
- work methodically, to a set pattern, usually from your left to right
- maintain separate containers for all trimmings
- keep your working area clean at all times, cleaning and washing as you go
- when preparing large quantities of food, organise the food so that lifting and moving items is reduced to a minimum
- have all equipment ready to hand
- arrange all food in containers, trays or bowls at all times. This will help to keep your work area clear and reduce the risks of cross-contamination
- conserve fuel. When not required, gas or electricity should be turned down or off as required
- develop a positive mental attitude to do the job to the best of your ability, improving performance by taking less time to do better work
- plan the best sequence to adopt when several things need to be done.

There are distinct advantages to be gained by planning your time rather than reacting to a potential crisis caused by a lack of careful consideration. You will become a more efficient food handler by taking time to plan, developing skills and knowledge in the process.

MEMORY JOGGER

Why is it important to plan ahead when working in kitchens?

Why plan?

- To be more efficient in production.
- To maximise work output.
- To meet production targets and customer needs.

How?

- Knowledge of tasks required.
- Knowledge of techniques.
- Knowledge of machinery and equipment.
- Production of an efficient *mise-en-place*.

What do you need to analyse?

- Jobs, tasks and menus.
- Check recipes or supervisor's directives.
- Work in a logical and sequential fashion, i.e. longest preparation and cooking times are approached first.

What do you need to be aware of?

- Complete procedures: this means being aware of any necessity to prepare one item in order to produce another, and any collation of items necessary to complete the task.

What do you need to organise?

- Yourself: self-management is important to ensure constant improvement.
- Materials and equipment.
- Your workplace.

Knowing when advance preparation should stop without sacrificing food quality is really the essence of preparation and planning.

DRAWING UP A PRODUCTION PLAN

At this stage you can begin to allocate the time needed for each stage of preparation and handling. Many factors influence a time plan:

- protection of quality. Time planning prevents a crisis from arising because too many items demand attention at the same time;
- efficient use of equipment and resources. You will need to plan when to use equipment in order to avoid conflict or over-utilisation of specialised machinery;
- protection of quantity. Make sure you measure ingredients accurately;
- cooking methods. Always follow technically correct procedures;
- using the correct tools for the task. Always use appliances designed for a specific purpose; remember the rule: *use the correct tools for the job.*

Why should materials and equipment be assembled before starting preparation?

In order to ensure that all items are available so work can progress without interruption and with less chance of error.

On what principles should work plans be based?

Proper planning and sequencing to achieve optimum quality with minimum expenditure of unnecessary effort and time.

How can work be done quickly and easily?

By having supplies and equipment arranged for a smooth work flow, so that each motion can be made in the easiest way with the fewest steps.

The basic time plan: an example

Task:	Braised beef: Burgundy style
	(Pièce de boeuf braisé bourguignonne)
Number of portions:	20 covers
Time required:	12.30 p.m. (luncheon service)
Ingredients:	As per recipe
Cooking method:	Braising
Service style:	Table d'hôte, full silver service

Step 1   *2 days prior to requirement:*
- acquire relevant raw materials and check purchasing availability.

Step 2   *1 day prior to requirement:*
- prepare, cook, chill and store brown beef stock
- prepare, trim and lard (with fat) the selected joints
- marinade for 24 hours in a red wine marinade as per selected recipe
- prepare, cook and chill sauce demi-glace or jus lié as required.

Step 3   *Day of requirement*:

0900 hours   Ensure workplace is ready and assemble raw ingredients to prepare and cook.

0930 hours   Seal and prepare joint, commence the braising process at approximately Gas Mark 6 (200 °C/400 °F) with a lid.

1000 hours   Baste joint with cooking liquor through cooking process.

1030 hours   Prepare appropriate garnish and retain for further cooking.

1100 hours   Remove lid and continue to baste the joint with cooking liquor to achieve desired glaze.

1130 hours   Cook and hold appropriate garnish of turned mushrooms, bacon lardons and glazed brown button onions.

1200 hours   Remove cooked joint and cover, reduce sauce until desired consistency is obtained, adjust seasoning and strain. Immerse joint in prepared sauce to keep moist.

1215 hours   Hold joint and garnish in readiness for service.

1230 hours   Service commences, slice joint to order, sauce and garnish as appropriate.

Identifying time gaps

The gaps in the time plan allow other items of *mise-en-place* to be undertaken, or other tasks as denoted by your job requirement or supervisor's directive.

Remember:
Advance planning is essential: failing to plan is planning to fail.

Do this

- Plan a comprehensive time plan for a complete menu. Indicate purchase requirements and recipes using the format and information in this chapter.
- List three ways you could save time doing your job without sacrificing quality.
- List the relevant information you require to do your job effectively.

The cookery processes and healthy eating

INTRODUCTION

The cookery processes are the *methods* of cooking which are common to all dishes, whether regional or international. Each process requires knowledge of basic skills and techniques which can be transferred throughout different types of cookery.

This chapter outlines each process, giving: a definition of the process, the reasons for using it, the methods used, the food items suitable, the equipment needed and key points to remember for each process.

The principal cookery methods are:
- Boiling
- Poaching
- Steaming
- Stewing
- Braising
- Roasting
- Grilling
- Shallow-frying
- Deep-frying
- Baking
- Cold preparations.

BOILING

Boiling is a moist method of cooking where prepared food is cooked in a liquid which contains water (water, aromatic cooking liquor, stock, milk). The boiling action may be quick and rapid (as when cooking green leaf vegetables); or slow, with a gentle surface movement known as *simmering* (used when boiling most foods).

Reasons for boiling foods

Food is boiled in order to:
1. make foods tender, by breaking down and softening starch, cellulose, protein and fibrous material
2. make foods more palatable and digestible
3. make foods safer to eat, by destroying bacteria which can cause food poisoning
4. produce a particular quality in food, of colour, flavour and texture (e.g. boiled cabbage)

Methods of boiling foods

These are divided into two groups:
1. *Food is placed into cold liquid*, brought to the boil and cooked. You would use this procedure in order to:
   (a) achieve a clear cooking liquid. Scum and impurities rise to the surface as the liquid comes to the boil and can be skimmed off. This is important when preparing stocks and clarified liquids such as consommes and jellies
   (b) work as safely as possible. It is safe and easy to cover food with cold liquid then bring to the boil (see also *Cookery myths*, page 6).

2 *Food is placed in boiling liquid* and cooked. You would use this procedure in order to:
(a) keep cooking times as short as possible
(b) retain as much nutritional value and colour as possible, by keeping the cooking time as short as possible
(c) reduce vitamin loss when cooking vegetables by destroying oxidative enzymes
(d) reduce the risk of burning cereals and starch mixtures such as rice and pastas.

Cookery myths
It is often stated that placing food in very hot or boiling liquid seals in the juices and therefore retains goodness and reduces weight loss. This is a myth which should be ignored.

Food items suitable for boiling

A wide range of foods can be boiled:
1 *Meat and poultry.* Boiling is used for the tougher joints and birds, e.g. silverside of beef, rolled brisket and hens. It is a suitable method for producing plain dishes, e.g. boiled gammon with cabbage and parsley sauce
2 *Fish and shellfish.* Although it is more desirable to poach most fish, there are some classic dishes which are boiled. Lobsters are usually cooked by boiling
3 *Eggs and pastas.* E.g. boiled eggs and fresh and dried pastas, e.g. noodles, spaghetti and macaroni
4 *Fresh and frozen vegetables.* E.g. cabbage, cauliflower, turnips, peas, green beans and potatoes
5 *Dried cereals and pulses.* E.g. barley, oats, marrowfat peas, lentils and various dried beans.

Equipment used when boiling foods

Types of equipment include saucepans, stockpots, fast boiling pans, bratt pans and boilers.

Boiling: key points

- Many boiled dishes have long cooking times (e.g. stocks, boiled meats and pulses); you will need to allow for this in your time plan.
- Arrange saucepans of boiling food on the stove so that the correct cooking speed is maintained, i.e. rapid boiling or simmering. Also check saucepans regularly to ensure the correct speed of cooking, to determine the degree of cooking and to ensure saucepans do not boil dry.
- Be careful when draining foods with boiling liquid. Stand back from the saucepan, avoiding splashes of hot liquid.
- To avoid food poisoning, cool liquids and foods quickly then store chilled until required for use. Never leave boiled foods and liquor standing in a warm kitchen.
- Store boiled foods at temperatures below 5 °C/40 °F, for as short a time as possible.
- Thoroughly cook dried beans as under-cooked beans contain a poison which can cause sickness. Dried beans should therefore be boiled rapidly for a minimum of 10 minutes and then simmered for the remaining cooking time.
- Always keep liquid content to a minimum when boiling food to ensure that valuable nutrients are not lost, but do not boil dry or contents will burn. Serve the cooking liquor with the food whenever possible.
- Avoid soaking or storing vegetables in water (except pulses). Also start the cooking of vegetables in boiling liquid whenever possible.

- Cook vegetables in batches and as near to service as possible. Avoid cooking and re-heating vegetables.
- Remove fat from the surface of stocks and sauces as it forms.
- Soak out as much salt as possible from salted joints prior to cooking e.g. hams and gammons.

POACHING

Poaching is a moist method of cooking where prepared food is cooked in a liquid containing water (water, milk, stock, wine or court-bouillon). The food is cooked at temperatures below boiling point (75–93 °C / 167–200 °F) with little or no liquid movement.

Reasons for poaching foods

Food is poached in order to:
1 make foods tender, by breaking down starch, cellulose and protein
2 set or *coagulate* (gel) protein when poaching eggs
3 make foods more palatable and digestible
4 make foods safer, by destroying bacteria which can cause food poisoning
5 produce a particular quality in food of colour, flavour and texture.

Poaching is a gentle method of cooking which is used to cook food items which would break up or lose shape if boiled, e.g. poached eggs, poached fish, delicate fruits.

Methods of poaching foods

Methods of poaching are divided into two groups: deep-poaching and shallow-poaching.

Deep-poaching
Food is covered with the minimum quantity of liquid then gently cooked. In most cases the food is placed in very hot liquid. Large whole fish are an exception: e.g. salmon, which is covered with cold liquid then brought to poaching temperature (to reduce the distortion of the fish when applying heat). Deep-poaching is a plain method of cooking, producing dishes such as poached fruits.

Shallow-poaching
Food is partly covered with the poaching liquor (to two-thirds the height of the food item) and then cooked gently under cover in an oven. This is a more complex method of cooking as the cooking liquor is reduced down and forms the base of the accompanying sauce. Many classic fish dishes are produced in this way.

Food items suitable for poaching

Deep-poaching
Whole fish, portioned fish, shellfish, whole chickens, eggs, fresh and dried fruits.

Shallow-poaching
Small whole fish, e.g. trout, sole, plaice; cuts of fish such as fillets and fish steaks.

Equipment used when poaching foods

1 When *deep-poaching*: saucepans, shallow-sided pots, fish kettles.
2 When *shallow-poaching*: use *plat à sauters* and shallow-sided cooking dishes. For fish, oval fish-cooking dishes can also be used.

Poaching: key points

- Allow sufficient time to prepare poached foods which are to be cooked and then served cold. For example, a whole salmon for a cold buffet has to be cooked then thoroughly cooled before it can be moved from its poaching liquor. After this it must be skinned, decorated and garnished.
- Fish may be prepared 1–2 hours prior to cooking. For example, fish for fillets of sole bonne-femme may be kept raw in a chiller, trayed up and covered with the cooking paper without any recipe liquid. This reduces the preparation time for the dish, especially during service time.
- Poached eggs are often cooked and kept chilled in ice water. When required for service, the eggs are re-heated and then finished as required.
- Check regularly to see that the food is being poached and *not* boiled; this is important to maintain good quality.
- Always keep liquid content to a minimum when deep-poaching food to ensure that valuable nutrients are not lost.
- Remove any fat from the surface of food as it forms.
- Use reduced sugar syrups when poaching fruits.

STEAMING

Steaming is a moist method of cooking where prepared food is cooked in steam (water vapour) at varying degrees of pressure.

Reasons for steaming foods

Food is steamed in order to:
1 make foods tender, by breaking down and softening starch, cellulose and protein
2 make foods more palatable and digestible
3 make foods safer to eat, by destroying bacteria which can cause food poisoning
4 produce a particular quality in food of colour, flavour and texture (e.g. steamed sponge pudding)
5 keep the loss of soluble nutrients to a minimum, e.g. in vegetables.

Methods of steaming foods

This is divided into two groups: low-pressure and high-pressure steaming.

Atmospheric or low-pressure steaming
Food is cooked at atmospheric pressure or under low-pressure moist steam, usually of $0-17$ kN m^{-2}/ $0-2$ lb in^{-2}. This is the traditional method of steaming food: eggs, root vegetables, shellfish and steamed puddings are examples of food items cooked by low-pressure steaming.

High-pressure steaming
Food is cooked at high pressures, usually $70-105$ kN m^{-2}/$10-15$ lb in^{-2}. High-pressure steaming is fast and ideally suitable for most food except steamed puddings and sponge puddings. This type of steaming is a good method of cooking vegetables because there is very little water and air in the cooking chamber and this helps to retain valuable nutrients.

Food items suitable for steaming

- Eggs.
- Fish and shellfish.
- Vegetables (including potatoes).
- Savoury and sweet puddings (low-pressure steaming only).

Equipment used when steaming foods

Types of equipment include atmospheric and low-pressure steamers, high-pressure steamers and jet steamers.

Steaming: key points

- Switch on the machine in good time if pre-heating is required.
- Always turn off the steam before opening the door unless using a low-pressure steaming cabinet (which is not switched off during cooking).
- Always be careful when opening the door after use. Stand behind the door and use it as a shield against escaping steam.
- Cook vegetables as near to service time as required. A high-speed steamer is ideally designed for this purpose.
- Avoid over-cooking food, especially with high-speed steaming where even short periods of over-cooking will destroy nutrients.

STEWING

Stewing is a moist method of cooking where prepared food (cut into pieces) is cooked in a minimum quantity of liquid. Both the food and the liquid form the stew, so they are always served together. Stewing is an ideal method of cooking for the tougher cuts of meat, poultry and game; and since you are cooking and serving them in their cooking juices, the process also saves valuable nutrients. Stewing is also a term used when slowly cooking fruits to a pulp (e.g. stewed apples).

Reasons for stewing foods

Foods are stewed in order to:
1 make foods tender, by breaking down and softening starch, cellulose, protein and fibrous material
2 make foods more palatable and digestible
3 make foods safer to eat, by destroying bacteria which can cause food poisoning
4 produce a particular quality in food, of colour, flavour and texture (e.g. stewed beef).

Methods of stewing foods

Methods of stewing are grouped according to the following factors:
1 *Type of commodity*; e.g. fish, meat, vegetable stews.
2 *Colour of stew*; e.g. white and brown stews.
3 *Method of preparation*:
   - stews cooked in a prepared sauce (e.g. fricassées)
   - stews where the liquid is thickened at the end of the cooking process (e.g. blanquettes).

Food items suitable for stewing

1 *Fish and shellfish.*
2 *Red and white meats.* E.g. beef, mutton, lamb, veal and pork. The tougher cuts of meat are used for stewing.
3 *Poultry and feathered game.* E.g. chicken, duckling, partridge and pheasant.
4 *Vegetables.* Several vegetables are usually cooked together to form the stew, e.g. onions, garlic, courgettes, aubergines and tomatoes in a ratatouille.
5 *Fruits.* Stewing apples, pears and rhubarb forms a coarse pulp.

Equipment used when stewing foods

Types of equipment include saucepans, boilers and bratt pans.

Basic techniques of stewing

Blanching
This is done to remove impurities from meat when preparing blanquettes. It is done as follows:
1   Cover the prepared meat with cold water and bring it to the boil
2   Remove from the stove and place under cold running water to rinse off all the scum which has formed.
3   Drain, then prepare the stew.

Liaising
This is a method of finishing a white stew, using a mixture of egg yolks and cream (*à liaison*). This increases the fat content.

Searing
This is the initial shallow-frying of flesh when preparing brown stews. It is carried out to develop colour and flavour. It is often stated that this procedure seals in the juices and therefore retains goodness and reduces weight loss. This is a myth which should be ignored.

Setting
This is the method of lightly cooking or *stiffening* flesh in fat without developing colour. It is used when preparing fricassées.

Stewing: key points

● Most stews have long cooking times, so make sure that you allow for this in your time plan. For example, beef stew made with shoulder steak may require 2–3 hours cooking before the meat is tender.
● Arrange saucepans on the stove so that the food is only simmering. Stir the stew regularly to prevent burning, and skim off surface fat and impurities.
● Check liquid content of stews during cooking and top up with additional stock as required.
● Remember that stews may be cooked in the oven under cover and this can provide much needed stove space for other items.
● Pay special attention to portion control. Estimating the number of portions from a large quantity of stew is difficult. Use ladles or spoons of standard sizes which will provide the correct portion size and number of portions expected.
● Avoid re-heating stews but if they must be reheated, cool quickly and store in a chiller below 5°C (40°F) for as short a time as possible. When reheating stews, bring to the boil and simmer for 15–20 minutes to avoid food poisoning.
● Trim off as much visible fat from meat, poultry and game as possible before cooking. Also skim the stew regularly during cooking to remove surface fat.
● Where possible reduce the red meat content of stews and increase the quantity of foods which provide fibre, e.g. use vegetable garnishes of beans, brown rice, sweetcorn kernels and low-fat dumplings made with wholemeal flour.

BRAISING

Braising is a moist method of cooking, where prepared food is cooked in a covered container with a quantity of stock or sauce in an oven. The food to be braised is usually placed on a vegetable base (*mirepoix*) and the liquid or sauce added to approximately two-thirds the height of the food item. This rule does not apply when braising small cuts of meat and offal such as chops, rump steaks and sliced ox liver, where the food is completely covered with the cooking liquor or sauce to maintain even cooking. When the food is cooked it is portioned and served with the finished sauce or cooking liquor.

Reasons for braising foods

Foods are braised in order to:
1 make foods tender, by breaking down and softening starch, cellulose, protein and fibrous material
2 make foods more palatable and digestible
3 cook and serve foods in their own juices, thus conserving valuable nutrients
4 make foods safer to eat, by destroying bacteria which can cause food poisoning
5 produce a particular quality in food, of colour, flavour and texture (e.g. braised celery).

Methods of braising foods

Methods of braising are grouped according to the colour of the finished dish and the foods to be braised:
1 brown braising of meat, poultry, game, offal and vegetables
2 white braising of sweetbreads
3 braising rice.

Food items suitable for braising

1 *Fresh butcher meats:* including beef, veal and venison.
2 *Fresh offal:* including ox liver and sweetbreads.
3 *Pickled meats and offal:* including ham and pickled tongue.
4 *Poultry and feathered game:* including duck, duckling, pheasant and partridge.
5 *Vegetables:* including cabbage, celery, leek and onion.
6 *Rice.*

Equipment used when braising foods

Types of equipment include braising pans, casseroles, lidded cooking vessels, *plat à sauters* with lids and bratt pans.

Basic techniques of braising

Basting
This is the process of coating the food with the cooking liquor or sauce during cooking. It ensures that the food item cooks evenly and it also keeps the surface of the item moist during cooking. A glazed shiny appearance on the surface of meat, poultry or game can also be produced by basting occasionally near the end of the cooking period while uncovered.

Blanching
This applies to braising pickled meats, ox liver, sweetbreads and vegetables and means something different in each case.
1 *Blanching pickled meats* (ham or tongue): cover with cold water, bring to the boil and simmer for 20 minutes approximately. This is done to remove excess salt from the pickled meat.
2 *Blanching ox liver:* cover with cold water, bring to the boil, then refresh under cold water. This removes impurities and scum from the liver which would otherwise be present in the sauce.
3 *Blanching sweetbreads:* cover with cold water, bring to the boil and simmer for 10–15 minutes. Refresh the sweetbreads under cold running water and drain.

When blanched, the tough membranes and tissue which surround the sweet-breads are trimmed off with a small knife.

4   *Blanching vegetables*: place the prepared vegetables in boiling water, simmer for a specified period of time then refresh under cold running water. Vegetables are blanched for the following reasons:
   ● crisp vegetables become limp and easy to shape
   ● the process helps to retain colour in vegetables
   ● bitterness is reduced in certain vegetables (e.g. mature celery)
   ● the process reduces cooking time.

Larding

This process consists of inserting strips of bacon or pork fat through flesh with special needles. It helps to produce a moist, rich eating quality but does increase the fat content.

Marinading

This process consists of soaking meat, poultry or game in a liquid (e.g. wine) with herbs and vegetables. The reason for marinading is to add flavour and increase tenderness. However, increasing tenderness by marinading has been found to be less effective than was previously thought. Marinading times vary depending on type of flesh, size of joint and taste; varying from 2–18 hours.

Searing

This is the initial shallow-frying of flesh when preparing brown braisings. It is carried out to develop colour and flavour. It is often stated that this procedure seals in the juices and therefore retains goodness and reduces weight loss. This is a myth which should be ignored.

Braising: key points

● Special care is required when removing braising pans from the oven, especially when they contain large joints. The pan should be lifted carefully (with 'correct body posture and movement') using a thick, dry, folded oven cloth on each handle, remembering that the joint may move about as the pan is lifted.
● See also *Stewing: key points* (page 10).

ROASTING

Roasting is a dry heat method of cooking, where prepared food is cooked with the presence of fat in an oven or on a spit.

Reasons for roasting foods

Foods are roasted in order to:
1   make foods tender, by breaking down and softening mainly protein, but also starch, cellulose and fibre
2   make foods more palatable and digestible
3   make foods safer to eat, by destroying bacteria which can cause food poisoning
4   produce a particular quality in food, of colour, flavour and texture (e.g. roast venison).

Methods of roasting foods

1   *Oven roasting.* This is the cooking of food in an oven, mainly by convected heat or forced air convected heat. However, other forms of heat application may also play an important function when roasting: e.g. conducted heat from a roasting tray when roasting potatoes, and radiated heat from the sides of an oven; both of which help to develop colour on the surface of the food. In addition, combination

ovens which combine microwave energy or steam with forced air convected heat are also used when roasting.

2 *Spit roasting.* This is the original form of roasting which involves cooking the food by dry heat on a spit which is slowly turned over a heat source such as a charcoal fire, electric elements or gas flames. The main form of heat application is direct radiated heat, but convected heat (hot air) is also present. Conducted heat from metal spit bars may also aid cooking in some instances.

3 *Pot roasting* (poêler). This is included in this section although it is not strictly a form of roasting, being closer to a form of casserole cooking. The food is cooked under cover in an oven with (traditionally) butter as the cooking fat. An important procedure with this method of cooking is the removal of the lid during cooking to allow the food to develop colour. After cooking, the vegetable base together with the cooking juices provide the basis of the accompanying sauce.

Food items suitable for roasting

Good quality joints must be used when roasting meat, poultry and game.
1 *Butcher meats and furred game:* e.g. beef, veal, lamb, mutton, pork and venison.
2 *Poultry and feathered game:* e.g. chicken, turkey, duckling, grouse and pheasant.
3 *Potatoes and parsnips.*

Pot roasting
Good quality butcher meats, poultry and game (as above) are required for this type of cooking.

Equipment used when roasting foods

1 Types of ovens: general purpose oven, forced air convection oven, combination ovens (e.g. microwave and convection ovens), steam and convection ovens.
2 Spit and rotisserie racks.
3 Small equipment: roasting trays, trivets, temperature probes.

Pot roasting
Various types of casserole dishes or similar cooking utensils can be used.

Basic techniques of roasting

Barding
This involves covering the surface of the roast with slices of pork or bacon fat. This is to prevent the flesh drying out during cooking; but because it increases fat content, it should only be used where necessary, normally with feathered game (grouse, partridge and pheasant).

Brushing with oil and basting
Both of these processes involve lightly brushing the joint with fat before and during cooking. This is done to prevent the surface of a joint drying out and becoming hard (especially lean joints). Basting is the traditional practice of coating the item with the fat. In order to keep the fat content to a minimum, brush with fat rather than baste.

Carry-over cooking
This is the further cooking which takes place after the joint has been removed from the oven.

Larding
See page 12.

Placing in the roasting tray
Butcher meats and furred game: Joints of meat should be placed onto a roasting tray

with the fat top upwards. Never place a joint directly onto a roasting tray: always place it onto a bed of bones or vegetables, or onto a trivet.

Poultry and feathered game: Birds should be placed on their sides with the breast downwards then turned during roasting to ensure even cooking.

Searing
This involves starting the cooking of the roast in a hot oven, or shallow 'frying the item prior to roasting. It is carried out to develop colour and flavour, especially with meat roasts. It is often stated that this procedure seals in the juices and therefore retains goodness and reduces weight loss. This is a myth which should be ignored.

Speed of cooking
The temperature at which an item should be roasted is related to the size of the food item. The larger the item, the lower the cooking temperature. High temperature roasting should be avoided as it increases shrinkage and weight loss. The temperature range when cooking roasts of average size is usually 175–200 °C (350–400 °F).

Resting, standing or settling a roast
This refers to removing a roast from the oven after cooking and leaving it in a warm place for a short period (5–15 minutes depending on size). This is to reduce the risk of someone being burned when portioning or carving the joint. The food is also easier to carve or portion after resting.

Roasting: key points

- Remember that roasts are served at a particular degree of cooking, i.e. underdone, medium, well done. This must be carefully considered when preparing your time plan.
- Always keep your hands well protected and wear your sleeves long to avoid burns from spurting hot fat. Take care when removing roasts from the oven. Special care should be taken with large roasts which may move when the tray is lifted.
- Where possible, use lean joints such as rump and good quality topside, and trim off surface fat before serving.

GRILLING

Grilling is a dry heat method of cooking where prepared food is cooked mainly by radiated heat in the form of infra-red waves.

Reasons for grilling foods

Foods are grilled in order to:
1 make foods tender, by breaking down and softening mainly protein, but also starch, cellulose and fibre
2 make foods more palatable and digestible
3 make foods safer to eat, by destroying bacteria which can cause food poisoning
4 produce a particular quality in food, of colour, flavour and texture (e.g. grilled lamb cutlets).

Methods of grilling foods

1 Grilling foods *over* a heat source which may be fired by charcoal, electricity or gas, e.g. steak grills and barbecue type grills.
2 Grilling foods *under* a heat source fired by gas or electricity, e.g. salamander type grills.
3 Grilling foods *between* electrically heated grill bars.

In Methods 1 and 2 above, most of the cooking is done through radiated heat, although some cooking occurs by convection from hot air currents and conduction (where the food is touching hot grill bars). In Method 3, most items of equipment cook the food between very hot ridged metal plates with conduction being the main cooking method.

Food items suitable for grilling

Good quality cuts must be used when grilling meat, poultry and game.
1 *Butcher meats and furred game*: various types of steaks, chops, and cutlets.
2 *Offal and bacon*: e.g. sliced liver, kidneys and gammon steaks.
3 *Poultry and feathered game*: various small birds prepared ready for grilling; e.g. spring chicken, grouse and partridge.
4 *Fish and shellfish*: various small whole fish (sole, plaice, trout); cuts of fish (fillets and steaks); and shellfish such as lobster, large prawns and scampi.
5 *Vegetables*: mainly mushrooms and tomatoes.
6 *Made-up items and convenience foods*: e.g. burgers, bitoks, sausages and sliced meat puddings.

Equipment used when grilling foods

1 Steak grills and barbecue units fired by charcoal, gas, or electricity.
2 Salamanders fired by gas or electricity.
3 Contact grills, infra-red units and toasters.

Basic techniques of grilling

Brushing with oil
This involves lightly brushing the item with fat before and during cooking. It is done to prevent the surface of the item drying out and becoming hard. Basting with fat (coating the item) should be avoided as this increases the fat content.

Flouring items to be grilled
Coating foods with flour prior to grilling only applies to items which do not develop a good colour when cooking. Whole fish, cuts of fish and liver are usually lightly coated with flour when they are to be cooked under a salamander.

Searing
This involves starting the cooking of the item (plain flesh only: not sausages, puddings or breaded items) on a hot part of the grill to develop colour and flavour. It is often stated that this procedure seals in the juices and therefore retains goodness and reduces weight loss. This is a myth which should be ignored (see *Speed of cooking* below).

Speed of cooking
High-temperature grilling produces the most suitable infra-red waves to cook food. However, the heat exposure and speed of cooking should cook the food to the correct degree without burning the outer surface. When cooking thick items, such as large steaks and chops, the item may be seared to develop some colour, then the speed of cooking reduced while the item finishes cooking. With thin items such as flattened steaks, small chops and cutlets, the item is usually cooked so that colour and the appropriate degree of cooking are reached at the same time.

Turning an item
Foods being grilled should be turned with tongs or a palette knife. Never stab or pierce foods with a fork *at any stage* of preparation or cooking. This applies to all foods including sausages.

Grilling: key points

- Remember that grilled foods are served at a particular degree of cooking depending on the type of food item and customer choice; i.e. rare, underdone, medium and well done. The time at which you should begin to cook these items is therefore dictated by the service requirements.
- Ensure that foods which can cause food poisoning (e.g. chicken, pork and made-up items such as sausages) are thoroughly cooked. Knowing when food has reached a specific degree of cooking is an important skill which must be learned. One way of quickly determining the degree of cooking is to use a temperature probe. The internal temperature ranges which indicate the various degrees of cooking are as follows:

Red meats:	underdone:	55–60 °C	(130–140 °F)
	just done:	66–71 °C	(150–160 °F)
	well done:	75–77 °C	(167–172 °F)
Chicken, turkey:	cooked through:	77 °C	(170 °F)

- Use salt sparingly on grilled foods. This is necessary not only to reduce salt in the diet, but also because by adding salt to an item being grilled you will slow down colour development.
- Where possible, use lean cuts of meat and trim off excess fat before cooking. Also drain the food to remove as much surface fat as possible prior to service.

SHALLOW-FRYING

Shallow-frying is a dry-heat method of cooking, where prepared food is cooked in a pre-heated pan or metal surface with a small quantity of fat or oil. Shallow-frying is a fast method of cooking because heat is conducted from the hot surface of the cooking pan directly to the food.

Reasons for shallow-frying foods

Foods are shallow-fried in order to:
1. make foods tender, by breaking down and softening protein, fat, starch, cellulose and fibre
2. make foods more palatable and digestible
3. make foods safer to eat, by destroying bacteria which can cause food poisoning
4. produce a particular quality in food, of colour, flavour and texture (e.g. sauté potatoes).

Methods of shallow-frying foods

Meunière
This method is commonly used for shallow-frying fish and shellfish. The fish is lightly coated with flour before frying and is served with lemon slices and chopped parsley. Nut-brown butter or margarine is poured over the fish when serving; remember that the quantity used should be kept to a minimum to reduce the fat content.

Sauter
This term has three meanings:
1. it is often used as an alternative term for *shallow-frying*, especially when referring to the shallow-frying of small cuts of butcher meats, poultry or game
2. it can refer to a particular type of shallow-frying where you use a tossing action to turn the food while frying, e.g. when cooking sliced potatoes or mushrooms
3. it can be used when preparing a high quality meat, poultry or game dish served with a sauce. Here a good quality item is shallow-fried to a specific degree of cooking, then removed from the pan while the pan is swilled with stock, wine or sauce. This procedure (known as *déglacer*) uses the sediment lost from the item being cooked, thereby increasing the flavour and aroma of the sauce.

Griddle

This involves cooking items on a lightly oiled metal plate (*griddle plate*). A *ridged surface* is used for cooking small cuts of meat, game and poultry to allow the fat to drain from the meat; while a *flat plate* is used for bakery items such as griddle scones.

Stir-fry

This is the quick-frying of pieces of fish, meat, poultry and vegetables with fat or oil in a wok.

Sweat

This involves slow-frying items in a little fat, using a lid, and without allowing colour to develop. Sweating is usually a preliminary procedure used when making certain soups.

Food items suitable for shallow-frying

Good quality cuts must be used when shallow-frying meat, poultry and game.
1 *Butcher meats and furred game:* e.g. various types of steaks, chops, cutlets, escalopes and medallions.
2 *Offal and bacon:* e.g. sliced liver, kidneys and gammon steaks.
3 *Poultry and feathered game:* cuts for sauter and supremes.
4 *Fish:* various small whole fish (sole, plaice, trout) and cuts of fish (fillets and steaks).
5 *Made-up items and convenience foods:* e.g. burgers, bitoks, sausages and sliced meat puddings.
6 *Eggs:* mainly scrambled eggs and omelettes.
7 *Vegetables:* sliced potatoes, mushrooms, onions, tomatoes and courgettes.
8 *Fruits:* e.g. bananas, peaches, apple and pineapple slices.
9 *Batters and doughs:* e.g. crêpes, scones and pancakes.

Equipment used when shallow-frying foods

Equipment used includes frying pans, omelette pans, crêpe pans, plat à sauter pans, sauteuses, bratt pans, griddle plates and woks.

Basic techniques of shallow-frying

Searing

This involves starting the cooking of the item (plain flesh: not sausages, puddings, breaded items or batters) in a hot pan to develop colour and flavour. It is often stated that this procedure seals in the juices and therefore retains goodness and reduces weight loss. This is a myth which should be ignored.

Speed of cooking

The speed of cooking varies with the item being cooked, but as a general rule, the thicker the item the lower the frying temperature. A common mistake is to fry at too high a temperature resulting in over-cooking, fat breakdown and off-flavours.

Turning an item

Foods being shallow-fried should be turned with a palette knife: never stab or pierce foods with a fork *at any stage* of preparation or cooking. This applies to all foods including sausages.

Shallow-frying: key points

● Remember that certain shallow-fried foods, e.g. beef dishes, are served at a particular degree of cooking; i.e. rare, underdone, medium and well done. The decision on when to start cooking a particular item must be made in keeping with service requirements.

- Always preheat the frying utensil to reduce both fat absorption into the food and the risk of the food sticking to the pan.
- Place the foods with the longest cooking times into the pan first, e.g. chicken *legs* before *wings*.
- Ensure the presentation side of the food item is fried first so that the item does not become discoloured or marked with sediment.
- Keep the frying fat to a minimum and if possible dry-fry on a non-stick surface.
- Use lean cuts of meat and trim off excessive fat before cooking. Also drain the food to remove as much surface fat as possible prior to service. To reduce fat content, cook foods by grilling rather than shallow-frying. This applies to meat, poultry, game and made-up items such as sausages and hamburgers.

DEEP-FRYING

Deep-frying is a dry heat method of cooking, where prepared food is cooked in preheated fat or oil. Deep-frying is a fast method of cooking because all the surfaces of the food being fried are cooked at the same time, with temperatures of up to 195 °C (383 °F) being used.

Reasons for deep-frying foods

Foods are deep-fried in order to:
1 make foods tender, by breaking down and softening protein, fat, starch, cellulose and fibre
2 make foods more palatable and digestible
3 make foods safer to eat, by destroying bacteria which can cause food poisoning
4 produce a particular quality in food, of colour, flavour and texture (e.g. apple fritters).

Methods of deep-frying foods

Partial cooking or blanching
This is the deep-frying of foods until tender, but without developing colour. The reason for blanching foods is that they can be stored on trays until required for service then fried quickly in hot fat until crisp and golden brown. Chips are usually blanched in this manner; fruit fritters and battered vegetables may also be blanched prior to service.

Complete cooking
This is the deep-frying of foods until fully cooked, where serving takes place immediately, to maintain a crisp, dry product.

Pressure frying
This is the frying of food under pressure in special fryers. Pressure fryers are usually automated and work on a timed cooking cycle. These fryers are fast at producing high-quality fried foods and are safe to use.

Food items suitable for deep-frying

1 *White fish:* e.g. some small whole fish (haddock) and fillets of fish.
2 *Chicken or turkey:* portions of poultry.
3 *Made-up items and convenience foods:* e.g. Scotch eggs, savoury cutlets, croquettes and cromesquis.
4 *Vegetables:* raw (e.g. aubergines, courgettes); or cooked (e.g. prepared celery, fennel and cauliflower).
5 *Potatoes.*

6 *Fruits:* e.g. bananas, peaches, apple and pineapple slices.
7 *Batters and doughs:* e.g. choux paste (fritters), bun dough and doughnuts.

Important: Some foods are less suitable for deep-frying because they contain fats or oils which will contaminate the frying medium. Examples of these foods are oily fish, fatty meats and meat products such as bacon, gammon, ham, sausages and meat puddings.

Equipment used when deep-frying foods

1 Fritures (old-fashioned frying vessels: see *Deep-frying: key points* below).
2 Free-standing fryers (electric or gas) with manual thermostat control.
3 Automatic fryers.
4 Continuous fryers.
5 Pressure fryers.

Basic techniques of deep-frying

Draining foods to be fried
Wet foods should be thoroughly drained and dried as much as possible before being cooked. Placing wet foods into hot fat is very dangerous as the fat reacts violently and rapidly increases in volume.

Coating foods to be fried
Many fried foods are coated with batter or breadcrumbs prior to frying. This not only produces a crisp, coloured surface but also reduces the juices and fat from the item entering and contaminating the frying medium.

Battered foods
Foods which are battered are passed through the batter (usually after coating with flour), and then placed directly into the hot fat. The food should be placed carefully into the fat to avoid splashes of fat which can cause burns. A basket should never be used when frying battered foods.

Breaded foods
Foods coated with breadcrumbs are usually fried on trays or in baskets.

Speed of cooking
Most foods are fried at a temperature which will cook, colour and crisp the food all at the same time. Avoid low-temperature frying as this increases fat absorption in the food.

Draining fried foods after cooking
Fried foods should be drained thoroughly after cooking to remove surface fat. In addition it is standard practice in many establishments to serve fried food on dish-papers which absorb surface fat.

Hot storage of fried foods
To produce high quality fried food for the customer, the food should be served immediately after frying. Never use a lid to cover fried foods as this produces condensation and softens the crisp coating.

Deep-frying: key points

● Always wear long sleeves to avoid burns to the arms from splashes of fat.
● Always use a well-designed fryer with a thermostat and never an old-fashioned friture.
● Never exceed a maximum frying temperature of 195 °C (383 °F).
● Never fry too much food at once as this is not only dangerous but will reduce the frying temperature and increase fat absorption.

● Check the accuracy of the thermostat at regular intervals.
● Strain the fat regularly to remove food particles. Keep the number of fried foods offered on your menus to a minimum.

BAKING

Baking is a dry-heat method of cooking where prepared food and food products are cooked by convected heat in a pre-heated oven.

Reasons for baking foods

Foods are baked in order to:
1 make foods tender, by breaking down and softening protein, fat, starch, cellulose and fibre
2 make foods more palatable and digestible
3 make foods safer to eat, by destroying bacteria which can cause food poisoning
4 produce a particular quality in food, of colour, flavour and texture (e.g. Victoria sandwich).

Methods of baking foods

Baking fruits, vegetables and potatoes
This is a form of simple oven cooking where the food items are cooked in an oven until tender.

Baking within a bain-marie *(water bath)*
This involves placing the item to be baked in a water bath, so that low temperatures may be maintained during cooking. The baking of egg custard mixtures is an example of this type of cooking, where a gentle oven heat is maintained by a bain-marie, reducing the likelihood of the mixture curdling.

Baking flour products
This is often a more complex form of cooking than the methods given above. When baking flour products such as cakes, the dry heat of the oven is usually modified with steam which has developed within the oven from the cake mixture during baking. The oven conditions in this instance should not only provide the correct temperature but also the correct humidity.

Cooking eggs
Cooking shirred eggs (*Oeufs sur le plat*) is also a form of oven cooking.

Food items suitable for baking and oven cooking

1 *Fruits:* e.g. apples and pears.
2 *Potatoes.*
3 *Milk puddings and egg custard products.*
4 *Flour products:* e.g. cakes, sponges, pastries and yeast goods.
5 *Vegetables* prepared in vegetarian bakes.
6 *Meat and vegetable hotpots* which are oven cooked.
7 *Eggs* which are oven cooked.

Equipment used when baking foods

Types of equipment used include: general purpose ovens, pastry ovens, forced-air convection ovens, baking ovens with steam injection (for bread) and specialist ovens (e.g. pizza ovens).

Basic techniques of baking

Traying-up items to be baked
Certain categories of food require the baking tray to be prepared in a particular way. Lightly greasing trays or tins with white fat (rather than butter or margarine which may cause the food to stick to the tray) is essential for cakes and sponges. However, with some foods (e.g. brandy snaps) it may be advisable to use silicone paper to avoid this problem. Allowance must be made when traying-up foods which will expand during baking (e.g. choux paste and yeast goods).

Marking foods to be baked
Some products, such as short pastry items (e.g. flans, pies and tarts) have their top edges neatly marked to produce an attractive finish. This is sometimes referred to as *notching* and may be done with the thumb and forefinger or special tweezers.

Gilding or coating with egg-wash
Many items which are to be baked, especially pastry and yeast goods, are lightly brushed with egg-wash just prior to baking so that a good colour will develop on the surface of the item.

Speed of cooking
Most items are baked so that the product rises (if appropriate), develops colour and cooks through at the same time. It is therefore important that the oven is set to the correct temperature and pre-heated before inserting the food.

Proving
This is the final fermentation of yeast goods after they have been shaped and placed on the baking tray. It is usually carried out at 28–30 °C (82–86 °F) in a moist atmosphere to prevent the surface of the goods developing a skin.

Cooling
Many baked items are very delicate when hot (e.g. cakes and pastries) and should be cooled or allowed to cool slightly prior to use. This is usually done on a cooling wire designed for the purpose, which allows the air to circulate under the food and prevents condensation and softening of the product.

Baking: key points

- When preparing your time plan, remember that many baked goods have long preparation times; such as yeast goods, large cakes and gateaux. In addition they may have to be served cold and you will therefore need to allow for cooling time.
- Ensure that you allow sufficient time for the oven to reach the correct baking temperature. Do not create a situation where a sponge is ready for the oven but cannot be cooked because the oven is not hot enough.
- Take care to measure and weigh foods accurately. When baking cakes, even small errors can have disastrous consequences; when weighing baking powder ensure the exact amount is used or the cake may be useless.

COLD PREPARATIONS

Cold preparations are cold items which have been prepared and assembled and are either raw, or cooked then cooled.

Reasons for making cold preparations

1   To make foods more palatable and digestible.
2   To produce a particular quality in food, of colour, flavour and texture (e.g. Florida cocktail).
3   To make foods visually attractive (e.g. whole decorated salmon).

Methods of producing cold preparations

Cold savoury items

These may be accompanied or finished with appropriate sauces or dressings. Categories include:

- *different types of hors d'oeuvre:* including single item, selection (various) and cocktail types
- *different types of salad:* including simple, mixed, fish, meat and poultry salads
- *cold decorative items:* e.g. fish, shellfish, meat, poultry and vegetables
- *different types of sandwiches:* plain, rolled and pinwheel types.

Cold sweet items

These may be garnished and decorated. Categories include: cold mousses, bavarois and charlottes; table jellies; trifles and condés; fresh fruit salads and coupes; syllabub.

Food items suitable for cold preparations

1 *Fresh vegetables and salad vegetables.*
2 *Cold cooked fish, shellfish, meat, poultry and game.*
3 *Convenience and processed foods:* e.g. canned, jarred, frozen, smoked and foods in brine.
4 *Fresh fruits.*
5 *Dairy foods:* including cream, fromage frais and yoghurt.
6 *Baked goods:* such as sponges and finger biscuits.

Equipment used when producing cold preparations

1 Small equipment, e.g. bowls, whisks, spoons, cutters.
2 Motorised equipment, e.g. mixers, blenders, food processors.
3 Large equipment, e.g. refrigerators, chillers and freezers.

Basic techniques of cold preparations

1 *Dividing skills:* such as slicing, dicing, shredding, chopping.
2 *Combining skills:* such as mixing, binding, dressing, garnishing.
3 *Artistic/creative arrangement of food:* attractive presentation and decoration of different food materials.

Cold preparations: key points

Always use good hygienic practices when handling and storing cold foods and remember the golden rules:

- *keep it clean,*
- *keep it cool,*
- *keep it covered.*

HEALTHY EATING

Most health professionals believe that there has been an increase in ill health and disease which is directly related to our eating habits. There have been several* reports on the subject of food and health which link the types and quantities of foods we eat

* The National Advisory Committee on Nutrition Education (NACNE) 1983.
Government report on coronary heart disease by the Committee on Medical Aspects of Food Policy (COMA): *Health and Social Subjects* No 28, 1984 HMSO.
Department of Health. *Dietary Reference Values for Food Energy and Nutrients for the United Kingdom*. London: HMSO, 1991 (Report on Health and Social Subjects, 41)
Department of Health. *The Health of the Nation*. London: HMSO, 1991.

with coronary heart disease, cancer of the colon, bowl disorders, constipation and tooth decay. The Government has also set specific dietary targets for the population in its *Health of the Nation* White Paper.

CURRENT DIETARY ADVICE

The common message which is fundamental to reports on diet and health is to:

- *Eat less fat, especially saturated fat.*
  Why? Because, too much fat in the diet is linked to coronary heart disease. Eating too much fat can also contribute to the problem of being overweight or obese. *Saturated fats.* These are hard fats usually provided by animal foods such as meat, butter, lard and milk products. However, they are also found in plants and in particular coconut and palm oil.
- *Eat less sugar*
  Why? Because eating too much sugar is one of the main causes of tooth decay. Eating too much sugar can also contribute to the problem of being overweight or obese. Remember that honey, golden syrup and treacle are all types of sugar. Sugar is also present in large quantities in some pickles, jarred sauces and condiments.
- *Eat less salt*
  Why? Because eating too much salt may result in increasing blood pressure. Note that most stock bouillons, jarred pickles and sauces and cured foods such as bacon and ham are high in salt.
- *Eat more fibre*
  Why? Because fibre aids in the prevention of bowl disorders such as constipation, cancer of the colon and diverticulitis. Soluble fibre is also believed to prevent coronary heart disease.
  1 *Insoluble fibre*: Good sources are wheat, rice, pulses (various beans) and products such as wholemeal bread and breakfast cereals such as bran flakes.
  2 *Soluble fibre*: Good sources are pulses, oatmeal and pectin in fruits.

Healthy eating is basically about being *light handed* with fat, sugar and salt and *generous* with fibre. It is also about eating sufficient vitamins and minerals. This simple message should also result in a diet which maintains a person's ideal body weight – not being too thin or too fat.

USING HEALTHY EATING PRACTICES WHEN BOILING, POACHING, STEWING AND BRAISING

These cookery processes apply to: sauces, soups, fish dishes, pasta dishes, stews, braised dishes, vegetables, potatoes, and sweet items.

General preparation

- Ensure that all the fat has been trimmed off any bones or meat prior to cooking.
- When preparing vegetables, never soak the vegetables in cold water as valuable water soluble vitamins will leach out and be lost.
- Always cut vegetables with a sharp knife. A blunt knife bruises the vegetable and causes a loss of vitamin C brought about by oxidative enzymes.
- Start the cooking of vegetables, wherever possible in a minimum quantity of boiling water to reduce nutrient and flavour loss.

Reduce fat

- Skim fat from the surfaces of liquids. Remember trace fat can be removed using a piece of clean kitchen paper floated on the surface of the liquid.
- Thickening paste can be used in place of roux.

- Replacing butter with lower-fat spreads will reduce fat, especially saturated fat.
- Use fatty foods sparingly e.g. cheese added to sauce (less cheese may be added if strong flavoured cheese is used).
- Do not liaise with cream or cream and eggs unless it is necessary.
- Do not enrich with butter (*monter au beurre*) unless necessary.
- Avoid tossing items (e.g. pasta and vegetables) in butter.
- Avoid garnishing the dishes with fatty garnishes e.g. shallow-fried or butter/sugar glazed items.

Reduce salt

- Cut down on the amount of salt you use when cooking.
- Where possible, use herbs and spices to flavour food instead of salt.
- Avoid seasoning food after cooking: leave this to the customer.
- Use convenience foods low in salt; read the label to determine the salt content.

Reduce sugar

- Reduce the quantity of sugar in syrups and sauces wherever possible.
- Poach fruits in natural unsweetened fruit juice or low sugar syrups; *Remember* this may affect the keeping quality.
- Use convenience foods which have no added sugar, such as canned fruits and sauces, yogurt and fruit purées

Increase fibre

- Use wholemeal flour instead of white flour wherever possible, e.g. brown sauces, soups and stews.
- Use wholemeal pastas and brown rices.
- Extend vegetable garnishes to include high fibre items such as wholegrain cereals and pulses e.g. brown rices, lentils, various beans and peas.
- Accompany items or dishes with products which provide fibre e.g. wholemeal, bread, toast or rolls.
- Wherever possible, do not remove or strain out commodities which provide fibre e.g. vegetables.

USING HEALTHY EATING PRACTICES WHEN GRILLING, FRYING, ROASTING, OVEN COOKING AND BAKING

These cookery processes apply to: grilled items/dishes, fried items/dishes, roast items/dishes, fish dishes, casseroles/hotpots, cakes, sponges and puddings.

General preparation

- Select lean joints of meat.
- Ensure that as much fat as possible has been trimmed off any joints or cuts of meat prior to cooking.

Reduce fat

- Methods of cooking may be altered to produce dishes with less fat, e.g. oven cooking may be used as an alternative to grilling or frying. Alternatively, grill foods instead of frying foods.
- Use non-stick frying utensils wherever possible, although this may be unrealistic in many commercial situations.

- Avoid using lard or dripping when cooking. Use an oil low in saturated fatty acids.
- Wherever possible, avoid food sitting in fat when roasting or oven cooking. Keep basting to a minimum.
- Always drain the surface fat from items after cooking. Use absorbent kitchen paper to remove surface fat after cooking wherever possible.
- Remove excess fat when portioning or carving food; removing the skin from poultry and feathered game after cooking will considerably reduce the fat content.
- Thoroughly skim surface fat from gravy.
- Avoid garnishing the dishes with fatty garnishes e.g. shallow-fried or butter/sugar glazed items.
- Wherever possible, use lower-fat recipes for pastry items, sponges and cakes.
- When baking, using soft margarines instead of butter should reduce saturated fatty acids.
- Use yogurts, fromage frais and fruit purées as alternatives to cream and pastry cream wherever possible.
- Use whipping cream instead of double cream when garnishing desserts.
- Use lower-fat ice-creams and sorbets.

Reduce salt

- Cut down on the salt you use when cooking.
- Where possible, use herbs and spices to flavour food instead of salt.
- Avoid seasoning food after cooking: leave this to the customer.

Reduce sugar

- Use reduced sugar recipes wherever possible.
- Cut down on the sugar you use when sweetening creams, fillings, puddings and garnishes.
- Use garnishes which are low in sugar e.g. fresh fruits or items cooked in natural unsweetened fruit juice or low-sugar syrups.
- Use convenience foods which have no added sugar or are low in sugar, such as reduced-sugar jams and jellies.

Increase fibre

- Wherever possible use wholemeal flour for baking, e.g. fruit crumbles. Mixtures of white flour and wholemeal flour can be used for pastry, cakes and sponges; 25–50% of the white flour in a recipe may be replaced with wholemeal flour.
- Interesting recipes for toppings, pastries and crumbles can be prepared using oats, porridge oats and muesli mixtures.
- Leave skins on fruits when preparing fillings or garnishes.
- Wherever possible, do not remove or strain out commodities which provide fibre, e.g. fruits.

USING HEALTHY EATING PRACTICES FOR COLD BUFFET

General Preparation

- All cold buffet items should be served as fresh as possible:
  1 To ensure quality of taste and texture. *Remember:* the attractive flavours and crisp textures of all salads deteriorate during storage.
  2 To retain nutritional value. *Remember:* valuable vitamins are lost if buffet items are prepared too early for service, especially with vegetables and fruits.

3   To reduce the risk of food poisoning. *Remember*: ensure hygienic practices are used when preparing, storing and serving all buffet items. It is also important to note that lower-fat sauces and dressings usually contain no added preservative and therefore they must be kept in a refrigerator and used as quickly as possible.

- Never soak salad vegetables in cold water. *Remember*: valuable water soluble vitamins will leach out and be lost.
- Always cut vegetables with a sharp knife. *Remember*: a blunt knife bruises the vegetable and causes a loss of vitamin C brought about by oxidative enzymes.

Reduce Fat

- Use commercially made lower-fat salad dressings, salad creams and mayonnaise instead of mayonnaise and traditional vinaigrette. *Remember*: reduce the risk of food poisoning, always make traditional mayonnaise with pasteurised egg yolk – never use raw egg.
- Prepare lower-fat vinaigrette by using 3 parts wine vinegar and 1 part olive oil.
- Try using yogurt, vegetables or fruit purées, herbs and spices to make excellent low-fat salad dressings and cold buffet sauces.
- Use small spoons for the service of sauces and dressings to help keep portion sizes to a minimum.
- Cut the vegetables for crudites as thick as possible; this is to ensure that more vegetable than dip is eaten.

Reduce salt

- Avoid seasoning buffet items during preparation: leave this to the customer.
- Remember that seasoning of sauces, salad dressings and dips can be done with herbs and spices instead of salt.
- Keep to a minimum the use of pickles and cooking liquors which are high in salt.

Reduce sugar

- Reduce the use of ketchup and honey in salad dressings and sauces.

Increase fibre

- Remember that the traditional green salad does not contain much fibre. To increase the fibre in salads, add cooked pasta, pulses such as kidney beans and chick peas, brown rice or cracked wheat.
- Use a selection of side dishes which are a good source of fibre e.g. pasta, pulse and rice dishes.
- Leave the skins on potatoes, vegetables or fruits whenever possible.
- Ensure that a good selection of wholemeal breads are available; this also offers a good source of fibre to customers.

Prepare and cook basic meat, poultry and offal dishes

This chapter covers:
ELEMENT 1:   **Prepare basic meat, poultry and offal for cooking**
ELEMENT 2:   **Cook basic meat, poultry and offal dishes**

What you need to do

- Ensure preparation, cooking areas and suitable equipment are hygienic and ready for use.
- Check that meat, poultry or offal is of the type, quality and quantity required.
- Report any problems identified with the quality of meat, poultry, offal or other ingredients promptly to the appropriate person.
- Ensure meat, poultry or offal is prepared and cooked correctly using appropriate basic preparation and dry or wet cooking methods and is combined with other ingredients to meet dish requirements.
- Ensure that meat, poultry or offal dish is finished using appropriate finishing methods to meet dish requirements.
- Ensure that prepared and cooked meat, poultry or offal not for immediate use is stored correctly.
- Report any problems identified with the quality of the dish promptly to the appropriate person.
- Ensure that preparation and cooking areas and equipment are cleaned correctly after use.
- Ensure all work is prioritised and carried out in an organised and efficient manner in line with appropriate organisational procedures and legal requirements.

What you need to know

- What safe working practices should be followed when preparing and cooking meat, poultry and offal for cooking.
- What signs might indicate that oil or fat is reaching 'flashpoint' and what procedures should be followed if fat or oil reaches flashpoint.
- Why it is important to keep food preparation and cooking areas and equipment hygienic when preparing and cooking meat, poultry and offal.
- What the main contamination threats are when preparing, cooking and storing meat, poultry and offal.
- Why time and temperature are important when preparing and cooking meat, poultry and offal.
- Why prepared and cooked meat, poultry and offal should be stored at a safe temperature before, during and after cooking or cooled rapidly.
- What quality points you should look for in fresh meat, poultry and offal dishes.
- What basic preparation and cooking methods are suitable for different types of meat, poultry and offal and how you might identify when meat, poultry and offal dishes are cooked.
- Which products and cooking methods and equipment could be used to substitute and contribute to reducing high fat ingredients when preparing and cooking meat, poultry and offal.
- Why increasing the fibre content of meat, poultry and offal dishes contributes to healthy eating practices.
- Why reducing the amount of salt added to meat, poultry and offal dishes contributes to healthy eating practices.

ELEMENT 1:   Prepare basic meat, poultry and offal for cooking

INTRODUCTION

Meat, poultry and offal are important foods providing much of the protein people need for the growth and repair of our bodies while at the same time providing a source of energy. Offal provides a rich source of protein, vitamins and minerals.

Meat, poultry and offal are cooked by a wide range of different cookery methods, these being divided into wet or dry methods. Different cuts, joints and pieces of meat, poultry and offal will require varying methods depending on the individual meat, poultry or offal. The knowledge and skill surrounding this area of food preparation and cooking is significant and will take time to understand.

Some meat can be cooked quickly because it does not require a prolonged cooking method to tenderise it, it is already tender as a cut or joint e.g. fillet steak, rump or sirloin from beef, leg of lamb or loin or leg of pork. Even so these cuts will need a certain degree of cooking before they are safe to serve.

What is meat?

Generally it helps to try and understand where on the animal the cut or joint comes from and what its function is. For example, the fillet is from the muscle which provides a balancing mechanism and does no mechanical work other than provide stability; this cut is one of the most tender from animals i.e. fillet of beef, lamb, pork, veal or venison. In shin or shank of beef, however, these parts have to provide support for the animal and are strained by the sheer weight and work required of them. These cuts are tough with strong sinews and need prolonged cooking. These cuts are used for a limited number of dishes such as soups or stocks.

When cooking meat, think about the structure of the food you are preparing for cooking. Lean flesh of meat is composed of fibrous muscles, bound together by connective tissues. The size and thickness of the fibres in the muscle will determine the grain and texture of the meat. Younger animals, with less developed muscle fibres, provide a more tender meat.

The connective tissues binding these fibres also affects the tenderness of the meat. There are two kinds of connective tissues: one (*elastin*) which must be broken up by pounding or mincing, while the second (*collagen*) can be broken down by the cooking process.

The amount, condition and distribution of fat on a meat carcass will also affect tenderness and flavour. Where fat is found between the muscle fibres, the meat is said to be *marbled*. This type of meat will be more tender and moist and flavourful. These three qualities are also enhanced in all meats by a process of *hanging*, which matures the meat before the carcass is dissected.

Meat covers the following types prepared for cooking (at this basic level):
● beef
● veal
● lamb
● mutton
● pork
● bacon.

What is poultry?

Poultry is the name given to all domestic fowl bred for food (their meat and eggs). It is more easily digested than meat and contains less fat. The tenderness and flavour depends on the type and age of the bird: older laying hens are tougher than younger ones, and need to be cooked by a wet process (e.g. boiling) to enhance tenderness. You may often use frozen poultry: when defrosting poultry ensure you follow the safe practices relating to defrosting of high-risk foods (see Unit 2ND16 p. 339).

Because it has less fat poultry has become a more popular meat to use on the menu. This rise has produced a wide range of chicken-based products and dishes, from supremes, chicken nuggets, burgers and pre-cooked prepared meals.

Poultry covers the following types prepared for cooking (at this basic level):
- chicken
- turkey.

What is offal?

Offal is the term applied to parts of animals found inside the animal carcass. Offal has gained in popularity in good class restaurants and has become used more widely on the menu in recent years. Offal covers the following range of cuts:

- liver
- kidney
- tripe
- head
- brains
- oxtail
- tongue
- heart
- lights
- sweetbreads
- suet
- bones and marrow.

QUALITY AND AROMA

Beef delivered for preparation or meat that has already been prepared should have a clean fresh aroma or smell. If meat, in this case beef, has an unpleasant aroma or smell then you need to question the quality of the order and/or delivered product. If you are unsure, refer the problem to the person you are responsible to. When in doubt always check with the supervisor or chef or stores person. *Remember* – you have a responsibility to your customers and yourself, to ensure food is of the best quality. Ensure that the supplier understands that you will return sub-standard meat that is unfit for the purpose for which it is intended.

Beef, as an example, is not a cheap meat. Many of the cuts popular in modern catering are expensive and only disreputable suppliers will try to pass on meat which is not fresh. Do not confuse meat which is hung, or has matured by being hung correctly in a fridge, with meat left to 'sweat' on a blood soaked tray in a wrapping.

APPEARANCE

Not only should all meat smell fresh, without trace of a stale or putrid aroma, it should also have a clean smooth appearance. All meat should be free from stickiness; this occurs from bad or incorrect storage.

Some examples commonly found are meat that has been stored on trays in its own blood juices; these deteriorate quickly. The meat will develop a poor colour and sticky surface together with an unpleasant odour. Meat that has been washed and placed back into storage will also very quickly become smelly and sticky; in this case a strong odour can be detected. This meat should not be used but discarded.

Fresh quality meat should have a clean finish, a good even colouring without any tinges of 'greying' which might indicate poor storage. Matured meat will have a deeper purple colour, especially beef, which indicates correct hanging/storage

> ### MEMORY JOGGER
>
> What quality points indicate that meat is fresh?

FRESHNESS

When you order meat and take delivery it is important that all orders are checked on arrival. Take time to see that meat is 'fresh' and not tainted in any way. Competent chefs and cooks will always make a point of examining daily deliveries, especially of meats. These commodity items are costly and can be the cause of problems if contaminated. Some of the points of quality concerning meat have already been described (see p. 29). Pork needs to be very fresh, with a clean smell and clear, clean surface.

Hang meat on hooks in a walk-in fridge or place on drip trays covered with oiled paper. Never leave meat to sweat in a plastic bag. Suppliers often use plastic bags to prevent the blood juices from seeping. Remove meat immediately from any plastic or bag wrapping, check for all quality points and store correctly. Butchers will in most cases ensure quality meat is delivered; sustaining a good relationship between butcher and chef will improve the end quality service for the consumer.

PROBLEMS WITH MEAT

<aside>
MEMORY JOGGER

Why should meat, poultry and offal deliveries be checked carefully on arrival?
</aside>

Every chef needs to ensure meat deliveries are the correct quantity (i.e. number or weight) when delivered. You will be able to check against the order sheet that the beef, lamb, pork, bacon, poultry or offal is of the right quality, cut, trim or joint.

It is not difficult for delivery staff to short-weight meat for their own personal benefit, or resale. This is known as shrinkage. Always weigh delivered meat on the scales in front of the delivery person; match these against the order delivery sheet.

When ordering for a function or service, the correct quantity of meat needs to be ordered taking into account the trim loss, cooking loss and cooked portion weight to be served. Under-calculating meat requirements might mean customers being disappointed: over-ordering could result in waste and loss of gross profit percentages.

Over a period of time the chef can judge the customer flow to make certain sufficient stocks are held without carrying excess meat stock which does have a limited shelf life. Talk with the chef and ask them how they determine the quantities required for each of the meats discussed in this element.

PREPARATION OF MEAT, POULTRY AND OFFAL

Defrosting

Food which has been frozen needs to be defrosted in the correct way to avoid problems. Frozen foods that have been purchased already processed will usually have defrosting directions which must be followed. Foods which you have frozen yourself need to be defrosted in good time, to ensure the meat, poultry or offal is no longer frozen in the centre.

Food should never be cooked from frozen unless specified by the packaging directions. Some foods are cooked straight from the freezer, e.g. scampi, chips and breaded fish items. Some meat items will be already prepared, or may be whole joints requiring preparation. Remove these from the deep freeze, place on a plastic tray and place in the fridge.

The larger the item the sooner it needs to be taken out to thaw. *Never thaw in warm water*: this produces conditions in which bacteria thrive and might in some cases be the cause of food poisoning. If you are unsure how long food items take to defrost always ask the chef or cook for advice. A good chef will always keep a freezer log of foods listing: when they were frozen, their weight and details about the food itself, e.g. 23 lamb cutlets – panéed – frozen 21st May 1996.

Skinning

Skinning is a term more usually connected with fish preparation. However some meat is skinned as a basic preparation method prior to cooking. Loin of pork for example is skinned to remove the tough outer layer of skin, leaving the fatty layer intact to aid basting of the meat as it cooks.

Lamb loins or best-ends that have been hung correctly will have the skin removed. This is called de-barking: the dry outer skin is peeled away using a cloth and should come away in one piece if hung correctly.

Bacon is generally skinned prior to the joint being rolled and chilled for cutting. Bacon can be purchased with skin on pre-sliced. Legs of bacon for boiling e.g. gammon ham, will only be skinned once, cooked and chilled. Then the joint is often rolled in breadcrumbs for decorative purposes.

Beef sirloin will have the skin already removed; only the fat layer is left on. This is trimmed further to remove the sinew which runs from the lower end of the sirloin. Some beef joints do have tough sinews which should be trimmed or removed or the meat will be tough when cooked. The reason for this is that the sinew shrinks and is not tenderised by the cooking process but toughened, making it similar in texture to an elastic band.

Chickens are skinned when the supremes are removed from the main carcass; the skin is lifted gently back toward the wing bone and pulled over the bone. You will have to make a small cut to remove the skin from the small winglet bone.

Offal is also skinned. Liver has a fine membrane skin covering which is carefully removed before being sliced. Kidneys also have this fine skin covering which you should remove before cooking.

Trimming

Trimming is a key preparation technique. It is used to remove those pieces of meat, skin, fat or sinew which will not enhance the meat product. Often excess fat will be trimmed to leave some fat for basting, appearance or flavouring purposes.

Sinews are trimmed to remove them completely in most cases as these will shrink and toughen when cooked. Meat is also trimmed to improve the shape or size of the portion, cut or joint.

Trimming can be done with a cook's knife or boning knife depending on the trim required. To bone a leg of lamb, use a boning knife, whereas to trim a pork escalope use a slim cook's knife. Trimming is used to prepare joints for roasting; a good example of this is the best-end of lamb. Trimming is only for removing small pieces of the meat and should not be confused with general butchery where you are cutting to produce particular cuts or small joints.

Trimming in the case of bacon can be done effectively with a small office knife as you need to ensure all the cartilage or sinew and fine small bone fragments are removed. When trimming generally, try to avoid damage to the main eye of the meat.

Remember: *Always take care when using knives.*

Healthy eating

Health has become a major factor in the eating styles, habits and practices in the 1990s. Leaner meat with less fat can be produced by genetic farming; sauces and the commodity composition of dishes can be based upon less harmful ingredients.

Seasoning

Seasoning is one of the most important skills chefs will learn or develop during their training, which will last a lifetime. To over-season can ruin a dish which has probably taken a long time to cook: to under-season is to not finish the story or the painting!

Salt and pepper are used as basic seasoning agents; some foods need less or more of each depending on the food. Bacon for example is already fairly salty. But it is not only salt and pepper that are used as seasoning agents, many spices and herbs can be used to season or flavour the dish or product in the preparation, production or finishing stages of the cooking process.

Seasoning skills develop as you gain in confidence. Always use a clean spoon to taste sauces and soups to determine if the seasoning is correct. These skills do take time to establish; it is always a good idea to discuss how much or little seasoning is required with experienced chefs or cooks. When you are cooking, never eat mints, which dull or kill the ability to taste. Seasoning can mean the difference between a satisfied or unhappy customer.

Try to understand the flavour development of each dish, recipe or product. How should it taste? Remember you can always add a bit more but it is not so easy to take it away.

Washing

Hygiene is very important when handling meat or meat-based products. Food handlers, especially in industry, do not pay enough attention to this basic yet potentially dangerous task.

When washing meat you need to ensure that cross-contamination risk is minimised. You should wash your hands when handling different meats.

Also ensure that, between handling each different meat, all surfaces are cleaned correctly before preparing the next product.

Washing of meat is safe as long as the meat is prepared and cooked straight away. Meat that has been washed and then returned to storage will soon develop a strong odour, especially poultry which carries a dangerously high risk if used.

Only wash meat when it is needed for cooking. Sometime blood juices need to be washed off the meat piece; rinse in cold water in a clean sink and dry with the correct disposable paper. Never use a cloth to dry meat.

Never wash meat when it is delivered and then store it in the fridge. Always hang meat where possible, order for one or two days in advance. Try and plan for the routine cleaning of meat fridges and general maintenance of meat fridges or chill rooms. Keep them clean and tidy – always check them *daily*.

Remember: *Moist surfaces encourage bacterial growth.*

Dicing

Dicing of meat is a basic skill used to portion meat without bone or gristle into a uniform size. The size of the dice depends upon the type of dish or recipe being prepared. Small, fine-diced cooked meat might be appropriate as a garnish. Medium-sized diced meat could be used for a hot or cold sauce-based dish e.g. a ragout or fricassée. A larger dice of meat might be used for a steak and kidney dish or curry.

Dicing using a knife can be dangerous, always follow basic safety rules for handling knives described in Unit 1ND2, pp. 56–57 of the Core Units book.

Foods can be diced when raw or cooked. Raw foods such as soft or unevenly shaped meats need to be cut carefully. Try to maintain a uniform size. Maintaining the size of cut is important if all pieces of diced food are to be cooked at the same time. Where the dice of meat is uneven then small pieces will cook before large pieces and the large pieces might be undercooked. As you will be aware, this is a risk which needs to be avoided.

Remember to dice cooked meat or poultry evenly. Poultry is generally diced when cooked as a garnish or filling, or as the main ingredient for hot or cold dishes.

Slicing

Slicing is a skill which can be done by hand with a knife or by machine. You can slice meat and poultry when either raw or cooked, hot or cold.

Take great care to make certain you do not cut yourself when slicing food. Where slicing machines are concerned *you are not allowed to use the machine if under the age of 18 without supervision and over 18 you must be trained in the correct use of any dangerous piece of equipment or machinery.*

Types of food sliced include: hot cooked meats such as roast beef, lamb or pork; hot boiled bacon; cold cooked sliced meats including game and formed cold products such as pies and galantines.

Slicing is a skill which needs to be practised to become safe and efficient.

An expensive joint sliced by someone who is not competent will reduce the quality and cost effectiveness of the dish. Watch an expert slice meat; see how they hold the joint securely. Always use the correct knife to slice cooked and raw meats. Always hold the food firmly and in a safe manner. Never talk while slicing; concentrate on what you are doing.

Coating

Coating is a technique used in a wide range of dishes and products. 'Coated' can refer to a dish being covered with a sauce, panéed with flour, egg and breadcrumbs or coated with a meat glaze or similar preparation. Use wholemeal breadcrumbs wherever possible to increase the fibre content of the dish.

Coating means to 'cover over'. Minced beef is made into Durham cutlets which are floured with seasoned flour and then dipped into egg-wash and breadcrumbs to provide a protective coating to prevent the fat being absorbed by the mince.

Many prepared frozen foods are coated in this way, ready to be deep or shallow-fried. Coating can also mean 'covering with a sauce', which can be hot or cold. In this technique the aim is to cover the product with the sauce to enhance the presentation of the dish. Too much sauce used in coating will look untidy and too little might not cover or provide the effect required. The consistency of sauces used for coating is important: too thin and the sauce will not hold on the meat, too thick and the dish will be unsightly.

Meat can also be coated with farces and wrapped in caul or thinly batted bacon, or blanched vegetable leaves which provide more fibre.

When coating using flour, egg and breadcrumbs, always use different preparation surfaces for different meats to avoid cross-contamination.

WORKING CLEANLY AND IN A HYGIENIC AND SAFE MANNER

'Ensure that preparation areas and suitable equipment are hygienic and ready for use' means you should:

- Work cleanly and in a methodical manner. These principles are at the core of good working practices in any trade or craft.
- Clean as you go. Cleaning after one and before subsequent tasks are undertaken is essential to producing safe food.
- Know what equipment to use.
- Make sure the equipment surfaces are clean.
- Have the correct knives sharpened.
- Check the storage trays or containers are clean.
- Check you have the correct quantity of trays or storage containers.
- Work in the correct area.
- Find out how long you have to prepare the task you are about to start.
- Be sure you know what it is you need to do.
- If necessary ask the chef to recap before you begin.
- Remember a good chef is always prepared and always willing to ensure safety, cleanliness and craftsmanship.

IS MEAT, POULTRY AND OFFAL OF THE TYPE, QUALITY AND QUANTITY REQUIRED?

Understanding how to identify the quality of meat, poultry or offal comes with practice. When training make a point to discuss the merits of quality on a daily basis. Ask questions of your chef, cook or supervisor, who should be able to pass on useful pointers.

BEEF

Notable beef cattle breeds: Aberdeen Angus, Welsh Blacks, Hereford, Sussex, Beef Type Shorthorn.

The main season for home-killed beef is from August to March with the lowest prices being in the spring. Fresh meat includes all meat not salted or cooked. Chilled and frozen meat is imported from Europe in line with current problems with British beef and beef products.

Chilled beef is imported from Argentina and Uruguay and after slaughter, the beef is graded and quartered and hung during transit in a non-freezing temperature in a sterile refrigerated container. It must be sold quickly after arrival in port. Storage temperature for chilled beef when packed in layers in refrigerated ships is $-20\ °C$ $(7\ °F)$.

Quality of carcass

Carcass quality is judged by three criteria:
1   *Quality:* the texture of the meat which is dependent upon the development of the muscle and amount of connective tissue; marbling and juices or sap should also be taken into account.
2   *Conformation:* the proportion of meat to bone.
3   *Finish:* the outer covering of fat, which should be smooth, creamy white and evenly distributed over the carcass.

Quality of beef may be judged from the following points:
1   The meat should be firm and bright red.
2   It should have a good show of dots or flecks of white fat (marbled).
3   The fat should be firm and brittle in texture, creamy white in colour.
4   Yellowish fat is a sign that the animal is older or a dairy breed.
5   Beef should be fresh or chilled; frozen beef is never as good.

Conformation points to look for:
1   Short plump carcass

2 Deep chest
3 Full buttocks
4 Well-covered loins
5 Thick full shoulder pieces
6 Short shanks.

Finish – points to look for:
1 Fat creamy white (except Scotch Beef which should be a richer colour)
2 Evenly distributed fat
3 Fat firm to the touch.

Quality of beef

Points to look for in good quality meat are:
1 Flesh should be smooth and moist not wet on freshly cut surfaces
2 Cherry red and marbled colouring
3 Bones should have a bluish tingle (old animals' bones are white and shiny).

Terms used:
● Steer: an ox bullock
● Heifer: 2/3 year old animal. These are the most widely used; good quality.

Hind Quarter of Beef (Approximate weight 82 kg/180 lb)

	English term	French term	Approx. weight	Uses
1	Shin	Gite/Jambe	6.5 kg/14 lb	consommé, stewing
2	Topside	Tende de Tranche	9 kg/20 lb	braising, stewing, 2nd class roast
3	Silverside	Tranch grasse (Ronde)	13 kg/28 lb	pickled in brine, boiled
4	Thick Flank	Gite à la noix	11 kg/24 lb	braising, stewing
5	Rump	Culotte	9 kg/20 lb	grilling, frying, braised in piece
6	Thin Flank	Flanchet (Bavette)	9 kg/20 lb	stewing, boiling, sausages
7	Sirloin	Aloyau	8 kg/18 lb	roasting, grilling, frying (steaks)
8	Wing Ribs	Cotes d'aloyau	4.5 kg/10 lb	roasting, grilling, fried steaks
9	Fillet	Filet	2.5 kg/6 lb	roasting, frying grilling, sauté

Fore Quarter of Beef (Approximate Weight 80 kg/175 lb)

	English term	French term	Approx. Weight	Uses
10	Fore Rib	Côtes Premieres	7 kg/16 lb	roasting, braising
11	Middle Rib	Côtes	9 kg/20 lb	roasting, braising
12	Chuck Rib	Côtes du Collier	13 kg/30 lb	stewing, braising
13	Sticking Piece	Collier	8 kg/18 lb	stewing, sausages
14	Plate	Hampe	9 kg/20 lb	stewing, sausages
15	Brisket	Poitrine	17 kg/38 lb	pickled in brine, boiled, pressed
16	Leg	Macreuse	10 kg/22 lb	braising, stewing
17	Shank	Jarret	5.4 kg/12 lb	consommé

Offal

The term refers to: tongue, heart, liver, kidney, sweetbreads, tripe, tail, suet, bones, marrow.

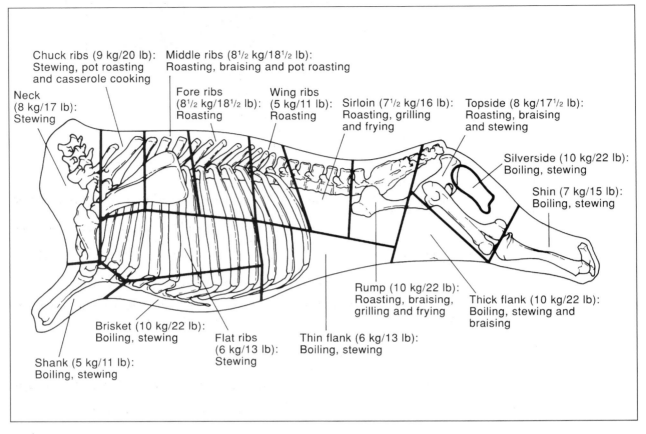

Chuck ribs (9 kg/20 lb):
Stewing, pot roasting
and casserole cooking

Middle ribs (8½ kg/18½ lb):
Roasting, braising and pot roasting

Neck
(8 kg/17 lb):
Stewing

Fore ribs
(8½ kg/18½ lb):
Roasting

Wing ribs
(5 kg/11 lb):
Roasting

Sirloin (7½ kg/16 lb):
Roasting, grilling
and frying

Topside (8 kg/17½ lb):
Roasting, braising
and stewing

Silverside (10 kg/22 lb):
Boiling, stewing

Shin (7 kg/15 lb):
Boiling, stewing

Brisket (10 kg/22 lb):
Boiling, stewing

Flat ribs
(6 kg/13 lb):
Stewing

Thin flank (6 kg/13 lb):
Boiling, stewing

Rump (10 kg/22 lb):
Roasting, braising,
grilling and frying

Thick flank (10 kg/22 lb):
Boiling, stewing and
braising

Shank (5 kg/11 lb):
Boiling, stewing

Beef carcass

PREPARING MEAT

This section covers the preparation of:
- Beef
- Lamb
- Veal
- Pork
- Bacon
- Ham
- Poultry
- Offal.

BEEF (*LE BOEUF*)

Beef is hung for up to 14 days to increase its tenderness and develop the flavour of the meat. It should smell fresh i.e. odourless, and have a good red colour or bloom. Beef cattle are slaughtered around the age of 18–21 months, and the meat from younger animals is generally more tender and brighter in colour; if the flesh has a deep red colour is has probably come from an older animal and might be tougher.

The colour of the meat is also affected by the length of time the meat has been hanging: the longer the meat is hung, the darker the meat will be in colour. You should be able to see flecks of fat (marbling), especially in the prime joints such as sirloin, fillet and rump. The outer layer of fat should be firm and brittle with a creamy-white colour.

Sirloin (*L'aloyau*)

The sirloin is used whole for roasting. When prepared whole, you will need to remove the chine bones (the T-shaped bone running from the bottom of the meat towards the fatty top).

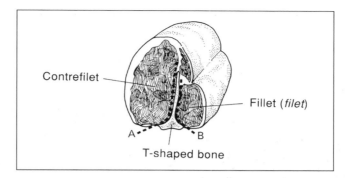

Preparing sirloin

Preparing sirloin:
1 Cut down between the meat of the fillet and the right-hand side of the chine bone, starting just above the top of the bone (**B**).
2 Cut down between the meat of the contrefilet and the left-hand side of the chine bone, again starting just above the top of the bone (**A**).
3 Pull back the cut away part of the contrefilet and saw or cleaver through the bone.
4 Remove the sinew (under the top layer of fat) and trim off any excess fat.

When roasting, the bone can be replaced and the sirloin tied onto it with string. The fillet may be cut away entirely, as it can be easily overcooked.

Cuts from the whole sirloin
- *Contrefilet* (see below)
- *Fillet* (see below)
- *T-bone steak* cut through the whole sirloin from the rib end: this contains a large piece of fillet
- *Porterhouse steak* as for T-bone but cut from the rump end of the sirloin; contains less fillet.

Contrefilet

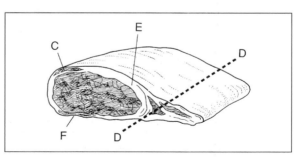

Preparing contrefilet

This is prepared from the sirloin, following the steps given above. To remove the contrefilet from the chinebone completely, follow the steps given below.

Preparing contrefilet:
1 Cut away the bottom flap (containing little meat) along the dotted line marked (**D**).
2 Remove the sinew and nerve under the fat at (**C**).
3 Trim any excess fat and sinew from (**E**) and (**F**).

Cuts from the contrefilet (suitable for grilling or frying):
- *Sirloin (entrecôte) steak* a piece 1–1.5 cm ($\frac{1}{2}$ in) thick from contrefilet, weight: 150 g (6 oz).
- *Double sirloin (entrecôte double)* a large sirloin steak: 2 cm (1 in) thick, approximate weight 300 g (12 ozs).

- *Minute steak*   a sirloin steak flattened (batted) to approximately 5–8 mm ($\frac{1}{4}$ in) thick.

Fillet (*Le filet*)

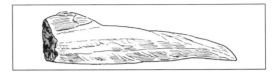

Fillet

Cut the fillet from the sirloin following step 1 of *Preparing Sirloin*, but cut the meat away from the sirloin entirely. Trim the meat by cutting away any sinew (running along the length of the fillet) and any excess fat.

Cuts from the fillet (suitable for grilling or frying)

- *Filet steak*   cut from the middle of the fillet: 1.5–2 cm ($\frac{1}{2}$ in) thick.
- *Chateaubriand*   cut from the head of the fillet as a double fillet steak: 3–10 cm (1–4 in) thick.
- *Tournedos steak*   cut from the middle of the fillet: 2–4 cm (1–1$\frac{1}{2}$ in) thick. Usually tied with string and barded with fat.
- *Médaillons*   small slices of steak cut from the tail end of the fillet.
- *Bâtons*   small slices of steak cut from the tail end of fillet.
- *Filets mignons*   cut from the tail end of fillet, so small that if used as fillet steaks, two should be used per portion; can be diced finely e.g. for beef stroganoff.
- *Paillard steak*   a flattened fillet steak.

MEMORY JOGGER

Which steaks are cut from the fillet?

Wing and fore rib

Remove the chine bone and sinew (under the top layer of fat) following the same method as for the preparation of sirloin (see p. 37). The fat and flesh from the bottom of the ribs may be trimmed away to expose the rib bones.

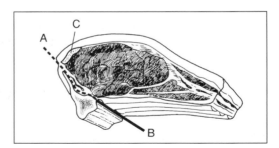

Wing and fore rib

Wing ribs are roasted whole or cut into steaks for grilling of frying.

Rump (*La culotte*)

This is cut away from the hip bone, and any sinew or excess fat removed.

Cuts from the rump

- *Rump steak*   2 cm (1 in) thick
- *Point steak*   cut from the triangular section of rump; 2 cm (1 in) thick.

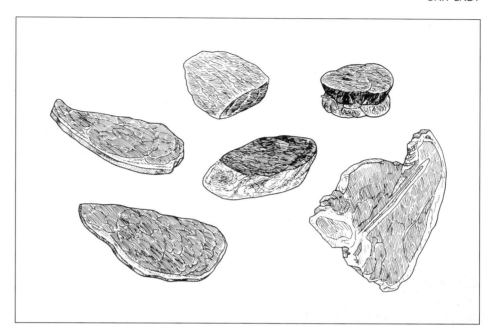

Beef steaks (clockwise from top left): entrecôte steak, fillet steak, tournedos, T-bone steak, chateaubriand, minute steak

Topside and silverside (*La tranche tendre and La gite à la noix*)

These are from the hindquarter of the carcass. To prepare, carefully cut and remove the bone and trim off any sinew or excess fat. Topside is jointed and tied with string for roasting and braising, or cut into dice or steaks for stewing.

Thick flank (*La tranche grasse*)

This is also cut from the hindquarter of the carcass. To prepare, remove any excess fat and cut as required. The thick flank is used for braising and stewing.

Shin (*La jambe*)

Another cut from the hindquarter, shin is prepared by boning-out then removing any excess sinew. It can be cut, chopped or minced as required. It is used generally for consommé or stewing.

LAMB AND MUTTON (*L'AGNEAU AND LE MOUTON*)

Lamb meat comes from a sheep that is less than 12 months old when slaughtered; if the animal is over 12 months old the meat is classed as mutton. Lamb flesh should be a dull red colour, while mutton flesh should be a slightly darker, dull brownish-red colour. Both should have a fine texture and grain.

The fat should be clear white, brittle and flaky, and evenly distributed across the carcase. Lamb bones should be pink and slightly porous.

Best end of lamb (*Le carré*)

This can be roasted whole or cut into cutlets for grilling or frying.
1   Cut away the chine bone: cut down following the lines marked (**A**) on the illustration, then use a saw or cleaver to cut away the bone (**B**) joining up to (**A**).

2 You now have two cuts of best end. Remove the skin (bark) from both and the blade bone (**C**).

3 Remove the tough sinew lying just below the fat at the top of each best end.

4 Cut along the length of each best end, allowing you to trim away any flesh or fat between the bones. Scrape the bones clean with the point of the boning knife.

5 If necessary, shorten the rib bones using a cleaver.

Cuts from the best end: cutlets (cut from between the rib bones) and double cutlets (each having two rib bones).

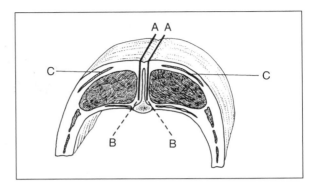

Best end of lamb

Loin (*La longe*)

This is half a saddle. Split the saddle through the middle (i.e. through the backbone) using a cleaver and then remove the skin. The bone can be removed to allow the loin to be stuffed or used for cuts.

Saddle (*La selle*)

This can be roasted whole or cut into fillet, loin and chump chops for grilling and frying.

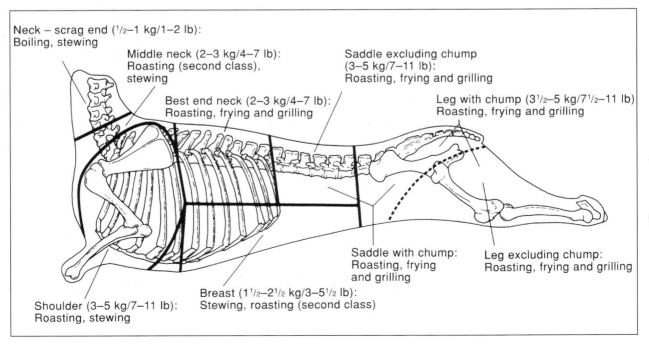

Lamb carcass

Preparing saddle of lamb
1 Pull away the skin.
2 Trim off any sinew or excess fat.
3 Trim the fatty ends from the flaps and tuck them under the saddle.
4 Remove the aitch bone.
5 Score the fat. Tie with string before cooking to keep the shape intact.

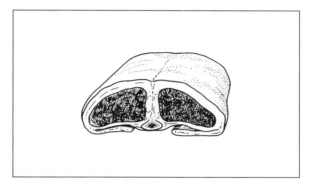

Saddle of lamb

Cuts from the loin and saddle

● *Single loin chops*	cut across the unboned loin; each chop 100–150 g (4–6 oz) in weight.
● *Noisettes* (French style)	cut from a boned loin at an angle of 45°; cuts are 2 cm (1 in) thick; flattened out and trimmed of excess fat.
● *Rosettes*	cut from a boned saddle (i.e. across two loins); 2 cm (1 in) thick; ends rolled in and secured with string to achieve a flat heart shape.
● *Barnsley chops*	cut from the unboned saddle; 2 cm (1 in) thick.
● *Cutlets* (*cotelette or cotellettes double*)	Prepare as for roasting, excluding the scoring and divide evenly between the bones; or the cutlets can be cut from the best-end and prepared separately. A double cutlet consists of two bones; therefore a six bone best-end yields six single or three double cutlets.
● *Saddle*	A full saddle includes the chumps and the tail. For large banquets it is sometimes found better to remove the chumps and use short saddles.

Leg (*Le gigot*)

This is generally boned or partly boned for roasting. Leg of mutton is usually boiled.

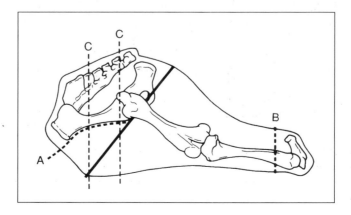

Preparing a leg of lamb

Preparing a leg of lamb
1 Cut along line (**A**), following the line of the aitchbone and through the ball and socket. Remove the aitchbone.
2 Saw off the bottom knuckle and bone (**B**).
3 Remove any excess fat, and tie with string before cooking.

Cuts from a leg of lamb
● *Gigot chops*   cut from the centre of the leg
● *Chump chops*   cut from the chump end of the leg

Shoulder (*L'épaule*)

Skin, then trim and clean the knucklebone, leaving 3 cm (1½ in) exposed. It can then be boned, stuffed and rolled if necessary.

Terms used with lamb:

Cut/point	French term	uses
Saddle	la selle	roasting, pot roasting (poêler)
Loin	la longe	roasting
Fillet	le filet mignon	grilling, frying
Loin chop	chop	grilling, frying, stewing
Chump chop	chump chop	grilling, frying, stewing
Kidney	le rognon	grilling, sauté

VEAL (*LE VEAU*)

Veal comes from the flesh of the calf (usually about 3 months old). The meat should be pale pink, with a fine, evenly-grained texture, and moist with no sign of stickiness. It should be covered by a fine layer of creamy-white fat. Any bones should be pinkish-white and quite soft.

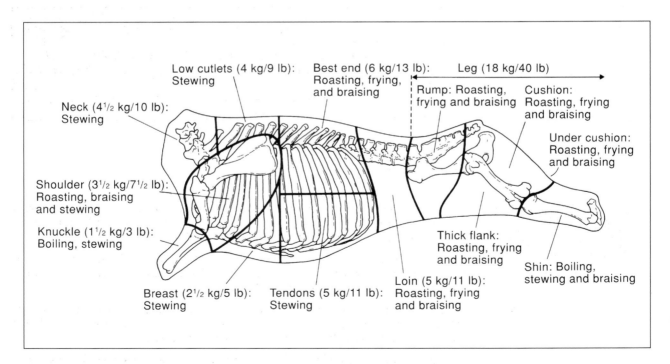

Veal carcass

Best end (*Le carré*)

This is a prime cut from a veal calf, and is prepared in the same way as for best end of lamb.

To prepare veal for roasting
Bone out, trim, roll out stuffing and then tie with string to secure shape.

Cuts from the best end of veal
● *Veal cutlets* (cut from between the rib bones).

Saddle and loin (*La selle and La longe*)

A saddle of veal is prepared following the same methods as for saddle of lamb (see p. 41). The loin can be cut from the saddle and roasted whole or cut into veal chops for grilling or frying.

Leg (*Le gigot*)

The leg is the leanest cut of veal. It is boned to produce three large joints called the cushion, under-cushion and thick flank. These can all be cooked whole or used to obtain: escalopes, grenadins, fricandeaus or medaillons.

Cuts from the cushion, under-cushion and thick flank
● *Escalopes*   large slices cut against the grain; 50–75 g (2–3 oz) in weight; batted out if required.
● *Grenadins*   small, thick slices cut across the grain; 10 cm (4 in) long and 2 cm (1 in) thick.
● *Fricandeaus*   thick slices cut from along the muscle 17 cm (7 in) long and 2 cm (1 in) thick.
● *Médaillons*   small round slices cut against the grain; 5 cm (2 in) diameter and 4 mm ($\frac{1}{4}$ in) thick.

Do this

● Watch a sirloin being boned and prepared and take note of how the fillet and con-trefilet are removed and trimmed.
● When a topside joint is delivered see how it is rolled and tied with fat.
● Find out why lamb loins and best ends should be hung well before removing the skin or bark.
● Investigate the best way to flatten out veal escalopes in a clean and hygienic way.

PORK (*LE PORC*)

MEMORY JOGGER

Why should pork be well cooked?

Pork keeps less well than other meats, and needs very careful handling, preparation and cooking. It may contain parasitic worms, which are destroyed by thorough cooking. Always serve pork well done, *never under-cook pork*.

Pork should be cooked for 25 mins per 450 g (1 lb) weight and 25 mins over. E.g. to calculate the cooking time of a 7 lb (3 kg) joint: $7 \times 25 + 25 = 200$ mins; therefore it will take 3 hours and 10 mins to cook the joint.

Pork joints should be well fleshed without excessive fat. The flesh should be pale pink, firm, finely textured and not too moist. Look for smooth skin and pliable bones. There should not be any unpleasant smell or odours.

The handling of pork should be efficient and hygienic, i.e. always wash your hands

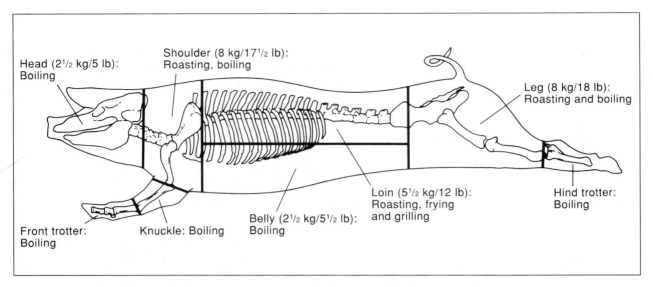

Head (2½ kg/5 lb):
Boiling

Shoulder (8 kg/17½ lb):
Roasting, boiling

Leg (8 kg/18 lb):
Roasting and boiling

Hind trotter:
Boiling

Loin (5½ kg/12 lb):
Roasting, frying
and grilling

Belly (2½ kg/5½ lb):
Boiling

Knuckle: Boiling

Front trotter:
Boiling

Pork carcass

after handling the meat; all equipment and tools should be cleaned and washed after touching pork.

Quality of pork

1 Lean flesh should be a nice pale pink colour.
2 Pork fat should be firm, white and smooth.
3 Pork has fine pink bones which are small.
4 Surface skin should be smooth and without hair.

Loin (*La longe*)

This can be boned or left unboned. If leaving unboned: saw off the bottom of the chine bone as for beef: wing rib (see p. 38), trim away any sinew and excess fat and score diagonal strokes across the top.

To bone: remove the *filet mignon* (tail of the fillet), cut away the bone completely, remove any sinew and excess fat. Neaten the flap and score as before. The filet mignon can be replaced before the meat is rolled and tied for roasting.

The loin can be roasted whole or cut into chops for grilling or frying.

Cuts from the loin
● *Chops*   cut from the unboned back loin; 2 cm (1 in) thick.
● *Cutlets*   cut from the unboned fore loin.
● *Escalopes* prepared from the fillet; flattened steaks.

Leg (*Le cuissot*)

Prepare as for leg of lamb (see p. 41), removing the trotter. Leg of pork is usually roasted.

Shoulder (*L'épaule*)

Bone the shoulder by removing the rib bones, shoulder blade and backbone. Remove any sinew and excess fat then score across the skin. Roll the joint (stuffed if required) and tie with string. The shoulder can be roasted, cut into spare ribs or used for making sausages or pies.

Cuts of pork

Cut/Joint	French Term	Uses	Approx. weight
Head	La tête	brawn (whole for buffets)	3.6 kg/8 lb
Spare Rib	La basse Côte	roast, pies	1.3 kg/3 lb
Loin	La longe	roast, fry, grill	5.4 kg/12 lb
Leg	Le cuissot	roast, boil	4.5 kg/10 lb
Shoulder	L'épaule	roast, sausages, pies	2.7 kg/6 lb
Hand/spring	Plat de côtes		
Belly	La poitrine	boiling, braising	1.8 kg/4 lb
Trotter	Le pied	grilling, boiling – brawn	1.8 kg/4 lb

Pork and lamb chops
From left: loin chops, cutlet, chump chop, noisette, Barnsley chop, rosette

BACON (*LE LARD*)

Bacon differs from pork in that it comes from a different, usually larger breed of pig called a *baconer pig*, and the meat is cured (salted in brine) and sometimes smoked. Green bacon is a name often used to describe unsmoked bacon. Ham comes from the hind leg of a baconer pig, which has been cut away from the carcass and cured or pickled in brine, and sometimes smoked. Rear baconer legs are sometimes boned and boiled to produce ham. When cold they can be covered in pastry and baked in the oven or covered in brown sugar, cloves and cherries and roasted.

Bacon should have no sign of stickiness and no unpleasant smell. The rind should be thick, smooth and free from wrinkles. Check that the fat is white, smooth and not excessive in proportion to the lean meat (flesh) which should be deep pink in colour and firm.

Quality of bacon

Flesh should be pink and fresh smelling, moist but not wet. Fat should be creamy white with no yellow or dark patches. Skin colouration is chiefly determined by the degree of smoking (light or heavy) and the type of sawdust used. Best grades are knows as 'As' or 'Is'.

A good side should have a light fore end, a long back and a plump meaty gammon. Baconer pigs are generally 6–8 months old when slaughtered.

```
Cuts of bacon

Joints                Uses in Cooking                    Weight
Gammon               boiling, braising,                 6.3 kg/14 lb
Rashers
Back                 rashers (245 slices if cut on 5)   6.3 kg/14 lb
Streaky              rashers (190 slices if cut on 6)   4.5 kg/10 lb
Collar               boiling rashers                    4 kg/9 lb
Fore Hock            boiling pressing                   4 kg/9 lb
Gammon               ● corner gammon
                     ● middle gammon
                     ● gammon slipper
                     ● gammon hock
```

Healthy eating

Grilling bacon is a healthier option to that of shallow frying.

Joints and cuts of bacon

Back bacon is cut from the loin of the pig while streaky bacon is cut from the belly, and gammon steaks cut from the hind leg. The hock and collar are cut from the shoulder and neck (these are tough but full flavoured cuts) usually boiled. The right temperature for storing bacon is 1–4 °C (38–40 °F), in a well ventilated carton wrapped in muslin to protect it from flies.

If small cuts of bacon are kept in the lower half of refrigerator, they should be well wrapped in greaseproof paper and on the lowest shelf, as far from the freezing box as possible, otherwise the moisture content of the bacon will be extracted, leaving only the salt. Much of the bacon used today is purchased pre-butchered.

Bacon can be boiled and served with parsley sauce, cabbage and potatoes. Bacon today contains more water than traditional bacon used to.

HAM

Ham is the hind leg of a prime pig, cut off round on the bone and cured by the dry salting method. It is usually unsmoked, except for Belfast Ham.

Four popular British hams are:
1 York
2 Brade Ham
3 Cumberland
4 Belfast.

Continental hams include:
1 Bayonne
2 West Phalian
3 Prague
4 Parma (eaten raw).

Cooking hams and gammons

Hams and gammons must be soaked before cooking to remove excess salt. Hams should be soaked for at least 24 hours: gammons overnight. Weigh the soaked joint, scrub off any 'bloom' (green mould on meat face) which is the hallmark of a naturally cured ham in perfect condition.

Place the ham in a pan of fresh, cold water, bring slowly to the boil, reduce heat to 85 °C (185 °F), simmer according to chart, matching the time to the soaked weight of the meat. At the end of the cooking period turn off the heat and leave the ham or gammon in the stock for one hour, or until cool.

POULTRY

A great many caterers now use oven-ready poultry and this now means that the quality of poultry purchased is consistent, owing to the factory quality control employed. When the UK joined the Common Market in the early seventies the market required all poultry to be cleaned and dressed by European standards and mostly to be frozen. Whilst this is a widespread practice it is still possible to obtain fresh quality poultry from reputable farmers and specialist mongers.

Quality of fresh poultry

1 Breast should be straight, firm and well fleshed with the point of the breast bone being pliable.
2 Legs, short and well fleshed with small scales and spurs.
3 Skin, white to yellow (depending on breed) with blue tinges.
4 Legs/breast free of cuts, sores, blood patches or bruises.
5 Fat, light yellow in colour, not too plentiful, especially in the cavity.

The use of fresh chickens should not present any particular problems, other than the normal points of care in preparation and cooking. With frozen, oven-ready birds the most important factor is correct defrosting.

This should be carried out slowly at normal refrigeration temperature 2–3 °C (35– 38 °F). The more slowly this operation is carried out, the less damage will occur to the flesh of the chicken as a result of the ice crystals rupturing the cell tissues of the meat. The thawing of frozen poultry should never be accelerated, for this very reason.

Poultry types available

Type	French term	Size	Portion
(Chicken)			
Single baby	Poussin	240 g (8–10 oz)	1
Double baby	Poussin double	300–480 g (10–16 oz)	2
Young chicken	Poulet de grain	900 g (1.5–2 lb)	3/4
Medium chicken	Poulet reine	1–2 kg (2– 4 lb)	4/6
Large roasting	Poularde (male)	2–3 kg (4–6 lb)	6/8
Large boiling	Poularde (female)	2–3 kg (4–6 lb)	6/8
Capon	Chapon	3–4 kg (6–9 lb)	8/12
Old boiling	Poule	2–4 kg (5–8 lb)	240 g per portion
(Fowl)			
Turkey cock	Dindon	5–12 kg (1–30 lb)	240 g
Turkey hen	Dinde	4–11 kg (10–25 lb)	240 g
Young turkey	Dindonneau	3–5 kg (6–12 lb)	240 g
Guinea fowl	Pintarde	0.8–3 kg (1–8 lb)	240 g
Duck	Canard	2–3 kg (4–6 lb)	4
Duckling	Caneton	1–2 kg (3–4 lb)	3/4
Goose	L'Oie	4–6 kg (8–14 lb)	240 g
Gosling	L'Oison	2–3 kg (4–6 lb)	240 g
Pigeon	Pigeon	360–480 g (12–16 oz)	1

Advantages of using pre-packed birds

1 Avoids using skilled labour in plucking and drawing thus saving time and money.
2 Standardisation of weight and quality for portion control.
3 Hygienically packed and easily stored in deep freeze unit, which also allows bulk purchasing and low purchase price.

Trussing

For roast:
The legs are blanched in boiling water for a few seconds and the scales removed with the aid of a cloth. The outside claws are removed leaving only the centre ones, and these are lightly trimmed. The leg sinew is then severed below the joint and the legs then inserted into these incisions. To facilitate carving, the wish bone should be removed. The bird is then trussed, using two strings: the first string passes through the winglets, skin of the neck and returns between the thigh and drumstick joints. Secure it firmly. A second string is passed over the legs and under the white breast meat and returned through the carcass of the bird and secured, to leave the prepared legs protruding beyond the rear of the chicken.

For entrees:
The preparation begins in the same way as for roasting. The leg sinew is then severed below the joint and the legs then inserted into these incisions. The first string of the truss is then made as for roasting, the second string remains the same, except that the prepared legs are made to lie forward, parallel with the breast.

The quick trade method is a figure-of-eight truss, which is made with one string and passes through all of the necessary points of the bird in order to maintain a good shape for final presentation. This truss should only be used when the cooked chicken is to be portioned in the kitchen as opposed to carved in the dining room.

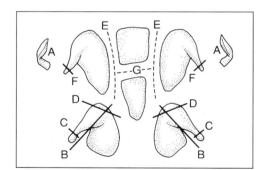

Trussing a bird

Jointing a bird

Cuts – Sauté
This is the jointing of a chicken from the raw state. The cuts are made mostly through the natural joints to produce two wings, two pieces of breast meat, two winglets, two drumsticks and two thigh pieces. The carcass can also be divided and is used in some recipes. When cut this way, a chicken will lend itself to many preparations i.e. fricassée, blanquette, sauté, curry, pies, etc.

OFFAL

Offal is the term used to describe edible parts of an animal taken from the inside of the carcass. The most commonly used offal are kidneys and liver, though this category also includes sweetbreads, tongue, brains, heart, tripe, trotters and tail.

The term 'offal' comes from the words 'off-all' i.e. the parts cut away when the carcass is being prepared for food.

Offal now includes the following:
(a) head
(b) feet
(c) lights
(d) liver
(e) kidneys
(f) stomachs
(g) sweetbreads
(h) tongue
(i) brains
(j) tails
(k) fat and suet
(l) horn/hoof/bone.

Liver (*Le foie*)

Liver should look fresh, moist and smooth and have a pleasant smell and colour. The liver from lamb, mutton, veal, pork and chicken can be used for cooking. Calf's liver is considered to be the most tender and flavoursome, while lamb's liver is also very tender but with a stronger flavour. The difference in quality is demonstrated in the vast price differentials.

Liver is reddish brown in colour, although pigs' is more mottled and has five lobes, as compared to three for both lambs' and ox liver.

Weight of liver per animal:
- Ox   5–6 kg   (12–14 lb)
- Sheep   0.5–1 kg   (1–2 lb)
- Pig   1–2 kg   (2–4 lb)

Ox liver is coarse and therefore cheaper, pig and lamb livers are used more widely in hotels and restaurants, but even today calf's liver is a delicacy. Liver and onions is a traditional British dish.

Preparing liver
1 Cut away any tubes and gristle.
2 Remove the outer membrane.
3 Cut as for recipe, usually thin slices cut on the slant.

Kidneys (*Le rognon*)

The kidneys from lamb, mutton, beef (calf and ox) and veal can be used for cooking, although calf's kidney is far superior in quality. Ox kidney requires longer cooking and is often blanched prior to cooking to remove excess uric acid. All kidneys should be moist, with any fat being brittle, and should smell pleasant.

Kidneys of most animals are put to good use, particularly that of ox and sheep. Ox kidney is the largest, the average weight 0.5 kg (1.25 lbs) each, divided into sections or lobes; lamb's and pig's kidneys are bean shaped and do not have lobed sections like the ox.

Lamb's kidney are 2–3 oz, and the pig's kidney are slightly larger. Pig's kidney is higher in calorific value but less than that of calf's kidney.

Preparing kidneys
1 Remove the outer membrane skin and cut away all fat and tubes.
2 Cut through the centre of the kidney without cutting right through: you should be able to open it out but keep it in one piece.
3 Trim off any fat or gristle found.
4 Cut or skewer whole as for recipe; if cutting, cut at a slant into thin slices, or dice.

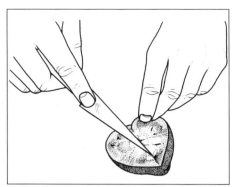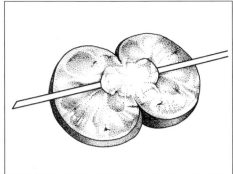

Left: slitting a kidney
Right: skewering a kidney

Tongue (*La longue*)

Ox tongues and lamb's tongues may be used in cooking. They should smell pleasant, and not require too much trimming from the root end. Both types may be used fresh, but ox tongues are also often used salted. They are suitable for boiling or braising.

Tongue is sometimes sold fresh but is now more common to purchase it in tins or pickled. The average weight of a tongue is 2–2.5 kg (4–5 lb). Ox tongue is the most popular and is used widely as a cold meat for sandwiches and salads; it is decorated as a joint for buffets.

Preparing tongue
1 Remove any bone and gristle from the throat end underside of the tongue.
2 If pickled, soak in cold water for 4–6 hours; if fresh, soak for 24 hours.

Sweetbreads (*Le ris*)

Neck and heart sweetbreads are commonly used. The heart bread is generally considered to be superior to neck sweetbreads. Both kinds should be fleshy, large and creamy-white with a clean pleasant smell. They can be braised or fried. As with kidneys, calf's sweetbreads are recognised as being of the highest quality, while ox-breads are not normally used except in the food processing industry.

Sweetbreads from sheep and calves are found in two sections. The *thymus* gland from the throat and the *pancreas* from beneath the stomach. Cream coloured ductless glands are large in young animals and reduce in size as the animals grow older.
● Calf's sweetbreads average 0.05 kg (1 lb).
● Lamb's sweetbreads average 100 gm (3–4 oz).

Sweetbreads are a good source of protein (17%).

Preparing sweetbreads
1 Soak in cold, salted water (2–3 hours) to remove any visible blood (disgorge).
2 Wash thoroughly under cold water.
3 Blanch, refresh and trim, removing the thin outer membrane.

Tripe

After being processed, stomachs are sold as tripe, usually from the ox. The ox and sheep are endowed with 4 stomachs and, in catering, the bleached tripe is used. The first 2 stomachs are used only, the smooth tripe and the honeycombed tripe.

The pig has only one stomach. The northern classical dish of tripe and onions is still eaten today, but is not as popular with the younger generations as it is with their grandparents. It has a low food value and requires long, slow cooking to render it digestible.

Essential knowledge

1 The main contamination threats when preparing and storing meat are caused by the following:
- storing uncooked and cooked meat and/or poultry together: this allows food poisoning bacteria to pass between the foods
- using the same preparation areas, equipment and utensils for preparing cooked and uncooked meat and/or poultry: this also allows food poisoning bacteria to pass between the foods
- using unhygienic preparation areas, equipment and utensils for preparing meat and poultry: food poisoning bacteria can pass from these to the foods
- leaving food uncovered: this allows pests carrying bacteria to contaminate the food
- inadequate personal hygiene: food poisoning bacteria can pass from your hands, mouth, nose or any open wounds to cooked or uncooked meat
- incorrect storage temperature: any meat or poultry stored at a temperature above 10 °C (50 °F) will become contaminated
- incorrect waste disposal.

2 You must always keep preparation, storage and cooking areas and equipment in a hygienic condition because:
- this prevents the transfer of food poisoning bacteria from working areas or equipment to food
- this prevents pest infestation in storage areas
- you are obliged by law to comply with food hygiene regulations.

Case study

Your meat fridge is full and does not seem to have any system of control, food is put in without careful wrapping and expensive meat, poultry and offal items are not dated or separated correctly.

1   *What steps need to be taken to store the meat, poultry and offal correctly?*
2   *How might the preparation be improved to maintain quality and minimise the risk of cross contamination?*
3   *Why should an effective system of control be implemented immediately?*
4   *What problems can occur through poor wrapping and hanging of meat and poultry?*
5   *Why should great care be taken with offal products when prepared and kept chilled until required.*
6   *Why should the fridge temperature be monitored twice daily?*

What have you learned

1   What safe working practices should be followed when preparing basic meat, poultry and offal dishes?
2   Why is it important to keep preparation and equipment clean and hygienic when preparing basic meat, poultry and offal dishes
3   What are the main contamination threats when preparing basic meat, poultry and offal dishes?
4   Why are time and temperature important when preparing and storing basic meat, poultry and offal?
5   What quality points should you look for in fresh meat, poultry and offal?
6   What basic preparation methods are suitable for different types of basic meat, poultry and offal dishes?
7   Which products could be used to substitute high-fat ingredients when preparing basic meat, poultry and offal dishes?
8   Which types of fats and oils contribute to healthy eating?
9   How does reducing the amount of salt in basic meat, poultry and offal dishes contribute to healthy eating practices?

| **ELEMENT 2:** | **Cook basic meat, poultry and offal dishes** |

The recipe is a guide and list of instruction on how to prepare and cook meat, poultry and offal dishes. Many excellent books have been produced to act as a professional guide to the trainee chef: Ceserani and Kintons' *Practical Cookery* is hailed as one of the best practical guides to professional cookery.

Cooking methods are divided into dry or wet methods of cookery:

Dry methods of cookery include:
- roasting
- grilling
- frying
- baking.

Wet methods of cookery include:
- boiling
- steaming
- combination cooking
- braising
- stewing.

> **MEMORY JOGGER**
>
> What are the dry methods of cookery

> **MEMORY JOGGER**
>
> What are the wet methods of cookery?

DRY METHODS OF COOKERY

Roasting

Roasting is cooking in dry heat with the aid of fat in an oven or on a spit. The purpose of roasting is to make the food easy to digest, safe to eat, palatable and to add variety to the menu.

True roasting is to expose meat or poultry to the radiant heat of an open fire e.g. spit-roasting. The spit constantly revolves to ensure even cooking and fat is used for basting to avoid the meat drying and burning. Owing to the many disadvantages of spit roasting, oven roasting has been developed in its place.

Oven roasting is the application of:
- applied dry heat
- forced air convected heat
- convected heat combined with microwave energy.

The initial heat seals the surface protein, adding colour and flavour. The heat is then reduced to prevent the outer surface over-hardening. Basting also has a softening affect.

Oven roasting is suitable for the following:
- Lamb: Best end, chump chop, leg, saddle and shoulder.
- Beef: Sirloin, wing rib, fillet, topside, fore and middle rib.
- Veal: Cushion, under cushion, thick flank and best end.
- Pork: Leg, loin, spare rib, belly and shoulder.
- Poultry and game: Chicken, duck, turkey, and venison if young and of high quality
- Vegetables: Potatoes, parsnips and onions.

Advantages of roasting
1 High quality foods are tender and succulent when roasted.
2 Foods take on a very distinctive and agreeable flavour.
3 Accurate temperature control is possible.

Time and temperature control

- Shelves and temperature must be set.
- Oven must be pre-heated.
- Bone proportion, shape, size and quality of food will affect cooking times.
- Internal temperature of food is critical in the roasting process.

Probes are used regularly in industry today to ensure that internal cooking temperatures are actually achieved. The tip of the probe is inserted into the meat or joint and the meter will display a digital or analogue reading of the temperature at the tip of the probe.

Meat such as pork must be thoroughly cooked, as proof, an accurate probe reading of 70 °C (158 °F) is required at the centre of the pork joint. Always visually check the juices are running clear.

Degree of Cooking

Beef	15 min per 450 g/1 lb plus 15 min over –	Underdone
Lamb	20 min per 450 g/1 lb plus 20 min over –	Cooked through
Lamb	15 min per 450 g/1 lb plus 15 min over –	Cooked pink
Mutton	20 min per 450 g/1 lb plus 20 min over –	Cooked through
Veal	20 min per 450 g/1 lb plus 25 min over –	Cooked through
Pork	25 min per 450 g/1 lb plus 25 min over –	Well cooked

English term	*French term*
Rare	au bleu
Underdone	saignant
Medium	à point
Well done	bien-cuit

Testing for degree of cooking when roasting
By pressing the surface of the meat, juice will be released. You can judge the degree of cooking by the appearance of this juice. If the juice is:

- Red = underdone
- Pink = medium
- Clear = cooked through.

Techniques associated with roasting

Boning	The removal of bones from raw meat to facilitate carving.
Tying	The securing of meat with string to retain shape.
Trussing	The tying of poultry with string to retain shape.
Trivet	A trivet is a metal grid used to lift the joint above the fat and the base of the cooking dish. The term is also used when the joint is lifted by using chopped bone or flavouring vegetables.
Basting	Frequent moistening of the joint with the cooking fat and juices is essential to prevent food drying and aid glazing (colouring).

Do this

- Find out how temperature probes work when fitted to combination ovens. How are they used to determine when meat or poultry are cooked?
- When using a meat probe fitted to an oven, what hygiene precautions need to be taken? Ask your chef to demonstrate what procedures are required.

Equipment maintenance

1   Trays should be strong, with handles, and in good repair.
2   Trays should be thoroughly washed, dried and placed upside-down on clean racks.
3   Ovens should be cleaned whilst warm with hot soapy water and a mild abrasive.
4   Oven trays and spits need to be thoroughly soaked before washing.
5   Ovens are inspected regularly and any fault discovered by the user must be reported immediately.

Safety when roasting
● Roasting trays should be of suitable size; if too small, basting becomes difficult and dangerous; if too large, fat in the tray will burn or catch fire spoiling the flavour of the dish.
● Handle hot roasting trays as little as possible; use a dry oven cloth.
● Do not carry hot dishes any further than necessary.
● Ensure you have made a space on the work bench to put the hot roasting tray onto before removing it from the oven.

GRILLING

Grilling is a fast method of cookery using radiant heat and is sometimes known as broiling (USA).
● Grilling makes food safe to eat, digestible and palatable.
● The speed of the cooking process introduces distinctive flavour, colour, texture and eating quality.
● Grilled food brings variety to the menu.

Methods of grilling

There are three methods of grilling:
1   Over heat (true grilling): charcoal, barbecues, gas or electrically-heated grills.
2   Under heat: gas or electric salamanders (oven-fired grills).
3   Between heat: electrically heated grill bars or plates.

Because grilling is such a rapid process using intense heat it is only suitable for certain cuts of the best quality meats; inferior produce would just toughen and become inedible. The effect of fierce radiated heat seals and coagulates the surface protein giving maximum flavour and appetising colour.

Meat, poultry and offal cuts are buttered with clarified butter or oil and then seasoned, turned over and the preparation repeated.

Care needs to be taken when seasoning such food to prevent the item from being made too salty or peppery.

Take account of the thickness and size of the food to be grilled. If the food is thick, then it would be wise to lower the grill tray setting to avoid burning or charring the top surface as this can become easily carbonised, resulting in waste.

Grilling is suitable for the following:
● Beef: Hind: rump, sirloin, wing rib and fillet. Fore: none.
● Lamb: Best end, saddle and kidney.
● Veal: Loin and best-end.
● Pork: Loin, trotters and kidney.
● Bacon: Collar, hock and gammon.
● Poultry: Chicken.
● Offal: Liver, kidneys.
● Fish: Cod, herring, mackerel, plaice, sole, whiting, salmon etc.
● Vegetables: Mushrooms, tomatoes.

Healthy eating

Grilling is a healthy alternative to frying as grilled food absorbs less fat.

MEMORY JOGGER

What are the three methods of grilling?

Testing for cooking when grilling
The colour of juices indicates how well done the grilled food is

English term	French term	Juices look:
Rare	(au bleu)	Red and bloody
Underdone	(saignant)	Reddish pink
Just done	(à point)	Pink
Well done	(bein cuit)	Clear

Grilled meat cuts

Techniques associated with grilling

1 *Basting:* All grilling equipment must be greased before and during cooking. Foods must be brushed with oil before and during cooking, this will stop them drying out.
2 *Flouring:* This is the passing of fish through seasoned flour.
3 *Crumbing:* Fish can be passed through flour, egg and breadcrumbs (pané) or butter and crumbs before traying up.

Charring and Searing

This is the marking of food with the aid of very hot grill bars or a hot iron, that gives the food its colour and flavour.

Equipment used for grilling

Grilling equipment includes: tongs, slices, palette knives and skewers. All equipment should be washed in hot soapy water after use, dried and stored. Check all equipment is safe and free from faults. Electrically or gas heated grills and salamanders should be inspected regularly by a qualified engineer.

General rules for grilling

1 Smaller, thinner items cook more quickly.
2 Seal and colour on hot, cook on cool part of equipment.
3 Food will dry out if cooked too slowly.
4 Basting and oiling of bars and equipment prevents drying out.

Safety when grilling

● Take care when moving hot parts of a grill or salamander.
● Take care when transporting cooked foods from a grill or salamander.
● Never place equipment on top of a heated salamander.
● If flames burn out of control due to a mixture of oil and water based juices, turn the gas or power supply off.
● Take care not to put yourself or others at risk.
● Clean the grill or salamander after use.
● When lighting a gas grill or salamander, take the lit wax taper to the grill and then turn on the gas supply, not the other way around.

Meat suitable for grilling

Beef grills

Entrecôte	Cut from a boned sirloin.
Entrecôte double	As above but twice as thick.
Entrecôte minute	Entrecote batted out.
Plank	Whole slice of boned rump (2 portions).
Rump	Whole portion cut from the plank.
Point	From the triangular end of the plank.
Chateaubriand	Cut from the head of the fillet (2 portions).
Filet (Fillet)	From middle fillet (untrimmed).
Filet minute	As above, but batted out.
Tournedos	From middle fillet, fat trimmed and strung.
Mignon	Tail of fillet, usually used for sauté.
T-bone	Slice of sirloin including bone and fillet.
Porterhouse	Slice of sirloin including bone.

Lamb grills

Chop	Cut from the loin (*côte*).
Chump chop	Cut from the top of the leg.
Cotelette (cutlet)	Cut from the best end.
Cotelette double	As above, but with 2 bones.
Filet mignon	Small strip from inside loin.
Noisette	From boned loin, batted pear shape.
Rosette	From boned loin.
Kidney (*rognon*)	Skinned, split and skewered.
Liver (*foie*)	Skinned, cut on slant-floured.

Pork Grills

Chop	As for lamb.
Fillet	As for filet mignon.
Kidney	As for lamb.

Bacon Grills

Back	Cut from loin (eye of meat).
Streaky	Cut from belly.
Gammon	Cut from top of leg.

Veal Grills

Chops	All as for lamb.
Cutlets	
Liver	
Kidney	

Poultry Grills

Whole small split birds (*poussin*).
Legs of larger birds coated with devilled mixture.
Livers, used for breakfast and savouries.

FRYING – SHALLOW-FRYING, SAUTÉ, GRIDDLING AND STIR FRYING

There are four main methods of frying used with meat:

Shallow-frying

Shallow-frying is the cooking of food in pre-heated shallow fat, oil or butter or a mixture or these commodities.

Foods are shallow-fried:

- to make foods safe, palatable, digestible and to add variety to the menu.
- to brown food giving it an interesting and attractive flavour.
- as a fairly quick method of cookery that can be used with tender foods which do not require too much cooking; a useful method to use for fast service styles or à la carte.

The food is placed presentation side down first in the pan to preserve the appearance; when this side is cooked it is turned uppermost. The fat is replaced each time. This method is applied to high quality small cuts of meat, poultry and offal as well as fish, whole or filleted cuts. Eggs, pancakes and some vegetables are also cooked by this method.

Effects of shallow-frying

The rapid cooking of shallow-fried items causes almost instant coagulation of surface protein, thus retaining all the juices. An agreeable colour and flavour are imparted to the food.

Techniques associated with shallow-frying

Proving: is the heating and oiling of a pan to stop sticking.
Coating: used to protect certain foods when cooking.
Browning: is achieved by the careful selection of pan, fat and temperature.
Tossing/Turning: is achieved by wrist and hand manipulation.
Holding: is to allow food to be kept hot after being cooked.
Draining: to allow surplus fat to be absorbed by kitchen paper prior to service.

Sauté

Sauté is a French term meaning to jump or leap. The first cooking stage is as for shallow-frying, where both sides are cooked or partly cooked. The fat is discarded and the sauté pan is de-glazed with one of the following:

1 Stock
2 Wine
3 Sauce
4 Liquor

This liquid forms an important contribution to the flavour of the eventual sauce as it is then combined with the cooked or part-cooked meat, poultry or offal and the cooking process is continued until the meat, poultry or offal is tender.

Only good quality cuts and small joints should be used. Vegetables and fish are cooked by this method. They can be finished or actually cooked by the sauté method.

Advantages of sauté

Sauté is a quick method of cooking high quality foods without burning, provided suitable fats and oils are available.

Time and temperature control

Foods that are cooked sauté must have a golden brown colour, this can only be achieved if the fat is very hot to start with and gradually reduced after turning the food.

Griddling

Foods are cooked on a pre-heated solid metal plate or griddle turning them regularly. Care needs to be taken not to over-cook one part of the food. This method is also used to cooked drop scones, pikelets, crumpets and fast food items such as bacon, burgers and eggs.

Stir-frying

This involves fast-frying in a wok or frying pan and is used extensively for vegetable and meat or poultry combinations. Oil is heated very hot and the ingredients are cooked in stages. It is a fast, ethnic form of shallow-frying. It is also sometimes used for deep-fried items.

Healthy eating

Less fat, in the form of polyunsaturated or low-fat spreads are used more widely in cooking, in restaurants and in the home. The public are more aware than they have been about the need to control their intake of high fat, high salt and low fibre foods.

BAKING

Baking is a dry method of cookery and food items are prepared and produced, baked in dry heat in a standard baking oven or forced air convector oven which reduces the time the food takes to cook.

Baking works by means of the convection and conduction of heat in a dry atmosphere, within a closed or confined chamber. The temperature of the baking process is directly related to the nature of the food to be baked.

High-sugar foods require a lower temperature to prevent caramelisation, whereas high-fat foods such as puff pastry used in en-croute dishes require a much higher temperature.

Foods are baked:
● to make foods crisp and coloured
● to reduce the percentage of fat or oil used in the cooking process
● to render food attractive by means of the colour and texture derived from the glazing and baking process
● to achieve the correct formulation of ingredient balance in complex recipes e.g. quiches, pies, tartes, en-papiotte dishes.
● to add variety to the menu

Methods of baking

1 Low crown bakers oven in dry heat.
2 High crown bakers oven in dry heat.
3 Baking in a roasting or standard oven.
4 Baking in a forced air convector oven.
5 Baking in a pastry oven.
6 Baking in a pizza oven or chamber.
7 Baking in a tunnel or rack oven.

Origins of baking

Baking food in a confined space using dry heat is the oldest method of cookery know to us. Aboriginal clay or earth ovens were used thousand of years ago. Baking is the application of heat energy which sets off or triggers chemical, mechanical and physical changes in the ingredients in the product being baked.

Ovens are pre-heated, with the temperature set according to the type of product being baked before products are placed in the oven. It is usual to set the oven slightly hotter than the required temperature at the start, to allow for the drop in heat as the foods to be baked absorb heat. This is especially true in baking of bread and fermented goods.

Principle of baking

Baking in an oven is in dry heat, food items are placed on baking trays, in baking tins or moulds or in special containers. Baking ovens can be fuelled by gas or electricity; bakers generally prefer to use electric ovens due to the constant temperature, as it is not subject to gas pressure fluctuations.

Dry heat convects as hot air within the confined space; this can be driven or assisted by a fan at the rear of the oven unit. Radiant heat is also given off from heat elements and from the wall linings of the oven. Food items also take in conducted heat via the container or tray they are in contact with.

Each product reacts in different ways and will require a specific baking temperature to produce the required colour and finish. A trained chef will know from experience how long and at what temperature the food should be baked.

During the baking process moisture is given off from most food items.

Types of food that are baked
- Quiches and tartlets
- Beef in pastry
- Ham in pastry
- Savouries
- Meat pies and pasties
- Hand raised pies, tarts and flans
- Fish
- Hot desserts, baked desserts served cold
- Bread, cakes and biscuits

WET METHODS OF COOKERY

Bacon cuts suitable for boiling

Boiling (*bouillir*)

Boiling is the cooking of prepared food in sufficient liquid at boiling point, this can be water, stock, milk or *court bouillon* (meaning 'short boil') a highly flavoured cooking liquor.

The purpose of boiling is:
● to make food safe to eat
● to make food digestible
● to make food palatable with a suitable texture.

Methods of boiling

1   Place food in boiling water and simmer.
2   Place food in cold liquid, bring to the boil, reduce heat and simmer.

Boiling is a suitable method of preparing the following:
● Stocks: fish, mutton, beef, chicken, veal, vegetable.
● Sauces: white, fawn, brown, curry, apricot.
● Soups: tomato, green pea, broths.
● Eggs: boiled egg
● Farinaceous: spaghetti, noodles, rice.
● Fish: skate, turbot, cod, salmon.
● Meats: silverside, brisket, leg of mutton, thin flank, leg of pork and gammon (bacon), chicken.
● Vegetables: carrots, potatoes etc. (almost all vegetables can be boiled).
● Desserts: milk puddings, sugar solutions.

Effects of boiling

Gentle boiling helps to break down the tough connective tissue (*collagen*) and turn this into soluble gelatine. This takes time and thus releases the fibre and makes these tender.

If food is boiled too rapidly the fibres fall apart and can make the meat tough, stringy or unsightly if very overcooked. Gentle heat will ensure coagulation of the proteins without hardening.

Advantages of boiling

● A quick, safe and simple procedure which takes advantage of cheaper, tougher joints or cuts of meat and poultry and renders them tender.
● Low in labour costs, producing nutritious and generally good flavoured stocks.
● Fat is driven off by this method of cookery and can be removed by skimming the liquor. This will enhance the healthy nature of the finished dish.

Remember: Boiling liquids can present a danger when the container is moved, or whilst boiling is in progress. Never allow the pot handle to protrude from the stove where it might be knocked by someone passing by.

Time and temperature control

Take care to ensure that a boiling temperature is maintained at all times and that you replace liquid as the volume evaporates.

You should understand the degree of cooking required for each particular meat, poultry or offal item being cooked. This involves a calculation based on the weight of the piece or pieces of meat, poultry or offal.

Techniques associated with boiling

Soaking
This involves covering the food with cold water prior to boiling vegetables. Soaking extracts salt from salted meats e.g. ham joint and softens dried vegetables and pulses.

MEMORY JOGGER

Why is boiling considered a healthier method of cookery?

Skimming
Skimming enables you to remove fat and impurities from the liquid surface.

Blanching
1   Place food into cold water, bring to the boil, remove from stove and run under cold water until clean e.g. sweetbreads, bones etc.
2   Plunge into hot water and refresh as above, used to remove tomato skins, blanch vegetables and cold buffet decorative media.

Equipment for boiling

● Stock pots and saucepans
● Boiling pans and bratt pans
● Sugar boilers and broiler pans

All equipment should be cleaned after use and dried well: stale water can be the cause of contamination. Handles, as already indicated must be secure at all times. It only takes a second to injure yourself or a colleague.

General safety rules when boiling

● Select pans that are not too small or too large.
● Skim frequently during cooking.
● Liquid should usually simmer and not boil – this will minimise shrinkage and evaporation.

STEAMING

Food is cooked by steam (moist heat) subject to various degrees of pressure, i.e. pressureless, low or atmospheric pressure or high-pressure steam units.

Steaming is the cooking by heat transfer using *conduction* and *condensation* (often known as latent heat). This can be either using a saucepan of water, low pressure or atmospheric steamer, high-pressure steamer or pressureless convection steamer.

Water is heated and turns to steam, this re-condenses and as it does so the heat from the steam (latent heat) is transferred to the food items and cooks it. It is important to ensure that the food is evenly set out on the tray or trivet.

Food cooked by the steaming method can be heated directly or indirectly by steam. Direct contact would be, for example, where food is cooked in a low pressure atmospheric steam unit, and indirect, such as sous-vide, where food is encapsulated in a plastic bag and all the oxygen removed.

Steaming is used as a method of cookery to preserve the nutritional content of the food. It also makes food easily digestible. Steamed food is generally associated with special diets, for the elderly or people with digestive disorders.

Steaming renders food safe to eat, providing the correct cooking times are followed.

Low-pressure or atmospheric steamer

Many catering establishments use low pressure or atmospheric steamers. In these a water reservoir at the base of the unit is heated, usually by gas. At 101 °C (214 °F) the water turns to steam. A ball valve mechanism returns the water to prevent the unit from drying out. Prepared food is placed in the steamer in stainless steel trays which are perforated with holes. These allow moisture to pass or drain back to the reservoir and prevent food from becoming soggy.

> **MEMORY JOGGER**
>
> Name the two types of pressure steamer?

Safety considerations

Take great care when opening this type of steamer. A door locking mechanism prevents the door from being opened directly. A wheel spindle handle is tightened down to create a pressure seal. Once the cooking time has lapsed the wheel is undone slowly allowing the built-up steam to dissipate slowly. When safe to do so the door lock is disengaged and the door opened. Some residual water will still be at or near boiling point so be very careful when removing the steamer trays.

This unit requires annual servicing and daily cleaning to prevent the build-up of fat and grease, which can cause problems with the ball valve mechanism and drain pipes. Where this type of steamer is built in it would be usual to have floor scupper drains to take away any water. This type of steamer also has an overflow outlet to prevent a build-up of water.

High-pressure steamer

High-pressure steamers are not as common as low-pressure units. They are expensive and require specialist installation. Only reputable contractors should be enlisted to install these units as they can be dangerous if incorrectly fitted.

The unit generates very high steam pressures in a sealed vessel or chamber. Food is cooked extremely quickly, only taking seconds to cook in some cases. The unit is filled, then switched on and the cooking time set by a dial. The food is placed in trays and the door is closed to seal a flexible diaphragm. The start button operates the high-pressure steam into the unit and once the set time elapses the steam is vented, via a special pipe assembly for safety.

High-pressure units vary in design but operate at approximately 10 (minimum) to 15 (maximum) lbs per sq. inch (70–105 kN/m^2) as opposed to the low-pressure unit only operating at a pressure of around 3 lbs per sq. inch (17 kN/m^2).

The high-pressure steamer is usually subject to special insurance conditions, e.g. being serviced and checked by a registered engineer. Insurance inspectors check to ensure this has been carried out correctly.

Cooking foods by the steaming method has some clear benefits over other methods:
- retention of nutrients
- flavours remain unaffected by colouring which occurs with grilling or frying
- food less likely to break up or shrink, as with other methods such as boiling
- little or no further action is required by the operative until the cooking process is complete.

High-pressure steam units retain the vitamins and nutrients and cook very quickly, making steamed food a healthy option. It is usually easier to digest, particularly for older people or customers with special diets. This seems to be an area which chefs are now required to know more about, e.g. fat-free diets and gluten-free diets are now more common. Steaming offers the chef the opportunity to cook a wide variety of vegetables, fish poultry and pudding items.

Steamed meat such as steak and kidney pudding are tenderised by this cooking process.

Steaming is suitable for the following:
- meat
- vegetables
- shell fish
- poultry
- fish (white)
- puddings
- stuffing.

COMBINATION COOKING

Combination cookery involves a number of cookery methods. Steaming is used with a convection oven; the oven or unit can be used conventionally as a roasting oven, roasting convector or, with the injection of low-pressure steam, a combination oven. Moisture loss from meats is reduced by the injection of steam during the cooking process.

Many different makes of combination oven are available. These ovens are also likely to be computerised so that the chef can pre-select the cooking temperature, steaming periods and convection periods as well as enabling the oven to hold the food items once cooked. A probe can also be inserted into the food to ensure the internal temperature is achieved.

Combination cookery harnesses the benefits of steaming with those of convection and roasting. Shrinkage of meat in particular improves the profitability of a joint such as sirloin of beef which is an expensive cut to purchase. Any saving made by using this type of cookery is a useful benefit to both the chef and proprietor.

Combination ovens are fairly costly but many more caterers are opting for this type of unit. More hotel and restaurant kitchen operations will opt for a combination cooker when replacing a traditional oven.

BRAISING

Braising is a combination of stewing and pot roasting that takes place in an oven-proof dish in liquid and combines conduction and convection. The purpose of braising is to make food safe, to add variety to the menu and to enhance flavour, texture and eating quality.

Methods of braising

There are two methods of braising:
1   Brown braising (*brun*)
2   White braising (*blanc*).

Brown braising
The joints of meat are firstly larded and marinaded, then sealed in hot fat and placed on a lightly fried bed of roots to which liquid is added in the form of brown stock, jus-lie or demi-glace. These are covered and cooked gently in oven. If braised in stock the sauce is formed by a reduction of the cooking liquid with equal quantities of demi-glace, reduced by half.

White braising
Except for sweetbreads and vegetables which are blanched, white braises are sealed in butter very lightly, as are the vegetables that form the bed of roots in the braising pan. White or veal stock is added with the meat in a covered pan and cooked in a moderate oven.

The accompanying sauce is made either by reducing the cooking liquor and adding demi-glace for a brown sauce or a velouté or cream for a white sauce.

Brown braising is suitable for the following:
● Lamb: hearts, chops, sweetbreads.
● Beef: olives, certain joints, liver, heart.
● Veal: leg joints and shoulder.
● Poultry and game: ducks, pheasants, venison.

White braising is suitable for the following:
● Sweetbreads, turkey, chickens, veal.
● Onions, leeks, cabbage, celery etc.

MEMORY JOGGER

What are the two main types of braising?

● Rice, as in a pilaff, can be braised using a different method.

Braising causes the breakdown of tissue fibre (*collagen*) in the structure of certain foods which softens the texture thus rendering the food tender and edible.

Braising is achieved in two stages:
1 The juices are driven to the centre of the meat, where pressure due to steam builds up (at this first stage the meat is still tough but appears cooked).
2 The juices then force their way out, causing the total breakdown of the almost indestructible fibre (collagen) .

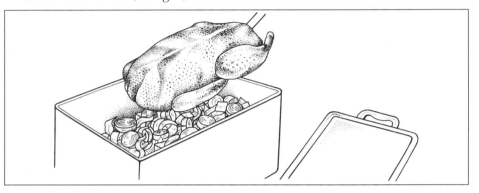

A braising pan with mirepoix

Advantages of Braising

● Advantage can be taken of the tougher and less expensive joints of meat and poultry which are rendered tender.
● The maximum nutritional value and flavour are retained.
● Variety and flavour can be added to a dish: the liquid will usually contain the marinade from the prepared joint.

Braising terms

Sealing:	the application of heat to the surface of the food to add colour and flavour.
Larding:	the insertion of pieces of pork fat into the grain of the meat to prevent drying out.
Marinading:	a highly flavoured pickling liquid that gives flavour and helps to moisten and tenderise: It contains wine, (red or white, according to colour of meat), carrot, onion, celery, parsley, herbs, oil and stock.
Sweating:	to cook and extract flavour from the food without colouring it.
Basting:	the frequent spooning of the cooking liquid over the food to moisten and prevent it drying out.
Refreshing:	to cool down food under running water.
Browning or sauté:	the application of heat to the surface of the food being cooked.

Equipment used for braising

An ovenproof dish or pan with a tight-fitting lid is essential for braising. Bratt pans are used for this in large kitchens. Rules for care of pans and soaking are as for roasting equipment.

General rules when braising

● It is not always possible to test braised meats in the same way as you would for roasting, as the juice will run clear at the end of the first stage and this will leave the meat very tough. You must also test the texture of the meat for tenderness.

- Braises should not be over-thickened; the sauce should be light with only the correct proportion of thickening agent used.
- The cooking liquor may need to be adjusted during the cooking.
- Avoid overcooking as this will break up the texture of the food, spoil the flavour and make the meat very dry and unpalatable.
- By removing the lid near the end of cooking and basting with the cooking liquor a glaze can be built up to aid presentation.
- Safety precautions to be taken when braising are as for roasting (see p. 54).

STEWING

Stewing is the slow cooking of small pieces of meat in the minimum of liquid (water, stock or sauce) in a suitable pot with a tight-fitting lid on top of the stove. The purpose of stewing is to produce an acceptable flavour, texture and eating quality in cheaper and tougher cuts of meat. Stewing is both economical and nutritional.

Methods of stewing

All stews are thickened by one of three methods:
1 The unpassed ingredients (i.e. those not strained out) in the stew (e.g potatoes in Irish stew).
2 Cooking in a thickened sauce (brown stew i.e. ragout or navarin).
3 Thickening the cooking liquor after cooking (white stew i.e. blanquette).

Stewing is suitable for the following:
Lamb: shoulder, breast, middle neck and scrag end.
Beef: (hind): shin, topside, thick flank; (fore): chuck rib sticking piece, plate, leg of mutton cut and kidneys.
Veal: shoulder, neck end, scrag, breast and kidneys.
Poultry: chicken and hare (cooked in e.g. jugged hare, fricassées and curries).
Vegetables: mixed vegetables in e.g. marrow provençale, ratatouille.
Fish: mixed fish and/or shellfish e.g. French fish stew (*bouillabaisse*).

(Pork is not generally a suitable meat for stewing.)

Effects of stewing

1 Stewing causes the breakdown of connective tissue fibre (*collagen*). This becomes gelatinous and allows the fibres to fall apart and become digestible.
2 Unlike with boiling, the protein in food is coagulated without becoming tough.
3 If a stew is left to cook for too long a period the base of the stew in the pan can burn, and the meat, or poultry in particular, will fall apart and be stringy.

Stewing terms
Blanching and refreshing:	Food is covered with cold water and brought to the boil, then rinsed under cold water until clean and cold.
Sealing and browning:	Food is shallow-fried in fat to enhance flavour and colour.
Blending:	Gradually mixing in the warm liquid to the main ingredients of the stew.

Equipment used for stewing

Sauce, boiling and bratt pans can all be used for stewing. Ovenproof dishes can be used to stew food in the oven. Care of pans and cleaning is as for roasting (see p. 54).

MEMORY JOGGER

Why is stewing used for poorer quality cuts of meat, poultry and offal?

Advantages of stewing

- Makes good use of the tougher and less expensive cuts of meat.
- The maximum nutritional value and flavour are retained.
- A variety of flavours can be added to the menu.
- Economical in labour as bulk cooking lends itself to stewing.
- Leaner trimmings or cuts of meat can be used, reducing the fat percentage contained in the recipe.
- Portion control can be maintained by accurate measurement of the stew using portion control utensils.
- Stews can be bulked out, e.g. with root vegetables, potatoes etc, thus adding to the fibre content of the dish.
- Less wasteful, (compared to a carved slice or portion of meat such as leg of lamb or chicken).

Healthy eating

The modern chef can use a wide range of healthier food ingredients to maintain a good balance in the diet for their customers, adding fibre wherever possible, reducing the salt and fat or replacing sauces with more healthy options. Stewing techniques provide the chef with options to reduce the oil and fat intake, preserve essential vitamins and nutrients and trace elements.

General rules when stewing

- Over-cooking causes the spoilage of texture and flavour, over- evaporation of liquid, breaking up of the fibre and discolouration.
- Stews should be light in consistency so great care should be paid to the use of thickening agents. The consistency should be checked during the cooking process.
- Safety precautions should be taken, as for roasting (see p. 54).

FINISHING METHODS

Garnishing

When a chef has taken a long time and used costly ingredients to produce a dish then the finishing of that dish needs to be high quality and done with care and attention to detail. Each dish needs to be cooked according to the recipe instructions and customer preferences. But the most essential part of the sales of food is how it looks and tastes; garnishing the food provides the finishing touch to complete the preparation and cooking process. Garnishing adds small delicate colours, flavours or textures to add to the overall presentation and provides added value to the food picture.

Many of the classical dishes prepared and cooked have standard garnishes recognised across the world. Food should not be over-dressed or this will spoil the desired effect. Stand back from the dish, close your eyes and open them in front of the dish. What impression does it give? Experience will develop your skills in this important area of finishing dishes.

Glazing

Glazing adds a colour, shine or finish to a dish, achieved by brushing with clarified butter, basting with fat and juices or by brushing with oil.

Coating

Coating means covering the dish or food item with a prepared sauce to aid the flavour and look of the finished dish. Preparing the sauce to produce the right consistency is vital if the sauce is to hold on the food and not run off before the dish reaches the table (see p. 33).

QUALITY POINTS WHEN COOKING MEAT, POULTRY AND OFFAL

Finished dishes should be of the best quality when completed in line with the standard of the establishment, the price charged and the availability of good produce. Many businesses have strict training to ensure the staff understand how each dish is completed prior to service.

- *Aroma:* the smell of food is part of the sales portfolio and provides a unique atmosphere to alert the customer of the experience awaiting them. The combination of flavours entices customers and provides an indication of quality.

- *Texture:* Getting the cooking right to produce the right sort of texture according to the food being cooked is crucial, especially where meat is concerned. Over-cooked and the dish can be tough and unpleasant to eat, under-cooked and blood juices might put the customer off. Use texture to maximise the eating experience; training will develop the skill and knowledge required to get this essential area of cooking right.

- *Flavour:* Producing flavour is sometimes the hardest aspect of cooking and is closely linked to time, temperature and preparation phases in the cooking process. Tasting dishes hygienically to develop your powers of flavour is a basic fundamental aspect of any chef's training and requires practice.

- *Appearance:* The overall look of the meat, poultry or offal depends on the presentation of the finished dish: colours, garnishing and saucing are integral parts of the appearance of each individual dish. Getting this right is important if repeat business is to be maintained and developed.

Do this

- Watch steaks being prepared and cooked rare, underdone, medium and well done. Notice the differences in the appearance of the cooked steaks.
- Find out how long and at what temperatures you would expect to roast, a leg of lamb, a top side of beef and a loin of pork.
- Find three example recipes for boiled meat dishes. Notice the differences. How long does each need to be boiled for? Is the meat started in cold or hot water or stock? Are the final dishes served hot or cold?

Essential knowledge

Always cook meat and poultry for the correct time and at the correct temperature. Failure to do so may result in:

- food poisoning. High risk foods such as chicken and pork must always be thoroughly cooked, to kill off bacteria or worms that may be present
- an incorrectly cooked meat or poultry dish. The finished dish depends on your achieving the right degree of cooking at each stage
- food shrinkage. Some foods will shrink if cooked for too long a time or at too high a temperature
- loss of moisture. Food will become dry if cooked for too long or too fast using a dry process
- an uncooked stuffing. The temperature must be high enough to cook the stuffing and prevent bacteria from multiplying, while not so high that the outside (meat) is burned.

What have you learned

1 What safe working practices should be followed when cooking basic meat, poultry and offal dishes?
2 Why is it important to keep cooking areas and equipment clean and hygienic when preparing and cooking basic meat, poultry and offal dishes?
3 What the main contamination threats are when cooking basic meat, poultry and offal dishes?
4 Why are time and temperature important when cooking and storing basic meat, poultry and offal dishes?
5 What basic cooking and finishing methods are suitable for different types of basic meat, poultry and offal dishes?
6 How does increasing the fibre content of basic meat, poultry and offal dishes can contribute to healthy eating practices?

Get ahead

- Obtain a copy of the *Advanced Practical Cookery* by Ceserani, Kinton and Foskett. This book contains many interesting ethnic and vegetarian dishes for Level 3 NVQ and is a useful reference source for extending your skills and knowledge from Level 2 toward Level 3.
- Investigate other recipe and text books and obtain a copy of the Level 3 National Standards to find out more about the training requirements at this level.

Prepare and cook basic fish dishes

This chapter covers:
ELEMENT 1: **Prepare fish for cooking**
ELEMENT 2: **Cook and finish basic fish dishes**

What you need to do

- Prepare preparation and cooking areas and equipment ready for use. then clean correctly after use.
- Prepare fish correctly and as appropriate for individual dishes.
- Combine prepared fish with other ingredients ready for cooking where appropriate.
- Cook fish dishes according to customer and dish requirements.

- Finish and present fish dishes according to customer and dish requirements.
- Plan your work, allocating your time to fit daily schedules, and complete the work within the required time.
- Carry out your work in an organised and efficient manner, taking account of priorities and any laid down procedures or establishment policy.

What you need to know

- The type, quality and quantity of fish required for each dish.
- What equipment you will need to use in preparing fish.
- Why time and temperature are important when preparing and cooking fish.
- Why it is important to keep preparation, cooking, storage areas and equipment hygienic.

- What the main contamination threats are when preparing, cooking and storing raw fish and cooked fish dishes.
- How to satisfy health, safety and hygiene regulations, concerning preparation and cooking areas and equipment, and how to deal with emergencies.

INTRODUCTION

The catering industry in the UK is well supplied with a wide range of both salt and freshwater fish. A highly organised fishing industry distributes its catch in prime condition. either fresh, frozen or chilled. Extensive farming of freshwater fish has also increased the availability of certain species, so that certain types of fish are no longer regarded as luxury commodities. However, exotic species of fish from other parts of the world are also readily available and appear regularly on menus.

Fish is an important contributor to a well-balanced diet, being high in protein, rich in certain vitamins yet low in fat and easy to digest. It does, however, require careful handling and cooking to maximise its benefits to the consumer.

The correct place of fish on the formal menu is as a separate course directly before and as a contrast to the meat course. Today fish is often used in other sections of the menu, for instance as an hors d'oeuvre or as part of a salad, savoury or farinaceous dish. In modern menus fish is frequently offered as a main course choice suitable for luncheon or dinner and this reflects its popularity with the modern palate.

ELEMENT 1:   Prepare fish for cooking

CLASSIFICATION OF FISH

Fish are normally classified for culinary purposes as *round* or *flat* fish. This very broad classification may be sub-divided into *white* and *oily* fish, encompassing the freshwater and sea-water varieties.

The following tables give examples of some fish in general use and a comparison of white and oily fish.

Fish classifications		
Flat white	*Round white*	*Round oily*
Brill	Cod	Anchovy
Dover sole	Haddock	Eel
Halibut	Hake	Herring
Lemon sole	Huss	Mackerel
Plaice	Whiting	Red mullet
Turbot	Monkfish	Salmon
		Salmon trout
		Sardine
		Trout
		Tuna
		Whitebait

A comparison of white and oily fish

White fish	*Oily fish*
White flesh	Dark flesh
Oil is stored in the liver	Oil is distributed throughout the flesh
May be round or flat	Always round
Vitamins A and D found only in the liver	Vitamins A and D dispersed throughout the flesh

> **Healthy eating**
>
> Oily fish e.g. trout, herring, mackerel, inevitably contain amounts of fat, but the fat is rich in the essential polyunsaturated fatty acids which help protect against heart disease.

> **Healthy eating**
>
> Fish contains a fat called monounsaturated fat. This has no influence on cholesterol levels and can be included in diets without detrimental effect.

QUALITY POINTS

Absolute freshness is essential when purchasing fresh fish to ensure a high quality dish. The flavour and appearance of fresh fish quickly deteriorates if it is stored incorrectly or not used within a short space of time. This means that fish must be purchased daily from a reputable supplier if standards and quality are to be maintained.

Frozen fish, if properly processed, defrosted and prepared, is a useful substitute when the fresh item is not available. Note, however, that it is not suitable for all

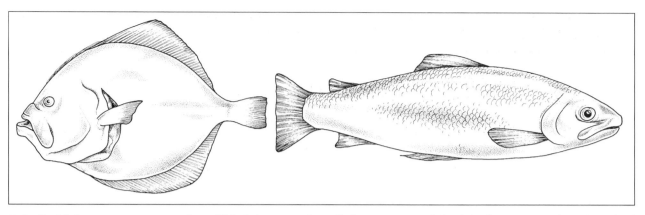

Left: 'flat' fish
Right: 'round' fish

recipes. This is because the cellular structure of the fish changes as it freezes. When preparing mousselines for example, it is difficult to achieve good results with fish that has been frozen because the protein needed to bind the cream with the fish is broken down during the freezing process.

Factors indicating freshness in whole wet fish
- Scales: plentiful, firmly attached, moist and shiny.
- Eyes: bright, clear and full (not sunken).
- Skin: bright, with a sheen and evidence of slime.
- Gills: bright when lifted, deep pink in colour, not sunken or dry.
- Flesh: firm to the touch (the flesh should spring back to its original shape when pressed).
- Smell: wholesome and pleasant, no hint of ammonia or any offensive odour.

Factors indicating freshness in cuts of wet fish
- The flesh should be firm to the touch.
- The fish should have a clean and pleasant smell.
- There should not be any areas of discolouration (through bruising or blood clots).

Factors indicating quality in frozen fish
- There should not be any evidence of dehydration or freezer burn.
- The packaging, if applicable, must be undamaged.
- There should be minimum fluid loss during thawing.
- Once thawed the flesh should still feel firm.

STORING FRESH FISH

Fresh fish should be purchased and used daily where possible. However, due to fluctuations in business you may need to store fish for short periods.

When storing fish:
- wash the fresh fish thoroughly under cold running water and store in a refrigerator designed specifically for storing fish
- place the fish in a container with holes at the base. Cover the fish with crushed ice to prevent any surfaces from drying, allowing the drips from the ice to drain away through the holes in the container. Change the ice daily
- store the fish immediately after delivery at a temperature of 1–2 °C (34–36 °F); just above freezing point
- store whole fish separately from fillets to minimise the risks of cross-contamination
- store frozen fish at −18 °C (0 °F) or below and use it in strict rotation
- store ready-prepared, cooked fish products separately from raw products to minimise any risk of transference of harmful bacteria from raw to cooked foods
- follow a strict rotation policy on all purchases of fish to ensure maximum freshness.

> **MEMORY JOGGER**
>
> At what temperature should fresh fish be stored?

STORING AND THAWING FROZEN FISH

Frozen fish must be purchased commercially, frozen and then stored in an appropriate freezer at −18 °C (0 °F). The length of storage will vary according to the product and the type of packaging (certain products have recommended storage times of one, two or three months, which is stated on the packaging).

Frozen fish must be be defrosted in a refrigerator (preferably overnight) to ensure that it is evenly thawed prior to cooking. Forced defrosting (i.e. in water or at room temperature) is a potentially dangerous practice as bacteria multiply in a warm environment.

Once defrosted, frozen fish must be used quickly, but should be stored as for fresh fish before use.

Under no circumstances should defrosted frozen fish be re-frozen. This is potentially hazardous to health.

Do this

- Identify and categorise four flat white fish, four round white fish and four oily fish currently stored in your establishment.
- Prepare a written checklist for inspecting a delivery of fresh fish.
- Check a delivery of fish against your checklist and discuss the results with your supervisor.
- Check the current operating temperature of your fish refrigerator using a thermometer.
- List the items currently in stock in the fish refrigerator and check their dates of purchase to ensure a strict rotation policy is being observed.

HEALTH, SAFETY AND HYGIENE

Observation of the basic rules of food safety and hygiene (as outlined in Units NG1 and 2ND11 of the Core Units book) are critical when handling fish as fish is a high risk food.

Note the following points before you start to prepare or cook any fish dishes:
- always use the correct colour-coded board for preparing raw fish, using a different board for cooked items
- do not work directly on the table. Keep your chopping board clean by using fresh disposable wipes
- use equipment reserved for the preparation of raw fish. Where this is not possible, wash and sanitise equipment before use and immediately after use
- work with separate bowls for fish offal, bones and usable fish; never mix them together as the risk of contamination from the offal is high
- store fish correctly at the correct temperatures (see *Storing fresh fish*, page 71)
- work away from areas where cooked foodstuffs are being handled
- keep your preparation area clean
- wash your equipment, knives and hands regularly and use a bactericidal detergent or sanitising agent to kill bacteria
- dispose of all swabs immediately after use to prevent contamination from soiled wipes.

Essential knowledge

It is important to keep preparation and storage areas and equipment hygienic in order to:
- prevent the transfer of food poisoning bacteria to food
- prevent pest infestation in storage areas
- ensure that standards of cleanliness are maintained
- comply with food hygiene regulations.

PLANNING YOUR TIME

When preparing fish, certain preparations and cooking methods are more time-consuming than others. Some dishes may require only minutes and can be undertaken at a specific time (i.e. cooked to order *à la carte* style), while others may either require lengthy preparation before cooking or use fish stocks or court-bouillons which must be prepared in advance.

Before starting any procedure, identify the basic culinary preparations required to complete the dish to the required establishment standard. Plan your approach to the dish carefully, addressing the longest and most time-consuming jobs first. Make sure that you have everything in place before starting to prepare a dish. Familiarise yourself with all ingredients and cooking and storage methods necessary.

EQUIPMENT

Before starting to prepare fish, decide what equipment and utensils you will need to complete the process. Place them ready to use, making sure they are clean. You may need to use mechanical equipment such as mincers or food processors; do not use these unless you have received instruction from your supervisor on how to use them and you are familiar with the safety procedures outlined in Units 1ND1 and 2ND17 in the Core Units book.

Knives

You will need a variety of cook's knives to prepare fish efficiently. Read Unit 1ND2: *Maintain and handle knives* in the Core Units book and make sure that you are familiar with the types of knives and the safety points listed there. Remember that you are less likely to have an accident using a sharp knife than when using a blunt one.

You will need to be familiar with the following types of knives and cutting implements when preparing fish:
- *filleting knife:*   a thin, flexible blade ideal for following bones closely
- *fish scissors:*   used for trimming fins and tails in fish preparation
- *fish steak knife:*   a long, firm blade with a curved end ideal for slicing through the skin, flesh and bones of fish
- *carving knife:*   a long, thin, slightly flexible blade used for portioning both raw and cooked fish.

Do this

- Prepare a simple written *do's and don'ts* list of procedures when working with fresh fish.
- Prepare two working time plans: one for fish cooked *à la carte* style (to order), and a second for a fish cooked *table d'hôte* style or for a banquet or function.
- Identify:
  - all tools from a knife set that may be used in fish preparation
  - three pieces of mechanical equipment that may be used in fish preparation.

PREPARATION METHODS

Washing

It is essential to wash all fresh fish under cold running water in order to:
- remove any coating of slime which may be present
- facilitate ease of handling.

MEMORY JOGGER

What procedures should be undertaken immediately after completing the gutting of fish?

Washing should be carried out:
● before any preparations commence
● during the preparation process (particularly when removing scales)
● after removing the intestines, to ensure that no traces of blood are left on the bone.

Fish should be washed at all stages of preparation and cutting and immediately before cooking. The most notable exception is when preparing fresh river trout for the classic dish *Truite au bleu* (Blue trout), where the natural skin slime is essential to maintain the distinctive colour achieved in cooking. In this case only the belly cavity should be washed.

Trimming

This is the removal of surplus items such as the gills, fins, eyes (where necessary) and head (if appropriate). Trimming is also an essential part of the fish filleting process, necessary to achieve a neat, well presented piece of fish ready for cooking.

Fish scissors are used to trim fish. The technique involves cutting along the natural line of the fish fin where it joins the body. If scissors are not available a cook's knife may be used.

Removing the fins and scales: cut off the fins using fish scissors. Hold the fish by its tail, preferably over the sink or clean paper, then scrape away the scales. Work towards the head.

Essential knowledge

The main contamination threats when preparing and storing uncooked fish are as follows:
● contamination through incorrect storage temperatures. Fish must be stored at temperatures of 1–2 °C (34–36 °F) and packed in ice which is changed daily
● cross-contamination between cooked and uncooked food during storage. Fish must be stored in separate refrigerators to any other foods and the cooked and uncooked fish kept away from each other
● cross-contamination from unhygienic equipment, utensils and preparation areas
● contamination from inadequate personal hygiene, i.e. from the nose, mouth, open cuts and sores or unclean hands
● contamination through incorrect thawing procedures when fish is prepared from frozen
● contamination through the fish being left uncovered
● contamination through incorrect disposal of waste.

Gutting

Many of the fish commonly found in culinary use such as cod, haddock, sole, place and whiting are delivered already opened and gutted; inspect these carefully to ensure they are thoroughly clean. Further minor cleaning may be necessary, such as scraping any congealed blood from under the spinal vertebrae or removing any hard membrane from the inner surface of the abdominal cavity. Many round fish such as herrings, mackerel, salmon and trout may be delivered whole and these require gutting. A general procedure may be followed as given below.

Method
1 Remove the gills and fins using fish scissors (see above).
2 Make an incision from the anal vent along the belly of the fish to two-thirds the length of the fish.
3 Remove the gut or intestines, pulling them out with your fingers or the handle of a spoon (for large fish use the hooked handle of a small ladle).

4   Remove any congealed blood lying under the vertebrae or backbone and wash the fish thoroughly.

Certain preparations may require the belly to be left intact. If this is the case the gut may be removed through the gills slits. This requires skill and care in handling the fish, and should not be attempted unsupervised.

Gutting a round fish

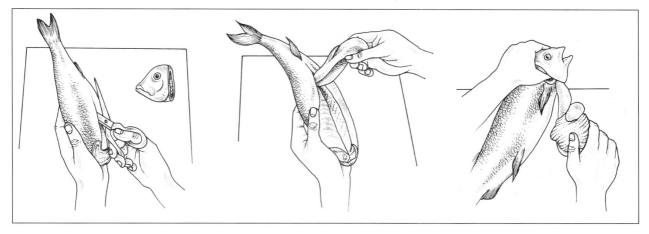

Filleting

Filleting is the neat removal of the flesh of the fish from its skeleton to yield sections of fish flesh free from skin and bone, making the fish easier to eat. Correctly removed fillets are evenly shaped and smoothly cut without ridges. There should not be any flesh remaining on the skeleton of the fish.

Flat fish yield four fillets (two from each side) which are known as *quarter-cuts*. Small flat fish are sometimes prepared into two fillets (one from each side) which are known as *cross-cuts*. Round fish only yield two fillets (one from each side of the vertebrae). These also require further trimming to remove all bones; many of the smaller bones are removed using stainless steel pliers (kept specifically for that purpose) or tweezers.

Filleting a flat fish
1   Lay the fish flat on the appropriate chopping board.
2   Cut down the natural centre line of the fish to the bone. Make your initial incision as close to the head as possible to minimise loss of flesh; finish at the tail.

> **MEMORY JOGGER**
>
> How many fillets are obtained from
> (a) flat fish
> (b) round fish?

Filleting a flat fish

3 Work from the centre, cutting with smooth sweeping strokes to the left, keeping the knife pressed against the bone. Detach the fillet from the bone, lifting the fillet away from the bone as you cut.
4 Repeat the process for the second fillet.
5 When the fillets have been completely removed, turn the fish over and repeat on the underside to yield the four fillets.

Filleting a round fish
1 Lay the round fish on the appropriate chopping board (the fish must be prepared for filleting: i.e. cleaned, gutted and trimmed).
2 Working from the head to tail, cut down the backbone following the vertebrae and over the rib cage. Lift the fillet as you cut so that you have more control over the action of the knife.
3 Detach the fillet at the tail and the head.
4 Turn the fish over and repeat to yield two fillets. (The head may be removed before filleting to make it easier to detach the fillets.)

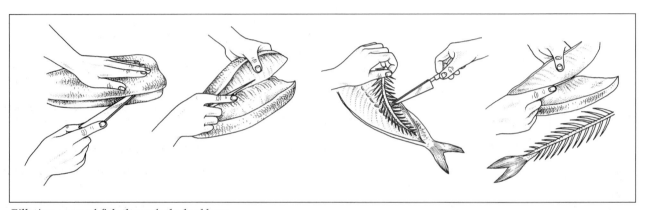

Filleting a round fish through the backbone

Boning a round fish without separating the fillets
This process is necessary where the recipe requires the fillets to still be attached for presentation purposes. It is commonly used with small round fish such as trout or herring or where the fish is to be filled with a stuffing (farce), when the head and tail are also left attached.

Method
1 Clean the fish in the normal manner but remove the intestine through the gill slits at the back of the head.
2 Lay the fish on the appropriate chopping board with the tail close to you.
3 Using the point of a filleting knife, open the back halfway through on the left side of the fish, following the bone closely. When this is complete, turn the fish over and proceed in the same way on the right side, separating the flesh from the bone halfway through the fish.
4 Hold the backbone between two fingers, then draw the tips of your fingers along the backbone from head to tail, separating the flesh from the bone.
5 Using fish scissors, cut the backbone at the head and the tail.
6 Pull the bone out by gently lifting it up with one hand while supporting the flesh with your other hand.

This is a difficult procedure requiring some practice and supervision to perfect the technique. The benefits of this method are in the final presentation of the fish dish, the most common example being *Truite meunière Cleopatre*.

Do this

- Wash and descale a round fish and a Dover sole. How do the two preparations differ?
- Trim a flat fish and a round fish before filleting. Compare the trimmings for quantity, style and ease of removal.
- Gut and clean a fresh salmon or trout. Weigh the fish prior to gutting and again after; compare the weight loss.
- Fillet any flat fish and any round fish. Note the difference in the techniques used and compare the length of time taken to fillet both.
- Prepare a herring or trout leaving the fillets intact and identify a suitable culinary use.

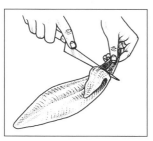

Skinning a fillet of fish

Skinning

It is normal culinary practice to remove the skin from most fillets of fish where this can be done without harming the flesh. The skin should also be removed from whole flat fish, and in all cases the dark skin must be removed before cooking.

Skinning a fillet of fish

1 Place the fillet skin-side down on the appropriate chopping board.
2 Cut through the flesh to the skin at the tail or tip end of the fillet.
3 Hold the fillet firmly by the tail with one hand.
4 Turn the fish filleting knife to an angle of 45 ° and push and cut forwards with the knife using a sawing motion, at the same time pulling the skin of the fish with the other hand until the skin and flesh are detached from each other.
5 Keep the blade as close to the skin as possible, but do not cut through it: the skin of the fish must be taut at all times to minimise loss of flesh in the skinning process.
6 Trim carefully as required to achieve a neat and sharp appearance.

Flat fish (e.g. lemon sole or plaice) may be skinned whole from head to tail using your thumb and fingers to detach the skin without damaging the flesh.

Dover sole is skinned tail to head with the edges loosened first by the thumb to minimise the risk of tearing the flesh. Dover sole is always skinned before filleting.

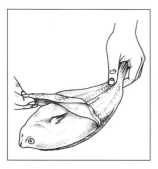

Skinning a whole Dover sole

Portioning fish

The amount of fish allowed per person will depend on the following:
- the type of fish being served
- the degree of preparation
- the method of cookery and, if appropriate, the sauce or garniture which will accompany it
- the cost of the raw commodity
- the pricing structure or policy of the establishment
- the customer requirements
- the menu type the fish appears on; i.e. *table d'hôte*, *à la carte* or banquet
- whether it represents a separate course as part of a menu or a main course choice.

You will need to discuss portion size with your supervisor in order to avoid making costly mistakes, taking into account the points listed above. Fish is portioned not only for effective cost control but importantly for *standardisation of cooking times*. By dissecting the fish into similar muscle tissue forms we control and select the most appropriate method of cookery to maximise the quality and flavour of a delicate product.

The *three P's* are essential for achieving excellent results in fish preparation:
- Purchasing
- Preparation and
- Portioning.

MEMORY JOGGER

Why is fish portioned?

The quality of every finished fish dish depends upon the quality of preparation prior to cooking.

Stuffing fish

Whole round fish
When a round fish has been boned with the head and tail intact (see page 76), the cavity in the belly forms an ideal pocket for filling with a stuffing to enhance the flavour of the fish and gives an added dimension to the concept of fish cookery.

The filling or *farce* may be a simple mixture of breadcrumbs, herbs and spices; a duxelle (such as a simple mushroom duxelle); or a more sophisticated fish mousseIine or quenelle mixture (where a purée of fish is bound with egg white, cream and seasoning to form a light forcemeat).

The basic rules are simple:
● ensure the belly cavity is thoroughly clean and dry
● do not over-fill the fish with any farce or stuffing as this may cause the fish to burst or distort in shape
● allow a longer cooking time for stuffed fish to ensure heat penetration and correct cooking
● select the cooking method appropriate to the type of farce used.

Flat fish
Flat fish may also be boned and stuffed, normally with a mousseline type of forcemeat. This is a complex procedure and requires skill and practice to achieve high quality results both in preparation and in cooking.

Fish fillets
Fillets of fish may also be stuffed. This is simply done by placing a little filling on the skin side of the seasoned fillet and rolling the fillet from head to tail. This is called a *paupiette* (see below).

FISH CUTS AND PREPARATIONS

Whole fish may be divided into smaller pieces to accommodate various cookery processes, to maximize cost efficiency and to standardize cooking times (see *Portioning fish*, page 77). Importantly, these cuts often also add to the overall presentation of the dish and usually make the fish easier for the customer to eat.

Cuts of fish. From top left (clockwise): paupiette, en goujons, tronçons, délice, darne

Case study

In the unforeseen absence of a supervisor, a young chef feels sufficiently confident to order the salmon required for the following day's function.

The function is for 100 people and the salmon is the main course dish. He phones the fishmonger direct and places the order for fresh salmon, knowing that he requires approximately 125 g per head. He therefore orders $100 \times 125\ g = 12.5\ kg$ of fresh salmon.

The fishmonger duly delivers and the chef diligently prepares and portions the fish correctly, yet finds that he is a considerable number of portions short.

1   In what ways did the young chef act incorrectly?
2   What procedures should have been in place to prevent this occurrence?
3   Exactly why was the young chef short of portions and what should be his future course of action for re-ordering to prevent a repetition of the shortfall?

Common cuts identified in fish cookery and menu terminology include:
- fillet or *filet*: the flesh of the fish free from skin and bone, presented as long flat fillets
- *délice*: a fillet of fish which has been trimmed and neatly folded for presentation prior to cooking
- *paupiette*: a small fillet of fish lightly flattened, usually spread with a stuffing or fish farce, rolled from head to tail and wrapped in a buttered paper (to retain the shape and protect the flesh from drying out during the cooking process)
- *goujons*: strips of fish cut at an angle diagonally from a fillet approximately 6–8 cm (2½–3 in) long and 15 mm thick
- *suprême*: a section of fish cut across and on the slant from a large fillet of fish
- *médaillon*: cut as for a supreme (above) but further trimmed to a neat oval or round shape
- steaks –
  - *darne*: a section of fish cut across and through the bone of a whole round fish
  - *tronçon*: a section of fish cut from a large flat fish through the bone.

Note that *darnes* and *tronçons* are cooked *with* the skin. The skin is removed just before service.

Do this

- Skin the fillets of any small flat fish (e.g. plaice or lemon sole) and any fillets of large fish (e.g. salmon). Compare the technique to that of skinning a Dover sole.
- Identify four fish that are filleted then skinned and one fish that is skinned then filleted.
- With your supervisor, prepare and cut *darnes* and *tronçons* of fish. Weigh them and record the weight. Prepare and cut *filets* or *délice* of plaice or sole, then weigh them and record the weight.
- Look at four or five fish dishes and compare the amounts of fish required for a portion. Identify the raw weight costs of the fish used.
- Prepare a fish forcemeat from whiting using a fish mousseline recipe, then prepare *paupiettes* of lemon sole or plaice. Record the length of time it takes you after the initial filleting stage.

What have you learned

1 What are the main contamination threats when preparing and storing uncooked fish?
2 Why is it important to keep preparation and storage areas and equipment hygienic?
3 Why is fish a contributor to a well-balanced diet?
4 How may fish be simply classified for culinary purposes?
5 How could you identify absolute freshness in fish purchases?
6 At what temperature should you store:
   ● fresh fish
   ● frozen fish?
7 What factors are involved when determining portion size?
8 Why must fish be used in a strict rotation policy?

ELEMENT 2:   Cook and finish basic fish dishes

THE COOKERY PROCESSES

All of the standard methods of cookery may be applied to most fish. To determine which cookery process to adopt you will need to consider the following:
● any dish, recipe specification, or menu demands
● any customer requirements and relevant establishment policies
● the type of menu on which the dish is to feature
● the quality, type and cut of fish being used
● the quantity of fish being cooked
● the equipment and resources you have available.

You will also need to plan your work to determine the shortest possible time between cooking and serving.

Points to consider

Having selected the most suitable cookery method for achieving the desired result, you will need to consider the points given below in order to ensure the quality of the dish.

● Excessive cooking will render any fish flesh dry and tasteless. Fish is composed of delicate muscle tissue and requires relatively little cooking in comparison to meat and poultry.
● Insufficient cooking may not destroy harmful bacteria that may be present, therefore care in timing and temperature control are essential to achieve a safe product.
● Handling should be kept to a minimum both before and after cooking as contamination can occur at either stage. Ensure that cooked fish is stored above 63 °C (145 °F) and that cooked cold fish is stored below 5 °C (41 °F), and preferably as near to 0 °C (32 °F) as possible without causing damage.
● Excessive time in hot storage will cause the fish to dry out.

Care in preparation and storage prior to cooking, and attention to detail to ensure correct cooking must constantly be observed if consistency in quality is to be achieved.

MEMORY JOGGER

Overcooking fish destroys flavour, succulence and nutritional value

The main contamination threats when preparing, cooking and storing fish dishes are as follows:
- contamination through incorrect storage temperatures. Fish stored in a warm environment for a prolonged period may provide a breeding ground for bacteria
- cross-contamination between cooked and uncooked food during storage
- cross-contamination from unhygienic equipment, utensils and preparation areas. Cooking, storage areas and equipment must be correctly cleaned before, during and immediately after use
- contamination from inadequate personal hygiene, i.e. from the nose, mouth, open cuts and sores or unclean hands
- contamination through incorrect thawing procedures when fish is prepared from frozen
- contamination through the finished fish dishes being left uncovered
- contamination through incorrect disposal of waste.

BAKING (OVEN-COOKING) FISH

Here fish is cooked by the controlled dry heat inside an oven. The delicate nature of fish flesh means that it requires some protection from the direct heat of the oven. This is achieved by retaining and protecting the natural moisture.

To achieve this you may use one of the following methods:
- cooking the fish in an ovenproof dish with a lid
- cooking it in a foil or greaseproof parcel or bag (this method is called *en papillote*)
- wrapping then cooking it in a protective pastry casing (known as cooking *en croûte*). Puff pastry, filo pastry or brioche dough may be used
- baking it in a protective coating, e.g. in a savoury custard for quiche or barquettes or within a savoury soufflé
- stuffing the fish with a moist mixture prior to baking and brushing or basting with oil or butter during cooking
- baking in a dish with an accompanying cooking liquor or complete sauce.

Fish suitable for baking
Whole fish: white or oily, round or flat. Cod, hake, bass, haddock, tuna, salmon and pike are amongst the fish most suited to the application of baking.

Cuts of fish: e.g. suprêmes, fillets or darnes.

Menu examples: Rouget en papillote, Baked codling fillet with parsley sauce, *Coulibiac de saumon*.

GRILLING FISH

Grilling is a dry method of cookery using the concentrated heat radiated by gas flames, electrical elements or glowing charcoal.

The heat may be directed:
- from *above* the food; as a salamander or overhead grill
- from *below* the food; as in a charcoal or simulated charcoal grill
- from *above and below* the food; as in some infra-red grills.

Key points to note when grilling fish

- Grilling radiates a fierce heat so the surface of the fish requires protection to prevent drying. In general, exposed areas of fish flesh will need to be passed through seasoned flour and brushed with oil or butter before cooking. Where the natural

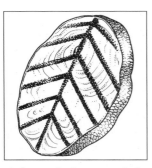

A darne of salmon marked with a hot poker (quadrillage) ready for grilling

skin covers the flesh the importance of using flour is reduced, although some chefs will flour the fish as a matter of course.

● When fish is grilled by the overhead method (i.e. by salamander), it is quite natural to mark the flesh of the fish with a very hot poker. This is to simulate the appearance of grill bar marks, enhancing the appearance of the fish when performed neatly. The culinary term for this is *quadrillage*.

● When grilling whole fish, score the thickest part of the flesh with 2–3 parallel cuts through the skin on either side. This allows the heat to penetrate for uniform cooking. This scoring process is known as *ciseler* (to score).

● Whole fish or thick cuts should be turned halfway through the cooking process to ensure even cooking. You may need to use special fish grilling wires to turn the fish. This reduces the risk of damaging the flesh and may be used in conjunction with a salamander or charcoal grill.

● Grilled fish is normally accompanied with a chilled savoury compound butter, e.g. parsley, red wine or anchovy butters or a warm butter sauce such as *béarnaise* or *choron*.

● Lemon and fresh parsley are the standard garnish.

● The bones of cuts of fish are normally removed after cooking and prior to service, although this will depend on establishment policy.

● Grilling is recognised as a quick method of cookery and is employed where the food is cooked to order. Grilled fish should be served to the customer as soon as possible after cooking is completed. Prolonged hot storage will allow the flesh to dry and spoil the dish.

Grilling breaded fish

A more gentle grilling procedure is applied to cuts of fish which are coated with breadcrumbs for protection prior to cooking. Unlike many breaded items, grilled fish uses flour and *melted* butter to adhere the crumb to the surface and a salamander is used to achieve a gentle, even cooking and colouring. Fish grilled by this method should not be turned during cooking as this would spoil the appearance. On menus this method of grilling often appears as *St Germain* or *Caprice*.

Fish suitable for grilling
Small to medium whole fish: round, flat, oily or white.

Cuts of fish: this includes darnes, tronçons and supremes.

Menu examples: Darne of salmon with bearnaise sauce (*Darne de saumon grillée, sauce béarnaise*), Fillets of plaice in breadcrumbs with béarnaise sauce and noisette potatoes (*Filets de plie St Germain*).

BARBECUING FISH

This method of grilling is often performed outdoors using the underheat method. The fish is barbecued over charcoal and wood, and the more informal way in which these dishes are eaten requires them to be less complex and relatively easy to cook.

Prior to cooking, barbecued items are placed in marinade to tenderise and improve flavour. The remaining marinade is brushed onto the fish during the cooking to keep it moist and improve appearance and taste.

Whole fish may have the belly cavity filled with branches of fresh herbs to give a distinctive flavour during cooking. They may also be wrapped in foil and baked over the barbecue.

Fish suitable for barbecuing
Small and medium whole fish, cuts of fish.

Example dishes: kebabs or brochettes (pieces of fish mixed with vegetables on skewers and grilled).

Healthy eating

Use polyunsaturated margarine or oil, instead of butter, for brushing grilled fish. Do not garnish with extra butters and serve accompaniments prepared from low-fat natural yoghurts.

Do this

- Watch your supervisor or chef baking a small cut of fish in puff pastry and in an oven-proof dish. Compare the preparation times and cooking times and examine the results for texture and flavour.
- Under supervision, grill a whole cleaned trout, recording the time it takes to cook. Examine the skin of the cooked fish for excessive dryness. If dry, how could you have protected it to preserve quality?
- Under supervision, grill a fillet of fish prepared by the melted butter and breadcrumb method. Note the position in the salamander required to achieve even cooking. Compare the cooking time to the conventional grilling method.
- Prepare a simple marinade for a fish kebab, then marinade and barbecue the kebab. Record the effects of the marinade in terms of texture and flavour and colour.

DEEP-FRYING FISH

Deep-frying is a process which cooks the food by entirely immersing it in hot oil or fat. The frying temperature should be 175–185 °C (347–365 °F) so as to bring sufficient heat into contact with the entire surface of the food at one time, enabling a golden brown and crisp surface to develop. The flesh of the fish will need a protective coating during cooking because of the high cooking temperature; this acts to protect the delicate flesh and to enhance the appearance and eating quality.

Protective coatings for fish

- Flour, egg-wash and breadcrumbs (*pané à l'anglaise*).
- Fresh breadcrumbs (*mie de pain*).
- Dry breadcrumbs or brown breadcrumbs (*chapelure*). Commercial golden-yellow rusk may be used in place of dried breadcrumbs.
- Batter (*pâté à frire*).
- Milk and flour (*pané à la française*).

Batter (pâté à frire)
This uses a combination of flour, liquids (milk, water), eggs (*à l'orly*), and an aerating agent (to give a lighter texture). The aerating agent may be yeast, baking powder or beaten egg whites; adding beer to some batters will produce a fermentation similar to that of yeast. To prepare fish in batter, flour the fish (in seasoned flour) then pass it through the batter, removing any surplus before deep-frying.

Milk and flour (pané à la française)
Here the fish is passed through milk and into seasoned flour to produce a thicker coating than by simply passing through flour. This gives better protection in cooking and assists in the quick colouring of the fish.

To improve the flavour of deep-fried fish it is advisable to marinade the cuts of fish for 1½–2 hours prior to cooking; the fish must remain in the fridge during this period. A simple marinade of cooking oil, lemon juice, crushed parsley stalk, salt and white mill pepper, will enhance the quality and flavour of any deep fried white fish dish.

Protective coatings for deep-fried fish, if administered correctly and cooked at the appropriate temperature, will:
- enhance the flavour
- help retain the shape of the fish during cooking
- enhance the colour and presentation
- reduce moisture loss in the flesh
- prevent excess absorption of the cooking medium.

Keep handling after cooking to a minimum; at this stage contamination can take place by bacteria being passed from the food handler to the fish. Use tongs and wire baskets or frying spiders.

MEMORY JOGGER

Why does fish require a protective coating before exposing to fierce heat?

Healthy eating

Deep-fry at the correct temperatures. Lower frying temperatures means longer cooking times and increased fat absorption.

MEMORY JOGGER

Why are correct frying temperatures and clean oil essential for obtaining good results when deep-frying?
What can happen if fish is fried at the incorrect temperature?

Key points to note when deep-frying

In order to present deep-fried fish at its optimum quality, observe the following:
- *draining*: allow the fish to drain well. The surface should be grease-free for presentation
- *seasoning*: season with a little salt immediately after cooking and draining away from the fryer. Season whilst hot so the salt sticks to the surface of the food
- *storage*: fried fish should be cooked and served as soon as possible. Do not hold quantities of fried fish for service as prolonged storage will cause the surface to lose its crisp texture. Never cover deep-fried fish as the moisture created will also cause the food to lose its crispness
- *garnishes*: keep these simple for deep-fried fish, using lemon crowns, lemon wedges (free from pips and pith) and sprigs of fried parsley
- *sauces*: these may be hot (as in tomato sauce for *Fish Orly*) or cold (as in *sauce tartare* for *Fish à l'anglaise*).

Safety precautions

Owing to the potential hazards when working with any deep-fryer it is essential to familiarise yourself with basic *do's and don't's* and to have a thorough knowledge of procedures for accidents and fires.

Follow the correct establishment procedures for filtering and changing oil in all fryers.

Never:
- over-fill the fryer with oil or fat
- over-heat the oil. If it begins to smoke, switch off the fryer and inform your supervisor
- plunge uncoated wet items into hot fat
- attempt to extinguish a fryer fire with water or sand
- leave fryers unattended whilst in use.

Make sure you know:
- where to find and how to sound the fire alarm
- who to inform in the case of an accident or fire and how they may be contacted quickly
- what type of fire extinguisher to use for a fryer fire, where the nearest is kept and how to use it
- where the switches are to turn off the gas or electricity to the fryer.

Fish suitable for deep-frying
Whole small round and flat fish, suprêmes, fillets and goujons are suitable for deep frying. Fish with a high fat content such as mackerel, tuna or salmon, do not suit this process as they taste unacceptably greasy after absorbing a percentage of the frying medium.

Menu examples: Fillets of lemon sole in batter (*Filets de limande à l'orly, sauce tomate*), Strips of plaice breaded and fried (*Goujons de plie frite, sauce tartare*), Devilled whitebait (*Blanchaille diablé*).

Do this

- Prepare four fillets of plaice, marinade in simple frying marinade and deep-fry:
  - in a frying batter made with yeast
  - in a frying batter made with egg white
  - pané à l'anglaise (flour, eggwash and breadcrumbs)
  - pané à la française (milk and flour).
- Note the differences in colour and variable cooking times.
- Examine for flavour and texture. Which do you prefer and why?

SHALLOW-FRYING FISH

Shallow-frying involves cooking the fish in a small amount of clarified butter or oil at high temperatures using a frying pan or special fish *meunière* pan.

Cooking *à la meunière*

This method is applied to small whole fish (trout, red mullet, Dover sole) or cuts of fish (fillets, suprêmes, médaillons, goujons) and produces quality results in white or oily fish.

After preparation the fish is passed through seasoned flour immediately before cooking and placed in the hot clarified butter presentation side first then cooked until it has developed a light golden brown colour. The fish is turned during cooking to even the process. Note that you may need to reduce the heat during cooking when cooking larger cuts and allow a prolonged period on the stove to ensure thorough cooking.

The amount of colour developed during shallow-frying fish is very important. Under-coloured fish may look insipid and unappetizing, while overcoloured fish may look as if it is burnt (and will probably be dry and over-cooked).

Finishing à la meunière *dishes*
A nut brown butter or *beurre noisette* is added to finish these dishes. To prepare beurre noisette, melt approximately 30 g (1 oz) butter per person in a clean pan and allow to cook to a light brown colour, sharpen with a squeeze of lemon juice and add a pinch of freshly chopped parsley at the last moment. Pour over the cooked fish whilst still bubbling.

Alternatively, season the cooked fish and squeeze lemon juice directly onto the surface. Sprinkle with chopped parsley and pour over the heated brown butter.

Fish meunière dishes are normally garnished with peeled lemon rings free from pips and pith. However, garnishes may vary from simple to complex depending on the requirements of the dish.

Simple garnishes
● *A la meunière Doria:*   peeled lemon, nut brown butter and blanched, turned cucumbers.
● *A la meunière aux amandes:*   peeled lemon, nut brown butter, chopped or flaked almonds.

Complex garnishes
● *A la meunière Murat:*   peeled lemon, nut brown butter, small turned potatoes, strips of artichoke bottom.
● *A la belle meunière:*   peeled lemon, nut brown butter, slice of peeled tomato, shallow-fried herring roe, turned mushroom head.

Key points to note when shallow-frying fish

● Shallow-frying is a quick process which lends itself to *cooking to order*.
● After cooking the fish should be served quickly as prolonged storage will allow the fish to become dry, or if stored with beurre noisette, soggy and unappetising. Timing in the execution of shallow-frying is critical.
● Make sure all equipment and commodities are ready to hand and all prior preparations are in place. Complete the task in a single action, cooking and presenting for service.

Fish suitable for shallow-frying
Small whole fish (trout, red mullet, Dover sole) or cuts of fish (fillets, suprêmes, médaillons, goujons). White or oily fish.

Healthy eating
Shallow fry in heavy duty pans with a minimum of oil. Substitute polyunsaturates for butter in sauces and garnishes.

Menu examples: *Filet de plie Grenobloise*, Shallow-fried Dover sole with cèpes, *Suprême de turbot meunière à l'orange et poivrons vert*.

POACHING FISH

Poaching is a process widely employed in fish cookery. It involves cooking fish in liquids at a temperature below boiling (approximately 90–95 °C/194–203 °F), creating very little or no movement in the cooking liquor.

Because of the gentle nature of this process, it is a most effective way of cooking most varieties of fish, particularly those with a delicate flavour or texture. Invariably the cooking liquid contributes to the quality of the finished dish by:
- imparting flavour to the food, and/or
- forming the basis of the resulting sauce.

Poaching may be divided into two categories: *deep-poaching* and *shallow-poaching*.

DEEP-POACHING

During deep-poaching the fish is totally immersed in a particular type of liquid: an *acidulated court bouillon*.

Vinegar court bouillon
This is used for salmon, salmon trout, trout and shellfish. It is made from: water, vinegar, carrots, onions, thyme, bay leaf, parsley stalks, salt and peppercorns.

Method
Bring the ingredients to the boil. Simmer for 25 minutes then strain, cool and use as required.

White wine bouillon
This is used for freshwater or oily fish. It is made from: dry white wine, water, lemon juice, sliced onions, thyme, bay leaf, parsley stalks, salt and peppercorns.

Method
Bring the ingredients to the boil. Simmer for 25 minutes then strain, cool and use as required.

Equipment for deep-poaching

The fish may be deep poached in a special fish kettle such as:
- a salmon kettle or saumonière
- a trout kettle or truitière
- turbot kettle or turbotière

Key points to note when deep-poaching fish

- The scales of the fish are removed but the skin is left on for protection during cooking.
- *Whole fish* is started in a cold court bouillon, to minimise the risk of distortion.
- *Cuts of fish* are started in a hot court bouillon to reduce the cooking time and prevent the natural juices escaping and coagulating into a white coating on the cut surface of the fish.
- Remember the importance of temperature control when deep poaching fish: excessive boiling will cause the flesh to shrink and distort and affect the texture of the flesh.
- Insufficient cooking may not destroy any harmful bacteria that may be present: check that poaching liquor temperatures reach 90–95 °C (194–203 °F).
- The cooking process is completed on top of the stove.

- The liquor contributes to the flavour of the food during cooking only.
- After deep-poaching, fish may be served with lemon, plain boiled turned potatoes, picked parsley and a suitable sauce (often a warm butter sauce, e.g. *sauce hollandaise*) or a beurre fondue.

Fish suitable for deep poaching
Larger whole fish and cuts of oily fish (especially where the fish is to be dressed for cold buffet use).

Menu examples: Saumon froid en belle-vue; Darne de saumon poché.

Whole fish cooked in a deep court bouillon

SHALLOW-POACHING

Fish is shallow-poached when it is to be coated with a sauce, and the cooking liquor is invariably used for finishing the sauce.

Shallow-poaching may be identified by definite procedures:
- poaching may take place in a sauteuse, shallow saucepan, deep sided tray or in a special fish poaching pan: a *plaque à poisson*
- the dish is lightly greased and any garnish (e.g. shallots, mushrooms, tomatoes) that requires cooking is placed on the bottom of the dish
- the seasoned fish is placed in the dish but kept slightly apart so that the poaching liquor heats evenly
- the poaching liquor is normally fish stock and dry wine. The stock is added at a cool temperature and to a level of two-thirds the height of the food
- the exposed areas of fish are covered with a buttered paper lid or cartouche, to prevent the fish from drying out during cooking
- pre-warming takes place on top of the stove (do not boil as this will cause shrinkage and distortion) and the poaching is completed in the oven on a medium heat to ensure even heat distribution
- once cooked, the fish is removed from the cooking liquor and kept covered to prevent the surface from drying. The cooking liquor is returned to the stove and reduced. The reduced liquor is then either:
  (a) added to the pre-prepared velouté sauce to improve flavour and quantity
  (b) reduced further (to a syrupy consistency), before cream is added and the liquid cooked to the desired sauce thickness and finished with unsalted butter to become the finished or complete sauce
- when dishing for service, place a little of the complete sauce on the serving dish to facilitate ease of service and to absorb any excess liquor, then arrange the fish neatly on the dish and coat it with the finished sauce.

MEMORY JOGGER

Why should poached fish not be boiled rapidly?

Healthy eating

Use half-fat cream instead of full-fat double cream in sauces. Utilise skimmed milk in sauce making. Use polyunsaturates in place of butter.

Glazing shallow poached fish dishes

Recipe requirements may demand that certain fish dishes are *glazed*. This refers to browning the surface of the completed sauce within its service dish under a salamander to enhance the appearance of the dish.

To achieve a good glaze, egg yolk (cooked to sabayon) and unsalted butter may be added to the velouté sauce. In the case of the fully reduced cooking liquor (Method (b) p. 87), the consistency of the syrup once the cream and butter is added should be sufficient to achieve a good glaze without any further additions.

It is advisable to check the glazing quality of the sauce prior to completing the dish; this may be done by pouring a little sauce onto a plate and testing glazing under the salamander. If an even glaze does not develop, rectify by adding sabayon.

Surface browning may also be achieved by the use of cheese, as dictated by the recipe. Breadcrumbs may also be used, but note that this method is called *gratinating* and should not be confused with *glazing*.

> **MEMORY JOGGER**
>
> How do gratinating and glazing methods differ?

Healthy eating

Do not enrich sauces with additional butter or employ the use of egg yolks to assist in glazing. If a glaze is required, a spoonful of half whipped, low-fat cream will achieve a suitable glaze.

Do this

- Under supervision, prepare two fillets of fish for cooking meunière with a simple garnish and two fillets of fish meunière with a complex garnish.
- Make a note of the time differentials in preparing the two dishes. Notice how the dishes differ in terms of colour, balance and presentation.
- Watch your chef or supervisor preparing a court bouillon.
- Under supervision, cook one glazed and one non-glazed dish of shallow poached fish. Compare the finishing of the sauces and the method employed to achieve a glaze.

Health and hygiene points

Owing to the relatively low temperatures at which fish is poached, it is important that the fish spends as little time as possible in a warm environment. Keep handling after cooking to a minimum, using the correct utensils. Arrange your timing so that cooked fish does not have to be held for long periods of time.

Fish suitable for shallow poaching
Small whole fish (sole, plaice, baby turbot) or cuts of fish (fillets, délice, suprêmes, paupiettes). This method lends itself to delicate or fragile types of fish flesh that would break up if deep poached.

Menu examples: Glazed shallow poached dishes: *Bonne femme, Brevale, Bercy, Marguery, Veronique*. Non-glazed shallow poached dishes: *Duglère, d'Antin, Dieppoise, Suchet, Vin-blanc*.

Essential knowledge

Time and temperature are important when cooking fish dishes in order to:
- prevent food poisoning. Insufficient cooking can cause food poisoning
- prevent shrinkage of fish
- ensure a correctly cooked fish or fish dish. Fish is a delicate food item which can easily be spoiled if cooked for too long or at the incorrect temperature
- prevent fat absorption during the frying processes.

STEAMING FISH

Small whole fish, fillets or other small cuts of fish can be cooked with excellent results by steaming. It can be carried out in a low-pressure steaming unit, high-pressure steaming oven or a pressureless convection steamer. All units give good results but cooking times vary, depending on the type of steamer you employ.

Steaming has the advantage of being easy to carry out, while offering rapid cooking with little loss of flavour, colour or nutrients. It is particularly useful when preparing large quantities for banquets as it reduces the number of times the fish is handled and allows the sauces to be made in advance. This reduces the amount of time the fish needs to be kept an a warm environment prior to serving; i.e. the fish is cooked immediately before it is required for service.

Many shallow poached dishes can be executed by the steaming process, where excellent results are obtained if the accompanying sauce is of the required quality.

Method
Prepare the fish for steaming by moistening it with a little fish stock, lemon juice or wine (or as recipe instruction). Season with a little salt and white pepper. Steam until just cooked (remembering that steaming is a rapid method of cookery). Prepare the accompanying sauce separately.

Fish suitable for steaming fish
Small whole fish, fillets or other small cuts of fish.

Menu examples: As for any shallow or short poached dishes.

Healthy eating

Steaming fish is considered a healthy method of cooking as no additional fats are required. The fibre content of steamed fish dishes can be increased by garnishing with lightly steamed vegetables or by thickening sauces with pulse purées.

Corrective action checklist for cooking fish

Fault	*Corrective action*
The fish is cooking too quickly	Reduce the heat, move to cooler part of the stove or oven.
The fish is not colouring	Increase the heat, cook less food at one time. Check whether you floured the fish (if required).
Service is unavoidably delayed	Cover with moist paper, keep hot but moist: brush with fish stock. Note that you should not add any sauce until required for service.
The sauce is too thick	Thin with the appropriate liquor.
The sauce is too thin	Reduce or correct the consistency prior to serving.
The fish is dry	Check whether you have cooked the fish for too long or at too high a temperature. Has it been badly handled or incorrectly stored?
Poached fish has a tough texture	Check whether you have cooked the fish too quickly. Has it boiled? At what temperature did you begin the cooking?
The fish sticks to the cooking dish	Check whether you greased the cooking dish.
The cream in the sauce separates	Check that the cream used was fresh. Did you shake and stir the sauce during reduction to ensure even heat distribution?
Steamed fish has a poor flavour	Check that the steamer was cleaned correctly before being used for cooking.

> ## Healthy eating
>
> The use of salt in a catering establishment varies according to the individual chef and is rarely measured, but high salt intakes are associated with hypertension which is a major risk factor for coronary heart disease. Therefore, to reduce salt intake, all stocks should be fresh (not bouillons) and seasonings can be achieved with herbs and spices.

STORING FISH DISHES

In order to prevent bacterial growth, hot fish dishes should be stored above 65 °C (149 °F); cold fish dishes should be stored below 5 °C (41 °F).

DEALING WITH UNEXPECTED SITUATIONS

If you have problems when preparing fish dishes, refer to the diagnostic corrective action list (above). This should help you to deal with any unexpected situations.

Make sure that you are familiar with all health and safety procedures; this will help you to respond appropriately to any emergencies. Keep a note of any emergency phone numbers (both within and outside of your organisation) that you will need to ring to obtain immediate assistance.

Case study

In a fashionable restaurant a chef prepares a poached sole dish for a party of twelve people at 8.30 pm.

He, quite correctly, shallow poaches the sole and uses the cooking liquor to make the resulting sauce. However, it is a very busy kitchen and, in order to be efficient and ready, he completes the task by 7.30 pm and stores the fish above the stove.

The party is served and the guests comment on the quality of the sauce but complain their fish was dry, too firm and lacked flavour. The result was that the cost of the fish dish was removed from their bill thus making this an ineffective cost exercise.

1   *Who was at fault in this situation?*
2   *What actions should have been taken to prevent this occurrence?*
3   *What alternative approach to poaching could the Chef have employed and still maintained the sauce quality?*
4   *What action would you take to prevent cooked fish from drying out?*

What have you learned?

1   What factors determine your choice of cookery process for cooking fish?
2   What effect will under-cooking or over-cooking have on fish dishes?
3   What are the main contamination threats when preparing, cooking and storing fish dishes?
4   Why are time and temperature important when cooking fish dishes?
5   Why does fish require protection during baking or grilling?
6   Name three protective coatings for deep-frying fish?
7   Why are oily fish not suitable for deep-frying?
8   What is the difference between deep-poaching and shallow or short poaching?
9   How is the cooking liquor used from shallow-poached dishes?

Get ahead

1 Research and prepare a list of fish used in other countries of the world. Many are readily available in this country. How would you cook them?
2 Find out how fish may be preserved other than by freezing. Note their culinary uses.
3 Visit a fish market and observe the variety of species, the handling and storage techniques and the current market prices. How and why does the fish reach you in first class condition?

Prepare and cook basic cold and hot desserts

This chapter covers:
ELEMENT 1: **Prepare, cook and finish basic cold desserts**
ELEMENT 2: **Prepare, cook and finish basic hot desserts**

What you need to do

- Check that preparation, cooking areas and suitable equipment are hygienic and ready for use.
- Ensure dessert ingredients are of the type, quality and quantity required.
- Report any problems identified with the quality of ingredients promptly to the appropriate person.
- Prepare and cook dessert ingredients using appropriate basic preparation and cooking methods.
- Finish desserts using appropriate finishing methods to meet quality requirements.
- Store finished desserts not for immediate consumption correctly.
- Check that preparation and cooking areas and equipment are cleaned correctly after use.
- Ensure all work is prioritised and carried out in an organised and efficient manner in line with appropriate organisational procedures and legal requirements.

What you need to know

- When preparing, cooking and finishing basic cold and hot desserts what safe working practices should be followed.
- When preparing, cooking and finishing basic cold and hot desserts why it is important to keep preparation, cooking areas and equipment hygienic.
- What the main contamination threats are when preparing, cooking and storing basic cold and hot desserts.
- Why time and temperature are important when preparing, cooking and finishing basic cold and hot desserts.
- What quality points you might look for in basic cold and hot desserts.
- Which basic preparation methods are suitable for different types of cold and hot basic desserts.
- Which basic cooking methods are suitable for different types of cold and hot basic desserts.
- What indications you might look for to identify that basic cold and hot desserts are cooked to dish requirements.
- What products might be used to substitute high fat ingredients when preparing basic cold and hot desserts.
- Which fats can contribute to healthy eating practices.
- Why increasing the fibre content of basic cold and hot desserts can contribute to healthy eating practices.
- Why reducing the amount of sugar in basic cold and hot desserts can contribute to healthy eating practices.
- Why basic hot desserts not for immediate consumption should be cooled rapidly or maintained at a safe hot temperature after cooking.

ELEMENT 1:   Prepare, cook and finish basic cold desserts

No meal is complete without a dessert; it is the conclusion of the meal experience and one which many customers look forward to the most. The sweet or dessert can cover a wide range of dishes, some classical, others created by the imagination of the chef. A good pastry chef is worth his or her weight in gold and thankfully this neglected area of catering is experiencing a revival in the 1990s.

TRIFLE

Trifle is a classic cold British dessert which can be made in a variety of ways. It is produced by combining jelly or jam, sponge and/or fruit with sherry or fruit juice and cold, set custard, finished with whipped cream. Trifles can be decorated with an array of decorating media. The custard can be either made from fresh egg yolks, cream or milk, sugar and vanilla, or by using custard powder with milk and sugar.

Trifle can be individually portioned in glass dishes or goblets, or multi-portioned in a glass bowl.

Sherry Trifle

How to prepare, produce and finish sherry trifle
1   Take a suitable glass bowl, either for single or multi-portions.
2   Spread the base with jam, smearing it with a spoon.
3   Place in some diced sponge pieces or fingers.
4   Soak with sherry
5   Pour over a warm fresh custard sauce and leave to cool.
6   Decorate with whipped fresh cream, toasted almonds and glacé cherries.
7   Chill until required.

Trifle

Fruit Trifle

How to prepare, produce and finish fruit trifle
1   Take a suitable glass bowl, either for single or multi portions.
2   Spread the base with jam, smearing it with a spoon.
3   Place in some diced sponge pieces or fingers.
4   Add some diced fresh or tinned fruit. *Do not use acid fruits.*
5   Pour over a warm fresh custard sauce and leave to cool.
6   Decorate with whipped fresh cream, toasted almonds and glacé cherries.
7   Chill until required.

Do this

Fruit trifle and traditional English trifle can be made with various recipes; look them up to find out about their history.
Work out the relative cost of the ingredients for each recipe.

EGG CUSTARD

Egg custard can be used as the basis for both savoury dishes and sweet desserts.

Liquid egg custard – sweet (*Sauce Anglaise*)

Method

1   Place the milk and vanilla pod or essence into a pan and bring to the boil. Remove the pan from the stove and allow the contents to cool for a few minutes. Remove the vanilla pod.
2   Whisk the eggs and sugar together in a mixing bowl.
3   Pour the cooled milk into the eggs and sugar, mixing well. The milk needs to be slightly cooled to prevent it from over-cooking the yolks, which can scramble if the milk is too hot.
4   Strain the mixture through a fine conical strainer to remove any shell particles.
5   Put the mixture into a clean pan and cook it on top of the stove until the custard is thick enough to coat the back of a spoon. Do not allow it to boil.
6   If necessary, keep the cooked sauce hot in a bain-marie until required for service.

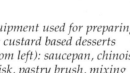

MEMORY JOGGER

Why is it important to strain a liquid egg custard before using it in a cold dessert product?

Equipment used for preparing egg custard based desserts (From left): saucepan, chinois, whisk, pastry brush, mixing bowl

Baked egg custard (*crème caramel*)

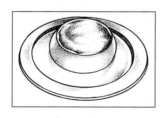

Baked egg custard

This classic baked egg custard has its own sweet caramel sauce. Caramel is a tasty nutty sugar sauce made from sugar and water used for crème caramel and as a flavouring agent for ice cream and desserts.

Method

1   Place the water in a clean copper or saucepan and add the sugar.
2   Heat gently to dissolve the sugar crystals. When dissolved boil over a full heat and cook until the sugar turns a rich chestnut colour. Wash down the sides of the pan during boiling with a clean wet pastry brush. The sugar will begin to smoke lightly.
3   Pour on some boiling water and shake to form the sauce.
4   While still hot pour into dariole moulds and allow to cool and set.
5   Pour and fill the dariole moulds with a sweet liquid egg custard and cook in a *bain-marie* (a tray half-filled with hot water) in the oven for 30–40 minutes or until set at approx 190–195 °C (360–380 °F).
6   When cool, press the edge of the cooked cream to allow air between the cream and the mould, turn out onto a plate and pour over any sauce from the base of the mould.

7 You can test the cream during cooking by inserting a small knife into the top of the cream; if liquid rises, then more cooking time is required. If the custard is cooked the knife will be clean when removed.

8 Serve plain, or decorated with some whipped fresh cream and biscuits.

9 Use within 48 hours of production.

Range of cold and hot desserts using egg custard

Baked egg custard	Crème brulée au chocolat
Crème caramel	Crème brulée aux fraise
Creme renversée	Queen of puddings
Creme Viennoise	Bread and butter pudding
Crème St Claire	Tarte d'orange
Creme beau-rivage	Crème Regence
Diplomat pudding	Flan Normande
Cabinet pudding	Baked egg custard flan
Petits pot de crème vanille	Custard tarts
Petit pot de crème café	Manchester flan
Petit pot de crème chocolat	Oeufs a la neige – (Sauce Anglaise based dessert)
Petit pot de crème praliné	Iles flottantes – (Sauce Anglaise based dessert)
Crème brulée vanille	

Basic cold egg custard desserts

Baked egg custard	Plain egg custard baked in the oven.
Crème caramel	Caramel topped baked egg custard.
Crème renversée	As for caramel cream without the caramel.
Crème St Claire	Baked egg custard with apricot sauce.
Crème Viennoise	Egg custard with the caramel dissolved into the mix cooked as for Creme renversée.
Diplomat pudding	Mould half filled with jam sponge pieces, glacé fruits and sultanas, filled with egg custard and baked, served cold with raspberry sauce.
Petits pot de crème vanille	Cream-enriched egg custard baked in small brown pots.
Petits pot de crème chocolate	Cream-enriched egg custard flavoured with chocolate baked in small brown pots.
Flan Normande	Flan cooked with cooking apples and egg custard.
Baked egg custard flan	Flan baked blind, filled with egg custard and seasoned with nutmeg and returned to the oven to complete cooking process.
Custard tarts	As above but in small individual tartlets. These can be lined and filled and cooked without baking pastry blind.
Manchester Flan	Flan lined and spread with jam, coconut and sultanas, filled with egg custard and baked
Crème Brûlée	Cream and egg enriched custard baked in a ramequin dish, dusted liberally with sugar and caramelised.

COLD RICE DESSERTS

Cold rice based desserts are used plain, with fruit or set to produce individual or multi-portion desserts. Some of the classical rice based dishes are:

Empress rice (Riz à l'impératrice)	Elaborate rice and gelatine mould, topped with jelly and whipped cream.
Rice condé (Riz condé)	Cold cooked rice, covered with apricot glaze,

	finished with angelica and glacé or maraschino cherries.
Pear condé (Poire condé)	Cold cooked rice, poached cored pears and apricot glaze decorated with angelica and glacé cherries.
Apricot condé (D'abricot condé)	Cold cooked rice, poached apricots and apricot glaze decorated with angelica and glacé or maraschino cherries.
Pineapple creole (Ananas créole)	Cooked cold rice formed on a flat in the shape of a pineapple. Mark to form a diamond pattern on the rice shape, place a currant in each diamond mark. Decorate with fruit and glaze with hot apricot sauce enhanced with kirsch. Complete the decoration with strips of tapered angelica to represent the pineapple leaves.

To make Riz à l'impératrice

1 Prepare some strawberry or raspberry jelly and cover the base of a charlotte mould with approximately 1 cm (½ in) depth of liquid jelly, refrigerate to set.
2 Soak some gelatine in cold water. Use 6–8 sheets per pint or half litre of milk.
3 Bring the milk to the boil and add the rice. Cook until the rice is soft.
4 Add in the vanilla essence, sugar and diced soaked chopped angelica and cherries previously soaked in kirsch.
5 Mix in the drained gelatine and cool stir the mix now and then to maintain an even cooling temperature.
6 When setting point is achieved fold in some whipped cream and firmly whipped egg whites; blend the two mixtures until clear, folding carefully.
7 Portion into the prepared charlotte moulds and chill for 1 hour.
8 Turn out by dipping the base of the mould in hot water, turn out the set rice onto a service dish and decorate with rosettes of cream.

JELLIES (GELÉES)

Jelly is purchased as small concentrated jelly slabs or as jelly crystals. These crystals are whisked into hot water in the required quantities. The jelly slabs are dissolved in hot water, with the remainder of the measured amount of water being added cold. Jelly is used as a dessert garnish or as a dessert base. Flavours include raspberry, strawberry, lemon, lime, orange, blackcurrant and greengage.

Gelée a la crème	Jelly served with freshly whipped cream.
Gelée Rubanée	Layers of different flavoured and coloured jelly.
Gelée Moscovite	Jelly served very cold, often whipped up.
Gelée Maltaise	Orange flavoured jelly served with orange fillets.
Gelée aux fruites	Fruit jelly and fresh whipped cream.
Gelée à la Russe	Whip the set jelly in a machine, pipe into moulds and set in the refrigerator.

To make *Gelée aux fruit*

Jelly can be made using prepared crystals or using leaf or powdered gelatine. It is usual to produce jelly in large quantities using jelly crystals.

Method
1 Follow the instructions suggested by the manufacturer and add boiling water, whisk the crystals well to ensure they dissolve.
2 Place some chopped fruits into the glass, mould or suitable container.

3 Add the cooling jelly and refrigerate when the jelly is cool but not set.
4 Decorate with whipped fresh or liquid cream and finish with a piped chocolate motif.

FLANS, TARTLETS, (SWEET AND SHORT PASTRY)

A wide range of desserts are made with pastry bases. When producing pastry always check that all equipment is clean before production begins. This is to minimize the risk of contamination and to maintain hygienic standards when handling food, especially dairy products, in a warm kitchen environment.

Short pastry *Pâte à brisée and Pâte à foncé*

Short pastry is made from soft flour, fat (50% lard and 50% margarine or butter), seasoning and bound with as little water as possible to prevent toughening the paste. It can be made by the rubbing in method for quick use, or the flour batter method if prepared in advance as this paste tends to be of a softer consistency and will need to be chilled before use.

When making paste by machine, take care when rubbing in the fat; if over-mixing occurs before the water has been added the paste will become crumbly and tough and off little use. Look for the 'crumb' developing and the change of colour as the fat is broken down. At this point add the water gradually. Always stop the machine to test the texture of the paste; you can always add a little more liquid if needed, this is better than adding more flour to tighten the paste for handling. Use just enough liquid to bind and bring the crumb together; the more water the more liable the mixture is to form gluten which will toughen the paste.

Fat shortening, a white commercial fat produces good results. A mixture of fat creates colour and texture; using butter increases the cost of the pastry and therefore the selling price should reflect an all-butter product. Fat from the fridge will be too cold and difficult to use; fat at room temperature will rub in well. Once the paste has formed, handle with care and bring the paste together to form a soft clear paste, wrap and cool in the fridge until required.

General rules for handling short pastry
● Make sure all equipment and work surfaces are clean.
● Ensure paste ingredients are at room temperature (21 °C/70 °F).
● Always sieve flour and salt to aerate the flour; disperse salt evenly.
● When rubbing in the fat lift the mix to incorporate air.
● Add the liquid gradually, checking the consistency.
● When making short paste by creaming, scrape down the sides of the machine or mixing bowl using a plastic scraper.
● When a clear paste is produced wrap well, chill and rest before use.
● Scraps of short paste should be worked into fresh mixes to reduce waste.
● Break eggs into a bowl in advance before preparing the paste to prevent contamination. Wash your hands after cracking eggs and before starting the next task.

Short pastry can be made using a range of recipes and production methods. Books such as the *International Confectioner and Complete Pastry Work Techniques* by Ildo Nicolello provide a useful array of recipes and professional techniques.

Moulding / Lining Pastry (*Pâte à foncer*)

This is used for pasties, quiches, savoury tarts and tartlettes, small individual pies, baked jam roll, baked apple dumplings.

MEMORY JOGGER

Why is it important to work in a clean and hygienic manner when producing pastry?

French pie pastry (*Pâte à pâté*)

This is used for pâtés, croustades and timbales, game and meat pies.

Short sweet pastry (*Pâte sucrée*)

Short pastry as described above is used for the production of savoury goods but short pastry can also contain small ratios of sugar (approximately 50 g of sugar to 500 g of soft flour) and is called *sweet pastry*. When the recipe contains a larger proportion of sugar at, say 125 g of sugar to 500 g of flour, then this is termed *sugar pastry*.

Pastries as desserts

The main types of pastry used for dessert tarts, tartlettes and flans are short sweet pastry (*pâte sucrée* and *pâte sablée*).

Sweet pastry is used to make flans, pies, bandes, tarts and tartlettes which are either baked blind and filled, or filled and then baked. Sweet pastry is made from soft flour, fat, sugar and eggs and/or water. The more fat used, the less egg will be required to bind the pastry together.

When the rubbing-in method is used the sugar is mixed with the egg/liquid and added once the fat has been finely crumbed into the sieved flour.

When produced by the creaming method the sugar is creamed with the fat until light and white, the eggs are added one at a time and finally the sieved flour is blended to form a clear smooth paste; this should not be over-mixed. The flour batter method can also be used and is often referred to as a secondary creaming method.

Cake margarines which have good emulsion properties are used in bakeries for the production of sweet pastes for tart stamping by machine, for custard or fruit-filled tartlettes. Sweet paste is best made the day before it is required and rested in the fridge, wrapped in cling film. Do not wrap in greaseproof paper or the paste will become dry and form a skin.

It is possible to purchase a tartlette stamp and cooking machine which uses a high-sugar paste recipe generally made from icing sugar. The paste is placed in the mould shape, the lid is closed, and the paste is cooked using the sandwich toaster principle which takes about 3 minutes. These goods have a good shelf life, although they are quite sweet.

Sugar in pastry has two functions. Firstly, it caramelises to produce the rich golden colour, the higher the sugar content the deeper the colour and generally a lower cooking temperature is required to prevent the product from burning. Secondly, sugar has a dispersing or solvent effect on the action of the gluten formed from the flour and liquid. High-sugar recipes such as shortbread produce a much shorter texture. Sometimes shortbread pastes can be difficult to work because of the high ratio of both fat and sugar in the recipe.

Sugar pastry can be used for fruit flans, sweet tartlettes and tarts, Bakewell goods, lemon meringue flans, barquettes, custard tarts, mince pies, tranche and bandes.

Shortbread pastry (*pâte sablée*)

This can be used for finger biscuits plain and fruited, small and large blocked shortbread biscuits and petit fours sec (dry small delicate baked biscuits plain or decorated), gateau and torte e.g. Gateau MacMahon bases.

Piped shortbread pastry (Sablés à la poche)
This can be used for petit four sec and tea biscuits, plain or fruited.

Sweet almond pastry (Pâte Allemande (or German paste))
In this, ground almonds are substituted for part of the flour content in the recipe. It is used for Linzer torte, torte bases, biscuits and petit fours or tartlettes.

PRINCIPLE OF SHORTENING

The principle of shortening is to coat the sub-proteins within the flour to prevent the development of gluten, which can toughen the pastry making it unpleasant to eat and difficult to digest.

To make a light short pastry the gluten strands that are formed should be short and easily break when eaten. This is achieved by coating the two sub-proteins so that when mixed with liquid, they come together to make the insoluble protein *gluten*. In dough you need to develop the gluten to form long elastic strands of gluten to hold in the expanding gases, with short pastry you need to do the exact opposite.

This is achieved by increasing the ratio of fat to flour: the standard ratio for pastry is 50% fat to 100% flour, which should be soft i.e. one with a low protein content (soft plain flour). As the ratio of fat is increased in the recipe, the pastry has a shorter texture. Shortbread has one of the shortest textures and 'melts in the mouth'. It is usually made with butter.

Short pastry can be made with a range of fats; butter is best for flavour and colour but is most expensive; margarine is widely used for cost, special fats such as shortening and cake margarines, which have very good creaming (emulsion) qualities, are used for commercial production .

PASTRY MAKING TECHNIQUES

Rubbing-in method (by hand)

Sieve the flour to aerate the flour and remove and small lumps or particles. Rub the fat into the flour by the hands to produce a fine textured crumb before the liquid is added. This action coats the sub-proteins and starch with fat which prevents gluten being formed: over-handling can toughen the pastry by forming long tougher strands of gluten. When the liquid, either egg, milk or water, is added bring the paste together gently with as little handling as possible to make a clear paste.

It is important to handle the paste lightly and work it as little as possible. Paste should be rested well before being used to allow the gluten to relax, which will improve the short texture and light eating quality required for good pastry bases.

Rubbing-in using a mixing machine

Mixing machines need to be controlled by the chef to determine when the fat is rubbed in sufficiently before adding the liquid to a pastry. Look for the crumb texture, the colour of the mix changing and the paste starting to come together as the fat content starts to re-join.

Very good results can be achieved using the machine for mixing large quantities, but many mixes are toughened because the operator does not pay attention.

Creaming method

Creaming is different from rubbing in because the fat and sugar are creamed together to form a light, white emulsion to which the liquid is added and then the sieved flour folded in, and cleared to a smooth paste. This method of production produces a softer and lighter paste but does require refrigeration to firm the paste before handling can begin. Special fats such as cake margarine and shortenings which have good creaming properties, are used in bakeries and kitchens. Butter needs to be at room temperature to enable creaming to take place successfully.

Flour batter method

Cream the fat with an equal quantity of flour, mix the sugar and liquid together and add slowly to the fat and flour mixture to form a smooth paste. Finally add the rest of the flour and mix to clear. Do not over-mix. This is called a secondary creaming method in some recipe books.

Basic pastry recipes

- Sweet moulding/lining paste (*pâte à brisée*)

100%	soft flour	500 g
50%	fat (butter, margarine)	250 g
12%	egg	2 × 60 g
10%	sugar	50 g
5%	water	25 ml
	pinch of salt	2 g

- Sweet paste (*pâte sucrée*)

100%	soft flour	500 g
50%	fat (butter, margarine)	250 g
12%	egg	2 × 60 g
25%	sugar	125 g
	pinch of salt	2 g

- Sweet almond paste (*pâte allemande*)

100%	soft flour	500 g
60%	fat (butter, margarine)	300 g
20%	sugar	125 g
15%	ground almonds	75 g
8–10%	egg yolks	4 or 5

- Suet paste (*pâte à grasse de boeuf*)

100%	soft flour	500 g
60%	water	300 ml
50%	fat (suet)	250 g
	baking powder	10 g
	pinch of salt	10 g

- Choux paste (*pâte à choux*)

100%	strong flour	500 g
120%	water	600 ml
50%	fat (butter or margarine)	250 g
1%	sugar (optional)	5 g
1%	salt (optional)	5 g

Healthy eating

Use wholemeal flour to make pastry to add fibre to the diet.

Brown/wholemeal pastry

Short pastry in particular can be made with wholemeal flour which provides useful fibre in the diet. More pastries today are made with wholemeal flour e.g. quiches and individual savoury tartlettes, meat and vegetable pies. For a lighter pastry wholemeal flour and white soft or strong flour can also be mixed 50/50.

Do this

- How are barquettes lined when produced in bulk ?
- How can quiche pastry be prevented from becoming wet or undercooked ?
- What is the difference between a pie and a tart ?
- Check the range of convenience products made with pastry, what types of pastry freeze well and for how long ?
- What are filo and strudel paste, how are they made ?

TARTS

Tarts can be open or closed, and cooked blind and then filled, or filled and then baked, depending on the dish and recipe. Fruit tarts, such as mandarin, strawberry or pineapple, can be filled, with or without a pastry cream base, finished with a clear glaze or boiled apricot purée. They can be either multi-portioned or individual.

Closed tarts such as apple tart are flan rings lined with a sweet or sugar paste and closed with a top, as in Dutch apple tart, which is flavoured with cinnamon and the apple mixed with sultanas. When cooked the flan ring or mould is removed and the tart is served whole on a round salver with semi-whipped fresh cream or hot *Sauce Anglaise*.

Tarts can be made on a plate with fresh, tinned or frozen fruits. It is important that any juice is kept to a minimum. Open tarts such as jam, treacle and lemon curd, apricot and fruit are made by lining the flan ring or tartlet moulds with sweet short paste and spooning in the filling. A lattice top can also be used as a decoration.

One of the most famous of tarts is the Bakewell tart, made from a flan of sweet paste, with jam spread over the inside base and frangipane piped or spread over, or done as a lattice. When cooked the top is brushed with boiled apricot purée and warm fondant is spread over this, with a decoration of piped chocolate or coloured fondant which is drawn with a fine point to form the typical spider's web decoration.

Types of tarts made with sweet short paste (some can be made using puff paste trimmings):

- Bakewell tart
- Treacle tart
- Dutch apple tart
- Congress tarts
- Strawberry cream tarts
- Assorted fruit tarts
- Linzer tart
- Jam tart
- Curd tart
- Conversation tarts.
- Brittany tart
- Belgium tart
- Maids of honour tarts

FLANS

A flan is a mould of pastry usually formed inside a 'flan ring'. Roll out the paste, lift it onto the rolling pin and gently place it over the flan ring. Lift the edges inside the ring and mould to the shape, ensuring the paste is pressed into the corners of the flan ring.

Trim away the excess and with floured fingers thumb up the sides to form a sharp ridge. The top edge of the flan ring should be visible, so that when the paste is cooked it shrinks away slightly from the flan ring edge, aiding the removal of the ring when cool. Crimp the ridge with the fingers or with the aid of a crimping tweezers, to produce a decorative top edge.

The pastry should not be too thin, otherwise the flan case will collapse once filled and spoil the finish.

Certain flans are baked 'blind'. To do this, line the flan ring, lift it onto a baking tray, dock the base of the paste with a fork, place a paper cartouche, which is 3 cm larger than the flan ring size, into the flan, and fill with baking beans. Cook the flan case until set but without colour, then remove the cartouche and beans. Wash the semi-cooked flan with egg and return to the oven to colour and finish cooking.

Banana, peach, cherry, pineapple or mandarin flans can be made with blind baked flan cases filled with pastry cream and topped with the drained tinned fruit, decorated with boiled apricot purée. Hot and cold process gel can be brushed or sprayed on to finished cool products.

Types of flans made with sweet short paste:
- Apple flan
- Normandy flan
- Apricot flan
- Alsacienne flan
- Cherry flan
- Jeanette flan
- Manchester flan
- Lemon meringue flan
- Pear flan bordalou

BASIC MERINGUE (SHELLS AND NESTS)

Egg white based desserts (*meringues*)

Apart from the range of egg custard based desserts (see p. 95), egg whites are used as a foam aerating agent for many dishes and desserts. Meringues are a popular product and add variety to a whole range of dessert items.

Care is needed when handling eggs to prevent contamination from the egg shell. Always wash your hands immediately after handling raw eggs and before even touching other surfaces or equipment. Bacteria from the egg shell is easily transferred to handles, equipment or other food.

The pastry kitchen should always have a stock of fresh egg whites, both from the kitchen and pastry production, where egg yolks are used for other recipes. You should take care using whites from the kitchen which might be tainted by the smell of fish or other strong odour foods. Egg whites that have been frozen produce good meringue foams.

Typical meringue dishes are:
- Cold plain meringue (*Meringue ordinaire*)
- Warm Swiss meringue (*Meringue Suisse*)
- Hot boiled Italian meringue (*Meringue Italianne*)
- Almond meringue (*Japonaise*).

The egg white to sugar ratio is 1 egg white to 60 g/2 oz sugar (caster or cube).

Piping meringues

Key points to producing meringues successfully
1 Use clean egg whites, free from yolk particles, shell or blood spots.
2 Make certain equipment is very clean by scalding with boiling water and drying thoroughly. Mixing machine bowls used for fat-based recipes and not cleaned properly can prevent the whites from whipping; the grease does not allow the albumen strands to bond and trap air bubbles, so always keep all equipment clean and grease free. Egg yolk has a fat content and this has the same effect as grease from equipment should any trace of yolk get into the whites.
3 A little acid e.g. lemon added to the whites will strengthen and stabilise the albumen foam; it extends the foam so producing more meringue.

Meringue can be either dried in a hot cupboard or above an oven range, or it can be baked in a very cool oven to produce a firm fawn coloured meringue product.

Cold basic meringue (*Meringue ordinaire*)

Place the egg white and acid (cream of tartar or lemon juice) in a clean machine bowl, whisk to a light foam and add the sugar slowly over 60 seconds, to produce a light firm meringue that has a pearly glow.

Technology tip
If the foam is over-whipped, so that the albumen strands on the outside of the bubble which hold the water molecules, are over-stretched, the water and sugar make contact and the sugar dissolves. This makes the meringue wet and heavy, but if you whip for another 10–15 minutes this will firm slightly, and will not have to be wasted.

Warm Swiss meringue (*Meringue Suisse*)

The method is the same as for cold meringue but the whites are first whisked to a foam over a bain-marie until very warm, approximately 50 °C (120 °F). Continue to whisk until cool and pipe into petit four shapes or dry meringues.

Boiled Italian meringue (*Meringue Italienne*)

This meringue is used for a wide variety of dessert, pastry and confectionery products. Cube sugar is used with a little water and is boiled to soft ball stage 118 °C (245 °F).

When the boiled sugar is nearly cooked, whisk up the egg white to half volume and pour on the boiled sugar while whisking on speed 3. If the whites are over-whipped the boiled sugar will cook the albumen foam structure and produce a coarse grain finish to the meringue. Continue to whisk until cool.

This meringue is used for Baked Alaska, soufflés, ice-cream, marshmallow, nougat de Montelimar, mousses, crèpe soufflé, buttercream, vacherin and fancy shapes, meringue tranche, shells, swans and figures. By adding gelatine to the Italian meringue you can make mallow; pipe this while still warm.

Almond semi-meringue (*Meringue Japonaise*)

Japonaise is a versatile mix produced by making a semi-meringue and mixing this with almonds and/or hazelnuts. Piped and cooked in the oven they are the basis of gateau, tea fancies, petit fours and biscuits.

Do this

- What type of egg white substitutes are available for meringue?
- How does the acid added to egg white work?
- Why is warm sugar best for producing basic cold meringue?
- How and when are meringues coloured and/or flavoured ?
- Why is care needed in the production of meringue japonaise? Look up a recipe?

MOULDED CREAMS

Pastry cream (*Crème Pâtissière*)

Crème pâtissière or pastry cream (confectioners custard) is the continental equivalent of fresh cream.

This cream or thick set sauce is the pastry chef's sweet equivalent of the béchamel sauce. It forms the basis of other creams and is used widely as a filling or ingredient in many pastry dessert dishes. Crème pâtissière is made from milk, egg yolks, flour sugar and vanilla flavouring.

Method
1 Mix the egg yolk and sugar well and stir in the flour, pour on the boiled milk into which the vanilla pod or essence has been infused (soaked).
2 Stir and mix well, return to the stove in a clean saucepan and cook the cream until it boils for approximately 1 minute or until the cream is thick.
3 If a thicker set cream for cutting is required, e.g. for *Flan aux bananes*, increase the flour content of the recipe or use a medium strength flour (50% soft and 50% strong).
4 When cooked, sprinkle with icing sugar or a buttered cartouche (round paper lid) to prevent a skin forming. When cool store in the fridge.
5 Crème pâtissière can be flavoured with chocolate, almond, coffee or with liqueurs, such as kirsch, Cointreau, brandy etc.

Crème pâtissière is used as a filling for pastries, flans, tartlets and barquettes, and as a base for soufflés.

Crème pâtissière can be made into *creme mousseline* by adding butter. One third of the butter is added to the hot crème pâtissière and allowed to cool. When cool this mixture is added a little at a time to the remaining two-thirds of the well-creamed butter. This can be used as a filling for desserts, biscuits and sponges. Store it for up to 4 days in the fridge; mix well before using.

Crème pâtissière is also used to make Crème St Honoré which is used for Gateau St Honoré and Crème Chiboust.

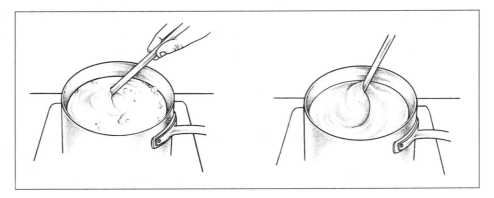

Cooking crème pâtissière
Left: pour the mixture into a saucepan and bring to the boil
Right: the cooked mixture is thicker and smoother

Cooked egg custard dessert creams and sauces

Crème ou Sauce Anglaise
Crème Bavarois
Crème St Honoré
Crème Danoise
Crème Mousseline
Sauce aux Amandes
Crème Pâtissière
Crème Charlotte
Crème Chiboust
Sauce Mousseline
Sauce Sabayon

Fresh custard sauce (*Crème/Sauce Anglaise*)

In France, custard (*Sauce Anglaise*) is a thinner sauce made from fresh eggs, milk, sugar and vanilla. Traditional English custard is a moderately thick convenience custard made by using custard powder. Many catering operations use this product as a garnishing sauce or for trifles and desserts.

Method
Infuse the vanilla pod with the milk and boil. Mix the egg yolks and sugar together well and pour the slightly cooled milk onto the yolks and sugar, mixing well. This prevents the heat of the milk overcooking the yolks, which can scramble if the milk is at boiling point. Return the mixture to the saucepan and cook on top of the stove until the sauce coats the back of a spoon, but do not boil.

If you over-cook Sauce Anglaise, do not throw it away; put it through a liquidiser and it will reform and can still be used. Cooked Sauce Anglaise can be kept hot in a bain-marie until ready for use. This sauce is very susceptible to bacterial growth due to the low coagulation temperature of the egg yolks, so it must be made fresh daily. Sauce Anglaise is used for icecream recipes, as an accompaniment for tarts, pies and puddings, or with fruit based desserts.

Convenience custard

Custard powder is also used to make custard. This is a flavoured cornflour-based powder that is mixed with a little cold milk and sugar and stirred into boiling milk. Always read the product instructions for ratio of powder to milk. If the milk is not hot enough and the dissolved powder is added, the sauce will taste of the uncooked custard powder and will probably burn before thickening.

> **MEMORY JOGGER**
>
> If you curdle a custard by over cooking it, how can you reverse the curdling effect to minimise wastage of costly ingredients?

Do this

● What effect will using more egg yolks in Sauce Anglaise have on the cooked sauce?
● Why does this sauce curdle if over-heated?
● What ratio of custard powder is required for 1 pint and 1 litre of milk.
● Sauce Anglaise is easily contaminated. Why is this, and how can it be prevented?

Bavarian cream (*Bavarois*)

Set custard based desserts
Bavarian cream has always been a standard dessert to produce. Today it is used extensively for Charlotte Russe and Royal, and bavarois desserts, which are made from either a Sauce Anglaise base or a fruit base. Every pastry and chef trainee should know how to produce this dessert.

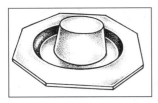

Bavarois

Sauce Anglaise based Bavarian cream – method
The ingredients are eggs, castor sugar, vanilla, milk, cream and gelatine. The gelatine is placed in cold water to soften. Use leaf sheet gelatine (8–10 sheets per 28 g/1 oz); while more expensive than powdered gelatine it is easier to use and works well in this type of product. It is available in gold, silver and bronze grades.

Mix the egg yolks and sugar together well, pour on the boiled milk into which the vanilla has been infused, stir well and return to the stove in a clean pan. Cook the custard sauce until it thickens slightly and coats the back of the spoon.

Remove from the stove and cool slightly; add the drained softened gelatine. Strain the custard into a clean stainless steel, glass or china bowl, leave to cool, or cool on a bowl of iced water. Semi-whip the cream, and when the custard begins to thicken and set, fold in the cream in three stages, clear and fill moulds or glasses.

To make a fruit bavarois using the Sauce Anglaise method, replace the milk with fruit purée, e.g. if the recipe requires 1 pint (500 ml) of milk and you are making a raspberry bavarois, use 50% milk and 50% raspberry purée. Add the purée only when the custard is setting or the acid of the fruit will denature (soften) the gelatine strands and prevent bonding, making the bavarois soft so that it will not set well enough to be de-moulded.

Fruit based Bavarian cream
Bavarois can be made using fruit purée, caster sugar with gelatine and cream. Mix the sugar with the fruit purée and bring to the boil, stir in the soaked, drained gelatine leaves and stir well. Strain the mixture into a stainless steel bowl and cool. Semi-whip the cream and fold into the setting fruit mixture. Use as required by the recipe.

MOUSSES

Mousses are an extension of bavarois, using more cream and less milk in the recipe, together with whipped cream, Italian meringue and fruit purée or a flavouring ingredient such as melted chocolate.

Mousses are traditionally produced by the bavarian cream method using Italian meringue and fruit with an appropriate liqueur or other flavouring commodities, e.g. chocolate, coffee etc. The basic Sauce Anglaise preparation is required with whipped cream and light, cool Italian meringue folded into it in two or three stages.

Add half of the cream, half of the meringue and so on to produce a very light mousse dessert for moulding and chilling in the fridge for 2–4 hours, or put it directly into a fine glass or dish and decorate with nuts, piped chocolate or crystallized fruits and flowers (roses, violets and mimosa). Serve chilled.

Mousses can also be produced using the fruit purée method as described for bavarian cream. Remember that high acid fruits will soften the gelatine and might cause problems with unmoulding this type of dessert.

Do this

Talk with your pastry chef about acid action on gelatine. Why does this happen and how can you prevent this reaction?

FRUIT BASED DESSERTS (BASIC BAKED AND STEWED FRUIT)

Baked apples

Take some medium sized cooking apples (Bramley are most commonly used), wash and core the apples with an apple corer making an incision or score mark around the centre of the apple. Place the prepared apples on a deep tray or dish suitable for baking in the oven. Fill the centre of the apple with white or brown sugar, a clove and a knob of butter; finally place a glacé cherry on top. Add a little water to the dish (about 150 ml), depending on the number of apples to be cooked. Bake in the oven at 210 °C (410–420 °F – Gas No 6) for 40–60 minutes, until just soft. Serve some of the cooking juice over the hot baked apples. Sauce Anglaise, cream, ice-cream or yoghurt can be served with this dish.

Stewed fruits (*compote of fruits*)

Stewed, poached or baked fruit is a popular dessert. It is good for a healthy eating diet and is full flavoured.

Fruits cooked in this way fall into a number of categories:

- Apples and pears — boil in sugared water with lemon juice.
- Soft fruits e.g. strawberries and raspberries — pick over, wash, cover with hot syrup and cool.
- Stone fruits e.g. damsons, plums, cherries and greengages — wash well, just cover with stock syrup and place a cartouche or lid over them. Cook slowly in a moderate oven until soft, take care not to overcook these fruits.
- Gooseberries redcurrants and blackcurrants — remove top and base stalk, gooseberries being larger and firmer are generally cooked as for stone type fruits. Cook blackcurrants and redcurrants for a shorter period of time.
- Dried fruits e.g. apricots, apples, pears and prunes — soak dried fruits overnight in cold water. Leave in the soaking liquid and cook gently with some sugar, cloves, orange and lemon slices, cardamom and bay leaf.

PROBLEMS WITH DESSERTS

In terms of freshness:

Food when purchased and stored correctly should not only be fresh but in good condition and of a good quality. More detailed information relating to purchasing and storage can be found in Unit 2ND11 in the Core Units book.

Where problems do occur it is important to minimise the disruption to production, to ensure the reason for the fault is identified to the supplier or notified or dealt with. Always inform your supervisor, chef of manager where this can be directly related to the quality of the delivered produce. If the problems occur in relation to storage or age i.e. through over-ordering, then this is an internal issue and management need to be aware of this.

Fresh produce directly relates to the quality and standard of your business and its reputation. Clearly if this is compromised by purchasing second rate commodities or through negligence then short, medium and long term profitability will suffer as a result.

In terms of quantity

Ordering of food and associated supplies is generally entrusted to experienced employees or in some cases the employer. The reason is to match the business production with the business and to minimise the stock in hand, keep products fresh and of good quality and to prevent shrinkage (pilfering). It is very important to check the foods ordered with those delivered and to weigh, count and measure the delivered commodities by checking the purchase order documentation.

BASIC PREPARATION METHODS

Piping

Piping with icing or chocolate
Piping with a nylon Savoy bag or a paper bag of icing or chocolate requires control, balance and co-ordination.

To produce designs both large and small, plain or complex requires one thing – practice. Start by trying to pipe a treble clef in chocolate on silicone paper, a gateau or individual petit four glacé.

To pipe a shape with flair and speed requires practice, but there are a few basic rules.
- Only fill the bag half full or less; if the bag is over-filled the chocolate will leak and become a problem, as you tend to concentrate on the leaking liquid rather than the design being piped.
- If the royal icing is too stiff and a fine nozzle is used, your hand can become cramped if the pressure is constant even for just a few minutes. Ensure basic preparations are carried out before piping occurs.
- Always try the design first on paper. When writing a name or message on cakes balance the words with your eyes, write the name on paper and compare the spacing with your cake.
- When filling paper piping bags, only half fill and fold tightly inwards and down toward the point of the bag.
- Make certain the paper is not creased as this can cause problems in both making up the bag and keeping a fine sharp point.

A good way of making decorations and giving yourself practice is to pipe icing onto waxed paper, letting it dry then transferring it to the cake. Chocolate can be thickened with a little glycerine, alcohol or stock syrup and piped onto silicone. These decorations set quickly and can be stored until required.

When you have some spare time prepare some of these mixtures and practise trying to keep neat rows of designs both large and small; try some little birds, butterflies or palm trees. Hand co-ordination is essential; always use your spare hand to guide the bag: it is not possible to produce high quality piping without using both hands.

Piping with cream
Fresh or synthetic cream can be used to finish cold desserts, cakes, puddings and pastries. Fresh cream if over-whipped will lose its buttermilk as the butter fat globules form together; this results in liquid dripping from the piping bag and spoiling the product as well as making it difficult to pipe. The cream will also look pale yellow and be coarse in texture. Never over-whip cream.

Piping can be done using a plain or star tube; these can be plastic or metal. Use nylon piping bags rather than cotton as nylon is more hygienic.

Never place too much whipped cream in the bag; half fill the piping bag and twist, at the same time work any trapped air from the bag to the top. When the bag feels comfortable to hold, pipe the shells by squeezing to apply an even and steady pressure as the shapes are formed.

Use your spare hand to guide the Savoy bag, it is always useful to practise icing using meringue and choux pastry, on a work bench, to develop control and accurate design.

Mixing

Mixing is the action of producing a recipe combination of different food commodities. Mixing can be done by hand, by using a spoon or with the aid of a food mixer e.g. a small hobart or food processor.

Aeration

Aeration is the action of trapping or creating oxygen bubbles in a mixture
● by chemical means, using baking powder
● by biological means, using yeast which produces carbon dioxide and ethyl alcohol (ethanol)
● by mechanical aeration using egg whites and eggs to trap air bubbles in the whisked mixture
● by lamination e.g. in puff pastry. The moisture turns to steam in the hot oven, the layers of fat and dough rise and set while the gluten blisters in the heat of the oven.

Combining

To combine means to bring together a number of different mixtures with the aim of producing one clear mix. A bavarois is a good example of this, where the Sauce Anglaise, cream and fruit mixes are combined to form a single set mixture.

Addition of flavours/colours

Adding flavour and/or colour to cold dessert mixtures requires care and practice. Too much colour and the dessert will look unsightly; too little and the presentation will be insipid. This also goes for flavours: too much and the dish will be spoilt, too little and the dessert will lack body. Follow recipe instructions when adding flavour and/or colour to any cold dessert product.

Puréeing

Puréeing is the action of pulping fruits, sauces or mixtures to produce a smooth texture. This is often done with a food processor, liquidiser or hand held tri-blade purée tool. Puréeing can also be achieved by hand with a fork or wooden spoon when foods are well cooked and break down easily when mixed, e.g. apples for apple purée (*marmalade de pommes*).

COOKING METHODS

Boiling/poaching

Cooking by the boiling or poaching method is generally applicable to fruits that are hot cooked and then cooled for service as a single fruit based dessert or composite 'compote'. Compote is a mixture of complimentary fruits poached in juices, wine or syrup until tender. These dishes can also be served hot. When served cold they should be offered with fresh cream and shortbread biscuits.

To poach fruit, just cover the fruit with the liquid and bring to the boil; reduce the heat so that the liquid just turns over but does not boil vigorously.

Pears are often cooked in this way with red wine (*poire au vin rouge*). When cooked they can be left in the cooking liquid to cool. This liquid is then served with the fruit.

Stewing

Use the method as for poaching. Use a cartouche or lid to trap the moisture and prevent evaporation during the cooking process.

Baking

Baking is a dry method of cookery and food items are prepared and produced, baked in dry heat in a standard baking oven, or forced air convector oven which reduces the time the food takes to cook.

Baking is the convection and conduction of heat in a dry atmosphere, within a closed or confined chamber. The temperature of the baking process is directly related to the nature of the food to be baked. High-sugar foods require a lower temperature to prevent caramelisation, whereas high-fat foods such as puff pastry, used in en-croute dishes, requires a much higher temperature.

Purpose of baking
- To make foods crisp and coloured, to add variety to the menu
- to reduce the percentage of fat or oil used in the cooking process
- to render food attractive by colour and texture derived from the glazing and baking process
- to achieve the correct formulation of ingredient balance in complex recipes

Methods of baking
- Low crown bakers oven in dry heat.
- High crown bakers oven in dry heat.
- Baking in a roasting or standard oven.
- Baking in a forced air convector oven.
- Baking in a pastry oven.
- Baking in a pizza oven or chamber.
- Baking in a tunnel or rack oven.

Effects of baking
Baking food in a confined space using dry heat is the oldest method of cookery know to us. Aboriginal clay or earth ovens were used thousands of years ago. Baking is the application of heat energy which sets off or triggers chemical, mechanical and physical changes in the product being baked.

The oven is pre-heated and the products are placed in the oven, the temperature set according to the type of product being baked. It is usual to set the oven hotter than the required temperature initially, to allow for the drop in heat as the foods to be baked absorb heat. This is especially true in the baking of bread and other yeast goods.

Baking ovens can be fuelled by gas or electricity; bakers generally prefer to use electric ovens which maintain a constant temperature, and are not subject to pressure fluctuations like those in gas ovens.

An oven provides a dry heat. Dry heat convects as hot air within the confined space, this can be driven or assisted by a fan at the rear of the oven unit. Radiant heat also is given off from heat elements and from the wall linings of the oven. Food items also conduct heat via the container or tray they are in contact with. Food items are placed on baking trays, in baking tins or moulds or in special containers.

A wide range of temperatures are used for baking, from cool settings to cook meringues up to very high temperatures for bread and Swiss roll sponges. Each product reacts in different ways and will require specific baking temperatures to produce the required colour and finish. Chefs learn from experience how long and at what temperature the food should be baked in their oven.

During the baking process moisture is given off from most food items. Crusty bread, for example, is steamed with water to produce a drier crust. Water in a tray is often placed in the oven when baking rich fruit cakes. Bain-marie trays of water are used to cook egg custard desserts, such as crème caramel and crème Viennoise.

High-sugar goods such as buns and Danish pastries require a lower setting than some other bread items to prevent caramelisation of the sugar. Foods change shape, size, colour and flavour when subject to baking. The changes are diverse, interesting and complex, too many to cover in this short space. Find out more by looking at some classical and contemporary books.

QUALITY IN DESSERTS

There are five main points to consider when checking a dessert for quality:
- *Texture* can be smooth, fine or coarse, relating to the general structure of the dessert. A balance is achieved when the constituent parts are combined correctly.
- *Consistency* This is the degree of viscosity or firmness of a dessert i.e. its ability to stick together to uphold a shape or form.

  Consistency also means to be able to produce similar quality over time with similar ingredients.
- *Appearance* refers to the overall presentation or look of a cold dessert item.
- *Aroma* is the distinctive, pleasant smell of a dessert dish which should be a subtle, pervasive quality or fragrance.
- *Flavour* is the balanced taste of a cold dessert, which should be not too little nor too much. Check the taste of the mixtures using a clean teaspoon to develop your skill in this vital area of professional cookery. *Always* use a clean spoon for each tasting. Never taste a mixture with a spoon already used once; this will cause cross-contamination and is very dangerous.

FINISHING METHODS

Cooling

When a basic dessert mixture or sauce is cooked it may need to be cooled, or a cooked dessert item such as poached fruits will need to be cooled prior to service. This can be achieved by natural methods, leaving it at room temperature to cool without the aid of ice or being placed into a deep freeze. Alternatively, you can place the hot food item on crushed ice in a tray or double bowl to speed up the cooling process. It is not advisable to cool hot food items in the fridge or freezer as this interferes with the safe operational temperature of the freezer unit. Most chefs cool food on a bed of crushed ice, or naturally in a cool room.

Filling

Filling is important, if only to make certain all the products have the same percentage of filling, not so much as to cause the pastry to burst or spill over e.g. in lemon curd tartlets, as this will spoil the finish and undermines professional standards of craftsmanship. Never over-fill, leave room for expansion, especially with products like turnovers, pasties, pithiviers and puffs.

When filling with fruit make sure the design produced is even in shape and colour, and balanced to make the dish attractive. Use complimentary colours and sizes, these are very important for customer satisfaction and therefore sales.

De-moulding

Cold desserts such as creams and bavarois-based desserts are usually moulded in an individual or multi-portion mould. When set and chilled the dessert must be de-moulded onto a plate or serving dish. Do this by first washing your hands well, then press the outside edge of the dessert where it meets the mould. This is to break the seal and allow air to enter between the mould and the dessert. Place the mould upside down on your hand and run it under hot water for 5 seconds. Press gently on the side of the dessert and the product should begin to come away from the mould. Place carefully onto the plate ensuring no moisture is left on the surface of the food. Decorate as required.

If de-moulding does not occur immediately then run under water for a further 5 seconds, but take care that this is not overdone as the dessert will begin to melt and affect the overall finish and presentation.

Chilling

Chilling can be done in a deep freeze, fridge or on a bed of crushed ice. The aim is to chill or lower the temperature of a dessert mixture or moulded dessert so that it sets which will enable you to de-mould or serve it as a chilled, cold dessert.

Glazing

Glazing of cold dessert dishes takes a number of forms; these can be glazing with hot and cold process gels, melting a fine dusting of icing sugar in a hot oven, using egg-wash glaze or boiled apricot jam to seal a glaze on fruit flans or applying a fondant glaze.

- *Hot process gel* is a clear gel boiled with a little water and brushed over dishes to both seal out oxygen and provide an attractive finish that has a high sheen. Hot process gels set while they are still hot. *Cold process gels* are used for the same reasons as hot process gels, but set when they are cold. Any air bubbles should be removed with a fine point of a knife or a cocktail stick.
- *Fine dusting of icing sugar* is done using a fine meshed sieve or muslin duster. The oven should be hot to melt the thin dust of sugar and produce a glorious shine and golden finish.
- *Egg-wash* is used to glaze most pastry products. The pastry goods are glazed by brushing with an egg yolk-and-water glaze. A little cream, salt and water mixed with the egg yolk is used to produce a high-gloss brown finish to puff pastry goods.
- *Salt added to egg-wash* helps denature the protein *lecithin* and improves the colour of the baked glaze. Do not leave egg-wash glaze out of the fridge when not in use; cover with cling film and only mix in small quantities.
- *Apricot jam*, boiled with a little water and strained if it contains fruit, will provide a good amber glaze and seal the dish from any oxidation, so improving the shelf life and appearance of the product.
- *Gum Arabic* is used to glaze English rout biscuits after drying and baking.

Rolling

Paste of any type should be rolled with care, puff paste needs careful handling when rolling so as not to destroy the fine lamination built up during production. Convenience sheets of puff pastry do not require rolling as they are manufactured to be used directly.

Rolling of pastry is often heavy-handed and if you do not dust and turn the paste as it is rolled the fat will be pressed against the bench surface and cause the paste to stick. Always roll soft paste lightly and heavier paste more firmly. Do not roll paste that is either too soft or still frozen as this will only cause problems.

When cutting a large number of shapes for tarts and tartlets, divide the bulk paste into a number of portions and roll, dust and turn the paste to prevent sticking. Roll paste by applying even pressure to the rolling pin with both hands spread slightly. Run your hand lightly over the paste to find out where it is thickest.

When rolling paste there is a tendency to a 'saddle shape' in puff pastry in particular because the paste has been rolled unevenly. Always roll the edges as well as the middle to prevent the saddle effect.

Remember: roll – dust – lift and turn, keep the paste on the move and dust lightly.

Defrost block paste or frozen pastry in the refrigerator to allow it to defrost naturally. Do not force it in a warm environment.

Piping

To pipe well you have to practise. Each product requires a particular skill in both holding the bag and controlling the flow by pressure of the hand to create the particular design required for each dish.

Fresh cream should not be too stiff for piping or the buttermilk will run, especially in a warm environment such as the kitchen, pastryroom or bakery.

Chocolate should be thickened with either a drop of stock syrup, spirit such as brandy, or best of all a few drops of glycerine. Melt the chocolate to approximately 43 °C/110 °F and stir in the glycerine; it takes a few minutes for the chocolate to thicken. Half fill a paper cornet bag and seal well, always folding into the centre to seal the liquid chocolate in the bag.

Practise piping to develop your skills; after a lot of practice you will be confident to pipe directly onto gateaux, desserts and pastries. Fondant is also a useful medium for piping; chocolate motifs can be made when you are not busy and stored in a cool place for decorating trifles, torten etc.

Dusting, dredging and sprinkling

The finish to any pastry product is important for a number of reasons. Firstly, all products should be the same size, finish and shape. The finish should appeal to the eye but still be good to the taste. Decoration should be delicate and balanced, colours should not be too bright and piping should be neat and tidy; strive for an artistic balance without overdoing the decoration which would detract from its saleability. This forms part of the skills of the contemporary chef, patissièr or baker.
- *Dusting* with icing sugar, icing sugar with cocoa, icing sugar with cinnamon etc. should be light and delicate, just enough to decorate the top of the particular dish. For fine finishing use a fine sieve or shaker or some muslin formed into a puff ball, especially for the famous Gâteau Pithiviers, where the fine glass finish is achieved by the fine dusting of sugar before placing it briefly in a very hot oven.
- Dust pastries and other dessert items to give them a sugar coating that forms part of the overall design, or glaze them in the oven or under a salamander. The sugar can be caster, icing or granulated for pies, biscuits or gateau. For an even dusting use a fine mesh sieve held about 20 cm (8 in) above the products. This will deposit an even dusting of sugar which should not be unsightly.
- *Dredging* is used where a heavier dusting is required e.g. with icing sugar for a white coated effect.
- When *sprinkling* with sugar scatter the sugar very lightly over the product just for effect, allowing the product surface still to be visible.

LEGAL REQUIREMENTS

You must be familiar with current relevant legislation relating to hygienic and safe working practices when preparing, cooking and finishing basic cold desserts.

You must ensure that cold dessert foods especially those containing dairy products are stored between 1 °C and 5 °C (34–41 °F).

It is advisable for you to display the full list of regulations updated from September

MEMORY JOGGER

What are the new regulations covering the safety of food?

1995 to ensure all staff are familiar with, not only the regulations, but their responsibilities in maintaining a safe and hygienic working environment. You need to comply with the *Food Safety Act 1990* and the updated *The Food Safety (General Food Hygiene) Regulations 1995* and *The Food Safety (Temperature Control) Regulations 1995*.

You need to know what company policy and procedures exist to comply with the Act and that 'due diligence' has been taken to maintain and prevent any contamination of food from delivery through storage and production.

Do you have forms for monitoring delivery temperatures of food, temperature log for refrigeration units and food service temperature log, if not – why not?

A very good reference book telling you about what procedures are required is *Croners Catering: Records and Procedures*.

Essential knowledge

It is essential that you:
- know how to prepare, cook, present and store cold dessert products in a safe and hygienic manner
- understand how each dessert dish is prepared according to recipe instructions
- can produce the dessert efficiently in the minimum amount of time to the highest standard
- know what the current food hygiene and health and safety regulations state, how they affect you and why it is important for all staff to follow these procedures.
- know how to work in a safe and hygienic manner in co-operation with fellow colleagues and to maintain work-based procedures for the benefit of the business and team spirit.

These factors contribute to the quality and standard of an establishment and are the building blocks of your own professional craft reputation.

Healthy eating

When cooking you should use substitute commodities that will improve the quality of your customers' health. Sometimes the dish cannot be produced exactly according to the recipe but wherever possible or appropriate you should substitute healthier ingredients. These might be:
- Brown flour instead of white flour
- Polyunsaturated or low fat spreads, margarines or butter substitutes
- Brown sugar or less sugar
- Reduced salt or no salt at all
- Sunflower oil rather than vegetable or hydrogenated oils or olive oil
- Less butter and margarine.

LOW CHOLESTEROL DIET

Cholesterol is a fatty substance occurring in all animal tissue and produced by the liver. We need cholesterol to carry essential fats through the bloodstream but in excess this can block arteries and reduce the blood flow to the heart.

The key is to reduce the level of animal fats in food and use polyunsaturated vegetable fats. Avoid products that contain 'hydrogenated fat' which can be vegetable fats that begin as polyunsaturated but become saturate type fats after the hydrogenation process.

You should use finishing methods to complete the production process for each dessert selected from the range listed in Healthy eating (above). Work in accordance with current relevant legal requirements.

1 What safe working practices should be followed when preparing and cooking cold desserts?
2 Why is it important to keep preparation areas and equipment hygienic when preparing and cooking cold desserts?
3 How can you minimise the risk of cross-contamination when preparing and cooking cold desserts?
4 Why are time and temperature important when preparing and cooking cold desserts?
5 Which products can be substituted for high fat ingredients when preparing and cooking cold desserts?
6 How does increasing the fibre content of cold desserts contribute to healthy eating practices?
7 Why does reducing the amount of salt and sugar in cold desserts contribute to healthy eating practices?
8 Why should high risk foods such as dairy products be stored in the fridge?

ELEMENT 2:   Prepare, cook and finish basic hot desserts

Hot desserts are a popular menu item; hot fruit pies, steamed and baked puddings or pancakes offer the customer a warm change to the usual cold dessert menu.

Basic preparation methods for hot dessert dishes

- *Creaming*   the action of mixing sugar and fat: the initial stages of beating a batter for the production of a cake or pastry recipe.
- *Moulding*   the forming of mixtures, pastes or batters into moulds, flan rings, tins or special moulds to produce the required shape of the dessert.
- *Mixing*   combining ingredients to produce a single uniform mixture.
- *Portioning*   dividing a product into equal quantities or pieces for the purposes of moulding or individual service portions.
- *Filling*   forming a product by adding a secondary ingredient or commodity, ie. filling a flan, mould, tart or pie, dish or glass.
- *Aeration*   incorporating air/oxygen by one of three methods:
  - mechanical/beating/whisking
  - chemical/baking powder/VOL
  - biological/yeast
- *Folding*   the action of combining two different commodities, i.e. flour into a batter, eggs into a panade, flavouring/colouring or liqueur into a hot mixture.
- *Peeling*   removing the outer skin of fruit.
- *Slicing*   cutting fruit into thin or appropriate slices.

COOKING METHODS

- *Boiling/poaching*   cooking in liquid syrup, water, wine or milk
- *Steaming*   cooking in a hot moist atmosphere under pressure
- *Baking*   dry cooking in an oven or enclosed space
- *Combination cookery*   a mix of steaming and baking in one unit
- *Bain-marie*   cooking in a bath of hot water

PANCAKES (CRÊPES)

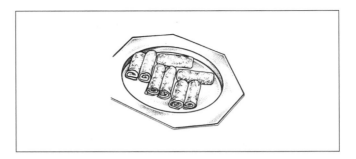

Filled pancakes

Pancakes are a reminder of Shrove Tuesday when people delight in making pancakes to eat and to toss in races for fun and for charity. This egg based dessert is made from milk, flour, eggs, salt, sugar and clarified butter.

For mass production, stack the crêpes between plates to keep warm in the hot cupboard until they are required. The classic dessert pancake dish is *crêpe suzette*.

Savoury pancakes are a popular dish, filled with vegetables, cheese and herbs for vegetarian diets, and for wrapping other food items in, as with the Russian pasties (*coulibiac*) and as a garnish for soups. Small trimmed pancakes called *pannequets* are used for sweet or savoury dishes and hors d'oeuvres.

A crêpe pan should be only used for the production of pancakes; this small flat handled pan should not be washed but wiped clean after cooking and stored cleanly.

> ### MEMORY JOGGER
>
> When producing pancakes how should you clean a crêpe pan?

Basic pancake batter recipe (*pâte à crêpe*)

Ingredients

Flour	300 g	(10oz)
Eggs	4	
Caster sugar	50 g	(2oz)
Milk	8 dl	(1¼pt)
Salt	5 g	pinch
Butter	100 g	(4oz)

This will produce about 36 pancakes depending on the size and thickness required.

Method
1 Mix the ingredients, except the butter, by whisking; strain the batter through a conical strainer.
2 Pour in the melted butter and stir.
3 Place a little butter in the pan to melt, pour off excess butter, heat the pan well and ladle in a portion of the pancake batter.
4 Swill the batter to just cover the base of the pan; this should set almost at once.
5 When no moist batter can be seen turn over (toss) to finish cooking.

Typical pancake dishes are:
● Lemon pancakes   (*crêpe au citron*)
● Orange pancakes   (*crêpe d'orange*)
● Jam pancakes   (*crêpe à la confiture*)
● Suzette pancake   (*crêpe Suzette*)
● Normandy pancakes   (*crêpe Normande*)
● Soufflé pancakes

Lemon pancakes (*crêpe au citron*)

Make the pancakes as directed above. Dust the pancakes with sugar and some lemon juice, fold neatly into four and arrange onto a serving dish, dust once again with more sugar. Colour under the salamander just before being served. Decorate with a trimmed neat wedge of lemon.

Orange pancakes (*crêpe d'orange*)

Make as for lemon pancakes, replacing the lemon with orange.

Jam pancakes (*crêpe à la confiture*)

Spread the hot pancake with raspberry or strawberry jam. Fold and dredge with fine icing sugar, mark with a hot poker to form a trellis pattern.

Suzette pancakes (*crêpe Suzette*)

These pancakes are a classic dessert, served re-heated in a hot, orange liqueur sauce.

Soufflé pancakes

These are hot pancakes freshly made and filled with a mixture of warm pastry cream with Italian meringue folded in, flavoured to the recipe requirements. Half-fill them with the mixture, fold over and dust with fine icing sugar. Place in a very hot oven to cook the meringue, serve immediately with an appropriate sauce.

SPONGE BASED DESSERTS (STEAMED/BAKED)

> **MEMORY JOGGER**
>
> What is the main aeration agent when producing steamed sponge puddings?

Steamed and baked sponge puddings are popular hot desserts especially during the autumn and winter months when the weather is cold. To produce hot light desserts from a wide variety of flavours, shapes and sizes, puddings are steamed. An essential ingredient is baking powder which produces carbon dioxide which, with the steam, aerates the product to make it light and easily digestible. Baking powder is made from two parts cream of tartar and one part bi-carbonate of soda, sieved 20 times to combine the two powders thoroughly.

These puddings can be classified into three main types:
1 steamed sponges
2 steamed suet pudding
3 baked suet roll.

Steamed sponges include:
- Cherry
- Currant
- Golden syrup
- Ginger
- Apple
- Apple and blackberry
- Sultanas
- Jam
- Lemon and/or orange
- Honey
- Almond
- Christmas pudding

Basic sponge recipe

Ingredients

Butter	250 g	(8 oz)
Sugar	250 g	(8 oz)
Eggs	5	
Flour	250 g	(8 oz)
Baking powder	15 g	($\frac{1}{2}$ oz)
Spice to taste	5 g	($\frac{1}{4}$ oz)

Method

1 Using either a sponge tin mould which comes in two halves or individual dariole moulds, brush the mould with melted butter and line with caster sugar.
2 Cream the sugar and butter well to form a light creamy mixture, scrape down the sides to incorporate any butter not creamed by the beating action.
3 Add the eggs one at a time. Ensure the eggs are at room temperature and beat each egg well into the batter before adding the next.
4 Sieve together the flour and baking powder at least five times to ensure the baking powder is well distributed throughout the flour.
5 Fold in carefully the sieved flour and baking powder and other dry ingredients e.g. spices.
6 Do not over-mix the sponge or vital aeration will be lost, gluten will also form resulting in a tight close crumb structure which will toughen the eating quality of the cooked sponge.
7 Fill the individual moulds two-thirds full, and the tubed sleeve mould half full. Place in a steamer tray and then into the pre-heated steamer.
8 Cover the moulds with greaseproof paper to prevent excess moisture from making the sponge wet.
9 Steam for 40 minutes for individual sponges and up to 90 minutes for larger multi-portion moulds.
10 Remove carefully from the steamer following all essential safety measures relating to operating a steamer.
11 De-mould the puddings and plate, or place on a serving dish.
12 Serve very hot with an appropriate sauce.

Puddings not required for immediate service should be kept in the steamer but without sealing down the door. The heat in the steamer chamber will maintain the product at a safe temperature without over-cooking the sponges.

Do this

Write up the recipe and methods for the following baked and steamed puddings:
● Baked suet roll
● College pudding
● Spotted Dick
● Summer pudding
● Baked jam roll
● Eves pudding
● Black cap pudding
● Canary pudding

HOT EGG BASED SET DESSERTS

This section covers any egg set dessert served hot. The following list covers the basic hot dessert dishes:
● Bread and butter pudding
● Queen of puddings
● Baked egg custard
● Cabinet pudding

When producing hot egg based set dessert dishes it is important to understand the cooking process for eggs to ensure the correct results are attained.

● You must maintain the water in the bain-marie in which the egg dishes are cooked at the same temperature as the egg custard itself.

● Egg custard will begin to coagulate at approx 83–85 °C (180–185 °F). Water boils at 100 °C (212 °F) and therefore you need to ensure the water *does not boil* so the cooking temperature is not excessive.

● Egg whites coagulate at approximately 58 °C (136 °F) and egg yolk at 68 °C (154 °F). The combined mixture of yolk and white coagulates at approximately 65 °C (150 °F). If the cooking process subjects the egg mixture to heat in excess of 83 °C (181 °F) then the custard will shrink and force out the liquid content resulting in a bubbled or curdled effect in the cooked egg custard.

Bread and butter pudding

Basic Recipe

Ingredients (8 portions)

Milk	1 lt	(2 pts)
Sugar	100 g	(4 oz)
Butter or low fat spread	50 g	(2 oz)
Sultanas	50 g	(2 oz)
Eggs	6	
Brown or white sliced bread	4 slices	
Vanilla essence to taste		

Method

1 Butter the base of a suitable pie dish, either metal or oven-proof china.
2 Wash the dried fruit and sprinkle over base of buttered dish.
3 Cut bread into small triangles, remove the bread crusts and dip in melted butter, then into sugar, both sides.
4 Neatly arrange the pieces of prepared bread so they overlap in the dish.
5 Prepare the egg custard. Ensure you strain the custard to remove any shell.
6 Pour over the bread and leave to soak for 20 minutes.
7 Cook in a cool oven until set.
8 Brush with clarified butter and serve hot.

BASIC CEREAL BASED MILK PUDDINGS

Cereal based desserts provide a nutritious alternative to cream or egg based hot and cold desserts. They are popular with elderly customers because they are easily digested and milk pudding are a useful alternative to less 'healthy' puddings.

This section covers the basic milk pudding desserts that are served hot. The list below is typical of the range of cereal based hot desserts:

● Rice pudding
● Sago milk pudding
● Ground rice pudding
● French rice pudding (*Riz à la Française*)
● Macaroni milk pudding
● Semolina pudding
● Tapioca milk pudding
● Flaked rice pudding

Basic rice pudding recipe

Ingredients (*8 portions*)

Carolina rice (short grain)	200 g	(8 oz)
Caster sugar	100 g	(4 oz)
Milk	1 lt	(2 pt)
Butter	25 g	(1 oz)
Vanilla and nutmeg to taste		

Method
1 Boil the milk in a thick based pan.
2 Put in the well-washed rice and stir until the milk boils.
3 Simmer and stir until the rice is cooked soft.
4 Add the sugar, butter and vanilla.
5 Place in a buttered pie dish, brown the top and serve hot.

Ratio of cereals to milk for hot cereal desserts:

Semolina	40 g $(1\frac{1}{2}$ oz)	per $\frac{1}{2}$ lt (1 pint) of milk
Ground Rice	40 g $(1\frac{1}{2}$ oz)	per $\frac{1}{2}$ lt (1 pint) of milk
Tapioca	50 g (2 oz)	per $\frac{1}{2}$ lt (1 pint) of milk
Sago	50 g (2 oz)	per $\frac{1}{2}$ lt (1 pint) of milk
Flaked rice	40 g $(1\frac{1}{2}$ oz)	per $\frac{1}{2}$ lt (1 pint) of milk
Macaroni	75 g (3 oz)	per $\frac{1}{2}$ lt (1 pint) of milk

HOT FRUIT BASED DESSERTS

Hot fruit based desserts are a popular item on the menu. When prepared and cooked correctly these desserts can be very profitable and provide healthy alternatives to the range of cream based desserts.

Typical hot fruit based desserts are:
● Baked apples
● Stewed rhubarb
● Pears in red wine
● Hot black cherries in kirsch
● Apple fritters
● Pineapple fritters
● Bananas fritters
● Apricot fritters
● Compote of hot plums and custard
● Grilled bananas with demerara sugar and double cream
● Apple strudel

Fruit fritters (*beignets*)

Ingredients
8 portions of apples, pineapple, bananas and apricots

Batter

Flour	500 g	(1 lb)
Sugar	50 g	(2 oz)
Yeast	25 g	(1 oz)
Salt	10 g	($\frac{1}{2}$ oz)
Water	5 dl	(22 fl oz)
Egg whites	3	
Egg yolks	3	

Method

1 Sieve the salt and flour into a clean bowl.
2 Dissolve the yeast in the warm water.
3 Make a bay in the flour and add the liquid and egg yolks.
4 Add the sugar and allow to dissolve.
5 Cover the liquid with the flour and beat to a smooth batter.
6 Leave to ferment until double in size (no more than 25 minutes).
7 Whisk the egg whites but do not over-whip or the whites will 'grain'. A little sugar may be added to the whipped whites to form a light meringue.
8 Fold the whipped egg whites carefully into the batter.
9 Always flour the fruit first before dipping into the prepared batter.
10 Place the coated fruit into a hot friture at approx 190–200 °C (375–400 °F). Cook until golden brown on both sides; do not over-colour.
11 Drain well onto kitchen paper and dredge in cinnamon or vanilla sugar.
12 Place on clean dish paper on a platter and serve hot with hot apricot or custard sauce.

PIES AND TARTS (SWEET AND SHORT PASTRY)

Pies and tarts, especially hot, are the backbone of traditional British hot desserts. Served with cream, custard or yoghurt they offer a wide range of seasonal and traditional puddings, popular with customers.

The most popular hot, or warm, pies and tarts are:

- Apple pie
- American apple pie
- Dutch apple pie
- Apple and blackberry pie
- Bakewell tart
- Jam tart
- Treacle tart
- Manchester tart
- Mixed fruit tart
- Gooseberry tart
- Plum tart
- Rhubarb tart

Dutch apple tart (*Tarte Hollandaise aux pommes*)

Ingredients

Short paste	200 g	(8 oz)
Cooking apples	500 g	(16 oz)
Sugar	100 g	(4 oz)
Sultanas	100 g	(4 oz)
Butter	50 g	(2 oz)

Zest of 1 lemon
Cinnamon to taste

Method

1 Produce the short paste either by the creaming or rubbing in method.
2 Roll out the paste to form a 24 cm circle to line a 20 cm flan ring. Rest in the fridge.
3 Melt the butter, lemon zest and sugar to form a light caramel in a frying pan or plat sauté.
4 Add the washed, peeled, sliced apples and sultanas; cook for a few minutes.
5 Allow the mix to cool and place neatly in the lined, rested flan case.
6 Roll out the remaining paste and cover the flan to form a tart.
7 Mark with a pattern using a small sharp knife.
8 Allow to rest for 30 minutes and bake in a moderate oven 205 °C (400 °C) until the top is a light golden colour.
9 When nearly cooked remove the flan ring and egg-wash the sides of the tart.
10 Return to the oven to complete the cooking process.
11 Serve hot cut into portions and serve with semi-whipped, fresh cream or custard sauce, or offer fresh Greek yoghurt as a healthier alternative.

MEMORY JOGGER

Which product can provide a healthy alternative to cream when serving pies and tarts?

FINISHING METHODS

Filling

When filling flans, pies or tarts do not put in too much fruit or filling which might spoil the overall appearance and presentation of a dessert. Take care when filling moulds; too little and the resultant dessert will look too small. Try and ensure all products are of the same size and shape. Filling using a ladle or portion scoop requires practice and patience.

Glazing

Pastry goods are glazed by brushing with an egg yolk-and-water glaze. If a little cream, salt and water are mixed with the egg yolk this produces a high-gloss brown finish to puff pastry goods.

Salt added to egg-wash helps denature the protein *lecithin* and improves the colour of the baked glaze. Do not leave egg wash glaze out of the fridge when not in use, cover with cling film and only mix in small quantities.

Dusting and dredging

Dust pastries and other dessert items to give them a sugar coating that forms part of the overall design. They can be glazed in the oven or under the salamander. The sugar can be caster, icing or granulated. An even dusting using a fine mesh sieve held about 20 cm (8 in) above the products will deposit an even dust of sugar which should not be unsightly.

Dredging is where a heavier dusting is required e.g. with icing sugar to give a white coated effect. You can also sprinkle sugar lightly over the product allowing the surface to be seen.

Portioning

When cutting or dividing desserts into portions it is important to maintain an even size and shape. This provides the same sized portion for each customer. If portions vary in size this can cause customers to complain, affect profit margins and actually cost the business money over time.

Portion dividers can be utilised to maintain an even size and shape for hot desserts. Flan rings, hoops or moulds provide the basis for portion control. Decide how many portions can be fairly cut from a dessert, if you are unsure seek advice from your chef or supervisor.

Types of portion aids:
● Dariole moulds
● Hoops
● Savarin rings
● Tartlet tins
● Pie dishes (metal or china)
● Flan rings
● Special individual shaped moulds
● Barquette moulds
● Torten dividers

KEY POINTS TO MAINTAINING QUALITY IN HOT DESSERT DISHES

- *Texture*   ensure pastry is short and not toughened by over-working
- *Appearance*   how a product looks is the key to sales
- *Aroma*   this enhances the quality of a dessert, attracts interest
- *Consistency*   this is essential to maintain your craft standard
- *Flavour*   as with appearance, this is vital to maintain repeat business.

LEGAL REQUIREMENTS

You should be familiar with current relevant legislation relating to hygienic and safe working practices when preparing, cooking and finishing basic hot desserts.

Hot dessert foods products should be kept above 70 °C (158 °F) prior to or during service periods. Some hot dessert products will obviously be ruined if left for long at such temperatures and care needs to be taken to maintain a safe hot temperature without destroying the essential quality of the hot dessert product.

It is advisable to display the full list of regulations updated from September 1995 to ensure all staff are familiar with not only the regulations but their responsibilities in maintaining a safe and hygienic working environment.

Do you have forms for monitoring delivery temperatures of food, temperature log for refrigeration units and food service temperature log, if not – why not?

A very good reference to know what procedures are required is provided by *Croners Catering 'Records and Procedures'*.

Healthy eating

Low salt and low sugar diets   Reducing the amount of salt (sodium chloride) and sugar (sucrose) in food has beneficial effects for health. Salt in the diet is essential to balance the degree of acid in the blood and to maintain the fluid content of the body cells. Without salt people are prone to severe cramp and their bodies might degenerate over time. The salt balance in the body is regulated by the kidneys. People become accustomed to high salt intake because of the way in which they usually season our food. If you aim to reduce salt in products by using unsalted butter or margarines, and use less salt in recipes, over time people will not notice the lack of salt.

Sugar is more difficult to reduce when preparing hot dessert items. Using more fresh fruits, reducing the amount of sugar in each recipe is worthwhile and it is possible to produce some low-sugar hot desserts without affecting the recipe balance too much.

Case study

You are required to provide a hot and cold dessert selection of dishes for a health club dinner. Some of the guests require low fat and high fibre dishes, some require non-sugar based desserts and a few can eat regular basic hot and cold desserts.
1 *Suggest a range of desserts that meet these requirements.*
2 *What information might you need from the health club regarding the dinner to be able to comply with the criteria set out above?*
3 *Once guest is allergic to egg dishes. Suggest three desserts appropriate for this person.*
4 *A number of guests are diabetic. What precautions need to be taken when preparing their desserts?*

What have you learned

1 What safe working practices should be followed when preparing and cooking hot desserts?
2 Why is it important to keep preparation areas and equipment hygienic when preparing and cooking hot desserts?
3 How can you minimise the risk of cross-contamination when preparing and cooking hot desserts?
4 Why are time and temperature important when preparing and cooking hot desserts?
5 Which products can be substituted for high fat ingredients when preparing and cooking hot desserts?
6 How does increasing the fibre content of hot desserts contribute to healthy eating practices?
7 Why does reducing the amount of salt and sugar in hot desserts contribute to healthy eating practices?
8 Above what safe temperature should hot desserts be maintained prior to and during service?

Get ahead

1 To extend your knowledge of basic cold and hot desserts read up on the types of more complex products from the following categories:
- complex egg based
- complex fruit based
- complex simple of single type desserts
- complex composite desserts e.g. Gateau Macmahon.
2 Look at other cold desserts where a number of basic dessert recipes are utilised to produce a complex dessert such as the example above.
3 Investigate the types of hot individual and composite desserts at level 3. These might include omelette soufflés, soufflé souprise, ruche, oeufs à la neige, poire d'aremburg etc.
4 Find out the range of text books available at your library that provide competent recipes and product information. Look for authors such as such as Kollist, Nicolello (*Complete pastry work techniques*), Barker and Hanneman.

Prepare and cook basic sauces and soups

This chapter covers:
ELEMENT 1:   **Prepare and cook basic hot and cold sauces**
ELEMENT 2:   **Prepare and cook basic soups**

What you need to do

- Prepare cooking and preparation areas and equipment ready for use and clean after use, satisfying all health, safety and hygiene regulations.
- Carry out your work in an organised and efficient manner taking account of priorities and laid down procedures.

- Prepare and cook sauces and soups according to customer and dish requirements.
- Finish and present sauces and soups according to customer and dish requirements.
- Store prepared sauces and soups in accordance with food hygiene regulations.

What you need to know

- The type, quality and quantity of ingredients required for each type of sauce and soup.
- How to plan your time efficiently, taking account of priorities and any laid down procedures.
- Why time and temperature are important when cooking sauces and soups.

- What the main contamination threats are when preparing, cooking and storing sauces and soups.
- Why it is important to keep preparation, cooking and storage areas and equipment hygienic.

INTRODUCTION

Sauces and soups are prepared and stored using similar methods and equipment.

STORING SAUCES AND SOUPS

Sauces and soups are known as *high risk foods*. This means that they are the foods most at risk from bacterial infection because they provide the nutrients that bacteria need to grow. If stored incorrectly, these items provide all the optimum conditions for bacteria growth: food, moisture, warmth and time.

If sauces and soups are to be stored, rapid cooking and correct temperature control are of vital importance in the prevention of food poisoning. The products required for storage should be placed in a clean pot, bucket or bain marie container. They must then be cooled down as quickly as possible, using one of the following methods:
- place the container in a large blast chiller (*see Unit 2ND16: Prepare cook-chill food, page 329*)
- place the container in a sink full of running cold water, stirring frequently
- rest the container on a wooden stand in a cool place so that the air can circulate under it.

If a blast chiller is not available, make sure that the cooling down process does not take more than 90 minutes before refrigeration. Once the product is cold, cover it and attach a clear label stating the contents and date produced. *It is essential to label and date every food product that is stored in the refrigerator*. Keep these products away from uncooked food; store in a separate refrigerator if possible. The refrigerator should be kept at a temperature below 5 °C (41 °F). If the product is to be stored in a freezer, make sure that the freezer maintains a temperature below −18 °C (0 °F).

Key points when storing sauces and soups

- Sauces and soups are high risk foods and bacteria will grow rapidly in the *danger zone*: 5–63 °C (41–145 °F). However, bacteria cannot grow at temperatures outside of this range, i.e. below 5 °C (41 °F) or above 63 °C (145 °F).
- Sauces and soups taken from storage must be boiled again for at least two minutes before use.
- Never reheat sauces or soups more than once.

EQUIPMENT

- Always use *clean* equipment to prevent food from becoming contaminated through harmful bacteria and dirt.
- Use the correct chopping boards for preparing meat, fish or vegetables for soups and sauces; check the colour coding system used in your kitchen. Do not use unhygienic wooden boards.
- When chopping vegetables, use the correct knife and correct techniques. (See Unit 2ND18: *Prepare and cook vegetables*, pages 336–37 and Unit 1ND2: *Maintain and handle knives*, pages 56, 57 and 63 in the Core Units book.)
- Do not use unhygienic wooden spoons or aluminium whisks for stirring soups or sauces. Utensils made from plastic or a similar polythene compound are more hygienic.
- Do not use mechanical bowl choppers or vegetable cutting and dicing machines unless you have received instruction from your supervisor on their use and you are familiar with the safety procedures outlined in Unit 2ND17: *Clean and maintain cutting equipment*, pages 90–96 in the Core Units book.

PREPARATION AND COOKING AREAS

Make sure you are familiar with the general points given in Unit NG1: *Maintain a safe and secure working environment* in the Core Units book. Remember that soups and sauces are *high-risk foods*.

The points below should all be considered when preparing soups and sauces.
- Make sure the vegetables for soups and sauces are thoroughly washed, peeled and rewashed before use.
- Only put out the tools and equipment you need; keep your work area uncluttered.
- Do not leave pots or pans on the floor.
- Keep cooking areas clean.
- Do not leave pan handles jutting over the edge of the stove where they could cause accidents.
- Remember that pan handles become hot when the pan is on top of a stove; always use a suitable dry cloth (*known as a rubber*) when lifting.
- Always mark hot pans or trays taken from the oven with something white such as a sprinkling of flour as a warning to others.
- Remember to seek assistance when lifting large, heavy pans and to lift them in the correct manner.
- Always mop up spillages immediately.

- When straining or passing sauces or soups into suitable containers, hold your face back and away from the hot products to avoid splashes from the hot liquid.
- When using an electric liquidiser, remember that they should never be more than two-thirds full. If they are filled above this level the initial power surge would send the contents over the top and you could suffer a serious scald or burn from the hot liquid.
- Make sure you are fully aware of what to do in the case of burns or scalds (see Unit NG1: *Maintain a safe and secure working environment* in the Core Units book).
- When tasting soups or sauces for seasoning, remember to use a clean spoon *on each occasion.*

Essential knowledge

It is important to keep preparation and storage areas and equipment in order to:
- prevent the transfer of food poisoning bacteria to the sauces and soups
- ensure that standards of cleanliness are maintained
- comply with statutory health and safety regulations.

ELEMENT 1: Prepare and cook basic hot and cold sauces

INTRODUCTION

The French word *sauce* comes from the Latin *saltus* or *salted*, reminding us that sauces were originally liquid seasonings for food. Sauces now have a much more important part to play as they are used to complement the flavour, texture and appearance of foods.

A sauce should never overpower the dish it accompanies but bring harmony and balance. A sauce may also aid digestion: traditionally acidic sauces often accompany fatty foods, orange sauce is often served with duck, and apple sauce with pork. Similarly, fatless foods such as fish and vegetables are often complemented by emollient sauces made with butter or oil. The strong taste of game is often balanced by a sharp, piquant sauce.

Today, due to increased public awareness of the relationship between health and diet, and our changing tastes and attitudes towards food, sauces that are natural, light and quick to prepare have grown in popularity.

Traditional sauces are often categorised or put into main classifications according to their method of preparation. During this element we will look at the following types of sauces: roux sauces, starch thickened sauces, egg based sauces, and meat, poultry and vegetable gravies.

ROUX-BASED SAUCES

A *roux* is generally defined as 'a type of thickening for sauces composed of cooked fat and flour to which liquid is added'. The type of fat and liquid used, and the degree to which the roux is cooked depend on the type of sauce being made.

Roux sauces are classified as *basic sauces*. This means that they are used as a foundation for other dishes or as a base for derivative sauces.

White roux

This is made from equal quantities of fat and flour. The fat used for the preparation of a white roux is usually butter or margarine, although a white roux can be made using vegetable oil.

Method: white roux
1   Melt the fat over a gentle heat.
2   Add the flour and mix well.
3   Gently heat the roux, cooking without developing colour.

Making a béchamel sauce using white roux:
4   Allow the roux to cool.
5   Gradually pour in some warmed, infused milk; i.e. milk that has been flavoured by being gently heated with an *onion clouté* or *studded onion*. (To make an onion clouté, press a number of cloves into a peeled onion, using one clove to staple a bay leaf to the onion.)
6   Cook the sauce for approximately 20–30 minutes.
7   Remove the onion and strain the sauce ready for use.

Healthy eating

White roux sauces: margarine high in polyunsaturates can be substituted for butter in the roux. However, the taste may be considered inferior.

Some à la carte chefs now prepare white sauces using only a reduction of cream, with the addition of the appropriate ingredients, which is sometimes finished with a little butter. This type of sauce provides a good taste but is not particularly good for health and should only be eaten on occasions rather than as part of a balanced diet.

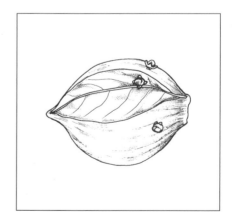

Left: preparing a roux
Right: an onion clouté

Ingredient ratios for basic white sauce	
Butter/margarine	100 g (4 oz)
Flour	100 g (4 oz)
Milk	1 litre (2 pt)
Small onion clouté	

Blond roux or yellow roux

A blond roux is prepared as for a white roux (above), but the roux is cooked for a little longer than for a white roux, until it develops a sandy texture and colour.

It may be used for *velouté* or velvet sauce and in the preparation of tomato sauce.

Method: blond roux
1 Melt the fat over a gentle heat.
2 Add the flour and mix well.
3 Gently heat the roux, cooking until it is light fawn in colour and has developed a sandy texture.

Making a velouté sauce using blond roux:
4 Allow the roux to cool.
5 Gradually add boiling white stock to the roux.
6 Cook the sauce for approximately 45 minutes–1 hour.
7 Strain the sauce through a conical strainer or chinois.
8 If a liaison is to be added (optional): mix a liaison of egg yolks and cream with a little of the sauce, then add the liaison to the main portion of sauce. Do not re-boil the sauce or the egg yolk will cook and *coagulate* (scramble), causing the sauce to develop a curdled texture and appearance.

Ingredient ratios for basic velouté sauce	
Butter/margarine/oil	100 g (4 oz)
Flour	100 g (4 oz)
White stock	1 litre (2 pt)
Liaison (optional):	
Cream	120 ml ($\frac{1}{4}$ pt)
Egg yolks	2

Brown roux

A brown roux is prepared as for a white roux (page 128), with the following differences:
● use lard or dripping as the fat
● add a little more flour than for a white roux, as the browning of the roux diminishes its thickening properties
● cook the roux over a gentle heat until it turns golden brown and smells of biscuits or lightly roasted hazelnuts.

Healthy eating

Brown roux sauces contain beef dripping which is high in saturated fats. Saturated fats raise blood cholesterol levels. The higher the level of cholesterol in the blood, the greater the risk of coronary heart disease. Reduced brown stock thickened with arrowroot, as described in the starch-thickened sauces, provides a healthy alternative which many consider to have a superior taste.

Making a sauce espagnole using brown roux:
1 Cook the roux until it turns golden brown. Allow it to cool.
2 Gradually add boiling brown stock to the roux over a gentle heat.
3 Add some browned vegetables, tomato purée and mushroom trimmings.
4 Cook the sauce for approximately 4–6 hours.
5 Strain ready for use.

Sauce espagnole can be refined to produce a *demi-glace* or *half-glaze* sauce. This is prepared by adding brown stock to the espagnole sauce, in equal quantities. The thinner sauce is then brought to the boil, simmered until it has reduced by half, and strained ready for use.

Ingredient ratios for basic espagnole sauce

Beef dripping	50 g (2 oz)
Flour	60 g (2½ oz)
Tomato purée	25 g (1 oz)
Brown stock	1 litre (2 pt)
Mirepoix (vegetables):	
Onions	100 g (4 oz)
Carrots	100 g (4 oz)
Mushroom trimmings	25 g (1 oz)

Beurre manié

This is an uncooked roux made from equal quantities of fresh butter and flour kneaded together into a paste. Small lumps are added to boiling liquids and beaten in with a spoon or whisk until the required consistency Is achieved.

PREPARING ROUX SAUCES

Keep the following points in mind when preparing roux sauces:
- the principle of the roux is that the flour (the thickening agent) is coated in fat and will not therefore clump together when mixed with a liquid
- always stir the roux when cooking so that it cooks evenly; do not allow it to catch in the corners of the pan where it might burn
- when preparing a sauce, it is important to have a cold roux and a hot liquid or a hot roux and a cold liquid. If the roux and liquid are mixed together when both are hot, the flour will cook and thicken immediately into lumps before being evenly distributed throughout the sauce. As the hot liquid meets the hot pan it will also cause some of the liquid to rapidly rise as steam, which can scald the face
- a smooth sauce is achieved by *gradually* adding the liquid, stirring thoroughly and continuously as the liquid comes to the boil. If you add the liquid too fast the sauce will become lumpy. Never use aluminium whisks for stirring sauces, as these are unhygienic and may discolour the sauce
- remember to cook the sauce for the correct period of time. Under-cooking will cause the sauce to be dull, lacking gloss and shine. The sauce may also have a raw flavour and grainy texture and it will not be the correct consistency
- remember that the sauce will only begin to thicken as the flour grains begin to swell up with moisture and eventually burst releasing starch. The sauce then needs to simmer for a further period to avoid a raw starch flavour
- when cooking the sauces, simmer gently and stir frequently to prevent the sauce settling on the bottom of the pan, developing a burnt taste. Sauces requiring long cooking times such as sauce espagnole can be gently cooked in the oven with a tight fitting lid to avoid the constant attention the sauce requires if it is cooked on top of the stove
- when the sauce is cooked it needs to be passed through a conical strainer or chinois into a clean container and kept at a temperature above 75 °C (167 °F)

MEMORY JOGGER

Why is it important to ensure that roux based sauces are cooked for the correct period of time?

- as basic sauces have many different uses it is best to keep the seasoning to a minimum. This can always be adjusted later. If the sauce is to be used immediately you will need to adjust the seasoning and consistency to suit the finished dish
- when preparing roux sauces, place some knobs of butter or a buttered greaseproof paper cartouche on the surface to prevent a skin forming.

Essential knowledge

Time and temperature are important when cooking sauces in order to:
- achieve the required flavour and consistency
- ensure that the finished product is correctly cooked
- prevent food poisoning.

Do this

- Watch your supervisor carry out general preparation on at least two types of roux-based sauces. Notice the equipment and techniques used.
- Find out the recipes and cooking times for each type of roux based sauce prepared in your workplace.
- Check today's menu and identify any roux-based sauces used in or with the various dishes.
- Find at least three different uses or derivatives for each type of basic roux sauce.
- Check the temperatures of areas in which basic roux sauces are stored in your kitchen.
- Find out if there are any 'convenience' basic sauces in your foodstores and ask your supervisor if you could arrange to make comparisons.

STARCH-THICKENED SAUCES

Sauces may be thickened by the addition of a starch such as rice flour, potato flour or arrowroot. Arrowroot is a very pure starch which has no taste and cooks very quickly. It is the refined starch from the root of the West Indian *Maranta* plant.

To thicken a sauce with a refined starch, first dissolve the starch in cold water. Take the liquid to be thickened off the boil and pour in the dissolved starch, stirring all the time. Return to the boil and simmer gently for 10–15 minutes. Pass the finished sauce through a conical strainer or chinois. Starch-thickened gravy (*jus lié*) made with gelatinous reduced stock is now widely used as a brown base sauce and is a modern alternative to traditional *demi-glace* sauce.

EGG-BASED SAUCES

Egg-based sauces are divided into two types.
1 Egg sauces that are served hot, made from emulsions of egg yolks and butter.
2 Egg sauces that are served cold, made from emulsions of egg yolks and oil.

Emulsion is the scientific name for a mixture of two substances that do not normally bind together. In cookery, an *emulsion* normally refers to fat and liquid bound together in a creamy mixture.

Preparing basic hot egg-based sauce

Sauce hollandaise is a hot emulsion sauce of egg yolks and butter and is prepared using the method below.

Method
1 Make a reduction of vinegar and peppercorns in a shallow saucepan or sauteuse by simmering the liquid until half has evaporated, making it more concentrated.

Gradually adding butter to hollandaise sauce

2 When completely reduced, add a little cold water.
3 Place some egg yolks and strained reduction into a clean mixing bowl.
4 Whisk up the yolks and reduction with a balloon whisk over a pan of hot water or over a gentle heat until the mixture becomes light and fluffy and thickens slightly. The cooked mixture, which should form stable peaks with the whisk is called a *sabayon*.
5 Remove from the heat and gradually whisk in warm, melted, unsalted butter a little at a time until the sauce thickens.
6 Season and strain through a fine chinois or through muslin into a clean bowl.

Ingredient ratios for hot egg-based sauce (sauce hollandaise)	
Vinegar	25 ml (1 fl oz)
Crushed peppercorns	8–10
Cold water	1 tbsp
Unsalted butter	400 g (1 lb)
Egg yolks	4

Healthy eating

Hollandaise sauce is high in saturated fat and cholesterol. The sauce has a characteristic taste of butter which cannot adequately be substituted by polyunsaturated margarines. Consequently it is advisable to be eaten only in small quantities as a treat and not part of a balanced diet.

Key points in preparing hot egg-based emulsion sauces

- Always use good quality ingredients.
- Take care not to overcook the sabayon mixture or the eggs will scramble.
- Make sure the butter is not too hot.
- Remember not to add the butter too quickly and always make sure all the butter has been incorporated into the sauce before adding any more.
- If your sauce should separate or split: put a tablespoon of hot water into a clean bowl and gradually add the separated sauce to it, whisking vigorously. Should this fail the yolks are probably slightly overcooked and cannot hold the butter, so you need to whisk up a fresh egg with a spoonful of water. Then repeat the procedure, adding the separated sauce.

Preparing basic cold egg-based sauces

Sauce mayonnaise is a cold emulsion of egg yolks and oil.

Method
1 Place the egg yolks, vinegar and mustard into a bowl and whisk together.*
2 Gradually whisk in the oil a little at a time.
3 Season to taste.

Key points in preparing cold egg-based emulsion sauces

- In order to reduce the danger of salmonella infection from raw eggs, use pasteurised egg. Remember that, pasteurised egg must still be handled and stored with care.

Making mayonnaise sauce by hand

* Some chefs like to add half the vinegar with the egg yolks and the remaining half when all the oil has been added.

MEMORY JOGGER

What factors could cause a mayonnaise sauce to curdle and how can the sauce be rectified?

- Keep all ingredients at room temperature. Gently warm the oil if it has been chilled.
- Add the oil very gradually at first, adding it in small drops until the egg yolks have had time to absorb the oil. The oil can be added more quickly as the sauce starts to thicken.
- If the oil is added too quickly or if the recipe balance is incorrect the sauce will curdle. If your sauce should separate or curdle: put a tablespoon of hot water into a clean bowl and gradually add the curdled sauce to it, whisking vigorously. Should this fail, whisk up a fresh egg yolk with a little cold water. Then proceed as before, gradually adding the curdled sauce.

Ingredient ratios for cold egg-based sauce	
Vinegar	1 tbsp
Dry mustard	$\frac{1}{2}$ tbsp
Oil	500 ml (1 pt)
Egg yolks	4

Storing hot egg emulsion sauces

Hollandaise sauce is usually held at a warm temperature rather than hot. If the sauce is allowed to become cold the butter will set and the sauce will split when reheated. Alternatively, if the sauce becomes too hot it will also split. The sauce cannot therefore be effectively stored outside the danger zone, i.e. the temperature range within which bacteria grow most quickly 5–63 °C (41–145 °F). The solution is to avoid storing the sauce: once prepared and it can only be kept warm for a *maximum* of two hours. Any remains must then be thrown away. It is strongly recommended that the sauce is prepared as close to the service time as possible and any surplus discarded.

Storing cold sauces

Cold sauces should be stored in a cool place away from extreme temperatures in airtight containers or screw top jars. If mayonnaise is stored in a refrigerator it must be allowed to come to room temperature slowly before it is stirred, or it will separate.

Do this

- Watch your supervisor carry out general preparation on a hot and a cold sauce. Notice the equipment and techniques used.
- Find at least three different uses or derivatives for each type of hot egg-based sauce and cold egg-based sauce.
- Ask your supervisor for the recipes and methods for hot egg-based sauces and cold sauces prepared in your workplace.
- Check the temperatures of areas in which egg-based sauces and cold sauces are stored in your kitchen.

Finishing and presenting sauces

If you have prepared your sauce correctly it should only require minor adjustments to finish and present. You will need to check the consistency and correct this if necessary, as shown in the following table.

Correcting sauce consistencies		
Type of sauce	**If the sauce is too thick**	**If the sauce is too thin**
Roux based	Gradually add more liquid to required consistency	Leave to simmer gently and reduce to required consistency *or*: thicken with *beurre manie* or refined starch (arrowroot)
Hollandaise	Add a little hot water	Gradually add sauce to fresh egg yolk which has been whisked over heat with a little water
Mayonnaise	Add a little hot water	Gradually add sauce to fresh egg yolk/s

You will also need to check whether the sauce is sufficiently seasoned; i.e. seasoned to capture the full taste. This comes with experience and you may need to check the seasoning with your supervisor when you first start to prepare sauces. Take care not to over-season, as it is easy to add more seasoning but virtually impossible to remove.

Make sure your sauce is served at the correct temperature and that any garnish is of the correct size and quantity and correctly cooked.

Serving sauces
Do not over-fill sauce boats. When serving hot sauce for plate service, do not over-fill the plate. Use a suitable jug with a lip for pouring the sauce to prevent unsightly drips on the plate.

COLD SAUCES

Vinaigrette

The basic blend of oil and vinegar, which is referred to as *vinaigrette* or French Dressing, can in addition contain mustard, either French or English, finely chopped garlic or herbs, according to choice.

Vinaigrette may be used to enhance the taste of leaf salads, vegetable, meat, pasta and fish salads and can also be used to compliment hors d'oeuvres and appropriate cold dishes.

Ingredient ratios for vinaigrette dressing
The proportion of oil to vinegar can be adjusted according to taste. However, a ratio of three parts oil to one part vinegar produces a good result

Ingredients for vinaigrette (using mustard)	
Oil	450 ml ($\frac{3}{4}$ pint)
Vinegar	150 ml ($\frac{1}{4}$ pint)
French mustard	1 tsp.
Salt and pepper	pinch

Different oils may be used for flavour such as vegetable oil, sunflower oil, walnut oil, olive oil, etc. Similarly, a range of different flavoured vinegars may be used as required.

Method
- Place salt, pepper, vinegar and mustard (if required) in a bowl
- Gradually whisk in oil with a balloon whisk to form an emulsion
- Alternatively, vinaigrette can be prepared in a food processor which will beat air into the emulsion if prepared just before service. This produces a frothy effect to the vinaigrette.

Healthy eating

Sunflower oil is high in polyunsaturates and can be used for vinaigrette or mayonnaise. Polyunsaturates in the diet reduce blood cholesterol levels. However the taste may be considered to be inferior.

Olive oil provides a good taste and is high in monounsaturates. Monounsaturate fatty acids are neutral in their affect on blood cholesterol, neither raising or lowering it.

Mint sauce

Mint sauce is a traditional English sauce suitable for serving with hot or cold roast lamb or mutton.

Ingredients for mint sauce	
Fresh mint	15 g ($\frac{1}{2}$ oz)
Vinegar	50 ml (2 fl oz)
Water	50 ml (2 fl oz)
Caster sugar	1 dessert spn.

Method
- Pick leaves from stalks and wash.
- Finely chop with a little caster sugar.
- Place in a bowl and add the vinegar and water – if the vinegar taste is too strong, add a pinch more sugar.
- If using dried mint, boil the water, pour over the mint and add the rest of the ingredients and leave to cool before using.

Horseradish sauce

Horseradish sauce is traditionally served as an accompaniment to roast beef, although it can also be served with smoked fish such as trout and eel or served warm as an accompaniment to Chicken Maryland.

Ingredients for horseradish sauce	
Horseradish	approx $\frac{1}{2}$ stick
Cream	300 ml ($\frac{1}{2}$ pint)
Salt and pepper	pinch
Vinegar	1 tablespn.

Method
- Wash, peel and re-wash the horseradish. Grate finely into a bowl.
- Lightly whip the cream and mix together with the horseradish.
- Add the vinegar and salt and pepper to taste.
- (Some chefs may also add white breadcrumbs soaked in milk, however, this is not essential.)

Essential knowledge	The main contamination threats when preparing, cooking and storing sauces are as follows:
	● food poisoning bacteria may be transferred through dirty surfaces and equipment
	● food poisoning bacteria may be transferred between yourself and food items through inadequate attention to personal hygiene
	● contamination can occur due to incorrect storage temperatures. Remember that bacteria will grow most rapidly in the danger zone: 5–63 °C (41–145 °F); bacteria growth will not occur above or below this range of temperatures
	● contamination can occur if items undergo prolonged cooling. Sauces must be rapidly cooled (within 90 minutes) before refrigeration
	● incorrect waste disposal procedures can lead to contamination
	● contamination can occur through items being left uncovered. Cooled sauces prepared for storage must be covered, labelled and dated before being placed in the refrigerator
	● cross-contamination can occur between cooked and uncooked food if these are stored together.

PLANNING YOUR TIME

Be aware of which sauces you will be preparing so that you know what equipment, ingredients and utensils you will need to use. Preparing a production time plan will help you think about priorities; make sure that you take account of the daily working schedules within your kitchen.

HEALTH, SAFETY AND HYGIENE

Make sure you are familiar with the general points given in Unit NG1 (*Maintain a safe and secure working environment*) of the Core Units book. Remember that sauces are high risk foods.

PREPARATION OF EQUIPMENT, PREPARATION AND COOKING AREAS

Refer to *Equipment* and *Preparation and cooking areas* (p. 126) for sauces and soups.

When making hollandaise sauce, use a copper or stainless steel pan (sauteuse) if possible, as this will conduct the heat evenly and retain the sauce's colour. It is important to ensure that any copper pans are well tinned to prevent the risk of contamination from the copper.

Use a thin, springy balloon whisk when making hollandaise, mayonnaise or vinaigrette sauce, as this will effectively combine the mixture. If mayonnaise is normally prepared in your workplace using a mechanical mixing machine, make sure that you have received instruction in its use and that you are familiar with the safety procedures before attempting to use the machine.

The wide surface area of a sauteuse makes it ideal for preparing sauces, especially those which need reducing

Case study

One evening in a small hotel kitchen a commis chef was asked by the chef to prepare a batch of béchamel sauce before the service commenced in forty minutes time.

The commis quickly went into action and to save time whisked the milk into the roux with an aluminium whisk. The sauce was presented to the chef within ten minutes, who immediately complained that it was unacceptable.

1   *Why do you think that the chef was unhappy with the sauce?*
2   *What possible faults can you list that may be wrong with the finished sauce?*
3   *If you had to instruct the commis to prepare a fresh batch of sauce, what key issues would you raise to ensure the finished sauce was of a high quality?*

Essential knowledge

It is important to keep preparation and storage areas and equipment hygienic in order to:
● prevent the transfer of food poisoning bacteria to the sauce
● ensure that standards of cleanliness are maintained
● comply with statutory health and safety regulations.

What have you learned

1   What are the main contamination threats when preparing, cooking, and storing sauces?
2   Why is it important to keep preparation, cooking and storage areas hygienic?
3   Why are time and temperature important when preparing and cooking sauces?
4   What faults can occur when preparing sauces? How can they be avoided and, in some cases, rectified?
5   What are the main classifications of sauces and how are they prepared?
6   Why are sauces served with food?

ELEMENT 2:   Prepare and cook basic soups

INTRODUCTION

Soups, unlike sauces, are a dish in their own right. Soups may be served as a snack meal, a meal in themselves, or more often, as a first course on a menu to stimulate the appetite. The place that soups have on the menu means that they are one of the first dishes to be eaten by a customer; this is important as they can influence the whole meal.

A good soup should be light and flavoursome, capturing the various flavours and aromas of the chosen ingredients. Soups can be classified according to their method of preparation. In this element we will look at the following types of soup: purée soups, cream soups, broths.

You will need to be familiar with the following culinary terms:
● *croûtons or sippets*: small cubes of shallow-fried bread served with soup. Additional flavours may be added to croûtons such as garlic or celery seeds
● *flûtes*: small circles of toasted French bread served with soup, e.g. minestrone
● *mirepoix*: roughly cut vegetables used for flavouring
● *bouquet garni*: herbs bundled together inside leek, celery or muslin, usually parsley stalks, thyme and bay leaf.

PURÉE SOUPS

These are soups where the main ingredients (usually vegetables, dried vegetables or pulses) are cooked with a stock and, as the name implies, puréed and strained. Where starchy vegetables and pulses are included as ingredients, these act as self-thickeners to the soup. Soups made using other types of vegetables need to be thickened by an extra ingredient: a starch-based thickening agent.

Purée soups are usually served accompanied by croûtons.

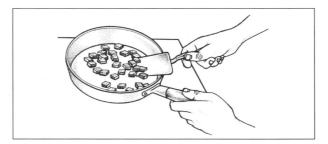

Frying croutons

Purée soups using starchy vegetables or pulses

Method
1 Place the main vegetables or pulses into a saucepan, add the stock and mirepoix.
2 Bring to the boil, reduce the heat and allow to simmer.
3 Add the bouquet garni and season as necessary. Skim off any impurities that rise to the surface.
4 Simmer for approximately 45 minutes, depending on the type of vegetable used.
5 Remove the bouquet garni and liquidise the soup.
6 Pass the liquidised soup through a chinois or conical strainer into a clean pan.
7 Adjust the consistency and seasoning, and add garnish required.

Recipe examples: Purée of haricot bean soup, Purée of lentil soup.

Purée soups requiring a thickening agent

Method
1 Sweat the main vegetable and mirepoix in fat.
2 Add flour to form a roux, and cook over a gentle heat without colouring.
3 Cool slightly and gradually add the hot stock
4 Bring to the boil, reduce the heat and allow to simmer.
5 Add the bouquet garni and season as necessary. Skim off any impurities that rise to the surface.

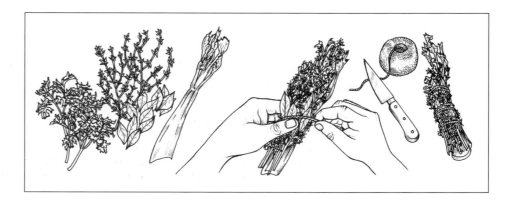

Tying a bouquet garni

6   Simmer for approximately 45 minutes, depending on the type of vegetable used.
7   Remove the bouquet garni and liquidise the soup.
8   Pass the liquidised soup through a chinois or conical strainer into a clean pan.
9   Adjust the consistency and seasoning, and add garnish required.

The soup can also be thickened by the addition of rice or potatoes (at Step 5) instead of flour. The roux is cooked a little longer to a sandy texture for some soups, such as mushroom and tomato soup.

Recipe examples: Purée of carrot soup, Purée of leek soup.

Healthy eating

Although some purée soups and sweated broths contain fat, this is relatively small in relation to the volume of the soup. Purée soups and sweated broths can therefore contribute to part of a healthy balanced diet.

VELOUTÉ SOUPS

Velouté soups are prepared from an appropriately flavoured white stock thickened by a blond roux (see page 129). The stock may be derived from meat, fish or vegetables according to recipe requirements.

Velouté soups without a vegetable content

Method
Gradually add the white stock to the blond roux and then gently simmer the soup until cooked, following the same procedures as for the preparation of velouté sauces (see page 129).

Recipe examples: Chicken velouté soup, Fish velouté soup.

Velouté soups with a vegetable content

Vegetable veloutés may also contain a vegetable content appropriate to the main character of the soup which is cooked separately and puréed into the soup. The vegetable content should not usually account for more than 25 per cent of the volume of the finished soup. A velouté soup can be thickened by the addition of the appropriately flavoured velouté sauce or thinned by the further addition of stock.

Method
1   Sweat the vegetable in butter, then cover with appropriately flavoured stock.
2   Add the bouquet garni and simmer until the vegetables are tender.
3   Remove the bouquet garni, add the prepared velouté to the vegetables and bring the soup back to a boil.
4   Liquidise the soup and pass it through a chinois or conical strainer into a clean allen pan.
5   Adjust the consistency and seasoning and add garnish if required.

Recipe examples: Asparagus velouté soup, Mushroom velouté soup.

Finishing a velouté soup

Velouté soups are finished by taking the soup off the boil and adding a liaison of egg yolks and cream which has been mixed with a little of the soup. The finished soup should have a light, smooth, velvet-like texture and a delicate flavour.

Healthy eating

The addition of cream and egg yolks to velouté soups adds fat and can raise blood cholesterol levels. Cream and egg yolks can therefore be omitted from the finished soup. Traditionalists, however, may consider this option to be an unacceptable compromise to the dish.

Essential knowledge

It is important to keep preparation and storage areas and equipment hygienic when preparing soups in order to:
● prevent the transfer of food poisoning bacteria to the stock soup
● ensure that standards of cleanliness are maintained
● comply with statutory health and safety regulations.

CREAM SOUPS

MEMORY JOGGER

Why is it important to keep preparation and storage areas and equipment hygienic when preparing soups?

The classical cream soup is a purée soup made with the addition of béchamel sauce and stock, where the béchamel sauce acts as the main thickening agent. However, purée soups finished with the addition of cream or velouté soups finished with the addition of cream (rather than cream and egg yolks) can also be identified as cream soups on a menu.

Method
1 Place the main vegetables or pulses into a saucepan, add the stock and mirepoix.
2 Bring to the boil, reduce the heat and allow to simmer.
3 Add the bouquet garni and season as necessary. Skim off any impurities that rise to the surface.
4 Simmer for approximately 45 minutes, depending on the type of vegetable used.
5 Remove the bouquet garni, add the béchamel sauce, mix well.
6 Bring back to the boil.
7 Liquidise the soup.
8 Pass the liquidised soup through a chinois or conical strainer into a clean pan.
9 Adjust the consistency and seasoning, and add garnish required.

Recipe examples: Cream of cauliflower soup, Cream of celery soup.

Key points

● If the soup is too thin, you can thicken it with a little refined starch; if it is too thick, you can add more stock. A thickened soup should have the consistency of single cream.
● Take care when seasoning: salt is easy to add but difficult to remove.
● If using convenience stock, remember that these products often have a high salt content.
● Always closely follow the recipes given to you by your supervisor.
● Remember: if you add cream to a soup, you must not re-boil the soup or it will separate. The same rule applies if you add a liaison to a velouté soup: do not re-boil the soup or the egg yolk will cook and scramble (*coagulate*), causing the soup to develop a curdled texture and appearance.

BROTHS

Broths are made from unthickened stock, finely cut vegetables and either meat or fish. They often contain a cereal such as pearl barley or rice which, due to the release of starch during cooking, slightly thickens and clouds the soup. A distinguishing feature of broths is that they are not strained or passed.

Broths can be divided into two main types of preparation:
● sweated broth type
● unsweated broth type.

Sweated broths containing fish or shellfish are usually referred to as *chowders* (see page 142).

Unsweated broths

Method
1 If using meat, blanch and refresh it. This is not necessary with chicken.
2 Place the meat in a clean pan and add appropriately flavoured stock or water. Bring to the boil and skim any impurities rising to the surface.
3 Add the bouquet garni, seasoning and cereal. Simmer until the meat is nearly cooked.
4 Add the washed and cut vegetables, then simmer until cooked.
5 Remove the meat, cut it into neat dice and return it to the soup.
6 Remove the bouquet garni, adjust the seasoning and skim again if necessary. Add chopped parsley.

Recipe examples: Chicken broth, Mutton broth.

<aside>
Healthy eating
Unsweated broths are low in fat, particularly fish and chicken broths and contain protein and unrefined carbohydrates in the vegetables and cereals.
</aside>

Sweated broths

Method
1 Sweat the washed and cut vegetables in fat without developing colour.
2 Add appropriately flavoured stock then bring to the boil, skimming if necessary.
3 Add the bouquet garni, season and simmer until the vegetables are nearly cooked.
4 Add any garnish and simmer until cooked.
5 Remove the bouquet garni and adjust the consistency and seasoning.

Some recipes for sweated broths contain vegetables (e.g. potatoes, peas or beans) that would overcook if they were sweated with the other vegetables. These vegetables are therefore added to the simmering broth at Step 3.

Recipe examples: Minestrone, Leek and potato soup (*Potage bonne femme*), Cock-a-leekie soup.

Key points

● Broths should not be too thick; the thickness can be adjusted by the addition of stock.
● Cream may be added to finish a broth. The soup must not then be reboiled or the cream will separate.
● It is possible to omit meat from most broth recipes for vegetarian preparations.

Healthy eating
If preparing meat broths, use only lean meat. The meat content in broths is relatively small. Broths are therefore low in calories and can be eaten as part of a healthy balanced diet.

CHOWDERS

These are sweated broths containing fish or shellfish. Chowders may also contain diced salted pork which needs to be blanched and refreshed before use.

Method
1. Sweat any diced blanched pork in fat, then add the vegetables and continue to sweat without developing colour.
2. Add the fish stock then bring to the boil, skimming as necessary.
3. Add the bouquet garni, season and simmer until the vegetables are nearly cooked.
4. Add the cut fish or shellfish then simmer until cooked.*
5. Remove the bouquet garni and adjust the consistency and seasoning.
6. Finish with chopped parsley and cream.

Optional ingredients: Some recipes for chowder also include tomato concassée, which would be added at Step 4. Water biscuits (whole or broken into small pieces) may be served separately.

* If using shellfish such as clams, cook them until the shells open. Remove and dice the meat. Add the diced meat and retained liquor from the shell, at Step 4.

FINISHING AND PRESENTING SOUPS

If you have prepared your soup correctly it should only require minor adjustments to finish and present.

Check the consistency and adjust if necessary following the guidelines given in the table below.

Correcting sauce consistencies

Type of sauce	If the sauce is too thick	If the sauce is too thin
Cream/purée	Add more stock or milk	Leave soup to simmer gently and reduce to required consistency *or*: thicken with a refined starch
Broths	Add more stock	Strain some stock from the soup

Check the seasoning: soups should be seasoned to capture the full taste. You will recognise this with experience; check the seasoning with your supervisor when you first begin to prepare soups. Take care not to over-season the soup, as it is easy to add more salt or pepper but virtually impossible to remove them. Ensure that any garnish in your soup is of the correct size and quantity and is correctly cooked.

Serving soup

Soup may be served using a ladle, which also provides a method of portion control. Where a large number of customers require serving at the same time (e.g. at banquets and functions) it is often easier to use a large jug with a lip for pouring the soup.

Garnishes

The main garnish may be added to the finished soup or kept separate and placed in each bowl before the liquid is added. This method has the advantage of ensuring that each customer receives an equal amount of garnish and so provides an effective method of portion control.

It is important to ensure that the garnish is kept at the correct temperature prior to service.

Purée soups may be finished with a small swirl of cream which is added when the soup is in the bowl. Croûtons and flûtes on traditional menus are served separately in sauce boats and offered to the customer. However, for bistro-style service, they may be sprinkled on top of the soup prior to service.

A purée soup may be finished with a swirl of cream

STORING SOUPS

See *Storing sauces and soups* on page 125. If the soup is to be used immediately it should be kept at a temperature above 75 °C (167 °F). Soups should be served very hot, at 90 °C (194 °F) in heated cups or bowls. Cold soups should be served at 3 °C (37 °F) in ice-cold bowls.

If a cooked garnish is added separately to a soup, ensure that the correct temperature control is maintained for both the garnish ingredient and the soup. Take care to avoid cross-contamination occurring between raw garnishes and cooked soup. Refrigerate raw garnishes which are cooked at the last minute (such as quenelles) until they are required.

MEMORY JOGGER

Why should soups required for storage be cooled rapidly before refrigeration?

Essential knowledge

The main contamination threats when preparing, cooking and storing soups are as follows:
- food poisoning bacteria may be transferred through dirty surfaces and equipment
- food poisoning bacteria may be transferred between yourself and food items through inadequate attention to personal hygiene
- contamination can occur due to incorrect storage temperatures. Remember that bacteria will grow most rapidly in the danger zone: 5–63 °C (41–145 °F); bacteria growth will not occur above or below this range of temperatures
- contamination can occur if items undergo prolonged cooling. Soups must be rapidly cooled (within 90 minutes) before refrigeration
- incorrect waste disposal procedures can lead to contamination
- contamination can occur through items being left uncovered. Cooled soups prepared for storage must be covered, labelled and dated before being placed in the refrigerator
- cross-contamination can occur between cooked and uncooked food if these are stored together.

PLAN YOUR TIME

Be aware of which soups you will be preparing so that you know what equipment, ingredients and utensils you will need to use. Preparing a production time plan will help you think about priorities; make sure that you take account of the daily working schedules within your kitchen.

Do this

- Watch your supervisor carry out general preparation on a purée soup, a cream soup and a broth. Notice the equipment and techniques used.
- Check today's menu and see if any purée, cream or broth type soups are featured. Ask your supervisor for the recipes. What methods of preparation are used?
- Check the temperatures of areas in which soups are stored in your kitchen.
- Find out if there are any convenience soups used in your work place and ask your supervisor if you may make comparisons.
- Find a suitable soup garnish where the main ingredient of the soup is:
  - vegetables
  - pasta
  - meat
  - fish
  - cheese.

HEALTH, SAFETY AND HYGIENE

Make sure you are familiar with the general points given in Unit NG1 (*Maintain a safe and secure working environment*) of the Core Units book.

Remember that soups are *high risk foods*.

PREPARATION OF EQUIPMENT, PREPARATION AND COOKING AREAS

Refer to *Equipment* and *Preparation and cooking areas* page 126 for sauces and soups.

DEALING WITH UNEXPECTED SITUATIONS

Unexpected situations usually fall under two categories: those that affect the safety of yourself or your colleagues and those that affect the product you are preparing. Kitchens are busy environments where people are often working to deadlines; if an unexpected situation arises, remember not to panic. Tackle each situation in a professional manner using the knowledge you have learnt in this unit.

An example of an unexpected situation might be a saucepan spillage. If this happens:
- mop and dry the area where the spillage has occurred immediately
- warn your colleagues
- make sure that you are familiar with the procedure for scalds (see Unit NG1: *Maintain a safe and secure working environment* in the Core Units book).

Case study

During preparation for a lunch service in a busy industrial kitchen, a chef carrying a large pan of hot soup slipped on a wet patch of the kitchen floor, all of the soup spilled over the floor and the chef scalded one of his hands.

1   Who was at fault in this situation?
2   What immediate action is required to deal with the situation?
3   What actions would you have taken
    ● *to prevent the incident occurring*
    ● *to deal with the incident?*

What have you learned

1   What are the main contamination threats when preparing cooking and storing soups?
2   Why is it important to keep preparation cooking areas and storage areas hygienic when preparing soups?
3   Why are time and temperature important when cooking soups?
4   How should you prepare and serve cream broth and purée types of soup?
5   What faults can occur when finishing soups and how they can be rectified?

Get ahead

1   Certain soups are unclassified. Find out what they are and how you might prepare and cook them.
2   Use recipe books to find examples of hard butter sauces. How are these made? What dishes are they usually served with?
3   Ask your supervisor if you have any coulis type sauces on your menu. Find out how they are prepared and cooked.
4   Small pieces of butter are sometimes shaken into finished sauces (*monter au beurre*). What effect does this have on the sauce?
5   Find out about classifications of soup not included in this unit, such as consommés and shellfish bisques. How might you prepare and cook them?
6   Find out what types of soups are made using a brown roux as a thickening agent.

Prepare and cook basic pulse dishes

This chapter covers:
ELEMENT 1: **Prepare basic pulse dishes**
ELEMENT 2: **Cook basic pulse dishes**

What you need to do

- Prepare cooking and preparation areas and equipment ready for use and clean after use.
- Combine pulses correctly with other ingredients according to customer and dish requirements.

- Prepare, cook, finish and present pulses according to customer and dish requirements.
- Work in an organised and efficient manner taking account of priorities and laid down procedures.

What you need to do

- The type, quality and quantity of pulses required for each dish.
- What the main contamination threats are when preparing and cooking pulse dishes.
- Why it is important to keep preparation, cooking and storage areas and equipment hygienic.
- Why time and temperature are

important when cooking pulses.
- How to satisfy health, safety and hygiene regulations concerning preparation and cooking areas.
- How to plan your time efficiently, allocating time appropriately to meet daily schedules.
- How to deal with unexpected situations.

ELEMENT 1: **Prepare basic pulse dishes**

INTRODUCTION

Pulses is the name given to the edible seeds of the legume family of plants. Peas, beans, chickpeas and lentils are all types of pulses. They are an important part of our diet as they are high in fibre, protein, iron and Vitamin B and contain no saturated fat. This makes them a healthy alternative to meat and especially useful for vegetarians, who need to rely on non-meat sources for protein. Our bodies can make the best use of the protein in pulses if they are served either with a cereal like wheat (bread) or rice, nuts or dairy products (milk, yoghurt, cheese or eggs).

There are many hundreds of varieties of pulses used throughout the world. They are harvested in warm temperate climates, so most pulses used in the UK are imported. They can be purchased in a variety of forms: fresh, dried or canned. Fresh pulses, like fresh peas and beans, can be treated like vegetables *(see Unit 2ND18, pages 350–91)*. Canned pulses have already been cooked and can be used immediately as an ingredient, while the dried varieties need to be prepared before they can be eaten.

Healthy eating

Pulses are a naturally healthy food and they are becoming increasingly more popular every year as people become more conscious of their diets. They are naturally high in fibre and this can aid digestion.

Pulses are very flexible and can easily be used to replace meat or fish on the menu. Some suggestions for using pulses on the menu are given below:

Starter: Lentil and mushroom pâté
Soup: Split green pea soup
Pasta: Lentil lasagne
Main course: Kidney bean moussaka
Vegetables: Stir fried butter beans
Salad: Chickpea beansprout and apple salad
Dessert: Adzuki bean dumplings.

TYPES OF PULSES

Pulses can be divided into three types: peas, beans and lentils.

Peas

Dried peas contain a large amount of starch and they disintegrate easily when cooked. This makes them especially useful when making soups. and they are often used as an ingredient in soups and broths. Chickpeas are an exception to the rule: they keep their shape even after 1½ hours of cooking.

The most commonly used peas are listed below:
- *Marrowfat (blue) peas:* these have a sweet flavour. Their skin is tough, but they have a floury texture when cooked.
- *Split green peas:* these are used to make traditional English pease pudding, served with boiled pork. They disintegrate when cooked and are used to make thick purée soups.
- *Split yellow peas:* these are cooked to a purée and served as a vegetable. They are also used to make thick purée soups.
- *Chickpeas:* these have a nutty taste and will absorb other flavours easily. They are widely used as a vegetable in Middle Eastern and Asian cookery. Chickpeas are also milled into gram flour.

MEMORY JOGGER

Which pulses break up during cooking?

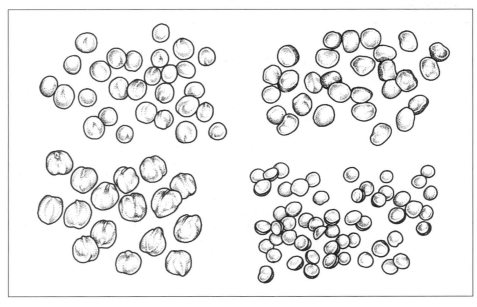

Clockwise from top left: Marrowfat (blue) peas; split green peas; split yellow peas; chickpeas

MEMORY JOGGER

Why do you need to rapidly boil red kidney beans for the first 10 minutes?

Beans

Beans are the largest group of pulses: in some Mexican markets you can find over 25 different varieties, each suited to a different local dish.

Examples of some beans now commonly available in this country are listed below.
- *Red kidney beans:* these have a floury texture and sweetish flavour. They contain an enzyme which needs to be destroyed by rapid boiling for the first ten minutes of cooking time. This is essential: failure to do this will cause food poisoning.
- *Mung beans:* these are mostly used in stews. They are very popular in their sprouted form, which can be used as a vegetable.
- *White haricot beans:* these are by far the most popular bean in the UK. Most of us will have eaten them as baked beans, where they are cooked with a tomato sauce. They are also used as an ingredient in soups.
- *Green flageolet beans:* these have a delicate taste and can be served hot as a vegetable or cold in salads. They are actually haricot beans which have been picked when still young and tender.
- *Lima beans* (butter beans): these come from Peru in South America and have a sweet buttery flavour which is why they are sometimes called butter beans.
- *Black-eyed beans:* these have a savoury flavour and succulent texture, and are popular in traditional North American cookery.
- *Adzuki beans:* these have a strong, nutty, sweet flavour and can be served as a savoury side dish. In the Far East they are sweetened with sugar and used in cakes and desserts.
- *Borlotti beans:* these are a member of the kidney bean family and can be substituted in any dish that requires kidney or haricot beans. They have a pleasant flavour and a moist and tender texture.
- *Broad beans:* these are most often eaten when fresh, but are also available dried. The tough skin of the dried beans needs to be removed before serving. They have a fine texture and can be used as a vegetable, in salads, or as a thickening agent for sauces in some modern recipes.
- *Soya beans:* these are very high in nutrients, especially protein and fat. They are available in many forms: ground to make soya flour; processed into chunks and granules for use as a meat substitute (TVP); processed into bean curd (Tofu); pressed and used to make soya oils and margarines; processed to form soya milk; and processed to make condiments such as soy sauce.

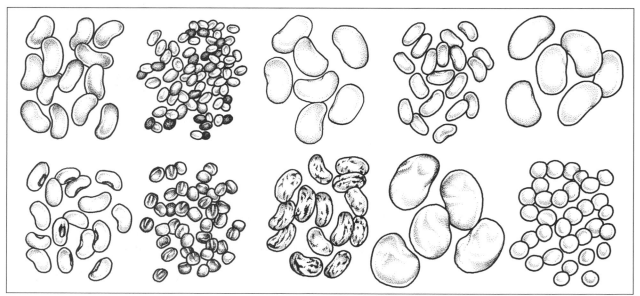

Top row: red kidney beans, mung beans, white haricot beans, green flageolet beans, lima beans
Bottom row: black-eyed beans, adzuki beans, borlotti beans, broad beans, soya beans

Lentils

Lentils are rich in protein and do not have to be soaked before cooking; the different types are identified and named by their colour. They are available whole or split.
- *Red and yellow lentils:* like peas, these disintegrate when cooked and are used to make soups, stews and vegetable loaves.
- *Green and brown lentils:* these stay whole when cooked and can be served as a vegetable or used in salads.

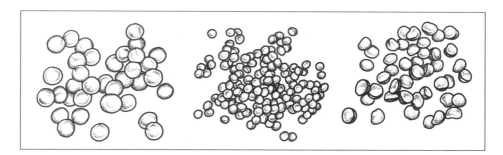

From left: green lentils, red lentils, yellow lentils

STORING PULSES

When storing pulses, make sure that wherever they are stored, they are part of a stock control system so that stocks will be rotated. Check the 'sell by' dates regularly and remember the rule: first in, first out. If pulses are stored for too long they become hard and inedible. Check the conditioning of their packaging regularly: any pulses in damaged packaging should be discarded as they may have become contaminated by food pests. Any cans showing signs of rust, dents or bulging should also be discarded.
- Fresh pulses should be stored in a refrigerator at a temperature below 5 °C (41 °F).
- Frozen pulses should be stored in a freezer at a temperature below −18 °C (0 °F).
- Dried or canned pulses should be stored in a dark, cool, dry and well ventilated place (the dry store). They should be kept in airtight containers placed off the floor and out of direct sunlight.
- If you notice any signs of pest infestation (*see Unit 2ND22 pages 102–3 in the Core Units book*) report it to your supervisor immediately.
- If any part of the packaging has been damaged you must discard the whole batch.

PLANNING YOUR TIME WHEN PREPARING PULSES

In order to work efficiently and effectively you need to plan ahead. Take the time to work out a schedule before you start: this will save you considerable time and trouble during preparation and cooking.

Use the following guidelines when planning to prepare pulses:
- identify the dishes you will be required to prepare. How many portions are needed? What time do they need to be ready by?
- make sure that all your equipment is ready, including your utensils and pans
- make sure that space is available on the stove or in the oven
- check the soaking time and the cooking time for the pulses that you will be preparing
- make sure that you have all the ingredients ready for the dishes you have to prepare
- check whether you will be cooking any pulses that need longer cooking times. This time could be used to prepare other ingredients for your dish.

HEALTH, SAFETY AND HYGIENE

Make sure that you are familiar with the general points given in Unit NG1: *Maintain a safe and secure working environment* in the Core Units book. The following points are especially important to remember when preparing pulses:

- pulses can be very dusty and need to be checked for food pests, like flour moths. Always wash the pulses in plenty of cold water and check for any foreign matter such as bits of wood or little stones
- cooked pulses contain both moisture and protein and can easily become contaminated by bacteria. Always keep them covered and at temperatures either below 5 °C (41 °F) or above 63 °C (145 °F)
- cooked pulse dishes must be stored separately from raw foods to prevent cross-contamination
- high standards of personal hygiene must be maintained at all times. Wash your hands frequently, avoid touching your hair, nose and mouth, and cover any open cuts or sores with visible waterproof dressing
- use of unhygienic preparation areas, utensils and equipment can cause contamination
- all waste must be disposed of in a hygienic manner.

Essential knowledge	The main contamination threats when preparing and cooking pulse dishes are as follows:
	● cross-contamination between cooked and uncooked food during storage
	● contamination of food through inadequate personal hygiene, where bacteria are transferred from the nose, mouth, open cuts or sores or unclean hands to the food
	● cross-contamination from unhygienic equipment, utensils and preparation areas
	● contamination through products being stored at incorrect temperatures
	● contamination through incorrect waste disposal
	● contamination through products being left uncovered and foreign objects (e.g. pieces of string, ash, etc.) falling into them.

PREPARING COOKING AREAS AND EQUIPMENT

Make sure that your preparation area is clean and tidy. Only put out the tools and equipment you need: large bowls for soaking, a colander for draining and pans for cooking. You may also need special equipment, such as a food processor to blend or purée pulses, or a loaf tin for baking certain dishes.

To prevent cross-contamination, check that all your equipment is clean and in good working order (e.g. none of the handles are loose). Report any damage or malfunction to your supervisor.

Keep your cooking area clean and always consider the safety of both yourself and your colleagues. Make sure that pan handles do not jut out over the edge of the stove, as this may cause accidents. Take care when carrying pans of boiling water; make sure that your path is clear. Lift any heavy loads correctly to avoid straining your back.

When you have completed each task wipe down and clean your preparation area and equipment.

PREPARATION METHODS

Soaking

All dried pulses benefit from an initial soaking before cooking. This makes them more digestible and shortens the cooking time.

Cover the pulses in twice their volume of cold water and leave for 4–8 hours. Pulses that are not adequately soaked will take longer to cook. The best place to do this is in the refrigerator, so that you keep them below 5 °C (41 °F) and therefore out of the danger zone.

Always rinse the pulses after soaking as this removes some of the sugars which make them difficult to digest.

Preparing dried pulses

Most pulses need to be thoroughly cooked before they can be used either as a vegetable or as an ingredient in a dish. Dried pulses need to reabsorb moisture, and the high percentage of starch they contain needs to be cooked before our bodies can digest it. As many beans take over an hour to cook (see below), they are normally cooked separately so that the other ingredients in the dish are not over-cooked.

1 Put the pulses into a large pan and cover them with double their volume of water or stock. You can add some flavourings (e.g. roughly cut carrots, onions and celery and a bouquet garni of parsley stalks, bay leaf and thyme).
   Do not:
   ● add any salt; this toughens the outside of the pulses and prevents them from cooking properly. Avoid using salty convenience stocks as a cooking liquid
   ● add any acids, such as lemon juice, vinegar or tomatoes. This will also toughen the pulses
   ● add any bicarbonate of soda; although it may speed up the cooking time it destroys the nutritional value and flavour.
2 Cook the pulses on top of the stove or in the oven. Check the amount of liquid in the pan regularly: there should always be enough liquid to cover the pulses. This will prevent them from burning.
3 When the pulses have come to the boil, reduce the temperature to a simmer. Prolonged rapid boiling will cause them to break up.
4 Test the pulses as they are cooking to ensure that they do not overcook; some varieties will become very soft and difficult to use.

Important: remember that red kidney beans contain an enzyme that must be destroyed by rapid boiling for the first ten minutes of the cooking time, otherwise food poisoning may result.

Cooking times for pulses

The cooking times for pulses will vary from batch to batch. The times given below can be used as a guide.

Pulse cooking times

Pulse	Cooking time	Pulse	Cooking time
Adzuki beans	30 minutes	Black-eye beans	30–45 minutes
Borlotti beans	1 hour	Broad beans	$1\frac{1}{2}$ hours
Chickpeas	1–$1\frac{1}{2}$ hours	Green/brown lentils	
		soaked	30–40 minutes
		unsoaked	1–$1\frac{1}{2}$ hours
Haricot beans	1–$1\frac{1}{2}$ hours	Kidney beans	1 hour
Lima beans	45–60 minutes	Mung beans	
		soaked	20–30 minutes
		unsoaked	30–40 minutes
Peas	45 minutes	Red split lentils	
		soaked	15–20 minutes
		unsoaked	20–30 minutes
Soybeans	3–4 hours	Split peas	
		soaked	30 minutes
		unsoaked	40–45 minutes

MEMORY JOGGER

Why should salt never be used in the initial stages of cooking pulses?

Do this

- Find examples of three different pulses used in your place of work.
- Note down how they are stored; how long they need to be soaked; and any other preparation needed.
- Find a recipe for each of three different types of pulses. Write down which utensils you would need to prepare them, and how the pulses are cooked.

What have you learned

1 What are pulses?
2 Why are pulses important in the diet of vegetarians?
3 How are pulses sold?
4 How should the different types of pulses be stored?
5 Why do you need to cook dried pulses before you can serve them?
6 What danger should you be aware of when cooking red kidney beans?
7 What are the main contamination threats when preparing and cooking pulses?
8 Why is it important to keep your preparation, storage areas and equipment hygienic?

ELEMENT 2: Cook basic pulse dishes

Healthy eating

When cooking pulses you should not use any salt as this will toughen them and make them difficult to eat.

Healthy eating

You always have the opportunity to reduce the amount of salt when finishing the dishes by adding more flavour in the form of herbs and spices.

COOKING PROCESSES AND EXAMPLE DISHES

Stewing and braising: Casseroles and curries

Red kidney, black-eye, mung and white haricot beans become very tender when cooked and are suitable for these long, slow methods of cooking because they can easily absorb the flavours of the other ingredients.

Stewing or casseroling is a moist method of cooking, where the pulses are gently simmered in a small amount of liquid which becomes part of the dish. They can be cooked with other vegetables (carrots, onions, leeks, garlic, tomatoes, celery, peppers, mushrooms); fruits (lemon, apple, dried apricots, sultanas, raisins); herbs (thyme, bay, parsley, coriander); and spices (cummin, caraway, ginger, chilli, turmeric, paprika).

Always check that there is enough liquid in the pan to prevent sticking or burning. Control the temperature of the stove or oven during cooking, so that it is not too hot or too cold.

Example recipe: Mung bean and chickpea curry

Mung bean and chickpea curry

152

Ingredients

Pulses:

200 g (7 oz)	green mung beans
200 g (7 oz)	chickpeas

Cooking ingredients:

400 g (14 oz)	tinned tomatoes
400 ml (14 fl oz)	cooking liquid from the chickpeas
2 tbsp	vegetable oil

Flavouring:

1 bunch	fresh coriander
100 g (4 oz)	fresh ginger
3 cloves	garlic
2	fresh green chillis
1 medium sized	onion (roughly chopped)
1 tsp	turmeric
1 tsp	ground coriander
1 tsp	ground cummin
$\frac{1}{2}$ tsp	chilli powder

To finish:

50 g (2 oz)	fresh yoghurt
25 g (1 oz)	creamed coconut

To accompany:

200 g (7 oz)	Basmati rice

Method

1 Cook the chickpeas and mung beans separately in water flavoured with the coriander stalks and some roughly chopped onion, using the guide on page 151.
2 Make the curry mix, by placing all the remaining flavouring ingredients into a food processor and blending them into a paste.
3 Cook the paste in the oil with a little salt and pepper to help extract the flavour of all the spices. Cook the paste out until it is almost dry.
4 When the paste is dry, add the tinned tomatoes, the creamed coconut and the cooking liquid. Then add the cooked pulses.
5 Gently simmer the curry for approximately 30 minutes, stirring occasionally to prevent sticking. Cook until the beans are tender, removing them from the heat before they begin to break up and become mushy.

This example is a very basic curry. By altering the amounts of the spices and the types of pulses you can make infinite variations on this theme. Whichever type of pulses you use, it is always best to choose a variety that will not break up during the cooking.

You can add vegetables to this recipe. Cauliflower, okra, courgettes or sweet capsicum peppers blend well into this type of dish. For authenticity, you can finish the curry with a couple of tablespoons of fresh yoghurt.

GRILLING OR BARBECUING: RISSOLES AND BURGERS

Grilling is a dry cooking process, using radiated heat generated by infra red waves which come from gas fired or electrically heated elements. It is a very quick method of cooking because of the high heat involved. You can adjust the heat by turning down the gas or electricity, or you can lower the tray so that the food is further away from the heat. However, the burgers and rissoles need to be of an even size and not too thick, so they will cook evenly and not burn on the outside before cooking through.

A barbecue has hot and cool zones: some positions on the grill bars are hotter than others. This allows you to start the food off in a hot zone and then place it in a cooler position to cook through.

Split peas and lentils are commonly used to make rissoles and burgers. They need to be cooked in just enough liquid to be absorbed in the cooking time. It is important not to make the burgers or rissoles too wet or mushy, or they will lose their shape and fall apart during frying or grilling. Other pulses can be used; they should be cooked and drained as normal then dried on a cloth before being blended with other ingredients. During grilling you will need to brush the food with oil to prevent if drying out.

BAKING: LOAF OR BAKE

Baking is a dry cooking process, where food is cooked by convected heat in an oven. As for rissoles and burgers, pulses should be cooked in as little water as possible during their initial cooking. The cooked pulses can then be mixed with other ingredients and flavourings. The pulses' natural starchy texture helps the mixture bind together, although some recipes use eggs as an additional binding agent.

Loaves and bakes are covered with a lid or aluminium foil for most of the cooking time to prevent the food drying out. The covers can be removed towards the end of the cooking to allow a crisp browned fop to develop, adding flavour to the dish.

Example recipe: Lentil and cider loaf

Lentil and cider loaf

Ingredients

150 g (5 oz)	dry red split lentils
250 ml (9 fl oz)	dry cider
100 g (4 oz)	sunflower margarine
50 g (2 oz)	dried breadcrumbs
100 g (4 oz)	chopped onion
100 g (4 oz)	carrots
1 stick	celery
1 clove	garlic (chopped)
3g	dried thyme
50 g (2 oz)	roasted ground hazelnuts
50 g (2 oz)	Parmesan cheese
$\frac{1}{2}$ tsp	chopped parsley
1	egg (for binding)

Healthy eating
You can increase the fibre content of this dish by using brown breadcrumbs in the recipe.

Method

1   Wash and drain the lentils, then put them in a saucepan with the cider and just enough water to cover them. Bring the pan to the boil and cook the lentils until they are almost tender and all the liquid has been absorbed. (If you are using pre-soaked lentils, they will cook more quickly and need less liquid.)
2   Line a 400 g (14 oz) loaf tin with silicone paper, brush the paper with melted sun-flower margarine and sprinkle with breadcrumbs.
3   Melt the rest of the margarine and use it to cook the onions, carrots and celery which should be cut into large brunoise or dice.
4   When the vegetables are soft and just beginning to brown, add the garlic and lentils and mix them together well.
5   Mix in the thyme, nuts, cheese, parsley and beaten egg, then taste for seasoning.
6   Add salt and pepper to taste, then put the loaf mixture in the prepared tin and cover with greased aluminium baking foil. Bake it in a preheated oven at 180 °C (350 °F) for approximately one hour.
7   Ten minutes before the end of cooking, remove the foil to brown the top. This helps to develop more flavour.
8   To serve the lentil and cider loaf, turn it out onto a warm plate and garnish with picked parsley.
9   Served with apple sauce, this loaf is perfect for vegetarians.

SHALLOW, DEEP AND STIR-FRYING: RISSOLES, BURGERS, FALAFEL

Shallow-frying

This is a dry cooking process, where the food is heated through contact with a hot cooking surface, using hot fat or oil.

Heat the pan until the fat is at the correct temperature: 175–195 °C (325–380 °F). This is important because if the fat is too cool the food items will absorb too much fat and become greasy while if it is too hot they will burn.

When frying burgers or rissoles, lower the temperature when they are browned on the outside to allow them to cook thoroughly. Take care when turning them to prevent them breaking up.

Essential knowledge	Time and temperature are important when cooking pulse dishes in order to: ● prevent food poisoning ● prevent toughening ● ensure that the dishes are cooked correctly ● maintain customer satisfaction.

Example recipe: **Falafel**

Falafel are Mediterranean fritters, made from broad beans or chickpeas which have been formed into either flat little cakes which are shallow-fried, or small balls which are deep-fried.

Ingredients

200 g (7 oz)	dried broad beans (skinless)
6	spring onions (finely chopped)
1 tbsp	fresh parsley (chopped)
1 tbsp	fresh coriander (chopped)
1 clove	garlic (crushed)
pinch	cummin, salt, pepper
small pinch	bicarbonate of soda (optional)

Falafel

Method

1 Soak the skinless broad beans for at least 8 hours.
2 Drain and dry the beans off carefully by patting them dry with a clean cloth, then put them through a mincing machine or processor to produce a grainy paste.
3 Add the spring onions, parsley, coriander, garlic, cummin, salt, pepper and bicarbonate of soda. Mix all these ingredients together to make a fine paste, then put it in the refrigerator to chill.
4 When the paste has hardened, shape it into mini-burgers or small balls and put them back in the refrigerator to set.
5 The shapes can then be shallow-fried until they are golden brown on the outside (approximately 5 minutes each side). As always when frying, take care not to have the fat too hot or the outside will be burnt before the inside is cooked.

Serve the falafel in the Middle Eastern way, with fresh natural yoghurt, a mixed salad and pitta bread.

DEEP-FRYING

Deep-frying is also a dry process, where food is cooked by being completely submerged in very hot oil or fat. Deep-fryers should never be filled over half-full with fat or oil, as the oil can easily boil over. Take care not to put too much food into the deep-fryer, as this can lower the temperature of the oil and/or cause the fat to boil over. Make sure your oil-to-food ratio is correct.

Always use clean, fresh oil. Oil deteriorates each time you heat it; any that has started to turn dark or frothy should be discarded. Follow the instructions for your particular fryer, draining and straining it regularly to remove any debris. Food particles left from a previous batch of frying will burn if they are left in the fryer, giving an unpleasant taste to the new batch.

Take all reasonable safety precautions whilst deep-frying:
● keep your sleeves rolled down to protect against any splashes of fat
● make sure all the necessary cooking utensils are to hand before you start
● use a clean, dry, thick cloth when handling the fryer
● make sure that the correct fire prevention equipment is to hand and that you are familiar with fire drill procedures
● keep a close eye on the temperature, and allow the fryer to regain heat before adding a new batch of food
● report any fault in your fryer immediately, as it is potentially a very dangerous piece of equipment

Deep-frying the falafel

If you are deep-frying your falafel, use a spider or basket to place them gently into the hot oil, which should be preheated to a temperature of 175 °C (330 °F). The falafel are cooked when the outside turns golden brown and they begin to float to the surface of the oil.

When they are cooked, drain them well and put them onto a tray with kitchen paper underneath to absorb any excess fat. If you need to store them for a few minutes, put them onto an open tray. Do not enclose them in any way, e.g. by placing them in a covered container, as they will turn soggy from their own steam.

Do this

- Find an example of a vegetarian casserole and note the pulses used.
- Find an example of a vegetarian loaf and note which pulses are used and how they are prepared.
- Find another example of a baked pulse dish and note how it is finished.
- Ask your supervisor what sort of foods usually accompany pulse dishes so that their nutritional value is maximised.

STIR-FRYING

MEMORY JOGGER

What precautions do you need to take when stir-frying pulses?

This is a dry cooking process very similar to shallow-frying, where the food is heated through contact with a hot cooking surface (usually a wok), using hot fat or oil.

When stir-frying pre-cooked pulses, make sure they are well drained and dried. Excess moisture will make them stick to each other and to the pan and may cause them to go mushy. Stir-fry in small batches: if you add too many pulses at once the pan will cool down and not fry properly. Only use the pulses that keep their shape well after this method of cooking (e.g. green and brown lentils; lima; flageolet; black-eye beans and chickpeas).

STORING COOKED PULSES

Once the pulses are cooked it is always best to use them immediately. If this is not possible, cool them rapidly. All cooked food needs to be cold within 90 minutes to avoid the potential growth of bacteria and the risk of contamination from other foods.

Cool the pulses by spreading them out on a large shallow tray and covering them with a sheet of greaseproof paper. You can also use special equipment like a blast chiller which cools food very quickly.

When the pulses are cold, place them in a covered container in the refrigerator or freezer, to avoid cross-contamination. Always check that the refrigerator is at the right temperature (below 5 °C/41 °F).

Essential knowledge

It is important to keep preparation and storage areas and equipment hygienic in order to:
- prevent contamination of food
- prevent pest infestation in storage areas
- ensure standards of cleanliness are maintained
- comply with the law.

Case study

You are making a chickpea curry and the recipe stipulates that you need to pre-cook the chickpeas for 1–1½ hours until they are soft.

You taste them after 1½ hours and they are still very hard so you give them another ½ hour. Even after 2 hours of cooking they are still hard so you give them another ½ hour ... but they are still hard!

● What may have caused this?
● What can you do to prevent this happening another time?

What have you learned

1 Why are time and temperature important when cooking pulse dishes?
2 What precautions do you need to take when cooking casseroles or curries with pulses?
3 Which pulses are best for stewing and why?
4 What precautions do you need to take when using pulses for rissoles and burgers?
5 Why is it so important to check that your cooking oil is at the right temperature?
6 What precautions do you need to take when stir-frying pulses?

Get ahead

1 Find out about pulses *not* listed on pages 147–9. How long do they need to cook? What type of dishes are they most suitable for?
2 Find out which pulses are most suitable for soups. Find recipes for two soups thickened with pulses.
3 Certain types of flour are made from pulses. Find out what these are and how they are used.
4 Visit some vegetarian restaurants and study the menu. Notice how pulses are used as a fundamental ingredient.

Prepare and cook basic rice dishes

The chapter covers:
ELEMENT 1:   Prepare basic rice dishes
ELEMENT 2:   Cook basic rice dishes

What you need to do

- Ensure preparation and cooking areas and suitable equipment are hygienic and ready for use.
- Check that rice and other ingredients are of the type quality and quantity required.
- Report any problems identified with the ingredients or rice dishes are reported promptly to the appropriate person.
- Ensure rice and other ingredients are prepared and cooked using appropriate basic preparation and cooking methods.

- Ensure rice dishes are finished to meet quality requirements.
- Ensure rice dishes not for immediate use are stored correctly.
- Ensure cooking areas and equipment are cleaned correctly after use.
- Ensure that all work is prioritised and carried out in an organised and efficient manner in line with appropriate organisational procedures and legal requirements.

What you need to know

- What health and safety practices should be followed when preparing and cooking basic rice dishes.
- Why it is important to keep food preparation areas and equipment hygienic when preparing and cooking basic rice dishes.
- What the main contamination threats are when preparing, cooking and storing basic rice dishes.
- Why time and temperature are important when preparing and cooking basic rice dishes.
- Why rice not for immediate consumption should be cooled rapidly or maintained at a safe temperature after preparation/cooking.
- What quality points you should look for with basic rice dishes.

- What basic preparation method and cooking are suitable for different types of rice dishes.
- What factors indicate that a basic rice dish is cooked correctly according to dish requirements.
- Which products could be used to substitute high-fat ingredients when preparing basic rice dishes.
- Which types of fats and oils can contribute to healthy eating practices.
- How increasing the fibre content of basic rice dishes contribute to healthy eating practices.
- Why the reduction of salt in basic rice dishes is beneficial.

ELEMENT 1:   Prepare basic rice dishes

TYPES OF RICE

There are four main types of rice:
- long grain
- brown rice
- short grain
- wild rice.

Rice is grown mainly in wet hot countries such as the Far East, Southern America, USA and especially India. Rice is a staple diet for many of the populations of these countries and has grown in popularity in Europe over the past 20 years.

Rice can be purchased in a wide variety of forms: frozen, pre-cooked, par-boiled and de-hydrated. It is used as a snack food, as a side dish or as an accompaniment to dishes, usually, but not always, in a sauce, curry, fricassée etc. Rice needs to be cooked correctly and can be a high risk food if not kept below or above critical temperatures.

Rice can be eaten as a farinaceous course prior to the main meal, braised in the oven, cooked on top of the stove as a savoury risotto, as milk pudding, desserts hot and cold, or used to garnish soups. The uses of rice are wide ranging, used for desserts as well as savoury recipes, the growth in healthy eating has made popular brown, Basmati and wild types of rice grain. In all there are over 2000 varieties of rice, these are generally divided into two categories: long grain and short grain.

Long grain rice

Rice that is known as long grain is slim and oval in shape and longer than short grain rice. Long grain traditionally was used as a plain boiled rice to accompany curry or hot sauce or pasta based dishes.

Long grain Indian and American rice
This is one of the longer grain types with dry, flaky, loose characteristics. Rice historically has been associated with India but America produces very good quality long grain rice especially for savoury recipes, a well known label being that of 'Uncle Ben's'.

Italy has a tradition of recipes for rice based dishes: pilaff and risotto being two famous styles or methods of cooking rice.

Japan also is associated with rice, but this is a short grain rice which is soft and sticky in texture. The sticky nature of this short grained rice is due to the high percentage of starch granules that make it waxy. This rice is used for the Japanese 'suchi': the rice is packed to form a shaped parcel and eaten with raw fish and vegetables.

Brown rice

This can be any rice which has the outer covering removed but retains its bran, making the grains look brown, hence the term brown rice. This rice has the benefit of being more nutritious than white rice. Brown rice can take longer to cook than white rice and generally is used only for savoury recipes. With the advent of healthy eating practices in the early 1990s, brown rice is now quite popular with chefs and the retail market.

Basmati rice
This is mainly grown in the foothills of the Himalayas. It is a long grain rice which is narrow in shape and reputed to be one of the best quality rice grains available.

This rice benefits from being soaked prior to cooking. It is usually eaten with Indian cuisine.

Carolina rice
This long grain rice, or patna rice as it is known, is grown widely across the globe and is very popular because of its versatility. Maintaining a firm and loose texture when cooked it is ideal for many savoury dishes.

Short grain rice

Short grain rice is sometimes thought of as just the rice which is used for sweet rice-based desserts. However, white Italian short grain rice is used for the classical Italian savoury dish *risotto*. The grain can be white or brown and has a short, round, plump shape.

Short grain pudding rice is a polished short grain rice which when cooked is soft in texture. It takes 50 g of short grain rice per 50 ml of milk to make rice pudding.

Converted rice
This is the term given to rice which has been par-boiled to remove some of the starch, while preserving vital vitamins and nutrients. Many catering operations use this form of rice, although it is more expensive than untreated long grain rice.

Glutinous rice
This can be black or white in colour. Glutinous rice is used widely in Chinese cookery and, despite its name, it is gluten free. This is of benefit to the growing number of people affected by the need for a gluten-free diet.

White glutinous rice has had the rice hull removed. It is used for confectionery and baking because of its sticky and sweet characteristics. This grain is sometimes used in the brewing of rice beer.

Wild rice

This has a nutty flavour and is of a grey-brown colour. It is not strictly a grain, but a water grass found as a native plant in North America. Wild rice is a long grained rice type used in cooking as a farce for game, poultry and as a cold salad in its cooked form.

INGREDIENTS COOKED WITH RICE

Rice has many uses in cookery. It is used as a garnish ingredient for soup, as a farinaceous course or as the base of main course dishes. Rice can also be cooked and cooled, mixed with cold dressings and chopped vegetables as an hors d'oeuvre

Rice is better slightly undercooked rather than over-cooked which results in a starchy pulp as opposed to loose light grains.

When preparing rice for cooking always wash it well in cold water prior to boiling or braising in the oven.

Vegetables used with rice

Vegetables commonly used with rice include:
● mushrooms
● peas
● green beans
● peppers
● celery
● carrot
● onions

- leeks
- tomatoes (fruit)
- sweetcorn
- garlic
- cucumber
- pimento
- beanshoots
- spring onions
- truffle.

Vegetables are used to garnish and flavour rice, generally when it is cooked or when it is cool. Wash all vegetables well to ensure they are clean and free from grit or dirt. Vegetables used with rice must be able to be cooked quickly and are usually prepared in a size that matches the rice dish, i.e. not cut too large. The vegetables should be chopped or cut small to aid quick cooking, sliced or shaped according to the recipe instructions.

Pimento needs only heating as its is cooked already. Peppers should be diced and mixed in with the rice when cooked or cooled. Mushrooms are used a lot with rice dishes; these are sliced and cooked in the butter, added to the rice, then finished in the oven.

Stocks used to cook rice

Stock is used to cook and moisten rice and rice dishes. It imparts flavour and colour to the rice dish. The stock needs to be fresh and strained before being used. Stocks used to cook rice include:

- chicken stock
- vegetable stock
- water
- saffron stock
- fish stock
- white stock
- mushroom stock
- consommé
- veal stock.

The ratio of stock to rice for cooking is *twice as much stock as rice* i.e. a ratio of 2 :1, stock to rice. This may need adjusting according to the type of rice used, the cooking time and the cooking temperature.

Fresh or convenience stock can be used but where stock cubes are employed careful seasoning is required as the stock can be salty in its own right.

When using saffron stock do not use too much or the colour will be too bright.

Cheeses used with rice

- Parmesan (Parmigiano)
- Cheddar
- Ricotta
- Mozzarella
- Fontina
- Provolone
- Pecorino

Although many of the Italian cheeses listed above are normally used for hot pasta dishes they can also be used in some risotto dishes.

Parmesan is the most famous cheese for service with hot rice dishes. This cheese is very hard and is grated by hand or by machine to form a fine powder. Parmesan is full-flavoured and used to cohere or top rice dishes prior to service. The cheese can be gratinated under a grill to induce a nutty flavour with a good brown colour. Cheddar does not have the same quality as Parmesan and should only be used when Parmesan is not available. Grate the cheese to produce a fine or small size powder. Parmesan is normally purchased pre-grated in 500 g units; you can purchase an electric grating unit especially for this cheese.

Herbs used to flavour rice dishes

- parsley
- oregano
- marjoram
- tarragon
- coriander
- basil
- fennel
- chervil
- thyme (lemon or common)

Fresh herbs provide a wealth of flavour and colour to rice dishes. The range of fresh herbs today is extensive with specialist growers able to provide herbs all year round. Care needs to be taken when flavouring with herbs to avoid overpowering the delicate flavours of the rice and other ingredients used in the recipe.

Spices used to flavour rice dishes

- garam masala
- bouquet garni
- cayenne
- nutmeg
- mace
- paprika
- cloves
- saffron
- turmeric
- chilli (handle with care)
- curry powder

Spices are used less often than herbs for preparation of rice dishes. Because spices can be very highly flavoured they need to be used sparingly. Often they will be used for sauces served with cooked rice or rice based dishes.

Fungi used with rice

MEMORY
JOGGER

When using fungi for rice dishes what can be done with excess fungi?

Fungi prepared and cooked with rice offer a unique flavour experience. For the modern chef, access to supplies has eased with specialist suppliers able to fly in wild fungi from all over the world. Boxed selections or fresh and dried fungi are available daily from suppliers. Because the cost of these foods is high the dish cost and selling price must reflect this. Excess fresh fungi can be dried or pickled for future use.

Cep (cèpe) Summer and autumn fungus sometimes called the flat mushroom, it is fleshy, flat and brown. Choose the smaller young ceps with no mechanical damage.

Chanterelle (Egg mushroom) Usually found in beech woods, summer to winter. It has a tinge of apricot aroma with an irregular funnel shape, egg-yellow in colour; the fragile structure needs careful handling and storage.

Morel (Sponge mushroom) It has a conical pitted cap with a brown to yellow colour; best when young and fresh.

Mushroom (cultivated as small button, cup or open flat mushroom) Firm and white when small becoming deeper brown in colour as they open to cup and flat forms, these should be unblemished and unbroken with no damage.

Truffle (White or Black) Black truffles have a rough hard skin with a strong aroma; they should be even in size. White truffles have a more pronounced flavour, usually Piedmont with a strong scent and taste.

Shiitake (Chinese mushroom) Flat top mushroom with a small stem underside, it is egg-yellow in colour, an Eastern tree fungus of oak and Skii trees.

Boletus (Yellow mushroom) Found in conifer woods it has a strong fruity aroma.

Field mushroom (Wild mushroom) A meadow and pasture land fungi common in late summer and autumn, large and small, brown and white in colour.

Eggs used with rice

- hen
- quail
- duck
- gulls
- bantam
- guinea fowl

Eggs are used to flavour and garnish rice dishes. The eggs can be used hard boiled such as for kedgeree or mixed as a seasoned liquid and cooked with the prepared rice such as with egg fried rice.

Care is needed when handling raw egg shell and rice together, both of which present a contamination potential. After handling egg shell wash your hands well with a sanitiser hand soap.

Fish and shellfish used with rice

Fish can be used to flavour or accompany rice dishes, the most famous being *paella* from Spain. Fish can be prepared by cooking first and all the skin and bone being carefully removed. The fish is flaked and cohered with the cooked rice or can be added raw at the beginning of the cooking process.

Shellfish should be clean, washed and drained well before being cooked with rice. Paella is a mixture of shellfish, chicken and saffron rice cooked in a flat wide pan.

Prawns are used with rice for Chinese dishes and are pre-cooked before being added to the cooking rice dish. Always wash prawns well before using, check for signs of decay, damage and dirt. Most shellfish can be prepared for use with raw or cooked rice dishes.

Meat and rice based dishes

Many different types of meat can be prepared for use with rice dishes, a few are listed below:
- lean bacon / smoked / green
- ham / raw Parma / cooked
- kidneys / liver / sweetbreads
- lamb / beef / pork / veal
- chicken / turkey / duck
- sausage / pepperoni / garlic

Any meat prepared for use with rice dishes should be handled carefully. Only better cuts are prepared such as chicken breast, rather than the legs, and smoked ham or fillet of beef.

Cheaper cuts which require prolonged cooking are not suitable for use with rice dishes. Cooked meat such as chicken would be prepared by dicing into a small neat size prior to adding to a cooked or cooking rice dish.

MEMORY JOGGER

Why is hygiene important when handling eggs?

Kidneys can be cooked after trimming and preparation and finished with an appropriate sauce for use with the rice e.g. turbigo or devilled kidneys.

Thin or small cuts of meat are preferable to larger cuts as they cook quickly. Rice is used as a base for many meat based dishes such as curry, fricassée, blanquettes, navarins, or any meat based dish served in or with a sauce.

Do this

- Find out what a rice socle is and how it is used.
- What is 'suchi' and which country does this dish come from?
- Apart from rice grains how else can rice be purchased?

QUALITY POINTS TO CONSIDER WITH RICE

MEMORY JOGGER

Why can rice be dangerous if stored or handled incorrectly?

Safety when preparing and cooking rice dishes
Prepared rice should be stored safely as rice can be a potential danger when left uncovered in a cooked state out of the fridge. Many chefs do not realise the problems that can occur with cooked or prepared rice if it is left in a warm kitchen.

All rice dishes should be freshly prepared; where a problem arises advice should be sought from your chef or line manager. The main risk is from *bacillus cereus* which results from rice not being kept at the correct temperature or in the correct storage conditions.

Vomiting and abdominal pains with diarrhoea can be indications of bacillus cereus infection. Thorough cooking and rapid cooling in cold water are essential in preparing rice.

Re-heating rice should be avoided where possible. Where this does take place ensure that the temperature of re-heating exceeds 70–75 °C (160–170 °F) for at least 5–8 minutes to ensure the rice is heated thoroughly. It is better to cook fresh rice from scratch than make a habit of re-heating cooked rice: because the preparation time is short, this potentially dangerous practice can be avoided.

Rice dishes should be freshly prepared and cooled rapidly if not required for immediate service. Never take risks: when in doubt – throw it out! Rice is relatively cheap and is not worth the difficulties that arise from someone developing bacillus cereus through lack of care.

PORTION SIZES AND PORTION CONTROL

The quantity of rice for a farinaceous course would be approximately 50 g of uncooked rice per portion and 75 g for a main course.

Where multi-catering operations require large quantities of cooked rice for curries or hot dishes then it is sensible to weigh the rice before cooking using the quantities given above.

When preparing rice for cooking always allow some extra portions for unexpected situations such as chance customers or where a choice is offered.

STORING RICE

Once prepared, always cover rice to prevent contamination from other foods, cool rapidly once cooked and store in the refrigerator at 3–5 °C (37–41 °F).

Excess quantities of prepared rice can be used for salads and hors d'oeuvres or as a filling for samosa. Rice can also be used as a garnish for soups.

Always check stored uncooked rice for infestation in the store. Check to see packaging is not broken or damaged and ensure stock rotation occurs. Stock items near the use-by date should be used first or the stock becomes dead stock and is wasted.

PREPARATION METHODS WITH RICE

Washing rice before cooking

Rice should be washed when raw to remove any dust and dirt especially when stored unsealed in a container. Once cooked, remove rice from the stove and refresh in cold running water to cool the rice as rapidly as possible.

Draining rice after cooking

Rice should be drained well after cooking when used as plain rice. Place the rice in a large stainless steel chinois or conical sieve and leave to drain until excess moisture is removed from the rice. This is also important when rice is stored ready for use as it prevents the rice from becoming too swollen.

Mixing rice with other ingredients

MEMORY JOGGER

Why should rice not be over-cooked?

Rice when prepared for pilau or risotto should be mixed well using a wooden spoon. When adding other ingredients such as vegetable or meat garnish mix into the rice carefully. When rice has been over-cooked care is needed to prevent the rice from sticking together during the mixing process. When rice is used as a filling, thorough mixing with other ingredients is important to maintain product consistency.

Moulding hot and cold cooked rice

Cooked rice can be moulded into shapes when hot or cold. The rice needs to be cooked correctly if hot moulding is required. This ensures the rice can be de-moulded onto the plate e.g. using a small savarin ring. The garnish is then placed in the centre.

Healthy eating
Rice has become more popular as a healthy replacement for potatoes and some fatty foods as it provides carbohydrates without the fat.

Essential knowledge

- When preparing and cooking rice it is essential to:
  - cool the rice as soon as possible and drain well, place in a suitable container and store until required in a fridge below 8 °C (46 °F).
  - keep hot rice dishes at or above 65 °C (150 °F) prior to and during service.
- Excess rice once reheated should not be used again.
- Rice can cause food poisoning. The main risk is from *bacillus cereus* which results from rice not kept at the correct temperature or in the correct storage conditions.
- Vomiting and abdominal pains with diarrhoea can be indications of bacillus cereus infection.
- Thorough cooking and rapid cooling in cold water are essential in preparing rice.

What have you learned?

1 What health and safety practices should be followed, when preparing basic rice dishes?
2 Why is it important to keep food preparation areas and equipment hygienic when preparing basic rice dishes?
3 What are the main contamination threats, when preparing storing rice and basic rice dishes ?
4 When preparing basic rice dishes, why are time and temperature important?
5 After preparation why should rice not for immediate consumption be cooled rapidly or maintained at a safe temperature ?
6 When preparing basic rice dishes, what quality points should you look for?
7 What basic preparation methods are suitable for different types of rice dishes?
8 When preparing basic rice dishes which products could be used to substitute high fat ingredients?
9 Which types of fats and oils can contribute to healthy eating practices?
10 How does increasing of fibre content of basic rice dishes contribute to healthy eating practices?
11 Why is the reduction of salt in basic rice dishes beneficial?

ELEMENT 2:   Cook basic rice dishes

TYPES OF COOKED RICE DISHES

- boiled
- pilau / pilaf
- risotto
- mixed fried / stir-fried
- steamed

Plain boiled rice

MEMORY JOGGER

Why should rice not be kept for longer than 24 hours once cooked?

Rice is purchased pre-washed in catering-sized units of 5 kg, 10 kg or 25 kg bags. Plain boiled rice should be measured in the appropriate quantity and placed in boiling salted water to cook.

Always stir the rice well in the initial cooking stages to prevent it sticking on the base of the saucepan. Cook until the rice is swollen but slightly nutty inside i.e. *al-dente*. Do not over-cook rice or it becomes soft and will stick together.

Rice not required for immediate use should be refreshed under cool running water, drained well and stored in a suitable container – not aluminium – and placed in the fridge immediately. Always cover cooked cooled rice before refrigeration.

Keep cooked plain rice for not more the 24 hours without using it, or throw it away and cook a fresh batch. Never leave rice in a warm kitchen (*see Element 1 p. 165*)

Serving suggestions
Plain boiled rice can be coloured with saffron or turmeric placed in the boiling water as the rice is cooking. Rice used plain for hors d'oeuvres can be mixed with vinaigrette to add flavour and keep the rice moist. Plain rice can be used to garnish soups such as Crème Portugaise / Crème Crecy / Mulligatawny.

Plain rice can be flavoured with lime pickle or chutney and wrapped in filo pastry for deep frying.

FOOD PREPARATION AND COOKING: COOKERY UNITS

Essential knowledge	Rice may become contaminated through:

Essential knowledge

Rice may become contaminated through:
- use of unhygienic equipment, utensils or preparation areas
- inadequate attention to personal hygiene (where bacteria passes from unclean hands, open cuts or sores, the nose or mouth to the rice)
- incorrect storage temperatures (cooked rice should always be stored below 5 °C/41 °F)
- incorrect waste disposal procedures
- being left uncovered at any stage
- excessive handling.

It is important to keep preparation and storage areas and equipment hygienic in order to:
- prevent the transfer of food poisoning bacteria to the rice
- prevent pest infestation in storage areas
- ensure that standards of cleanliness are maintained
- comply with statutory health and safety regulations.

Riz pilaf (cooked in the oven)

Used for farinaceous courses and as an accompaniment for main dishes.

Ingredients

Butter	100 g (4 oz)
Rice	200 g (8 oz)
Onion	50 g (2 oz)
White Stock	400 ml ($\frac{3}{4}$ pt)
Seasoning	salt and white or mill pepper to taste
Cartouche	

Method

1 Sweat the finely chopped onion in half the butter in a shallow pan or sauteuse.
2 Add the washed drained and dry rice to the butter and onions.
3 Cook for 2–3 minutes without colouring the onion or butter.
4 Pour on twice the volume of white stock, season and cover with the paper cartouche which has been buttered well.
5 Bring to the boil and cook in the oven for 15 minutes at 230 °C (450 °F).
6 When cooked stir in the remaining butter, re-season and serve.

Risotto (cooked on top of the stove)

Ingredients

Butter	100 g (4 oz)
Rice	200 g (8 oz)
Onion	50 g (2 oz)
White Stock	360 ml (chicken) (12 fl oz)
Parmesan cheese	50 g (2 oz)

Seasoning – salt and white or mill pepper to taste

Method

1 Sweat the finely chopped onion in half the butter in a shallow pan or sauteuse.
2 Add the washed drained and dry rice to the butter and onions.
3 Cook for 2–3 minutes without colouring the onion or butter.
4 Pour on the white stock, adding this in stages cooking with a lid partially on the pan. Keep adding stock until the rice is cooked. When the rice is cooked all the liquid should have been absorbed by the rice producing a moist dish unlike pilaff which has a drier texture.
6 When cooked stir in the remaining butter and cheese, re-season and serve.

MEMORY JOGGER

What is the basic difference between pilaff and risotto?

Stir-fried rice

Rice can be and has been used in ethnic cookery styles as a fried ingredient mixed with other foods to produce a stir-fried rice dish. This is eaten on its own or as part of a mixed meal with meat, fish or vegetables.

The rice is always pre-cooked and drained well to produce a free grain rice base which should not be over-cooked or the rice is starchy. Basmati rice is good for this type of cooked rice dish.

The rice is cooked in hot oil or butter or a mixture of oil and butter. Thinly sliced and chopped vegetables are cooked in the oil, the rice added and cooked through. Sesame seed oil is used for flavour although this is more expensive than sunflower or other vegetable oils.

A wok can be used to cook stir-fried rice in, when cooking the rice it is kept stirred or agitated to prevent it from sticking in the pan. After cooking each service of rice, wipe out the wok with a clean dry cloth or disposable paper. Re-oil and heat the pan to repeat the process.

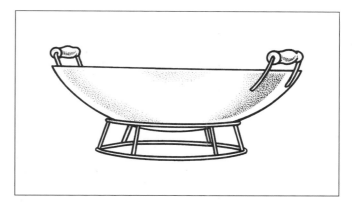

A wok

Stir-fried rice is a popular dish in Chinese and Eastern cookery. Many food outlets in Europe produce fried rice dishes using chicken, prawns, pork and eggs; any food which can be cooked quickly can be used.

Steamed rice

Rice can be cooked not just by boiling but can be steamed from raw or steamed for re-heating purposes. The rice should be covered with a buttered cartouche to prevent moisture from collecting in the dish or tray.

When re-heating rice by this method it is important to ensure the rice is re-heated correctly to prevent problems. Always ensure the steamer has been pre-heated and is at operational temperature.

Rice can be purchased in sealed bags which can be steamed or boiled. Place the punctured bags in a steamer tray and follow the manufacturers' instructions for cooking times.

TYPICAL RICE BASED RECIPES

- Riz pilaf au saffron
- Riz pilaf aux champignons
- Riz Espagnol
- Risotto Milanaise

- Risotto Piedmontaise
- Risotto al forno
- Egg fried rice
- Vegetable stir-fried rice
- Prawn fried rice
- Chicken fried rice

COOKING METHODS USED FOR RICE DISHES

Boiling/Steaming

This is the principal method of cookery for plain boiled rice used to accompany main dishes or as a garnish: also when cooked rice is required for cold rice salad.

Braising

This is the principal method of cookery for rice cooked in the pilaf style. Cooking is started on top of the stove with hot stock, a lid is placed over, often a buttered cartouche, and the rice cooked or braised in the oven for approximately 10–15 minutes.

Stewing

This is the principal method of cookery for risotto where the rice is stewed in stock on top of the stove. The liquid content is added as evaporation occurs and the rice swells up.

Stir-frying

This is the principal method of cookery for pre-cooked rice which is then subject to the stir-fry method, in a pan or wok. Rice is not cooked by the stir-fry method when raw, only when the rice is cooked and drained, used hot or refreshed in cold water drained and re-heated as required.

Do this

- Which soups are garnished with cooked rice?
- How could cooked rice be used for a finger buffet?
- Find out what black rice is and which diet it is suitable for.

TEXTURE OF COOKED RICE

The texture of any rice dish is generally affected by the cooking time and cooking temperature. If rice is not cooked for long enough it will be hard and gritty with an unpleasant bland flavour.

If however it is over-cooked then it becomes starchy and stodgy, producing a bound texture that is unpleasant to eat.

Always follow the cooking instructions determined by the recipe and follow the methods of preparation and production. These have usually been tried and tested to produce a good quality dish with optimum texture. It can follow that food styles affect this tradition at times but classical cookery has been with us for a long time and should remain so.

APPEARANCE OF RICE DISHES

If the texture has been optimised then the appearance of a rice based dish should only require common sense to finish the dish neatly and simply. With or without a sauce the food should look attractive, be very hot, or well chilled if served cold.

If the texture is wrong and the appearance is not good the dish will still lack quality. People eat with their eyes – this is a persistent quality to maintain when dealing with the appearance of any food dish.

Aroma

People eat not only with their eyes but also with their sense of smell. The rich aroma of herbs and spices, garlic and fresh tomato sauces are essential parts of the sales portfolio with food. Good quality aroma where food is concerned will entice customers to investigate and discuss particular dishes. The aroma of wild mushrooms and fresh parmesan cheese in particular provide a rich smell to attract the nose and activate the customer's palette.

Consistency

When you cook the first and last dish should be maintained at the same quality threshold: this is called consistency. Cooking requires effective preparation and persistent attention to consistent quality. This is important to maintain those customers who are loyal and return because of good meal experiences. They recommend these to their friends and return. If they find this consistency has altered in some way then they are embarrassed and will withdraw their custom in favour of your competitor.

Imparting flavour

People judge food by its appearance but only when they taste food can they judge its flavour – good flavours promote regular custom, poor flavours undermine the reputation of a business and damage the profitability of a business.

Flavour is developed by understanding recipes, following recipe instructions, cooking times and cooking temperatures while using only the best quality ingredients. You get out from a dish what you put in – buying cheap or poor quality foods cannot usually result in good competent flavours unless masked by lots of high flavoured ingredients such as garlic.

Flavour with rice based dishes needs to be subtle and delicate, not over powering or so bland as to be plain. Over or undercooking rice can affect the overall flavour – use butter not margarine to improve the flavour and colour of hot pilaff or risotto. Saffron has a special flavour when used with rice but should not be over-done by using a strong flavoured herb or spice. Garnish and add to the dish with prawns or chicken or fish, but not curry or harsh flavoured foods.

Flavours should complement one another, no one flavour should predominate but blend to highlight the quality of each ingredient.

> **MEMORY JOGGER**
>
> Why is care needed when seasoning rice dishes with herbs or spices?

Case study

You are asked to provide a stir-fry of oysters and rice with vegetables for the local oyster fair in July. You have to set up and plan the service, prepare all ingredients and use woks to cook and finish the dishes for customers by the local harbour side.
1 *What are the most important aspects to consider before agreeing to set up this event?*
2 *What prior cooking might need to be done before setting up the stand?*
3 *What precautions need to be organised when using open gas burners?*
4 *What form of insurance will you need to cover yourself and your organisation before executing the event?*

What have you learned

1 What health and safety practices should be followed when cooking basic rice dishes?
2 Why is it important to keep food preparation areas and equipment hygienic when cooking basic rice dishes?
3 What are the main contamination threats, when cooking and storing basic rice dishes?
4 When cooking basic rice dishes, why are time and temperature important?
5 After cooking, why should rice not for immediate consumption be cooled rapidly or maintained at a safe temperature ?
6 When cooking basic rice dishes, what quality points should you look for?
7 What basic cooking methods are suitable for different types of rice dishes?
8 What factors indicate that a basic rice dish is cooked correctly according to dish requirements?
9 Which types of fats and oils can contribute to healthy eating practices?

Get ahead

1 Visit oriental food stores and find out what other types of rice are available. what cooking processes and dishes might they be suitable for?
2 What vegetables other than those listed on pp. 161–62 might be suitable for cooking with basic rice dishes? How are they prepared and served?
3 Visit some local restaurants and find out what rice dishes they offer and what ingredients are used.

Prepare and cook basic dough products

This chapter covers:
ELEMENT 1: **Prepare basic dough products for cooking**
ELEMENT 2: **Cook basic dough products**

What you need to do

- Check that preparation and cooking areas and suitable equipment are hygienic and ready for use.
- Ensure dough ingredients and products are of the type, quality and quantity required for use in appropriate cooking methods to meet quality requirements.
- Report any problems identified with the quality of ingredients and dough products promptly to the appropriate person.
- Prepare dough using appropriate basic preparation methods to meet quality requirements.
- Ensure prepared and cooked dough and dough products not for immediate consumption are stored correctly.
- Check that preparation and cooking areas and equipment are cleaned correctly after use.
- Ensure all work is prioritised and carried out in an organised and efficient manner in line with appropriate organisational procedures and legal requirements.

What you need to know

- When preparing and cooking basic dough products what safe working practices should be followed.
- When preparing and cooking basic dough products why it is important to keep preparation, cooking areas and equipment hygienic.
- What the main contamination threats are when preparing, cooking and storing basic dough products.
- Why time and temperature are important when preparing and cooking basic dough products.
- How to identify when oil/fat is approaching 'flashpoint'.
- What action needs to be taken if oil/fat reaches 'flashpoint'.
- Why prepared and cooked basic dough products should be stored or held at the required safe temperature before and following cooking.
- What quality points you might look for in basic dough products.
- Which basic cooking methods are suitable for different types of basic dough product.
- How you can identify when basic dough products are cooked to recipe requirements.
- What products might be used to substitute high fat ingredients when preparing basic dough products for cooking.
- Why increasing the fibre content of basic dough can contribute to healthy eating practices.
- Which different types of flours could increase the fibre content of basic dough products.
- Why reducing the amount of sugar in basic dough products can contribute to healthy eating practices.

INTRODUCTION

What is dough?

Dough is a mixture of strong flour, water, salt and yeast, kneaded (mixed) together to the required consistency at a suitable temperature. This allows the yeast action to occur, which will produce the gases that aerate the dough piece so that when baked the products are light, digestible with a good flavour and colour.

- Basic doughs are made from strong flour, salt, yeast and water and generally are made into crusty bread products.
- When fat or milk powder is added this produces a softer range of products, as the fat content insulates the water molecules and prevents moisture loss during baking.
- When fat, sugar and eggs are added in a variety of combinations the dough is 'enriched', e.g. for buns, savarin and brioche.
- Enriched doughs which have the fat worked in by layering as in puff pastry, are called laminated doughs. These are used for Danish pastries and croissants.

The basic ingredients for making dough

FERMENTATION OF BASIC YEAST DOUGHS

Essential basic requirements for successful fermentation of dough

Yeast feeds on simple sugars (glucose) and produces carbon dioxide gas (CO_2) which aerates the dough making it light and digestible. Acids produced during fermentation also convey flavour to the baked bread products.

- *Food* – starch sugar is converted by yeast into alcohol and produces the distinctive flavour in bread. This aids the production of gas and provides the colour and bloom to the crust.
- *Warmth* – a good working temperature for the production of dough is between 22–30 °C (72–86 °F).
- *Moisture* – the temperature of water added can vary according to the kitchen temperature and weather. The water temperature should be approximately 38 °C (100 °F). Egg and milk may also be used as the liquid/moisture.
- *Time* – timing is crucial to produce good quality doughs. Hand-made doughs need approximately 45 minutes to ferment before 'knocking back' to expel the gases and re-introduce oxygen to continue the fermentation process.

Healthy eating

Dough based products add variety to the menu and have an important role in the daily diet. People need the roughage provided by brown wholemeal and wholewheat, granary or stoneground bread goods to keep their digestive system healthy. Flour based products also form a key part of the energy, vitamins, and minerals that are required every day to keep people's bodies fuelled and functioning.

Flour products are an essential part of the daily diet and flour products account for 56% of our carbohydrates, 25% of the protein and 9% of the fats in the average diet as well as essential vitamins and minerals. Bread contains essential nutrients that form part of the daily balanced diet providing energy (15%), calcium (13%), protein (16%), iron (19%) and vitamin B_1 (22%).

Brown breads can provide roughage but are less popular, although, in Britain, people are becoming more aware of the balance required in the diet. The choice and variety of high fibre and softgrain breads, speciality and new bread products has never been so great, particularly as Britain has become part of a single European market.

MEMORY JOGGER

Why is brown bread healthier than white bread?

WHERE DOES BREAD FEATURE IN THE DIET?

Bread is eaten:

- for breakfast as toast
- for luncheon as sandwiches or filled rolls
- as light snacks as hot filled rolls such as burgers and hot dogs
- cold filled rolls such as French sticks
- with dinner, sliced and buttered, or as bread rolls with soup
- as an ingredient in bread and butter pudding, apple Charlotte and bread sauces
- as filled croissant (a popular snack); filled bridge rolls are widely used for parties and weddings.

BASIC AND ENRICHED DOUGH

Freshly baked products like bread, buns, Danish pastries, croissant and brioche goods can be found in many catering outlets, hotels, restaurants, fast-food operations where these goods entice customers with the sweet, fresh smell and quality finish of such goods.

There is a wide variety of dough products produced from each main dough type e.g. bread goods can be white or brown, soft or crusty, baked in tins or shaped and cooked in the direct heat of the oven. Bread is one of the oldest products known, it is made all over the world in many shapes, sizes, flavours and textures.

Bread can be made without yeast, this is known as *unleavened* bread and is a flat bread product, such as Russian *blinis*, *pitta* or Indian *nan* bread. Bun doughs are produced by adding improvers such as fat, sugar, milk powder and flavouring to the basic bread ingredients. More yeast is required to ferment bun doughs because increased fat levels inhibit yeast activity, or longer fermentation time can be given with the same amount of yeast.

ELEMENT 1:   Prepare basic dough products for cooking

BASIC DOUGH TYPES

White basic dough – crusty products

One type of basic white dough is used for crusty products e.g.:
- White crusty bread
- White crusty rolls

Crusty white rolls being trayed before baking

These products are made from refined wheat flour mixed with water, salt and yeast sometimes with a little added bread fat and milk powder. Generally cooked on open trays or on the oven bottom, these types of basic dough products are referred to as 'oven bottom breads', e.g. crusty cottage loaf, crusty Coburg or bloomer. Oven bottom doughs need to be tighter or firmer than tin doughs as they have to support their shape but not be too firm.

Softer basic doughs are made for baking in bread tins. These are often called 'strapped tins', i.e. a row of tins joined together for ease of handling.

Because the tin supports the dough, a softer dough is used which rises more quickly due to less resistance, resulting in a larger loaf product. Crusty rolls are made from a similar soft dough. These should be spaced on perforated baking trays with small holes in them to allow the heat to pass upward and produce a brown, even dry-crust finish to the roll or loaf.

Damp humid weather or bad storage can soften crusty rolls and loaves. The oven is steamed to aid the lift as the bread begins to bake and assist the bloom finish through dextrinisation (the colouring of the starch sugar *dextrin*).

White basic dough – soft products

A different type of basic white dough is used for soft products e.g.
- White soft bread
- White soft rolls

MEMORY JOGGER

What is the main difference between soft and crusty doughs?

These products are made from refined wheat flour called *strong* flour (which has approx 75% of the wheat grain) mixed with water, salt, yeast, fat and milk powder, the amount of fat and milk powder is greater than that used for basic crusty doughs.

The addition of fat and milk powder prevents moisture loss and upon cooling results in a softer loaf or roll product. When a dough contains 6% or more of non-fat milk solids it is called *milk bread* and is subject to trading standards regulations.

Many kitchens do not have special bakery ovens but use roasting ovens to bake bread in. If using a roasting oven you might need to brush dough products with egg glaze or decorate with rice cones, flour or seeds to provide a decorative finish.

Good colouring of bread occurs when bread is steamed, which should only be done in ovens designed for such use. Never steam bread in an electric oven such as a convector oven if it is not specifically designed for steaming; it can be dangerous.

Brown dough

Wholemeal or wheatmeal bread or rolls
The flour used for these contains 100% of the bran and germ of the wheat with nothing added or taken away. This is referred to as 100% extraction.

Wholemeal flour is rich in vitamin B. Doughs made from wholemeal flours need less proving as the bran enzymes and germ react with the gluten to ripen the dough more quickly.

These doughs will also need more water due to the absorbing properties of the bran. Less gluten is formed when using wholewheat and wholemeal flours and therefore products have less volume.

White flour contains more gluten forming proteins with an average extraction rate of some 70% being mostly the crushed endosperm (starch). If wholemeal doughs are over-proved the dough will collapse resulting in poor volume and a dense texture. Wholewheat and wholemeal flour will not keep as long as white flour and should be used as soon as possible to ensure good quality baked dough products.

Because there is less gluten to develop the doughs tend to be softer in texture and require a softer moulding. However if the water content is low and a tight dough is produced the bread will lack volume and result in a heavy texture.

Healthy eating

When producing dough products we have an opportunity to promote healthy catering practices by utilising high fibre commodities. These can be cereal based using brown, wholemeal and wheatmeal flours rather than bleached white flour.

White flour has only approximately 70% of the grain remaining after the milling process. In contrast wholewheat flour has 100% of the grain after the husk is removed. Wholewheat is a high fibre flour that will assist in preventing bowel disorders later in life. Promote the use of wholewheat and wholemeal flour where possible.

Brown bread or rolls.
A flour that has at least 85% of the wheat berry included will also have all of the endosperm (starchy) and most of the bran. A brown loaf must contain at least 0.6% of fibre calculated on the dried weight of the flour. Many of the sliced brown breads and soft brown roll products found in modern bakeries are produced from fine wheatmeal flours where the flour has been ground finely and the crushed bran gives it a light brown colour.

Stoneground flour is simply wheat crushed between two stones in the mill. Brown flour generally refers to a finer ground *wheatmeal flour*. *Granary flour* is brown flour with malted grains of rye and barley added and is a popular dough product used for granary loaves, rolls or pizza bases. Many mixed-grain flours are now available adding to the variety of breads available.

Bun dough

Basic bun dough is made from strong flour, water, yeast, salt, eggs, sugar, fat, milk or milk powder and lemon flavour or bun spice. Bun dough is the same as basic bread dough with less salt and enriched by the added ingredients above. Buns can be made in a variety of shapes and sizes, many of which are traditional and have local historical origins. A bun dough should be clear and slightly sticky. More yeast is often used in bun doughs to counteract the enriching ingredients – butter and eggs.

Many of the bun range of dough products are sold from bakeries, hot bread units and instore bakeries, although some hotels and cafes will offer these dough goods as 'morning goods' with coffee.

Bun spice should only be added when the dough has been mixed and proved once because bunspice has a narcotic effect on the yeast and retards the fermentation process.

Lemon oil or more usually lemon flavour is used for certain bun dough products and unlike bunspice does not effect the yeast. It provides the distinct flavouring in hot cross buns.

Fruited bun dough

When fruit is added to the basic bun dough an extended range of bun dough products can be made. Fruit should be added to the dough after mixing has taken place as this avoids the fruit being crushed which would spoil the colour and appearance of the bun dough products. Currants, sultanas, cherries and mixed chopped peel can be used.

These fruits add flavour colour and texture to the basic bun dough for making Chelsea, currant and Belgian buns, fruit loaves, plaits and bun rounds. Cornish saffron loaves, lardy cake and decorated fruit bread are regional specialities that are delicious when eaten fresh with morning coffee or afternoon tea.

Do this

- Find out what fermentation is, how it works, why it works and what are the ideal conditions for fermentation to occur.
- What types of fat and other ingredients are added to bread? Why and what effect do they have on fermentation?
- State the importance of the recipe in breadmaking.

ENRICHED DOUGHS

Enriched dough is the basic bread dough to which extra ingredients have been added. These can be eggs, butter, sugar and dried fruits. These ingredients enrich the basic dough, improving the colour, flavour, texture and shelf life. They are used to make:
- Baba
- Savarin
- Brioche

Baba

This is a rich fermented yeast sponge made from a medium (50% soft/50% strong flour mix) or just strong flour, yeast, eggs, butter, milk, sugar and currants. The baba paste is made by mixing the flour, yeast, milk and sugar for ten minutes until a smooth sticky paste results. The mix is then scraped down well and the melted butter poured over and covered. This is left to double in size (approx 45 mins) and then mixed carefully to incorporate the butter which will have sunk to the bottom as the paste ferments. When mixed again well, using a paddle or dough hook, the currants are added and the mix is piped into baba moulds, which must be well greased to prevent sticking, to fill one third. This is proved until two third risen in the mould and then baked which will then expand the baba to the top of the mould. When cool, the baba is trimmed level and soaked in a rich fruit-and-spice syrup.

Savarin

Savarin can be made from the same recipe as for baba, but without the fruit. When ready and mixed the paste is piped into well greased moulds called savarin rings; these can be individual or multi-portions. The paste can also be piped into a charlotte mould, baked and sliced, dusted with sugar and toasted, then decorated with fruit and glazed to produce *croute aux fruites*. When cooked in a barquette mould these are called *marignans* and are finished as for savarin with soaking syrup, apricot glaze fresh fruit and cream, decorated with almonds or pistachio nuts.

Brioche

Brioche is the rich yeast dough paste that has a high butter and egg content. Brioche are made extensively in France and eaten for breakfast with coffee. Many supermarkets stock a limited range of brioche products but they are best eaten freshly baked. The dough is soft and difficult to handle and benefits from being placed in the fridge overnight to aid handling. The dough is moulded into small rounds and placed in well-greased fluted brioche tins; these can be individual or multi-portion moulds.

LAMINATED DOUGH

Laminated dough is used to make croissant and Danish pastries.

Croissant

Croissant, meaning 'crescent', are made from a dough into which fat has been layered (laminated) as it is in the production of puff pastry.

The basic dough is made from flour, yeast, milk, sugar and salt. When this has developed it is rested and then rolled into a rectangle shape.

The butter or fat is spread over two thirds of the dough which is then folded as for puff pastry, giving three half or single turns. When completely rested the paste is rolled out to a 2–3 mm($\frac{1}{10}$ in) thickness and cut using a knife, or special croissant roller, into triangular shapes measuring approximately 10–12 cm (4–5 in) wide at the base and 20–24 cm (8–9 in) long. They are rolled up from the widest part of the base and then formed into a crescent shape for proving.

The proving stage should be in dry heat and not in a moist prover as for bread and bun products. This is because of the high fat content; moisture would cause a poor finish to croissant. Croissant are eaten for breakfast. They are best made with butter and are good served with coffee. Today they are widely used instead of bread rolls and are filled with fish, meat and salad.

Danish pastries

Like croissant, Danish pastry dough is a laminated dough. The paste is made using medium-strong flour, yeast, chilled milk, egg and cardamom spice. The basic dough is made and rested before the fat is added, as for croissant paste.

When being rested, rolled and folded, after the three single or half turns the paste is cut into shapes and formed into Danish pastry bases. These are then filled with fruit, frangipane, apple, mincemeat and other ingredients to produce a popular array of morning pastries.

When formed, the pastries are again dry proved and then baked. When cool, an apricot glaze is brushed over the baked goods which are then finished with water icing and/or toasted nuts. Good piping of the fondant icing will add artistry to these popular goods and will improve sales.

BASIC INGREDIENTS IN PREPARING DOUGH

Knowledge of the ingredients used to prepare dough and dough products is essential if quality products are to be produced. While many catering operations use bought-in products, convenience mixes or frozen pre-formed goods, it is still worthwhile knowing how to prepare and produce your own dough products.

MEMORY JOGGER

Why should the salt and sugar be kept away from the yeast when placed in the mixing bowl?

The basic ingredients are:
- *Flour* – strong flour contains approximately 11–12% protein and when the flour is mixed with water the protein is formed into *gluten*. This is an elastic substance that holds the gas within the dough; this process is called aeration.
- *Yeast* is either fresh or dried. Fresh yeast is fawn in colour with a pleasant smell. It should be stored in a refrigerator. When using dried yeast only half the quantity is required.
- *Water* should be warm. If mixing doughs by hand dissolve the yeast in the water; if you use a mixing machine put the yeast in dry, but keep it away from any salt and sugar as direct contact with salt and sugar can kill yeast.
- *Salt* provides the dough with flavour, acts as a preservative, improves the quality of the crumb and crust and strengthens the gluten. Check recipes for the correct quantity of salt in each type of dough.

Types of Yeast

Yeast is available as:
- Fresh compound yeast
- Dried granular or powdered yeast

Yeast can be used in either fresh or dried form. Fresh compressed yeast is fawn in colour with a pleasant smell, and should be stored in a refrigerator. Dried yeast may be granular or powdered, and is also fawn in colour with a slight yeast smell.

Yeast is the agent responsible for the fermentation of dough and dough products. It is a living, single-cell micro-organism. When it is combined with food in a warm and moist atmosphere it ferments, producing carbon dioxide and ethanol (a type of alcohol), while at the same time reproducing itself.

The optimum temperature for yeast activity in dough making is 26–27 °C (79–81 °F).

Do this
- Check the storage temperature of fresh yeast and what one block of yeast weighs.
- Find out the difference between the quantity of yeast needed when fresh yeast is used and when dried yeast is used.

Fat and oil

The addition of fat or oil to a basic bread dough has the effect of enriching the dough product. When fat is added to the basic dough recipe it prevents moisture in the form of steam from being evaporated from the dough pieces as they bake. The fat traps moisture so that when the product cools the dough piece retains a soft texture. Milk powder is often added to doughs to produce a soft roll or soft loaf. Buns are a good example of this.

Oil is added to certain breads to enrich and moisten the bread such as with black olive bread. Lard, shortening, butter or margarine are also used in dough production. Fat gives the cooked dough product a softer crumb and assists in preserving the freshness of the bread or bun product.

Eggs

Used generally only in enriched doughs, eggs improve the flavour, colour and food value of the dough product whilst increasing the production costs. Eggs help to make the dough product lighter. Brioche has butter and eggs added to produce a rich, silky, light dough product.

Sugar

Sugar is present in large quantities in the flour, held in the starch from which the yeast feeds and converts into *ethanol* (ethyl alcohol). Some sugar is added to dough to kick-start the yeast, or to sweeten the dough for bun production. A larger quantity of sugar is employed in the production of lardy cakes and Portland dough cake. Keep sugar away from direct contact with the yeast or the yeast will begin to die. This also applies to salt as salt also kills yeast.

Milk and water

Milk enriches basic doughs and preserves the moisture content; water is used in most dough products at blood temperature (37 °C /98.6 °F). When the weather is colder outside, bakers will often increase the temperature of the water to compensate for the colder flour.

Do this

- Why do enriched dough baked products have a longer shelf life than basic dough products?
- Find out why skimmed milk powder is more suitable for use in doughs.
- What is meant by 'the extraction rate of flour' ?
- List 10 varieties of flour which may be used in breadmaking.

EQUIPMENT FAILURE WHEN PREPARING AND PRODUCING DOUGHS

A common problem in catering is the failure of equipment. This can be attributed to a number of factors:
- human error
- mechanical failure
- electrical failure
- accidents
- wear and tear.

Human error

Every member of staff needs to be trained in the safe and proper use of machinery and equipment. All staff should be aware or be made aware of the *Health and Safety at Work Act*. Employers are legally bound to take reasonable precautions to protect their employees where machinery and the working environment are concerned.

Staff using machines where they are untrained in the use of the machine not only present a potential hazard but can damage machines costing the business vital lost production time and replacement or repair costs to bring the equipment back to a safe operational condition.

Mechanical failure

Mechanical failure can occur for a number of reasons. This might be human error, improper use of the machine or a part failing because of fatigue, weakness in the design or construction of the part. Effective business practice is to have a service contract for expensive machinery to insure against failure. This might be for the parts, loss of production or for a replacement, covering both parts and labour.

MEMORY JOGGER

When a problem is noticed with equipment, what action should be taken immediately and who should be informed about the problem?

Where a part or machine fails the equipment should be isolated from the electricity supply, or the gas turned off immediately. Always stop production and advise your superior of the problem.

If you suspect a problem, e.g. an unusual noise or smell, then stop the equipment immediately and ask for a second opinion to confirm your suspicions. Never work on a machine you suspect of being faulty, even if asked to do so by your employer. This is a breach of the *Health and Safety at Work Act* regulations.

Always be trained, be careful, be vigilant, and look, listen and smell to try and pre-empt any failure. This could save time and money and ensure the personal safety of other employees and yourself.

Electrical failure

Electrical failure is a rare problem but can occur on occasions. Where this does happen, always isolate the equipment; seek advice or assistance from your superior. Serious problems must be dealt with by a qualified electrical engineer. Never attempt to rectify electrical problems; you place yourself and others at risk.

Where you smell burning, switch off the machine immediately. Each machine should have an isolation switch. Advise your employer of the problems; he or she is responsible to ensure the equipment is maintained and repaired safely.

Accidents

Generally, accidents only happens where people are either negligent or fool around when they should be concentrating on their work. With accidental damage all of the above points are relevant. When working be careful to prevent accidental damage to equipment and yourself and fellow colleagues.

Never play about near or in work areas. Incidents can lead to serious injury or loss of life. Always be professional, careful and considerate. It takes only a second to remove a finger or limb, but you live with the consequences for the rest of your life – so be careful and be safe.

Wear and tear

Where machines are used constantly parts will wear either from mechanical damage, heat damage or just fatigue. Get to know the equipment, how it usually sounds and operates. Any change can be detected before damage occurs. Sometime this happens without warning and the problem parts need to be changed and the machine checked for other problems or weak points.

PROBLEMS WITH FOOD

The delivery and storage of food

When preparing or cooking dough you need to be aware of problems that can and do occur with food commodities related to dough and dough products. Flour can be contaminated with weevil; flour bags might have been damaged and contaminated by vermin, flies or dirt. Always check flour bags are sound and fit for the purpose for which they are intended. When receiving a delivery check the details e.g. that the flour is bakery strong flour and not soft plain flour.

Where a problem with flour is identified, notify your supervisor and inform the supplier, noting the nature of the problem. Ask what action they will take, and when, and check that you have sufficient flour to meet production deadlines.

Where any dough ingredient is concerned you need to check all deliveries and ensure they are stored correctly.

- Check the use-by date of all deliveries.
- Move older stock such as flour, fats, yeast, sugar to ensure they are used first and newest stock last.
- Check dried fruit for stalk, stones and foreign bodies.
- Check fondant and other perishable commodities for mould growth or infestation from ants, especially when the weather is warm.
- Be vigilant when handling all dough and dough product ingredients to maintain quality production and minimise the risk of contamination or problems resulting from infestation.
- Clean and check storage areas regularly, every store should be tidied each day at the conclusion of production and deep cleaned each week to maintain a clean and safe environment for the storage of food ingredients.

REPORTING PROBLEMS

Where a problem cannot be resolved, always report the difficulty to your line manager, supervisor or person you are responsible to.

Never leave a problem to develop into a major difficulty; this in time will cost money and might affect production or the quality of products and services, especially where baking ovens, fryers or dough moulders are concerned. These are costly pieces of equipment and will have a major impact on production if broken, prevention is better than a cure.

Where problems with deliveries are noticed, having checked the delivered items carefully you should bring the problem to the attention of the delivery person.

It is also advisable to inform the company supplying the items to prevent any misunderstanding. Where the delivery is urgent or needed the same day it is important to make sure the driver understands a replacement is required.

If the item is not urgent, then always ensure a replacement is sent shortly afterwards. Where a replacement cannot be provided a credit note should be given by the supplier. Never accept food or packaged goods that are not fit for the purpose for which they are intended.

Where flour is not producing the right results, which does occur from time to time, this might be due to the protein content being low and therefore producing bread or dough products with low volume. Inform the supplier immediately and demand an immediate replacement to maintain production.

QUALITY INDICATORS FOR BASIC DOUGHS

Texture

When dough is produced, unless the correct texture is achieved a number of problems can occur.

- If the dough texture is too slack the dough pieces will not be easy to handle or to maintain in the desired shape prior to proving; as the dough piece proves it will lose its shape quickly.
- If the dough is too tight the dough will not prove quickly as the gluten will be tight and tough and the dough will not expand and grow, holding in the gas produced.
- To maintain the correct dough texture comes with practice and understanding what it is you are trying to do when producing dough.

Appearance

If the texture is wrong then it is likely the appearance of the dough will be wrong. When producing white or brown dough the dough should have a clean, smooth, silky appearance and be free from contamination i.e. there should be no pieces of white dough or fruit in brown doughs and vice versa.

Where the dough pieces are 300 g or more, each dough piece produced should be the same shape and size as the next to maintain an even standard and to conform to trading standards regulations.

Aroma

When a dough is under-proved then the dough will smell very yeasty and will lack colour and be of poor volume. The aroma given off by the dough is distinctive and indicates the dough is unripe.

When a dough is over-proved it develops a pungent smell of alcohol as the yeast continues to produce ethanol from the starch sugar but has no oxygen remaining to produce carbon dioxide. This aroma is unmistakable and this kind of dough is called over-ripe.

Consistency

When preparing and producing dough for baking or deep-frying it is important to maintain consistency with production. The reasons for this are more common sense than anything else:
- to be able to produce the same standard of product for repeat custom and to maintain cost effective production.
- to be able to ensure the balance of recipe in producing individual doughs and product in line with trading standards regulations.

Maintaining consistency is a vital part of training. Ensure all trainees understand why the term consistency is used.

The term consistency is also used in the context of texture, where a dough has the correct consistency for the product or process. It would be no use placing a dough with a slack consistency into a hydraulic divider or placing a dough with a very firm consistency in a chain moulder.

> **MEMORY JOGGER**
>
> Why is consistency an important quality indicator when preparing and cooking dough products?

PREPARATION OF DOUGH

The tables below provide: a list of ingredients (metric) required, the order of addition, and a check list for the products being produced.

Ingredients for white dough recipes

	Tin	Crusty	Bloomer	Enriched	Milk
Strong flour	1 kg	1 kg	1 kg	1 kg	1 kg
Water	570 ml	530 ml	530 ml	585 ml	585 ml
Yeast	30 g	30 g	30 g	30 g	30 g
Salt	20 g	20 g	20 g	20 g	20 g
Fat shortening			20 g		60 g
Butter				20 g	
Skim milk powder			20 g	30 g	60 g
Sugar			5 g		
Dough temperature 24–25 °C (76–78 °F).					

Ingredients for brown dough recipes

	Wholemeal Tin	Wholemeal Crusty	Wheatmeal Tin	Wheatmeal Crusty	Granary Cracked wheat
Wholemeal	1 kg	1 kg			
Wheatmeal			1 kg	1 kg	720 g
White flour			140 g		
Cracked wheat					140 g
Water	720 ml	695 ml	640 ml	610 ml	640 ml
Salt	15 g	15 g	15 g	15 g	20 g
Fat shortening	20 g	20 g	20 g	15 g	
Sugar	10 g	10 g			10 g
Yeast	30 g	30 g	35 g	35 g	30 g

PREPARATION METHODS

There are a number of preparation methods which you will need to use:
- Mixing
- Kneading
- Portioning
- First proving
- Folding
- Moulding
- Rolling
- Shaping
- Second proving
- Glazing

Mixing by hand

This is used for small dough mixes.
1 Weigh and check ingredients.
2 Place dry ingredients into mixing bowl.
3 Dissolve yeast in warm water/milk (37 °C/98 °F).
4 Make a bay in centre of flour and add warm liquid.
5 Mix with one hand and knead to a smooth dough. Dough should be soft and smooth in texture but not sticky.

Dough being mixed by machine

Mixing by machine

This is used for large dough mixes and quick dough development.
1 Weigh and check ingredients, checking that all equipment is clean.
2 Place all ingredients into mixing bowl; keep salt and sugar away from yeast.
3 Ensure the bowl and machine are set correctly.
4 Mix the dough for required length of time, or until a tough elastic dough has been produced.
5 If dough is slack or tight adjust as necessary.
6 Stop mixer and remove dough, only if safe to do so.
7 Handle dough cleanly, placing it onto the bench for dividing and weighing.

Kneading

This is used to make the dough pieces smooth.
1 When the dough has formed together, squeeze and rub the dough on the bench (*knead*) to form a smooth and silky finish to the dough piece.
2 Machine-made doughs only need a light kneading to produce a clean smooth surface.

Dividing and scaling dough

Portioning – dividing and scaling

This means to cut or divide a shaped or formed dough product to produce individual pieces for traying or tinning. An example would be Belgian buns where the rectangular piece of prepared dough is rolled up to form a Swiss roll shape and then portioned with a knife or dough scraper.
1 Once the dough has been mixed and kneaded the dough is cut by using a dough divider which can be a hand scraper or hydraulic cutting machine.
2 Divided dough pieces are cut and scaled to the required weight. All dough pieces exceeding 300 g are subject to trading standards regulations.
3 Scaled dough pieces are rested for a short time.

Proving

In the initial proving stage, the dough is placed in the warm prover and left for the yeast to ferment and produce carbon dioxide gas and ethanol (ethyl alcohol). The smell given off is a good indicator of the right degree of proving. If the dough smells yeasty, it is under-proved: if it smells of alcohol it is over-proved.

Folding

Once it has been rested for the initial proving stage, the moulded piece of dough is flattened to remove the carbon dioxide and ethanol, replacing the oxygen content of the dough piece. This preparation is generally related to dough pieces prepared for bread loaves, either tinned or oven-bottom bread.

To fold dough:
1 Weigh a piece of bread dough e.g. 980 g.
2 Mould the dough piece into a round ball. Try to get a smooth surface.
3 Rest the dough for 10 minutes.
4 Turn the dough piece upsidedown onto a lightly floured clean bench and flatten with a clenched fist, so the gas is expelled. Then oxygen is re-introduced for the secondary proving stage.
5 Fold the two outer opposite edges into the centre, roll and mould from a single edge toward yourself making a cylinder shape, to form a bread loaf.
6 Place folded dough in tin.

 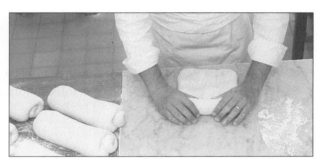

Top left: Folding the two outer edges of the dough into the centre

Top right: Rolling the dough into a loaf shape

Right: Placing the dough tins for baking

Moulding

This is to form the dough piece into a round shape to produce a smooth surface prior to shaping.
● When dough has been rested for a short time, mould dough piece into a round ball shape and rest again for a short time prior to shaping.
● Bread rolls can be moulded by hand or using a roll moulder. Each bread product is moulded to get a very smooth silky finish.
● The smoother the moulding, the better the proved and cooked product will look. If dough pieces have a rough mould they will develop a rough finish when proven and baked.

Rolling

Rolling is typically used for Chelsea and Belgian buns, baps, lardy cakes, pizza bases and unleavened bread. Dough is rolled (pinned) to make it flat prior to shaping.

1 Divide and weigh a piece of dough to get the required weight.
2 Dust the dough piece lightly and using a rolling pin roll out to the required shape.

Shaping dough

Shaping

This is used to form the dough piece prior to the second or final proving stage.
1 Check that the moulded dough piece has been rested for sufficient time.
2 Knock back the moulded, proved dough piece to expel the gas.
3 Check what shape is required.
4 Shape according to product requirement.

Second proving

The second proving stage occurs after the goods have been moulded and shaped. They are put into the proving cabinet (or warm place) for a second time, to double in size.
1 When you have shaped the dough place goods on to tray on silicone paper, spacing them evenly.
2 Place them in the prover. If you do not have a proving cabinet place the tray of rolls in a warm place and spray with water to prevent a skin forming. Ideally the temperature should be 30 °C (104 °F) with Relative Humidity (RH) of 85–90%.
3 Prove until double in size; the rolls should be light to touch and smell fresh. An over-proved (over-ripe) dough smells of alcohol !
4 Remove carefully from the proving cabinet or warm shelf and place in the oven.

Glazing

Glazing with egg-wash is carried out on raw unproved yeast goods to provide a brown colour. A sugar glaze (bun wash) is applied to baked goods to provide a shiny finish and seal the product (to prevent it drying out too quickly).

You need to know what type of glazing is required.
● Egg-wash glaze is the washing of the yeast product before and after proving. A little salt added to the egg-wash breaks down the protein and produces a better colour and glaze.
● Sugar or bun glazing is done by brushing on a boiled sugar syrup (bun wash), which can be flavoured, e.g. lemon.

KEY POINTS IN PREPARATION OF DOUGH

● Check that ovens are pre-set and switched on, or that the deep-fryer has clean oil, filled to the correct level and pre-set. Bread tins should be kept clean but not washed, use a bread emulsion to grease tins for bread. Baking trays should be kept clean and any carbonised food removed and the tray cleaned.

- Use silicone paper for trayed buns, Danish or croissant and individual items. Cut a sheet of silicone into 6 pieces and oil if you are making doughnuts, and do not have a doughnut fryer. Silicone can be used a number of times, this reduces costs but replace if it begins to break up. Keep mixers and oven clean, make sure you give them a good clean each day after production.
- Divide, scale, knead, mould, shape and prove dough product according to product requirements. Remove the mixed dough cleanly onto a work bench and divide into the required weights. Scale each dough piece and check the weight carefully. Knead each dough piece into a smooth round ball and rest. Mould the rested dough piece into the required shape and tin or tray according to the product requirements. Prove the product for the required length of time, do not over or under-prove.

Essential knowledge

Clean and hygienic preparation areas and equipment are important because:
- They can prevent cross-contamination of basic dough products.
- They can minimise the risk of dough ingredients and products being contaminated.
- They can prevent the risk of infestation by reducing the opportunity for vermin and insects to feed on dirty equipment and surfaces.

Do this

- Watch the chef or baker producing a dough.
- Check the mixing times and make a list for each different dough from the range.
- Find out how they know when the goods are proved. What indicators do they use?
- Check the cooking times and oven temperatures for each dough type.

LEGAL REQUIREMENTS

In September 1995 new regulations were brought into effect to add to the *Food Safety Act 1990*. These new regulations cover the standards of premises; raw materials; quality of water in food; personal hygiene for food handlers; preventing food contamination and training and supervising food handlers.

At the same time the detailed temperatures as set out in the 1990 Act have been updated to include *The Food Safety (Temperature Control) Regulations 1995*. All food premises, under *The Food Premises (Registration) Regulations 1991*, must be registered with their local Environmental Health Office if they wish to prepare or produce food in any shape of form.

Do this

1 What regulations are currently in force to cover food hygiene?
2 Obtain a copy of the *Food Hygiene Regulations* from your local Environmental Health Office.
3 In the act, highlight those legal considerations that directly effect the storage and temperatures of food.
4 What are the implications for a business that does not currently have resources or equipment in place to comply with the legal obligations enforced under the act?
5 What are the consequences for a business if they do not meet with these legal requirements?
6 What powers do Environmental Health Officers have to force an employer to comply?
7 What temperatures are you required to check where food is concerned?
8 Why must you record these temperatures and what action should be taken where differences to the required temperatures are found?

ELEMENT 2:   Cook basic dough products

BAKING DOUGH PRODUCTS

Oven bottom breads and rolls are generally cooked on trays without any tin moulds. The dough used for these breads needs to be firm enough to support the shape during baking. Softer basic doughs can be baked in bread tins, where the tin supports the dough. The softer dough rises more quickly due to its lower resistance during baking, resulting in a larger loaf. These loaves are often baked in *strapped tins*, i.e. a row of tins joined together for ease of handling.

Crusty rolls should be evenly spaced over baking trays which have small holes in to allow the heat to pass upward and produce a brown, even, dry-crust finish to the roll or loaf. The oven is *steamed* to aid the lift as the bread begins to bake and to assist the bloom finish.

Brown breads such as wholemeal are usually baked in bread tins or formed into rolls. If you are baking buns, tray them according to their type and bake them at a reduced heat to allow for the enriched dough. Always check the baking temperature for each individual bun product.

KEY POINTS WHEN COOKING DOUGH PRODUCTS

- When the products are proved, handle them carefully and put them into a pre-set oven for the required period of time.
- Remember that some baked goods need to be piped, cut or marked before baking.
- Try to fill the oven space when baking by planning your production carefully. This saves time, energy and money.
- Always remove baked products carefully and cleanly, making sure you have cleared a space to place the hot goods for hygienic storage while cooling.
- Many kitchens do not have special bakery ovens but use roasting ovens for baking bread. If using a roasting oven, you might need to brush dough products with egg-wash or decorate with rice cones, flour or seeds to provide a decorative finish.

● Bread achieves a good colour when cooked by steaming, but this should only be done in an oven specifically designed for such use. Never steam in an electric oven (such as a convector) if it has not been designed for this: *it can be dangerous*.

BAKING AND DEEP-FRYING OF DOUGH PRODUCTS

Baking and frying makes dough edible; the correct temperature for the appropriate length of time ensures a product that is of pleasant colour and good volume. Under-baked or over-baked dough products do not sell well. Deep-fried doughnuts should be an even colour and not greasy, but light with an even golden colour.

Cooking doughs – Baking

Once the dough has been proved the next stage is the baking process. The bread rolls, loaves or yeasted goods are placed carefully into the oven. This is crucial so as not to disturb the light delicate structure of gas held by the developed dough and formed by the structure of the gluten.

Bread should be baked in an oven set at least to 230 °C (450 °F), when the bread is placed in the oven the gas (carbon dioxide and ethanol) is heated and expands, this expansion to the stage where the protein coagulates is called the 'oven spring'.

The temperature range for baking bread is from 230–260 °C (450–500 °F). When bread is placed in the heated oven the temperature drops, so it is customary to put the bread in at a slightly higher temperature initially, to compensate for this. The time it takes to bake bread will depend on the size of the product and the volume being cooked at any one time.

Tinned loaves being placed in the oven

Guide to the baking times for bread loaves		
400 g	loaf	30–40 minutes
800 g	loaf	35–40 minutes
1600 g	loaf	40–45 minutes

When baked, the loaf should be of a good colour and sound hollow when tapped. Rolls and small dough items vary little in baking time. They should be baked for between 8–12 minutes until the required colour is achieved.

Bun goods that contain sugar need a lower baking temperature or the sugar will caramelise, spoiling the finish. Approximately 226–232 °C (440–450 °F) is the temperature for most bun products.

Deep-Frying

Doughnuts are not baked but deep-fried in oil in a special doughnut fryer or standard friture. The moulded dough pieces are placed on oiled silicone paper, allowing enough room for the pieces to expand without touching. When proved the doughnuts are placed in the hot fat which should be at 193 °C (380 °F). The doughnuts will float and colour on the underneath side; when a golden brown colour use a palette knife to turn the doughnuts over. *Be very careful when working with hot fat.*

Special doughnut fryers are used by bakers. The dough pieces are trayed onto special perforated trays and the tray is lowered into the hot fat. When cooked on both sides the tray is lifted removing all the doughnuts at once. The cooked doughnuts are left to drain off any excess oil and stored in a rack until cool enough to be filled with jam.

The doughnuts are filled with a seedless jam by using a doughnut jam injector; this can be manual or electronic. The filled doughnuts should be rolled in vanilla or cinnamon sugar. Special fat can be used that has a low smoke point and low absorption properties to prevent the doughnut from being greasy. The cooking temperature is important; if too hot the centre of the doughnut will be raw and the outside over-coloured, if too low the doughnut will absorb the fat and become greasy.

Remember: Take care when frying and always strain the warm fat or oil each day after use.

KEY POINTS WHEN DEEP-FRYING DOUGH PRODUCTS

- Deep-fry dough products for the required time at the correct temperature.
- When the products are proved, handle them carefully and place in the deep-fryer for the required period of time.
- Some baked goods need to be piped, cut or marked before baking. Do this now.
- Handle doughnuts carefully in the deep fryer and turn when golden brown.
- Try and fill the deep-fryer when baking by planning your production carefully; this saves time, energy and money.
- Remove fried products carefully and cleanly, make sure you have cleared a space to place the hot goods for hygienic storage while cooling.

FINISHING DEEP-FRIED DOUGH PRODUCTS

- Finish, present and store deep-fried dough products according to the product requirements, meeting food hygiene regulations.
- Ensure the cooked products are cool before finishing, dusting or filling (except bun goods that are bun washed while still warm).
- Finish by filling, dusting or decorating the deep-fried cool products according to requirements e.g. with icing, sugar, jam or cream.
- Present and store the finished cooked products according to the *Food Hygiene (Amendments) Regulations 1995.*

Remember: Never use cream to fill a product that is still warm. Warm cream breeds bacteria and can cause food-poisoning.

> **MEMORY JOGGER**
>
> Why should you never pipe cream into warm dough products?

MAINTAINING HYGIENE STANDARDS

Waste materials should be disposed of cleanly and efficiently, to prevent contamination of uncooked and cooked dough products and ingredients and to prevent health hazards. Work in a clean and organized manner attending to any priorities and laid down procedures in the event of unexpected situations, this might be a rush order, customer request or emergency.

Know your responsibilities, if in doubt ask your supervisor. As you work clean up after yourself. Wipe down between each task or job: do not use glass or oven cloths to wipe down work surfaces; this causes contamination.

SPECIALITY DOUGHS

Pizza bases

Pizza requires a basic bread dough made with cold water, less yeast and some oil added before the dough is mixed well.

There is no need to develop this dough fully as the base should not be too thick, although deep pan pizza generally has a thicker base. When rested the dough is weighed and portioned and moulded into round shapes (or large rectangles if making large quantities for buffets), brushing with oil to prevent the tomato topping from softening the dough below.

Cover with cheese and top with appropriate toppings, then oil is again sprinkled over and the herbs added. These products are generally baked at high temperature in a special pizza oven which is very shallow. The baked pizza is one of the most popular baked dough based products. Granary base dough adds a nutty flavour and texture topped with a rich tomato pulp, tomato purée, garlic, onion, oregano, basil and marjoram herb mix.

Pitta / Nan breads

- *Nan bread* – Indian flat bread.
- *Pitta bread* – Middle Eastern and Greek in origin. In Greece pitta is eaten with houmous and taramasalata.
- *Chapati* – Indian unleavened bread made from *ata*, a fine ground wholewheat flour.
- *Tortilla* – Mexican unleavened bread made from *masaharina* (a fine ground cornmeal flour ground from white maize soaked in lime water) or wholewheat flour doughs.

Blinis

Russian in origin, this pancake is served with caviar and is made from flour, warm milk, a little yeast, eggs and salt. When fermented the mixture is lightly mixed and whipped egg whites are added, sometimes with cream also. The blinis are then cooked in special small blinis pans; they resemble tiny pancakes.

Do this

- Find out which countries produce strong flours and how and when they are grown.
- Why do enriched dough baked products have a longer shelf-life than basic dough products?
- Ask why skimmed milk powder is more suitable for use in doughs.
- What is meant by 'the extraction rate of flour' ?
- List 10 varieties of flour which may be used in breadmaking.

FINISHING DOUGH PRODUCTS PRIOR TO BAKING

Removing baked dough products from the oven

Decoration by using a sharp blade, knife or scissors

Bread dough products can be finished by cutting the fermented dough piece just before it is baked. A sharp blade is used to cut a decorative pattern on top of the dough product. Bloomers are cut to form a herringbone, diagonal cut or horizontal cut. The baker will make a light score with the blade by drawing the cutter lightly over the top of the fermented dough piece.

Coburg loaves are scored with a sharp blade to form a cross, sometimes called 'knotching'. Cottage loaves and rolls are marked by small cut marks from the top down at regular intervals around the product, this is done when the dough has been formed into shape but prior to the proof stage. Bread can be decorated with cuts using scissors to produce a decorative pattern to the baked bread.

Decoration by using flour, seeds, grains or wash

Doughs can be decorated by dusting with flour just prior to baking, this produces a decorative finish to the baked product. Rolls and loaves can be dipped in seed when moulded e.g. blue poppy seed or sesame seeds. When baked these add a distinct flavour and colour to bread.

Rolled oats are used also as a decorating media for dough products, sprinkled over the bread just prior to baking. Egg-wash is used to produce a sheen and colour to dough products, a double wash, once before, and once after the second fermentation, will give the bread a glossy golden colour. Steam injected into the oven during baking also gives the bread a decorative shine.

MEMORY JOGGER
What ways are there of marking or decorating bread prior to baking?

Do this

- How do you clean a deep fat fryer and why is oil strained daily after use?
- Where is the cool zone in a deep fat fryer?
- Make a list of fats or oils suitable for deep frying.
- Why is clarified butter used for deep frying, but not ordinary butter?

QUALITY POINTS FOR COOKED DOUGH PRODUCTS:

Texture – cooked dough products should be completely cooked through. Where the internal texture appears uncooked the dough product or products should be cooked

Cooked bread placed on wire racks for cooling

further to complete the cooking process. Always follow the cooking times and temperatures recommended by the recipe.

Appearance – this is the most important aspect of marketing dough products. All products should be clean of a similar size and finish. Never display products where the size, shape or finish are different unless this is intentional.

Flavour – Each cooked dough product should taste of the appropriate flavour. When frying oil ages, the flavour of doughnuts can be tainted. Change the oil after the recommended period.

Take care when mixing garlic bread mixes that the flavour is not transferred either by equipment or hand to other dough products.

Aroma – The smell of a cooked dough product is pleasant, distinctive, a subtle pervasive quality or fragrance.

Consistency – see Element 1 page 184.

PROBLEMS WITH DOUGH BAKING OR FRYING EQUIPMENT

Equipment failure

It can happen that equipment can fail and presents a real danger to staff working in the immediate environment. The piece of equipment that presents the greatest risk is the deep-fat fryer, used when frying doughnuts or other deep-fried foods.

Always cook at the recommended temperatures. Change the oil regularly and ensure the fryer is maintained on a service contract by a qualified engineer.

Flashpoint of oil

Different fats and oil reach their smoke point at different temperatures. The smoke point is the point at which the fat or oil bursts into flames and is extremely dangerous.

Generally, every fryer should be fitted with a thermostat control mechanism that prevents the fryer from heating the oil higher than set by the regulator switch. Oil can reach flashpoint temperature if the regulator has been accidentally turned on to full or the thermostat fails.

When fat or oil reaches smoke point – the point where pungent fumes and smoke is given off – the fat changes chemically, producing unpleasant flavours that transfer to any food being cooked. This food is then not fit for consumption.

MEMORY JOGGER

What signs might you look for when fat or oil approaches 'flashpoint'.

MEMORY JOGGER

What action needs to be taken immediately you suspect oil of reaching 'flashpoint'?

When you notice these conditions building up, turn off the unit both at the mains and on the unit itself. Leave the unit to cool completely before removing the oil and investigating the problem.

Important: Do not use the fryer until a qualified engineer has passed the machine as safe.

If oil or fat reaches flashpoint never put yourself or others at risk, withdraw from the area and isolate the fryer by turning off the mains power or main gas valve. Withdraw from the area, evacuating all staff as you go. Do not return until the unit has cooled. If flash point is reached you will need to call the fire brigade by dialling 999. Close all doors as you leave. *Do not re-enter* the kitchen for any reason.

Freshness

Dough products are prepared fresh daily. Only certain products can be kept for longer than 24 hours and if kept longer should be sealed and wrapped to prevent them drying or being contaminated during storage.

Quantity

Where products are unused these can be deep frozen provided they do not contain sugar, such as bun goods. Bread can generally be frozen for up to 1 month or dried and used as breadcrumbs or rusk for sausages and stuffing.

Essential knowledge

When baking dough products you must
- Know why time and temperature are important in the preparation of dough products.
- Ensure the dough is mixed and proved for the required amount of time in order to prevent faults in the dough products when being cooked.
- Ensure that the dough goods are correctly cooked, baked or deep fried.
- Know how to identify and deal with oil or fat that reaches 'flashpoint'.
- Know why it is necessary to maintain hygienic cooking practices at all times when cooking food for public consumption.

Case study

A batch of bread rolls is produced for a dinner; the bread doughs are prepared and baked. The rolls are cooled and stored correctly in preparation for the dinner later that evening. On cleaning down at the end of the production and nearing closing time you notice some splinters of plastic on one of the dough trays.
1 What action needs to be taken to deal with this discovery?
2 Should the dinner rolls be used or discarded?
3 How might you ensure fresh rolls are provided for the dinner given the time of the day and suggest how this type of contamination can be prevented?
4 What responsibility do you and your employer have in these circumstances?

What have you learned

1 What safe working practices should be followed when cooking dough products?
2 Why is it important to keep cooking areas and equipment clean and hygienic?
3 What are the main contamination threats when cooking and storing dough and dough products?
4 Why are time and temperature important when cooking dough and dough products?
5 What quality points should you look for in cooked dough and dough products?

Get ahead

1 Find out about different types of baking ovens. Combination ovens are used widely in catering operations, what are the benefits of this type of oven?

2 What are computerised deep fat fryers, what types of fryers are available and how much do they cost?

3 Look into the range of enriched dough products such as *croutes* and *poponettes*. Why do they have a longer shelf-life than basic dough products and what types of uses do they have on the catering menu.

4 Find out what other types of flours are used in breadmaking, and what different types of brioche doughs are produced.

5 Look up the types of roll shapes that can be prepared and what quality convenience ready-to-bake products are available on the market.

6 Investigate how doughs are mixed in vacuum mixers now that bread improvers have been banned from use. How does the process work, who developed this method and what firms produce machinery that uses this technology?

Prepare and cook basic pastry dishes

This chapter covers:
ELEMENT 1: **Prepare basic pastry**
ELEMENT 2: **Cook basic pastry dishes**

What you need to do

- Check that preparation and cooking areas and suitable equipment are hygienic and ready for use.
- Ensure pastry ingredients are of the type, quality and quantity required.
- Report any problems identified with the quality of the pastry or pastry ingredients promptly to the appropriate person.
- Prepare pastry and combine with other ingredients using appropriate basic preparation methods to meet quality requirements in preparation for cooking.
- Ensure pastry dishes are cooked using appropriate cooking methods to meet quality requirements.
- Ensure prepared pastry not for immediate consumption is stored correctly.
- Ensure pastry dishes are finished using appropriate finishing methods.
- Check that preparation and cooking areas and equipment are cleaned correctly after use.
- Ensure that all work is prioritised and carried out in an organised and efficient manner in line with appropriate organisational procedures and legal requirements.

What you need to know

- What safe working practices should be followed when preparing and cooking basic fresh pastry dishes.
- Why it is important to keep preparation, cooking areas and equipment hygienic when preparing and cooking basic fresh pastry dishes.
- What the main contamination threats are when preparing, cooking and storing basic fresh pastry dishes.
- Why time and temperature are important when preparing and cooking basic fresh pastry dishes.
- Why prepared fresh pastry should be stored or held at the required safe temperature before, during and after cooking.
- What quality points you might look for in different types of basic fresh pastry and cooked pastry dishes.
- Which basic cooking methods are suitable for different types of basic fresh pastry dishes, and how you can identify when basic pastry dishes are cooked to recipe requirements.
- What products might be used to substitute high-fat ingredients when preparing and cooking basic fresh pastry.
- Why increasing the fibre content of basic fresh pastry can contribute to healthy eating practices.
- Which different types of flours could increase the fibre content of basic fresh pastry.
- Why reducing the amount of sugar in basic fresh pastry can contribute to healthy eating practices.

ELEMENT 1:   Prepare basic pastry

INTRODUCTION

What is pastry?

Pastry is the basis of good patisserie; basic pastes form the foundations of the art and craft of patisserie. This covers short sweet (sugar paste) and savoury pastry (short paste), laminated pastry (puff pastry), suet pastry and boiled pastry including English pie pastry and choux pastry, French pie pastry and German pastry.

Pastry is the combination of ingredients such as flour, fat, salt and/or sugar, water, milk and/or eggs. A wide range of recipes are used to produce flans, pies, tarts, tartlets, pastry cases, shells and other shaped baked and steamed pastry products.

To make good pastry that is tasty, light and looks appetising takes time, practice and understanding of the essential principles and processes of the preparation, production and cooking of pastry.

Why is pastry important?

Pastry provides a useful range of baked and steamed products that when combined with fresh fruits, dairy and decorative commodities are the 'paint and canvas' of the contemporary cook-craftsperson.

Fresh cream strawberry tarts, apple pie, quiche Lorraine, fresh French pastries, chocolate eclairs and many others are traditional products popular for morning coffee, afternoon tea, as a sweet or savoury snack food or as the finish to a balanced luncheon or dinner.

Pastry has a tradition of its own, from basic short pastry flans to the rich almond speciality biscuits from Italy, Denmark or Britain. In Britain, an enormous array of sweet biscuit and pastry products are consumed on a daily basis, from fruit tarts and pies to Easter biscuits.

Where does pastry feature in the diet?

People eat pastry that is both savoury and sweet, in pasties and meat or vegetable pies as a snack lunch item or as the main evening meal. Sausage rolls, quiches, fruit pies and tarts, tartlets, mince pies, slices and biscuits all use pastry to encase a wide variety of fillings and flavourings.

The convenience of purchasing sweet and savoury types of pastry based food items from modern supermarkets has in many cases replaced the traditional skills of home baking which were such a cornerstone of European culinary practice. Convenience premixes which just have water added to them remove the need for the skill of making short light pastry.

Essential knowledge	General rules for handling short pastry:
	• Make sure all equipment and work surfaces are clean.
	• Ensure paste ingredients are at room temperature (21 °C/70 °F).
	• Always sieve flour and salt to aerate the flour and disperse the salt evenly.
	• When rubbing in the fat lift the mix to incorporate air.
	• Add the liquid gradually checking the consistency.

- When making short paste by creaming, scrape down the sides of the machine or mixing bowl using a plastic scraper.
- When a clear paste is produced wrap well, chill and rest before use.
- Scraps of short paste should be worked into fresh mixes to reduce waste.
- Break eggs into a bowl before preparing the paste which prevents contamination. Wash your hands after cracking eggs and before starting the next task.

TYPES OF BASIC FRESH PASTRY

There are four basic types of pastry:
- short
- sweet
- suet
- boiled/hot pastry (choux)

SHORT PASTRY (*pâte brisée*)

As the term implies, short pastry should be easily broken when cooked and melt in the mouth. It should be tender, light and dry to eat; a complete absence of toughness should be evident. The balance of fat and flour together with the correct production method will ensure a good paste is made.

Toughness in pastry is caused by the hydration and formation of insoluble proteins in the flour known as *gluten*, an elastic substance which is more or less tough depending on the type of flour used, and the degree of handling given once the pastry is mixed.

If the same recipe is given to a number of trainees/commis chefs it is likely to produce a range of different pastry due to their varying degrees of knowledge of pastry production and handling techniques.

Short pastry differs from short sweet pastry in that it contains no sugar and is used for the basis of savoury products. Flans, tartlets and barquettes are prepared using thinly rolled short pastry, either baked 'blind' (see p. 208) or filled and then baked.

Short pastry is made with a range of fats; butter is best for flavour and colour but is the most expensive. Margarine is widely used, mainly for reasons of cost, but special fats are used for commercial production e.g. shortening and cake margarines, which have very good creaming (emulsion) qualities.

The shortening principle is used with both sweet and savoury short pastry which are produced by either the rubbing-in method, the creaming method or the flour batter method. These are the basic pastry-making techniques.

Short pastry is made from soft flour, fat (50% lard and 50% margarine or butter), seasoning and bound with as little water as possible to prevent toughening the paste. If it is for immediate use it is best made by the rubbing in method, but by the batter method if prepared in advance as the paste tends to be of a softer consistency and will need to be chilled before use.

When made by machine, care needs to be taken in rubbing in the fat; if over-mixing occurs before the water has been added the paste will become crumbly and tough. Watch for the crumb stage occurring and the change of colour as the fat is broken down. Add the water gradually and always stop the machine to test the texture of the paste; you can always add a little more liquid rather than adding more flour to tighten a soft paste for handling. Use only enough liquid to bind the crumb and bring the paste together; the more water the more liable the flour is to form gluten which will toughen the paste.

Fat shortening A white commercial fat produces good results; a mixture of fat improves both colour and texture; using butter increases the cost of the pastry and therefore the selling price should reflect an all-butter product.

Fat taken straight from the fridge will be difficult to use as it is too cold and hard. Fat at room temperature will rub in well. Once the paste has formed, handle it with care and bring the paste together to form a soft clear paste; wrap it and cool it in the fridge until required.

Short pastry can be made using a range of recipes and production methods. Books such as *The international confectioner and complete pastry work techniques* by IIdo Nicolello provide a useful variety of recipes and professional techniques.

Moulding/ Lining pastry (pâte à foncer)
Uses: pasties, quiches, savoury tarts and tartlets, small individual pies, baked jam roll, baked apple dumplings.

French pie pastry (pâte à pâté)
Uses: pâtés, croustades and timbales, game and meat pies.

Short sweet pastry (*pâte sucrée*)

Healthy eating
Reduce the amount of sugar in sweet pastry recipes.

Basic short paste as described already is for the production of savoury goods but short paste can contain a low ratio of sugar, approximately 50 g of sugar to 500 g of soft flour: this is called *sweet pastry*. When the recipe contains a larger proportion of sugar e.g. 125 g of sugar to 500 g flour then this is termed *sugar pastry*.

Sweet pastry is used to make flans, pies, bandes, tarts and tartlets which are either baked blind and filled (see p. 218) or filled and then baked. Sweet pastry is made from soft flour, fat, sugar and eggs and/or water. The more fat that is used will mean less egg will be required to bind the pastry together. To make good sweet pastry, the same basic rules as for the production of short paste should be followed.

When the rubbing in method is used the sugar is mixed with the egg/liquid and added once the fat has been finely crumbed by rubbing with the sieved flour.

When produced by the creaming method the sugar is creamed with the fat until light and white, the eggs are added one at a time and finally the sieved flour is blended to form a clear smooth paste: this should not be over-mixed. The flour batter method can also be used and is often referred to as a secondary creaming method.

Cake margarines which have good emulsion properties are used in bakeries for the production of sweet pastes for tart stamping by machine, for custard or fruit filled tartlets. Sweet paste is best made the day before it is required and rested in the fridge, wrapped in cling film; do not wrap in greaseproof paper or the paste will become dry and form a skin.

It is possible to purchase a tartlet stamp-and-cooking machine which uses a high-sugar paste recipe usually made from icing sugar. The paste is placed in the mould shape and the lid is closed while the paste is cooked. This uses the sandwich toaster principle and takes about three minutes to cook. These goods have a good shelf-life, although they tend to be quite sweet.

Sugar in pastry has two functions:
1   It caramelises to produce the rich golden colour – the higher the sugar content, the deeper the colour. Generally a lower cooking temperature is required to prevent the product from burning.
2   Sugar has a dispersing or solvent effect on the action of the gluten formed from the flour and liquid.

Uses: fruit flans, sweet tartlets and tarts, Bakewell tart, lemon meringue flans, barquettes, custard tarts, mince pies, tranche and bandes.

Shortbread pastry (*pâte sablée*)

High-sugar recipes such as shortbread produce a much shorter texture. Sometimes shortbread pastes can be difficult to work because of both the high ratio of fat and sugar in the recipe. Shortbread is usually made with butter.

Uses: finger biscuits plain and fruited, small and large blocked shortbread biscuits and petit fours sec (dry small delicate baked biscuits, plain or decorated), gateaux and torten e.g. Gateau MacMahon bases.

Piped shortbread pastry (sablée à la poche)
Uses: petit four sec and tea biscuit, plain or fruited.

Sweet almond pastry (pâte Allemande or German paste)
Uses: Linzer Tart, torten bases, biscuits and petit fours or tartlets.

PRINCIPLES OF SHORTENING

The principle of shortening is to prevent the development of gluten which can toughen the paste making it unpleasant to eat and difficult to digest.

When making dough you need to develop the gluten to form long elastic strands of gluten to hold in the expanding gases, but with short pastry you need to do the opposite. To make a good-eating light, short pastry the gluten strands that are formed should be short and break easily when eaten. This is achieved by coating the sub-proteins in the flour with a fine layer of fat so that when mixed with the liquid they form together to make the insoluble protein gluten. In short pastry, the standard ratio of fat to flour is 2 to 1, i.e. half as much fat as flour. The flour should be a soft one with a low protein content (soft plain flour). As the ratio of fat is increased in the recipe, the pastry has a shorter texture; shortbread has one of the shortest textures and 'melts in the mouth'.

MEMORY JOGGER

What effect does increasing the ratio of fat to flour have when producing pastry?

Suet pastry (*pâte à grasse de boeuf*)

Suet is the protective fat that surrounds the kidneys of cattle and sheep. The fat is covered with a fine membrane (skin) which is removed along with any traces of blood or kidney. Suet is used for puddings and as an ingredient of sweet mincemeat and suet pastry. Fresh suet is made by mincing the cold suet through a mincing machine on slow speed; it is available pre-shredded in commercial units.

Suet paste is generally produced by mixing or blending the fat into the flour then the water added and the paste mixed.

Uses: steamed fruit and jam roll, steamed steak and kidney pudding and steamed fruit puddings. Golden syrup roll, orange or lemon and almond roll can also be made using suet pastry.

BOILED/ HOT PASTRY

Choux pastry (*pâte à choux*)

Choux pastry is made from boiling water, fat, salt and sugar, strong flour and eggs. It is made by boiling the water and fat with the salt and/ or sugar then stirring in the sieved strong flour and cooking for approximately one minute on top of the stove. The heat 'gelatinises' the starch in the flour, which swells, absorbing the water to form a type of roux known as a *panade*. Making a panade in this way involves the process known as 'the principle of gelatinisation'.

The panade should readily leave the sides of the pan when shaken. It is then cooled by spreading onto a clean plastic tray. When cool, the eggs are cracked into a bowl or jug and mixed with the panade to form a smooth paste of medium dropping consistency. The eggs should be at room temperature (21 °C/ 70 °F); if too much egg is added the choux paste will be soft and not hold its shape when piped. If the paste becomes soft, rather than waste this mix, a new panade should be made and the soft choux paste added to the cool panade.

The best way to remember how to produce good choux products is to think of the following three 'B's.
● Boil well – i.e. the water, fat and salt/sugar, but do not evaporate the water as this will alter the recipe.
● Beat well – beat the panade well and cook for one minute on top of the stove, stirring well.
● Bake well – the choux goods should be crisp baked, do not open the oven for at least 20–25 minutes for most goods such as eclairs or choux buns. Small piped items such as swans' heads or petit profiterole only take 15 minutes to cook. Opening the oven too soon causes the product to collapse and under-baking will result in soft products that will not keep well.

English pie pastry (*pâte à l'Anglaise*)

This uses the same method of gelatinisation of the starch as does choux paste but when the flour is added the paste is used warm to mould pie shapes either by hand blocking around traditional wooden blocks, or by lining tins which are hinged, or blocked on a pie stamping machine which can be manual, semi or fully automatic. In the latter, the paste is pressed by a hot metal dye to form the shape of the pie base, as with individual pork pies.

Hot savoury pastry

Unlike the English boiled pie pastry used for pork pie goods, hot pastry is made by fat being rubbed into the flour to form a fine crumb and the boiling water is added to this flour and fat mixture, which is then cleared to a smooth paste. This paste is not used warm but is cooled and then formed into shape, filled and topped to make pies and savoury goods.

Essential knowledge	The main contamination threats when preparing and producing pastry and pastry products are as follows: ● cross-contamination can occur between cooked and uncooked food during storage ● food poisoning bacteria can be transferred through preparation areas, equipment and utensils if the same ones are used for preparing or finishing cooked, baked goods and raw, uncooked pastry and foods ● food poisoning bacteria may be transferred from yourself to the food. Open cuts, sores, sneezing, colds, sore throats or dirty hands are all possible sources ● contamination will occur if flour or any foods are allowed to come into contact with rodents (such as mice or rats), insects (house flies, cockroaches, silver fish, beetles). Fly screens should be fitted to all windows ● food poisoning bacteria may be transferred through dirty surfaces and equipment. Unhygienic equipment (utensils and tables, trays, mixers, moulds, pastry brakes) and preparation areas (particularly egg and cream based mixes) can lead to contamination ● contamination can occur through products being left opened or uncovered. Foreign bodies can fall into open containers and flour bins, e.g. sack tape, metal objects, machine parts, string, egg shell, cigarette ends, etc.

- cross-contamination can occur if equipment is not cleaned correctly between operations
- contamination can occur if frozen doughs are de-frosted incorrectly (always check the manufacturer's instructions)
- incorrect waste disposal can lead to contamination.

PROBLEMS WHEN PREPARING BASIC FRESH PASTRY

Freshness of basic pastry

The main problems with fresh basic pastry are:
- when it has either been made without care and is tough or it has been incorrectly stored and has discoloured. When the pastry has been made it should be wrapped in cling film and dated to indicate what type of pastry it is and when it was produced
- by mixing strong flour with soft plain flour. This often happen where the containers are not clearly marked
- the contamination of flour by foreign bodies; old flour can be contaminated by weevil or foreign matter. Always keep flour bins covered at all times when not in use.

Quantities for making basic pastry

Write down the number and types of pastry products to be produced, work how much pastry will be required for each range of dishes and then determine how much pastry needs to be made.

Over time you will develop the skill of production without having to work it out on paper but can do it quickly in your head. Always allow some extra mix for unforeseen circumstances, e.g. extra sales not planned for or spoilage in the oven during the cooking process.

Do this

- Find out what types of convenience pastry products are purchased frozen.
- What is meant by the term 'baking blind' and what are baking beans used for?
- What type of fat is high-ratio shortening? How does it differ from the other fats mentioned and what special properties does it have? What type of flour is it used with and why?
- How are flans crimped, why are they crimped and what tool is used?
- Draw up a chart of faults that can occur with pastry from any of the standard text books available.

PASTRY MAKING TECHNIQUES

The basic preparation techniques for producing pastry are:
- rubbing in/creaming/batter method
- mixing
- relaxing
- kneading

Rubbing in method

The flour is sieved to aerate the flour and remove any small lumps or particles. The fat content is rubbed into the flour with the fingers or mixed using a paddle on a mixing machine to produce a fine textured crumb before the liquid is added. This coats the sub-proteins and starch with fat which prevents the gluten being formed; over-handling can toughen the pastry by forming long tough strands of gluten. It is important the pastry is handled lightly and worked as little as possible as over-handling will also increase toughness. To allow the gluten to relax, pastry should be rested well before being used, or the items prepared or shaped. This will aid the short texture and light eating quality required for good pastry bases.

MEMORY JOGGER

Why is it necessary to sieve flour before preparing fresh basic pastry?

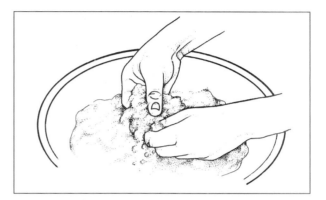

Rubbing in by hand

Rubbing in using a mixing machine

Mixing machines cannot think for themselves; the chef needs to determine when the paste is rubbed in sufficiently before adding the liquid to a pastry. The trainee must learn what signs to look for, such as the crumb texture, the colour of the mix and the paste starting to come together as the fat content starts to re-join.

Very good results can be achieved using a machine for mixing large quantities, but unless used carefully, paste mixes may be toughened because the operative does not pay attention to the mixing; this wastes food commodities and time.

Creaming method

Creaming is different from rubbing in because the fat and sugar are creamed together to form a light white emulsion to which the liquid is added and then the sieved flour folded in, and cleared to a smooth paste. This method of production produces a softer and lighter paste but does require refrigeration to firm the paste before handling can begin.

Special fats, such as cake margarine and shortenings which have good creaming properties, are used in bakeries and kitchens. Butter needs to be at room temperature to enable creaming to be successful.

Flour batter method

This is described as a secondary creaming method in some recipe books. In the flour batter method you cream the fat with an equal quantity of flour, then the sugar and liquid are mixed together and added slowly to the fat and mixture to form a smooth paste. Finally, add the rest of the flour and clear, do not over-mix once all the flour has been added.

MEMORY JOGGER

What are the three main methods of producing basic fresh pastry?

Mixing pastry

When mixing pastry care is needed to avoid toughening the pastry by over-handling or over-mixing once any liquid content has been added. When rubbing in fat do not over-rub or the fat will begin to come together and the gluten will form with the small amount of liquid in the fat to create a very tough mixture indeed.

When this happens the pastry is wasted and you need to start from the beginning. Take care when mixing in flour to develop the mixture only sufficiently to bind the ingredients to a clear mixture. This does come with practice although some trainees do find it difficult to make light pastry that melts in the mouth.

Mixing methods for different types of pastry

Rubbing in	short and sweet pastry
Creaming	short and sweet pastry
Flour batter	short and sweet pastry
Blending/mixing	suet pastry
Folding by layering dough and fat layers	puff pastry
Boiling	choux and English pie pastry
Hot mixing	savoury pastry

Relaxing pastry

The action of mixing paste develops the gluten and toughens the mixture. To overcome this you should rest or relax the paste in the fridge before working with it to form the pastry products. Wrap the paste before chilling, if the paste has been rested overnight you will need to allow it to come to room temperature to be able to use it effectively.

Most pastry benefits from relaxing before being cooked. Short types of pastry can be produced in their shape and then rested; when the paste is formed together it should be wrapped to prevent a skin forming and rested/relaxed in the fridge. Paste is best made the day before it is required for use.

Short paste if tough or tight when made will not become less so by relaxing, but if made correctly short paste items will relax within an hour. Puff paste items benefit from resting for approximately 1 hour prior to baking. All paste items should be rested in a cool environment, preferable in the fridge.

Convenience puff pastry is more widely used because of the relaxing/resting time required before the paste can be used or baked. The making of fresh puff pastry is more limited today but should be mastered, you never know when you might need to prepare this useful paste fresh!

Kneading pastry

Kneading is not really a term connected with pastry, but with dough development. Where a paste is kneaded this must be very carefully carried out to prevent the paste from toughening. Kneading is done with the base of the palm of your hand very lightly to clear a mixture prior to rolling or relaxing.

METHODS OF PROCESSING PASTRY

The main techniques for processing pastry are:
- cutting
- rolling
- shaping
- lining

Cutting

Pastry once rested is rolled out, lightly dusting it with flour. Dust, roll and give the pastry a quarter turn to the right, repeating the process until the required thickness results. Then cut the pastry using various tools:

- plain or fluted ring cutters
- flan ring
- knife or dividers
- lattice cutters

Lightly dust cutters before cutting to prevent the pastry from sticking to the cutter. Always wash and dry cutting equipment well before putting away.

When cutting pastry, clean even cutting is required. If cutting raw paste use a damp clean knife with a sharp edge such as a cook's knife. For trimming pastry from pies, tarts or flans then a small office knife will do.

When cutting short paste discs for tartlets use a lightly floured ring cutter, ensuring the cutter is floured every two or three cuts to keep the cut sharp and neat. If using a fluted cutter there is a tendency for paste to become lodged in the gap between the ring frame and the flute; this is a serious point as contamination can occur if the cutter is left unclean. When cutting puff pastry use a warm damp knife or preferably, a hot, oiled cutter to melt the layers rather than pressing them together.

When using a lattice cutter, only roll the lattice roller over pastry that is cool and firm, or problems will occur if the paste is too soft when trying to lift the cut latticed paste into position.

When cutting cooked pastry, especially mille-feuille slices, use a sharp pointed cook's knife, wiping the blade between each cut.

When preparing barquettes the rolled pastry is cut into rectangles slightly larger than the boat, or roll the pastry out thinly, pick it up on the rolling pin and place it over the rows of barquette moulds. Use a small lump of paste to depress the rolled pastry into the moulds and then, with two rolling pins held together, roll these over the top of the moulds to cut the pastry.

Each boat should be 'thumbed-up' using thumb and first index finger to finish shaping the boat shape. This thumbing-up also applies to tartlets lined with short paste, either sweet or savoury. As a general rule plain edges are for savoury goods while fluted edges are used for sweet goods; the same applies to plain dish papers and lacy doilies as underliner decoration for dishes.

Rolling

Pastry is rolled out using a wooden, plastic, marble, glass or metal rolling pin. Trainees often fail to adopt the dust–roll–quarter-turn technique and the paste sticks to the worktop. This happens because you are pressing the pastry and forcing out fat and moisture which adheres to the work bench. Lightly dust the bench with flour, lightly dust the top of the pastry then roll the pin over the top of the paste lightly, turn and roll again. Repeat this technique until the paste is of the required thickness and size without being stuck to the bench.

Problems can occur if the paste is too short and rolling becomes difficult. Knead the pastry lightly to toughen it slightly if it is too short.

Only handle sufficient pastry for each flan or pie. Form the paste into a circle for flans, dusting lightly and pressing with your hands to flatten prior to rolling. Roll lightly and evenly and keep the rolling pin free from paste, turning and dusting the pastry regularly.

Puff pastry will require a firmer rolling pressure because of the toughness of the gluten in the dough together with the plastic pastry margarines used.

Shaping

Once pastry has been rolled out and cut you need to be able to form it into the required shape. This is done by placing the rolling pin at the far edge of the paste, picking up the edge and rolling it back towards yourself, lifting up the paste on the pin. Lift the paste and position it over the mould, dish or flan ring. Let the paste down gently unrolling it as it drops. Press into place using floured fingers to form the required shape determined by the dish, mould or flan ring.

A key technique in shaping pastry is known as 'thumbing up'. This is where circles of pastry are cut and placed in the tartlet tin or mould and the paste is pressed into shape using the thumbs to raise the paste to form a neat edge around the top edge of the tin.

Make sure no air bubbles are trapped between the paste and the tin, thumbing up should remove these. Paste can then be docked with a fork or small knife and filled with baking beans or filled prior to baking.

Flans, barquettes, tartlets, horns, Banbury cakes etc. require skilful handling to form the required shape. In commercial kitchens this needs to be done neatly, quickly and efficiently to ensure the batch of products being shaped are identical. You will develop the knack as you practise these techniques.

Always keep work benches clean and fingers lightly dusted with flour when shaping short paste goods; ensure that cream horn tins are greased and set before attempting to shape puff paste strips onto the mould.

When hand-raising pies, shape the paste first on your hand, transferring the paste to the floured mould and shape so as to keep the base of the pie thicker to support the weight of the filling and top.

When shaping by crimping use the back of a small knife and the thumb technique; ask your chef to demonstrate this. Or you can use the finger and thumb of one hand and the first finger of your other hand to flute a crimp shape on pie, flan or tart edges.

When cutting plain round shapes or more difficult shapes handle the cut paste with care; the shape is easily lost by heavy handling.

Lining flans

A flan is a mould of pastry usually formed inside a flan ring. Roll the pastry, lift it onto the rolling pin and gently place it over the flan ring. Lift the edges inside the ring and mould it to the shape, ensuring the paste is pressed into the corner between ring and base. When pressed into place, trim away the excess and with floured fingers thumb-up the sides to form a pointed ridge. The top edge of the flan ring should be visible, so that when the pastry is cooked it shrinks away slightly from the flan ring edge, aiding the removal of the ring when cool.

The pointed ridge is crimped with the fingers or with the aid of a crimping tweezers, to produce a decorative top edge.

The pastry should not be too thin otherwise the flan case will collapse once filled and spoil the finish.

Certain flans are *baked blind*. To do this line the flan ring and edge, slide the flan onto the baking tray, dock (prick) the base of the paste with a fork, place a paper cartouche, which is 3 cm larger than the flan ring size, into the flan and fill it with baking beans. The flan is cooked until set but without colour, then the cartouche and beans are removed, the semi-cooked flan is washed with egg and returned to the oven to colour and finish cooking.

Quality indicators when preparing fresh basic pastry

The indicators of quality are:
● texture
● appearance
● consistency

The three concepts above are better understood if you know something about the commodities used to prepare basic fresh pastry. Only when you understand what each commodity is and how it is used will you be able to recognize correct textures and bake to produce the right appearance consistently over time. Pastry should have a light crumbly texture with a clean fresh-baked appearance. By following the basic principles set out for producing basic fresh pastry you will be able to maintain consistent standards.

Essential knowledge

Time and temperature are important in the preparation of paste products in order to:
● ensure the paste is mixed and rested/relaxed for the required amount of time, in order to prevent faults in the paste products
● ensure that the pastry dishes are correctly baked or steamed
● prevent food poisoning from direct and indirect contamination
● eliminate the possibility of shrinkage
● promote and maintain customer satisfaction by the production of consistent standards of quality.

PASTRY COMMODITIES

Flour

Short pastry, sweet pastry, suet, flan, German, French and almond pastry use soft weak flour, one with a low weak protein content approximately 7–8%. This is milled from wheat grown in milder climatic conditions such as the UK. Strong flour with a higher protein content is used for the production of puff and choux paste. In choux paste the starch is gelatinised when added to boiling water and fat, usually butter or margarine.

Fats

Healthy eating
Use low-fat margarines and polyunsaturated fats instead of butter, lard or ordinary margarine where possible.

Pastry is made with a range of fats, either a single type, or in a combination.

Butter provides good flavour and a rich colour when used for pastry; shortbread paste is best made with unsalted butter. Pastry can be made with butter but this does make it more costly for many catering operations.

Margarine is produced for particular purposes and is a blend of oils and fats which have been hydrogenated (pumped with hydrogen gas and set with a catalyst). It is then subjected to further processes and can be mixed with up to 10% butter fat, but no more than 16% water.

Cake margarine is widely used for its emulsion properties, again up to 10% butter fat can be added, which is the legal maximum. This margarine creams well and is quite soft at room temperature.

Pastry margarine was developed for use in the production of puff pastry as a substitute for butter which is expensive in comparison and more difficult to handle. The margarine is a tough plastic or waxy fat which lends itself to being formed into fine layers essential for puff pastry.

Pastry margarine also melts at much higher temperature than butter and commercial pastry margarines are tough and flexible. Sometimes called flex, this fat is used for fat sculpturing, now a reviving art in culinary circles.

One type of machine-made pastry is made by creaming the fat and sugar together, adding cold water to this emulsion and then blending in the sieved flour. This makes a good commercial paste for manual or semi-automatic pie machines, large fruit slices or individual tarts and sweet pies.

Shortening is a white edible oil manufactured for the production of 100% fat shortening or compound that has no protein content or salt and is hydrogenated. Developed originally as a substitute for lard, the modern forms of shortening have an excellent shelf-life and produce good results when used for savoury pastry.

Lard is the rendered fat of the pig, and is used for savoury pastes such as hot water paste or hot savoury paste. It is also a main ingredient of lardy cakes where the lard fat is mixed with sugar and fruit.

Sugar

It is usual to use caster sugar in pastry because of its fine grain and good creaming properties when mixed with fat. Some pastes can be made with icing sugar but it is unusual to use granulated sugar for the production of pastry.

Eggs

Fresh whole egg is mixed with sugar and/or water and added at the emulsion stage when using the creaming method of production.

Water

This should be cold and added while mixing on a slow speed; the aim is to add as little water as possible but just enough to bind the paste. It is usually used for savoury paste, but also with commercial machine-made sweet paste used in the bakery trade.

Salt

Salt should be used with great care. It assists in the colour and finish of pastry. If using salted butter or margarine, less salt is required, but as shortening does not contain salt it will be required for savoury pastry made with this type of fat.

Healthy eating

When using butter or margarine do not add extra salt for flavour, this will reduce the salt intake without detracting from flavour to any great extent.

Do this

- Check the storage temperature of pastry products that are fresh and frozen.
- Find out the range of different pastry fats used in your kitchens.
- What function does salt play in pastry?
- Why do fats become rancid? How can this be avoided, especially with butter?

BASIC PASTRY RECIPES

(metric weights and ingredient ratios: expressed in percentages in relation to amount of flour)

Short pastry: savoury, sweet, sugar

Savoury moulding/lining paste (pâte à foncer)

100% soft flour	500 g	(1 lb)
50% fat (butter, margarine)	250 g	(8 oz)
30% water	150 ml	(6 fl oz)
salt	2 g	pinch

Sweet moulding/lining paste

100% soft flour	500 g	(1 lb)
50% fat (butter, margarine)	250 g	(8 oz)
12% egg	2×60 g	(2×2 oz)
10% sugar	50 g	(2 oz)
5% water	25 ml	(1 fl oz)
salt	2 g	pinch

Sweet paste (pâte sucrée)

100% soft flour	500 g	(1 lb)
50% fat (butter, margarine)	250 g	(8 oz)
12% egg	2×60 g	(2×2 oz)
25% sugar	125 g	(5 oz)
salt	2 g	pinch

Sweet almond paste (pâte Allemande)

100% soft flour	500 g	(1 lb)
60% fat (butter, margarine)	300 g	(10 oz)
20% sugar	125 g	(4–5 oz)
15% ground almonds	75 g	(2–3 oz)
8–10% egg yolks	4 or 5	

Suet paste (pâte à grasse de boeuf)

100% soft flour	500 g	(1 lb)
60% water	300 ml	(10 fl oz)
50% fat (suet)	250 g	(8 oz)
baking powder	10 g	($\frac{1}{2}$ oz)
salt	10 g	($\frac{1}{2}$ oz)

Choux paste (pâte à choux)

100% strong flour	500 g	(1 lb)
120% water	600 ml	(1 pt)
50% fat (butter or margarine)	250 g	(8 oz)
1% sugar (optional)	5 g	($\frac{1}{4}$ oz)
1% salt (optional)	5 g	($\frac{1}{4}$ oz)

Boiled pastry

Hot water paste (pâte à l'Anglaise) (Boiling method)

100% medium flour	500 g (50% soft/ 50% strong)	(1 lb)
50% fat (lard)	250 g	(8 oz)
25% water	125 ml	(6 fl oz)
3% salt	15 g	($\frac{3}{4}$ oz)

French pie paste (pâte à pâté) (Rubbing in method)

100% medium flour	500 g (50% soft/50% strong)	(1 lb)
50% fat (lard or butter)	250 g	(8 oz)
25% water	125 ml	(6 fl oz)
12% egg (whole)	1×60 g	(1×2 oz)
3% salt (optional)	15 g	($\frac{3}{4}$ oz)

Brown/Wholemeal pastry

Short pastry in particular can be made with wholewheat or wholemeal flour which provides useful fibre in our diet. More pastries today are made with wholemeal flour, e.g. quiches and individual savoury tartlets, meat and vegetable pies. Wholemeal flour and white soft or strong flour can be mixed 50/50.

Healthy eating

When producing pastry the availability of wholewheat flour provides the opportunity to increase the fibre content of basic pastry recipes. Use wholewheat flour where appropriate to do so.

Do this

- How are barquettes lined when produced in bulk?
- How can quiche pastry be prevented from becoming wet or undercooked ?
- What is the difference between a pie and a tart?
- Check the range of convenience products made with pastry. What types of pastry freeze well and for how long?
- What are filo and strudel paste and how are they made?

LEGAL REQUIREMENTS

Current relevant legislation relating to hygienic and safe working practices when preparing and storing basic pastry state:.

- When working to produce pastry or any food production you need to work in a safe and secure manner to prevent accidents and be able to demonstrate 'due diligence', in the prevention of food poisoning or complaints arising from problems with products and services.
- Your work place should have a food safety policy statement setting out procedures for:
  1. Monitoring – deliveries, storage temperatures and service temperatures.
  2. Control/Prevention – Food safety, risk assessment, food safety audit, food sampling, training and possible medical screening in certain areas of work.

What have you learned

1. What safe working practices should be followed when preparing basic fresh pastry and pastry dishes?
2. Why is it important to keep preparation areas and equipment clean and hygienic when preparing basic pastry and pastry dishes?
3. How do you identify problems with pastry and pastry ingredients and why do problems need to be reported?
4. What are the main contamination threats when preparing and storing pastry?
5. Why are time and temperature important when preparing and storing basic pastry?
6. What quality points are there to look for in different types of basic fresh pastry?
7. Which products could be used to substitute high-fat ingredients when preparing pastry and pastry dishes?
8. Which types of fats and oils contribute to healthier catering practices?
9. How does increasing the fibre content of basic fresh pastry contribute to healthy eating practices?
10. How does reducing the amount of salt and sugar in basic fresh pastry and pastry dishes contribute to healthy eating?

ELEMENT 2:   Cook basic pastry dishes

INTRODUCTION

Cooking short savoury and sweet pastry

Short savoury pastry is baked in a medium oven at approximately 205 °C/ 400 °F. For sweet pastry, because of the sugar content which will caramelise at 170 °C/ 325 °F, the baking temperature is lower at approximately 193 °C/ 380 °F.

After working with ovens for some time you will become familiar with the heat of the oven. You will learn where your oven has hot or cool spots and know how often the pastry requires to be checked to prevent the pastry burning.

Steaming suet pastry puddings

Suet pastry is usually steamed in a low-pressure steamer. Products such as steak and kidney pudding or steamed suet roll are steamed for approximately 90 minutes. The smaller the product the less time it requires in the steamer. Where individual portions are cooked by the steaming method the cooking time will be approximately 45 minutes.

You must ensure that any puddings in bowls are covered prior to steaming or the pastry will become soggy from the condensing steam vapour. Steamers need to be pre-set and heated long before cooking starts.

Once the dish has been steamed for the required length of time, undo the locking mechanism on the front of the steamer unit. Do not open the door until all the pressure of the steamer unit has been released. Only then should you release the door mechanism.

Baking choux pastry

The piped choux products should be *baked well*; if under-cooked the products will become soft and collapse. With most items never open the oven before 20 minutes has passed, except for very small items such as swans' heads or petit profiteroles for soup garnish.

Choux pastry expands in the oven as the water and fat liquids are converted into steam and the egg and flour proteins set. Unless choux goods are well baked, the inside will be moist and will make the case go soft when cool, resulting in a collapsed product that will not keep very long.

Pre-baked choux eclairs and choux buns with a six-month shelf life can be purchased and are used extensively in the bakery and catering industry.

Convenience pastry (Frozen/ Convenience/Puff or flaky pastry)

Puff pastry today is mostly purchased frozen in sheet or block form. Because it takes time and skill to produce good fresh puff pastry many kitchens use frozen puff or pre-formed puff products. This saves time and consistency of standard is now available from quality sheet puff such as Gold Cup Express.

Sheet puff pastry
The quality of lift and cost effectiveness of sheet puff pastry is far superior to many of the frozen block puff goods available. It is widely used in the bakery industry for turnovers, cream slices and scraps are used to make e.g. Eccles, Coventry's etc.

> **MEMORY JOGGER**
>
> Why should basic pastry containing high sugar be cooked at a lower temperature than pastry with a low sugar content?

213

Convenience pastry dishes

There is a wide range of convenience pastry products which can prove very cost-effective. The range of frozen pre-formed pastry products includes tarts, pies, flans and puff pastry shells and slices available both ready-to-bake and cooked at competitive prices. Frozen pre-formed products such as cooked puff horns with a long shelf-life can also be purchased and used to achieve good results if well finished. This can improve profitability by reduced labour costs while providing consistent quality at a time of great skill shortages in the industry.

The provision of such goods enables the contemporary craftsperson to concentrate on the flavour and decorative display of food items without having to spend long hours in production or investing in a large variety of specialist equipment. While puff pastry made with butter has no equal when freshly made and baked, the place of convenience pastry products is well established and must be used alongside, combining the skills of traditional craft and contemporary innovations.

Bake-off products are now widely available in stores, shops and supermarkets bringing a more diverse and interesting range of pastry products to the public. People readily use convenience pastry based products from frozen. It is essential for all trainees to avail themselves of the best selection of such goods, seek out the best suppliers and promote the best classical craft skills with this new technology.

COOKING METHODS

The two basic pastry cooking methods are:
- baking
- steaming.

Baking pastry and pastry products

Baking pastry and pastry products needs to be done at the correct temperature and for the appropriate amount of time. Each recipe will suggest the best times and temperatures for each item.

If the temperature of the oven is too high the pastry will shrink and over-colour, too low and the pastry will drop as the fat melts, and lose its shape. When baking, aim to produce a balanced golden colour to each product, the higher the sugar content of the recipe the lower the oven temperature setting should be as the sugar will caramelise at 170 °C (325 °F).

Timing needs to be checked and monitored constantly when baking especially if the oven is prone to fluctuations in temperature brought about by rises and falls in gas pressure, or if it has hot spots which over-colour part of the product.

Steaming pastry

Steaming applies to suet pastry cooked for steamed suet roll. The pastry is cooked in a moist atmosphere, usually in a low-pressure steamer for 90 minutes for sleeved puddings and 30–40 minutes for individual puddings.

For detailed instructions on how to cook basic hot and cold desserts, see Unit 2ND3 pages 97–102, 110 and 121.

FINISHING METHODS

The three basic techniques for finishing are:
- dusting
- piping
- filling.

The finish to any pastry product is important for a number of reasons. All products should be the same size, finish and shape. The finish should appeal to the eye but still be good to taste. Decoration should be delicate and balanced, colours should not be too bright and piping should be neat and tidy; you should strive for an artistic balance not overdoing the decoration which would detract from the product's saleability. Finishing techniques form part of the skills of the contemporary chef, patissiere or baker.

Dusting

Dusting with icing sugar, icing sugar with cocoa, or icing sugar with e.g.cinnamon should be light and delicate but just enough to decorate the top of the particular dish.

A fine sieve or shaker is usually used, or you can form some muslin into a puff ball for very fine finishing, especially for the famous Gâteau Pithiviers, where a fine glass finish is only achieved by the fine dusting of sugar before being put into a very hot oven.

Piping

To be able to pipe well you need to practise. It requires a skill in both holding the bag and controlling the flow by pressure of the hand to create the particular design required for each dish.

Fresh cream should not be too stiff for piping or the buttermilk will run, especially in a warm environment such as the kitchen or bakery.

Healthy eating

Reducing your intake of cream and using more yoghurt will contribute to healthy eating practices. Customers do not always want the healthy alternative but you should try to improve everyone's diet by looking at the ingredients you use and consider the likely benefit from using healthier alternatives.

Chocolate should be thickened with either a drop of stock syrup, spirit such as brandy or, best of all, a few drops of glycerine. To do this, melt the chocolate by heating it to approximately 45 °C (110 °F), then stir in the glycerine; it takes a few minutes for the chocolate to thicken. Half fill a paper cornet bag and seal well, always folding into the centre to seal the liquid chocolate in the bag.

Practise piping to develop your skills. After a lot of practice you will be confident to pipe directly onto gateau, desserts and pastries. Fondant also provides a useful medium for piping; chocolate motifs can be made when you are not busy and stored in a cool place for decorating trifles, torten and so on.

Filling

Filling is important if only to make certain all the products have the same percentage of filling, not so much as to cause the pastry to burst or spill over so spoiling the finish and undermining professional standards of craftsmanship. Never overfill, leave room for expansion, especially products like turnovers, pasties, pithiviers and puffs.

When filling with fruit make sure the design produced is even in shape and colour, balanced to make the dish attractive; use complimentary colours and sizes, these are very important for customer satisfaction and therefore sales.

When filling with cream try to pipe an even design using star pointed tubes, remember star tubes have different numbers of teeth for a variety of piped designs, as do royal icing tubes.

PASTRY DISHES

Pastry dishes include:
- pies
- tartlets
- tarts
- puddings

Pies and pasties

Fruit pie

Pies can be either sweet or savoury, with a base or without a base.

Fruit pies – apple pie
Apple pie, the classic of all English pies can be made with sweet or sugar pastry, preferably using the creaming method of production. Place the fruit in a china, earthenware or metal pie dish, filling it to just above the rim of the dish. Sprinkle the fruit with caster sugar and wet the rim edge of the pie dish.

Place a 2 cm band of pastry around the rim and seal well to the rim of the pie dish. Egg-wash this rim and roll out the sugar pastry evenly to just slightly larger than the dish size. Pick up the pastry on a lightly dusted rolling pin, place this at one end of the dish and gently unroll the pastry across the top of the dish, making sure the pastry covers the egg-washed rim. Seal by pressing the two pastes together and mark with the finger and thumb technique, then brush with milk or egg-wash and sprinkle with sugar. Finally make a hole in the centre of the pie to allow the steam to escape during baking.

When formed allow the pies to rest for 20–30 minutes, bake in an oven pre-set at 200–205 °C (395–400 °F), until light or golden brown. Test using a small sharp knife by inserting it into the hole in the centre of the pie to check that the fruit is cooked.

Serve with an underliner on a doily and pie frill, with *sauce Anglaise*

When using apples early in the season (September -December) the cooking apple is sharp and will require more sugar; as apples age the natural sugars develop producing a less sharp taste.

Other fruit pies include: apple and blackberry; blackberry; cherry; plum; rhubarb; blueberry; pumpkin; gooseberry; blackcurrant; greengage; apple and raspberry; damson; quince.

Pork pies
These can be hand raised using hot boiled pastry which is moulded around a wooden pie block while still warm, using either individual-size or larger 500 g and 1 kilo blocks. Most pork pies however are moulded by machine where the paste is stamped into a pie mould with a warm dye stamp on a rotating pie stamp machine.

Veal, egg and ham pies (Gala pies) are made by lining a hinged metal frame mould with hot water paste, filled with the appropriate filling just below the top edge of the lining. The top is sealed with a strip of paste and a second finishing layer is added and decorated. Holes are cut using a hot, oiled, plain cutter and pie funnels are used with kitchen paper to absorb any excess juices during the cooking process.

Steak and kidney pies, meat or vegetable pies
Unlike the pork pie, classic meat pies do not have a base. Put the meat e.g. steak and kidney or chicken, into the pie dish with some seasoning, chopped onion and stock, line the edge of the pie dish with a 2 cm strip of pastry and cover the dish with cold

Pork pie

savoury pastry. Seal well and make a hole in the centre. For a 500 g (1 lb) steak and kidney pudding, cook in a low pressure steamer for about 2–3 hours if the filling is raw, or for 1–1 ½ hours if the filling has been pre-cooked.

If preferred, make a slightly thickened filling, having first cooked the meat slowly and corrected the seasoning and colour. Then cover in the usual way and bake in a moderate oven until a light golden crust results. The British prefer this thickened filling in their meat pies rather than the classical stock.

Meat and potato pies, lamb and mutton pies can also be produced. Vegetable pies are very popular for vegetarian diets, using a crisp seasoned mix of vegetables bound with a light cream sauce or vegetable velouté, Portugaise or other flavoured sauces.

Meat and vegetable pasties

Meat pasties must contain at least 12.5% of the total weight of the pasty, by law (*Meat Pie and Sausage Roll Regulations 1967*).

- Pork, mutton, veal and ham pies: total meat content 25% minimum.
- Steak and kidney pies: total meat content 25%, kidney 15–20% of total steak weight.
- Meat and potato pies and pasties: total meat content 25% (this refers to the weight of raw meat before processing).

Pasties can be made using either a good short cold savoury pastry or, more generally today, puff pastry, using scotch rough puff or three-quarter puff pastry.

The pasty has a special place in culinary history. Tin and copper miners would take pasties down the mines for their main meal. Filled originally with fish, but later with a meat and potato filling, one end contained a sweet fruit filling, generally apple. The pasty needed to be strong enough to take down the mine and it was said that if dropped down the mine shaft it should not break!

Today mince beef, potato and onion is the standard filling; pasties are made from either puff pastry or savoury short pastry and eaten as a snack food item. The raw minced meat, seasoning and potato are placed in the centre of a 13–16 cm circle of savoury short pastry, one half of the edge of the pastry is egg-washed and a traditional way of sealing pasties is to fold the doubled outer edge back on itself. This type of pasty should be baked at 180–200 °C (350–390 °F) for 30–45 minutes.

Pasties can also be made from brioche pastry or puff pastry e.g. the Russian pasty *coulibiac* can be filled with fish, meat or vegetable.

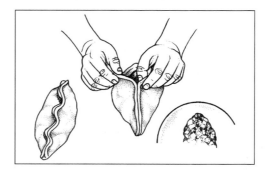

Folding the outer edges to seal the pastry

Sweet tarts, tartlets or flans

Tarts can be open or closed, and cooked blind and then filled, or filled and then baked, depending on the dish and recipe. Fruit tarts can be either multi-portioned or individual with fillings such as mandarin, strawberry or pineapple, with or without a pastry cream base, finished with a clear glaze or boiled apricot purée.

Preparing a flan for baking blind

Filling a baked flan

MEMORY JOGGER

Which type of basic fresh pastry could be used to produce fruit tarts?

Left: using a rolling pin to lift and place the pastry over the flan ring
Right: adding fruit to the pastry base

Closed tarts, such as apple tart, are made in flan rings lined with a sweet or sugar pastry and closed with a pastry top. Dutch apple tart is flavoured with cinnamon and the apple mixed with sultanas. When cooked the flan ring or mould is removed and the tart is served whole on a round salver with semi-whipped fresh cream or hot *Sauce Anglaise*.

Tarts can also be made on plates using fresh, tinned or frozen fruits but it is important to keep the juice to a minimum. Open tarts such as jam, treacle and lemon curd, apricot and fruit are made by lining a flan ring or tartlet moulds with sweet short pastry and spooning the filling in. Sometimes a pastry lattice can be used as a decoration.

One of the most famous of tarts is the Bakewell tart, made from a flan of sweet pastry, with jam spread over the inside base and frangipane piped or spread over that; a lattice top can be used but is not essential. When cooked the top is brushed with boiled apricot purée and warm fondant is spread over. A decoration of piped chocolate or coloured fondant is then applied and the fondant is drawn with a fine point to form the typical spider's web decoration.

Types of tarts made with sweet short pastry: Bakewell tart, Linzer torte, Brittany tart, treacle tart, jam tart, Belgian tart, Dutch apple tart, curd tart, maids of honour tarts, Congress tarts, conversation tarts, strawberry cream tarts and assorted fruit tarts.

Some short pastry tarts can be made using puff pastry trimmings.

Types of flans made with sweet short pastry: Fruits used include: banana, peach, cherry, pineapple or mandarin. The blind baked flan cases are filled with pastry cream and topped with the drained tinned fruit, decorated with boiled apricot purée; hot and cold process gel can then be brushed or sprayed on to finished cool products.

Traditional types of sweet flan made with short pastry are: Alsacienne Flan, Manchester flan, Normandy flan, cherry flan, lemon meringue flan, apricot flan, Jeanette flan and pear flan Bordalou.

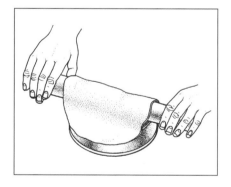 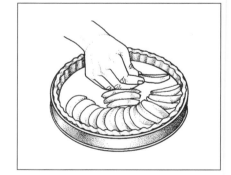

Savoury Flans

The most famous savoury flan is *Quiche Lorraine*, a cheese, bacon and onion flan which is served hot or cold as a snack, luncheon or buffet savoury, individual or multi-portioned.

A good short pastry is used to line a flan ring; the pastry should be thin. The lightly cooked, sweated onion is spread over the base and small ham or bacon pieces placed over with grated cheese, then a savoury strained egg custard is poured over and the flan cooked in a medium oven at approximately 180–185°C (340–350°F) until the custard is set and of a light brown colour.

If the oven is too hot the custard will boil and the displaced water content will soak the base of the flan, producing a wet and unpalatable waxy pastry.

<table>
<tr><td>

Case study

</td><td>

A batch of savoury tartlettes is produced for a buffet. These are to be filled with cold fillings. Also a batch of sweet paste barquettes are made for filling with pastry cream and fruit to be finished with a glaze.

When checked by the chef the savoury tartlettes had shrunk considerably and the barquettes were undercooked.
1 *Give reasons for these faults in both cases.*
2 *Suggest how these problems can be avoided.*
3 *What problems might have occurred if these errors were not checked or found?*

</td></tr>
</table>

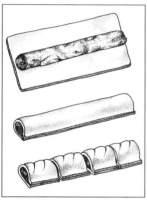

Top: pipe sausage-meat down the centre of the pastry strip
Middle: roll the pastry to form a tube
Bottom: cut into individual sausage rolls

PUFF PASTRY GOODS

Sausage or vegetarian rolls

Puff pastry is used for a very wide range of patisserie and bakery products. Sausage rolls use rough or Scotch puff pastry, as this is quicker to produce but does not have the quality of lift essential for products such as vol-au-vents and bouchées.

To produce sausage rolls in quantity, roll out the puff pastry into lengths approximately 1 metre in length and 10 cm wide, egg-wash a 3 cm strip at one side of the length of pastry and pipe the appropriate filling of sausage-meat or vegetarian filling down the centre.

Roll up the pastry from the side that is not egg-washed and form into a tube length, flatten slightly with a pin and, if they are to be baked immediately, egg-wash the tops of rolls. Mark these and cut into the required lengths. If not egg-washed these can be frozen and stored provided the meat or vegetable filling was not frozen previously.

Products made from full virgin puff pastry include: vol-au-vents, bouchées, petit bouchées, oval vol-au-vents (filled with fish), palmiers, papillon turnovers, cream puffs, Gâteau Pithiviers, jalousie.

Products made from trimmings, Scotch or rough puff pastry include: sausage rolls, cheese straws, fleurons, mille-feuille, Eccles, Banbury, Dartois, mince pies, bande aux fruits or tranche aux fruits, meat/vegetable pies, pasties, meat or fish en croûte, chausson, allumettes glacées, cream horns.

Vol-au-vents and bouchées

Vol-au-vent means 'puff of wind' in French and they are made from good full virgin puff pastry given four full book/double turns or six single turns. The vol-au-vents are cut from thin 5 mm sheets of puff pastry and when baked form a light case for sweet or savoury food items. They can be served as entrée with fish, meat or vegetable/salad fillings.

Oval shaped vol-au-vents are used for the service of fish, usually sole or salmon. Circles are cut using a plain or fluted ring cutter which has been dipped in hot oil. This is to melt the layers rather than press them which is the result of using an ordinary floured cutter.

Egg-wash one of the circles and place a second circle on top, seal gently. With a cutter approximately 5 mm smaller dipped in hot oil, carefully cut half way through the top disc of puff pastry. Then egg-wash the tops carefully, making sure the wash

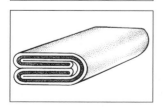

Layering puff pastry
Top: single or half turn
Bottom: double or book turn

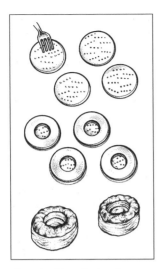

Top: docking the pastry circles
Middle: the double layered circle ready for baking
Bottom: baked vol-au-vent cases

does not flow down the sides of the pastry as egg protein coagulates at a lower temperature and glues the pastry, preventing an even rise.

For best effect and even lift, vol-au-vents should be placed close together on the baking tray to help keep each other up.Cover them with a sheet of lightly oiled paper, preferable silicon; this controls the lift of the paste and prevents any from flying off. All puff pastry items once formed should be rested for about 30 minutes prior to baking and be cooked in a hot oven at 220 °C (425 °F) until light and golden. If puff pastry is not rested sufficiently prior to baking the pastry is likely to be miss-shapen and shrink. To produce good results the gluten needs to relax once handled.

The lid and inner part of the baked vol-au-vent is removed while the pastry is still hot. Bouchées and petits bouchées are smaller in size: bouchées are about 5 cm in diameter and petits bouchées approximately 3–4 cm in diameter.

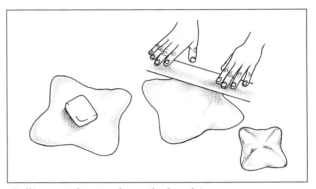

Rolling out the star shapes for bouchées

MEMORY JOGGER

Why do pastry dishes made using puff pastry benefit from being rested prior to baking?

SWEET PASTRIES

Sweet pastries can be produced using sweet short paste, sugar paste, almond short paste or biscuit paste. Alternatively puff pastry is used for a range of French pastries. The range of such goods is vast and many have already been mentioned. It is useful to look at the following sweet pastries to extend your knowledge:

Puff pastry products: Dartois, mirliton, lampions, allumettes, cornets à la crème (cream horns), puits d'amour (wells of love), chaussons (turnovers), mille-feuilles (thousand leaves), palmiers (pigs' ears),batons glacés (iced sticks), papillon (butterfly), ramequins, mince pies.

Sweet short pastry products: Congress tarts, sablés à la poche, fruit barquettes, fruit tartlets, egg custard tarts, honey and almond barquettes, Tartlette Lorraine, Evesham tartlets, tartlettes forestaire, jam tarts, curd tarts, ramequins, treacle tart, mince pies.

SUET PUDDING

Suet pastry is the combination of suet fat, flour, water and baking powder. The paste is used for sweet and savoury dishes such as steamed suet roll or steamed steak and kidney or steak and mushroom pudding. Sieve together the flour, salt and baking powder and mix in the shredded suet fat. Make a well in the fat and flour and add the cold water then mix lightly to a firm paste. Rolled this out and spread it with jam, roll it up and place it in a buttered and sugared steaming sleeve and steam for 60–90 minutes. Serve warm with a jam and/or custard sauce.

Fruit such as apple, sultanas or currants can also be cooked in the suet roll. Suet paste is used to make dumplings which are small pastry pieces poached in the sauce of the stew or plain boiled in salted water.

If the steaming temperature is too low when cooking suet pastry, it will be heavy and soggy, or if the paste is over-handled it will become tough. Always use fresh baking powder, or mix your own using one part bicarbonate of soda to two parts cream of tartar. This mixture must be sieved at least 10 times and stored in an air-tight container.

Self-raising flour at sea level or in damp conditions will liberate its carbon dioxide and weaken the power of the baking powder.

GLAZING PASTRY

Glazing of pastry dishes takes a number of forms; these can be glazing with hot and cold process gels, or melting the fine dusting of icing sugar in a hot oven. Egg-wash glaze, boiled apricot jam used to seal a glaze on fruit flans, or a fondant glaze can be used.

Hot process gel is a clear gel boiled with a little water and brushed over dishes to both seal out oxygen and provide an attractive finish that has a high sheen. Hot process gels set while they are still hot. Cold process gels are used for the same reasons as hot process gels but set when they are cold; any air bubbles should be removed with a fine point of a knife or a cocktail stick.

A fine dusting of icing sugar as already mentioned should be done using a fine meshed sieve or muslin duster; the oven should be hot to melt the thin dust of sugar producing a glorious shine and golden finish.

Pastry goods can be glazed by brushing with an egg yolk and water glaze. If a little cream, salt and water are mixed with the egg yolk this produces a high gloss brown finish to puff pastry goods.

Salt added to egg-wash helps denature the protein *lecithin* and improves the colour of the baked glaze. Do not leave egg-wash glaze out of the fridge when not in use; cover with cling film and only mix in small quantities.

Apricot jam boiled with a little water, and strained if it contains pieces of fruit, will provide a good amber glaze and seal the dish from any oxidation, so improving the shelf-life and appearance of the product. Gum Arabic is used to glaze English rout biscuits after drying and baking.

LEGAL REQUIREMENTS

Current legislation relating to hygienic and safe working practices when cooking and storing basic pastry dishes covers the following points:
● Has your employer done a hazard analysis of the potential food hazards in your food business operation. They will need to identify the critical points in their food operation where food hazards may occur. They will need to decide which of the points identified are critical to ensuring food safety i.e. 'critical points'.
● Are you aware of the control and monitoring procedures for your work place where the critical control points have been identified. How often does monitoring occur? By whom and how is the information held?
● Food premises must be kept clean and maintained in good repair and condition, this is a legal requirement for all businesses working with food.
● Have you been trained in basic food hygiene skills appropriate to the tasks or levels of responsibility undertaken by you?

Do this

Obtain a copy of *The Food Safety (General Food Hygiene) Regulations 1995.*

What have you learned

1 What safe working practices should be followed when cooking fresh pastry and pastry dishes?
2 Why is it important to keep cooking areas and equipment clean and hygienic when cooking basic pastry and pastry dishes?
3 How can you identify problems with pastry and pastry ingredients and why do problems need to be reported?
4 What are the main contamination threats when cooking and storing basic pastry and pastry dishes?
5 Why are time and temperature important when preparing, storing and cooking basic pastry and pastry dishes?
6 What quality points should you look for in different types of cooked pastry?
7 What basic preparation cooking and finishing methods are suitable for different types of basic fresh pastry and pastry dishes?

Get ahead

You can extend your knowledge of making pastry by reading up on some of the more complex recipes used in the preparation and production of composite desserts i.e. where a dessert utilises a certain type of pastry in its composition.

- Look up recipes and methods for puff pastry and some of the shortbread and continental spice pastry recipes. Find out how they are made, how they are produced and what uses they have on the pastry menu.
- To extend your knowledge for Level 3 NVQ look at the complex range of hot and cold desserts that use basic and more complex pastry recipes in their composition. These might include spiced pastry, pastry made with ground almonds or special biscuit pastes such as Dutch and English rout pastes. Look at specialist biscuit pastes e.g. tuille paste, wafer pastes and cornet mixtures for Cat's and Bull's tongue biscuits. Read about the sablé pastes for shortbreads, piped or block-formed, and find recipes for German pastry.

Prepare, cook and finish basic cakes, sponges and scones

This chapter covers:
ELEMENT 1:   **Prepare basic cakes, sponges and scones**
ELEMENT 2:   **Cook and finish basic cakes, sponges and scones**
ELEMENT 3:   **Decorate basic cakes and sponges**

What you need to do

- Check that preparation and cooking areas and suitable equipment are hygienic and ready for use.
- Ensure cake, sponge and scone mixture ingredients are of the type, quality and quantity required for preparation, cooking and finishing basic cakes, sponges and scones.
- Report any problems identified with the quality of ingredients, mixtures and products promptly to the appropriate person.
- Prepare cake, sponge and scone mixture using appropriate basic preparation, cooking and finishing methods to meet quality requirements.
- Ensure decorations, fillings or toppings are suitably prepared to meet quality requirements.
- Ensure prepared, cooked and finished cake, sponge and scone mixture not for immediate consumption is stored correctly.
- Ensure cakes and sponges are decorated, topped or filled using appropriate decorating media.
- Check that preparation and cooking areas and equipment are cleaned correctly after use.
- Ensure all work is prioritised and carried out in an organised and efficient manner in line with appropriate organisational procedures and legal requirements.

What you need to know

- What safe working practices should be followed when preparing, cooking and finishing/decorating basic cake, sponge and scone mixtures and products
- When preparing basic cake, sponge and scone mixtures, why it is important to keep preparation, cooking areas and equipment hygienic
- What the main contamination threats are when preparing, cooking, finishing and storing basic cake, sponge and scone mixtures and products
- Why time and temperature are important when preparing basic cake, sponge and scone mixtures and why it is essential that the oven should be set at the correct temperature before baking commences
- Why it is essential to follow safety procedures when using ovens
- Why basic cake, sponge and scone mixtures should be stored at the required safe temperature before and after cooking
- What quality points you might look for in different types of basic cake, sponge and scone mixtures
- What basic preparation methods are most suitable for different types of basic cake, sponge and scone mixtures
- How to identify when different cakes, sponge and scone products are cooked and finished to dish requirements
- What basic decorating methods are suitable for different types of cakes and sponges

- What products might be used as substitutes for high fat ingredients when preparing basic cake, sponge and scone mixtures
- Why increasing the fibre content of basic cake, sponge and scone mixtures can contribute to healthy catering practices
- Which different types of flours could increase the fibre content of basic cake, sponge and scone mixtures
- Why reducing the amount of sugar in basic cake, sponge and scone mixtures can contribute to healthy catering practices

---

ELEMENT 1:   Prepare basic cakes, sponges and scones

INTRODUCTION

What are cakes and sponges?

Many books have been written about cakes and sponges; each product range covers a multitude of gateaux, torten, biscuit and sponge goods.

Cakes can be made by a variety of methods from light fruit cakes to rich wedding and celebration cakes, from individual cup cakes to layered cakes such as high ratio angel and Battenburg.

Sponges of all shapes, sizes, flavours and finishes are produced and vary from country to country, each area of each country has regional speciality recipes indicative of their own particular tradition and practice. Sponges form a light alternative to cakes and can be produced from egg foams, such as the range of Genoese sponges, creamed, such as the Victoria sponge or blended batters, such as high-ratio sheet sponge.

These products and dishes can be very complicated or extremely simple, but whichever are produced all will require knowledge of preparation and production techniques, and skill in formation and artistry in order to complete a decorative, appealing cake that will tempt the taste buds of all your customers.

CAKES AND SPONGES

Cakes and sponges and the products made from each range make up the sweet dessert, confectionery and snack elements of our daily diet. We compliment and convey to our digestive systems all manner of sweet, cream and fruit cakes, dessert biscuits, cookies and biscuit nibbles with tea and coffee and consume for shear enjoyment and self-satisfaction sponge gateau, torte, buttercream and dairy cream cake.

Where do they feature in our diet?

Cakes and sponges are not conducive to a balanced nutritional diet but do support the contentment of a modern day fast food market and life style. People are satisfied less today than in years gone by when on Sunday 'Baking Day' such delicacies were offered at afternoon tea and were part of the social communication and interaction of the family unit. Today, people simply eat and enjoy the vast production capability supplied by supermarkets, bakeries and patisserie shops, tea and coffee houses, by munching cakes, biscuits and sponges of all types at all times of day.

Ready-made products

The fast food and snack market has delivered us a vast range of cake, sponge and biscuit products with good eating quality both fresh, frozen and ready-to-mix. These goods have extended shelf life with modern high sugar and technical preservation methods. Many more types of continental cakes and sponges, biscuit and cake products adorn the supermarket shelf and the list of specialist wholesalers and retailers to the bakery, catering and hospitality industries. Light, fine Swiss roll sponges from high-ratio fats and flours, assorted cup and fairy cake goods, almond cake and fruit biscuits fill the display cabinets to tempt us for mid-morning coffee, with cakes for luncheon and evening dessert of pastry or gateau.

BAKING CAKES AND SPONGES

The baking of cakes should be done to cook the cake as quickly as possible with the optimum colouring of the cake crust while being cooked in the centre. Many factors will influence the baking of a cake and need to be understood if good baked cakes are to result.

Shape and size

The shape and size affect the degree of cooking required to ensure the centre of the cake is cooked. Smaller cakes take less time to cook than larger or deeper cakes. Larger cakes need a lower baking temperature and a longer baking time to make certain the middle of the cakes are not undercooked or still raw. The shape of a cake will also determine the cooking time and temperature, the temperature range is wide from 175 °C (350 °F) for rich fruit or wedding cakes to 230 °C (450 °F), for small sponge cakes such as fairy cakes or Swiss roll.

Richness

Where cake mixtures contain a high proportion of sugar in the recipe the cooler the oven temperature the longer the cooking time will be. This results from the caramelisation of the sugar in the mixture; sugar forms a caramel at approximately 155 °C (320 °F). When the cake has coloured sufficiently it should be covered with sheets of silicone or greaseproof paper.

Steam / Moisture

A major fault in many cakes is that they become dry because the oven temperature is too hot and the atmosphere dry. The ideal baking atmosphere should have a quantity of steam present as this delays the formation of the crust until the cake batter has become fully aerated and the proteins have set. A full oven of cakes will generate sufficient moisture to steam the oven but if small batches are baked, a tray of hot water should be placed into the oven carefully.

If the oven is too hot this will cause the cake crust to form early and the rising cake batter will form a peak and break through the peaked centre.

Additions to the basic mixture

When the tops of cakes are covered with almonds or sugar this enriches the cake. As a result the baking temperature should be lowered to prevent over-colouring of the cake crust: generally a reduction in temperature between 5–10 °C (10–20 °F) will compensate for such enriching.

Glycerine, glucose and invert sugar, honey or treacle added to cake mixtures all colour at much lower temperatures than sugar. When these commodities are used to improve the moisture and flavour of the cake, then a temperature reduction will be necessary.

Always check the accuracy of your oven temperature and the required baking heat for each individual type of cake mixture.

Cake-making ingredients

Flour A soft, low-protein flour is best for cakes and a proportion of the soft flour can be replaced by substituting with cornflour. Flour should always be sieved before use and any spices or dry ingredients can be mixed with the flour to ensure even distribution in the cake mixture.

Sugar To ensure a good batter results, caster sugar is used for its fine grain and dissolving properties, essential for a good quality cake batter. Rich fruit and celebration cakes can use soft light or dark brown sugar for colour and flavour.

Fat Butter provides good flavour and imparts a natural yellow to cakes, but has poor creaming properties. To produce quality cakes which have good volume, even structure with a fine and balanced crumb and texture, then modern cake margarines take some beating !

Butter has largely been replaced by these cake margarines and shortening agents which trap more air in the cake batter and are manufactured to have very good creaming qualities. Butter and cake margarine can be used together to balance the cake mixture for both cost and aeration; use 50% butter and 50% cake margarine and/or shortening.

Dried fruit

Many cake mixtures contain fruit which is mainly dried. Such fruit needs careful preparation to ensure the fruit cake is moist with the fruit evenly set in the baked cake. Fruit should be washed and drained well, the drained fruit should be laid out onto a clean working surface and checked for stalks, stones and foreign bodies: cheap fruit needs especially careful attention. Hard dried fruit such as currants, raisins or sultanas can be soaked in hot water for 10 minutes but must be left to drain for at least 12 hours before use.

Methods of producing cake mixtures

- *Sugar batter method:* Dundee, slab, angel, fruit and cup cakes
- *Flour batter method:* Madeira, slab, angel and fruit cakes
- *Blending method:* high-ratio Genoese, angel, slab, fruit and Madeira cakes

When producing cake batter mixtures the temperature of the batter is crucial and a working temperature of 21 °C (70 °F) is achieved by ensuring the ingredients are at room temperature.

TYPES OF CAKES AND SPONGE

Sponge mixtures

Sponges are light, medium or heavier mixtures usually produced by a foam of eggs, sugar and flour. They can be whole-egg sponges or separate yolk and white based sponges. Sponges form the basis of gateaux, torten, sponge fingers, sponge drops, Swiss rolls, roulardes and other sheet and layer sponge products.

Sponges tend to be light aerated mixtures where the egg (white) content of the recipe traps air bubbles by forming a semi-rigid membrane structure. As the eggs and

Whisking by machine

sugar are whisked the liquid mixture thickens, when this stage reaches peak volume the sieved flour is 'cut in' using a stainless steel spoon.

When folding or cutting in the flour it is essential to lift the flour without stirring the mix and prevent it from reaching the bottom of the mixing bowl; if the flour falls to the base of the mixture it will become lumpy and difficult to clear.

SPONGE MAKING INGREDIENTS

Flour should be soft and well sieved. When producing coffee or chocolate sponges the powder should be sieved two or three times to evenly blend the two powders.

Sugar should be caster for foam sponges because of its aeration properties and fine grain. Sugar can become damp and develop a crust or lumps; such sugar should be warmed in the oven and sieved to produce a free-flowing fine grain.

Eggs Hen eggs produce good results when fresh; as eggs age the white can become watery as the egg shell is porous, and this can affect the volume of the foam. If eggs are left for any time before mixing begins the yolk can develop a skin.

Glycerine is a clear, syrupy, colourless, odourless liquid added to some sponges to prevent the sponge from drying out. Glycerine is very *hygroscopic* (attracts moisture) and can be derived from the fermentation of molasses by the addition of an alkaline medium.

Stabilisers are added to sponges to assist in preventing the sponge from collapsing e.g. EMS (ethyl methyl cellulose or Edifas), GMS (glycerol monostearate); these are flakes or powder or a ready prepared gel which are added to the eggs and sugar prior to whisking. Egg yolk (Lecithin) is a natural stabiliser and is used in sponges to stabilise the foam.

Methods of producing sponge mixture

- *Foaming:* Swiss roll, Genoese and plain sponge
- *Melting:* Genoese
- *Boiling:* Genoese
- *Blending:* high-ratio sheet, cup cake and layer sponge
- *Creaming:* Victoria
- *Separate yolk and white:* sponge fingers, drops and Sacher torte

Foaming method

Equipment such as trays, tins and moulds for sponge making should be prepared before mixing begins. All equipment such as bowls and whisks should be cleaned well and preferably sterilised to remove any traces of fat or grease which would

MEMORY JOGGER

What are the six basic methods of producing sponges?

Eggs and sugar prepared for whisking

prevent the egg from trapping air. This occurs because the grease or fat prevents the membrane structure from forming bonds.

Weigh the ingredients carefully and mix the egg and sugar together in the machine bowl with a hand whisk and warm to 32 °C (90 °F). This can be over a pan of boiling water, or the sugar can be heated on a tray in the oven. Do not overheat the sugar and egg mixture which might cause the eggs to begin to coagulate and cook.

The warm eggs and sugar are then whisked on speed 3 until cool and the foam is light and of a thick cream consistency. When dropped on itself the foam should leave its own mark. Foams can be over-whisked. Any colour or flavour is added at this stage prior to the flour being folded or cut in.

The sieved flour and dry ingredients are now carefully folded in by hand using a stainless steel spoon; the flour is sieved evenly over the top of the foam to distribute the weight and then cutting-in begins.

It is important to keep cutting, preventing the flour from reaching the base of the bowl as this would cause lumps to occur. Cut and fold by turning the mixing bowl with one hand and cutting from the centre base of the foam in an upward, circular motion.

When the flour is clear, always tap the spoon which usually has a pocket of flour trapped. The sponge mixture is then put in the tin or spread and baked according to the type of sponge product being produced.

Melting method

French Genoese sponges use the foam production method but when the flour has been carefully folded and cut in, melted butter is added in the same manner. The mixture is carefully blended to incorporate the melted butter. The addition of the melted clarified butter will enrich the sponge, improving the flavour, texture and crumb structure but also extending the shelf life of the Genoese.

Boiling method

Boiled Genoese sponges have a stable crumb texture that is stronger than foam type sponge recipes. The boiled sponge method produces a product that when cut does not crumb so readily. This is particularly suitable for *petit fours glacé* and the sponge will keep longer than plain foam sponge mixtures.

The eggs and sugar are heated to 37 °C (98 °F) and whisked to a thick sponge; the butter is heated until boiling and placed in a mixing bowl. The flour is then stirred in with the glycerine and beaten to form a smooth paste. The egg and sugar sponge is then added to the butter and flour paste in three or four portions, beating each portion well to ensure a clear, smooth batter void of lumps. The mix is then poured into a lined baking tin or sheet according to the recipe and product requirements.

Bake this type of mixture at 190 °C (375 °F) for approx 35–40 minutes.

Blending method

High-ratio mixtures apply to sponges as well as cakes, the method of blending the batter is the same and produces a sponge with a fine stable crumb, with good shelf-life, a freeze-thaw stability and fine even texture. Many catering operations do not use such mixtures but they are very easy to produce if the mixing rules are followed. Because the sponge mixture has a high sugar liquid content the sponges will keep well for a long time if stored correctly.

Many of the confectionery cakes made with sponge are of this type. High-ratio flour and high-ratio fat must be used according to recipe specifications.

Creaming method

Victoria sponge is produced by the creaming method. Flour and baking powder are sieved and, after the eggs, are added to the well-creamed butter and sugar, glycerine may also be used. The Victoria sandwich is a traditional mixture where the two sponges are sandwiched together with jam, jam and cream, or butter cream.

Creaming the butter and sugar

Preparing equipment and ingredients for baking cakes and sponges

Separate yolk and white method

Biscuit à la cuillier, *biscuit perlés*, sponge drops, sponge brickettes for trifle; these continental sponges are made by using the egg yolk and egg white separately.

This sponge needs careful preparation; all equipment should be to hand and trays or tins prepared with silicone paper, or buttered and floured, before production begins. The egg yolks are beaten well with half the sugar to form a light mixture.

When the yolks and half the sugar are well mixed the whites are made into a meringue with the rest of the sugar. Half of the meringue is folded carefully and lightly with the egg yolk and sugar mixture, all of the flour is sieved onto this mix and carefully cut in.

Finally the rest of the meringue is folded in to lighten the mixture. As much volume as possible should be preserved by careful folding and cutting using a stainless steel spoon. If this mixture is handled by stirring or vigorous action when folding then the mixture will collapse and become soft.

When mixed it should be piped to form sponge fingers, sponge drops, or sponge shapes depending on the recipe being produced. This type of sponge is very useful for many different pastry dishes: *Charlotte Russe* uses sponge finger biscuits, *Othellos*, *Desdemonas*, *Jagos* and *Rosalinds* use sponge drops sandwiched with fresh cream or pastry cream as a tea fancy, coated with boiled apricot jam and covered with warm fondant.

Special sponge such as the *Sacher torte* relies on a separate yolk and white sponge mixing method to produce a light delicate sponge.

Do this

- Check the range of pre-mix sponges available.
- Investigate types of stabilisers used. How do they work and why ?
- Why is care needed when mixing chocolate based sponges ?
- What is *biscuit jaconde*, how is it made and what is it used for ?

SCONES AND SCONE PRODUCTS

Scones are part of the British tradition; a cream tea featuring freshly made scones embodies the true ideal of a country tea. Scones are produced for a range of uses, as fresh cream morning goods sold in bakeries, as an afternoon accompaniment for tea with clotted cream and jam, or commercially in supermarkets – plain, fruited and wholemeal varieties being popular.

Scones are aerated with baking powder made from two parts cream of tartar and one part bi-carbonate of soda. These should be sieved together at least eight or ten times to ensure they are thoroughly combined.

Baking powder starts to liberate carbon dioxide as soon as the ingredients are mixed as, once moisture comes into contact with the baking powder CO_2 gas is given off.

Fresh scone mixture, once made, needs to be baked within 20 minutes of production to maintain the liberated gas within the scone itself. After this time the gas produced by the baking powder will be lost and the eventual lift of the scone limited, producing a close texture.

Basic scone recipe

Ingredients

Flour	500 g (1 lb)
Baking powder	40 g (1½ oz)
Butter or margarine	100 g (4 oz)
Sugar	75 g (3 oz)
Salt	small pinch (3 g)
Milk	6 dl (½ pt)

Method

1 Sieve the flour salt and baking powder at least four times.
2 Rub in the butter or fat to form a fine crumb texture.
3 Make a bay in the flour and pour in the milk and sugar.
4 Add the flour and mix the ingredients to form a clear soft paste.
5 Do not over-handle or over-mix at this stage.
6 Lightly dust the formed paste and roll out to about 2.5 cm (1in) thickness.
7 Dust a plain or fluted round cutter with flour and cut out the required number of scones.
8 Place on silicone paper and wash with egg-wash. Try not to let the wash run down the sides of the scone or the egg protein with coagulate at a lower temperature than that of the flour and hold down the edge, producing an uneven top to the baked scone.
9 Bake in an oven set at 215–230 °C until the tops and bases are lightly browned.

Scone products cover the following types of goods

- Plain tea scones
- Fruited scones
- Scone rounds
- Wholemeal scones
- Scone topping (cobbler)
- Potato scones
- Raspberry buns
- Rice buns
- Coconut buns
- Rock cakes

MEMORY JOGGER

What two ingredients are combined to make baking powder?

Scones can be purchased pre-baked, or as a convenience powder mix to which water is added, or they can be made fresh.

PROBLEMS WITH CAKES, SPONGES AND SCONES

Freshness

A dry store should have a relative humidity of R.H. 60–65%, be cool, well lit and ventilated with adequate storage space to enable effective stock rotation. Generally cakes that are moist products i.e. finished or filled with buttercream, sugar based filling, fudge icing etc. need to kept cool; fresh cream products need to be refrigerated below 5 °C to prevent contamination and spoilage.

Dry cake and biscuit products such as sponges, sweet and savoury biscuits should be stored in dry storage at a temperature of 5–10 °C. Frozen cakes need to be de-frosted in the fridge and not in ambient conditions.

Cake mixtures that are powder based (convenience) should be stored at least 45 cm off the floor in the dry food storage area. Storing cakes and biscuit is made simple by following the storage instructions on the packaging for each individual food item. Never over-order in this area as many cake and biscuit commodities have a limited shelf life; use in strict stock rotation and keep a log of the use by dates for each range of cake or biscuit food.

Quantity

When producing cakes, sponges and scones you need to check that you have sufficient quantities of each basic ingredient to meet production requirements: flour, sugar, eggs, fat, fruit or other fillings. Check stock and place orders, especially before a busy weekend or bank holiday.

Refer to Unit 2ND3, 2ND7 and 2ND8 for more detailed information relating to quantities for cold and hot desserts, dough products and pastry dishes.

Essential knowledge	It is important to keep preparation and storage areas and equipment hygienic in order to: ● comply with food hygiene regulations ● prevent the transfer of food poisoning bacteria to food ● prevent pest infestation in preparation and storage areas ● prevent contamination of food commodity items by foreign bodies.

STAGES IN CAKE PREPARATION

● creaming
● blending
● rubbing in
● machine-mixing
● greasing tins/trays
● glazing
● portioning

Creaming

Sugar batter method

Cake margarine, butter or shortening are beaten to a light emulsion with the caster sugar using a machine paddle. Always scrape down the sides of the mixing bowl to incorporate any fat and sugar that has not been mixed. Any colour, essences or flavourings can now be added to the light batter.

The liquid egg is added in a steady flow over approximately two minutes. If the eggs are added too quickly the mix can curdle; a little flour can be added to bring the mixture back to normal. The sieved flour is then added carefully to the batter mixture. This should be mixed in slowly to produce a smooth, clear cake mixture, free from lumps and not over-mixed.

Any other ingredients in the form of milk, fruit and nuts can be blended slowly to distribute them evenly throughout the batter.

Flour batter method

In this method the eggs and sugar are whisked to a half foam; this is to foam the two ingredients until half the potential volume is achieved, next the colour and or flavour of the cake mixture is added.

The cake margarine is then creamed with an equal quantity of flour from the recipe to make a fat-and-flour batter.

The half foam mixture is then folded into the fat-and-flour batter in three or four equal portions, each portion being folded and blended carefully. Lastly the remainder of the flour is folded in to produce a smooth cake mixture. Again all other ingredients such as fruit and milk or nuts are blended in last to evenly distribute them throughout the cake mixture.

Dry ingredients such as cocoa, coffee powder, ground almonds or baking powder are always blended with the flour before mixing begins. Glycerine is usually added to assist in moisture retention during baking as it has high *hygroscopic* properties (attracts moisture).

Blending method

The blending method is suitable for making high-ratio cake mixtures. The special flour used is fractionated to very small particle size to increase its surface area and the ability of the flour grains to absorb liquid, and it is fully bleached.

High-ratio fat or shortening is a very soft white fat that has been fully hydrogenated and superglycerinated. This produces a fat that will hold and balance the high level of liquids in the form of milk and dissolved sugar, which gives this type of cake a fine stable crumb, extended shelf-life and good eating quality with good freeze-thaw characteristics.

The flour and dry ingredients i.e. baking powder are sieved together. The fat is crumbed into the flour in a mixing machine. Next the egg, milk and sugar are added, often in two stages: the sugar dissolved in the milk and added over 1 minute, on slow speed, scraped down and then mixed for 2 minutes on medium speed; lastly the liquid eggs are added in the same way over 1 minute, scraped down well, and mixed on medium speed for 2 minutes. It is essential that each stage of the batter is blended into the next to produce a smooth batter free from any lumps.

Rubbing in method

This method is usually related to the production of basic pastes but it is used for the production of scone mixtures (see p. 210).

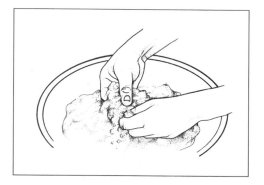

Rubbing in

Mixing cake mixtures in a machine

When beating a cake mixture in a machine the paddle attachment is used on a medium speed; when blending, the paddle attachment is used on a slow speed. With high-ratio blended mixes, always scrape the mix from the bottom of the machine bowl to ensure any first and second stage batter does not remain.

Greasing or lining tins and trays

Preparation of cake tins and hoops
Cake tins come in all shapes and sizes, usually round or square, and are now available for wedding cakes and celebration fruit cakes or sponge in heart, oval, hexagonal and horseshoe shapes.

Cake tins, hoops and baking trays should be lined with paper to protect light, medium or heavy fruit cakes during baking. If the tin is of the hoop type with no base, just a hoop of metal, then the tray should be covered in two or three sheets of paper with silicone paper or greaseproof on top. The cake hoop is then lined in the same way using fat to glue the layers of trimmed paper into place.

Once the tin is prepared, the cake mixture can be produced and the cake tin or hoop filled. Wooden frames for square and slab fruit cake used to be used, but cake tins are now made from a light steel or aluminium.

Another way to prepare tins, trays and moulds is to grease the tin with fat and dip it straight away into flour. This provides a protective lining to the sponge or cake. When sponges or cakes have been turned out the tin should be wiped clean and stored. If sponge or cake tins are washed or scoured then the coating which prevents the mixture from sticking is destroyed and the cake or sponge will stick to the tin.

Glazing

Glazing of cakes, sponges and scones takes a number of forms; these can be glazing with hot and cold process gels, or melting the fine dusting of icing sugar in a hot oven. Egg-wash glaze or boiled apricot jam can be used to seal a glaze on fruit cakes, or a fondant glaze can be used.

Hot process gel is a clear gel boiled with a little water and brushed over dishes to both seal out oxygen and provide an attractive finish that has a high sheen. Hot process gels set while they are still hot. Cold process gels are used for the same reasons as hot process gels but set when they are cold: any air bubbles should be removed with a fine point of a knife or a cocktail stick.

Fine dusting with icing sugar as already mentioned should be done using a fine meshed sieve or muslin duster. The oven should be hot to melt the thin dust of sugar and produce a glorious shine and golden finish.

MEMORY JOGGER

What machine attachment is used to produce cake mixtures?

MEMORY JOGGER

Suggest three types of glazing used to finish cakes, scones and sponges?

233

Egg-wash will glaze most pastry products. The pastry goods are glazed by brushing with an egg yolk and water glaze. If a little cream, salt and water are mixed with the egg yolk this produces a high gloss brown finish to puff pastry goods.

Salt added to egg-wash helps denature the protein 'lecithin' and improves the colour of the baked glaze. Do not leave egg-wash glaze out of the fridge when not in use; cover with cling film and only mix in small quantities. When glazing with raw egg, always ensure the product is well baked to cook the egg glaze thoroughly.

Portioning

Cakes, sponges and scone products are portioned to provide control over the size and cost of production. This is done to determine the selling price. A number of important factors need to be learned when considering portioning products:

- individual portions
- multi-portions
- cost of production
- production control and shrinkage
- standardisation of recipes and weight / size ratio.

When producing sponges the sponge tin will be of a certain size e.g. 10, 20 or 30 cm, and different quantities of the mixture will be required to fill each size of tin. When making sponge sheet the tray size will determine the number of portions.

For cakes, as with sponges, the cake tin or hoop will determine the eventual number of cooked portions resulting.

Where scones are concerned the size of the cutter and the weight of mixture will influence how many portions are produced; also, the thickness of the scones produced will either mean more or less portions.

Practice and careful recipe calculations can provide accurate portion information. You can use portion control tools to assist in this area. A torten divider marks either 8/10/12/14/16/ or 18 portions onto the top of a prepared cake or sponge. This indicates the number of equal portions to be cut.

Portions should not be too small or too big, but sufficient to provide value for money so that customers return time and time again.

Healthy eating

Cake, sponge and scone items or portions should be neither too small, thus tempting customers to take a second, nor too large, encouraging them to over-indulge on sweet foods which should only form a small part of a balanced nutritional diet.

Do this

- Test the accuracy of your oven with a thermometer at different temperatures.
- What are sultanas, currants and raisins made from and how are they made?
- Find out more about high-ratio recipes and products made from them.
- Check the range, shape and sizes of cake tins and hoops in the kitchen.
- What is the reason for fruit cakes being so costly. Investigate the cost of celebration cakes from bakery and cake artistry outlets in your area.

Essential knowledge

The main contamination threats when preparing and producing cakes, sponges and scones are as follows:

- cross-contamination can occur between cooked and uncooked food during storage
- food poisoning bacteria can be transferred through preparation areas, equipment and utensils if the same ones are used for preparing or finishing cooked, baked goods and raw, uncooked mixtures, icings, creams and toppings
- food poisoning bacteria may be transferred from yourself to the food. Open cuts, sores, sneezing, colds, sore throats or dirty hands are all possible sources

- contamination will occur if flour or any foods are allowed to come into contact with rodents (such as mice or rats), or insects (house flies, cockroaches, silverfish, beetles). Fly screens should be fitted to all windows
- food poisoning bacteria may be transferred through dirty surfaces and equipment. Unhygenic equipment (utensils and tables, trays, mixing bowls and tins) and preparation areas (particularly egg and cream based mixes) can lead to contamination
- contamination can occur through products being left opened or uncovered. Foreign bodies (e.g. sack tape, metal objects, machine parts, string, cigarette ends, etc.) can fall into open containers and flour bins
- cross-contamination can occur if equipment is not cleaned correctly between operations
- contamination can occur if frozen cakes and sponges are not de-frosted correctly (always check the manufacturer's instructions)
- incorrect waste disposal can lead to contamination

LEGAL REQUIREMENTS

Current relevant legislation relating to hygienic and safe working practices when preparing basic cakes, sponges and scones.
Look at your work area. Does it meet with the legal requirements of the *Food Safety (General Food Hygiene) Regulations 1995*?

The legal requirement covers premises … *premises shall be so sited, designed, constructed and kept clean and maintained in good repair and condition, as to avoid the risk of contaminating foodstuffs and harbouring pests, so far as is reasonably practicable. …*

Look at the 1995 Act in relation to some of the following areas:
- Personal hygiene facilities
- Work surfaces
- Cleaning equipment and materials
- Storage facilities for cleaning equipment and materials
- Facilities for the disposal of waste.

What have you learned?

1 When preparing basic cake, sponge and scone mixtures what safe working practices should be followed?
2 When preparing basic cake, sponge and scone mixtures why is it important to keep preparation, cooking areas and equipment hygienic?
3 What are the main contamination threats when preparing basic cake, sponge and scone mixtures and products?
4 Why are time and temperature important when preparing basic cake, sponge and scone mixtures and products?
5 What quality points might you look for in different types of basic cake, sponge and scone mixtures and products?
6 What basic preparation methods are most suitable for different types of basic cake, sponge and scone mixtures?
7 What products might be used to substitute high fat ingredients when preparing basic cake, sponge and scone mixtures and products?
8 Why should tins be lined? What extra precautions should you take with rich fruit cakes?

ELEMENT 2: Cook and finish basic cakes, sponges and scones

BAKING CAKE MIXTURES: PLAIN CAKE TYPES

Plain cake mixes benefit from being produced by the flour batter or high-ratio blended method of production.

Madeira cake

Using unsalted butter for Madeira cake recipes is best. It is either a round cake baked in a cake tin or produced in slabs and cut into 500 g or 1 kg pieces.

A lemon flavoured plain Madeira cake should be baked at approximately 180–185 °C (360 °F) for 40–50 minutes according to the size and shape.

Test by depressing the top of the cake which should feel resistant but slightly springy, or pierce through the centre with a needle; if withdrawn clean without any mix adhering to the pin, the cake should be cooked.

A slice of lemon can be used to decorate the cake prior to baking.

Slab cake

Slab cake is the term given to plain or fruited cakes cooked in frames, usually rectangle in shape. The cake is divided into portions by cutting the baked cake slab across to form bars of cake 10 cm wide and 20 cm long.

Madeira cake can be produced in this shape. Slab cake can be sliced and sandwiched with jam or buttercream when cool or the top decorated with almonds or sugar prior to baking.

Slab cakes are baked at 177 °C (350 °F); tops should have a light golden crust. You can also make a fruited slab – sultanas, currant, mixed fruit or cherry, or flavoured with coffee and walnut, chocolate, coconut, orange or lemon.

Angel cake

Angel cake refers to a light, plain cake mixture baked in colours, white, pink, yellow, orange or chocolate. These are layered usually white, yellow and pink, and sandwiched with buttercream. Angel cake is baked at 171 °C (340 °F).

Cup cakes

Made by using the sugar batter method the mixture is piped into paper cases using a Savoy bag and plain 12 mm tube. Cup cakes can be plain or fruited and the tops of plain cup cakes are usually finished with an icing or fondant; chocolate, lemon, orange, coffee or vanilla. The piped filled cases are baked at 204 °C (400 °F) for 15 minutes. Plain cup cakes can be stored for future use. Commercial cup cakes today are produced using a high-ratio blending method and mixture.

Queen or fairy cakes

Produced by the sugar batter method, these can be plain or fruited. Fairy cakes have the centre removed, filled with buttercream and the top replaced. For Butterfly cakes, the top is cut into two pieces to form the wings of the butterfly.

Queen cakes can be made by placing a little prepared dried fruit in the base of the paper cup and the mixture piped on top. Baked at 204 °C (400 °F) for 20 minutes.

BAKING CAKE MIXTURES: FRUITED CAKE TYPES

Light fruit cake

Dried fruit is expensive to buy and many cheap brands are available, but this is false economy as they often contain more stalk, stone and foreign body matter. Good quality dried fruit, while being more expensive, is more reliable.

Light fruit cake can be made with mixed fruit, sultanas, currants or be the Genoa type. The type of light fruit cake is determined by the ratio of total fruit weight to that of the total batter weight. Fruit cakes are produced by the sugar batter method; fruit should be added last of all.

The fruit cake mixture is deposited into the prepared cake tin and then the tin is dropped onto the work bench to dispel any air pockets. The top may be levelled with a damp hand or plastic scraper. Bake at 182 °C (360 °F) for approximately 75 minutes depending on the size and depth of the cake. Remember to place a tray of hot water in the oven when cooking fruit cakes.

Fruit ratio for fruit cakes

Lightly fruited: 125 g of fruit per 500 g of batter.
Medium fruited: 250 g of fruit per 500 g of batter.
Heavily fruited: 500 g of fruit per 500 g of batter.

Weight of batter and fruit per size of cake tin or hoop.

Batter	Hoop or tin size
500 g of batter	14 cm hoop or tin
700 g	15 cm
1 kilo	17.5 cm
1.5 kilo	20 cm
2 kilo	22.5 cm
2.5 kilo	25 cm

Medium fruit cake

See the scale for quantity of fruit to batter: as more fruit is added the baking temperature should drop slightly to compensate for the denser mixture during baking.

Heavy fruit cake

Heavy fruit cake should use a medium flour as this provides greater strength in the mixture to support the fruit and help prevent it from sinking during baking. Also, the temperature of baking is reduced to prevent the outside of the cake from burning. Always protect heavy or rich fruit cakes well with layers of paper as lining inside and outside the cake tin. Heavily fruited cakes are baked at 170–175 °C (340–350 °F).

Dundee cake

Traditionally a Scottish cake, Dundee is medium to heavily fruited and has a delicate moist brown crumb texture. It is produced by the sugar batter method, split almonds,

MEMORY JOGGER

Why do heavy fruit cakes require longer baking times and lower temperatures?

round side facing up, are used to decorate the top of the cake prior to baking. Black treacle is sometimes used to deepen the colour of this cake: use this carefully.

Cherry slab or cherry cake

Cherry cake is difficult to make without the cherries sinking to the base of the mixture during baking. Whole or chopped glacé cherries are first washed in warm water to remove the preserving syrup, and dried thoroughly. They can be coated in flour or ground rice to keep them up in the cake mixture during baking. Using a medium strength flour will help to prevent the fruit sinking. The cake batter can also be slightly over-mixed before the cherries are added, to partially toughen the mixture, but this is not really recommended. The addition of an acid will help strengthen the batter to prevent the cherries from sinking: use cream of tartar.

This cake benefits from being set quickly in a hot oven 200 °C (400 °F) and then the heat reduced to 180 °C (350 °F). This starts to coagulate the egg and flour proteins and prevents the cherries sinking through the melted liquid batter.

Sultana slab

See details for slab cakes (page 236).

Genoa

This is a mixed fruit cake or slab using mixed peel, currants, sultanas and cherries. The top of the cake is finished with slivers of flaked almonds and baked in a humid oven set at 171 °C (340 °F).

Wedding cake, birthday or celebration cake

Made from a rich fruit cake mixture these three types of cake can be the same recipe although many recipe books provide particular recipes for each. The cost of producing rich fruit cakes is high and they require a long slow bake, having prepared the ingredients well in advance.

Prepared from the traditional sugar batter the cake mixture is tinned and flattened with a slight depression made in the centre top. This will counteract any rising in the middle and produce a flat surface. Bake at 177 °C (350 °F) for medium sized cakes; but reduce the oven heat to 165 °C (330 °F) for larger cakes. During baking the cakes need to be covered with silicone paper to prevent the tops from burning.

When cooked and cool the cakes are best stored for 6–8 weeks minimum to mature. Any brandy or rum added to the cakes is best done after baking, as alcohol will evaporate during baking. The cakes should be brushed with a warm solution of stock syrup and brandy or rum every 3–5 days and wrapped in greaseproof paper.

When the paper becomes wet then this indicates the cake will not absorb more liquid. Never store cakes in a damp atmosphere; they will mature if lightly wrapped in greaseproof paper and stored in a cool, dry place until required for decoration.

Christmas cake

A traditional measurement for a good quality Christmas cake is the pound-all-round-ratio. This is where a pound of all main ingredients are used for the recipe. Many good reliable Christmas cake recipes can be found in pastry, confectionery and bakery text books. Christmas cakes can be soaked with rum and stock syrup while maturing. Baking should be slow, as for celebration cakes.

Other cake types to consider:
Simnel cake; Date and Walnut; Ginger cake; Farmhouse cake; Coconut; Date and honey; Diabetic; Seed cake; Walnut; Banana cake and Cider and Apple cake.

FAULTS THAT CAN OCCUR IN CAKES

There are nine common errors made when baking cakes which create various unsatisfactory results such as the cake sinking, or rising too much.

Cake sinking in the centre

1 **Too much aeration**
    - Excessive sugar in the recipe, noted by over-coloured crust
    - Over-beating of batter before adding the flour or beating on fast speed
    - Too much baking powder.

2 **Too much liquid**
    - The sides and top of the cake cave inwards after being removed from the oven; there will be a seam above the base crust which is indicative of moisture re-condensing to water and sinking to the base of the cake, and as a result the texture collapses.

3 **Undercooked**
    - A sticky wet seam below the top surface of the crust denotes the cake has not been baked for the right length of time, or was baked at too low an oven temperature.

4 **Cake batter is knocked during baking**
    - The result of the tin being disturbed before the cake is set is that the mixture will cave inwards, particularly the top of the cake, also caused by cool air rushing into the oven when the door is opened.

Peaked top

5 **Toughened cake mixture**
    - Over-mixing once the flour and dry ingredients have been added results in the development of *gluten*. The liberation of gas or oxygen is prevented by the toughened mixture and results in a peaked surface. This will also affect the quality of crumb structure and its eating quality.

6 **Strong flour used for mixture**
    - This has the same effect as over-mixing but this time the mixture already contains too high a level of gluten. Weak low-protein flour is required for cake mixtures.

7 **Oven too hot and insufficient steam during baking**
    - If the oven temperature is too hot then the surface proteins coagulate and set before the cake has completely risen. The uncooked internal mixture cooks and expands breaking through the baked surface resulting in a peaked top.

Bound appearance: little volume

8 **Lack of aeration**
    - Cake batter has not been beaten sufficiently prior to the addition of the flour
    - Not enough sugar in the recipe
    - Lacking in baking powder.

Sinking fruit

9 **Cake batter too soft to hold weight of fruit.**
    - Too much baking powder used
    - Too much sugar used
    - Batter was not toughened sufficiently
    - Flour was too soft/weak
    - Wet fruit which was soaked too long and poorly dried
    - Cooking temperature was too low, this melts the batter fats and sugar letting the fruit slip or slide in the mixture to the base of the cake.

Do this

- Find out more about high-ratio cake recipes.
- Investigate the range of cake products available from local shops.
- Why are cake products usually expensive to buy and produce?
- How are commercial cake products packaged?
- Where should rich cakes be stored, for how long and why?
- What is an 'M' fault, why does it occur ?
- What is an 'X' fault, how can it be prevented ?

BAKING SPONGE MIXTURES

Sponge mixtures are produced by the following methods

- Foaming   Swiss roll – English and French Genoese
- Boiling   Genoese
- Blending   High ratio sheet, Cup cake and Layer sponges
- Creaming   Victoria
- Separate yolk and white   Sponge finger, Drops and Sacher torte

Swiss Roll – *Biscuit Roularde*

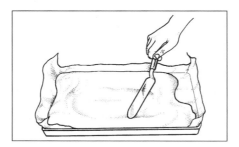
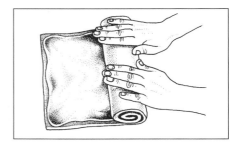

Left: spread the mixture on the baking tray
Right: rolling up a Swiss roll

Made from equal quantities of egg, sugar and soft flour and a little glycerine the eggs and sugar are whisked over hot water to produce a light, thick foam. The sieved flour is carefully folded or cut in and the mixture spread thinly onto a Swiss roll tray or baking sheet prepared with silicone paper.

Bake at 238 °C (460 °F) for 3–4 minutes. When baked, remove from the oven and sprinkle with caster sugar and turn upside down on to a sheet of silicone or grease-proof; leave the tray on top until cool. By baking quickly in a sharp oven the sponge will not be dried out and should be soft when cool. Do not roll the sponge when it is warm, as this will cause it to stick to itself and the sponge can sweat and become sticky.

When cool, trim the edges and spread with jam, using the sheet of paper it was turned out on to roll up tightly. Fine, small Swiss roll is used for Charlotte Royale, chocolate Swiss roll for yule logs, and Swiss kirsch roularde tea fancies. Fruit and cream-filled Swiss roll is used as a dessert or pastry. They can also be made from high-ratio sheet mixtures.

Genoese

Genoese sponge is used as a base for gateaux, torten and petit fours glacé bases. A range of sponges can be made using a variety of production methods. Sheet Genoese can be used for layer cakes, fancies and Battenburg.

Light English Genoese

Whisk the eggs and caster sugar on speed 3 over a bain-marie to blood heat until a light foam occurs at the 'ribbon stage'. Fold in the sieved soft flour and deposit the mixture into a lined gateau tin or tray, either buttered and floured, or lined with silicone paper. Bake at 180 °C for 30–40 minutes, test the top by pressing with a finger; this should spring back, leaving no finger mark, when baked. Cool in the tin for 10 minutes and turn out the Genoese onto a cooling wire, leave the lining paper on until cool.

French Genoese

This can be produced in the same way as for English Genoese, but when the flour has been carefully cut in, melted clarified butter is folded into the sponge. This should be done with care to avoid loss of volume. Deposit the mixture in the tin and bake, cool and store until required. This sponge has an enriched texture and flavour by the addition of butter, and an extended shelf-life.

Boiled Genoese

This type of sponge is stronger than English or French Genoese sponge, so is suitable as sheet sponge for petit four glacé, layer and Battenburg fancies.

The eggs and sugar are made into a foam in the usual way. Melt the butter and boil, then stir in the flour and glycerine and beat to a smooth paste. The sponge foam is then cut into the flour and fat paste in three portions, mixing well as each portion is folded in. Pour into the prepared trays or tins and bake at 191 °C (375 °F) for 35–40 minutes.

Boiled Genoese can be flavoured and coloured with chocolate, walnut, almond, coffee, lemon or orange etc. This sponge freezes quite well for up to one month; wrapped in greaseproof it will keep fresh for one week. Dry sponge trimmings can be used as a substitute for ground almonds or used in queen of puddings.

High-ratio Genoese

This blended batter makes an excellent sponge which has a long shelf life, is stable and used for many commercial sponge products, mini rolls, Swiss rolls, fondant fancies, gateaux and layer cake goods. High levels of liquid and sugar are absorbed by the special fat and flour. If made following accurate mixing speeds and times, the batter colours and flavours well for Angel or layer sponges, Battenburg or sheet sponge for petit fours and tea fancies. High-ratio mixes are also used for cup cakes and layer sponges, but each recipe is different and cannot be made using standard flour or fat.

Sponge made with separate yolk and white – *Biscuit à la cuillier*

Biscuit à la cuillier (spoon biscuits) are sponge fingers made by separating the yolks and whites as described in the methods of production (see p. 229). Using a Savoy bag and 1 cm plain piping tube, pipe finger shaped biscuits 5–6 cm long. Dust with caster sugar and bake at 190 °C (375 °F) until lightly golden. Cool before they are removed from the paper. These store well if left attached to their baking paper until required.

Used for *Charlotte Russe*, sponge fingers can be served with mousses, creams and fools. With the ends dipped in liquid chocolate and sandwiched with cream or ganache they make dumbell biscuits. Small biscuits of vanilla or chocolate are used to decorate the sides of gateaux and torten. Sponge drops are the base for Othellos, Jagos, Rosalinds and Desdemonas. Sponge brickettes can be baked in special tins for trifle sponge.

Biscuit perlés

These are made as for *biscuit à la cuillier* but are dredged with icing sugar instead of caster sugar. They are left to stand until the sugar dissolves and given a light dusting of icing sugar prior to baking. When baked they have a fine pearl finish; they can be used as for sponge fingers and drops and as a *petit four sec*.

Essential knowledge	Time and temperature are important in the preparation and baking of cakes, sponges and biscuits in order to:
	● ensure that the cake or sponge mixture is mixed for the required amount of time in order to prevent faults during baking
	● ensure that the cake or sponge mixtures are correctly baked to impart the correct degree of colour, at the same time as cooking the mixture in the minimum period of time
	● eliminate the opportunity for shrinkage during baking
	● promote and maintain customer satisfaction by producing goods of consistent standards of quality.

Do this

- What difference is there between a gateau and torten ?
- Draw up a list and index of gateau and torten products.
- What type of sponge is best for frozen sponge products and why?
- In what ways can dried or excess sponge be used up?
- How are striped sponges produced?
- What method is used for flavouring sponge with liqueur?

FINISHING METHODS

There are nine basic finishing methods:
- spreading
- turning out
- cooling
- glazing
- trimming
- rolling
- basic piping
- sprinkling / dusting / dredging
- filling

Spreading and smoothing

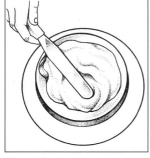

Spreading

The skill of spreading and smoothing mixtures to either fill or coat a sponge or gateau requires practice and patience. To obtain a clean buttercream or icing finish where no air bubble or scratches are evident you must prepare the mixture by stirring and working with a small cake palette knife to remove the air. The technique of spreading is best learnt by watching an expert. How do they hold the palette knife? How do they place the mixture to be flattened onto the cake surface? What technique is used to distribute the icing or cream or topping on the cake evenly?

Turning out baked cakes

When cakes are cooked and removed from the oven, fruit and slab cake benefit from being left to cool in the tin. Cakes such as these are fragile while still hot and are liable to break or crack if turned out straight from the oven. Leaving the cakes in the tin or cake frame will also help retain moisture.

When a celebration cake is cool the top should be trimmed if slightly risen, then turn the cake upsidedown, check that it is level and use the base as the top surface for decoration purposes.

Cooling of baked cakes

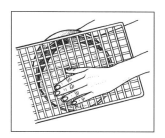

Turning out the cake

Light plain or lightly fruited cakes can be turned straight out from their tins and placed on cooling wires. They should be stored on cake racks with any lining paper left on until the cake is required, this helps retain moisture and protects the cake during storage. Many pound cakes are sold wrapped in clear film with the baking paper, usually corrugated, still intact.

Cake should be cooled naturally at room temperature; if stored in an enclosed environment while still warm, cake will become sticky and create mould growth over time. When cool, cakes should be film-wrapped if possible, or wrapped in greaseproof paper.

Glazing

For details about glazing cakes, sponges and scones see Element 1 pages 233–234.

Trimming

When finishing cakes, sponges or scone products, especially those which require the construction of layers or a number of different fillings and finishes, take care to shape the product as you go i.e. pressing down to produce a flat shape when spreading and filling cream in cakes and sponges.

Slicing a cake into layers

When cutting to shape sponges for decorating use a sharp serrated knife and use a sawing action to form the shape required. Allow sponges in particular to cool well before attempting to shape or cut them.

Trimming of sponges and cakes or biscuits should be carried out in a safe manner, taking care to hold the knife correctly and trim effectively according to the product requirements. Trimming is required for both cooked and uncooked products. When trimming pastry use a cook's knife. Always ensure the bench where trimmings is done is clear, hold the cook's knife with a firm grip with the hand clasped around the knife handle, on no account should you cut near where someone else is working. Keep the point of the knife on the bench and use the knife to trim raw pastry or foods with a guillotine action.

Trimming of cooked sponges and cake should be done with a serrated carving knife. When trimming the edges of a sponge keep a firm grip on the sponge or cake keeping the spare hand behind the knife edge. Cut with a sawing action using the length of the knife to saw, do not press the sponge or cake.

Cutting small portions is safer than trying to cut a large section in one action. If you are trimming a sponge by cutting it into slices, say for a gateau, take the serrated knife in your hand and hold it with a firm safe grip; all fingers should be tucked around the knife handle.

Make a small cut into the side of the sponge to mark the required thickness, then using a slow sawing action, score this cut around the outside of the sponge to a depth of 2.5 cm until you return to the starting cut. When this has been marked continue with a gentle sawing action following the initial cut as a guide.

Your other hand should be held flat on top of the sponge to hold it in place and turn the turntable. Continue to cut until the slice of sponge is completely cut through; repeat this for subsequent slices.

When trimming delicate items such as meringue bases, use a cook's knife with short slow guillotine cuts using the heel of the blade without lifting the blade too far from the bench.

Rolling

When rolling mediums such as sugar paste, marzipan or other decorating media make certain the work surfaces are clean and that the rolling pin is clean. Flour brought into contact with marzipan or covering pastes can create fermentation and spoil the product. Great care and cleanliness in required when rolling costly pastes such as sugar paste, pastello, marzipan or other covering media.

Basic piping

To be able to pipe basic items you will need a Savoy piping bag or make a paper cornet from greaseproof or silicone paper and use a plain or fluted piping tube.

Never overfill a piping bag or the mixture will be difficult to pipe, half filling the bag is sufficient. Seal the bag well when closing the top by folding inwards towards the tip of the bag. Use both hands to pipe. Ask your chef or supervisor to demonstrate basic piping techniques and designs.

Sprinkling, dusting and dredging

When finishing cakes, sponges and scones use either caster or icing sugar to complete the product. This might be caster sugar over small cakes and sponges, icing sugar on Victoria sponges, and fresh cream on scones. You can use a number of aids to apply sugar:
- a fine muslin pouch filled with sugar
- a fine-meshed sieve
- a sugar shaker
- a sugar dredger
- sprinkle by hand using your fingers
- apply sugar by dipping a hot or moist product into a bowl or tray of sugar.

Filling

Cakes and sponges can be filled with a variety of mixtures, cream based, fruit based or paste based, such as *chocolate ganache*. The basic principle to follow when filling any product is that it is sufficient to flavour and compliment the cake or sponge, pleasing to the eye but not so full that it is difficult to handle or divide into portions, over-power the flavour balance or detract from the appearance, all of which might affect sales and service to customers.

Healthy eating

For a healthier alternative use fresh fruit instead of jam or chocolate as a filling, and substitute whipping cream, fromage frais or yoghurt for whipped double cream.

What have you learned?

1 When cooking and finishing basic cake, sponge and scone mixtures what safe working practices should be followed?
2 What are the main contamination threats when cooking and storing basic cake, sponge and scone mixtures and products?
3 Why are time and temperature important when cooking and finishing basic cake, sponge and scone mixtures and products?
4 How should basic cake, sponge and scone mixtures and products be stored at the required safe temperature before cooking?
5 How can increasing the fibre content of basic cake, sponge and scone mixtures contribute to healthy eating practices?
6 Which different types of flours could increase the fibre content of basic cake, sponge and scone mixtures?
7 What causes a cake to sink in the centre during baking?
8 What are the causes of the fruit sinking during baking?
9 When is it advisable to place a tray of water in the oven?
10 How should cakes, sponges and scones be stored after baking?

ELEMENT 3:   Decorate basic cakes and sponges

DECORATIONS, FILLINGS AND TOPPINGS

These may include one or more of the following:
- water icing
- butter cream
- whipped cream
- jam
- fruit filling/fresh fruit
- chocolate

Water icing

Water icing is used to decorate or glaze with a thin layer of opaque icing on cakes and sponges. The water is boiled and the icing sugar stirred in to form a smooth icing free from lumps. Small sponges can be dipped into the icing which forms a crust within minutes and then sets.

Cherries or other decorations should be added before the icing sets; this holds them in place. Water icing can be coloured and flavoured; if chocolate is added this can sometimes thicken the icing and a little stock syrup will soften it to the required consistency for dipping or topping.

Buttercream

This term can only be used for mixtures where the fat content of the buttercream is at least 22.5%. Buttercream can be made with icing sugar and butter or other fat. Fresh unsalted butter and sieved icing sugar are beaten well together until light and free from any lumps. The cream can be spread or piped to fill, sandwich or decorate cakes and sponges.

Buttercream is susceptible to contamination and should be stored in the fridge. It also easily picks up odours from strong smelling foods; always keep the buttercream covered with cling film. Many recipes are available for the production of these

Healthy eating

Use buttercream sparingly as it is high in saturated fats. Consider using whipping cream, fromage frais or yoghurt as an alternative.

MEMORY JOGGER

Why is it important to handle, use and store fresh cream hygienically?

creams and all can be flavoured and coloured according to the product and dish requirements.

Boiled buttercream is less sweet than the beaten variety. Beat the yolks and boil the sugar to 150 °C (300 °F). Then pour the boiled sugar on gradually to the beaten yolks and mix until cool. Add the softened butter in small portions while beating the mixture of yolks and boiled sugar. Because the sucrose has been dissolved and boiled, the sweetness is less evident and produces a far better cream than the standard mix of butter and sugar.

Italian meringue can be blended with softened butter to produce an equally useful cream that is not as sweet but takes up flavours well to produce a continental type of buttercream.

Many commercial recipes are available that use marshmallow, margarine and shortening rather than butter, some stabilised, others made with fondant or pectin.

Healthy eating

Whipping cream is a healthier alternative to double cream as it has a lower butterfat content and also gives more volume.

Whipped cream

The term 'cream' can only be applied to products filled, finished, topped or decorated with *fresh dairy cream*.

Cream for whipping should be either double or whipping cream; double cream is more expensive and contains a higher butterfat content (48%) than whipping cream (35%) which takes slightly longer to whip to a piping consistency. When fully whipped, whipping cream will give more volume than double or other fresh creams.

Because of the higher butter fat content, double cream is more stable which is useful when you need to add liqueur or liquid flavours.

Essential knowledge

- Whipping can be done by hand or machine.
- Never whip cream in aluminium bowls or with aluminium whisks.
- All equipment should be very clean.
- Over-beating will turn the cream to butter and butter milk.
- Cream should be stored at 4 °C (40 °F).
- Always use cream and dairy products in strict date rotation.
- Always return cream containers to the fridge; do not leave them standing in a warm environment.
- If using a machine to whip cream clean it correctly, including splashes, after mixing.
- Whipped cream should be piped using a clean sterilised nylon piping bag rather than the older cotton variety.

Jam

Jam is used to flavour, fill and decorate a range of cake and sponge products. Seedless jam is often used, spread onto sponges prior to being spread with buttercream or whipped cream. Fresh cream scones often have a small bead of jam piped onto the scone before the cream is piped. Swiss rolls are spread with jam and rolled. Jam needs to be mixed to soften its texture to aid piping. Small cakes are often piped with free-flowing jam and gels to aid decoration and add flavour.

Fruit filling / Fresh fruit

A range of fruit fillings, toppings and decorating gels are available; some are relatively cheap, others made with quality fruits can be more expensive. Fruit fillings are used to flavour gateaux, torten, small and large cakes and sponges. Alternatively, fresh fruit is used extensively as a garnish or as a main flavouring ingredient for sponge and cake items.

Never over-decorate with any filling, fruit or gel. Use complimentary flavours and colours i.e. kiwi and orange, mandarin and strawberry, black grapes and pineapple are just a few options. When placing fruit on a cake take care to centre the fruit and position it to prevent it from falling off its base.

Chocolate

Coating with chocolate or ganache
Ganache is a rich mixture of fresh cream and chocolate; the chocolate can be good quality 'couverture' or cheaper baker's compound chocolate. The cream is boiled and the chopped chocolate stirred in to form a thick glossy sauce. This is used while warm as a coating for individual cakes, sponges and gateaux.

The cakes or gateaux should be sandwiched and then placed on a wire rack. Using a large ladle, 'nappe' two or three ladles of chocolate over the product, or one if on individual cakes. The rack can be agitated by shaking it gently to ensure the coating covers the top and sides evenly; excess should drip off onto a clean plastic tray. If possible, always use the force or gravity to allow the weight of the coating to flow over the product. If you need to use a palette knife this can spoil the finish if not done quickly.

The ganache will have a thicker consistency as it cools, so to obtain a glass-like finish, coat products as soon as the mixture has been stirred sufficiently to melt all the chocolate.

Compound chocolate made with vegetable fats and oils instead of cocoa butter should be melted to 52 °C for milk chocolate and 55 °C for plain coating chocolate.

PROBLEMS WITH DECORATING

When decorating cakes and sponges problems may occur:
- in terms of freshness
- in terms of quantity.

Problems that can occur result mainly from poor or weak decorating skills, lack of care when finishing, or incorrect preparation of decorating media. For example do not overheat fondant or chocolate as this will result in a waste of costly commodities.

If you are unsure always ask for help; competent staff will not mind showing you how to decorate to produce clean results of good quality, but they will be annoyed if you ruin products or produce goods not up to the establishment standards.

Always prepare sufficient goods to cover service requirements; spare bases of cake and sponge can be stored in tins or airtight storage trays until required, or frozen. If frozen wrap sponges in plastic bags and mark the date they were made, the quantity frozen and what the sponges are. This will help other members of staff who might need to use this stock when you are off duty.

DECORATION METHODS

Decoration methods include:
1 trimming
2 filling
3 spreading and smoothing
4 icing
5 coating
6 piping icing or chocolate
7 piping with cream
8 dusting, dredging or sprinkling
9 topping

Trimming

See Element 2 p. 243 for details about how to trim basic cakes and sponges.

Filling

Cream based fillings include: Fresh semi- or full whipped cream (double or whipping); clotted cream; pastry cream; buttercream, set creams and mousses.

Fruit based fillings include: Apple and assorted fresh fruit purée; tinned fruit pie fillings; fruit pastes and conserves such as raspberry or apricot confit, jams and preserves; whole fresh fruit or portioned sliced fruits; fruit creams; mousses and set custards.

Flavoured fillings include: Chocolate ganache; fondant and pastry cream pastes; nut pastes; powders and products such as praline, coconut or almond pastes; fudge; caramel; butterscotch sauces and pastes; mallow; curds and gels of assorted flavours and textures.

<aside>
Healthy eating
Fruit based fillings are a healthier alternative to cream, chocolate or rich, flavoured fillings.
</aside>

Spreading and smoothing mediums

Some simple procedures can be followed when spreading or smoothing soft surfaces. If fresh cream is the medium being used, never over-whip the cream, a softer, semi-whipped cream for covering gateaux and torten will smooth easily when worked.

If cream is over-whipped the action of smoothing only causes further coagulation of the butterfats that is difficult to spread effectively producing a rough and unsightly finish that is anything but smooth.

When spreading fondant or chocolate mixes the tools need to be clean, the action must be swift and skilled to spread and smooth such mixtures before they set and without causing crumbs or partially set areas to drag and spoil the finish.

Smoothing

Icing

Royal icing
Royal icing made from egg whites and icing sugar is used to decorate wedding, birthday or celebration cakes. For traditional royal icing mix 2 egg whites with 400 g of sieved fine icing sugar; beat for 20 minutes to form a stiff light icing mixture.

Today, powdered egg white called 'albumen' or 'albumen substitute' is widely used to make royal icing. Mix albumen powder with water in the ratio of 75 g per 400 ml of water; this is best mixed and left overnight to extract maximum strength from the albumen. Strain the solution and stir in the sieved sugar and mix on a high speed for 20 minutes, a little blue colour added to the royal icing will improve the whiteness. When mixed, cover the bowl with a damp cloth or place in an airtight container.

Royal icing should be a day old before being used to coat cakes, the marzipan on celebration cakes having been done a few days prior to flat icing, to prevent oil from the paste rising through the wet icing and spoiling the finish.

Use plastic scrapers for smoothing sides of gateaux and torten or other cake products. Keep scrapers wrapped in cling film to protect them from being scratched; when drawing royal icing a scratch will leave a mark or line in the smooth surface.

<aside>
MEMORY JOGGER

Why should decorating tools and equipment be cleaned and stored correctly after use?
</aside>

Fondant icing
This should be warmed slowly over time and not made too hot as this produces large sugar crystals which set quickly with a dull finish. Never try to smooth a very large surface on cakes unless you are confident; always ask for help and advice.

Steel straight edges are available for flat coating buttercream and icing, again protect them from being scratched. They are best used slightly warm by rinsing with warm water and drying just before use. Sugar paste which is rolled out can be effective in achieving a smooth sugar surface on celebration cakes. It can be polished with a clean soft cloth to buff the paste once in place, and trimmed, crimped or fluted to add decoration to the edges.

Coating

Coating products with liquid mixtures such as fondant, chocolate or hot jam requires basic preparation and special techniques to be effective. Having spent time producing a good quality cake, sponge or biscuit, the coating it receives should be clean, even thickness, provide a sheen and cover the food item without showing the base product.

MEMORY JOGGER

Why should care be taken when heating chocolate or fondant as a decorating medium?

Coating with royal icing

To coat a cake well with royal icing requires skill developed by constant practice. Royal icing should be at least 24 hours old before being worked to remove the air and form a smooth icing mixture. Cakes should be coated with three thin coats, using a plastic scraper for the sides and an icing ruler for the top. Cake dummies can be used to practise on; these skills are useful when coating with buttercreams to obtain a flat clean surface. A good flat surface will improve piping that is not quite accurate, but good piping will not enhance a poor surface, which is the most critical decoration in cake artistry, gateaux and torten production.

Coating with fondant

Fondant when prepared correctly will give a high gloss finish, an even smooth surface and provide a good foundation for the final decoration.

The fondant icing should never be heated above 38 °C (100 °F). Break the fondant into small pieces and place in a copper pan or saucepan, cover with hot water and leave to stand for 10 minutes. After this time pour off the water and stir the fondant well, this method is effective in warming the fondant sufficiently without overheating.

If it is overheated the fine small crystals in the fondant enlarge and reflect less light while setting quickly and producing a thick unpleasant coating. Sponge items to be coated should be first dipped or brushed with boiled apricot purée or covered in marzipan before the fondant coating is added.

Place the items to be coated on a fine wire rack evenly spaced. Having coated with jam pour over fondant and allow the icing to set, place the items evenly on the wire. Use a plastic tray under the wire to catch the excess fondant.

Using a small ladle 'nappe' (cover) the sponge shapes with fondant, always coating the furthest sponge from you first and working back towards yourself; this avoids dripping fondant on those already coated.

To improve the gloss, add a little piping jelly, gelatine, glucose, stock syrup or mallow; *on no account add raw egg white* – this is not recommended for reasons of possible contamination and/or fermentation which might occur. Food regulations do not allow raw egg whites to be added to uncooked food.

Spirit, liqueur, essence, chocolate couverture or baker's chocolate, coffee essence or powder, or essential oils can be added to fondant to add flavour and colour. Flavour compounds should be used with care, only a few drops are required and the bottle needs a good shake prior to using as some compounds can settle and separate when stood.

Organisation when coating

● Above all work cleanly, always wash your tools when they become sticky.
● Blend and work coatings and fillings before trying to achieve a smooth surface.

- Spread mixtures with an even pressure of the hand with a small palette knife.
- Never use too much or too little filling or coating to spread and smooth.
- Do not over-whip cream for coating, warm fondant correctly and rest royal icing before using it for coating wedding, birthday or celebration cakes.

Piping with icing or chocolate

Piping with icing

Piping with a nylon Savoy bag or a paper bag of icing or chocolate requires control, balance and co-ordination.

To produce designs both large and small, plain or complex requires one thing– practice. Piping a treble clef in chocolate on silicone paper, a gateau or individual petit four glacé is an easy design to start off with.

To pipe a shape with flair and speed, there are a few basic rules:
- only fill the bag half full or less. If the bag is over-filled the chocolate will leak and become a problem as you tend to concentrate on the leaking liquid rather than the design being piped.
- Ensure the icing is not too stiff. If the royal icing is too stiff and a fine nozzle is used, your hand can become cramped if the pressure is constant even for just a few minutes.
- Ensure basic preparations are carried out *before* starting to pipe.
- Always try the design on paper first. When writing a name or message on cakes, balance the words with your eyes (write the name on paper and compare the spacing with your cake).
- When filling paper piping bags, only half fill and fold tightly inwards and down toward the point of the bag. Make certain the paper is not creased; this can cause problems in both making the bag and keeping a fine sharp point.
- Icing piped onto waxed paper and dried then transferred to the cake is a good way of decorating and gives you practice.

Chocolate icing for piping can be thickened with a little glycerine, alcohol or stock syrup and piped onto silicone paper. These decorations set quickly and can be stored until required. When you have some spare time, prepare some of these mixtures and practise trying to keep neat rows of designs both large and small. Try some little birds, butterflies or palm trees.

Hand co-ordination is essential; always use your spare hand to guide the bag, it is not possible to produce high quality piping without using both hands.

Piping with cream

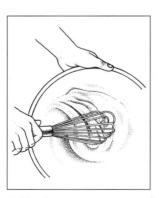

Whipping cream

Before using any cream, always check that it is fresh and not tainted with other flavours. Make sure that all the tools and containers you need to use are absolutely clean.

Fresh or synthetic cream can be used to finish cold desserts, cakes, puddings and pastries. Fresh cream if over-whipped will lose its buttermilk as the butterfat globules form together: this results in liquid dripping from the piping bag and spoiling the product as well as making it difficult to pipe. The cream will look pale yellow and be coarse in texture. Never over-whip cream.

Piping can be done using a plain or star tube; this can be plastic or metal. Piping bags should be of the nylon variety, rather than cotton, as the nylon is more hygienic.

Never place too much whipped cream in the bag, half fill the piping bag and twist, at the same time work any trapped air from the bag to the top. When the bag feels comfortable to hold, pipe the shapes by squeezing to apply an even and steady pressure as the shapes are formed.

Use your spare hand to guide the Savoy bag. It is a good idea to practise 'icing' with meringue and choux pastry on a work bench, to develop control and accurate design.

Dusting, dredging or sprinkling

Dust pastries and other dessert items to give them a sugar coating that forms part of the overall design, or if they are to be glazed in the oven or under the salamander. The sugar can be caster, icing or granulated for pies, biscuits or gateaux. An even dusting using a fine mesh sieve held approximately 20 cm above the products will deposit an even dust of sugar which should not be unsightly.

Dredging is where a heavier dusting is required such as icing sugar for a white coated effect. Sprinkling with sugar is done just to very lightly dust the product for effect, allowing the product surface still to be seen.

Topping

Top dressings are added both prior to baking and to finish the decoration of desserts, cakes, pastries, sponges and biscuit products. The topping added to products before baking can over colour, therefore the oven setting should be reduced. Check the goods while baking to achieve the required finish.

Toppings added to sponges, cakes or pastries should be balanced, in proportion to the size of the base, and be complimentary in colour and flavour. If toppings such as toasted coconut or vermicelli are used, this should be added carefully. A plain ring cutter pressed through a card and positioned on the gateau can provide a useful frame into which topping can be placed without spilling it over the whole surface.

Essential knowledge

The main contamination threats when preparing and using cake decorations are as follows:
- food poisoning bacteria can be transferred through to the cake decorations through use of unhygienic preparation areas, equipment and utensils
- food poisoning bacteria may be transferred from yourself to the food. Open cuts, sores, sneezing, colds, sore throats or dirty hands are all possible sources
- contamination will occur if flour or any foods are allowed to come into contact with rodents (such as mice or rats), or insects (house flies, cockroaches, silver fish, beetles). Fly screens should be fitted to all windows
- contamination can occur if products are stored at incorrect temperatures
- contamination can occur through products being left opened or uncovered. Foreign bodies (e.g. sack tape, metal objects, machine parts, string, cigarette ends, etc.) can fall into food, open containers and flour bins
- cross-contamination can occur if equipment is not cleaned correctly between operations
- incorrect waste disposal can lead to contamination.

DECORATION AND DESIGN

The rule is *moderation with design, moderation with colour and flavour*. The aim is always to top a product to enhance the overall picture for your clients and customers. Your reputation and standard are constantly judged by the quality of finish, flavour and eating quality of your work. Keep this in mind and your knowledge, understanding and crafts skills will continue to develop. We can all do better.

Case study

You run a small bakery but have recently been asked to supply cakes to a neighbouring teashop.

Preparing and producing cakes, sponges and scone products can be a costly investment. Skilled staff are required to produce ranges of cakes, sponges and scone products and the commodities used in their production can be expensive.

● *Suggest some advantages for purchasing convenience cakes, sponges and scone products?*
● *Suggest some disadvantages in purchasing convenience cakes, sponges and scone products?*
● *If you were asked to prepare a selection of afternoon tea fancies of 6 types what cakes, sponge or scone products would you make and why?*

Healthy eating

● *Which products could be used to substitute high fat ingredients when decorating basic cakes and sponges?*
   Using low fat or polyunsaturated fats will assist in reducing the amount of saturated fat consumed by customers. One problem with this is that the flavour base might need to be masked to improve or cover the blander taste of these fats.
● *How can reducing the amount of sugar when filling basic cakes and sponges can contribute to healthy catering practices?*
   Where possible we should all strive to use less sugar in all pastry products. Our tastes have over recent year been invaded by high sugar levels and the true taste of good food is often lost.

What have you learned

1 When decorating basic cakes and sponges what safe working practices should be followed?
2 When decorating basic cakes and sponges why is it important to keep preparation areas and equipment hygienic?
3 What are the main contamination threats when decorating and storing basic cakes, sponge and scone mixtures and products?
4 Why are time and temperature important when decorating basic cakes and sponges with royal icing, fondant and chocolate?
5 What decorating methods are most suitable for different types of basic cakes and sponges?
6 How can reducing the amount of sugar in basic cake, sponge and scone mixtures contribute to healthy eating practices?
7 How can you adjust the consistency of water icing?
8 What precautions should you take with whipped cream?
9 What products can be used as a substitute for cream when decorating basic cakes and sponges?
10 What products can be used as a substitute for buttercream when decorating cakes and sponges?

Get ahead

- Once you are competent in cooking and finishing basic cake, sponge and scone products write up a list of more complex products that will provide evidence for this element at Level 3 NVQ. Does the range of products and services offered by your establishment allow you to extend your practical skills to cover more complex dishes? Look at tea fancies, morning and afternoon goods. Are there any alternative product ideas that you can research and try on the menu to enhance the quality and range of products offered.

- To develop your knowledge of this unit you might also research tea fancies, French pastries both classical types and contemporary variations. Investigate types of friandise, petit four and individual dessert dishes using cake or sponge bases as composite ingredients.

- Read up on fruit cake recipes, both commercial and everyday recipes. Where you come across ingredients you are unfamiliar with look these up in any text books available to you or visit your local Further Education college and join their library. This will give you access to a wide range of catering text books and multi-media information regarding food subjects.

- Look at prepared ready-to-use products for cakes, sponges and scones. Many companies now produce high quality products, convenience mixes and frozen produce. This can be labour saving, be easy to cost and work out selling prices, and have a better shelf-life than freshly prepared goods.

- Look at different types of cakes, regional specialities, types of sponges such as high-ratio and powdered mixes.

- Producing sponges using special comb scrapers is now popular. How much do they cost what types of designs can be produced and who sells these specialist tools?

Prepare and cook basic egg dishes

This chapter covers:
ELEMENT 1:   **Prepare basic egg dishes**
ELEMENT 2:   **Cook basic egg dishes**

What you need to do

- Prepare eggs by a variety of methods.
- Understand the correct use of equipment when preparing egg dishes.
- Appreciate the need for hygienic storage of eggs.
- Cook egg dishes by a variety of methods.
- Identify any problems with the quality of any ingredients used in the cooking of egg dishes
- Select the appropriate method of cookery for the egg dish to meet dish requirements.
- Understand the correct equipment used for cooking egg dishes.
- Clean cooking areas and equipment correctly before and after use.
- Store egg dishes not for immediate service correctly.

What you need to know

- The types of eggs used and the quality points associated with them.
- Correct equipment to be used in a safe and hygienic manner.
- Preparation methods used in egg cookery.
- How to combine eggs with other ingredients.
- Why it is necessary to work in an efficient and organised manner.
- Why it is important to keep cooking and service areas and equipment hygienic when cooking and finishing egg dishes.
- What the main contamination threats are when cooking and storing egg dishes.
- Why time and temperature are important when cooking egg dishes.
- What basic cooking methods are suitable for different types of basic egg dishes.
- Which fats and oils encourage healthy eating.
- What effect reducing the salt content will have on a person's diet.

INTRODUCTION

Eggs are an extremely nutritional form of food and easily available, contributing to a well-balanced diet. They can be used in a variety of ways ranging from an omelette as a main meal to a meringue on a sweet trolley. Usually, they are quick to prepare and cook as well as lending themselves to a variety of cooking methods.

You need to be able to judge the quality points associated with eggs. Correct storage of eggs is also extremely important, especially as they can absorb strong odours from other foods. At the same time you should have an understanding of the various types of equipment used when producing egg dishes.

As well as being a menu item in their own right eggs are frequently combined with other commodities to make dishes more appealing, attractive and digestible. Apart from the use of hens' eggs it is also necessary to have an understanding of ducks' and quails' eggs in cookery.

ELEMENT 1:   Prepare basic egg dishes

QUALITY POINTS IN EGGS

There are various aspects to determine the quality of an egg. For several egg dishes it is important that the egg is of a good quality. These are primarily boiling, poaching and frying as here it is important to have the yolk in the centre of the white.

As an egg ages the white becomes watery, the yolk is less pronounced and more to the side of the shell within the white. For this reason you must know what quality points to look for in a fresh egg. They are:
● the shell should be clean, a good shape and the surface slightly rough
● when placed into a brine solution (100g of salt to 1 litre of water) heated to 23 °C (73 °F) a good quality egg will float near the bottom. As the egg becomes older the air sac inside increases and the egg floats nearer the surface of the water.
● commercially, egg are passed over a strong light which shows the placement of the yolk within the egg and the size of the air sac
● when cracked open the yolk, which should be of a good yellow colour, will sit proud and in the centre of the 'white'. The 'white' itself should be firm and clear with very little watery white around the outer edge.

While different breeds of hen produce different coloured shells and some people prefer one colour to another, once cracked open there is no difference between eggs in terms of quality or content.

STORAGE

The shell of an egg is porous which allows it to absorb strong smelling odours. Therefore it is important for them to be stored away from foods such as fish, onions and strong smelling cheese that could affect the taste of the egg or the dish they are used in.

At the same time it is necessary to store them in a cool but not too dry place. A refrigerator is an ideal place with a temperature of 4–5 °C. In storage, the eggs should be point end down in the tray because the air sac within the shell is at the rounded end.

> **MEMORY JOGGER**
>
> What is the ideal recommended temperature to store eggs at?

> ### Healthy eating
> The type of salmonella in eggs can result from a specific organism called Salmonella enteridis. The bacteria infects the ovaries of the chicken and from there moves into the yolk. The white is not effected as it has a defence mechanism against the bacteria, unlike the yolk. Therefore eating under-cooked egg dishes, especially those with running yolks or in mousses, can cause this type of infection.

Chickens are subject to a variety of bacteria; some are harmful. The contents of eggs can become contaminated by bacteria such as *salmonella* through the birds' feed or the laying process, or even through handling. Refrigerated eggs keep well for up to two weeks. For those susceptible to or anxious about infection, pasteurised eggs, heat treated to kill any potentially harmful bacteria, are available, either in a dried form as whole egg, or as yolks or whites only.

Eggs are purchased by number and still retain the imperial unit of a dozen or half dozen. The wholesale unit of hens' eggs is in boxes of 360, which is 12 trays of 30 eggs. It is perfectly acceptable to store them in the box and the trays they are delivered in.

MEMORY JOGGER

Why can eggs be an important part of our diet?

Nutritional content of a hen's egg

Eggs are a basic and important food as a form of protein, vitamins A, B and D and several important minerals: iron, calcium and iodine.

A plainly cooked size three egg contains just over 80 kilocalories.

Composition of an egg

Shell 12%   albumen (white) 58%   yolk 30%

	Water	Protein	Fat	Minerals
Whole egg	73–75%	12–14%	10–12%	1–1.2%

Nutritional content of the white and yolk of an egg

White	86–87%	12–12.5%	0.25%	0.8–1.5%
Yolk	50–50.5%	16–16.5%	31–32%	0.8–1.5%

- 1 litre of whole egg is equivalent to 16 eggs
- 1 litre of egg whites is equivalent to 30–32 eggs
- 1 litre of egg yolk is the equivalent to 54–56 eggs

Healthy eating

During recent times the overall death rate attributed to heart disease has fallen but it is still comparatively high. One cause of this, especially in Europe, is the amount of saturated fats consumed in the diet. These come mainly from the consumption of red meats, dairy products and processed foods available on the market. Saturated fats encourage the build-up of fatty deposits within the arteries around the body and also increase the level of cholesterol within the blood itself.

Eggs, by their very nature, are high in cholesterol and therefore potentially harmful. The consensus of opinion is that the *maximum* number of eggs that should be eaten per week should not exceed four. This, with a reduced intake of salt and the use of polyunsaturated fats in the diet will support a healthy eating approach.

Other ingredients used in the preparation of egg dishes

Ingredients	Preparation		Uses
Vegetables	Tomato:	blanch, deseed, dice	Omelette, *sur le plat*, *en cocotte*, scrambled eggs
	Onion:	peel, shred, shallow-fry	Omelette, *sur le plat*, *en cocotte*
	Peppers:	skin, deseed, dice, shred	Omelette, *sur le plat*
	Potato:	peel, dice, shallow-fry	Omelette
	Peas:	boil, refresh	Omelette
Ham	Cook and dice		Omelette, *sur le plat*, *en cocotte*, scrambled
Bacon	Grill or fry		Omelette, *sur le plat*
Cooked smoked fish/shellfish	Ensure thoroughly cooked and normally combine with appropriate sauce. Smoked salmon is the exception. It is normally cut into thin strips and used as a garnish.		Omelette, *sur le plat*, *en cocotte*, scrambled eggs

Ingredients	Preparation	Uses
Rice (plain)	Boiled	Use as a base for presenting soft boiled, poached or hard boiled eggs with an appropriate sauce such as curry.
Fungi	Wash, slice and/or quarter; lightly shallow-fry	Omelette, *sur le plat*, *en cocotte*, scrambled eggs
Herbs	Pick, clean and chop	Omelette, scrambled eggs

TYPES OF EGGS

Hens' eggs

These eggs are graded according to weight in grams.

Grade 1	70 g and over,
Grade 2	70–65 g,
Grade 3	65–60 g,
Grade 4	60–55 g,
Grade 5	55-50 g,
Grade 6	50–45 g,
Grade 7	under 45 g.

Eggs are also graded A, B, C. A is the freshest and so on down to C, which are only sold to food manufacturers. Boxes of pre-packed eggs are stamped with the packing date and size of egg and, sometimes, the sell-by date.

Over 90% of eggs in Britain come from the battery system or other intensive systems such as deep litter and perchery.

Commercially raised free-range eggs come from hens that have continuous daytime access to open air runs which are limited to 404 birds per acre.

There is no difference in flavour or nutritional value between white or brown eggs. The colour depends on the breed of hen, not on how it is fed. For example, specialist breeders sometimes have surplus eggs and the eggs that come from a breed of hen called *Aracana* give a medium-sized egg with a bluish cast to the shell, not unlike a duck egg. You would use this in the same way as a normal hen egg.

Duck eggs

These are available all the year round but are at their best between spring and summer. Duck eggs should always be well-cooked and never eaten raw, or with the yolk runny. Because of their size which is larger than that of a hen's egg, they are usually used for baking. Duck eggs also have a stronger and richer flavour than hens' eggs. Types available are: Barbary or Muscovy, Blue, Khaki Campbell, and White.

Goose eggs

Because geese are not reared intensively but follow the natural breeding cycle and start laying from spring to midsummer, goose eggs are not easily available. They should always be well cooked and treated like duck eggs. They are generally used in baking.

Guinea fowl eggs

These are small brown eggs, not widely available commercially. They are rich, with an excellent flavour, and are usually served hard-boiled in salads.

MEMORY JOGGER

Which is larger: a Grade 1 or a Grade 3 egg? What is the difference in weight?

MEMORY JOGGER

What is the difference between a battery egg and a free range egg?

Gulls' eggs

Seagulls nest in very inaccessible places so that their eggs are generally difficult to obtain. They are slightly smaller than a hen's egg. Gulls' eggs are said to have a very delicate fishy flavour. They are usually hard-boiled and sprinkled with celery salt, or hard-boiled and served in salads. They are normally available from Scottish game farmers. They would feature as an *Hors d'oeuvre 'riche'* on a traditional *à la carte* menu.

Pigeon eggs

A pigeon's egg is a small white egg. They are often found on French menus, and are usually served lightly poached in a rich game consommé.

Quails' eggs

Quails' eggs are attractive small, dark speckled eggs. They can be eaten soft- or hard-boiled. Traditionally they were sprinkled with celery salt just prior to serving. These would feature on a menu as an hors d'oeuvre, as a garnish, or as part of the selection on a cocktail buffet menu.

Game eggs from such birds as the partridge and pheasant are also available from time to time. These can be used in the same way as quails' eggs.

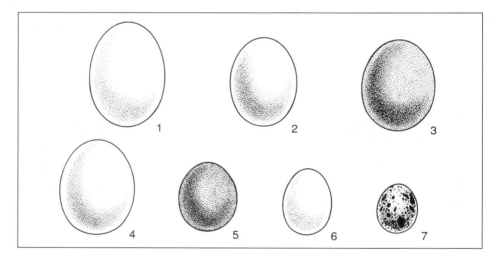

Different types of eggs Key: 1 Duck (white); 2 Duck (blue); 3 Hen; 4 Duck (Khaki Campbell); 5 Guinea fowl; 6 Pigeon; 7 Quail

EQUIPMENT

Most egg dishes are produced as and when the customer orders them. There are some exceptions where a certain amount of preparation can be done in advance such as a poached egg, a soft-boiled or a hard-boiled egg dish. These can be cooked in advance and then reheated as the customer orders them. It is necessary to have checked through the recipe and have all the cooking and service equipment at hand before you start to cook any egg dish.

You must also think ahead and place your omelette pan on the stove to heat up at the start of service so that when an order is taken for an omelette, the pan is ready and the dish can be cooked immediately. Likewise with the water to poach an egg which needs to be simmering as service starts. It is important to keep an eye on this equipment when it is on the stove, as you do not want to let the omelette pan get too hot, nor do you want the water to boil away in the poaching pan.

As egg dishes over-cook very quickly and loose their heat rapidly, it is important to have warmed service dishes ready and easily accessible to serve the egg dishes on.

Sur le plat dish: a small china dish with sloping sides and lipid handles on each side, 13–14 cm (5–6 in) diameter

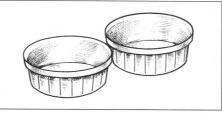

En cocotte dish: small dish similar to a small soufflé mould, approximately 7 cm (3 in) diameter

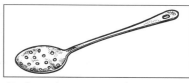

Perforated spoon: stainless steel spoon with holes through the bowl so that water and other liquids can drain away from the food

Omelette pan: heavy duty cast iron pan, similar to a frying pay, but with curved sides which help in the shaping of the omelette, usually about 20 cm (8 in) diameter

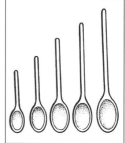

Long-handled spoon made of wood, used to mould deep-fried eggs

Sauteuse: shallow pan made of tinned copper, stainless steel or aluminium, with sloping sides and a single long handle

Frying pan: usually made of cast iron, shallow with straight sides and a flat base, available in a variety of sizes

Proving an omlette pan

To prove an omelette pan, place it on the stove with a generous handful of salt in the base and heat. Then rub it with a thick cloth to remove any dirt and moisture. Pour away the salt and add a generous coating of oil and allow this to heat up slowly until it nearly starts to smoke. Carefully dispose of the oil and rub the pan out with a clean dry cloth. It is now ready to use.

Case study

Imagine you have the following egg dishes on your menu:
1 *Egg en cocotte with cream (cooked as a plain egg en cocotte and finished with cream).*
2 *Scrambled eggs with cornets of smoked salmon.*
3 *Egg sur la plat with bacon (served garnished with grilled bacon).*
   ● *Draw up a list of the equipment and ingredients you will need to produce the egg dish, prior to cooking them.*
   ● *Make a list with notes outlining hygiene aspects of preparation.*

POINTS OF HYGIENE

The following are recommendations for the caterer when storing, handling and serving egg dishes. They have been produced by the egg industry in association with the DHSS.

1 Eggs should be stored in a cool place preferably in a refrigerator.
2 Stocks should be carefully rotated on a first in – first out basis.
3 Cracked eggs should be thrown away and not used in the production of food items.
4 Eggs should be stored away from foods that might contaminate them, such as raw meat.
5 Persons who handle eggs should wash their hands before and after handling them, as they would do with any raw food product.
6 Whole eggs out of their shells should be covered, refrigerated, and used within two days.

Essential knowledge

To be able to prepare egg dishes correctly you must know:
● what points to look for when deciding the quality of an egg when it is in the shell and when it is cracked open
● correct storage of eggs prior to being used
● the types of eggs commonly used in cookery and what they are used for.

What have you learned

● How would you tell if an egg is fresh when it is still in the shell?
● Why should eggs be stored away from strong smelling foods?
● What is the ideal temperature at which to store eggs?
● What vitamins are found in eggs?
● Which is the larger, a Grade 1 or a Grade 3 egg?
● What food poisoning bacteria can sometimes be found in eggs?

ELEMENT 2: Cook basic egg dishes

EGG COOKERY

Boiled egg in shell (*Oeufs à la coque*)

1 Plunge the eggs into a saucepan of boiling water.
2 Eggs of an average size should be left for three-and-a-half minutes.
3 Drain and serve straight away in warm egg cups.
4 Serve at breakfast and tea-time.

Soft-boiled eggs (*Oeufs mollets*)

1 Place the eggs into boiling water; keep the water boiling for five minutes (boiling for longer means the egg will not shell easily).
2 Remove and immerse in cold runnmg water.
3 Shell carefully and keep in cold water or serve immediately. This method produces a soft yolk with a firm white.
4 If you are not going to serve the eggs immediately, reheat them for one minute in very hot but not boiling water to which a little salt has been added.
5 Serve as an egg course with a suitable garnish for lunch or dinner. On the continent these are served for breakfast.

MEMORY JOGGER

Why is it important to time a soft-boiled egg accurately? What may happen if you boil it for more than five minutes?

Hard-boiled eggs (*Oeufs durs*)

There are two acceptable ways of cooking hard-boiled eggs.
1   Have plenty of boiling water, place the eggs in the water, let the water re-boil and then cook the eggs for ten minutes gently on the side of the stove, making sure that the water stays at boiling point. Drain, then put the eggs into cold running water until completely cold before shelling.
    or:
2   Place the eggs into plenty of cold water, bring it to the boil and, according to the size of eggs, boil gently for seven to eight minutes, drain and place under cold running water until cold, then shell.

Serve as a hot hard-boiled egg dish, as an hors d'oeuvre, or in salads, buffets or as a garnish.

When serving eggs hot any of the recipes for poached or soft-boiled eggs are suitable.

Poached eggs (*Oeufs poches*)

1   It is best to use a shallow pan for poaching. Add the water to the depth of about 10 cm (3½ in), *acidulate* the water by adding 75 ml (3 fl oz) of white wine vinegar or lemon juice, add a little salt and bring to the boil.
2   Remove the pan to the side of the stove to bubble gently, then break the egg and pour it carefully into the water. In the gently bubbling water the egg will take about 3–4 minutes to cook.
3   When just firm to the touch, remove with a perforated spoon and place in iced cold water.
4   Trim the white with a small knife. Reheat in very hot salted water which should not be boiling.

Serve plain on toast or with smoked haddock for breakfast; or serve at lunch or dinner, with a garnish as hot hors d'oeuvre, or as a main course.

Egg cocotte (*Oeufs en cocotte*)

This is a combination of soft-boiling and poaching. The egg is cooked in a special mould or dish (see p. 259).
1   Heat the dish and butter well.
2   Place any cooked garnish on the bottom.
3   Break the egg into the dish and cook in a *bain-marie* for 3–4 minutes. The *bain-marie* should be covered with a lid, but leave a gap for the steam to escape, or the dish will also fill up with water from the condensation created by the steam.
4   When cooked, serve immediately on a warm service dish with a dish paper on it.
5   These can be served at breakfast, lunch, or dinner as hot hors d'oeuvre.

Moulded eggs (*Oeufs moules*)

As the name implies, moulded eggs dishes are cooked in a shaped mould. The moulds can be plain or fancy. The preparation of the mould and the cooking of the egg are the same as for egg cocotte, but these are unmoulded prior to service and can be served hot or cold. If they are served cold they are normally decorated and glazed with aspic jelly.

They can be served as for recipes for poached egg, or decorated and served cold as an hors d'oeuvre.

Scrambled eggs (*Oeufs brouilles*)

1 Crack the eggs into a suitable sized bowl and whisk until the eggs are well mixed.
2 Season with salt and pepper.
3 Place the mixture in a hot well-buttered sauteuse. Stir continuously with a wooden spoon or spatula over a gentle heat until firm but creamy.
4 Remove from the heat and add a little cream and mix well. The cream is added at the last minute to help to slow down the cooking process.
5 Serve at breakfast, as a hot hors d'oeuvre, as a main meal at lunch, dressed in a mould or tartlet, on toast, or as a savoury at the end of a meal e.g. Scotch Woodcock. This egg dish must be served immediately as it will carry on cooking and loose its heat rapidly.

Stirred eggs/baked (*Oeufs sur la plat*)

The dishes used for these egg dishes are made of a fireproof porcelain (see p. 259).
1 Heat the dish up with a generous knob of butter and season the dish with salt and pepper.
2 When the butter starts to foam, gently break the egg in.
3 Place the *sur la plat* dish onto a hot baking sheet in a pre-heated oven and allow to set. The egg is cooked when the white is opaque and the yolk just set.
4 Any garnish require should be added at this stage and served immediately. Serve at breakfast, or at lunch or dinner as a hot hors d'oeuvre.

Healthy eating

It has been established that eggs are a useful nutritional component of our diet. Some methods of egg cookery such as boiling and poaching support healthy eating, but when fats are used in the cooking process these have the ability to increase the level of cholesterol in the diet.

To produce a healthier product it is necessary to use polyunsaturated oil such as: corn oil, peanut oil, sunflower oil and safflower oil. This will help to lower the cholesterol levels in the diet.

French fried eggs (*Oeufs frits à la Française*)

1 Two-thirds fill an omelette pan with oil.
2 Place two wooden spoons in the oil and gradually heat up the oil.
3 Slide the egg into medium hot fat about 150 °C (300 °F) using the wooden spoons to shape the egg. The yolk should be enveloped by the white to keep it soft.
4 Remove from the fat when the white is firm. Place the eggs on kitchen paper to absorb any excess fat, then season.

Deep-fried eggs are normally served on toast or on *croute* or with half a grilled tomato and an appropriate sauce e.g. tomato sauce. They can also be used as a garnish to some entrées.

Healthy eating

Salt: when preparing food for today's health conscious public, remember, wherever possible, to cut down on the amount of salt used. People need an average of 3 g of salt per day which will normally come from eating processed food items.

It has been proven that there is a link between high salt intakes and higher resultant blood pressure, causing hypertension.

Omelette

Allow two to three eggs per portion depending on whether you are serving the omelette as a main course or an hors d'oeuvre.

1 Heat the omelette pan and add a knob of butter.
2 Beat the eggs with a fork until well mixed.
3 When the butter is foaming pour all the egg in at once.
4 Assuming that you are right-handed, use your left hand to hold the handle and twist and twirl the pan clockwise a couple of times at the same time stirring with the fork.
5 Bring the mixture from the sides of the pan towards the centre with the fork.
6 By now the base should have set and the remaining mixture should be starting to set; add the filling if required and/or start to roll up the omelette.
7 To roll up the omelette fold in the first few centimetre of the omelette at the back of the pan.
8 Tip the pan forward and then fold over the front of the omelette.
9 Keep easing the omelette forward in the pan and keep rolling it over until it becomes a fat cigar shape.
10 Turn it out onto the warmed service plate. Brush with melted butter and serve immediately.

Rolling up an omelette

Soufflé omelettes

Allow two to three eggs per portion depending on whether the soufflé is to be a starter or a main course.

1 Separate the yolks from the whites.
2 Beat the yolks with a little salt and pepper in a bowl.
3 Whisk the white until stiff (full peak) in a separate bowl. Take care not to over-whisk.
4 Fold the whites carefully into the yolks.
5 Making sure that both the sides and bottom of the hot omelette pan are coated with melted butter, add the eggs.
6 Shake the pan and stir lightly with a fork, at the same time easing the egg away from the sides of the pan. Do not stir too hard or too long.
7 Add a little more butter around the edge of the pan, now toss or turn the omelette over with a palette knife.
8 Carry on cooking and then turn out onto a warmed plate and serve. Again brush the surface with a little melted butter before serving.
9 Serve at breakfast or as a main course or as an hors d'oeuvre at lunch.

Case study

Your menu includes the following items:
- *Scrambled eggs*
- *Soufflé omelette*
- *Eggs en cocotte*
- *Egg sur la plat*

1   Can any of these dishes be prepared in advance?

2   For each dish, list which quality points would apply.

Essential knowledge

To be able to cook egg dishes correctly you must:
- be able to identify the equipment used in the cooking of egg dishes and how they are prepared and used correctly
- know the methods of cookery used to produce the various dishes described
- state the types of meal certain egg dishes are used for
- know the use of eggs in the diet and the effect they have.

What have you learned

- Why should the sides of an omelette pan be curved?
- Why is cream added at the last moment when cooking scrambled egg?
- What is the difference between an *Oeuf sur le plat* and an *Oeuf en cocotte*?
- Most egg dishes are cooked and served to order, name three egg dishes where this does not necessarily apply?
- Name two polyunsaturated oils that can be used to fry eggs in?
- Why is it important to reduce salt in people's diet?

Get ahead

This section has been an introduction into the basic methods of cooking eggs and some simple garnishes used with them. The number of dishes that can be created using eggs is enormous and a brief look in the '*Repetoire de la Cuisine*' illustrates how vast the number and variety of garnishes is. Research the use of eggs in cold dishes, both as a garnish and as a dish in their own right.

Whilst eggs as a course on menus is becoming less fashionable they still have a place on popular menus and can be both attractive and economical. Look at examples of older menus and see how they were used and try to adapt these to the more modem and healthier style of food preparation.

Prepare and cook basic pasta dishes

This chapter covers:
ELEMENT 1: Prepare basic pasta dishes
ELEMENT 2: Cook basic pasta dishes

What you need to do

- Check that preparation, cooking areas and suitable equipment are hygienic and ready for use.
- Check that pasta and other ingredients are of the type, quality and quantity required.
- Cook pasta dishes using appropriate basic cooking methods to meet quality requirements.
- Report any problems identified with the quality of pasta and other ingredients promptly to the appropriate person.
- Prepare and cook pasta using appropriate basic preparation and cooking methods to meet quality requirements.

- Ensure that pasta is combined correctly with other ingredients.
- Finish pasta dishes using appropriate finishing methods to meet quality requirements.
- Ensure that pasta and pasta dishes not for immediate consumption are stored correctly or held at a safe hot temperature.
- Check that preparation and cooking areas and equipment are cleaned correctly after use.
- Ensure that all work is prioritised and carried out in an organised and efficient manner in line with appropriate organisational procedures and legal requirements.

What you need to know

- When preparing and cooking basic pasta dishes, what safe working practices should be followed.
- When preparing and cooking basic pasta dishes, why is it important to keep preparation, cooking areas and equipment hygienic.
- What the main contamination threats are when preparing, cooking and storing basic pasta dishes.
- Why time and temperature are important when preparing and cooking basic pasta dishes.
- What quality points you might look for in fresh and or dried pasta and cooked pasta dishes.
- Why basic pasta dishes not for immediate consumption should be cooled rapidly or maintained at a

safe hot temperature after cooking.
- What basic cooking methods are suitable for different types of basic pasta dishes and how to identify when pasta is cooked to dish requirements.
- What products might be used to substitute high fat ingredients when preparing and cooking basic pasta dishes.
- What fats/oils contribute to healthy eating practice.
- Why increasing the fibre content of basic pasta dishes can contribute to healthy eating practice.
- Why reducing the amount of salt added to basic pasta dishes can contribute to healthy eating practice.

INTRODUCTION

What is pasta?

The basic ingredients of pasta are *wheat* and *water*, with small quantities of other commodities such as egg, oil, tomato, spinach and seasoning. Durum wheat which produces one of the strongest (hardest wheat) flours, is used in the production of fresh and commercial pasta. This strong or hard wheat is used because weaker flours would become soft and sticky when cooked as pasta, and they have a distinctly floury taste.

Pasta – Italian for 'paste'
Durum wheat is grown in mainly the southern and central regions of Italy, the Mediterranean basin, the Middle East, Russia, and the U.S.A. The wheat has a distinct yellow colour, with a protein content of approximately 15%. Durum wheat is made into a *semolina* flour; this is then mixed with water and the tough dough is manufactured by extrusion into an array of shapes and sizes. Much pasta today is dried for the convenience market.

Pasta has been produced since the times of the Middle Ages, the pasta can be made fresh and cooked or can be dried as a form of preservation. Many kitchens buy in dried pasta shapes which are cooked in boiling salted water and finished to the requirements of a particular recipe and dish. Fresh pasta has seen a resurgence of popularity in recent years. Pasta is easy to make, costs little to produce and provides a nutritious meal when combined with herbs, tomatoes, and other fresh vegetables, sauce and cheese.

As fresh pasta is easy and cheap to make, and with a growing awareness of quality fresh foods, many chefs have been prompted to make their own pasta for filling with traditional, classical fillings or to create new dishes. Fresh spinach pasta can have the finished appearance of rich marble and the flavour is distinct, whereas dried spinach and tomato pasta tends not to taste of very much.

There are two important points to remember about pasta:
1 fresh home-made pasta is known as *pasta fatta in casa* (home made pasta);
2 dried *pasta ascuitta*, best quality dried pasta, comes from Naples.

Recent years has seen a growth in the availability of fresh pasta, which takes less time to cook than the dried variety. Specialist producers make a range of fresh pasta, many high street supermarkets stock a good selection of freshly packaged pasta, and pasta products which just need a sauce adding with a few fresh vegetables to produce a true Italian meal.

Healthy eating

Pasta is a good commodity to use for healthy eating because it is low in fat and is a valuable source of fibre in the diet when *wholewheat pasta* is used. Wholemeal, spinach and tomato pasta have higher fibre percentages than ordinary white pasta made with bleached strong flour.

Use recipes with low-fat and high-fibre ingredients. Where a recipe uses flour-based white sauces, cream or cheese, try replacing these with Greek yogurt or low-fat alternatives, and use less salt when seasoning.

Why is pasta an important part of the diet?

Pasta is made from wheat flour (Durum wheat) which has a high protein content (15%). This high protein content makes pasta a good alternative to rice or potatoes, which contain less protein. It is a good food for vegetarian-based diets, where it is used with tomatoes, onions and mushrooms. Pasta also contains starch which is a carbohydrate which the body converts into energy.

Where does pasta feature in our diet?

People eat more pasta today because of the convenience products now available from the supermarket. These shops have used the classic craft of cookery and produced an array of ready-made classical and contemporary dishes to both tempt the customer and rival their competitors – domestic and professional cooks. Pasta is eaten as a daytime snack, light lunch or evening meal; it is used as a garnish for soups and broths; a garnish for main dishes of meat, fish and shellfish or as the essential main ingredient for many vegetarian recipes. In classical cookery pasta is used as a farinaceous course prior to the main meal, often with tomatoes, onion, garlic and fresh herbs such as basil, oregano and marjoram.

ELEMENT 1:   Prepare basic pasta dishes

Organisation when preparing fresh pasta

Equipment used in preparing pasta

Prepare appropriate cutting and shaping equipment ready for use:
- Check that the pasta cutting and shaping equipment is clean and in working order.
- Pasta machines should be kept clean, dry and well brushed: if of the cheaper variety, they are likely to rust if washed. Stainless steel pasta machines should be cleaned after each production or between different types of pasta, i.e. spinach – tomato – white pasta.
- Pasta trays should be kept clean and dusted with semolina to prevent the pasta sticking.
- Use cling film to wrap pasta doughs while resting prior to rolling out.
- If a cloth is used to stretch pasta it should be clean and not one used for trays or wiping down.
- Small cutting and preparation equipment should be cleaned and dried after use before storing away.

- Keep mixers, range tops and ovens clean; make sure you give them a good clean each day after production.
- Prepare the pasta ingredients correctly for each individual dough.
- Check that your scales are accurate and meet existing regulations.
- When ingredient items are low in stock inform the chef or patissière, to re-order to prevent running out.
- Work cleanly and replace lids on storage bins to prevent contamination.

TYPES OF PASTA

- Prepared fresh/dried spaghetti
- Prepared fresh/dried macaroni
- Prepared fresh/dried stuffed pasta
- Prepared fresh/dried lasagne

Fresh and dried pasta

Refreshing pasta in hot water with a knob of butter

Fresh pasta has become more popular in this country over the past 15 years. It is easy, quick and economic to make fresh pasta. Pasta machines are available which enable you to make spaghetti and noodles easily. The availability of ready-made fresh pasta is now widespread and many different shapes, sizes, colours and flavours can be purchased.

GENERAL RULES FOR HANDLING PASTA

1 Use semolina or flour to dust the pasta
2 Pin out the pasta evenly for noodles, cannelloni, ravioli or lasagne.
3 Always rest the pasta well once made.
4 Pasta is best made the night before for the next day.
5 Pasta can be made by hand, or if using a machine, mix on a slow speed using a dough hook.

Do this

- Find out what types of pasta are available from your suppliers.
- Draw up a list of pasta types that require a machine for production and those that can be made by hand.
- Investigate the range of multi-portion ready-made pasta convenience products available to the commercial caterer.
- Why do the southern regions of Italy produce different pasta to the northern regions?

Other ingredients used in the preparation and cooking of pasta dishes:
- vegetables
- stock
- spices
- fish/shellfish
- meat
- cheese
- eggs
- herbs

Vegetables

Vegetables used with pasta can be:
- Mushrooms
- Green Beans

- Celery
- Onions
- Tomatoes (fruit)
- Garlic
- Pimento
- Spring onions
- Peas
- Peppers
- Carrot
- Leeks
- Sweetcorn
- Cucumber
- Beanshoots
- Truffle

Vegetables are used to garnish and flavour pasta, generally when it is cooked or when it is cool. Wash all vegetables well to ensure they are clean and free from grit or dirt. The vegetables should be chopped or cut small to aid quick cooking, sliced or shaped according to the recipe instructions. Pimento needs only heating as it is cooked already. Peppers should be diced and mixed in with the pasta when cooked or cooled.

Mushrooms are used often with pasta dishes; these are sliced and added when the pasta is cooked in the butter for braised rice, then finished in the oven.

Meat

Many different types of meat can be prepared for use with pasta dishes; a few are listed below:
- lean bacon; smoked / green
- ham: raw Parma / cooked
- kidneys: liver / sweetbreads
- lamb: beef / pork / veal
- chicken: turkey / duck
- sausage: pepperoni / garlic

Any meat prepared for use with pasta dishes should be handled carefully. Only better cuts are used, such as chicken breast rather than the legs and smoked raw ham or fillet of beef.

Cheaper cuts which require prolonged cooking are not suitable for use with pasta dishes. Cooked meat such as chicken is prepared by dicing it into a small neat pieces prior to adding it to a pasta dish which may already be cooked, or require further cooking.

Kidneys can be cooked after trimming and preparation and finished with an appropriate sauce for use with pasta e.g. *Turbigo* or *devilled kidney*.

Thin or small cuts of meat are preferable to larger cuts as they cook quickly. Pasta is used as an accompaniment for many meat-based dishes such as curry, fricassée, blanquettes, navarins, or any meat-based dish served in or with a sauce.

Stocks

Stocks are used to cook pasta and can be either:
- Chicken stock
- Water
- Fish stock
- Mushroom stock
- Veal stock

MEMORY JOGGER

When using convenience stocks for pasta and pasta sauces why should care be taken with seasoning?

- Vegetable stock
- Saffron stock
- White stock
- Consommé

Either fresh or convenience stock can be used, but where convenience stock cubes are employed careful seasoning is required as this stock can be salty in its own right. When using saffron stock do not use too much or the colour will be too bright.

Cheeses

Cheeses used with pasta include:
- Parmesan (Parmigiano)
- Cheddar
- Ricotta
- Mozzarella
- Fontina
- Provolone
- Pecorino

Although many of the Italian cheese listed above are used for hot pasta dishes they can also be used in some risotto dishes. Parmesan is the most famous cheese for service with hot pasta and rice dishes.

Parmesan cheese is very hard and is grated by hand or by machine to form a fine powder. This cheese is full-flavoured and used to cohere or top dishes prior to serving. The cheese can be gratinated under a grill to produce a nutty flavour with a good brown colour.

Cheddar does not have the same quality as parmesan and should only be used when parmesan is not available. Grate the cheese to a fine or small size. Parmesan can be purchased pre-grated. You can also purchase an electric grating unit especially for this cheese.

MEMORY JOGGER

Which cheese is usually served with many pasta dishes and why is it grated?

Herbs

Herbs used to flavour pasta dishes are:
- Parsley
- Marjoram
- Coriander
- Thyme (Lemon or common)
- Chervil
- Oregano
- Tarragon
- Basil
- Fennel

Spices

Spices used to flavour pasta dishes are:
- Garam masala
- Cayenne
- Mace
- Cloves
- Turmeric
- Curry powder
- Bouquet garni
- Nutmeg
- Paprika
- Saffron
- Chilli

Eggs

Eggs are used to flavour and garnish pasta dishes; the eggs can be used hard-boiled, as for kedgeree, or mixed as a seasoned liquid and cooked with the prepared pasta.

Care is needed when handling raw egg shell and pasta at the same time as together there is a risk of cross-contamination. After handling egg shells wash your hands well with a sanitiser hand soap.

Fish and shellfish

Fish can be used to flavour or accompany pasta dishes in a similar way to rice dishes, the most famous of these being *paella* from Spain. Prepare the fish by cooking it first and removing all the skin and bone carefully. The fish is either flaked and mixed with the cooked pasta or it can be added raw at the beginning of the cooking process.

Prawns are used with pasta for Chinese dishes and are pre-cooked before being added to the cooking pasta dish. Always wash prawns and all shellfish well before using; check for signs of decay, damage and dirt. Most shellfish can be prepared for use with raw or cooked pasta dishes.

Fungi

Fungi used with pasta can be:

Cep (cèps): a summer and autumn fungus sometimes called the flat mushroom, fleshy flat and brown; choose the smaller young ceps with no mechanical damage.

Chanterelle (egg mushroom): usually found in beech woods summer to winter, they have a tinge of apricot aroma with an irregular funnel shape, egg yellow in colour. The fragile structure needs careful handling and storage.

Morel (sponge mushroom): conical pitted cap with a brown to yellow colour; best used young and fresh.

Mushroom (cultivated as small button, cup or open, flat mushroom): firm and white when small becoming deeper brown in colour as they open to cup and flat forms. They should be unblemished and unbroken with no damage.

Truffle (white or black): Black truffles have a rough hard skin with a strong aroma. They should be even in size. White truffles have a more pronounced flavour, usually from Piedmont they should have a strong scent and taste.

Shiitake (Chinese mushroom): these have a flat top with a small stem, the underside is an egg yellow colour. They are an eastern tree fungus of oak and Skii trees.

Boletus (yellow mushroom): found in conifer woods, it has strong fruity aroma.

Field mushroom (wild mushroom): meadow and pasture land fungi common in late summer and autumn. They are large and small, brown and white in colour.

Mixed and prepared pastes

PROBLEMS WITH PASTA

Freshness
When fresh pasta is produced, keep it dusted with semolina flour and in a dry place. If the pasta is not dusted with semolina flour it will stick together and to the tray it is stored on. Pasta not used immediately can be stored in the fridge for 24 hours but after this time it tends to discolour. When producing any quantity of fresh pasta make the pasta in a number of batches to aid shaping and cutting.

MEMORY JOGGER

When storing fresh cooked or prepared pasta, at what temperature should it be kept?

When preparing dried pasta make sure you stir the pasta in the pan to prevent it sticking to the pan and sticking together. Do not cook more than is required. Pasta should be cooled and stored as soon as possible if it is not to be used immediately.

Quality
Check that the pasta and other ingredients are of the type, quality and quantity required. Prepare pasta using appropriate basic preparation methods to meet quality requirements. Check the date given on the packet by which dried pasta should be used. Any open packets of dried pasta should be stored in an airtight storage container. Fresh pasta purchased shrink-wrapped or vacuum-packed should be stored in the fridge below 8 °C (46 °F).

Essential knowledge

It is important to keep preparation, cooking and storage areas and equipment hygienic in order to:
- comply with food hygiene regulations;
- prevent the transfer of food poisoning bacteria to food;
- prevent pest infestation in preparation, cooking and storage areas;
- prevent contamination of food commodity items by foreign bodies;
- ensure work is carried out efficiently and effectively.

PREPARATION METHODS FOR PASTA

MEMORY JOGGER

Why should waste materials be disposed of cleanly and efficiently?

Mixing
When mixing cooked pasta with other ingredients do not over mix or the pasta can become stodgy. Mix or fold gently to combine sauces and other ingredients according to the recipe instructions.

Draining
When fresh or dried pasta has been cooked, drain using a colander or sieve; take care to drain shaped pasta well to remove excess moisture.

Chopping
When chopping herbs or vegetables always cut the garnish or ingredients to an appropriate size, in keeping with the size of the pasta being prepared. Avoid chopping vegetables and herbs too small or too large unless this is indicative of the style of the prepared dish, ie. ratatouille.

Grating
Grating cheese such as parmesan needs to be done with care and often requires an electric grater. When grating by hand, always allow the cheese to fall into a container from the grater to prevent it from compacting against the grater.

Slicing
Slicing vegetables or fungi should be carried out with care to produce even slices of the same thickness. If the preparation is uneven then some slices might be over cooked while others are still raw.

PASTA SHAPES

Dried pasta shapes (*Pasta Ascuitta*)

Acine di pepe	Peppercorns
Alfabeti	Letters and numbers
Anellini	Small rings

Capellini	Fine hair vermicelli
Cappelleti	Small caps/hats
Coralline	Seashells (small)
Cravatini	Bow-ties (small)
Denti di Cavallo	Tiny horses' teeth
Ditalini	Thimbles (small)
Diavolini	Tiny devils' teeth
Lumachini	Snails (small)
Nociette	Hazelnuts
Occhi de pernice	Partridge eyes
Pisellini	Pea shapes (small)
Semi di melo	Apple seeds
Stelline	Tiny stars
Risone	Grains of rice
Vermicelli	Fine spaghetti

Dried pasta

Long pasta

Fidelini	Very fine spaghetti
Spaghettini	Fine spaghetti
Spaghetti	Standard spaghetti size
Fusilli	Twisted spaghetti
Perciatelli	Macaroni rod (fine)
Perciatelloni	Macaroni cane (small)
Mezzani	Macaroni (medium)
Ziti	Standard macaroni
Zitoni	Large macaroni
Fettuchine	Noodles
Fettuchine verdi	Green noodles
Bavette fine	Noodles (fine)
Linguine	Tongue noodles (narrow)
Mafaldine	Twisted noodles / Small lasagne
Lasagnette	Lasagne (small)
Nastri	Lasagne ribbons (medium)
Lasagne verdi	Lasagne green/spinach
Lasagne	Standard lasagne (wide)

Short and shaped pasta

Occhi di lupo	Macaroni large cut
Gramigna rigata	Macaroni (bent fluted)
Pennini	Macaroni slant cut (pen nib)
Penne	Macaroni slant cut large
Tortiglioni	Spiral short plump
Ruote	Wheel shaped pasta
Farfalle	Butterfly plain or fluted

Filled pasta (after boiling)

Lumache	Snail shape, large
Canneloni – 1	Short fluted, large tube
Canneloni – 2	Flat square or rectangle
Marricotti	Large canneloni

Filled pasta (before boiling)

Agnolotti   Dome shaped stuffed small cushion
Ravioli   Square shaped stuffed cushion
Tortellini   Small stuffed round shape

CONVENIENCE PASTA PRODUCTS

The range of convenience pasta products available frozen, tinned, vacuum packed and dehydrated provides the consumer with a good and varied selection. Prepared fresh pasta can be purchased in large and small quantities, as can true Italian sauces. Multi-pack dishes for commercial and industrial catering are widely available from frozen food wholesalers. New products are appearing all the time as research kitchens compete to market a different selection of classical and contemporary dishes.

Oven-bake pasta dishes to be cooked from frozen are widely available in the ready-meal market, with pasta products across the range. *Pasta ascuitta* (dried pasta) is produced in many of the unusual shapes. Tomato, spinach and wholewheat pasta is readily available from wholesale and retail suppliers. The modern chef has a good supply of different pasta products to assist in the production of good food to satisfy their customers.

Do this

- Collect as many shapes of dried pasta as you can and produce a display with clear labels to denote each pasta.
- Wash out some strong flour to examine the resultant gluten.
- What is the name of the famous Italian sauce made from basil and pine kernels?
- Which three ways can gnocchi be made?
- Design a new filled pasta shape as a group; prepare and produce it and ask others to judge and provide a critical review.

LEGAL REQUIREMENTS TO CONSIDER

Current relevant legislation relating to hygienic and safe working practices when preparing basic pasta dishes states:

Store pasta prepared for cooking carefully and always covered to prevent cross-contamination. It is a legal requirement to. … .foodstuffs must be so placed as to avoid, so far as is reasonably practicable, the risk of contamination. …

HEALTH, SAFETY AND HYGIENE

When preparing pasta and pasta products the following points are particularly important:
- Machines must be set to slow speed before switching on.
- All safety guards must be in place and working correctly.
- Moving parts of machines must be stopped before pasta is removed from the mixing bowl.
- Do not attempt to remove any pasta while the machine is mixing.
- Spillages should be wiped up when they occur.
- Keep fingers away from the machine while forming pasta shapes.

ELEMENT 2:   Cook basic pasta dishes

COOKING FRESH AND DRIED PASTA

Cooking times

Fresh pasta can take between 3–5 minutes for fine pasta such as noodles and 8–12 minutes for cannelloni and ravioli. Dried pasta needs to be cooked longer, approximately 12–15 minutes. Always check the manufacturer's cooking times for dried pasta products. Pasta that is dried has an approximate two-year shelf-life if stored in the correct dry conditions.

General rules for cooking pasta

1   Use a very large pan of fast-boiling salted water.
2   Always add the pasta when the water is boiling and stir to prevent the pasta sticking.
3   Strain immediately after cooking.
4   Pasta is cooked *al dente*: this means 'to have a firm bite'.
5   Do not overcook pasta or the starch will become sticky and make it form a solid mass.

PORTION CONTROL

Allow 90–120 g (3–4 oz) per portion of fresh or dried pasta, smaller quantities for starter courses, less if used as a garnish for soups and other main dishes.

When cooked 90g (3oz) of dried pasta will produce three times the weight 270 g (9 oz).

PASTA DISHES TO BE PREPARED AND COOKED

● lasagne
● canneloni
● macaroni
● spaghetti

Lasagne

Roll the rested pasta as for canneloni (below) and cut into rectangular lengths approximately 10 cm × 15 cm (4 in × 6 in): sometimes the edges are crimped to produce a frill along the length. Cook in plenty of boiling, salted water and drain. All

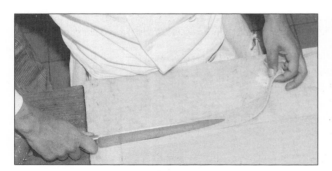

Cutting rolled pasta by hand

Cutting rolled pasta using a rotella

flat pasta benefits from being used as soon as it is cooked, although it is common practice to prepare this complete dish ready for finishing by baking in the oven.

Canneloni – *Pâte a Canneloni*

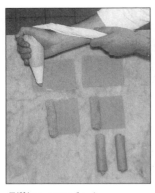

Filling canneloni

- Dust the pasta with flour or semolina and pin out thinly, for the canneloni cut the pasta into 6 cm × 6 cm (3 in × 3 in) squares
- Cook for approximately 12 minutes; drain well.
- Pipe on a suitable filling (see Fillings pp. 278–79) and roll up to form a cylinder.
- Finish the dish according to the recipe and serving requirements.

Spaghetti and macaroni

Both these pasta types are usually purchased in the dried form. Macaroni and spaghetti can be cooked by boiling in salted water in a flat pan and drained. Spaghetti and macaroni both can be finished with or without sauces and garnishes. Look in recipe books for ways in which both are cooked and finished.

Some popular recipe include:
- spaghetti Bolognese
- spaghetti Italienne
- spaghetti au fromage
- macaroni au gratin
- macaroni al forno
- macaroni carbonara

FLAT PASTA

Other types of pasta you will need to be aware of cover:
- noodles
- ravioli
- tortellini
- vermicelli
- fettuchini
- tagliatelli

Basic white egg pasta

Although durum wheat is required for true Italian pasta, pasta can be still be made successfully with a good strong bread flour. The flour is mixed with water, salt and sometimes eggs. Fresh noodle pasta – *Pâte a Nouilles Fraiches*, is also known as tagliatelle or fettuccine, depending on the width of the pasta.

To every 500 g of strong flour you will require 2 whole eggs, 8 egg yolks, 2 table-spoons of oil and 2 tablespoons of water or milk with salt to taste (some recipes only use egg without the water).

1 Sieve the flour and salt onto a marble slab and make a bay.
2 Pour in the mixed egg and/or water and oil.
3 Mix to a clear smooth dough.
4 Cover with a damp cloth or in cling film and rest for 1–2 hours in the fridge.
5 Roll out and dust with flour to prevent the pasta from sticking.
6 Cut or form into the required shape and size according to the pasta type.

Fine noodles cut and shaped by machine

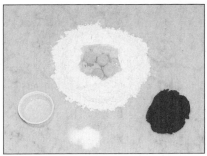

The ingredients for spinach pasta

Noodles

Noodle Paste – spinach (Pâté nouille alla spinaci)
This recipe can be made from the noodle paste using the following ingredients as a guide:

Ingredients
500 g (1 lb)	strong flour
5 g ($\frac{1}{4}$ oz)	salt
2	whole eggs and 8 yolks
75 g (3 oz)	cooked drained spinach (squeeze well).

Method
1 Add the spinach with the eggs as for nouille paste and clear to a smooth paste.
2 Knead this paste well.
3 Wrap and use as required, according to the dish requirements.

Noodle paste – tomato (Pâté à nouille de tomates)
To the basic noodle paste (above) add 50 g (4 oz) of tomato purée when the eggs are added in the bay. Clear to a smooth paste. This paste also needs to be kneaded well, then covered to rest. Cut the pasta into noodles. Mix these with spinach noodles and plain noodles to produce an attractive pasta mix.

Noodle paste with saffron (Nouille allo zafferano)
To the basic noodle paste (above) add 2–3 small sachets powdered saffron when the eggs are added. Work the paste until it is a rich golden yellow colour. Wrap and rest for 1 hour before cutting into noodles.

Noodle paste – wholewheat (Pâté à Nouille)
Wholewheat flour can be used instead of strong flour. Wholewheat pasta has a higher fibre content than basic white pasta, may require slightly longer cooking.

Lasagne pasta (*Pâté à Lasagne*)

The ratio of ingredients can be used for both of the above pasta types, to every 500 g (1 lb) of strong flour 3 eggs, 2 tablespoons of oil (olive or vegetable) salt to taste and 56 ml (2 fl oz) of water. Mix the dough as previously described, wrap and rest in the fridge for 1 hour.

Essential knowledge	When preparing and cooking pasta it is important to use appropriate basic preparation and cooking methods to meet quality requirements in order :
	● To ensure the pasta is mixed and rested for the required amount of time in order to prevent faults in the pasta products.
	● To ensure that the pasta goods are correctly prepared, produced, cooked and finished.
	● Frozen convenience pasta dishes should be thawed and or cooked according to the manufacturer's instructions: never re-freeze thawed convenience products.
	● Pasta for cook freeze should be *undercooked* before freezing.

FILLED/STUFFED PASTA

Meat-based fillings used with pasta

Ragu – (Bolognese)
Ragu is the original name for Bolognese sauce made from lean beef, chicken livers, bacon (fat and lean), carrot, onion, celery, tomato purée, stock and wine (optional), butter, salt and pepper. In this country, commercial chefs produce Bolognese without the livers or wine, according to the customer requirements. Bolognese is used as a sauce and with noodles, spaghetti, tagliatelle, as a filling for cannelloni and lasagne, or as stuffing for ravioli.

Cappelletti (filling)
Cappelletti are a form of small ravioli filled with a meat filling made from lean pork, lean veal, ham, veal brains, carrot, celery, wine or marsala, egg and parmesan cheese, seasoned with nutmeg and freshly ground salt and pepper. It is usual in this country not to include the veal brains. Another Cappelletti filling can be made with chicken breast, butter, mortadella and ricotta cheese, parmesan and egg with the above seasoning. This is put into small rounds of thin pasta, folded in the same way as for tortellini, poached and served either in a broth or on their own.

Any finely cooked minced meat fillings can be used for filling or stuffing; these could be made from soya for vegetarian tastes. Chicken, turkey, duck or game can be used. Many chefs today are experimenting with unusual fillings, as customers become more discerning about good quality food that is fresh, tasty and good value for money. To use sweetbreads as a filling, blanch the sweetbread and refresh, and remove the membrane skin before preparing a fine, seasoned mixture.

Vegetable-based fillings

Spinach and nutmeg – cook some fresh or frozen spinach, drain and squeeze out the moisture and season with salt, pepper and grated nutmeg.

Spinach and ricotta cheese – for filling *tortelli*, a ravioli made in the province of

Parma, approximately 180 g (6 oz) cooked, shaped spinach is mixed with an equal quantity of ricotta cheese, 30 g (1 oz) of fresh parmesan cheese, seasoned with salt, pepper and nutmeg and mixed together with 2 eggs.

Cheese and herb – for filling *Ravioli Caprese (Capri Ravioli)*, this is a mixture of 180 g (6 oz) parmesan cheese, with 180 g (6 oz) Caciotta cheese, a sheep's milk cheese from Tuscany and the southern regions of Italy, (you can use Gruyère instead); add a cupful of milk, 3 eggs, seasoning including nutmeg with basil and or marjoram. Fresh herbs may be used when available, or use freeze-dried which are now of a good quality and flavour.

Fish-based fillings

Fish and shellfish can be made into a *farce* (stuffing) for filling ravioli, cannelloni or tortellini. Seafood is now often used for filling ravioli and makes a tasty meal or starter course. Smoked fish can also be used to make interesting and full flavoured fish fillings for pasta.

Left: piping filling onto the rolled portion of paste
Right: sealing the ravioli
Bottom: cutting the squares using a jigger wheel

Ravioli paste (*Pâte à raviolis*)

The recipes to be found for the production of ravioli vary: some with eggs, some without.

Ingredients

500 g (1 lb)	strong flour
35 ml (1½ fl oz)	oil
100 ml (⅕ pt)	water (just under 95 ml/4 fl oz)
salt	to taste (approximately) 5 g (¼ oz)

Method
1 Sieve the flour and salt, add the oil and water and mix to a smooth paste.
2 Wrap as for noodle paste and rest for 30 mins–1 hour in the fridge.
3 Divide the paste into two equal portions and roll out each portion thinly.
4 Pipe a suitable filling, either spinach, meat or as dictated by the dish requirement, onto the rolled portions at 2.5 cm (1 in) intervals.
5 Wash the spaces between the piped filling lightly with water.

MEMORY JOGGER

Which pasta shapes are filled after cooking?

6 Place over the other rolled portion of paste.

7 Working from the middle, carefully seal down each ravioli removing as much air as possible.

8 When well sealed well cut between each ravioli with a 'jigger wheel' (*rotella*) – a serrated cutting wheel.

9 Dry the squares for approx 1 hour

10 Poach in boiling salted water for approximately 12 minutes, drain and finish according to the dish requirements.

Tortellini

A famous regional dish from Bologna, this filled pasta is shaped by filling with minced veal, chicken, pork, ham and cheese, seasoned with salt, pepper and nutmeg, moistened with melted butter.

The pasta is rolled thinly and cut into 2.5 cm (1 in) squares. The filling is placed in the centre of the square which is folded into a triangle which should be sealed well; fold the opposite ends of the triangle together and seal the ends to form the unmistakable tortellini shape. Cook according to the dish and customer requirements.

OTHER TYPES OF PASTA

Gnocchi

Gnocchi are small dumplings made from a variety of different ingredients.

Gnocchi – potato (Gnocchi di Patate – Gnocchi Piedmontaise)
Potato gnocchi are a speciality from Piedmont. Take 500 g (1 lb) of mashed potato; this can be creamed or, as in Italy, scooped out of a baked or steamed jacket potato, mix, while still hot, with 25 g (1 oz) of butter, 5 egg yolks and 120 g (4 oz) of flour.

Knead gently to form a dough and roll into a cylinder shape about 1 cm (0.5 in) thick).

Cut the gnocchi into small pieces about 1.5 cm long ($\frac{3}{4}$ in long), mould in the hand into small crescent shapes and finish with a fork to mark with a corrugated pattern, place onto a floured tray. Cook a few at a time in boiling salted water. Finish according to the dish requirements.

Gnocchi – semolina (Gnocchi alla Romana – Gnocchi Roman Style)
Made from semolina, milk, eggs, salt, pepper and nutmeg, this pasta is cooked to a thick paste and turned onto a buttered tray and left to cool and set firm; the gnocchi should be approx 2.5 cm (1 in) thick. When cool cut into crescent shapes using a plain 6 cm (3 in) cutter, finish according to the dish and recipe requirements. Plenty of butter is required.

Gnocchi – choux paste (Gnocchi Parisienne – Gnocchi Paris style)
Pipe cool choux paste into boiling salted water, cutting it into small tubes with a damp knife. Poach gently for 10 mins; drain and sautée lightly in butter. Finish according to the dish and recipe requirements.

Polenta

Polenta is made from cornmeal, a finely ground maize which can be yellow or white flour. Polenta resembles gnocchi but is made with water rather than milk.

Polenta can also be made from buckwheat flour grown in America and Europe. This flour contains 15% protein 64% carbohydrate and 13.5% water.

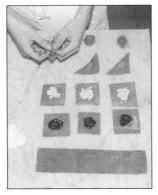

Producing tortellini

MEMORY JOGGER

Name two basic pasta that are stuffed with a filling?

Do this

- Find out about this traditional dish from the Lombardy and Piedmont regions of Italy.
- How is it served?
- What are the classical ways of serving polenta?

CLASSICAL GARNISHES FOR PASTA

Napolitain (Naples Style)	Tomato sauce, tomato concasse and parmesan cheese
Milanaise (Milan Style)	Julienne of ox tongue, mushroom, truffle and tomato sauce.
Bolognese (Ragu)	Tomato concasse, chopped shallots, minced beef, garlic, demi-glace.
Au Beurre	Butter and parmesan cheese
Au gratin	Mornay sauce, parmesan cheese and nutmeg
Niçoise	Tomato concasse, garlic, onion, olive oil, parmesan cheese.
Carbonara	Smoked bacon (*pancetta*) and eggs (sometimes ham and cream)
Romaine (Romana)	Melted butter and parmesan cheese
Norma	Tomatoes, olive oil, onion, garlic, ground pepper, aubergine, basil.
Al Forno	Ragu sauce, mornay sauce, parmesan cheese, layered and baked.
Florentine	Spinach and mornay sauce, parmesan cheese
Sicilienne	Butter, parmesan cheese, purée of chicken livers, chicken velouté.

MEMORY JOGGER

Which cheese is usually served with many pasta dishes and why is it grated?

Do this

- Make a list of the main types of Italian cheese. Find out about fresh parmesan. Why is it the hardest cheese. How is it so finely grated?
- Find out the difference in taste of *pasta verde* and fresh spinach pasta.
- Why should pasta be served as soon as it is cooked rather than re-heated ?

Essential knowledge

- Check the cooking times of fresh and dried pasta.
- Check flour for weevil and contamination from foreign objects; be vigilant, always sieve flour in a clean and hygienic sieve as these can be a source of cross contamination.
- Remember brown pasta will take more time to cook.
- Always use strong flour in the production of fresh pasta.
- Mix the prepared pasta ingredients according to the product requirements.
- Check the type of pasta being produced. Have you weighed the ingredients carefully?
- Remember to sieve the flour and seasoning together.
- If using dried pasta allow longer cooking time.
- If using a mixing machine observe the health and safety regulations.
- Knead, roll, cut by hand or machine, shape and store the pasta product according to product requirements.
- Remove the mixed kneaded pasta cleanly onto a work bench and divide into the required weights.
- Wrap and rest each pasta piece for the required amount of time to aid relaxation of the paste.
- Roll and dust each pasta piece into the required shape and/or thickness according to the dish requirements.

ORGANISATION WHEN COOKING PASTA

- Boil, grill or bake the pasta products for the required time and at the correct temperature.
- When the pasta is cooked, drain well and use immediately; finish according to the customer and dish requirements.
- When the pasta is cooked, drain and refresh in cold iced water, cover and refrigerate, until required.
- Finish, present and store cooked pasta products according to the product requirements, meeting food hygiene regulations.
- Ensure the cooked pasta is cool before storing or assembling with other ingredients and finished products are stored according to requirements.
- Store the finished cooked and cool unused products according to the *Food Hygiene (Amendments) regulations 1990.*

TIME AND TEMPERATURE WHEN STORING PASTA

Always ensure that cooked, finished pasta dishes not used are cool before storing and held below 5 °C (41 °F). Reheated pasta dishes must be heated thoroughly to 70–75 °C (158–167 °F). This temperature should be registered at the centre of the cooked pasta dish to ensure any harmful bacteria are killed.

Pasta to be used for cold salad foods should be cooled to below 5 °C (41 °F) within 90 minutes of being cooked, or sooner.

Do this

- Watch the chef or patissiere producing pasta, particularly filled pasta.
- Check the resting and cooking times and make a list for each different pasta from the range.
- Find out how to recognise when the pasta is *al dente*. What indicators are used?
- Check the classical garnishes and finishing methods for each pasta type.

CUTTING AND SHAPING PASTA

Cutting and shaping by hand
This is very important; each pasta product should be the same size, colour and shape. Dust ring cutters with semolina flour to prevent sticking, use knives carefully and ensure pasta pieces are of the same width and length. Cut and shape pasta in a cool area and store on trays dusted with semolina flour, covered and in the cool room or fridge until required for cooking. Pasta will stick together if not dusted and stored correctly.

Cutting and shaping by machine
Pasta machines must be used carefully according to the manufacturer's instructions and cleaned after each production session. When using small pasta machines roll out the pasta lengths by hand first, to speed up production. Keep fingers away from the shaping rollers. Dust the pasta rollers regularly during shaping to prevent the pasta sticking to the machine parts. Ensure that small pasta machines are secured to the workbench.

COOKING METHODS FOR PASTA

- **Boiling** Most pasta can be boiled in a shallow pan of boiling salted water. Always stir pasta in the initial cooking phase to prevent the pieces from sticking to each other and to the base of the pan.
- **Steaming** Pasta can be heated or re-heated using a low-pressure steamer or one of the new multi-cooker units which use a combination of boiling and steaming.
- **Combination cooking** Combination ovens are used widely to cook and heat pasta and pasta dishes either with steam and convected heat or just as a conventional oven. This might include combination microwave units in some catering businesses.
- **Grilling** Prepared and sauced dishes of pasta are often grilled to gratinate the cheese or sauce topping prior to service. This might be as individual portions or the grilling of multi-portioned trays which are then held at a safe temperature during service.

Cooking pasta

QUALITY POINTS TO CONSIDER WHEN PREPARING AND COOKING PASTA

- **Texture** Do not over-cook pasta or it will swell up and taste very stodgy, it is likely that any sauce used to flavour and garnish the pasta will thin and not appeal to customers. Equally, pasta that is undercooked will be too firm to digest with a leathery texture.
- **Appearance** A pasta dish cooked correctly will have a neat bright appearance, look appetising and entice customers.
- **Aroma** Pasta dishes flavoured with garlic, fresh herbs, tomato and or cheese will have a pleasant aroma. Where old or inferior products are used the pasta will be dull in flavour and appearance.
- **Consistency** Sauces and pasta dishes should have a medium consistency. If sauces are too thin the pasta dish will not be appealing: sauces that are too thick will have the opposite effect.
- **Flavour** The aim in cooking is to produce food that is well flavoured and has a balance of flavours and textures. These concepts develop over time, by trial-and-error you will become an effective cook providing you learn quickly.

FINISHING METHODS

- **Garnishing** Garnish needs to be in keeping with the recipe instructions not too much nor too little but balance overall the appearance of the cooked pasta dish.
- **Gratinating with cheese** Parmesan and mozzarella cheese are popular for gratinating although many operations use cheddar cheese for this purpose. Any

cheese capable of being grated can be used to finish dishes off. Cook under a salamander until the cheese is melted and a light golden brown.

● **Saucing** When adding sauce to pasta do not use too much or too little. Follow recipe instructions to determine how much sauce is required. When using dried pasta you will need to make the sauce thinner to compensate for the volume of moisture absorbed by the pasta during the cooking process.

Do this

- ● Check to see if any cooked and uncooked pasta is stored together. Find out why.
- ● Where is flour stored? How is it stored? Check to see if flour bins are used?
- ● How are pasta machines cleaned in the kitchen? Check to see if they need cleaning.

Case study

You are required to produce a new menu featuring pasta to offer freshly cooked pasta dishes aimed at attracting new customers.
1. *What are the main considerations in planning such a menu?*
2. *How can you utilise this event to gain a marketing advantage?*
3. *Would you use all fresh pasta, all dried pasta or a combination of each?*
4. *What would the equipment implications be for the menu you design? What have you learned?*

What have you learned

1. Why are time and temperature important when preparing, cooking and storing basic pasta dishes.
2. What products might be used to substitute high-fat ingredients when preparing and cooking basic pasta dishes?
3. What fats/oils contribute to healthy eating practices?
4. How can increasing the fibre content of basic pasta dishes contribute to healthy eating practices?
5. How does reducing the amount of salt added to basic pasta dishes contribute to healthy eating practices?

Get ahead

1. Look at ways in which pasta can be used to produce unusual or creative recipes for healthy eating. This could be for vegetarian or vegan diets or for use as menu alternatives.
2. In what ways can pasta be made attractive and appetising without adding extra saturated fat in the form of butter, butter-based sauces or using cheese.
3. How is pasta dried commercially and what types of machines are used to produce the array of unusual pasta shapes.
4. Read up on the provincial types of pasta cookery popular in Italy and Europe. Find out what cookery books are available on this subject.
5. Discuss with your chef how pasta is used to garnish other more complex dishes.
6. Find out what types of pasta machines and cooking systems are available for specialist pasta restaurants. Who supplies such equipment and how costly is it?

Prepare and present food for cold presentation

This chapter covers:
ELEMENT 1: **Prepare and present sandwiches and canapés**
ELEMENT 2: **Prepare and present cooked, cured and prepared foods**

What you need to do

- Prepare ingredients of the correct type, quality and quantity for canapés and sandwiches.
- Prepare the correct cooked, cured and prepared foods and garnishes in the quantity and of the quality required.
- Prepare and present food products according to customer and dish requirements.

- Prepare garnishes according to customer and dish requirements.
- Prepare and finish canapés and sandwiches according to customer and product requirements.
- Store canapés, sandwiches and prepared dishes in accordance with food hygiene regulations.

What you need to know

- What the main contamination threats are when preparing and storing canapés, sandwiches or any foods for cold presentation.
- How to satisfy health, safety and hygiene regulations concerning preparation areas and equipment both before and after use.

- Why it is important to keep preparation and storage areas and equipment hygienic.
- How to plan your work to meet daily schedules.
- How to deal with unexpected situations.

INTRODUCTION

Preparing foods for cold presentation covers a wide area of food preparation; from an *hors d'oeuvre* through to a decorated sweet. Nearly every course on a menu could include food of some description which could be served cold.

This unit is aimed specifically at illustrating the preparation, storage and service of cold canapés and open sandwiches, and the presentation of savoury cooked, cured and pre-prepared foods. It will illustrate the importance of careful and safe production and presentation to ensure the customer is served the best possible product.

ELEMENT 1: Prepare and present sandwiches and canapés

PLANNING YOUR TIME

Producing sandwiches and (especially) cold canapés can be time consuming and requires a great deal of patience and care. Always work in a methodical manner.

Take the following points into consideration.
1   What types of bases, fillings and toppings are to be prepared?
2   What garnishes are to be used?
3   How many of each variety do you need to produce?
4   What equipment will you need to produce and store them?
5   What service dishes will you need for presenting the finished canapés?

You also need to prioritise your order of work, by deciding which jobs you need to do first. Establish the appropriate sequence, then produce the canapés in a methodical manner, beginning with the most time consuming jobs.

PREPARATION AREAS AND EQUIPMENT

When producing canapés or sandwiches you should have all the equipment that you will need close at hand and ready before you start work.

Follow the guidelines given below.
● Make sure that any chopping boards, knives and any other equipment needed is thoroughly clean.
● As you finish each canapé you will need to place it on a tray; work out how many trays you will need and place these near your work bench, ready for use.
● If you are making canapés coated in aspic jelly, make sure you have racks clean and ready to hand for storing the canapés before coating them with aspic.
● When producing sandwiches, ensure that the bread is kept covered to prevent it from becoming dry.
● Make sure that all of the preparation work is completed before starting to make sandwiches. This means checking that the butter is softened, any purées are made, and any tomatoes, cucumber, meats, etc. are sliced ready for production. This will help your work flow and ensure that the sandwiches are made as quickly as possible.
● Remember that foods can be easily contaminated, especially through handling. In order to produce canapés you will need to handle them during production. keep this to a minimum and always work hygienically, using disposable gloves.
● Keep all cooked meat, fish, eggs and vegetables refrigerated until required at a temperature of not more than 4–5 °C (39–41 °F).
● Canapés require delicately cut garnishes, so make sure that knives are clean, sharp and organised tidily next to the cutting board before you start.
● Canapés can be served dressed on a clear set aspic jelly, a dish paper or a doily.

HEALTH, SAFETY AND HYGIENE

Cold canapés and sandwiches are produced from raw, cooked or preserved commodities and once they are made there is no further cooking process involved. For this reason it is essential that they are produced in a clean, safe and hygienic manner. Canapés and open sandwiches are high-risk foods that are easily contaminated by incorrect handling.

Make sure that you are familiar with the general points given in Units NG1, 1ND1 and 2ND22 of the Core Units book. Pay special attention to the section on cross-contamination and the storage of cooked and raw food items.

Remember that lettuce can contain live food poisoning bacteria: always wash it well before use to prevent any soil from contaminating sandwiches or your work area. Watercress must also be washed well, as the water in which it grew may have been contaminated by waste products.

Essential knowledge	The main contamination threats when preparing and storing canapés and sandwiches are as follows:
	● bacteria may be passed to the food from the nose, mouth, cuts, sores or unclean hands
	● cross-contamination can occur through the use of unhygienic equipment, utensils and preparation areas. Always use colour coded boards for chopping, slicing and cutting foods
	● foods stored at incorrect temperatures can become contaminated through the development of micro-organisms. Keep items refrigerated as much as possible
	● frozen foods can become contaminated during the thawing process. Make sure that any frozen foods you need to use are thoroughly and correctly defrosted
	● uncovered finished or partly prepared items can easily become contaminated
	● bacteria may be transferred to food, utensils or preparation areas unless waste is disposed of correctly.

SANDWICHES

Traditionally, sandwiches were two slices of bread and butter with a filling of some sort, but nowadays, due to the availability of many types of breads (continental and local), flavoured butters and a variety of fillings, both hot and cold, sandwiches have radically changed their role and image.

Categories of sandwiches
● Conventional or closed sandwiches;
● Buffet sandwiches;
● Tea sandwiches;
● Pinwheel sandwiches;
● Open sandwiches;
● Hot sandwiches;
● Continental or French sandwiches.

Conventional or closed sandwiches

These are also called lunch box sandwiches. They can be served on any occasion and consist of two slices of bread (either white or brown) spread with a flavoured butter and filled with slices of seasoned meat, poultry, game, fish, shellfish, cheese or eggs. They can be garnished with lettuce, tomato, cucumber, cress, mustard and cress. In the case of meat and fish, certain seasonings like made-up English or French mustard, salt and pepper and mayonnaise may be added where suitable. The sandwich is then cut into triangles (without removing the crust) and served with a suitable garnish.

Ingredients
Bread	Sandwich-bread, white or brown
Butters	Plain, mustard, anchovy, tomato, onion or garlic flavoured
Fillings	Smoked herring, sardines, smoked eel, smoked trout, smoked salmon, prawns, lobster, fresh salmon, boiled ham, smoked ham, tongue, corned beef, roast beef, pork or lamb, salami, liver sausage, roast chicken, duck, game, liver pâté, gammon, eggs and all dry and creamed cheeses.

Garnish   Lettuce, tomatoes, watercress, mustard and cress, spring onion, radish, gherkins, pickled and fresh cucumber, pickles, chutneys, parsley as well as mayonnaise, sauce and ketchup.

Conventional sandwiches are served in bars, cafés, snackbars and restaurants.

Buffet sandwiches

This sandwich is very much the same as the conventional sandwich and similar fillings are used. This sandwich is cut smaller than the conventional sandwich, into neat triangles, fingers or squares with the crust cut off. With these sandwiches, a combination of white and brown bread is often used. Sometimes these sandwiches are given fancy shapes by cutting them with different sizes of pastry cutter, but this method is very wasteful.

Ingredients

Bread	Sandwich-bread, white or brown.
Butter	As for conventional sandwich.
Filling	As for conventional sandwich, plus potted or tinned meat and fish.
Garnish	As for conventional sandwich.
Finish	Neatly remove the crust and cut into even fingers, triangles or squares, or cut with a fancy pastry cutter. Serve on a silver platter with a doily or dish paper; garnish with sprigs of parsley, watercress or mustard and cress.

Pinwheel sandwich

These are sandwiches which are made from loaves of brown or white bread which are sliced thinly lengthways, then spread with butter and filling. The fillings should be thin slices or pastes of meat, fish, vegetables or cheese. The sandwich is then rolled up, chilled and then sliced into individual 'wheels'.

Ingredients

Bread	Brown or white loaves, thinly sliced lengthways.
Butter	Creamy plain butter.
Filling	Thin slices of meat or fish, vegetable paste, cheeses.
Garnish	As for conventional sandwiches.
Finish	Served on a silver platter with doily or dish paper.

Open sandwich

These are also known as Scandinavian or Smorrebrod. Very much the same ingredients as for the conventional sandwich are used, but here the emphasis is on a very attractive and appetising presentation and as the name indicates, the sandwich is open and not covered with a second slice of bread.

Ingredients

Bread	White, brown, rye, olive, pumpernickel, Vienna, French sticks.
Butter	Plain, mustard, anchovy, tomato, onion or garlic.
Fillings	Smoked herring, sardines, smoked eels, smoked salmon, smoked trout, prawns, lobster, caviar, shrimps, boiled ham, smoked ham, tongue, brisket, salami, corned beef, liver sausage, chicken, pheasant, duck, turkey, chicken liver, gammon, eggs, dry and creamed cheese, or any combination of any of these ingredients.
Garnishes	Lettuce, tomatoes, watercress, mustard and cress, spring onion, radishes, gherkins, pickled cucumber, cucumber, pickles, chutney, parsley, mayonnaise, tartare sauce, tomato ketchup.
Service	With large open sandwiches, a knife and fork must be given to the guest who sits down. Where this is not possible, the open sandwich

can be made much smaller, similar to a canapé, or the finished large open sandwich can be cut across with a very sharp knife, without doing damage to its appetising looks.

Hot sandwiches

Hot sandwiches consist of a single or variety of fillings placed between two or more slices of toasted brown or white bread, spread lightly with butter, margarine or mayonnaise. The crusts are usually removed and the sandwich is cut into four triangles.

Toasted sandwiches are served in most catering establishments and fillings can vary from scrambled egg, bacon and fried egg, cooked ham and cheese to the more traditional fillings of chicken breast and minute steaks.

Hot sandwiches are served on a silver platter with a doily or dish paper. Traditionally cocktail sticks are placed in the corner of each triangle to keep the bread and filling in position for service.

Continental or French sandwich

This usually consists of a crusty French stick, cut in half and well buttered with either a single savoury filling and garnished with lettuce, tomatoes, cucumber, mayonnaise, or a mixture of savoury fllings of meat, fish, poultry, game, cheese and eggs, again garnished as above. Cut into small strips, it can easily be picked up with the fingers and eaten in this manner.

Ingredients

Bread	French stick or cottage loaf.
Butter	As for conventional sandwiches.
Fillings	As for conventional sandwiches.
Garnish	As for conventional sandwiches.
Finish	Cut into even, neat strips. Serve on a silver platter with a doily or dish paper and garnish with sprigs of parsley, watercress or mustard and cress.

Healthy eating

Fibre content: apart from people's awareness that they should be eating less animal fat, they are also aware they should be increasing their fibre intake. Therefore it is important that they are offered a choice of breads and bases for sandwiches and canapés. Good digestion is associated with a diet containing large quantities of vegetables, fruit and unrefined cereals. Recent studies have suggested that fibre plays an important role in the prevention of cancer of the colon and heart disease indicating that wholegrain bread and wheat bran bases are best for sandwiches and canapés. You should try to avoid standard white bread or highly-processed products when making sandwiches or canapés.

Case study

You notice that a group of employees preparing a large quantity of sandwiches are taking longer than you expected. When checking the quality of them you also notice that the bread is becoming dry and that some of the fillings are not as fresh as they should be.
1 *What is the possible reason for the bread becoming dry?*
2 *Why are they taking so long in preparing them?*
3 *What could be the cause of the deterioration in the quality of the filling?*
4 *What action would you take to speed the process up and ensure the quality is maintained?*

PREPARING COLD CANAPÉS

Canapés are attractive, bite-sized delicacies that can be served in a number of ways and on many occasions. They can be served as an appetiser before a meal, as accompaniments to drinks at receptions or cocktail parties or as part of a buffet display. Their delicate nature means that they often need to be prepared in advance and stored carefully to ensure that they remain attractive and appealing.

When producing cold canapés, you need to allow for many individual tastes and preferences, so you should aim to offer as wide a variety as possible. This applies both to fillings and toppings and the bases on which they are dressed. In this section we will look at how to produce canapés of different tastes, textures, finishes and garnishes, enabling you to produce an interesting and varied selection.

Dressed canapés

When making canapés we refer to *bases*, *toppings* or *fillings* and *garnishes*. *Bases* refers to the items onto or into which you place the *topping* or *filling*. *Garnishes* refers to the decorations you use to enhance appearance, vary texture and balance flavour.

CANAPÉ BASES

Bread

When bread is used as a base for canapés it is usually toasted, and the slice of toast may be referred to as the croûte. When preparing croûtes, remember the following points:
- once toasted, the bread must be allowed to cool before it is spread with butter. This prevents the butter from soaking into the toast and making it soft
- the butter will act as a seal to prevent any moisture from the topping soaking into the toast

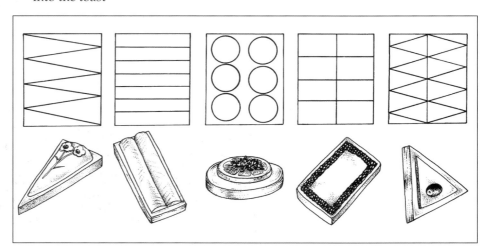

Cuts of toast and their resulting canapé shapes

- the croûte may be cut into shapes either before or after the topping is added; check which method you will need to use. Canapés topped with soft pâtés or cream cheeses may require the toast to be cut first, then the topping piped onto the different shapes. Smoked salmon canapés should be made by placing the salmon over the entire piece of toast, which is then cut to ensure that the croûte is totally covered.
- different types of bread can be used to produce croûtes; different breads give different flavours to the canapés. Likewise flavoured butters can be used to enhance the flavours of the toppings used.

Puff pastry

Puff pastry can be made in the kitchen or bought in either chilled or frozen form (*see page 213*). When purchased made up, the pastry may come either in a thin roll or as a thick block to be shaped and rolled as required. Specific shapes can also be purchased, such as *bouchées* and *vol-au-vent* cases.

Puff pastry is used to make bite-sized canapés in the form of bouchées. These use small vol-au-vent cases of puff pastry as a base for a variety of fillings. The vol-au-vent cases are usually filled with mixtures that have been puréed or diced and then bound with a suitable sauce or dressing. The fillings may be piped or spooned into the puff pastry base.

A puff pastry base, unlike toast, cannot be sealed with butter, so some fillings may cause the bouchées to become soft. Bearing this in mind, always add the filling just before service to keep the pastry as crisp as possible.

Short pastry

Short pastry can be made in the kitchen (*see page 200*) or purchased ready made in frozen or chilled forms. Short pastry is normally purchased in a block which must be rolled and cut to the shape and size required. Frozen pastry should be thawed at room temperature before use. Several pre-cooked items are available, such as small *tartlettes* and *barquettes*, which are ready for immediate use.

A savoury short pastry is used for canapés such as small tartlettes or barquettes. *Tartlettes* are round pastry cases while *barquettes* are 'boat shaped'. For both of these types of canapé the pastry is rolled out thinly and used to line the moulds which are then *baked blind* (i.e. without the filling). Once cooked, the pastry cases can be removed from the moulds, cooled and sealed with butter (which may be flavoured if required). The filling can then be puréed and piped into them; chopped and bound with sauce/dressing and spooned into them; or thinly sliced, rolled or folded and then placed into them.

Barquettes and bouchées

CANAPÉ FILLINGS AND TOPPINGS

Canapés are small, delicate and eaten with the fingers, which must be kept in mind when you are producing them. Sliced items should be thinly sliced and diced items should be finely diced, making them easier to eat.

Any sauces and dressings that you use in the production of your canapés should be used to complement the foods they are being used with; choose and use them carefully to avoid masking or hiding the flavour of the main ingredient.

Cooked and cured meats and poultry

Meats can be thinly sliced and either placed onto the canapé or rolled or folded onto one for attractive presentation. Poultry may be sliced, diced or puréed and then bound with an appropriate sauce to improve the overall texture. Meats and poultry can easily dry out, making them look unappetising: produce them as close to service as possible.

Examples of suitable meats and poultry: salami, pastrami, mortadella, liverwurst, Parma ham, liver sausage, smoked chicken, turkey, duck.

Cured fish and shellfish

As for meats and poultry. these can be sliced, diced or puréed and appropriate sauces used to enhance their appeal. Prawns bound with a cocktail sauce and placed in a bouchée or tartlette are a common feature in canapé presentations.

Examples of suitable fish and shellfish: rollmop herrings, bucklings, smoked oysters, soused herrings, smoked trout, prawns, smoked salmon, smoked fish roe, mussels.

Fresh vegetables and fruits

Fruits and vegetables can provide a variety of textures when used on cold canapés. When using cooked vegetables, it is essential that you ensure that they are well drained; if any liquid is left on the vegetables it will quickly make the canapé bases soft. Salad vegetables should be clean and crisp when used. They quickly become limp once prepared and stored and should therefore be added just before service.

When using fruits, remember that some will discolour very quickly and lose their appeal. Many fruits will also need to have skins, stones and pips removed where they are bitter and inedible.

Eggs

Eggs can be used hard-boiled and either sliced, cut into sections or diced and bound with a sauce such as mayonnaise. Scrambled eggs are also occasionally used for canapés. When using eggs, take care not to overcook and discolour them and remember that they dry out very quickly, so should be stored carefully and produced as close to service as possible.

Hens' eggs are generally used, but quails', plovers' and gulls' eggs are also acceptable and provide interest.

Cheeses

Cheeses, depending on the variety used, can be sliced, diced, grated or even piped onto or into canapé bases. Different types of cheese will provide you with different textures, flavours and colours.

MEMORY JOGGER

When using eggs, why must care be taken not to overcook them!

Do this

- Look at the variety of food items used in your establishment and decide which are acceptable for producing canapés and how they can be used.
- Find out the correct temperatures for storing the food items that you will be using for the production of your canapés.

FATS

The fats used in the production of sandwiches and canapés can vary from establishment to establishment and will depend upon many factors: e.g. the cost of the product, the marketing style of the establishment – vegetarian, healthy eating or traditional. There are many types of fats available today that are designed to look and taste like butter. Butter was the traditional spread used on bread-based products in this country. Margarine was invented in France in the nineteenth century and used as an inexpensive substitute for butter. By law margarine has to contain certain levels of Vitamin A and D.

One of the reasons that so many different types of spreads for putting on bread are available relates to healthy eating. Butter and spreads made from animal fats contain saturated fats which can increase the level of cholesterol in the blood. They are also not suitable for vegetarians.

Vegetable oil based spreads are, in the main, made from polyunsaturated fats which can play a vital role in helping to reduce the cholesterol in the blood. These are suitable to use in vegetarian products. You need to be aware that some margarine or soft margarine spreads contain as many calories as butter. Also some soft margarine spreads contain palm oil or coconut oil and are therefore high in saturated fats.

The reasons that butter or a butter substitute are used on bread-based products is to add flavour, and to add a coating that will stop the topping soaking into the base and/or top of a sandwich or canapé.

Healthy eating

People are now aware that they must reduce their intake of animal fats or saturated fats; so within catering polyunsaturated soft vegetable spreads or low fat mayonnaise are now used in place of butter or margarine, with ingredients such as pesto or mustard as flavouring on sandwiches and canapés. You must always check the contents of your soft spread margarine to make sure that it is made with polyunsaturated oils.

Polyunsaturated oils	Saturated oils
Safflower oil	Palm oil
Sunflower oil	Coconut oil
Corn oil	
Soybean oil	
Cotton seed oil	
Peanut oil	

GARNISHES

Any garnish or decoration used on a canapé should not only enhance the appearance, but should also complement the taste. Taste and flavours must be considered as well as visual appeal.

These decorations should be neat, small, attractive and obviously fresh at all times. Remember that they are to be eaten.

Flavoured butters and mayonnaise can also be used as garnishes: simply pipe them over the canapé.

Suggested combinations for cold canapés

Bases	Filling	Garnish
Toast	Smoked salmon*	Lemon and picked parsley
Toast	Creamed cheese*	Caper and cayenne pepper
Toast	Pâté*	Black olive
Tartlette	Prawn and mayonnaise	Sieved hard boiled egg and chopped parsley
Tartlette	Asparagus	Julienne red pepper
Tartlette	Diced chicken and mayonnaise	Fan of cocktail gherkin
Bouchée	Salmon mousse	Slice of stuffed olive
Bouchée	Creamed tuna	Red fish roe

* These canapés may be glazed with aspic jelly

PREPARING OPEN SANDWICHES

Open sandwiches are a speciality of Scandinavian countries, and make up part of a traditional Smorgasbord buffet.

Today they are served at many different occasions, from light snack, brunch type meals to cocktail receptions. Open sandwiches are usually fairly substantial, they are made from a thick slice of bread covered with a variety of toppings and decorations. The end result should be colourful and appetising. There is no set size for open sandwiches, as this depends on the occasions for which they are being used and the style of service.

Producing open sandwiches

Method

1   Advance preparation and organisation required:
    ● collect all ingredients, making sure that they are of the correct quality and quantity
    ● ensure that you have the correct equipment and that it is clean and any knives are sharp
    ● check that the work area is clean.
2   Cut a slice of bread 0.75 cm ($\frac{1}{4}$ in) thick and spread it with butter.
3   Cover the bread with a base of lettuce or similar ingredient, then cover with the chosen topping making sure that the bread is completely covered. (If you are using hot ingredients do not cover the bread with lettuce.)
4   Season the sandwich with condiments and seasonings.
5   Finish with a suitable decoration.
6   Arrange a dishpaper on a suitable flat service dish and place the open sandwich onto the dishpaper. You may also want to arrange some decoration on the dish. Serve.

A selection of open sandwiches

STORING CANAPÉS AND SANDWICHES

If at all possible, canapés and sandwiches should be made and served immediately. If you do need to store them for a short time, remember that these products are decoratively garnished and so the way you store them must prevent the finished appearance from being damaged.

1 Lay out the canapés or sandwiches on a dish and vacuum pack, making sure that the vacuum is not too great.
  or:
2 Cover the dish with cling film, making sure the film does not disturb the garnish.
3 Store in a chilled environment.

In the past, canapés and sandwiches may have been covered with damp greaseproof paper or cloths while stored for a short time. This practice should be avoided, as it causes the food product to become damp and then to dry out as the covering dries.

What have you learned

1 What are canapés? When might they be served?
2 What are the main contamination threats when preparing and storing canapés and sandwiches?
3 List five toppings or fillings that may be used in preparing canapés.
4 Why is it important to keep preparation and storage areas and equipment hygienic?
5 Suggest four sandwich fillings that might be used at a buffet.

ELEMENT 2: Prepare and present cooked, cured and prepared foods

Any presentation of cold foods should offer a wide range of choice, including fish, meat and poultry and prepared items. The dishes should all be attractively displayed and neatly garnished.

Most meat, poultry, game and fish items can be cooked and presented as part of a cold buffet presentation. Many of these can be cooked by traditional methods (such as roasting or boiling) or *cured*. Cured foods are preserved by methods such as smoking, drying and salting. Smoked fish is often seen on the menu, but smoked meat and poultry items are also becoming more common.

Also included in this Element are the many prepared items available to you as the caterer. These would normally include a wide selection of pâtés, terrines, sausages, salamis and pressed meats.

Stuffed loin of pork

Healthy eating

Salt. When preparing food for today's health concious public remember, wherever possible, to cut down on the amount of salt used. People need an average of 3 g ($\frac{1}{8}$ oz) of salt per day, which will normally come from eating processed food items.

It has been proved that there is a link between high salt intakes and higher resultant blood pressure causing hypertension.

PLANNING YOUR TIME

- Ensure your work area is clean, tidy and clear of all unwanted equipment.
- Collect dishes and any other items you will need for presenting food before you start work.
- Assemble all the required ingredients in a methodical manner.
- Prepare the ingredients according to the recipe you are using.
- Present the items on the service dishes as required.
- Garnish each dish and then store in the appropriate way or serve as required.

HEALTH AND SAFETY

As with any cold food there is always the possibility of contamination occurring. Always:
- ensure work surfaces and areas are kept clean
- handle food items as little as possible
- use plastic gloves when handling food
- keep food refrigerated for as long as you can
- display food under refrigerated conditions whenever possible
- remember and follow good personal hygiene practices and the health and safety regulations.

Refrigeration management

- Raw and cooked foods must be stored in separate areas to prevent cross-contamination and at a temperature not exceeding 4–5 °C (39–41 °F).
- Food should always be covered.
- Bacteria is present in all foods; remember that refrigeration does not kill bacteria, but does help to prevent its growth. It is therefore essential to refrigerate cold items for as long as possible before service.
- When displaying food for service, monitor the temperature to check that a safe temperature is being maintained.
- Ideally any food displayed in a restaurant should be placed behind a *sneeze screen* to protect it while customers make their choice.

Essential knowledge

The main contamination threats when preparing and storing foods for cold presentation are as follows:

- Bacteria may be passed to the food from the nose, mouth, cuts, sores or unclean hands.
- Cross-contamination can occur through the use of unhygienic equipment, utensils and preparation areas. Always use colour coded boards for chopping, slicing and cutting foods.
- Foods stored at incorrect temperatures can become contaminated through the development of micro-organisms. Keep items refrigerated as much as possible.
- Frozen foods can become contaminated during the thawing process. Make sure that any frozen foods you need to use are thoroughly and correctly defrosted.
- Uncovered finished or partly prepared items can easily become contaminated.
- Bacteria may be transferred to food, utensils or preparation areas unless waste is disposed of correctly.

Case study

Three hours before the start of a large garden party in July the head chef asks the staff to start to unload the food off the refrigerated vans. Some of the trays contained smoked salmon canapés, chicken and wild mushroom bouchés, brown bread and asparagus roulades and cheese ramekins all of which are unloaded into a marquee ready to add the final touches.

Approximately eight hours after the end of the party several guests are ill. The signs were diarrhoea and vomiting.

1 What could have caused the guests' illness?
2 What action should the guests take next and why?
3 When notified by a guest that several other guests were taken ill, what should the caterer do and why?
4 Did the caterers do anything that could have caused this problem whilst the food was on site? If so, what would you recommend they did to prevent it happening again?

FOOD ITEMS

Cooked and cured meats

These items include all butcher meats which are usually cooked by roasting or boiling or prepared by curing.

Roasted and boiled joints can be presented as a whole joint (such as a fore rib of beef or whole decorated ham) and carved on the buffet as and when needed. They can also be pre-sliced before service when a quicker service time is required. Cured meats are generally pre-sliced for display.

Cooked poultry

Poultry is normally roasted or poached for cold presentation. Traditionally, poached poultry was presented coated in chaud-froid sauce, attractively decorated and glazed in aspic jelly. This style of presentation is now thought to be unhygienic due to the amount of handling required and the need to keep moving the item in and out of the refrigerator whilst it is being coated and decorated. This means that today poultry is more often roasted and then cut into joints (for chicken or duck), or sliced (for turkey).

Some poultry is poached, removed from the bone, diced and then presented as a salad.

Fish and shellfish

Several fish and shellfish items are eaten cold. These are normally cooked by poaching in fish stock or court-bouillon or eaten in a preserved form, such as smoked, canned or pickled. Fish is a delicate type of food and so is often cooked and presented whole (e.g. salmon or trout). It can also be pre-portioned before or after cooking or prepared into a variety of mousses and terrines.

Preserved fish is generally served as a single hors d'oeuvre or as part of a selection of hors d'oeuvres.

Crustacean items (e.g. crab) are cooked by traditional methods such as poaching and can be served plain or bound with a sauce or dressing.

Some molluscs (e.g. oysters) can be served raw or cooked. For instance, oysters are eaten raw or cooked depending on the recipe you are using; some are even smoked.

Decorated cold salmon

Pre-prepared pâtés and terrines

Today there is a wide range of pâtés and terrines available ready-made, from traditional liver pâté to vegetable and fish terrines. These differ in both flavour and texture. You are able to choose from a very coarse mixture to a fine texture which can be easily spread on toast or biscuits.

For presentation these items can be left whole and garnished, or portioned by slicing or cutting into wedges and displayed on trays or dishes. Care must be taken when portioning to prevent the mixture from breaking and losing its appeal. The surface of pâtés and terrines will also become dry and unappetising if they are incorrectly stored.

All composite items like these are susceptible to contamination. It is essential to store, handle and present them in a safe and hygienic manner.

Healthy eating

Fats and oils. Wherever possible use polyunsaturated oils as opposed to saturated animal or vegetable fats or oils.
Common polyunsaturated oils used in place of saturated fats are: *soya bean oil, groundnut or peanut oil, sunflower oil, olive oil, blended vegetable oil, corn oil, grape seed oil*

Do this

- Visit a local delicatessen and list the variety of cooked and prepared items on offer.
- List joints of meat suitable for cold presentation and how each would be cooked and served.
- Find out which types of preserved fish and shellfish are suitable for cold displays.
- Look through recipe books to find examples of decoration used when displaying cold foods.
- Find out where cooked, prepared items are stored in your kitchen.
- Check the temperature of foods and the environment in which they are stored.

Pre-prepared basic salads

There is a wide variety of pre-prepared basic salads readily available to the caterer. When purchasing these items you should consider several points.
● The container should still be sealed and in a clean and hygienic condition.
● The product purchased should clearly display a sell- or use-by date which has not expired.
● The contents of the container should be easily identified by the label.
● There should not be any unpleasant aroma and the salad should have an attractive and appetising appearance.
● When delivered they should be stored in the appropriate refrigerated area.

Pre-prepared pies

Pre-prepared pies are easily available and offer a wide variety of tastes and flavours using meat, poultry, game, fish and vegetarian ingredients. They are sold as an individual item or in multi-portion sizes to suit you and your customers' needs.
● The pastry should be firm and totally enclose the contents. It should not be broken which would indicate damage and a possible deterioration of the filling.
● All of these items must be hygienically packaged when delivered.
● The temperature should be checked upon delivery and must not exceed 5 °C.
● When received these items must be immediately stored in the appropriate refrigerated area.
● All products should be clearly labelled and indicate a sell- or use-by date.

Herbs

Today it is possible to purchase many fresh herbs at reasonable prices. They are useful to add aroma, flavour and colour to many dishes. The flavour of the herb comes from the oils stored in the stems, flowers and leaves.

To get the best from them you must try to use herbs as soon as they are purchased. You can store them for a couple of days if you wrap them up in damp paper or keep them standing in a bowl of water, stored somewhere dark and cool.

When purchasing herbs it is important that they look fresh, bright in colour and do not show any signs of limpness or bruising as this is an indication that they have been picked some time ago or stored badly. Poor quality goods should then be returned to the supplier, and a credit note requested.

Fresh herbs can be dried to store them but you will loose the effect that you want to create if you try to use dried herbs as a garnish.

DISPLAYING FOOD

Dressings and garnishes

When presenting cold items of food you must ensure that they always look:
● attractive
● appealing
● fresh.

This may mean that if food is on display over a period of time it will need re-dressing and garnishing to maintain the appeal. You should bear certain factors in mind when displaying cold food:
● Look at the colour of the food items being displayed and the garnish being used. It is easy to get carried away and add garnishes that are so colourful the main item is lost.
● Provide a centre point to your display; even if you are only presenting one tray of food there should still be a focal point.

MEMORY JOGGER

What would happen to pre-prepared items if they were not refrigerated whilst being stored?

MEMORY JOGGER

Why is it important that you provide a centre point when displaying a tray of cold meat on a salad bar?

- Ensure your cutting and slicing is even. This makes a more attractive presentation.
- Think about how the customer is going to eat the food being displayed. Will they have a knife and fork, or is it a fork buffet? This will influence the size of portions.
- When decorating the dish ask yourself whether the decoration will be destroyed once the first portion is removed.
- Remember that often the simplest design and decoration is the most attractive and successful.

Types of garnish

Vegetables, salad items and fruits can be prepared and presented in many ways to garnish and decorate food items. They are used to make the presentation attractive but they are also part of the dish and should always be edible. Some vegetables and fruits can be shaped into flowers for an attractive presentation, such as radishes, tomatoes and certain root vegetables. This type of decoration helps to enhance the appearance and appeal of the dish they accompany. You should learn how to prepare some of the items shown below.

Decorative garnishes

STORING PREPARED DISHES

Prepared dishes must be stored in a way that helps to prevent them from becoming dry and unattractive. Store them at a temperature of 1–3 °C (34–37 °F) and keep them covered with cling film or in a vacuum pack.

Essential knowledge	It is important to keep preparation and storage areas and equipment hygienic, in order to: ● prevent the transfer of food poisoning bacteria to food ● prevent pest infestation in storage areas ● ensure that standards of cleanliness are maintained ● comply with the law.

DEALING WITH UNEXPECTED SITUATIONS

● Check that you know what to do in the case of accidents and emergencies. Note all the points given in Unit NG1 of the Core Units book: *Maintain a safe and secure working environment*.
● Be aware of your personal responsibilities within the kitchen. If in doubt, ask your supervisor.

What have you learned

1 What do you need to consider when displaying cold items of food?
2 Why is it necessary to keep cold food items refrigerated?
3 What are the main contamination threats when preparing and storing foods for cold presentation?
4 Why do you garnish cold foods in an attractive manner?
5 At what temperature should you store cold foods?
6 Why do you need to plan your work?

Get ahead

1 Look through the following books for details of particular types of cold canapés, open sandwiches and items that might be included in a cold presentation: *The Larder Chef* (M J Leto and W K H Bode); *Pâtés and Terrines* (F Ehlere, E Longe, M Raftael, F Wessel); *Chinese Appetisers and Garnishes* (Huang Su-Huei).
2 Look through supplier's catalogues to discover the range of convenience items that are available for using as canapé bases.
3 Research the number of slices/pieces you can obtain from various types of breads. This will help you with purchasing and portion control.
4 Look at the different types of hot canapés that can be produced. How do the production and storage methods differ from cold canapés?

Prepare and cook basic shellfish dishes

This chapter covers:

ELEMENT 1: **Prepare basic shellfish dishes**
ELEMENT 2: **Cook basic shellfish dishes**

What you need to do

- Prepare preparation and cooking areas and equipment ready for use, then clean correctly after use.
- Prepare shellfish correctly and as appropriate for individual dishes.
- Combine prepared shellfish with other ingredients ready for cooking where appropriate.
- Cook and finish shellfish dishes according to customer and dish requirements.

- Correctly store prepared shellfish not required for immediate consumption.
- Plan your work, allocating your time to fit schedules, and carry out the work within the required time.
- Carry out your work in an organised and efficient manner, taking account of priorities and any laid down procedures or establishment policy.

What you need to know

- The type, quality and quantity of shellfish required for each dish.
- What equipment you will need to use in preparing shellfish.
- Why it is important to keep preparation, cooking, storage areas and equipment hygienic.
- Why time and temperature are important when preparing and cooking shellfish.

- The main contamination threats when preparing, cooking and storing shellfish and shellfish dishes.
- How to satisfy health, safety and hygiene regulations, concerning preparation and cooking areas and equipment, and how to deal with emergencies.

INTRODUCTION

The coastal waters of Great Britain are rich in quantities of highly regarded shellfish: oysters from Colchester, Dublin Bay prawns, lobsters from Cornwall and Morecambe Bay shrimps. They offer a wealth of opportunity for caterers to express themselves, through exotic dishes or a simple snack. Shellfish are available throughout the year and are prized by gourmets and domestic cooks alike as they may be cooked simply with a minimum of fuss, or with great skill and technique to provide complex dishes; with both types giving maximum flavour and pleasure. Certain shellfish are even consumed in their raw state.

Shellfish may contribute to a well-balanced diet by providing a nutritious food rich in protein and trace elements. They are a consistent source of iodine and also provide calcium, iron and sodium.

Their diversity of use has led to them to appear on menus as appetisers and hors d'oeuvres, soups, fish courses, main courses and as garnishes for many other dishes. They also lend themselves well as delicate items for decorative techniques.

ELEMENT 1:   Prepare basic shellfish dishes

CLASSIFICATION OF SHELLFISH

Shellfish are divided into two main groups for culinary purposes:
- crustaceans
- molluscs.

Crustaceans

Crustaceans have jointed legs and a tough outer layer or shell covering the body known as an *exoskeleton*. The category includes: lobsters, crabs, prawns, shrimps, crawfish and crayfish.

Molluscs

Molluscs are soft-bodied creatures with protective shells which form their habitat. There are three main groups: *gastropods*, *bivalves* and *cephalopods*.

Gastropods have only one shell; this category includes whelks, cockles, winkles, and snails. *Bivalves* have two shells joined together; this category includes mussels, scallops, clams and oysters. The third group, *cephalopods*, are grouped as molluscs even though they have an internal transparent shell or bone (quill) instead of a hard, external shell. This category includes squid, octopus and cuttlefish.

QUALITY POINTS

Shellfish deteriorate quickly after death, making correct handling, storage and use essential if quality is to be maintained and the risk of contamination reduced.

They are best purchased live from a reputable supplier or direct from a wholesale market or port where the catch is landed daily, as this is the only way to ensure freshness. However, most shellfish can be purchased in a frozen state, and these are widely used in the catering industry.

Note that all shellfish must be *thoroughly washed* prior to preparation to remove any surface contamination from their natural habitat.

Live crustaceans

Look for the following points in live crustaceans:
- a fresh salty sea-smell
- a lustrous and fresh looking shell
- black and glossy eyes (not dull or pale)
- no missing claws (on lobsters or crabs)
- fish that are heavy in proportion to their size
- fish that react strongly when handled
- no signs of limpness. Limp-tailed animals should not be purchased as a limp tail is a sign of deterioration
- lobster tails that spring back into place after being uncurled.

Note that the hen or female lobster is distinguished from the cock or male lobster by the breadth of the tail. Hen lobsters have a wider tail to facilitate the carrying of eggs or coral.

Cooked crustaceans

Look for the following points in cooked crustaceans:
● fish that are heavy in proportion to their size
● intact shells, with no visible damage
● no signs of discoloration or unpleasant smells (especially ammonia).
● undamaged packaging (if applicable).

Molluscs

In general, when shellfish with two shells are purchased they must be live. Look for the following points:
● tightly closed shells (this indicates whether they are live or not). If shells are open and do not close when sharply tapped the mollusc is dead and *must be discarded*. This is because it is impossible to know how long the mollusc has been dead and whether or not it is contaminated
● a fresh sea-smell
● an absence of excessive barnacles.

STORING SHELLFISH

Shellfish are highly perishable food commodities requiring immediate storage upon delivery. It is essential to maintain high standards of storage procedures in order to minimise wastage and the risk of spoiling food. Spoilage can lead to the contamination of other foodstuffs and increase the risk of possible food poisoning. The fine eating quality of shellfish is dependant on *absolute freshness*.

Prolonged storage of cooked and raw shellfish must be avoided because of the danger of spoilage and contamination. This could lead to severe food poisoning if eaten, as a long storage period increases the risk of bacterial growth.

Key points

● Store live shellfish at a temperature of 1–5 °C (34–41 °F).
● Keep the live shellfish in its packaging to avoid moisture loss.
● Keep it covered with wet cloths or sacking to retain moisture.
● Do not over-purchase shellfish as the keeping quality is poor.
● Check that shellfish are alive prior to cooking; *reject any dead or dying specimens.*
● Store cooked and uncooked shellfish separately *at all times* to avoid any risk of cross-contamination. Ideally they should be stored in separate refrigerators.
● Cooked shellfish should be covered and stored at 0–3 °C (32–37 °F)
● Frozen shellfish should be defrosted in a refrigerator overnight and used within a short period of time (approximately 12 hours).
● *Never freeze shellfish:* this is a dangerous practice which could lead to severe food poisoning.
● Live lobsters can be kept for short periods of time in a specially aerated salt water tank. The water must be kept at a constant temperature suitable to the lobster.
● All live shellfish should be cooked and served as soon as possible after purchase.

HEALTH, SAFETY AND HYGIENE

The observation of the basic rules of food safety and hygiene as outlined in Units NG1 and 2ND22 of the Core Units book are critical when handling shellfish as you will be handling high risk foods.

Note the following points before you start to prepare or cook any shellfish dish:
● always use the correct colour-coded board for preparing raw shellfish and make

---

Healthy eating

Eating quality of shellfish depends on absolute freshness. Buy daily, store correctly. If in doubt – discard! Take no risks.

---

sure that you use a different board for cooked items. Do not work directly on the table
- keep your chopping board clean using fresh disposable wipes
- use equipment reserved for the preparation of raw shellfish. Where this is not possible, wash and sanitise equipment before use and immediately after use
- work with separate bowls for shellfish offal, bones and usable shellfish: never mix these as the risk of contamination from the offal is high
- always follow the correct storage procedures and temperature controls (see *Storing shellfish*, page 304)
- work away from areas where other cooked foodstuffs are being handled
- keep your preparation area clean. Wash your equipment, knives and hands regularly and employ the use of a bactericidal detergent or sanitising agent to kill bacteria
- dispose of all swabs immediately after use to prevent contamination via soiled wipes.

Essential knowledge

It is important to keep preparation and storage areas and equipment hygienic in order to:
- prevent the transfer of food poisoning bacteria to food
- prevent pest infestation in storage areas
- ensure that standards of cleanliness are maintained
- comply with the law.

PLANNING YOUR TIME

When preparing shellfish, remember that some preparations and cooking methods are more time consuming than others. Some procedures may require only minutes and will be undertaken at a specific time (i.e. cooked to order *à la carte* style), while others may require lengthy preparation before cooking and may employ the use of fish stocks or court bouillons which must be prepared in advance.

Before starting any procedure, identify the basic culinary preparations required to complete the dish to the required establishment standard. Plan your approach to the dish carefully, addressing the longest and most time consuming jobs first. Familiarise yourself with all ingredients, cooking and storage methods involved. Make sure that you have everything in place before you start cooking the shellfish dish.

Do this

- List the shellfish used in your establishment and group them under:
  - crustaceans
  - molluscs.
- Check with your supervisor how and where cooked shellfish and live shellfish are stored in your establishment.
- identify those currently stored as live, cooked or frozen.
- Select a shellfish dish that appears on your establishment menu. Prepare a written time plan, indicating recipe requirements, advance preparation and service requirements.

EQUIPMENT

Before starting to prepare or cook shellfish, decide what equipment and utensils you will need to complete the process. Arrange them, making sure they are clean and ready to use. You may need to use mechanical equipment such as mincers or food processors: do not use this equipment unless you have received instruction from your supervisor and you are also familiar with the safety procedures outlined in Units 1ND1 and 2ND17 in the Core Units book.

Knives

You will need a variety of cook's knives for efficient shellfish preparations. Read Unit 1ND2: *Maintain and handle knives* in the Core Units book, noting especially the safety points on handling knives.

You will need to be familiar with the following knives:

- filleting knife: a thin, flexible blade ideal for following bones closely used for trimming fins and tails in fish preparation
- fish scissors: used for trimming fins and tails in fish preparation
- oyster knife: (a) a round-nosed, short-handled knife with a rigid blade and guard, designed for separating the flat shell from the bowl shell of the oyster

  (b) a sharp pointed rigid short-bladed knife, designed for prising apart the shells of bivalve molluscs
- heavy duty cook's knife: a heavy bladed 25–30 cm (10–12 in) cook's knife for cracking and cutting through shells of crustaceans
- carving knife: a long, thin bladed knife used for portioning raw and cooked shellfish.

TYPES OF SHELLFISH

Crab (*Crabe*)

Edible brown crab

The brown edible crab is a large, powerful crab measuring over 20 cm (8 in) across the shell, although smaller ones are sometimes used. The large claws crack open to provide white meat, while brown meat is found in the shell.

Edible crabs are cooked in boiling salted water or *court-bouillon* (see page 86). Only the *dead man's fingers* (gills), the mouth and stomach bag cannot be eaten and must be discarded.

Crab is available all year round in fresh, tinned and frozen forms. Fresh crabs are best in summer.

Culinary uses
- Dressed crab: here both the brown and the white meat are arranged in the cleaned shell and usually decorated with sieved hard-boiled egg, chopped parsley, paprika, anchovy fillets and capers.
- Soup: bisque, bouillabaisse.
- Pâtés/mousses.
- Hot soufflés.

Lobster (*Homard*)

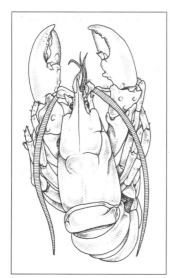

Lobster

Lobsters are a dark, bluish-black colour which changes to red when cooked. They may grow up to 60 cm (24 in) in length and have two powerful claws. The claws contain well-flavoured white meat, as does the tail/abdomen.

Hen (female) lobsters can contain eggs in the form of red roe or coral. Males and females contain creamy parts and greenish liver known as *tomalley*, which is used in soups and sauces. Raw lobster coral can be used for lobster butter to enrich sauces, while cooked lobster coral is often used for decoration and garnish.

The only part of the lobster which cannot be eaten are the intestinal tract and the gelatinous sac behind the eye, known as the *queen*. These parts are discarded because they impart a bitter flavour to the item being cooked.

Lobster is available all year round in fresh, tinned and frozen forms. Fresh lobsters are best in summer.

Culinary uses

- Soup: bisque d'homard.
- Sauce: sauce americaine.
- Grilled lobster: here the lobster is split lengthways before cooking.
- Boiled lobster: this is cooked in court-bouillon and served cold for salads or decorated for presentation on a cold buffet.
- Mouses: hot or cold.
- Soufflés: hot or cold.

Crawfish/spiny (*Langouste*)

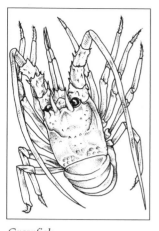

Crawfish are reddish-brown in colour, with tiny spines dotted over the shell and long antennae. They resemble lobsters except that they have no claws, and unlike lobsters, they do not change colour when cooked. Crawfish may grow to 4.5–5.5 kg (10–12 lb) in weight. Most of the flesh is contained in the tail.

They are available fresh (cooked or raw) and frozen. Fresh crawfish are best in summer.

Culinary uses
As for lobster (see above). They are particularly attractive in cold buffet displays.

Crawfish

Dublin bay prawn/scampi (*Langoustine*)

These are rose-grey to pink in colour, and resemble a miniature lobster, growing to 18 cm (7 in) in length. Note that only the tail is used. They are available in the shell or shelled, fresh or frozen raw (encased in an ice glacé), or egg-and-crumbed ready for deep-frying.

Culinary uses
- Deep-frying: egg-and-crumbed.
- Shallow-frying: meunière style.
- Poached: with an accompanying sauce.
- Cooked as for classical lobster dishes.

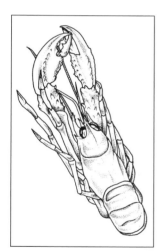

Common prawn (*Crevette rose*)

These prawns are a pale, semi-transparent pink colour when raw, turning an opaque pinkish-red when cooked. Caught from shallow inshore waters, they are 9–10 cm (4 in) in length. They are usually only available cooked (whole or the tail), shelled, frozen or tinned.

Dublin bay prawn

Culinary uses
- Cocktails: usually accompanied by a mayonnaise-based sauce.
- Salads.
- Soup: bisque de crevettes.
- Garnish: for fish, egg, chicken, veal, avocado and rice dishes.

Jumbo prawn/Mediterranean prawn (*Crevette rouge*)

These large prawns grow up to 20 cm (8 in) long and are light-pinkish to yellowish-grey in colour, turning pink-red when cooked.

Culinary uses
- Hors d'oeuvre: whole, unpeeled on a bed of crushed ice.
- Salads.
- Grilled or shallow-fried (raw tails only).
- Barbecued.

Jumbo prawn

Shrimp

Shrimps are smaller than prawns, semi-transparent grey in colour with dark spots, changing to reddish-brown when cooked. They are usually only available cooked, either shelled, smoked, frozen, tinned or dried.

Culinary uses
- Soup: bisque de crevettes.
- Potted in butter.
- Snack item.

Crayfish (*Ecrevisse*)

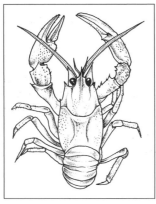

Freshwater crayfish

This is a freshwater crustacean that lives in the muddy banks of rivers, streams and lakes. In appearance it is like a miniature lobster. Crayfish are pale pink in colour, changing to a dark reddish-brown when cooked. Only the tails are eaten, after removing the intestinal tract (failure to do this will render the flesh bitter). This is done by depressing the centre of the tail carapace and removing the middle part of the tail, extracting the gut in one piece. This process should be undertaken while the crayfish is live, although an alternative is to plunge the crayfish in boiling water for two minutes to kill humanely prior to cleaning.

Crayfish are available whole and fresh (cooked and raw) and frozen.

Culinary uses
- Soup: bisque d'ecrevisses.
- Boiled or stewed.
- Mousse: hot or cold.
- Sauce: Nantua sauce.
- Garnish: hot and cold for fish and chicken.

Scallop (*Coquille St Jacque*)

Scallops have a fan-shaped, ribbed, pinkish-red convex upper shell, and a white and flat under shell. The edible parts of a scallop consist of the large, round, white muscle and the orange-red tongue or coral. The frill is discarded. Open (as illustrated below) or purchase opened in half shells.

They are available whole and uncleaned in their shells; freshly cleaned in a half shell or cleaned and frozen as king or queen scallops.

Culinary uses
- Ingredient for *Fruits de mer* mixture.
- Mousses: hot or cold.
- Stuffing for fish, supremes of chicken, escalopes of turkey.
- Poached: deep-poached in court-bouillon.
- Deep-fried and served with a suitable sauce or garnish.

*Left: opening a scallop
Right: separating the white part (muscle) from the pink part (roe)*

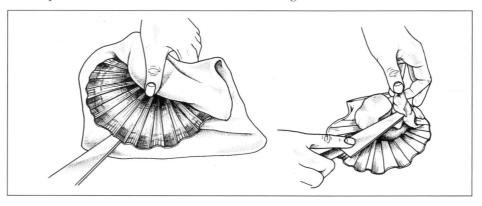

Mussels (*Moules*)

Mussels are bivalves with a bluish-black shell, which has a pointed hinged end.

To prepare mussels, scrape the shells with a knife or brush to remove the barnacles, then place them in clean salted water. They will stay alive for several hours expelling sand and grit. Mussels have a collection of fine hair-like strands, known as the beard, along the hinge of the shell; this must be removed with a knife prior to cooking.

Mussels are available fresh in the autumn and winter, and frozen and pickled all year.

Culinary uses
- Soup: as the main ingredient or as a garnish item.
- Garnish: for rice, pasta and fish dishes.
- Popular mussel dishes include stuffed, curried, grilled, poulette and marinière.

Oyster (*Huître*)

Oysters are the most highly valued of all the molluscs. They are greyish in colour with a rough ridged shell. A number of varieties are cultivated, including the native, Portuguese and Marenne. They should be eaten raw only when there is an 'R' in the month (i.e. they should not be eaten from May to August). Oysters are opened at the hinged end, turned, bearded, and placed into the convex upper shell. Use an oyster knife to open the hinged shell: this has a short broad blade and a large guard to protect the hand.

Culinary uses
- Raw: with lemon juice.
- Garnish: for steak-and-kidney pudding, carpet bagger steak, and fish dishes.
- Oysters can be steamed, poached, grilled and baked, and served with various sauces or garnishes, e.g. Huître florentine.

Do this

- Find examples of the following types of prawn: Dublin bay prawn, common prawn, jumbo (Mediterranean) prawn. Notice the difference in shapes and colour.
- Watch your supervisor preparing mussels.
- Under supervision, prepare some oysters to be eaten raw, using an oyster knife to open the shells.

What have you learned

1 What are the main contamination threats when preparing fresh shellfish?
2 Why is it important to keep preparation and storage areas and equipment hygienic?
3 Why must dead or dying molluscs be discarded? How can you tell if they are dead?
4 How should shellfish be stored?
5 Why is it essential to wash shellfish prior to cooking?

ELEMENT 2: Cook basic shellfish dishes

COOKING METHODS

Shellfish can be cooked by a variety of methods, including: poaching, grilling, barbecuing, boiling, steaming and frying; they are a very versatile food item.

Key points

- Shellfish cooks very quickly and can easily be over-cooked, resulting in loss of flavour and a tough chewy texture.
- If the shellfish is to be served hot, it must be very hot and not held in a cooked state for prolonged periods of time. This would result in dry flesh and poor eating quality.
- Shellfish are highly perishable; stock must be rotated frequently and kept at the correct chilled temperature prior to cooking
- Shellfish have a delicate flavour and lend themselves to simple preparations and garnishes, giving excellent results quite simply.
- Poached shellfish may be poached in fish stock or wine (see Unit 2ND2: *Preparing and cooking fish*, pages 86–9).

MEMORY JOGGER

What is the result of over-cooking shellfish?

Healthy eating
Shelfish are high in cholesterol and not recommended for people's controlled diets.

COOKING CRUSTACEANS

Boiling crustaceans

Lobster, crawfish, crayfish, Dublin Bay prawns and crabs are crustaceans that may be cooked by boiling. Many of the crustaceans purchased are already cooked by this method (or by steaming).

Crustaceans may be boiled in:
- boiling salted water with a little vinegar, or
- boiling pre-prepared court-bouillon (see Unit 2ND2: *Preparing and cooking fish*, page 86).

Key points

- Allow approximately 15 minutes per lb/450 g for the first pound and 5 minutes per lb/450 g thereafter for lobster, crawfish and crabs in the simmering liquid.
- Crayfish require cooking times relative to their sizes; approximately 5–7 minutes will ensure thorough but not over-cooking. Make sure that you have removed the intestinal tract before cooking.
- Crustaceans may be removed from the boiling liquor and allowed to cool, or may be allowed to cool with the cooking liquor. If cooling in the liquor: reduce the overall cooking time by 20 per cent.
- After cooking the crustaceans may be served hot or cold, although further preparation is required for dressing cold lobsters, crawfish or crabs.
- For application and processes of grilling, shallow-frying and poaching see Unit 2ND2: *Preparing and cooking fish*, pages 81, 85 and 86.

Essential knowledge

Time and temperature are important when cooking fresh shellfish in order to:
- ensure a correctly cooked dish. Over-cooking of crustaceans or molluscs will render the flesh tough and dry, and affect the eating quality. Hot shellfish should also be cooked and served immediately: if held for service the quality of the dish will be badly affected
- prevent food poisoning.

Preparing crab for cold presentation

Wash the live crab then plunge it into a boiling court-bouillon for 15–20 minutes according to size. Allow to cool in the liquor.

Dressed crab (illustrated below)

1 Remove the large claws and sever at the joints.
2 Remove the flexible pincer from the claw.
3 Crack carefully and remove all flesh.
4 Remove the flesh from two remaining joints with the back of a spoon. (This is known as *white meat*).
5 Carefully remove and discard the soft under-shell, mouth and stomach bag.
6 Discard the gills (*dead man's fingers*) and the sac behind the eyes.
7 Scrape out the whole of the inside of the shell and pass through a sieve.
8 Season with salt, pepper, Worcester sauce and a little mayonnaise sauce, then thicken lightly with fresh white breadcrumbs. This mixture forms the *brown meat*.
9 Trim the shell by tapping carefully along the natural line.
10 Scrub the shell thoroughly and leave to dry.
11 Dress the brown meat down the centre of the shell.
12 Shred the white meat, taking care to remove any small pieces of shell and then season with salt, pepper and a little vinaigrette sauce.
13 Dress neatly on either side of the brown meat.
14 Decorate as required, using any of the following: chopped parsley, hard-boiled white and yolk of egg, anchovies, capers, olives.
15 Serve the crab on a flat dish, garnished with lettuce leaves, quarters of tomato and the legs. Serve a vinaigrette or mayonnaise sauce separately.

Healthy eating

Use low-calorie mayonnaise for sauces or dressings to accompany shellfish.

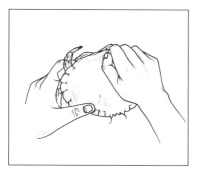

Loosen the shell by hitting the crab firmly on the back

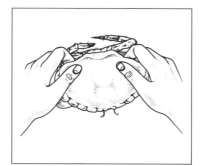

Stand the crab on one side with the shell facing you then force the body from the shell with your thumbs

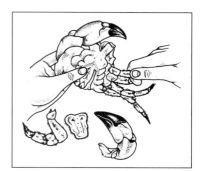

Twist off the tail, legs and claws. Crack open the legs and claws to remove the meat

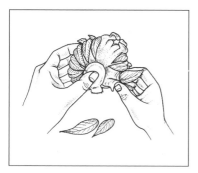

Pull off and discard the gills

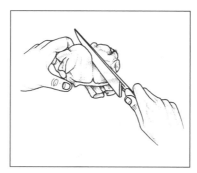

Split the body open down the centre and prise out the meat

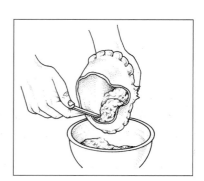

Scrape the brown meat from the shell

Preparing a cooked lobster for cold presentation

1 Twist and remove the claws, legs and pincers from the body.
2 Crack open the legs and claws with a mallet or heavy knife. Remove the flesh and set aside. Discard the blade cartilage in the centre of the claw meat.
3 Split the lobster in half using a large, heavy knife. Draw the knife through the head towards the eye; then reinsert the knife and draw in the opposite direction, cutting completely through the tail or carapace. Pull into two distinct halves.
4 Discard the gelatinous sac in the top of the head directly behind the eyes.
5 Remove and discard the intestinal tract or canal which runs through the middle of the tail flesh.
6 Scrape out the soft head meat and the greenish liver or *tomalley*, and reserve this for other uses (butters, soups or sauces).
7 Remove and discard the gills situated in the cavities to either side of the body.
8 Remove the tail flesh in one piece keeping the red skin-like coating intact. Wash the shells thoroughly, then replace the claw meat into the head cavity and the tail meat into the carapace (this may be sliced or left whole).
9 Garnish to establishment requirements: normally a light salad garnish and lemon, accompanied by a sauce mayonnaise. Chill and serve very cold.

> **MEMORY JOGGER**
>
> Which parts of
> (a) lobsters or
> (b) crabs
> should be discarded
> during preparation?

Preparing lobster for a complex hot presentation

Lobster thermidor (Homard thermidor)

1 Plunge the live lobster into a simmering court-bouillon, reboil and set to simmer gently for approximately 15 minutes per 500 g/1 lb, depending on the size of the lobster.
2 Remove and allow to cool.
3 Place the cooled lobster on a board and remove the claws, cracking and removing the flesh intact.
4 Split the lobster through the centre into two halves, then carefully remove the tail meat and creamy parts. Trim the fingers back to the shell and thoroughly clean.
5 Place on a baking tray and insert in a moderate oven to dry and heat lightly.
6 Slice the lobster tail and claw and reserve.
7 In a suitable pan, sweat some chopped shallots then add white wine, fish stock and bruised parsley stalks. Reduce to a syrupy consistency, remove the parsley stalks and add chopped parsley and double cream.
8 Reduce the mixture further, then add 2 or 3 dessertspoons of high quality Mornay sauce to the required consistency without allowing the mixture to boil
9 Put the pan to the side of the stove and cool slightly, *monter au beurre* (work up with butter) and add diluted English mustard to taste. Correct the seasoning.
10 In a minimum amount of butter, carefully sauté slices of lobster, gently binding with the prepared sauce off the heat.
11 Remove the shells from the oven and coat the base with the sauce. Arrange the lobster neatly in the shell or carapace, coat with sauce and place in a hot oven to glaze. Alternatively, finish under the salamander.
12 Remove the lobster from the tray and serve on a serviette on a polished silver platter

Notes
● At Step 8, a spoonful of hollandaise is often used in conjunction with the sauce Mornay.
● A slice of truffle may be placed on top of the finished lobster; or interspersed with carefully arranged slices of lobster before glazing.

Healthy eating

Use the lower-fat varieties of milk in sauce production.
Substitute polyunsaturates for butter.
Use half-fat cream or natural yoghurt instead of double cream.
Do not enrich sauces with extra egg yolks and butter but achieve glazing by the addition of a little half-whipped low-fat cream.

Grilling lobsters and crawfish

Lobsters and crawfish may be blanched in boiling salted water, split and then grilled, or split from raw, seasoned and grilled. If the lobster is split live the intestinal tract and stomach must be removed prior to seasoning and cooking. If the lobster has been blanched to kill and then split, the cord must be removed at this stage.

Serve grilled lobster with a warm butter sauce or a savoury butter made with lemon and parsley.

Healthy eating

The use of salt in a catering establishment varies according to the individual chef and is rarely measured, but high salt intakes are associated with hypertension which is a major risk factor for coronary heart disease. Therefore, to reduce salt intake, all stocks should be fresh (not bouillons) and seasonings can be achieved with herbs and spices.

Essential knowledge	The main contamination threats when preparing and cooking fresh shellfish are as follows:

The main contamination threats when preparing and cooking fresh shellfish are as follows:
- contamination from the food handler to the food due to inadequate personal hygiene; i.e. from the nose, mouth, open cuts and sores and unclean hands
- cross-contamination from use of unhygienic equipment, utensils and preparation areas
- contamination through products being stored at incorrect temperatures. Fresh, live shellfish are at risk if stored outside the range of 0–3 °C (32–37 °F). They will deteriorate quickly above that temperature and increase the risk of bacterial growth. Live crustaceans should be cooked and cooled quickly in court-bouillon and stored below 5 °C (41 °F) in a separate container away from any raw commodities to avoid cross-contamination
- contamination through incorrect thawing procedures when shellfish is prepared from frozen. Frozen shellfish must be defrosted in a refrigerator and never re-frozen; this is dangerous to health
- use of dead or dying shellfish. These are very likely to be contaminated and must never be used
- contamination through incorrect disposal of waste
- contamination through products being left uncovered.

Cooking shrimps and prawns

Most shrimps and prawns are purchased pre-cooked, the exception being king or *jumbo* prawns which are purchased, fresh or frozen, uncooked in the shell. *Remember:* in shrimps and prawns only the tails are edible.

As for other crustaceans, a court-bouillon may be used for king prawns although grilling, shallow-frying, deep-frying and barbecuing are excellent methods of cooking this delicacy. (See Unit 2ND2 pp. 81–86.)

Menu examples: Grilled king prawns with garlic and parsley butter; Shallow-fried king prawns with bacon and garlic; Deep-fried butterfly king prawns with tartare sauce; Marinaded barbecued king prawns.

The smaller shrimps or prawns are used in an enormous variety of ways, such as: stir-fried with rice and vegetables; cooked in a combination for paella, soups, mousses, soufflés; potted; or simply prepared as a chilled shrimp or prawn cocktail.

Healthy eating
Use natural yoghurt or fromage frais in place of double cream.

Scampi/Dublin Bay prawns

Scampi can be cooked in a number of ways:
- boiled in a court-bouillon and served hot or cold
- shallow-fried à la meunière
- grilled with a savoury butter,
- incorporated into a stir-fry mixture with rice and vegetables
- paoched with a sauce
- (most popularly) coated with flour, egg-wash, breadcrumbs and deep fried, eaten with a tartare sauce. (For deep-frying see Unit 2ND2 pp. 83–84)

When cooking frozen scampi, ensure that the flesh is defrosted thoroughly to permit even cooking, otherwise only surface bacteria may be destroyed.

In the shell, scampi make an excellent garnish and are most handsome on a cold buffet display. The peeled tails are used for kebabs, mousses, mousselines, terrines of shellfish and fish stews. The shells are reserved for use in bisque style soups or shellfish sauces.

MEMORY JOGGER

Why should frozen shellfish be defrosted slowly? How quickly should they be used?

COOKING MOLLUSCS

Cooking mussels

Mussels produce a large quantity of moisture as they cook, so you need only add a small proportion of liquid to assist cooking.

They are cooked or blanched in a pan over a fast direct heat. The mussels are cooked when the shell opens. Take care not to over-cook the mussels as this will affect the texture, rendering them tough and chewy.

The resulting cooking liquor may form the basis of an accompanying sauce, as in the case of the classic *moules marinière*, or the cooked mussels may form a garnish for another dish.

Health and safety
Mussels feed by filtering out nutrients from the water. This makes them subject to contamination by disease organisms and bacteria. It is essential to purchase mussels only from a reputable supplier and to *discard any open shells before cooking*.

MEMORY JOGGER

What should you do with dead or dying mussels

<table>
<tr><td>

Case study

</td><td>

Due to the breakdown of the delivery van, the local fishmonger delivers a batch of fresh mussels late to an hotel kitchen as service is about to commence.

The first order requested is a portion of moules à la marinière *and the young chef – confident the mussels are fresh – immediately cooks and serves the freshly delivered seafood.*

The customer consumes the mussels but telephones the hotel later to say he has been quite ill and the doctor has diagnosed possible food poisoning.

On investigation by the supervisor, it appears the chef cooked the mussels without showing the due diligence and procedures required when handling molluscs.

1   *Who was at fault for this incident?*
2   *What steps, irrespective of pressure of time, should the chef have taken when handling mussels?*
3   *Why are mussels susceptible to contamination by bacteria and how should any suspect shellfish be dealt with?*

</td></tr>
</table>

<table>
<tr><td>

Do this

</td><td>

● Read Unit 2ND2: *Prepare and cook basic fish dishes* (pages 69–91).
● Watch your chef or supervisor preparing a cooked lobster for cold presentation. Notice the equipment and techniques used.
● Find out whether grilled lobsters and crawfish are usually blanched before grilling in your establishment. Ask your supervisor why this decision has been made.
● Check the temperature of stored live shellfish. Does it fall within the correct range?

</td></tr>
</table>

Cooking scallops (*Coquilles St Jacques*)

Scallops may be shallow-fried, lightly grilled or poached and served with a wide variety of sauces. Note that if over-cooked, scallops become tough and chewy and completely spoiled. When poaching it is advisable to detach the orange roe to reduce the cooking time. Owing to of the delicate flavour of the scallop, care must be taken when selecting the appropriate sauce or garnish as the natural delicacy can be lost by the use of strong, over-powering flavours.

Cooking oysters (*Huîtres*)

Oysters are considered by gourmets to be at their best when consumed raw with a little lemon juice. When oysters are to be eaten raw they should not be prepared until they are required for service, in order to retain their flavour and natural liquids.

Preparing oysters
1   Hold the oyster in one hand in a cloth for protection.
2   Using a special oyster knife, prise the shells apart through the natural ligament that joins the shells (this is at the narrow part of the oyster).
3   Discard the flat shell, without spilling the juices, and loosen the oyster in the shell. Serve on a bed of crushed ice.

Oysters may be lightly grilled from raw, wrapped in bacon and used for a savoury (e.g. Angels on horseback), served on toast, or they may be lightly poached and served with an accompanying sauce, (e.g. Oysters florentine). Care is needed in cooking oysters as they become tough if over-cooked or from being stored for a long period at a high temperature.

<table>
<tr><td>

Healthy eating

The fibre content of shellfish dishes can be increased by garnishing with vegetables or pulses, or by thickening the sauces with purées of lentils or broad beans.

</td></tr>
</table>

What have you learned

1 What are the main contamination threats when cooking fresh shellfish?
2 Why are time and temperature important when cooking fresh shellfish?
3 When preparing cooked lobster and cooked crab, which parts are discarded?
4 What effect does over-cooking have on shellfish?

Do this

1 Find out about shellfish not covered by this unit. What types of shellfish are they? How might you prepare and cook them? What part of the world are they from?
2 Find out how long shellfish take to mature in their natural habitat until they are ready for eating. List the different types of shellfish and their growing time.
3 Some shellfish are farmed. Find out which ones are and which ones are not. Why is this?
4 Find out about preserving shellfish. Many shellfish may be frozen but some may be preserved by other methods. What are these methods and which types of shellfish are they used for? Find out how preserved shellfish may be used in menus.

Cook-chill food

This chapter covers:
ELEMENT 1: **Portion, pack and blast-chill food**
ELEMENT 2: **Store cook-chill food**

What you need to do

- Portion and pack food in accordance with laid down procedures.
- Blast-chill and store food in accordance with laid down procedures.
- Seal and label food containers correctly.
- Monitor and record food temperatures.
- Follow stock rotation procedures and maintain accurate records.
- Store cook-chill items under the correct conditions in accordance with laid down procedures.
- Keep accurate records of received, stored and issued food items.
- Carry out your work in an organised and efficient manner in accordance with current regulations.

What you need to know

- The required type, quality and quantity of food for cook-chilling.
- How and when food temperatures are monitored and recorded.
- Why food containers must be sealed and labelled correctly.
- Why food items must be handled carefully and remain undamaged at all stages.
- Why storage areas must be kept clean and tidy, and secure from unauthorised access.
- Why time and food temperatures are important when preparing cook-chill foods.
- How cook-chill food (in food containers) can be transported undamaged to storage areas within a required time.
- How to satisfy health, safety and hygiene regulations concerning preparation areas and equipment both before and after use.
- How to plan your work to meet daily schedules.
- How to deal with unexpected situations.

MEMORY JOGGER

What is the maximum time and at what temperature must food be stored in the cook-chill process?

INTRODUCTION

A cook-chill system is one where food is prepared before it is required, quickly chilled to 0–3 °C (32–37 °F) and stored at that temperature for up to five days until required for sale or consumption. It is a system that is widely used in institutional catering such as hospitals, schools and industrial catering. An increasing number of small commercial outlets within the hotel and restaurant, in-flight and catering-on-the-move sectors also pre-prepare and store finished dishes, and are therefore using the cook-chill system although this is not always recognised as such.

Advantages of the system

Cook-chill production and service offers a number of advantages to the caterer:
- *a cost-effective use of labour.* Food may be prepared within normal working hours when there is the most available labour, and served at times when labour is more expensive; e.g. very early mornings, evenings, weekends and holiday periods
- *flexibility in the menu.* A variety of stored food allows the caterer to offer a greater number of dishes without suffering the potential wastage of conventional cooking and serving systems
- *consistent standards.* A standard quality of dishes is more easily attained because the dishes are produced in bulk before being individually packed. This applies particularly where the production occurs in a large kitchen or Central Production Unit (CPU)
- *fresh-tasting food.* Cook-chilling does not allow ice crystals to form in the foods, so the regenerated (re-heated) dishes are closer to their original taste, colour and texture than is the case with some frozen foods or foods that have been kept hot for a long time
- *fast service times.* The regeneration (reheating) of chilled food is very quick in comparison with frozen products; dishes may be removed from chill cabinets only minutes before being served to the client
- *a lower equipment requirement* in the regenerating kitchen. The kitchens where regeneration takes place (known as satellite kitchens) may be some distance from the Central Production Unit (CPU), and these need less equipment than for conventional cooking and, provided there are strictly enforced guidelines, fewer skilled staff.

Disadvantages of the system

As in any system, there are also a number of disadvantages that have to be considered before adopting a cook-chill operation:
- *high equipment cost at production stage.* The cost of buying the quick chiller, packaging material, general equipment, chilled storage facilities and temperature control and monitoring equipment is considerable
- *the need for a large working space.* Cook-chill usually demands more space than conventional production, both for storage and packing
- *higher risk of food poisoning.* The potential for food poisoning on an epidemic scale is greater, since food is usually cooked in greater bulk than conventional cooking, temperature controls are more critical and there is a possibility of poor stock control. These factors can all cause contamination to take place in large quantities of food
- *risk of nutritional loss.* In addition to the food poisoning potential, if the highest standards of cooking and storage are not employed there is an added danger of nutritional and microbiological decay, reducing the flavour, texture, taste and food value of the dishes
- *detailed re-training* of management and production staff. This is needed to obtain maximum benefit from the system and to avoid the new range of hazards. Such training should include the adoption of Hazard Analysis Critical Control Point procedures in which each step of the process is analysed. This pinpoints potential hazards, allowing management to develop any procedures necessary to minimise risk.

ELEMENT 1:   Portion, pack and blast-chill food

SUITABLE TYPES OF FOOD

Meat and poultry

All meat, poultry, game and offal can be successfully chilled. Meat dishes that need to be sliced, such as roast beef, are cooked, chilled, quickly sliced and then packed for storage. It is not possible to serve rare (acceptably under-done) roast, fried or grilled meat dishes using cook-chill, because the regenerated food *must* be heated to an internal temperature of 70 °C (158 °F) for 2 minutes, thoroughly cooking the food.

Vegetables and fruits

Most cooked potato, vegetable and fruit dishes are suitable for cook-chill, with the exception of dishes containing a mixture of cooked and uncooked ingredients, such as composite salads. Salad items such as lettuce, watercress, radiccio, endive and other leaf salad vegetables should not be incorporated into dishes prior to chilling but added fresh before service.

Vegetables reheated and garnished ready for service

Fish

All pre-cooked fish dishes are suitable for cook-chill processing. However, if modern combination regeneration ovens are not available, deep-fried fish dishes are best cooked completely in the finishing kitchen for direct service to the client.

Sauces and soups

Most sauces and soups are suitable for cook-chill, although those using egg as a thickening agent and those with a high fat content (e.g. hollandaise, béarnaise, mousseline sauces) need particular care when regenerating to avoid curdling. Soups thickened with a liaison (cream and egg yolk), must have this added immediately before service rather than before being chilled.

Egg dishes

Most egg dishes are easily prepared on demand and cook-chill offers no great advantage to the caterer in this area. However, omelettes, scrambled, poached and fried eggs provide a satisfactory end product. Some caterers, particularly airlines, use eggs as part of meals provided as breakfasts.

Desserts

Basic cooked desserts chill well, with the exception of those that rely on batters lifted by eggs, such as soufflés. Mousses, jellies, pastry goods, yeast goods and fruits are all suitable for chilling. Composite sweet dishes that require a hot base with a raw fruit or cream topping are not suitable unless the two components are packed separately.

PREPARING, COOKING AND CHILLING DISHES

Guidelines for these are given in the table on pages 321–23.

HEALTH, SAFETY AND HYGIENE

Note all points given in the Core Units book concerning general attention to health, safety and hygiene. When chilling and storing foods, the following points are particularly important:
- *hygiene:* since the objective of chilling is to extend the life of cooked food, hygienic preparation and storage is of prime importance. The extended life of the product also extends the opportunity for dangerous bacteria (particularly *salmonella, stapylococcus aureus, clostridium perfringens, escherichia coli* and *listeria*) to contaminate and grow in the food
- *time and temperature:* the limits for these must be adhered to very strictly and accurate records of time and temperatures of stored goods must be kept
- *prevention of cross-contamination:* the possibility of cross-contamination between cooked and uncooked foods must be kept to an absolute minimum.

TIME AND TEMPERATURE

Some bacteria leave dangerous toxins in food even after they have been killed; other bacteria can protect themselves from the effects of heat. This is why the strict time and temperature controls exist and why they must be adhered to by all concerned. All of the following points are essential when carrying out preparation within the cook-chill process.
- The temperature of uncooked ingredients delivered from stores must not exceed 5 °C/41 °F for high risk foods such as poultry, fish, dairy produce and cooked and uncooked meat. The temperature of food must not exceed this level during the preparation process.
- The temperature of cooked food must reach a minimum of 70 °C (158 °F) for at least 2 minutes and chilling should commence within 30 minutes.
  Reason: this temperature will kill the majority of harmful bacteria which cause food poisoning. By chilling food quickly to a temperature which prevents bacterial growth, you prevent any remaining bacteria from having time to multiply.
- Food must be chilled down to 3 °C (37 °F) within a period of 90 minutes. Whole joints above 2.5 kg (5½ lb) may not be used for cook-chill processes.
  Reason: 90 minutes is the shortest practical time that the temperature can be achieved in a controlled way. Large joints (being dense and thick) cannot meet this requirement and so cannot be safely reheated.

  See *Temperature recording* in Element 2 on p. 331 for temperature control during the storage and transportation stages.

Preparing, cooking and chilling dishes for the cook-chill process. Source: Regethermic UK Ltd

Food item	Preparation	Cooking	Chilling/chilling times	Portioning plated and bulk
Fish:				
Fried meunière, fish cakes and fingers	Preparation of batter: make a thicker mixture or prepare mixture using an oil batter. By using this type of mixture the batter will not break away from the surface of the fish and it ensures a crisp result	In usual way. As fish is a delicate product do not overcook or flesh becomes flaky, difficult to handle and even dry	Place cooked fish onto cooling racks, lined with damp greaseproof paper (to prevent sticking). Ensure bottom side of fish uppermost. *Do not overlap,* but ensure even circulation of air around product. Time: 20 mins	Turn fish to correct way up and ensure that in both bulk/plated systems, battered goods do not overlap (this prevents sticking). This is not so important with fish cakes, etc. Brush fried fillets with butter for attractive glaze. Garnish with lemon wedges after regeneration. Do not place parsley on lemon, or parsley will turn yellow
Poached		In usual way, making sure fish does not break up during cooking process to spoil presentation	Chill in cooking liquor to avoid surface drying. Cover once chilled to 3 °C (37 °F). Time: 30 mins.	Place onto plate or in dish as usual. Garnish. If product is to be served with a sauce, chill fish and sauce separately and put together when cold.
Red/white meats:				
Roasted	Butcher joints into 2–3 kg (5–7 lb) units if chilling as whole joints	In usual way ensuring correct seasoning. Red meat should be cooked rare/medium rare	Allow meat to cool and place on clean dishes to chill. By chilling whole, meat juices are retained and there is little flavour loss. If chilling slices, chilling times will be reduced but meat liquor will need to be doubled. Time: whole 90 mins sliced 30 mins.	Cut medium slices. Bulk portion: place a few vegetables or meat trimming along one corner of dish. Lay first slice on top of this layer and place each successive slice overlapping the one below. *Never put thick gravy on meat:* use a stock or *jus lié.* Plated: arrange slices of meat to the side of vegetables: do not place them near the edge of the plate. Chicken joints: ensure a large surface area is in contact with the dish and that height of joint is not too great and so touching underside of lid
Boiled	Small joints 2–3 kg (5–7 lb) each	In usual way. Can be immersed in cold water to partly cool. Drain meat prior to chilling	Chill in trays until core temperature 2 °C (35 °F). Best results obtained from joints chilled whole. Time: whole 90 mins sliced 30 mins.	As for sliced roast meats. if required, coat with cold sauce when meat is cold

Food item	Preparation	Cooking	Chilling/chilling times	Portioning plated and bulk
Red/white meats: Grilled (chops, steaks, hamburgers, cutlets)	Ensure chops, etc. are not too thick: average 1–2 cm ($\frac{1}{2}$–$\frac{3}{4}$ in)	Seal under very hot grill to seal in the juices. Cook rare/medium rare. Hamburger mixture is best served the day after cooking	Chill on trays in single thickness to ensure fat drains to the bottom of the dish. Ensure product chilled immediately after grilling. Time: 30 mins	As for roast meat avoid direct contact with the plate/dish. Arrange overlapping items as for roast sliced meat. No food should touch the underside of the lid. Garnish: tomato, water-cress, etc. Do not add liquid
Fried (bacon, burgers, sausages)		In normal way ensuring product is fully cooked. Drain off fat	Chill in single layers to ensure fat drains to the bottom of dish. Once chilled, place in clean dishes to leave excess fat behind. Time: 30 mins.	Bacon: as for sliced meat. Sausages: single thicknesses in contact with the dish. Burgers: overlapped as for chops, steaks, etc.
Stewed/braised (casseroles, stews)	Cut meat into small portions and serve two small pieces instead of one large one to avoid undue thickness	In usual way. Check that flour based sauces are *fully* cooked out. If not, sauce will thicken during regeneration	Chill in bulk maximum thickness of 6 cm (2½ in). If a finer presentation is required, meat/sauce can be reportioned after chilling. Time: 60 mins	Bulk: already portioned prior to chilling. Plated: remove meat from sauce, re-plate then pour sauce over product after skin is stirred in
Offal: Liver, kidneys, etc.	Slice into 1 cm ($\frac{1}{2}$–$\frac{3}{4}$ in) units	Liver: with or without flour. Cook as normal. Drain	Chill on cooling racks to allow blood to drain away from product and thus prevent discolouration and tainting. Time: 30 mins.	As for roast, sliced meats. Coat with cold sauce or onion gravy if required
Binding sauces:	Make sauce thinner than usual (by approx. 15%)	Check that the sauce is fully cooked out. If not flour will absorb more liquid	Chill immediately in shallow bulk dishes. Agitate during chilling to ensure product is chilled to the centre. Time: 30 mins	Never portion sauce into bulk containers with no solid content. When sauce is cold, eradicate skin and nappe over item to be coated. Check none is in contact with lid.
Eggs: Scrambled	Season egg/milk mixture well	Cook until egg begins to scramble, remove from heat and allow heat of product to complete process to a soft/runny consistency	Transfer immediately to shallow dishes and chill. Stir during chilling. Consistency will thicken during chilling as temperature drops. Time: 20 mins	Place cold egg mixture onto cold buttered toast, in pastry case or on fried bread. Procedure is the same for bulk and plated. Depth 2.5 cm (1 in) or less in bulk dishes. If insulating layer not used, regeneration time must be reduced

Food item	Preparation	Cooking	Chilling/chilling times	Portioning plated and bulk
Potatoes: Mashed/creamed	Add more liquid to make product looser and less dense, thereby assisting the chilling and regeneration stages, as the potato absorbs more liquid when chilled. Season well	Bulk: 50–60 mins. Plated: (individual piped potato, etc.): 30 mins.	Prior to chilling either using a piping bag or by filling dish to maximum 2.5 cm (1 in) depth and fluting surface with palette knife or fish slice. Portion to ensure even heat penetration, e.g. by piping or fluting to expose maximum surface area
Roast/sauté/parmentier	Cut potatoes into quite small pieces ensuring adequate heat penetration in specified time	Blanch, finishing off in oven/frying pan/fryer until potatoes are golden brown and crisp. Season	Chill as quickly as possible, avoiding undue heaping of product in dish which extends chilling time. Time: 45 mins.	Ensure seasoning is correct and there is a single layer of potato in dish to ensure adequate heat penetration.
Baked jacket	When selecting potatoes for baking make sure they are not too large: 100–115 g (4–5 oz). This assists regeneration and ensures they are within recommended food depth	Wash/dry. Rub salt into skins as usual. Bake. Rub off excess salt	As quickly as possible avoiding undue heaping of vegetables to ensure product chills fast. If potato is to be filled, chill filling separately. Time: 45 mins.	In normal fashion ensuring potato is not in contact with underside of lid. If potatoes are large, cut neatly in half
Vegetables – rice, pasta, pulses and boiled potatoes: Green and root vegetables. boiled potatoes, boiled rice, pasta, pulses	In normal way. For boiled potatoes ensure potatoes are cut into small pieces (about the size of new potatoes)	In normal way using plenty of salt. Best cooked *en croquant* (with a bite). Once cooked, refresh under cold running water and glaze with a little melted butter/margarine (optional). Re-season.	Product can be chilled following portioning. Ensure rice and pasta are chilled in shallow layers to prevent bottom layers becoming starchy and to minimise chilling times. Time: 15 mins.	When portioning the heavier products, e.g. rice, swede, pasta, etc. remember to ensure depth in dish is within limits to ensure heat penetration. Any vegetable touching underside of lid will dehydrate and discolour. Once drained, re-season and chill
Tinned	Open tin and drain away any unwanted juice or liquid	No need for further cooking in service dishes after portioning.	Although vegetable is already cold it is very important that the item is chilled to 3 °C (37 °F). Time: 15 mins.	As above, reheated as a freshly prepared vegetable
Pastry goods: Savoury, fruit	Best results are obtained from pastry goods cooked in bulk and portioned or enclosed as individual items, e.g. Cornish pasties	In normal way. Maximum thickness 4 cm (1½ in). Check all pastry including crimped edges are contained within depth of dish (i.e. not standing proud)	Chill in bulk before cutting or portioning. Time: 1–2 hours (depending on density of content)	Cut when cold or shrinkage away from cut line will occur, exposing contents. Portion onto plates cold, so contents do not run over plate (they gel when cold). Do not pour sauce over pastry or it will be soggy.

PLANNING YOUR TIME

The time between cooking food, packing it and chilling it is very short. For this reason it is very important that every stage of the portioning-packing-chilling-storing cycle of the operation is planned with precision. Problems will arise if dishes are produced more quickly than they can be packed, or packed when there is not enough chilling or storage space available.

The Operations Manager is responsible for scheduling production so that none of the sections of the operation is required to work above its maximum capacity. Within the schedule, the staff responsible for each operation have to ensure that they have the necessary equipment to perform the task successfully.

Do this

- Find out the colour coding system for preparation equipment in your kitchen. List the colours used and the food items they refer to.
- Check and note the temperatures of your chiller and holding refrigerators. Do they comply with the regulations?
- Look at temperature records and note any changes that have occurred.

Production section

The manager will produce written schedules for each area. An example of a production section schedule is given at the top of the next page.

The volume of the production unit will vary according to the scale of the operation and will be controlled by the Unit Manager.

The production schedule will go to the stores so that the correct quantities of ingredients will be available to the cooks at the time required. The schedule will allow enough time between the preparation of dishes and the arrival of ingredients for the next batch of dishes for cleaning down and sterilisation of equipment and work areas. This is a necessary precaution against cross-contamination.

SELECTING CONTAINERS

When selecting the containers for cook-chill, you need to ensure that they are capable of withstanding both the chilling and reheating process without changing their structure or contaminating the food.

In order to be acceptable:
- containers should be a suitable size for the number of portions that they are required to contain
- the depth of the container should not exceed 5 cm (2 in). Deeper containers will not cool quickly enough

PRODUCTION SECTION: Schedule

DATE . . . . .5 June 1993

SHIFT LEADER . . . . .John Hurst

DISH PRODUCTION (1): BRAISED BEEF

RECIPE NUMBER 26

BATCH NUMBER 15131 E3

QUANTITY . . . . .50 × 5 portion
packs = 250

STORES DELIVERY . . . . .8.00 a.m.

TIME REQUIRED FOR PACKING .12.15 p.m.

DISH PRODUCTION (2): Beef stew and dumplings

RECIPE NUMBER 29

BATCH NUMBER 25132E5

QUANTITY . . . . .50 × 5 portion
packs = 250

STORES DELIVERY . . . . .9.30 am.

TIME REQUIRED FOR PACKING .13.45 am.

- containers should be stackable without compressing the food they contain in order to utilise space fully
- container lids should have an airtight fit or be capable of being sealed with a non-contaminating seal.

The principal packing materials are aluminium foil, paperboard cartons and plastics.

Aluminium foil containers
Aluminium foil containers are ideal for the majority of purposes, as they can withstand high and low temperatures, have excellent moisture retention properties, and are non-toxic, odourless and good conductors of heat. Modern plastic-coated foil is protected against acids and alkalines present in some foods, as the coating prevents the metal in the foil from coming into direct contact with the food. The coating also means that foil containers may be used in microwave ovens.

Paperboard cartons
Paperboard cartons are usually coated with wax, polyester or polythene, none of which are able to withstand the temperatures required for regeneration very effectively. Since this is the cheapest form of packaging it is often used for dishes that are to be served cold.

Plastic containers
Plastics have many of the properties of aluminium but cannot withstand very high temperatures (above 120 °C/248 °F). One particular advantage of plastic containers is that they are available in many attractive designs, enhancing the presentation of food.

PREPARATION FOR PORTIONING AND PACKING

Equipment and clothing

Assemble all the equipment and containers that you need in order to portion and pack the dishes being prepared. Never use the same equipment for portioning/packing and processing raw food as you do for cooking food: the equipment may be contaminated with harmful bacteria that will transfer to the cooked food.

Most establishments using a cook-chill system have colour-coded equipment with highly visible markings that identify the area in which the items are to be used. Make sure that you are familiar with these. The operations management should be very strict in ensuring that this equipment is not moved from one area to another.

This colour-coding is often also used for protective clothing so that staff are confined to one area of a production unit by the colour of the uniform they are wearing.

Before you start

You must have:
- sufficient containers of the correct type
- clean service/portioning equipment
- prepared labels listing the dish name, time, date and batch number
- adequate chiller space for the food you are packing
- adequate cold storage space for the food once it has been chilled
- a probe thermometer in order to check that the dishes are at acceptable temperatures within the required time.

There will be a schedule for the packing section, as for the production section. It will contain details as given in the example schedule at the top of the next page.

MEMORY JOGGER

What is the advantage of using coated foil containers for the packing of food?

PORTIONING, PACKING AND CHILLING FOOD

1 Place exactly the required quantity of food in each container in accordance with your establishment requirements. Scoops, ladles and spoons of the correct size will help you to control portion sizes and will speed up the process. If greater accuracy is required, you will need to use scales.
  Remember:
  - all constituents of the dish to be packed should be ready at the same time
  - you have only 30 minutes to portion and pack before the chilling process must commence
  - composite dishes or meals should be presented as you have been instructed.
2 Completely seal all containers as soon as possible to prevent contamination from the air and deterioration while in cold storage.
3 Fix labels to each container.
4 Pack the containers onto racks for chilling (see *Blast-chilling* on page 329). The size of the racks will depend on the type and capacity of the chiller you are using, but they are usually either transportable racks (e.g. they can be placed onto a trolley) or are specialist trolleys designed to fit completely into the chiller.
5 Check the temperature of the food using a probe thermometer. This should be done twice: once immediately before chilling starts, and then again after the food has been in the chiller for 90 minutes. These times and temperatures should be recorded on a document that is kept for reference.

PACKING SECTION: Schedule

DATE . . . . .5 June 1993

SHIFT LEADER . . . . .Peter Brewer

DISH TO PACK (1): Braised beef

BATCH NUMBER 15131 E3

QUANTITY 250

PACKS . . . . .50 × 5 portions

AVAILABLE TIME . . . . .12.15 p.m.

PACKED FOR CHILLING BY . . . . .12.40 p.m.

PACKING MATERIAL . . . . .Foil pack no. 14
(8 × 6 inches)

CHILLER . . . . .No. 1

CHILL STORE . . . . .East 3

DISH TO PACK (2): Beef stew and dumplings

BATCH NUMBER 25132E5

QUANTITY 250

PACKS . . . . .50 × 5 portions

AVAILABLE TIME . . . . .13.45 p.m.

PACKED FOR CHILLING BY . . . . .14.25 p.m.

PACKING MATERIAL . . . . .Foil pack no. 10
(8 × 8 inches)

CHILLER . . . . .No. 2

CHILL STORE . . . . .East 5

MEMORY JOGGER

How long is allowed between cooking finishing and packing and chilling down to 3 °C?

Essential knowledge

Food containers must be sealed correctly before storage in order to:
- protect the food from airborne contamination
- reduce the dehydration effects of chilling
- improve the presentation of the dishes
- prevent tampering with finished dishes
- prevent the evaporation of moisture when reheated.

Checking and recording the internal temperature of a batch of chilled dishes using a probe thermometer

Portioning and packing different types of food

Sliced meats
Layer the meat slices into the tray so they are overlapping, and continue until the slices completely cover the base of the dish. Keep the layers to a constant level: do not allow some areas to become much higher than others. Thick layers will take longer to reheat. Use gravy sparingly, making sure that some gravy runs under the meat slices. Too much direct contact between the meat and the container will cause the meat to dry out.

Meat, poultry and fish dishes with sauces
Chill both the meat, poultry or fish and sauce before combining. Place the meat or fish in the container and then add the cold sauce. Do not use excessive amounts of sauce: the final dish will be hard to serve and may be unacceptable to the client.

Meat steaks, chops and cuts
Place the meat into the container so that only the heel of the meat comes into contact with the container, making sure that the eye of the meat is protected by any bone.

Meat stews/casseroles
Portion after chilling so that the portions of stew do not form a skin. Do not fill the container too deeply: the food will take longer to re-heat. A depth of 4 cm (1½ in) is recommended.

Egg dishes
Never place cooked egg directly onto the base of a container. Eggs should be placed onto concassée (chopped tomatoes), vegetables or toast to prevent them from drying out.

Left: meat portioned for chilling. Right: chicken portioned for chilling

> **MEMORY JOGGER**
>
> What is the maximum recommended thickness that stews and casseroles may be packed into foil trays?

Vegetables
Place vegetables evenly into the dish, to a depth of approximately 4 cm (1½ in). Vegetables benefit from being tossed in butter or packed with small pats of butter. Make sure that any vegetables are fully drained before packing: any remaining cooking liquor will make the dish difficult to serve and quality will be badly affected.

Potatoes
Whole potatoes should be even in size and shape so that they will all take the same amount of time to reheat. Place them into the container so that all of them have some direct contact with the container. Mashed potatoes should be spread evenly across the base of the container, then fluted on top to allow as much surface area as possible to become exposed.

Pastries

Large pies may be cooked and chilled in the same dish. Individually portioned pies should be removed from their cooking containers and placed flat on the chilling container. Do not allow them to overlap. Make sure that pastry lids are at least 1.5 cm ($\frac{1}{2}$ in) below the lid of the container to prevent them from browning during regeneration.

Essential knowledge	Portions must be controlled when filling packages in order to: ● ensure efficient stock control ● control costs ● ensure that sufficient food is delivered to regenerating kitchens ● ensure that the standard regeneration procedures are safe to use.

Essential knowledge	Food containers must be labelled correctly before storage in order to: ● allow easy identification of the contents ● facilitate stock control ● ensure that correct stock rotation is carried out ● identify product and 'use by' information ● enable Environmental Health Officers to check that food safety laws are being complied with ● allow dishes and products to be tracked.

BLAST-CHILLING

Blast-chilling is a widely used and efficient method of reducing the temperature in cooked and, in some cases, raw food at a very rapid rate. Correctly packed food is stacked onto racks or trolleys designed to fit into the chillers. Powerful fans then circulate the air in the chiller over refrigerated elements and the food within the cabinet. The movement of the air reduces the insulating properties of the air on the surface of the food and allows the temperature of the food to be reduced very rapidly.

Sensors placed in the food and in the cabinets stop the cooling process as soon as the desired temperature is reached, at which point the chiller becomes a holding cabinet. In large scale operations chillers normally have two doors. The first connects the kitchen to the chiller, allowing the containers to be loaded into the chiller. The second leads from the chiller directly into the chill storage room, allowing the products to be removed from the chiller without any possibility of temperature variations occurring.

Left: blast chillers
Right: racks being withdrawn from a blast chiller

KEY POINTS IN THE PREPARATION OF FOOD FOR COOK-CHILL PRODUCTION

- Raw materials must be of the highest quality and freshness and must be stored separately from the finished product.
- Cooking must take place as soon as possible after preparation to avoid spoilage, deterioration or bacterial growth.
- Any cook-chill food bought in must always be constantly evaluated and checked to see that it meets quality control standards. Food must be received at the right temperature, date coded and transferred to the right temperature/conditions.
- Where appropriate, cook-chill food may be removed from cartons before storing. All cook-chill food must be transferred after production/transportation into hygienic storage containers.
- Every effort must be made to avoid the risk of cross-contamination during preparation and storage.
- The highest standards of personal hygiene must be maintained at all times.

<table>
<tr><td rowspan="7">What have you learned</td><td>1</td><td>What period of time is allowed between the completion of cooking and the start of the chilling process?</td></tr>
<tr><td>2</td><td>What are the critical temperatures for cooking and storing cook-chill food?</td></tr>
<tr><td>3</td><td>What are the particular hazards of the cook-chill system of catering?</td></tr>
<tr><td>4</td><td>What is the maximum length of time allowed between the cooking and the consumption of chilled foods?</td></tr>
<tr><td>5</td><td>Why must portions be controlled when filling packages?</td></tr>
<tr><td>6</td><td>Why are time and temperature important when preparing cook-chill food'?</td></tr>
<tr><td>7</td><td>Why must food containers be sealed and labelled correctly before storage?</td></tr>
</table>

ELEMENT 2:   Store cook-chill food

Trolley racks in the chill store awaiting despatch

TRANSPORTING THE CHILLED FOOD

The cooked food needs to be transported from the chillers to the regenerating kitchens. As mentioned earlier, the food will have been packaged and packed into racks designed to fit the chillers (*see Blast-chilling, page 329*). These racks are also used to move the stock from one location to another; i.e. into a holding store and then on to the satellite kitchen where the food will be finally prepared for service. This method reduces the handling of the actual containers to a minimum, which in turn reduces the possibility of damage occurring. When smaller quantities of prepared and chilled food have to be delivered to a store or kitchen, the batch is put together in the chill store on a suitable number of racks before being transported.

The speed of transportation is critical as every minute spent out of the cold store produces an increase in temperature in the food which can dramatically reduce the shelf-life of the product (see *Temperature recording, page 332*). Refrigerated vans or lorries must be used for any transportation other than a very short internal distance. Note that the same regulations apply to refrigerated vehicles as apply to non-mobile refrigerators; temperatures have to be checked and recorded regularly.

Chilled food must be transported correctly in order to;
● minimise temperature variations in the product
● reduce the risk of contamination
● eliminate loss of stock due to damage
● comply with hygiene and food safety legislation.

Accepting food for storage

No food other than chilled and packed food should be stored in a chill store, as to do so would create a risk of cross-contamination. It would also result in more people needing access to the store which can cause problems with temperature control.

Chilled food must not be accepted for storage unless it is properly labelled. The information on the label must include:
1 the description of the contents (i.e. the name of the dish)
2 the date and time of chilling
3 the batch number
4 the storage temperature
5 the use-by-date.
6 Additional information may include nutritional information which may be necessary for special medical diets (e.g. 'Salt free' or 'Gluten free') or for religious purposes (e.g. 'Kosher prepared' for those of the Jewish faith or 'Halal prepared' for Muslims).

Temperature control during storage, transportation and regeneration

The following points are essential during these stages:
● Food must be stored at 0–3 °C (32–37 °F) for no longer than five days. This includes the day that the food is re-heated.
  Reason: most, but not all bacterial activity stops at these temperatures. After five days there could still be some build up of harmful bacteria, which could dangerously contaminate the food when re-heated.
● When food is distributed from the cold store the temperature must be carefully monitored. If the temperature of the food exceeds 5 °C (41 °F) at any time, it must be consumed within 12 hours or discarded. If it exceeds 10 °C (50 °F) it must be either consumed immediately or discarded.
  Reason: food stored at 5–10 °C (41–50 °F) will allow bacteria to multiply slowly, but provided the preparation and packing is carried out under strict hygienic control the food will remain safe for a maximum of 12 hours. As soon as 10 °C (50 °F) is reached, the food rapidly becomes dangerous if not consumed immediately.
● When removed from chilled storage the cooked food must be re-heated to an internal temperature of at least 70 °C (158 °F) and held at this temperature for at least two minutes.
  Reason: this temperature will kill most dangerous bacteria present.

MEMORY JOGGER

What information should be recorded on the label of cook-chill food?

MEMORY JOGGER

Why should food that has reached a temperature of 10 °C be consumed immediately or discarded?

TEMPERATURE RECORDING

The temperature of cook-chill food must be monitored throughout the production and storage processes in order to keep the risk of contamination by food poisoning bacteria to a minimum. It also makes it possible to trace any problems back to a particular process or department.

The importance of accurate and continuous temperature monitoring cannot be stressed enough. Temperatures should be taken at the core (the centre of the thickest part) of the product using an accurate probe thermometer which should be cleaned with a special 'once-only' bactericidal wipe after each use. It is also essential that the thermometers used are recalibrated regularly to ensure that they are accurate. Records must be kept of these recalibration tests.

The temperature of food should be taken with an accurate probe thermometer at the following times:
- *on delivery* (maximum: 5 °C/41 °F for high-risk foods such as meats, poultry, fish, dairy produce, cooked meat)
- *when moved* from the stores to the cooking area (maximum: 5 °C/41 °F for high-risk foods such as meats, poultry, fish, dairy produce, cooked meat)
- *when cooked* (minimum 70 °C/158 °F for two minutes)
- *when chilled* (maximum 3 °C/37 °F)
- at regular intervals *whilst in storage* (maximum 3 °C/37 °F; if higher than this temperature see page 331 for action)
- *when moved* from chill to service area (maximum 3 °C/37 °F)
- *when re-generated* (minimum 70 °C/158 °F for two minutes)
- *whilst held for service* (minimum 70 °C/158 °F).

Under current hygiene regulations these temperatures must be recorded with dates, times and the name of the person responsible. Each establishment will have standard procedures to ensure that the records are maintained and filed for future reference for every batch of food that is stored and moved or served. These records must be made available to the Environmental Health Inspector on demand.

Essential knowledge	It is important to monitor and record food temperatures regularly in order to: ● prevent contamination from incorrect storage conditions ● ensure flavour and texture is maintained.

STOCK CONTROL SYSTEM

MEMORY JOGGER

What is meant by stock rotation when dealing with items stored in a chill cabinet or room?

All food must be booked into the cold store and the label details recorded. Items required for dispatch should be those that were first into the store (the oldest). An efficient stock rotation system should be in place to ensure this. No food should be held in the cold store longer than five days. Daily checks should be made both through records and actual stocks held to ensure that no out-of-date items are held.

The temperature of the cold storage unit, irrespective of size should not vary from the range of 0–3 °C (32–37 °F). If there is no continuous recording system for the cold store, the temperature should be checked at least twice a day and the time and temperature recorded on a log. These records should be safely filed in accordance with the established procedures of the cook-chill unit.

Before sending food for consumption, the chilling date should be recorded on an issue sheet. Food dispatched for consumption may need to be transported in refrigerated containers in order to keep the temperature below 3 °C (37 °F).

Stock rotation procedures must be followed in order to:
● prevent damage or decay to stock
● ensure that older stock is used before newer stock.

LIMITING ACCESS

Access to cold storage areas should be restricted to authorised people only. This can be achieved by using digital locks with special codes, personal keys or systems using a 'booking in and out' log. In large chill stores there must be some form of external indication that there is someone in the store and when they entered the store. This is essential as unnecessary opening of the cold store door would destabilise the temperature and could cause spoilage of the food. There is also, as with any store, the need to guard against the possibility of theft.

Remember that a cold store is a hazardous area and unauthorised people may become trapped inside with very serious consequences.

Storage areas must be secured from unauthorised access in order to:
● prevent pilferage or damage by unauthorised persons
● prevent injury to unauthorised persons
● prevent unnecessary opening of store doors, which would destabilise the temperature.

LEGAL REQUIREMENTS

A caterer or manufacturer should bear in mind the potentially dangerous (and expensive) outcomes that contravention of the *Food Safety Act of 1990* can entail. The labelling of products, recording of temperatures, attention to hygiene and training given to staff would all form part of a legal defence known as *due diligence*, should any legal action be taken. For this to be a successful defence, the caterer must convince the court that all the requirements of the law have been complied with and that the 'accepted customs and practices' of the trade have been carried out. It is also necessary to have documentary evidence to prove these facts.

Do this

● Find out how times and temperatures are recorded in your establishment, and how long the records are kept.
● Find out who is authorised to enter your cold store.
● What safety precautions apply to your unit?

KEY POINTS: CHILLING, STORING AND REGENERATING FOOD

● The rate of cooling will depend on a number of factors including container size, shape or weight, and food density and moisture content.
● The product must be labelled with the date of production and a strict system of stock control must be in operation. Temperature control during food distribution should be very closely monitored.

- For reasons of safety and palatability the food must be re-heated (regenerated) quickly. It must be heated to 70 °C (158 °F) for 2 minutes, maintained at a minimum temperature of 63 °C (145 °F) and consumed within 15 minutes.
- Food to be served cold should be consumed within 4 hours after chilled storage.
- No food, once re-heated, should be returned to the refrigerator. All uneaten, re-heated food should be destroyed.

DEALING WITH UNEXPECTED SITUATIONS

Establishments that operate cook-chill systems will have detailed operational procedures for dealing with every non-routine situation.

The most important of these will deal with refrigeration faults in chillers and storage, abnormal temperature variations in storage, below-specification deliveries from suppliers, and incorrect processing times.

It is your responsibility to be aware of these procedures and to follow them exactly; there is no margin of error.

Case study

Just before lunch is due to be served, a senior supervisor of a satellite kitchen of your cook-chill operation phones to tell you that a 4-portion tray of chicken casserole, delivered the previous evening, when opened after re-heating today smells 'off' and is very watery.

1   What instructions would you give the supervisor?
2   What would you do with the remainder of batch that is in your chiller?
3   How would you check to see what caused the problem?
4   What records would you have to assist you in tracking down the cause?

What have you learned

1   What temperature should chilled food be stored at?
2   What does *First in – First out* mean when referring to controlling stocks of chilled food?
3   Why must stock rotation procedures always be followed?
4   Why is it important to monitor and record food temperatures regularly?
5   Why must storage areas be secured from unauthorised access at all times?

Get ahead

1   Find out about the full legal requirements concerning the production of cook-chill food. You will find the relevant laws included in *The Food Safety Act 1990* and *The Food Hygiene (Amendment) Regulations 1990 and 1991*. You should also read the following government guidelines: *Guidelines on Cook-chill and Cook-freeze Catering Systems (Dept of Health 1989)*, *Guidelines on the Food Hygiene (Amendment) Regulations (Dept of Health 1990 and 1991)*.
2   You can find out more about cook-chill generally by reading *A Guide to Cook-chill Catering* by Lewis Napleton (International Thomson Business Publishing, 1991).
3   To increase your understanding of contamination threats and how to prevent these, you may like to read *Croner's Food Hygiene Manual* (Croner Publications, 1991).

Cook-freeze food

This chapter covers:
ELEMENT 1: **Portion, pack and blast-freeze food**
ELEMENT 2: **Store cook-freeze food**

What you need to do

- Portion, pack and cover food in accordance with laid down procedures.
- Blast-freeze and store food in accordance with laid down procedures.
- Seal and label food containers correctly.
- Rotate stock holdings and use stock according to date ordered.
- Monitor and record food temperatures in accordance with laid down procedures.
- Keep accurate records of received, stored and issued food items.
- Carry out your work in an organised and efficient manner in accordance with current regulations.

What you need to know

- The type, quality and quantity of food required.
- Why portions must be controlled when filling packages.
- Why time and temperature are important when preparing cook-freeze foods.
- Why food items must be handled carefully and remain undamaged.
- Why it is important to monitor and record food temperatures regularly.
- How to transport food containers undamaged to storage areas within a required time.
- Why food containers must be sealed and labelled correctly.
- Why it is important to follow stock rotation procedures and maintain accurate records.
- Why storage areas must be kept secure from unauthorised access and kept clean and tidy.
- How to satisfy health, safety and hygiene regulations concerning preparation areas and equipment both before and after use.
- How to plan your work to meet daily schedules.
- How to deal with unexpected situations.

INTRODUCTION

A cook-freeze system is one where food is prepared well before it is required, quickly blast-frozen to $-18\,°C$ ($0\,°F$) then stored at that temperature until required for sale or consumption (for up to 3 months). It is a system that has been adopted by many institutional caterers such as hospitals, schools and industrial catering facilities.

MEMORY JOGGER

What is the maximum temperature at which deep frozen food may be stored in a cook-freeze operation?

Advantages of the system

Cook-freeze production and service offers a number of advantages to the caterer:
- *a cost-effective use of labour.* Food may be prepared within normal working hours when there is the most available labour, and served at times when labour is more expensive; e.g. very early mornings, evenings, weekends and holiday periods
- *greater buying power.* Centralising production brings economies of scale and economies in buying supplies in larger bulk

- *flexibility in the menu.* A variety of stored food allows the caterer to offer a greater number of dishes without suffering the potential wastage of conventional cooking and serving systems
- *consistent standards.* A standard quality of dishes is more easily attained because the dishes are produced in bulk before being individually or multi-portion packed
- *fresh-tasting food.* Blast freezing does not allow large ice crystals to form in the foods, so the regenerated (re-heated) dishes are closer to their original taste, colour and texture than is the case with foods that have been kept hot for a long time. The large ice crystals that form when foods are frozen slowly (as in a domestic freezer) puncture the structures of foods and cause loss of texture, moisture and flavour. It is therefore essential to buy specifically designed fast-freezing equipment for this task
- *fast service times.* The regeneration (re-heating) of frozen food is relatively quick using microwaves and combination ovens; dishes may be removed from freezer cabinets close to service times
- *a lower equipment requirement* in the regenerating kitchen. The kitchens where regeneration takes place (known as satellite kitchens) may be some distance from the Central Production Unit (CPU), and these need less equipment than for conventional cooking. Provided there are strictly enforced guidelines, they may also need staff with fewer culinary skills.

Disadvantages of the system

As in any system, there are a number of disadvantages that have to be considered before adopting a cook-freeze operation:
- *high equipment cost* at production stage. The cost of buying the quick freezer, packaging material, general equipment, frozen storage facilities and temperature control and monitoring equipment is considerable
- *the need for a large working space.* Cook-freeze usually demands more space than conventional production, both for storage and packing
- *higher risk of food poisoning.* The potential for food poisoning on an epidemic scale is greater, since food is usually cooked in greater bulk than conventional cooking, temperature controls are more critical and the possibility of poor stock control can all allow contamination to take place in large quantities of food
- *high energy consumption.* The consumption of energy (i.e. electricity) for freezing and storage is considerable
- *high cost to prevent damage to ecology.* The refrigerant gases are not environmentally friendly (they contain CFCs) and the alternative less damaging refrigerants are considerably more expensive
- *detailed re-training* of management and production staff. This is needed to obtain maximum benefit and to avoid the new range of hazards. Such training should include the adoption of Hazard Analysis Critical Control Point procedures in which each step of the process is analyzed. This pinpoints potential hazards, allowing management procedures to be developed to minimise risk.

ELEMENT 1: Portion, pack and blast-freeze food

EQUIPMENT

The equipment used in the production of food for the freezing process can be the same as that for a conventional kitchen. Ideally, however, in order to reduce the possibility of cross-contamination between cooked and raw food, the kitchen should be designed so that the stores delivery point, stores and preparation areas are separate from the cooking, packing and freezing areas.

The packaging area can vary in size and complexity, from a full conveyor system for a large production unit to a table in a side room for a small system. Within the packaging area there must be a sealing system which will remove the air from the container holding food and then seal it. The sealers are usually manually operated, with the exception of large capacity cook-freeze operations. There are three methods of fast-freezing foods.

- The first method involves freezing food in a blast freezer, where sub-zero air is blown over the surface of the food to be frozen.
- The second method uses an immersion freezer, where the containers are immersed in a cabinet containing liquid refrigerant. Until recently the liquid refrigerant normally used was liquid nitrogen or carbon dioxide, but other special liquids have now been developed which are easier and cheaper to use.
- A third method which may be used for high capacity systems involves the use of tunnel freezers, which move the containers along a tunnel whilst they are sprayed with a very cold refrigerant.

The system used depends on the design capacity of the cook-freeze unit.

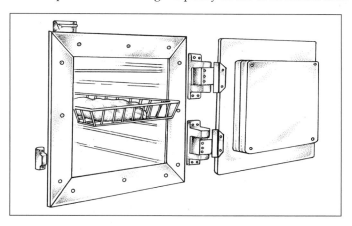

A blast-freezer

In order to set up a cook-freeze unit on a commercial basis, the unit must be capable of producing and selling around 5,000 meals per day. This inevitably means that a specialist fleet of vehicles will be required to distribute the meals at sub-zero temperatures to a number of geographical locations not necessarily very close to the production unit.

SUITABLE TYPES OF FOOD

Meat and poultry

Most meat, poultry, game and offal can be successfully frozen. Meat dishes that need to be sliced, e.g. roast beef, are cooked, chilled, quickly sliced and then packed for freezing and storage. It is not possible to serve rare (acceptably under-done) roast, fried or grilled meat dishes using cook-freeze because the food must be cooked to an internal temperature of 70 °C (158 °F) and held at this temperature for two minutes.

Cooked pork can be frozen but pork tenderloin has a very high water and internal fat content and a relatively short storage life (a maximum of eight weeks). Ground pork (e.g. sausages) and cured pork (bacon and ham) have a very short life even at the frozen temperature of −18 °C/0 °F (a maximum of four weeks). The preservatives used in these products can oxidise during their storage life and develop a rancid flavour or smell which is not dangerous but tastes unpleasant.

Vegetables and fruits

Most cooked potato, vegetable and fruit dishes are suitable for freezing with the exception of composite salads containing cooked and raw ingredients. Salad items that are to be eaten raw such as lettuce, watercress, radiccio and endive should be added fresh to dishes just before service, not added to dishes prior to freezing.

The delicate cellular structures and high water content of these leafy foods causes changes in the food during the harsh freezing process which badly affects the flavour and textural quality (they become limp). The use of conventional garnishing material after regeneration (re-heating) is recommended in order to prevent customers from becoming 'processed food fatigued'.

Fish dishes

All pre-cooked fish dishes are suitable for cook-freeze processing. Salmon, crab, lobster and shrimp/prawn dishes freeze well but have a shorter shelf life.

Sauces and soups

Most sauces and soups are suitable for cook-freeze although those with egg as a thickening agent and those with a high fat content (e.g. hollandaise, béarnaise, mousseline sauces) will need particular care when regenerating to avoid curdling. Soups thickened with a liaison (cream and egg yolk) must have this added immediately prior to service and not before being chilled.

There are specialist modified starches on the commercial market which can be used as thickeners for sauces and soups in place of a conventional roux (fat and flour). These solve the problem of curdling which can occur using a roux method. Waxy maize flour, cornflower and arrowroot are all acceptable thickeners of this type. This is one example of how conventional recipes have to be modified to allow for the hostile environment of the freeze/regeneration cycle.

Egg dishes

Most egg dishes are easily prepared on demand and cook-freeze offers no great advantage to the caterer.

Desserts

Basic cooked desserts freeze well, with the exception of those that rely on batters lifted by eggs, such as soufflés.

Mousses, jellies, pastry goods, yeast goods, cooked fruits and uncooked fruit are all suitable for freezing, although in many cases the high sugar content prevents hard freezing. This sometimes causes concern as it may lead you to think that the product is not cold enough or that the freezer is not operating at the correct temperature.

Composite sweet dishes that require a hot base with a raw fruit or cream topping are not suitable unless the two components are packed separately.

PREPARING AND COOKING DISHES

Most conventional recipes may be frozen successfully provided suitable thickening agents are used for accompanying sauces and soups. Waxy maize flour should be used to replace wheat flour as a thickening agent as it does not curdle when regenerated. Sauces thickened with cornflour and arrowroot will also reheat satisfactorily.

Do not garnish finished dishes until the food has been re-heated. This is particularly important for any fresh garnish, such as parsley sprigs, tomato or salad items. These do not freeze well as they have a high water content and become limp and unappetising when thawed.

The dishes outlined in the Unit 2ND15: *Preparing cook-chill food (pages 317–34)* would all be suitable for freezing using the cook-freeze methods of production.

Food preparation in a cook-freeze operation

HEALTH, SAFETY AND HYGIENE

Note all points given in the Core Units book concerning general attention to health, safety and hygiene. When freezing and storing foods, the following points are particularly important:
● *hygiene.* Since the objective of freezing is to extend the life of cooked food, hygienic preparation and storage is of prime importance. The extended life of the product also extends the opportunity for dangerous bacteria (particularly *salmonella, staphylococcus aureus, clostridium perfringens, escherichia coli* and *listeria*) to contaminate and grow in the food. For more detailed information on this subject see the further reading list at the end of this chapter
● *time and temperature.* The limits for these must be adhered to very strictly and accurate records of time and temperatures of stored goods must be kept
● *prevention of cross-contamination.* The possibility of cross-contamination between cooked and uncooked foods must be kept to an absolute minimum.

TIME AND TEMPERATURE

Some bacteria leave dangerous toxins in food even after they have been killed and others can protect themselves from the effects of heat. This is why the strict time and temperature controls exist and why they must be adhered to by all concerned. All of the following points are essential when carrying out preparation within the cook-freeze process.
● The temperature of uncooked ingredients delivered from stores must not exceed 5 °C/41 °F for high risk foods such as meats, poultry, fish, dairy produce and cooked meat. The temperature of food must not exceed this level during the preparation process.
● The temperature of cooked food must reach a minimum of 70 °C (158 °F) for at least two minutes and freezing should commence within 30 minutes.
Reason: this temperature will kill the majority of harmful bacteria which cause food poisoning. By freezing quickly to a temperature which prevents bacterial growth, any remaining bacteria do not have time to multiply.

MEMORY JOGGER

How long is allowed between the end of the cooking process and food being cooled to −5 °C?

● Foods must be chilled down to a temperature of −5 °C (19 °F) within a period of 90 minutes. The food should then drop again to −18 °C (0 °F). Whole joints above 2.5 kg (5½ lb) may not be used.

Reason: 90 minutes is the shortest practical time that this temperature can be achieved in a controlled way. Large joints (being dense and thick) cannot meet this requirement and so would not be safe when re-heated.

● However food is distributed from deep-freeze storage, if the temperature of the food exceeds 5 °C (41 °F) it must be consumed within 12 hours or discarded. If it exceeds 10 °C (50 °F) it must be consumed immediately or discarded.

Reason: food stored at 5–10 °C (41–50 °F) will allow bacteria present to multiply slowly. However, provided the preparation and packing was carried out under strict hygienic control and in accordance with the regulations, the food will remain safe for a maximum of 12 hours. Once 10 °C (50 °F) is reached the danger from bacteria increases dramatically and the food would become hazardous if not consumed immediately.

Remember: some bacteria leave dangerous toxins in food even after they have been killed, and others can protect themselves from the effects of heat. This is why the strict time and temperature controls exist and why they must be adhered to by all concerned.

See *Temperature control and recording* in Element 2 (*page 346*) for temperature control during the storage and transportation stages.

Essential knowledge

Time and temperature are important when preparing cook-freeze food in order to:
● prevent contamination from food poisoning bacteria
● prevent any bacteria present from multiplying
● kill bacteria susceptible to heat
● present the food to the consumer in the best possible condition.

Do this

● Find out the colour coding system for your preparation equipment and list the colours used and the types of food they are used for.
● Check and note the temperatures of your freezer and holding freezer cabinets. Do they comply with the regulations?
● Look at temperature records and note any changes that have occurred.

PLANNING YOUR TIME

Because of the short time that is required between the cooking of food and the packing and freezing it is very important that you plan every stage of the portion-packaging-freezing-storage cycle of operation precisely. You will create severe problems if you produce more dishes than you can pack, or pack more than you can freeze and/or store.

Production scheduling

The operations manager is responsible for scheduling production so that none of the sections of the operation is required to work above its maximum capacity. Within the schedule, the staff responsible for each operation have to ensure that they have the necessary equipment to perform the task successfully.

The manager will produce written schedules for each area. An example of a Production Section Schedule is given on page 325.

Packaging scheduling

The volume of the production unit will vary according to the scale of the operation and will be controlled by the Unit Manager.

The production schedule will go to the stores so that the correct quantities of ingredients will be available to the cooks at the time required. The schedule will allow enough time between the preparation of dishes and arrival of ingredients for the next batch of dishes for cleaning down sterilisation of equipment and work areas. This is a necessary precaution against cross-contamination.

The Packing Section Schedule may look like the one below.

SELECTION OF CONTAINERS

In selecting the containers for cook-freeze the person responsible needs to ensure that they are capable of withstanding both the freezing and re-heating process without any change in their structure or contamination of the food. The one common factor for all containers used for cook-freeze is that they must be able to maintain a near-vacuum (the exclusion of all air) in order to reduce the spoilage rate within the freezing storage.

PACKING SECTION: Schedule

DATE	5 June 1993
SHIFT LEADER	Peter Brewer
DISH TO PACK (1): Braised beef	
BATCH NUMBER	15131E3
QUANTITY	250
PACKS	50 × 5 portions
AVAILABLE TIME	12.15 p.m.
PACKED FOR FREEZING BY	12.40 p.m.
PACKING MATERIAL	Foil pack no. 14 (8 × 6 inches)
BLAST FREEZER	No. 1
FREEZER STORE	East 3
DISH TO PACK (2): Beef stew and dumplings	
BATCH NUMBER	25132E5
QUANTITY	250
PACKS	50 × 5 portions
AVAILABLE TIME	13.45 p.m.
PACKED FOR CHILLING BY	14.25 p.m.
PACKING MATERIAL	Foil pack no. 10 (8 × 8 inches)
BLAST FREEZER	No. 2

In order to be acceptable:

● containers should be a suitable size for the number of portions that they are required to contain
● the depth of the container should not exceed 5 cm (2 in). Deeper containers will not cool quickly enough
● container lids should have an airtight fit or be capable of being sealed with a non-contaminating seal.

The principal packing materials are aluminium foil, paperboard cartons and plastics.

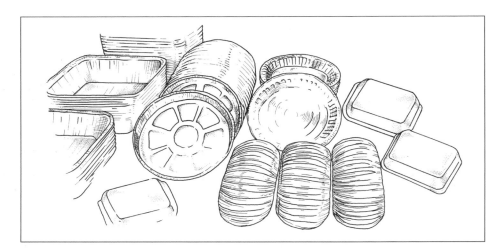

Containers for packaging cook-freeze food

Aluminium foil containers

Aluminum foil containers are ideal for the majority of purposes, as they can withstand high and low temperatures, have excellent moisture retention properties, and are non-toxic, odourless and good conductors of heat. Modern plastic-coated foil is protected against acids and alkalines present in some foods, as the coating prevents the metal in the foil from coming into direct contact with the food. The coating also means that foil containers may be used in microwave ovens.

Paperboard cartons

Paperboard cartons are usually coated with wax, polyester or polythene, none of which are able to withstand the temperatures required for regeneration very effectively. Since this is the cheapest form of packaging it is often used for dishes that are to be served cold.

Plastic containers

Plastics have many of the properties of aluminium but cannot withstand very high temperatures (above 120 °C/248 °F). One particular advantage of plastic containers is that they are available in many attractive designs, enhancing the presentation of food. Plastic can also be heat-sealed, allowing food to be packaged in heat-sealed bags, which is useful for small quantities of liquids and single portions of dishes that can be reheated in the bag.

PREPARATION FOR PORTIONING AND PACKING

Equipment and clothing

Assemble all the equipment and containers that you need in order to portion and pack the dishes being prepared. Never use the same equipment for portioning/packing and processing raw food as you have used for cooking food: the equipment may be contaminated with harmful bacteria that will transfer to the

MEMORY JOGGER

Have wax coated card containers any applications for cook-freeze production and service?

cooked food. Most establishments using a cook-freeze system have colour-coded equipment with highly visible markings that identify the area in which the items are to be used. The operations-management should be very strict in ensuring that equipment is not moved from one area to another. This colour-coding is often also used for protective clothing so that staff are confined to one area of a production unit by the colour of the uniform they are wearing.

Before you start

You must have:
- sufficient containers of the correct type
- clean service/portioning equipment
- prepared labels with the dish, time, date and batch number
- adequate blast-freezer space for the food you are packing
- adequate cold storage space for the food once it has been frozen
- a probe thermometer in order to check that the dishes are at acceptable temperatures within the required time.

PORTIONING, PACKING AND FREEZING FOOD

1   Place exactly the required quantity of food in each container in accordance with establishment requirements. Scoops, ladles and spoons of the correct size are an aid to portion control and will speed up this process. If greater accuracy is required, you will need to use scales.
    Remember:
    - all constituents of the dish to be packed should be ready at the same time
    - you have only 30 minutes to portion and pack before the freezing process must commence; i.e. to complete steps 1, 2, 3 and 4.
    - composite dishes or meals should be presented as instructed.
2   Completely seal all containers as soon as possible to prevent contamination from the air and deterioration while in cold storage.
3   Fix labels to each container.
4   Pack the containers into racks for freezing. The size of the racks will depend on the type and capacity of the freezer you are using, but they are usually either transportable racks (e.g. they can be placed on a trolley) or are specialist trolleys designed to fit completely into the freezer.
5   Check the temperature of the food using a probe thermometer. This should be done twice: once immediately before freezing starts, and then again after the food has been in the freezer for 90 minutes. These times and temperatures should be recorded on a document that is kept for reference.

Essential knowledge

Portions must be controlled when filling packages in order to:
- standardise the cost
- control costings
- facilitate stores control
- help service staff to serve the correct size portion
- standardise the thawing or reheating process
- allow the sealing to be properly accomplished.

Food containers must be labelled correctly before storage in order to:
- accurately identify the contents of a container
- enable stocktaking to be completed quickly and accurately
- indicate important information regarding the packing date and 'use by' date
- inform service staff of the number of portions contained in the package.

Food containers must be sealed correctly before storage in order to:
● prevent spoilage due to contact with the cold air
● prevent spillage prior to freezing
● allow safe stacking without damage to containers.

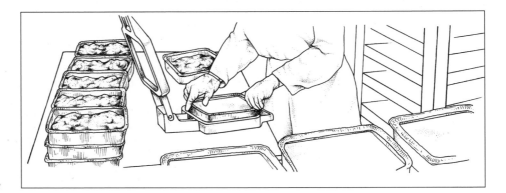

Packing food for cook-freeze

Portioning and packing different types of food

Follow the same procedures as for cook-chill food (see page 326).

Blast-freezing

Blast-freezing is the most widely used method for reducing the temperature of cooked food in medium to small scale operations. Freezers of this type are usually classified by the quantity of food that they can bring down to -5 °C (19 °F) within one hour.

Portioned and sealed dishes are loaded onto racks which allow air to circulate freely between the shelves. The racks are then pushed into the freezing chamber where sub-zero air is blown over the containers by powerful fans. The movement of the air reduces the insulating properties of the containers and lowers the temperature rapidly. Blast-freezers are not efficient as storage and the power consumption is very high, so the products should be removed from the cabinets and stored in deep-freeze storage as soon as the desired temperature is reached. The deep-freeze storage will then reduce the temperature still further to -18 °C (0 °F).

KEY POINTS IN THE PREPARATION OF FOOD FOR COOK-FREEZE

● Raw materials must be of the highest quality and freshness and must be stored separately from the finished product.
● Cooking must take place as soon as possible after preparation to avoid spoilage, deterioration of quality or bacterial growth.
● Any cook-freeze food bought in must always be constantly evaluated and checked to see that it meets quality control standards. Food must be received at the right temperature, date coded and transferred to the right temperature/conditions.
● Where appropriate, cook-freeze food may be removed from cartons before storing. All cook-freeze food must be transferred after production/transportation into hygienic storage containers.

- Every effort must be made to avoid the risk of cross-contamination during preparation and storage.
- The highest standards of personal hygiene must be maintained at all times.
- Times and temperatures must be carefully controlled and recorded.

ELEMENT 2:   Store cook-freeze food

PERSONAL SAFETY

Make sure that you:
- always wear protective clothing when entering a deep freeze store. Temperatures of $-18\,°C$ ($0\,°F$) and below can cause frostbite and respiratory illnesses very quickly
- follow your unit's safety procedures. Always notify your colleagues that you are working in the deep-freeze store: they may accidentally lock you in if you forget
- know where the alarm switches are inside the freezers in case you get into difficulties
- know what to do if the alarm is sounded by a colleague.

ACCEPTING FOOD FOR STORAGE

No food other than prepared frozen and packed food should be stored in a freeze store, as to do so would create a risk of cross-contamination. It would also result in more people needing access to the store which can cause problems with temperature control.

Frozen food must not be accepted for storage unless it is properly labelled. The information on the label must include:
1 the description of the contents (i.e. the name of the dish)
2 the date and time of freezing
3 the batch number
4 the storage temperature
5 the use-by-date.
6 Additional information may include nutritional information which may be necessary for special medical diets (e.g. 'Salt free' or 'Gluten free') or for religious purposes (e.g. 'Kosher prepared' for those of the Jewish faith or 'Halal prepared' for Muslims).

TEMPERATURE CONTROL DURING STORAGE, TRANSPORTATION AND REGENERATION

The following points are essential during these stages:

- Food must be stored at −18 °C (0 °F) for no longer than three months.
  Reason: although bacterial activity ceases at these temperatures, there is a tendency for food to dehydrate and change colour after eight weeks due to the absorption of oxygen by the surface of the food. This is known as 'oxidisation' and shows up as freezer burn. Freezer burn can be reduced by using good packaging which excludes air from the product.
- Ideally food should only be stored in freezers for eight weeks. This is not a hard and fast rule, and food is sometimes kept up to a maximum of six months.
  Reason: the nutritional content will be seriously affected if food is kept for longer than this. Foods with a high fat content may go rancid and become unpalatable.
- When food is distributed from the freezer the temperature must be carefully monitored. If the temperature of the food exceeds 5 °C (41 °F) at any time, it must be consumed within 12 hours or discarded. If it exceeds 10 °C (50 °F) it must be either consumed immediately or discarded.
  Reason: food stored at 10 °C (50 °F) will allow bacteria present to multiply slowly, but providing the preparation and packing is carried out under strict hygienic control the food will remain safe for a maximum of 12 hours. As soon as 10 °C (50 °F) is reached, the food rapidly becomes dangerous if not consumed immediately.
- When removed from frozen storage the cooked food must be re-heated to a core temperature of at least 70 °C (158 °F) and held at this temperature for at least two minutes (and served within 15 minutes). Some foods may be re-heated straight from the freezer. However, most food will need to be defrosted in a thawing cabinet to chill temperature 5 °C (41 °F) before re-heating begins.
  Reason: this temperature will kill most dangerous bacteria present.

> **MEMORY JOGGER**
>
> Food that has been re-heated must be served quickly. Within how many minutes must it be served?

Temperature recording

The temperature of cook-freeze food must be monitored throughout the production and storage processes in order to keep the risk of contamination by food poisoning bacteria to a minimum. It also makes it possible to trace any problems back to a particular process or department.

The importance of accurate and continuous temperature monitoring cannot be stressed enough. Temperatures should be taken at the core (the centre of the thickest part) of the product using an accurate probe thermometer which should be cleaned with a special 'once-only' bactericidal wipe after each use. It is also essential that the thermometers used are recalibrated regularly to ensure that they are accurate. (Records must be kept of these recalibration tests.)

The temperature of food should be taken with an accurate probe thermometer at the following times:

- on delivery (maximum: 5 °C/41 °F for high risk foods such as meats, poultry, fish, dairy produce, cooked meat)
- when moved from the stores to the cooking area (maximum: 5 °C/41 °F for high-risk foods such as meats, poultry, fish, dairy produce, cooked meat)
- when cooked (minimum 70 °C/158 °F for two minutes)
- when frozen (maximum −5 °C/19 °F after 90 minutes)
- at regular intervals whilst in storage (maximum −18 °C/0 °F; if higher than this temperature see pages 339–340 for action)
- when moved from freezer to service area (maximum −18 °C/0 °F)
- when re-heated (minimum 70 °C/158 °F for two minutes)
- whilst held for service (minimum 65 °C/149 °F).

Under current hygiene regulations these temperatures must be recorded with dates, times and the name of the person responsible. Each establishment will have standard procedures to ensure that the records are maintained and filed for future reference for every batch of food that is stored and moved or served. These records must be made available to the Environmental Health Inspector on demand.

Case study	*A case of food poisoning is reported from an industrial canteen which may have been caused by your cook-freeze operation that services the site. This canteen is 20 miles from your production kitchen and cold store. An average of 1,500 meals per day are served seven days per week.*
	1 What checks would you make in order to discover where and if your production and service operation was the cause?
	2 The kitchen supervisor has a temperature check list that shows that all food was re-heated to 70 °C (158 °F) or more before service. Is it correct to assume that it was therefore safe? Justify your answer.

Essential knowledge	It is important to monitor and record food temperatures regularly in order to:
	● prevent contamination from incorrect storage conditions
	● ensure flavour and texture is maintained.

STOCK CONTROL SYSTEM

All food must be booked into the cold store and the label details recorded. Items required for dispatch should be those that were first into the store (the oldest). An efficient stock rotation system should be in place to ensure this. No food should be held in the cold store longer than 12 weeks. Daily checks should be made both through records and the actual stocks held to ensure that no out-of-date items are held.

MEMORY JOGGER

How frequently should the temperature of a cold store be checked?

The temperature of the cold storage unit, irrespective of size, should not exceed −18 °C (0 °F). If there is no continuous recording system for the cold store, the temperature should be checked at least twice a day and the time and temperature recorded on a log. These records should be safely filed in accordance with the established procedures of the cook-freeze unit.

Before sending food for consumption, the freezing date should be recorded on an issue sheet. Food dispatched for consumption may need to be transported in refrigerated containers in order to keep the temperature below −18 °C (0 °F) if the food is to be held for some time on another site or kitchen.

Essential knowledge	Stock rotation procedures must be followed in order to:
	● prevent damage or decay to stock
	● ensure that older stock is used before newer stock.

LIMITING ACCESS

Access to cold storage areas should be restricted to authorised people only. This can be achieved by using digital locks with special codes, personal keys, or systems using a 'booking in and out' log. In large freezers there must be some form of external indication that there is someone in the store and when they entered the store. This is essential as unnecessary opening of the frozen store door would destabilise the temperature and could cause spoilage of the food. There is also, as with any store, the need to guard against the possibility of theft.

Remember that a cold store is a hazardous area and unauthorised people may become trapped inside with very serious consequences.

Essential knowledge	Storage areas must be secured from unauthorised access in order to <ul><li>prevent pilferage or damage by unauthorised persons</li><li>prevent injury to unauthorised persons</li><li>prevent unnecessary opening of store doors, which would destabilise the temperature.</li></ul>

LEGAL REQUIREMENTS

MEMORY JOGGER

What is meant be 'Due diligence'

A caterer or manufacturer should bear in mind the potentially dangerous (and expensive) outcomes that contravention of the *Food Safety Act of 1990* can entail. The labelling of products, recording of temperatures, attention to hygiene and training given to staff would all form part of a legal defence known as *due diligence*, should any legal action be taken. For 'due diligence' to be a successful defence, the caterer must convince the court that all the requirements of the law have been complied with and also that the 'accepted customs and practices' of the trade have been carried out. It is also necessary to have documentary evidence to prove these facts.

Do this ✔	<ul><li>Find out how times and temperatures are recorded in your establishment, and how long the records are kept.</li><li>Find out who is authorised to enter your cold store.</li><li>What safety precautions apply to your unit?</li></ul>

KEY POINTS: FREEZING, STORING AND REGENERATING FOOD

- The rate of cooling will depend on a number of factors including container size, shape or weight, and food density and moisture content.
- The product must be labelled with the date of production and a strict system of stock control must be in operation. Temperature control during food distribution should be very closely monitored.
- For reasons of safety and palatability the food must be re-heated (regenerated) quickly.
- Food to be served cold should be consumed within four hours after removal from chilled storage unless it is in a refrigerated display unit.
- *No food, once reheated, should be returned to the refrigerator.* All unconsumed, re-heated food should be destroyed.

DEALING WITH UNEXPECTED SITUATIONS

Establishments that operate cook-freeze systems will have detailed operational instructions for dealing with every non-routine situation.

The most important of these will deal with refrigeration faults in freezers and storage, abnormal temperature variations in storage, below-specification deliveries from suppliers, and incorrect processing times.

It is your responsibility to be aware of these instructions and to follow them exactly; there is no margin of error.

<table>
<tr><td rowspan="5">What have you learned?</td><td>1</td><td>What temperature should frozen food be stored at?</td></tr>
<tr><td>2</td><td>Why must stock rotation procedures be followed?</td></tr>
<tr><td>3</td><td>Why is it important to monitor and record food temperatures regularly?</td></tr>
<tr><td>4</td><td>Why must storage areas be secured from unauthorised access?</td></tr>
<tr><td>5</td><td>What does First in – First out mean when referring to controlling stocks of frozen food?</td></tr>
</table>

<table>
<tr><td rowspan="2">Get ahead</td><td>1</td><td>Find out about the full legal requirements concerning the production of cook-freeze food. You will find the relevant laws included in The Food Safety Act 1990 and The Food Hygiene (Amendment) Regulations 1990 and 1991. You should also read the following government guidelines: Guidelines on Cook-chill and Cook-freeze Catering Systems (Dept of Health 1989), Guidelines on the Food Hygiene (Amendment) Regulations (Dept of Health 1990 and 1991).</td></tr>
<tr><td>2</td><td>To increase your understanding of contamination threats and how to prevent these, you may like to read Croner's Food Hygiene Manual (Croner Publications, 1991).</td></tr>
</table>

Prepare and cook vegetables for basic hot dishes and salads

This chapter covers:
ELEMENT 1:   **Prepare vegetables for basic hot dishes and salads**
ELEMENT 2:   **Cook vegetables for basic hot dishes and salads**

What you need to do

- Ensure preparation and cooking areas and suitable equipment are hygienic and ready for use.
- Check that vegetables are of the type quality and quantity required.
- Report any problems identified with the quality of vegetables promptly to the appropriate person.
- Ensure vegetables are prepared, cooked and finished using appropriate preparation, cooking and finishing methods and correctly combined with other ingredients to meet quality requirements.
- Ensure prepared vegetables for immediate use or consumption are finished using appropriate finishing methods to meet quality requirements.
- Ensure prepared vegetables not for immediate consumption are stored correctly.
- Ensure preparation and cooking areas and equipment are cleaned correctly after use.
- Ensure all work is prioritised and carried out in an organised and efficient manner in line with appropriate organisational procedures and legal requirements.

What you need to know

- When preparing and cooking vegetables what health and safety practices should be followed.
- When lifting heavy or bulk items why it is important to use approved safe methods.
- When preparing, cooking and storing vegetables why it is important to keep food preparation areas and equipment hygienic.
- When preparing, cooking and storing vegetables what the main contamination threats are.
- Why it is important to thoroughly wash vegetables.
- Why vegetables should be loosened or removed from packaging.
- When preparing vegetables why they should be stored correctly before being cooked.
- List the main categories of vegetables.
- List all the basic preparation methods used in the preparation of vegetables for cooking.
- What quality points you should look for with cooked vegetables.
- Why time and temperature are important when cooking vegetables.
- List the main cookery methods applied to the cooking of vegetables.
- Why vegetables are boiled or simmered gently.
- Why you should sweat vegetables.
- Why vegetables not for immediate consumption should be cooled rapidly or maintained at a safe temperature after cooking.
- Which basic preparation methods can increase the fibre content of vegetable dishes.
- Of the cookery methods applicable to the cooking of vegetables which contribute most to minimal fat levels for healthy eating.
- Why the reduction of salt in vegetable cookery is beneficial.

ELEMENT 1:   Prepare vegetables for basic hot dishes and salads

VEGETABLES FOR HOT DISHES AND SALADS

Vegetables are available on a daily basis from suppliers and include a wide range of varieties. Divided up into different categories each group offers the chef a choice of quality fresh ingredients for the menu. Try to cook fresh vegetables as close to service time as is possible, or prepare them by blanching without over-cooking them.

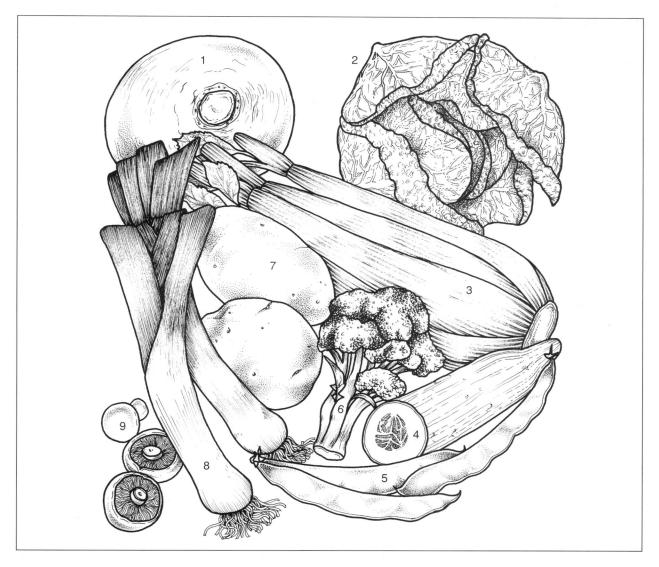

Examples of nine vegetable types:
1 swede (root)
2 cabbage (1 leaf)
3 celery (stem)
4 cucumber (fruit)
5 runner beans (legume)
6 broccoli (flower)
7 potatoes (tuber)
8 leeks (bulb)
9 mushrooms (fungi)

351

Healthy eating

Vegetables are a very important part of the diet. They provide a good source of vitamins, but only if prepared and cooked carefully.

Over-cooked vegetables loose their colour, but more importantly they loose their vitamin and nutrient content. Soaking vegetables in water diminishes the vitamin C content. Wash vegetables well and drain as soon as they are clean.

Vegetable categories include:
- roots
- tubers
- bulbs
- stems
- legumes
- aqueous (courgette, marrow)
- leaves
- flower heads
- fungi
- vegetable fruits (tomato)

ROOT VEGETABLES

MEMORY JOGGER

Why should root vegetables be washed well before being prepared or cooked and what two bacteria are carried in soil?

English term	French term
Carrots	Carottes
Turnips	Navets
Swede	Rutabaga
Parsnip	Panais
Beetroot	Bettrave
Celeriac	Céleri-rave
Radish	Radis
Salsify	Salsifi

Root vegetables need to be cleaned well to remove soil which can be a source of contamination. The bacteria *Clostridium perfingens* and *Bacillus cereus* are present in soil and are very harmful.

Carrots (*carottes*)

Healthy eating

Root vegetables are a good source of fibre which is an important element of the diet.

One of the most popular vegetables, available all year round, the carrot is a good source of vitamin A. Wash and peel carrots, top and tail, cut into required shape and size. They are usually boiled in salted water, mineral water, or sugared water for glacé carrots. Baby carrots or young new carrots require less cooking. Carrots are also used for a wide range of soups, sauces and salads and are one of the most important root vegetables used in cookery.

Celeriac (*céleri-rave*)

This is a celery-flavoured root resembling a large rough-skinned turnip. Choose the smoothest roots and cut them into pieces before peeling them so you can see what you are doing. As celeriac discolours quickly, when peeled, keep the pieces in water with a little vinegar added. Cook it in boiling water for 25–30 minutes and serve with white sauce, or fry in butter. Celeriac can also be used raw, grated and mixed with mayonnaise as a salad, but it is better sliced and blanched first.

Beetroot (*bettrave*)

Beetroot is not usually used as a vegetable, but boiled and pickled for use as a salad vegetable; crinkle cut, sliced or whole (baby). It can also be steamed, but avoid puncturing the flesh when preparing as beetroot will bleed and become pale in colour. Wash and scrub well prior to cooking. Beetroots are usually boiled in salted water and cooled in the cooking liquor. You can then peel the outer skin which should come away quite easily if cooked correctly.

Vegetable types

Vegetable	Type	Quality	General preparation	Examples of use and quantity
Artichoke (globe)	Flower	Stiff leaves, no dryness	Cut off the stalk and top third, trim off points of outer leaves. Rub cut surfaces with lemon to prevent discolouring; tie with string to hold shape. Remove choke before/after cooking; spread apart top leaves, remove furry choke	Globe artichokes (*Artichauts en blanche*): 1 per portion
Artichoke (Jerusalem)	Tuber	Should not be mis-shapen or small	Wash, thinly peel and wash again. Keep in salted water ready for cooking	Jerusalem artichokes in cream sauce (*Topinambours à la crème*): 500 g (1 lb) portions for 4
Asparagus	Stem	Tight, well-formed heads, stems not dry or woody. Graded by spear length and shoot width	Cut woody parts from base of stem. Remove tips (spurs) from leaves using back of a small knife. Thinly peel white part of stems downwards using small knife or French peeler. Wash well	Asparagus au gratin (*Asperges au gratin*): 6–8 pieces per portion
Aubergine	Fruit	Firm, no soft patches	Wash, peel, trim then slice as dish demands	Stuffed aubergine (*Augergine farcies*) 5 for 10 portions
Beans, French	Legume	Crisp, medium size, break crisply under pressure	Wash, top and tail. Leave small beans whole: cut large beans into 7 cm (2¾ in) pieces	Boiled French beans (*Haricots verts à l'anglaise*): 500 g (1 lb) for 3–4 portions
Beans, Broad	Legume	Young, tender pods of uniform size	Remove beans from pods	Buttered broad beans (*Fèves au beurre*): 500 g (1 lb) for 2 portions
Beans, Runner	Legume	Crisp, medium size, break crisply under pressure	Wash, top and tail, string. Cut into 4–7 cm (1¾–2¾ in) strips	Boiled Runner beans (*Fèves nature*) 500 g (1 lb) for 3–4 portions
Beetroot	Root	Firm, sound, blemish-free	Screw off green leaves; do *not* cut tapering root (this causes vegetable to bleed). Wash well	Buttered beetroot (*Betterave au beurre*)
Broccoli	Flower	Small, fresh-looking heads, crisp stalks	Wash thoroughly and drain. Cut off stalk and any damaged outer leaves	Broccoli with hollandaise sauce (*Brocolis hollandaise*): 1 kg (2 lb) for 8 portions
Brussels sprouts	Leaf	No limp, yellowing leaves; tightly grown leaves; compact	Trim stalks, cut off any discoloured leaves. Cut an 'X' in stem base to ensure even cooking	Boiled Brussels sprouts (*Choux de bruxelles à nature*): 1 kg (2¾ lb) for 10 portions

Vegetable	Type	Quality	General preparation	Examples of use and quantity
Cabbage	Leaf	No discoloured leaves, tightly grown, compact	Wash, cut away outer leaves, quarter and remove hard centre core	Cabbage (*Chou nature*): 1 kg (2 lb) for 5 portions
Carrots	Root	Firm, not too large	Peel, wash and shape as for recipe	Buttered carrots (*Carottes au beurre*): 500 g (1 lb) for 4 portions
Cauliflower	Flower	No discoloured leaves or damaged, discoloured curds	Wash, remove outer leaves, trim stem and hollow out using peeler	Boiled cauliflower (*Chou-fleur nature*): 1 for 4 portions
Celery	Stem	Firm, tightly grown. Thick, plump at base, smooth sticks	Remove outer stalks, trim heads and root, peel to remove fibres, wash well	Braised celery (*Céleri Braisé*): 2 heads for 4 portions
Chicory	Stem	Firmly packed, crisp, no discoloured or curling leaves	Remove outer leaves if necessary, trim stem, wash	Braised chicory (*Endives braisées*): 500 g (1 lb) for 3 portions
Courgettes	Fruit	Firm, straight, light green, blemish-free	Wash, top and tail. Cut as recipe demands	Stuffed courgettes (*Courgettes farcies*): 1 per portion
Cucumber	Fruit	Straight, firm	Peel, shape as recipe demands	Cucumber in cream sauce (*Concombres à la crème*): 3 for 10 portions
Leeks	Bulb	Well-shaped, curling leaves no discoloured or slimy leaves	Cut off roots and trim tops; remove any discoloured leaves. Cut lengthways, wash to remove any soil inside leaves	Braised leeks (*Poireaux braisés*): 500 g (1 lb) for 2 portions
Lettuce	Leaf	Leaves bright in colour, fresh look. No brown, slimy leaves or brown patches	Trim base, remove outer leaves. Leave whole for cooking; separate leaves for salad. Wash	Braised lettuce (*Laitue braisée*): 2 for 4 portions
Marrow	Fruit	Firm, well-shaped with soft skin	Peel, seed, cut as recipe demands	Stuffed marrow (*Courge farcie*)
Mushrooms	Fungi	Not limp, broken or sweaty-looking	Trim base of stalks, wash and drain. Cut as recipe demands	Grilled mushrooms (*Champignons grillés*): 500 g (1 lb) for 4 portions
Onions	Bulb	Firm, regular shape, no soft patches at neck	Wash, peel, trim roots. Cut as recipe demands	French fried onions (*Oignons frits à la française*): 500 g (1 lb) for 4 portions
Parsnips	Root	Firm, sound, blemish-free. No splits up root	Wash, peel, rewash. Remove hard core if mature. Shape as for recipe	Buttered parsnips (*Panais au beurre*): 500 g (1 lb) for 3 portions
Peas	Legume	Plump, crisp, bright green pea pods	Shell and wash (*mange-tout* are cooked whole, i.e. within pods)	Peas French style (*Petits pois à la française*): 1 kg (2 lb) for 4 portions

Vegetable	Type	Quality	General preparation	Examples of use and quantity
Potatoes	Tuber	Firm, sound, no signs of damage	Wash, peel, rewash and shape as recipe demands. New potatoes may be peeled after cooking	Plain boiled potatoes (*Pommes nature*): 2 lb for 4 portions
Salsify	Root	Young roots with fresh grey-green leaves, tapering roots	Wash, peel, rewash; cut off top and keep in water with lemon juice if not cooked immediately	Buttered salsify (*Salsifis au beurre*): 500 g (1 lb) for 4 portions
Seakale	Stem	Crips, not wilted; leaves bright in colour	Remove any discoloured leaves, trim roots, wash under running water	Seakale Mornay (*Chou de mer Mornay*): 500 g (1 lb) for 3 portions
Spinach	Leaf	Bright leaves, crisp	Remove stalks, wash several times in cold water to remove soil and grit	Leaf spinach (*Epinards en branches*) 1 kg (2 lb) for 4 portions
Swedes	Root	Firm, sound, free from spade marks	Trim stalk and root, peel thickly, wash. Cut as recipe demands	Buttered swedes (*Rutabaga au beurre*): 500 g (1 lb) for 2 portions
Sweet potatoes	Tuber	Firm, sound, no signs of damage	Scrub, peel if necessary	As for potatoes (above)
Tomatoes	Fruit	Firm, regular shape, bright colour, no blotches	Wash, remove eye using small knife	Grilled tomatoes (*Tomates farcies*): 1–2 per portion
Turnips	Root	Firm, sound, no signs of worm holes	Wash, trim stalk and root ends, peel thickly, rewash and shape as for recipe	Glazed turnips (*Navets glacés*): 500 g (1 lb) for 4 portions

Salsify (*salsifi*)

This is a root vegetable often known as the oyster plant due to its oyster-type flavour. Choose vegetables with regular tapered roots. Wash and scrape off skin, then cut into 5 cm (2 in) lengths and boil in salted water with a squeeze of lemon juice for 45 minutes.

Turnips (*navet*)

Turnips are generally available and at their best in May and June although they can be purchased outside these maincrop months. They should be green and white in colour; avoid spongy or soft turnips which will probably be woody in texture. Wash and peel the turnips, cut into the required shape for cooking and boil in salted water.

Swede (*rutabaga*)

Best between October and March or after frosty weather, hard outer skin, care is needed when peeling. Remove it by peeling or cutting the outer skin and cut into required shape or cut small for purée. Cook in salted water from cold and boil until tender. Some swedes will remain firm and not be suitable for purée until after a good frost has softened them.

Parsnip (*panais*)

This is a white tapered vegetable available between October and April. It has a sweet flavour. Avoid blemished and soft or discoloured parsnips. Wash and peel them, then re-wash, top and tail. They are usually boiled in salted water or served plain with melted butter. They can also be roasted, or puréed when young.

Radish (*radis*)

Radish is not usually cooked as a vegetable but used for salads and decoration. It has a hot flavour, and a red outer skin with a green leafy top. Top and tail, removing the fine root, wash and slice or trim for decorative flower presentation. Radishes are not usually cooked.

TYPES OF TUBER

- Potatoes
- Jerusalem artichokes
- Sweet potatoes

Healthy eating

Potatoes are an important source of carbohydrate – one of the essential nutrients.

Potatoes

Although potatoes are really vegetables (tubers) they are an important carbohydrate food. They were originally cultivated in Peru and Bolivia and were brought to England by Sir Walter Raleigh in the 16th century. They did not become popular for nearly two centuries, but by the end of the 18th century they had become the staple food of the Irish.

The composition of a potato
It you cut a potato in half you will see that it has distinct layers, these layers are interesting because their composition varies:
1 *Outer skin:* this has more protein than fat and more minerals than the main flesh.
2 *Thick fibrous layer under the skin:* this has more protein and minerals than the main flesh.

MEMORY JOGGER

Which minerals and vitamins are found in potatoes?

3   *Main flesh:* this has more carbohydrates and less protein, fat and minerals than the other two layers.

A potato contains 81% water, little protein or fat but is an important supplier of minerals, notably potassium and a little calcium, vitamins B and C. The food value of potatoes is not great but as they are eaten on a regular basis this value becomes very significant to the diet.

In grading potatoes for market, farmers must remove potatoes that are:
● unsound
● tainted, damaged or diseased
● badly mis-shapen.
● bruised or damaged by frost or pests
● affected by greening, hollow heart or water-logging.

As many as 40 varieties of potatoes e.g. King Edward, desirée, are grown by British farmers, 15 of these varieties are grown in large numbers; some of these are now offered in the shops by name. Each variety of potato has different properties and that affects its cooking ability. The Potato Marketing Board has made the labelling of potato sacks compulsory so that the type of potato and the farm of origin can be identified and action taken if the product is sub-standard.

Old Potatoes (Pommes de terre)
Old potatoes are available all year round and provide the basis for an array of potato dishes cooked by many different methods of cookery. These potatoes are at their best when free from blemish and smooth skinned. Many different varieties are sold wholesale in 25 and 32 kg units.

You can purchase ready washed and scrubbed potatoes from wholesale vegetable suppliers. It is also possible to buy in ready cut potatoes for chips, roast and turned products, these are labour saving but do cost more for obvious reasons.

Potatoes form a major part of the Western civilization's diet and the ways of preparing and cooking potatoes are numerous. In the catering industry potatoes can be purchased in various forms e.g.:
● fresh: old and new potatoes
● frozen: chips, croquettes, noisettes, sauté etc.
● dried: creamed or mashed potatoes
● tinned: new potatoes
● prepared: roast, chips, chateau, jackets

Potatoes are part of a main meal and are prepared using many different cookery methods:
● baking   (*Pommes au four*)
● steaming   (*Pomme vapeur*)
● boiling   (*Pommes naturelle*)
● roasting   (*Pommes chateau*)
● shallow-frying (*Pommes macaire, pommes sauté*)
● deep-frying   (*Pommes frit*)
● grilling   (*Pommes duchesse*)

Potatoes are made up mainly of starch and carbohydrate. They are most nutritious when their skins are left e.g. *en robe* and *au four*. Many people today eat jacket potatoes in a variety of ways, but to some extent rice is replacing potatoes in many daily menus.

Healthy eating
Always offer a healthier alternative for diet-conscious customers when roast, shallow-fried or deep-fried potatoes are on the menu. Both old and new potatoes can be baked or steamed in their jackets after being well washed.

MEMORY
JOGGER

What hazards do
you need to be
aware of when using
hand peelers or
potato rumblers?

Preparing potatoes
Prepared with a hand peeler or potato rumbler you need to be careful when peeling to prevent accidents to yourself or others. Look for stones in bags of potatoes and always follow the safety guidelines given when using a potato rumbler to minimise the risk of an accident.

Storage and lifting of heavy or awkward items
If buying potatoes in bulk, empty the sacks completely and use any which show signs of damage at once. If the rest are dry and reasonably clean, return to the sack and keep in a cool, dry, frost-free place, raised from the ground and in the dark.

Take care when lifting heavy or awkward bags of potatoes; establish how you will lift, carry and place the item before moving it. Do you know what manual handling skills are required? If not consult your chef or supervisor, ask them to demonstrate how such items can be moved safely. Remember to bend your knees and keep your back straight when attempting to lift large or heavy items. If you feel the task is dangerous, seek help from a colleague or use a trolley or truck wheels.

Potato seasons
● Early crop (May–August)
● Main crop (September–May)

Varieties of main crop potatoes:
Arran comet, Kerrs pink, Pentland javelin, Majestic, Pentland crown, Pentland ivory, Desirée, Maris Piper, King Edwards, Ulster sceptre, Pentland dell, Home guard, Redskins, Red criegs royal, Pentland hawk.

MEMORY
JOGGER

What care should
be taken when
attempting to lift or
move large or heavy
items?

Jerusalem artichokes

Trim the artichokes with a peeler to produce a smooth bowl shape and store in lemon juice and water to prevent discoloration. Boil in salted water until just tender. Serve in a cream sauce. They are also used to make soup.

Sweet potatoes (*eddoes*)

This is the edible tuber of a climbing plant, originally from South America which was brought to Europe in 1493 by Columbus. The tubers have pale reddish-brown skins and yellow flesh. Scrub well and peel if necessary.

Sweet potatoes can be used for stir-fry dishes or in sweet-and-sour recipes. They have a crisp firm texture which needs prolonged cooking to soften this product. They can weigh from 30 g/1 oz to 500 g/1 lb with flesh colour varying from white, yellow, pink to orange. The flavour is somewhat similar to the common potato with a slight nutty taste. Prepare and cook as you would the common potato i.e. bake, boil, fry or roast.

TYPES OF BULB VEGETABLE

● Onion
● Spring onion
● Shallot
● Leek
● Chives
● Garlic

Onions (*l'oignons*)

Onions should have a dry crisp outer skin, which is unbroken, and no signs of sprouting. They should be even in size and firm when pressed; softness and moisture are signs of decay and age. Used probably more than any other vegetables for a wide range of dishes and products, onions can be prepared for many different cookery methods but the most common are :

- Deep-fried (French fried onion rings)
- Sautéed sliced onions for lyonnaise
- Boiled button onions for garnish
- Carbonised for soups and sauces
- Braised onions
- Baked onions

Most of the onions used are home grown in Britain but some are imported, from Spain and France in particular.

Onions can be: sliced, diced, grated, puréed, whole or halved.

Leeks *(poireaux)*

Leeks are available all year round and have a white base stem which is green further up. Leeks should be clean, firm and plump; not limp or damaged with no signs of yellowness or wilting. If grown in soot or soil trenches leeks will need to be split and well washed before use. Leeks have a mellower flavour to that of onion and are used in soups and stocks or braised as a vegetable or plain boiled.

To prepare, trim to remove the root and cut away any damaged or inferior outer leaves. Split from approximately 3 cm (1½ in) from the base to the top with a cook's knife and wash well to clean away any grit or dirt.

Used for garnish in soups, the leek is not a popular vegetable but best when young and small – baby leeks are sweet flavoured and decorative. Used for cold buffet decoration.

Spring onion *(ciboule)*

Spring onions are used primarily as a salad ingredient. The Chinese use the spring onion for many different recipes whereas the European culinary tradition is to use it in salads and hors d'oeuvres. Prepare by trimming the base roots and top leaves, wash well and use whole or shredded. They are available from May to September.

Chives *(ciboulette)*

Chives are used as a garnish for salads and soups: the lush green stems which have a mild, onion flavour are finely chopped and shredded and sprinkled on top of salad preparations, hors d'oeuvres and soups. Although used in some main dishes, chives are not served alone as a vegetable. Chives are available from May to August.

Shallot *(l'échalote)*

The shallot is the queen of the bulb family, available in September and October it is red in colour with a distinct prominent flavour. Many classical recipes use the shallot instead of onion because of its delicate flavour. Shallots can be used whole or finely chopped, but are slow and difficult to peel where a large quantity is needed. Prepare with a small office or turning knife. Remove the roots and stem, peel to remove the outer skin and use as required.

Garlic *(l'ail)*

This is available all year round, and can be either standard, jumbo or elephant garlic. The best garlic comes from France. It is used to flavour all manner of dishes, soups sauces and salads. Peel and crush, slice or finely chop, macerate in olive oil or used in mayonnaise and many sauce recipes.

MEMORY JOGGER

When preparing and cooking leeks why should they be washed well?

AQUEOUS VEGETABLES

Courgette (*courgette*)

Courgettes should be firm and crisp and not too large, and should show no signs of softness or skin blemish: look for signs of decay. Available from May till August, this vegetable is 15–20 cm in length and has green skin with a white/yellow flesh. Courgettes are small baby marrow's and are used for a number of dishes such as *ratatouille*.

Wash courgettes well and trim. They can be cooked plain with the skin on or sliced and sautéed or deep fried. Courgettes can be prepared provençale or portugaise style.

Marrow (*courge*)

Marrow should be firm with a good green colour; avoid marrows with very tough skins. They are usually cut in half lengthways and the soft pithy seed mass removed, then poached in salted water, drained and stuffed and finished in the oven.

Marrows are not a popular vegetable, but are available from July to September.

To cook as a vegetable the marrow should be peeled to remove the tough outer skin, washed and gently boiled. The marrow is 80% water and needs careful cooking to prevent it becoming soft and difficult to handle.

HYGIENE AND CLEANLINESS

Always wash all vegetables before you prepare or cook them, many are sprayed with insecticides and chemical sprays to manage and control damage from pests. By cleaning vegetables correctly you will minimise the risk of contamination.

MEMORY JOGGER

Why should vegetables be cleaned before being prepared or cooked?

LEAF VEGETABLES

- Cabbage
- Curly kale
- Sprout tops
- Sorrel
- Chard
- Lettuce
- Chicory
- Watercress
- Endive
- Sprouts
- Spinach

Types of cabbage

Green (chou vert)
Red (chou rouge)
Chinese (salade de chine)
Spring Greens (chou de printemps)

Cabbage should have a good colour with no rust or damage to leaf structure, and it should be crisp – not limp or yellowing. White cabbage should be heavy and compact with a very close leaf structure. Red cabbage should be reddish-purple in colour, be firm with a closed leaf structure; look for signs of limpness or dehydration. Trim away any discoloured or decayed outer leaves. Cut into four pieces and trim the centre stalk. Shred the quarters into the required size and wash well.

Healthy eating
Green leafy vegetables should be prepared quickly and carefully to preserve their useful vitamin content.

Never over-cook cabbage or the vitamin content is destroyed. Red cabbage can be pickled. Spring greens should be de-stalked and lightly cooked to maintain the colour and iron content. Remember not to soak vegetables in water as this destroys the vitamin C content.

Chard

Chard should be firm, dark green with a white coloured stem. It is best when young; large leaves denote old age and are usually tough when cooked.

Endive

This has tightly packed leaves which are long and blanched. They should be very firm and unopened; any signs of browning on the outer edge of the leaves denotes age and decay.

Curly kale

This should be crisp without too much stalk and be unblemished. It has very dark green leaves without a heart structure.

MEMORY JOGGER

What do you need to check leaf or salad leaf vegetables for?

Lettuce

This should be crisp, with a firm heart and no rotting or decaying leaves. Check for fly infestation and slug or caterpillar damage to leaves or heart. Check for mechanical damage during storage and transportation. Check for brown rust disease.

Many different types of lettuce are in wide use today:

Radiccio, Rocket, Iceberg, Lollo Rosso, Oak leaf, Cos, Frisee, Lamb's tongue, Webbs, Curly endive and Romaine.

Sprouts and sprout tops

Sprouts and sprout tops should be small, compact, with a tight leaf structure and with a bright green colour. Browning on the leaf edge denotes prolonged storage. If delivered in green nets, always open and check the actual leaf condition as the netting masks the true colour of the sprouts. Use sprout tops as for cabbage.

Chicory (curly-leaved)

Curly-leaved chicory should be crisp with a fresh appearance, no traces of browning or blemish. Use as for lettuce in salads.

Spinach

Spinach should be fresh with deep green leaves and no signs of decay. Small stalks are preferred to larger, hard tougher stalks. Wash well in salt water and drain.

Sorrel

Sorrel should be green with fresh crisp leaves and no trace of discoloration. Wash well in salt water and drain. Use in salads or cook as for spinach.

Watercress

Watercress should be fresh with bright green leaves, packed in bunches with grower's label. Trim roots and wash, pick over individually, store in a bowl of iced water.

Do this

Draw up a chart or table using a computer and classify all vegetables into the following headings:
- type of vegetable
- salad or vegetable or both
- methods of cookery applicable
- eaten cooked or raw or both

FLOWER HEAD VEGETABLES

Cauliflower (*Chou fleur*)

Cauliflower has a compact white head which should be well formed with a close, tightly-packed structure. Look for signs of decay in the head itself; it should not be soft but very firm. They are available from March to December, and are now also available frozen or as baby miniature cauliflower.

Broccolli (*Brocoli*)

Broccoli should be firm and of good colour; they are available as green or purple heads. The broccoli should be clean and look fresh without discoloration or yellow-brown wilt. It is also available frozen.

Broccoli stems have grown wild for centuries. They have been cultivated and are now very popular.

Celery (*celeri*)

Celery should be white, firm and very crisp without signs of rust or mechanical damage; check for insect damage and decay. Trim the top and base of the stem to separate the individual sticks. Celery is often gritty and soiled with dirt and needs to be scrubbed in clean running water. Use celery for bouquet garni, soups and sauces, salads and as a braised vegetable or hors d'oeuvre.

Asparagus (*d'asperges*)

Asparagus should have long narrow stem with a tight closed flower head. Check for signs of browning or wrinkling at the ends of the stalk which indicates the asparagus is not fresh.

The difficulty encountered in cooking asparagus arises from the fact that the tips, being much more tender than the stalks, cook more quickly. The answer is cook asparagus in an asparagus kettle (a special pan with a rack) but failing this they may be cooked tied together in bundles in a wide pan.

Sea kale (*chou de mer*)

Sea kale has a bright whitish stem colour with a firm crisp texture; check for blemish and discoloration, dirt and damage. Wash well in salt water and drain. Cook as for cabbage.

Fennel (*fenouil*)

This is a bulb-like vegetable with stalks similar in appearance to celery on the top. The vegetable may weigh up to 500 g (1lb) and gives off a strong aroma of liquorice. Fennel should have a firm swollen base with a bulbous shape; check for signs of browning or split damage to the base. Remove any woody upper stalks, cook whole, halved or quartered by steaming, boiling or braising. Cooking times vary depending on size and quality. Fennel may also be sliced and used raw in salads.

Globe artichokes (*Topinambours*)

When preparing artichokes cut off the stalk and all the base leaves. Remove the furry centre of the artichoke; this part is actually known as the choke. It can be cooked and removed after cooking if preferred.

Some vegetables discolour when exposed to the air and during cooking so it is necessary to rub them with lemon juice or plunge them into acidulated water immediately after peeling. These vegetables include Globe and Jerusalem artichokes, celeriac and salsify.

The Globe artichoke is best cooked, with a piece of lemon attached to its base.

EDIBLE FUNGI

MEMORY
JOGGER

Why is care needed when purchasing fungi?

Only purchase fungi from a reputable supplier. Do not purchase fungi you do not recognise, especially if you do not know the person selling them. Some fungi are poisonous and great care needs to be taken to avoid them. Because of the high prices wild fungi attract, people pick them but are not always competent at distinguishing the edible ones from those that are dangerous.

Fungi include:
Cep, chanterelle, morel, mushroom, truffle, shiitake, boletus, wood ears, rubber brush, field mushroom, parasol mushroom and blewit, beefsteak fungus.

Cep (*Cèpe*) Summer and autumn fungus sometimes called the flat mushroom; fleshy, flat, brown. Choose the smaller young ceps with no mechanical damage.

Chanterelle (*Egg Mushroom*) usually found in beech woods summer to winter; tinge of apricot aroma with an irregular funnel shape, egg-yellow in colour; fragile structure needs careful handling and storage.

Morel (*Sponge mushroom*) conical pitted cap with a brown to yellow colour, best young and fresh.

Mushroom (cultivated as small button, cup or open flat mushroom) firm and white when small becoming deeper brown in colour as they open to cup and flat forms; should be unbroken with no damage and unblemished.

Truffle (*White or Black*) Black truffle has a rough hard skin with a strong aroma; should be even in size. White truffle has a more pronounced flavour; usually piedmont variety with a strong scent and taste.

Shiitake (*Chinese mushroom*) flat top with a small stem underside which is an egg-yellow colour; an Eastern tree fungus of oak and Skii trees.

Boletus (*Yellow mushroom*) found in conifer woods, has strong fruity aroma.

Wood ears (*Chinese black fungus*) from China, gelatinous with an irregular shape white underside with a black topside.

Rubber brush (*Wood hedgehog*) woodland fungi with underspines cream to white in colour, needs careful handling: useful for white stews, fricassée and blanquettes.

Field mushroom (*Wild mushroom*) a meadow and pastureland fungi common in late summer and autumn; large and small, brown and white in colour.

Parasol mushroom (*Umbrella mushroom*) summer and autumn fungus picked when young, found on grassy hillsides usually near to trees.

Blewit forms a blue to violet cast near conifer or deciduous trees or on grassy pasture land.

Beefsteak fungus beef-like flesh found on oak trees; large with a reddish brown colour.

TYPES OF VEGETABLE FRUITS

- Tomato
- Aubergine
- Capsicum
- Cucumber
- Sweetcorn
- Avocado

Tomatoes

Tomatoes should be ripe with a bright red colour and a firm even shape. Tomato varieties change throughout the season. Many are imported or grown in the Channel Islands. Varieties include Moneymaker and Cherry red. Beefsteak tomatoes are large and coarse compared to salad varieties.

Prepare tomatoes by washing and slicing, or remove the skin for concasse (chopped tomato). They can be used as a vegetable, stuffed, or used in soups, sauces, salads and hors d'oeuvres.

Avocado

This is the fruit of a tropical tree, originally from South America. Avocados are generally used as a starter in Britain, but solely as a dessert in South America. An avocado must be ripe before eating and should yield to light pressure on the skin. To prepare, cut in half, remove the stone and serve with a vinaigrette dressing or prawn or crab salad; alternatively slice the flesh and arrange with alternate slices of grapefruit.

Healthy eating
Avocados are very nutritious. They are the only fruit to contain carbohydrate, protein and fat.

Aubergine

Originally from India, these are now grown all over the world and particularly associated with Mediterranean cookery. The skin is usually purplish-black but may be green/yellow or pale brown. The shape varies from round to an elongated egg-shape.

As aubergines contain a large percentage of water it is best to sprinkle the insides or cut slices liberally with salt. This draws the excess water out and helps to remove any bitterness. Rinse salt off after 30 minutes and pat dry before use. Both the flesh and the skin are edible in a cooked form, but remove the inedible, spiny stalk before cooking. Bake aubergines with tomatoes, or slice to make fritters.

Cucumber

Cucumber should be firm and crisp; choose long, straight, narrow ones as opposed to curled, wide fruits. Feel for signs of limpness. Wash the cucumber and slice it into thin slices for salads, dice for hors d'oeuvres or decorate with a canele tool and slice.

Cucumber can be cut into portions for dips and crudités, scooped or hollowed out and garnished with assorted fillings. The cucumber is not usually cooked but generally used for cold preparation work.

Baby cucumbers are called dills i.e, dill pickle.

Capsicum (sweet pepper)

These are green, red or yellow and should show no sign of softness, wrinkling or blemish. To prepare for salads, remove stalk and seeds and slice. Peppers are sometimes blanched and served stuffed with rice and other ingredients.

Sweetcorn, baby

Recognisable by their light yellow kernels, baby corn cobs are 5–8 cm (2–3 in) in length and are eaten whole. They have a delicious sweet nutty taste and are a good source of vitamins C and B_1 as well as being high in fibre.

Marrows and *courgettes* are also vegetable fruits. (See *Aqueous vegetables* p. 360).

TYPES OF LEGUMES AND SEED VEGETABLES

- Broad bean
- Runner bean
- French bean
- Mangetout
- Kenya bean (fine)
- Peas

Broad bean

Broad beans should have a firm broad pod which should be a good green colour and not too limp. Keep in the pods until required, then shell and cook beans in salted water until just soft. Very young beans can be added to salads, raw.

French bean (*haricot vert*)

French beans should be a crisp, firm, straight bean, not too large with a good green colour. Wash, top, tail and slice or cook whole if young, in salted water.

Runner bean

Runner beans are best when young and small with a good green colour: large wilted beans are tough and stringy. Wash, top and tail and remove string, slice diagonally and cook in salted water.

Mangetout

Mangetout are crisp flat, undeveloped peas used whole with the shell. They should have a bright green colour. They are available fresh or frozen. Wash well, top and tail. Cook lightly for just a few minutes immediately prior to service as they tend to turn mushy.

Peas

Peas should be crisp and firm with a plump shape. Usually purchased frozen they cook quickly. When available fresh in season, they require longer cooking. Sugar snap peas should be treated like mangetout.

Kenya bean

This is a variety of the French bean which is picked young. It is extensively grown in Kenya. To prepare, wash, top and tail and tie in bundles. Cook quickly in boiling salted water for about 8 minutes until tender but still crisp. Use either hot or cold in salads.

QUALITY POINTS OF VEGETABLES

Texture

When checking vegetables it is sometimes difficult to check for the texture of a vegetable item. As you become more used to checking deliveries you will notice certain traits or signs that might indicate a woody texture, a firm or under-ripe texture. These items once discovered should either be returned and replaced or kept to ripen if under-ripe, but ensure you have sufficient quantities of vegetables for service.

At certain times of the year vegetables become woody or do not have a prime texture, generally due to either being premature in the season or as the vegetable goes to seed. Where a consignment of vegetables is found to be of a poor texture you should return them directly to the supplier having informed your superior, chef or manager first. A credit note should be issued if these items have been invoiced. It is the chef's job and responsibility to see all credit notes and returns tally at the end of each month or audit period.

When prices for vegetable are high, out-of-season vegetables will be imported but these do not have the flavour or texture of main crop produce.

PREPARING VEGETABLES

Vegetables can be prepared in a variety of ways depending on the dish to be cooked. Vegetables should be washed well and peeled with a hand peeler. Use a bowl to place all peelings and debris in to maintain a clean and hygienic work bench. Remove rubbish to the bin when the bowl is full. Clean down all work surfaces when preparation is complete and before starting a new task.

> ### Healthy eating
> Peel vegetables thinly or leave unpeeled where possible. The skin adds fibre to the diet and the most nutritious part of many vegetables lies just under the skin.

- *Peel* with a peeler
- *Cut* with a cook's knife or office knife
- *Shell* peas and beans by hand
- *Chop* with a large cook's knife
- *Shred* using a food processor or mandolin
- *Cut* with knives and processors or mandolin
- *Slice* with a carving or cook's knife or mandolin
- *Trim* with a cook's knife or office knife
- *Grate* with a grater or processor

MEMORY JOGGER

When washing vegetables in a sink used to clean equipment what precautions need to be taken to prevent contamination?

Keep knives sharp and clean at all times, replace them in their storage place when not being used. Some vegetables benefit from being peeled by removing the skin in boiling water; tomatoes and peppers are two examples. When washing vegetables in a sink used to clean equipment, ensure it is sanitised before being used to wash and clean food.

TYPES OF VEGETABLE CUTS

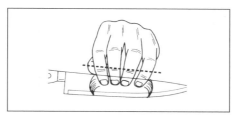

The correct way to hold a vegetable while cutting

The correct way to slice a vegetable

- *Paysanne* (thin sliced 1 cm/$\frac{1}{2}$ in shapes)
- *Brunoise* (fine dice)

- *Mirepoix* (roughly chopped)

- *Julienne* (thin strips)

- *Macédoine* (5 mm/$\frac{1}{4}$ in dice)

- *Jardinière* (15 × 4 mm/ $\frac{1}{4} × \frac{1}{2}$ in batons)

Thinly sliced rounds, squares, triangles or rough-sided rounds all 1 cm ($\frac{1}{2}$ in) in diameter.
The vegetable is cut into 2 mm ($\frac{1}{10}$ in) slices, these are cut to form 2 mm ($\frac{1}{10}$ in) strips and the strips cut to form 2 mm × 2 mm ($\frac{1}{10} × \frac{1}{10}$ in) small dice (cubes).
Chopped root vegetables 1–2 cms ($\frac{1}{2}$–1 in) roughly cut
Cut thin slices of vegetable 2–4 mm ($\frac{1}{10}$ in) thick, cut these slices to form 3–4 cm (1–1$\frac{1}{2}$ in) strips.
Cut the vegetable into slices 5 mm ($\frac{1}{4}$ in) and cut the slices into 5 cm ($\frac{1}{4}$ in) dice.
Cut the vegetables into 15 mm ($\frac{1}{2}$ in) slices and the slices to form 4 mm × 15 mm ($\frac{1}{4} × \frac{1}{2}$ in) pieces.

Basic cuts of vegetable

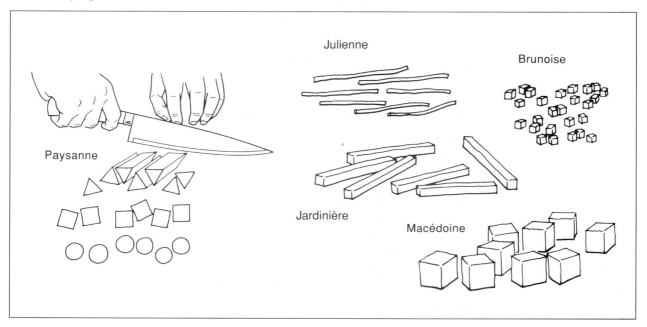

Essential knowledge

You should work in a safe, clean and hygienic manner when preparing and cooking vegetables:
- To minimise the risk of injury from equipment and tools used to prepare vegetables.
- To maintain a safe and secure working environment for yourself and those you work with.
- To prevent accidents by being vigilant and careful when moving heavy or awkward shaped items and following laid down procedures for manual handling.
- To remove the risk of contamination from soil by washing all vegetables correctly.
- To check vegetables for infestation from flies, slugs and caterpillars or any other insect and wash all leaf and salad vegetables to remove traces of spray or chemical insecticide.
- To use only those salad and vegetable foods you know to be safe, fresh and fit for consumption.

What have you learned

1 What healthy and safety practices should be followed when preparing vegetables?
2 Why is it important to use an approved safe method when lifting heavy or bulk items?
3 Why is it important to keep food preparation areas and equipment hygienic when preparing and storing vegetables?
4 What are the main contamination threats when preparing and storing vegetables?
5 Why is it important to thoroughly wash vegetables?
6 Why should vegetables be loosened or removed from packaging?
7 When preparing vegetables why should they be stored correctly before being cooked?
8 What are the main categories of vegetables?
9 Which basic preparation methods are used in the preparation of vegetables for cooking?
10 Which quality points should you look for in vegetables when delivered?
11 What basic preparation methods can increase the fibre content of vegetable dishes?

ELEMENT 2: Cook vegetables for basic hot dishes and salads

MEMORY JOGGER

When cooking vegetables why is time important?

COOKING VEGETABLES

Vegetables are cooked by a wide range of single or combination cooking methods prior to being served. Many are boiled or blanched to initiate cooking then finished by shallow-frying, roasting or grilling to complete the process.

Vegetables generally, should not be under or over-cooked. The chef needs to understand also that not all customers like their vegetables hard or *al dente* – nor soft and mushy. By minimising the time between preparation and cooking you will maintain the vitamin and mineral value of vegetables and prevent deterioration in texture, colour and flavour.

MEMORY JOGGER

Why are carrots an important part of a balanced healthy diet?

Carrots (*carottes*)

Carrots are usually boiled in salted water, mineral water or sugared water for glacé; baby carrots or young new carrots require less cooking. Serve carrots buttered with chopped parsley. They can also be creamed or puréed and are also used for a wide range of soups, sauces and salads. Eating carrots is important in providing *carotene*; the liver converts carotene into vitamin A and is an important factor for a healthy and balanced diet.

Typical carrot dishes are:

Carottes au beurre	buttered carrots
Carrotes glacées	sugared water, reduced to glaze
Carrotes Vichy	cooked in Vichy mineral water
Purée de carrotes	cooked and puréed, finished with butter and cream (or skimmed milk or yoghurt for healthier eating).

Typical cuts for carrots for cooking and salads are:

Whole	baby carrots
Jardinèire/baton	vegetable and garnish
Rondel	vegetable
Turned (barrel shaped)	vegetable and garnish
Fingers	vegetable
Macédoine	vegetable
Julienne	soups and sauces and garnish
Paysanne	soups and sauces
Brunoise	soups and sauces and garnish
Grated	for salads

Celeriac (*céleri-rave*)

Celeriac should be placed in lemon water prior to cooking to prevent it from turning black. Cook in boiling water for 25–30 minutes and serve with white sauce, or fry in butter. It can also be used raw, grated and mixed with mayonnaise as a salad, but it is better sliced and blanched first.

Typical celeriac dishes are:

Céleri-rave nature	plain boiled
Céleri-rave au beurre	buttered
Céleri-rave à la crème	cream or yoghurt
Céleri-rave aux fines herbs	fresh herbs / parsley

Beetroot (*bettrave*)

Beetroots are usually boiled in salted water and cooled in the cooking liquor, then peel off the outer skin which should come away quite easily if cooked correctly. Smaller beetroot are better than medium or larger beetroot which can have a rather firm texture.

Typical ways of serving beetroot are:

Steamed or boiled
Shredded for sauces and garnish
Whole baby pickled for salads
Crinkle cut beetroot slices on a mandolin for salads
Shredded for beetroot soup

Salsify (*salsifi*)

Boil in salted water with a squeeze of lemon juice for 30–40 minutes: serve with butter, hollandaise or a white sauce.

Salsify is best cooked in a blanc (see p. 370), as for artichokes, but should not be cooked too much.

Typical ways of serving salsify are:

Battered and deep fried in baton shapes
Nature – plain boiled in a blanc
Au beurre – served with butter
Served with finely chopped parsley
A la crème – with cream, yogurt or skimmed milk

The use of blanc
25 g/1 oz flour to 1 litre/2 pints water plus salt and lemon juice if required. Certain vegetables are best kept cooked in a blanc (made with this recipe) which helps them to keep their pure white colour. This applies especially to Salsify and can apply to Artichokes and Mushrooms.

Turnips (*navet*)

Boiled in salted water, turnips can be cut in a variety of shapes for plain boiling or steaming. Early season turnip take longer to cook but once subject to a good frost the vegetable is tenderised.

Typical ways of serving turnips are:

Nature – (barrel shaped) plain boiled
Au beurre – buttered
Shallow fried in butter
Finished with chopped parsley
Glacé – cooked in sugared water
Purée de navet – puréed
Used in soups and as a vegetable garnish.

Swede (*rutabaga*)

Swedes are cooked in cold salted water and boil until tender. Some swede will remain firm and not be suitable for purée until after a good frost has softened them.

Typical ways of serving swedes are:

Nature – (barrel shaped) plain boiled
Au beurre – buttered
Shallow fried in butter
Finished with chopped parsley
Glacé – cooked in sugared water
Purée de rutabaga – puréed
Used in soups and as a vegetable garnish.

Parsnip (*panais*)

Parsnips are usually boiled in salted water, and roasted or served plain boiled with melted butter. They can be puréed when young. Do not over-cook parsnips especially when roasted; they will shrivel and be tough to eat.

Typical ways of serving parsnips are:

Au nature – quartered and plain boiled
Panais rôti – quartered, blanched and roasted
A la crème – with cream, yogurt or skimmed milk
Steamed
Roasted with honey
Aux fines herb – served plain boiled with fresh herbs

Potatoes

Key points when cooking potatoes:
● Potatoes should be started in cold, salted water and brought to the boil (except new potatoes).
● They absorb water but loose vitamins and minerals.
● They are best cooked in their skins if possible.
● Maximum food value is retained if the potatoes are barely covered with water.
● They can be roasted, boiled, baked, steamed, deep and shallow-fried, cooked by combination methods, braised and microwaved.
● They can be served hot or cold e.g. potato salad.

Potato purée dishes

Name of dish	Method
Gratinée	Purée, place into a buttered dish, sprinkle with cheese and glaze.
Mousseline	Purée with the addition of whipped cream.
Biarritz	Purée with the addition of diced ham, capsicum and parsley.
Algeriènne	Purée of sweet potato with the addition of chestnut purée and egg yolk, shape as quoit, pane Anglaise (coat in flour, egg and breadcrumbs) and fry in clarified butter.

Duchesse potato dishes

Name of dish	Method
Duchesse	Sieve cooked potato, mix with butter, cream egg and seasoning. Pipe onto greased tray in individual portions. Glaze with egg-wash and brown in hot oven.
Brioche	Prepare as for Duchesse, shape like cottage loaf, egg-wash and glaze.
Galette	Prepare as for Duchesse, make medallion shape, make trellis pattern, egg-wash and glaze.
Rosette	Prepare as for Duchesse, pipe onto tray in rose shapes, sprinkle with clarified butter and glaze.
Marquise	(1) Prepare as for Duchesse, mix with reduced tomato sauce, shape as for medallion, egg-wash and glaze.
Marquise	(2) Prepare as for Duchesse, pipe into nests, egg-wash fill nests with tomato concasse and glaze.
Berny	Prepare as for Duchesse with the addition of chopped truffle, shape as an apricot, pane with sliced almonds and deep fry.
Croquette	Prepare as for Duchesse, shape like small sausages, pane Anglaise and deep fry.
Royale	As for croquette, with the addition of chopped ham, pane with vermicelli, then deep fry.
Dauphine	Mix two parts of Duchesse with one part choux paste. Shape as for croquettes and pane Anglaise and deep fry, or make into shapes with two spoons (as for Beignets) and deep fry.
Lorette	As for Dauphine, but shape like small cigars.
Busy	As for Lorette with the addition of chopped truffle and parsley.
Elizabeth	As for Dauphine, stuffed with spinach, shaped and deep fried.

Potatoes which are deep-fried need to be drained well and placed on kitchen paper to absorb as much excess oil as possible. Always deep-fry at the correct temperature and ensure potato coatings are sound before cooking.

Baked potato dishes

Name of dish	Method
Arlie	Scoop out baked potato, mix with butter, cream and chives then refill skins, brush with butter and sprinkle with cheese, glaze and reheat.
Gratinées	Scoop out baked potato, mix pulp with butter and season, refill shells sprinkle with cheese and gratinate.
Menagère	As for gratinée with the addition of chopped ham and onions cooked in butter.
Surprise	Scoop out baked potato through small hole, mix pulp with butter and cream, refill skins and brush with butter.
Macaire	Scoop out baked potato, mix with 30 g/1 oz butter per $\frac{1}{2}$ kg/lb of potato, shape medallion, trellis the top and shallow fry in clarified butter.
Byron	As for Macaire, then hollow the top, sprinkle with cheese and cover with cream.
Robert	As for Macaire, then mix chopped chives and 3 egg yolks per $\frac{1}{2}$ kg/lb of mix. Finish as for Macaire.
Alphonese	Peel, slice, add *Beurre Maitre d'hotel* (parsley butter), sprinkle with cheese, glaze.

Dishes using turned (barrel shaped) potatoes

Name of dish	Method
Fondantes	Turned, cooked in stock in the oven, brush with butter during cooking.
Champignole	As for fondant, glaze with cheese in the oven.
Berrichonne	As for fondant with addition of lardons and button onions during the cooking.
Cretan	As for fondant with the addition of powdered thyme.
Flamade	Cook in consommé with the addition of small onions and carrots.
Chateau	Blanch for 3 minutes, sauté, finish by roasting in oven.

Cocotte	Turn pieces half the size of Chateau, cook in same way.
Bonne-femme	As for Cocotte with the addition of small braised onions.
Noisette	Cut with a scoop the size of a hazelnut, cook as for Chateau.
Parisienne	Make twice the size of Noisette, cook as for Chateau, roll in *glace de viande* (meat stock) to finish.
Quelin	As for large Noisette, then boil or steam, roll in butter and parsley to finish.

Sliced potato dishes

Name of dish	**Method**
Anna	Cut lengthways, slice, wash and dry, set in layers in a buttered mould; butter and season as layers build up, butter and cook in the oven, remove from mould to serve.
Vision	As for Anna with cheese. Also known as *Ambassadeur*.
Mirelle	As for Anna mix with Jerusalem artichoke and truffle.
Darphine	Cut Julienne strips of potato, cook as for Anna.
Ideale	As for Darphine, with truffle.
Jetée-Promenade	As for Darphine with Julienne strips of Jerusalem artichoke and truffle.
Nana	As for Darphine, cooked in a dariole mould.
Paysanne	Slice thick, cook in butter and consommé with garlic, sorrel and chervil.
Normade	Slice with leek and onion, toss in butter, flour and milk, season, place in gratin dish, brown in oven.
Dauphinoise	Slice raw, cook in the oven with milk and Gruyère cheese.
Boulengère	Slice raw, mix with sliced onions, (3 parts potato to 1 part onion) moisten with consommé, butter, and cook in the oven.
Savoyarde	As for Boulangère with lardons and cheese. Also known as *Chambery*.
A la crème	Boil, slice and cook in cream in the oven.
Maire	As for à la crème.
Schnider	As for à la crème with consommé and meat glaze, finish with butter and parsley.
Delmonico	Dice raw, cook as for à la crème, finish with breadcrumbs and brown or gratinate.
Villa des Fleurs	As for Delmonico, with cheese.
Sable	Dice raw, toss in butter, add breadcrumbs when nearly cooked.

Fried potato dishes

Name of dish	**Method**
Cheveu	Fine julienne strips of potato, deep-fry.
Julienne	Julienne strips of potato deep-fry.
Paille	Large julienne strips, deep-fry.
Allumette	Matchstick size pieces of potato, deep-fry.
Mignonette	Double the size of allumette, deep-fry.
Frites	Double the size of mignonettes, blanch in fat, deep-fry.
Chips	Slice potatoes very thinly, deep-fry till golden.
En liard	Cut potato into cork shape, slice and deep-fry,
Gaufrettes	Cut in a trellis using a mandolin, deep-fry till golden. Also known as *Loulou*.
Soufflées	Trim square, cut 3 mm ($\frac{1}{8}$ in) thick, blanch in cool fat, finish in hot fat
Chatouillard	Cut ribbon shape, cook as for soufflées.
Au nid	(1) Soufflés potato dressed in a nest of *pommes pailles*.
	(2) In the same nest fill with *pomme parisienne*.
Benedictine	Cut in a spiral, deep-fry.
Copeaux	Cut ribbon shape, deep-fry.
Collerette	Cut cylinder shape, groove, blanch in fat, finish in hot fat.
Bataille	Dice and deep-fry.
Cendrillon	Shape like a sabot, pane, deep-fry, fill with pulp mixed with cream.

Sauté potato dishes

Name of dish	**Method**
Sauté	Boil or steam in skins, peel, slice, toss in butter till brown.
Allemande	Sauté potatoes cut thick and buttered.

Lyonnaise	Sauté potatoes mix with sauté onions. (3 potato to 1 onion).
Columbine	Sauté raw potatoes, garnish with julienne strips of pimento.
Provençale	Sauté potatoes with garlic.

Steamed potato dishes

Name of dish	Method
Vapeur	Shaped and steamed. Also known as *Anglaise*.
Irlandaise	Cut in ribbons and steamed.
Menth	Steamed with mint.
Robe de Chambre	Wash and steam in skins.
Jacquette	Wash, cut round the skin, steam in skins

Other potato dishes

Name of dish	Method
Bignon	Small boxes of potato, filled with sausage meat, mix with breadcrumbs, cook in the oven. Serve with Madeira sauce.
Farcis	Scoop out potato, fill with forcemeat, braise in stock.
Au lard	Cut potato in quarters, cook with bacon and braised onions in consommé.
Gastronome	Shape like corks, blanch, and cook in butter, roll in meat glaze and chopped truffle.
Grillées	Slice 12 mm ($\frac{1}{2}$ in) thick, butter and grill.
Hongroise	Large rounds of potato cooked in consommé with onions, tomatoes and paprika, reduce and finish with butter and parsley.
Mirette	Dice, cook in butter add julienne strips of truffle, roll in meat glaze and sprinkle with grated cheese, cook in oven.
Persillees	Shape, steam, roll in butter and chopped parsley.

Portion sizes (raw weight)
- 1 kg ($2\frac{1}{4}$ lb) of old potatoes will produce approximately 8 portions.
- 1 kg ($2\frac{1}{4}$ lb) of new potatoes will produce approximately 12 portions.

New potatoes are new season crop potatoes and begin very small, commanding high prices until the main crop begins to be harvested. They are imported first from the Channel Islands – Jersey and Guernsey, and are also imported from Europe in large quantities. The new potato is cooked starting in boiling not cold water, or cooked in their skins in the steamer.

Typical new potato dishes are:
Pommes nouvelles au menthe
Pommes nouvelles au beurre
Pommes nouvelles rissolées
Salade de pommes de terre (potato salad)
Salade Niçoise
Soups
As potato starch (fecule) used to thicken sauces.

Sweet Potato (Eddoe)

Prepare and cook as you would the common potato. Sweet potato can be stir-fried or sautéed from raw providing the cut is small i.e. julienne or baton strips.

Typical sweet potato dishes are:
Nature – boiled
Sauté – stir fried
Vapeur – steamed

COOKING BULB VEGETABLE DISHES

Onions are cooked as a vegetable dish and also used in salads and recipes for main dish productions.

The main onion vegetables dishes are:

Oignons braisés	Braised onions
Oignons frit à la Française	French fried onions
Oignons sautés	Fried onions
L'oignon hacher	Mince or finely chop
L'oignon émincer	Thinly cut slices.
Oignons Lyonnaise	Fried and used to compliment a dish i.e. potatoes or liver.

Leeks

Leeks are related to the onion family and are cooked as a vegetable in their own right. Younger leeks are preferred to larger older leeks which can be stringy even when cooked. Choose slim tender leeks for use as a vegetable dish, having prepared the leeks and checked they are free from grit and dirt place them tied in a bunch into boiling salted water to blanch for 5–7 mins, when required for braising, and 8–15 minutes when plain boiled.

Braised leeks are cooked in a braising pan or tray on a bed of chopped root vegetables, covered with stock and cooked with a faggot of herbs (*bouquet garni*). Cover them with a lid and cook in the oven for 20–40 minutes. Finish the stock with a thickened gravy and check the consistency and seasoning of the finished sauce. Dress the hot leeks in a vegetable dish and coat with sauce. Allow two small leeks per portion or one medium sized.

Leeks are used in many stocks, soups and sauces, hors d'oeuvres and savoury products e.g. leek and potato pie or tartlettes.

Typical leek dishes are:

Poireaux braisée	braised leeks
Poireaux au beurre	buttered leeks
Poireaux nature	plain boiled leeks
Poireaux au gratin	with a cheese sauce

You can now get tiny miniature leeks which are tender and very decorative. Leeks are used for cold buffet aspic work to decorate joints and poultry, game and fish. The small leeks are blanched and cut into shapes, dipped in aspic and dressed to form neat artistic patterns.

Spring onion (*ciboule*)

Spring onions can be finely chopped and added to sauces, hors d'oeuvres and cold preparations. They are not cooked as a vegetable in European cookery but do have a key place in Chinese cookery methods where they are often deep fried in sesame seed oil or used as a composite ingredient of traditional dishes.

Shallot (*l'échalote*)

The shallot is generally used as a flavouring agent for a sauce, soup or main dish. The firm texture and delicate flavour is a favourite especially in September and October when they are at their best. They can be cooked and served as a vegetable but this is not usual. They are also used as a shredded or finely chopped addition to salads and hors d'oeuvre preparations.

Garlic (*l'ail*)

Available all year round, garlic can be either standard, jumbo or elephant garlic; the best garlic comes from France. It is used to flavour all manner of dishes, soups sauces and salads. Peel and crush, slice or finely chop, macerate in olive oil or use in mayonnaise and many sauce recipes. Garlic is cooked as a composite ingredient. Garlic has a strong flavour and should be used sparingly when very fresh.

Courgette (*courgette*)

Courgettes require very little cooking because they are tender. They are often not peeled and have no seeds to speak of. They can be sliced or cooked whole.

Typical courgette dishes are:

*Courgettes sautée*s	fried courgette
Courgette nature	plain boiled
Courgettes au beurre	with butter
Courgettes frites	deep fried
Courgettes provençale	provençale style
Courgettes portugaise	portugaise style

Marrow (*courge*)

Marrows are cooked by steaming in trays or by brief blanching in boiling water, draining well and brushing with melted butter and chopped parsley.

The skin of the marrow is tough and is not cooked but peeled. De-seed the marrow before cooking. Marrow is 80% water and when ripe does not need a lot of cooking, so do not over cook or it will be difficult to handle; they often break up when over-steamed or boiled too long.

Typical marrow dishes are:

Courge provençale	provençale style
Courge nature	plain boiled
Courge farcie	stuffed with farce

MEMORY JOGGER

Why must marrows not be cooked for too long?

COOKING LEAF VEGETABLES

Where green leaf vegetables are cooked it is important to retain both the colour for appearance, and the natural nutritive value by not cooking too much. Cook in the minimum volume of water.

Remove the outer green leaves and cook whole, chop up the paler inside of the cabbage or greens and cook separately. Use the blanched outer leaves as a wrapping for the chopped centre parts of the cabbage or greens. Season well and form a ball with the outer leaves. Butter well and steam or re-heat in the oven.

This method can be used with a variety of stuffing e.g. rice or meat, duxelles or provençale type fillings. Equally you can cover the ball of leaf vegetable with a mornay sauce and gratinate.

Healthy eating

Cook leafy vegetables for as short a time as possible to maintain the maximum nutritional value.

Green/White Cabbage (*chou vert*)

Typical cabbage dishes are:

Chou vert nature	plain boiled
Chou vert farcie	stuffed
Chou vert braisés	braised cabbage
Sauerkraut	pickled cabbage
Coleslaw	sliced raw cabbage salad

Red Cabbage (*chou rouge*)

Chou rouge nature	plain boiled
Chou à la flamande	braised red cabbage
Chou salade	pickled in vinegar (for hors d'oeuvres or salad)

Chard

Use only the youngest leaves which are tender; cook as for cabbage.

Chicory (*endive*)

Prepare with lemon and sugar. Do not cook any discoloured or wilted leaves. Cook in the minimum volume of water and save butter; cook in a pan by steaming or in the oven covered with a buttered cartouche for approximately 45 mins. It can also be braised and served with a thickened stock or shallow fried in butter, chopped parsley and lemon juice.

Curly kale (*chou-frisé*)

Served as a hot vegetable dish, curly kale is cooked as for cabbage.

Typical curly kale dishes are:

Chou-frisé nature	plain boiled
Chou-frisé au beurre	with butter

Lettuce (*laitue*)

Lettuce should be crisp, with a firm heart and no rotting or decaying leaves. It can be braised and is used to garnish certain dishes as well as salads.

Braised lettuce is cooked on a bed of roots and covered with white stock, cooked in the oven and finished with jus-lié.

Sprouts and sprout tops

Young sprouts are cooked briefly in boiling salted water; do not over-cook or they will lose colour and vitamins. Serve with butter and nutmeg. Sprouts can be cooked as for cabbage recipes but do not need as much cooking time. Always remove the stem.

Typical sprout dishes are:

Chou de Bruxelles	brussel sprouts
Chou de Bruxelles au beurre	buttered
Chou de Bruxelles au lard	with bacon
Chou de Bruxelles au muscade	with nutmeg

Spinach

You need a large volume of spinach to produce reasonable portions when cooked fresh; 90% of spinach is water and when cooked much of the mass volume is lost. Cook in boiling salted water for 2–5 minutes, drain well and squeeze out the moisture before finishing with butter and seasoning.

Typical spinach dishes are:

Epinard nature	plain boiled
Epinard en branche	leaf spinach
Epinard en purée	spinach purée
Epinard à la crème	with cream, yogurt or skimmed milk.

Spinach is used in many different dishes such as fish, eggs and savoury tartlets, salads and hors d'oeuvres.

When used as a garnish the name referring to spinach is *Florentine*.

Cauliflower (*chou fleur*)

Cauliflowers are either cooked whole or as florettes. It can be fresh or frozen. When frozen it is usual to purchase them as florettes. Cook in boiling salted water for about 15–20 minutes depending on the size and volume being cooked. Remove the stalk heart before cooking.

Typical cauliflower dishes are:

Chou-fleur nature	plain boiled
Chou-fleur au beurre	with butter
Chou-fleur frit	deep fried in batter
Chou-fleur à la crème	with cream, yogurt or skimmed milk.
Chou-fleur au gratin	with a cheese sauce
Chou-fleur mornay	with egg yolk and cheese not gratinated
Chou-fleur polonaise	finished with a mixture of fried breadcrumbs, sieved egg yolk and white and chopped parsley.

Cauliflower can be used for crudités, i.e. raw vegetables washed and trimmed and served with a selection of savoury dips.

Broccoli (*brocoli*)

All broccoli recipes, both cooking and finishing are as for cauliflower. There are two types of broccoli, the standard green, and purple sprouting broccoli. It can also be used as a crudité vegetable.

Globe artichokes (*artichauts*)

Globe artichokes are best cooked in a *blanc* made from flour, water and lemon juice. The artichoke goes brown or oxidises because of the enzymic action with oxygen resulting in a discolouration which does not enhance the presentation of the dish.

Blanc recipe
1 litre (2 pt) of water
25 g (1 oz) flour
juice of 1 large lemon
salt and pepper.
1 Blend the flour and water
2 Stir in the lemon juice and seasoning
3 Bring to the boil, stir well as it comes to the boil.

Typical artichoke dishes are:

Artichaut en branche	globe Artichokes
Artichaut hollandaise	with hollandaise sauce
Fonds d' artichauts	artichoke bottoms
Fonds d' artichauts	with butter (au beurre)

Artichokes are also used in soups and as a garnish for certain dishes. Bottoms can be purchased in brine in tins. They can be used as an hors d'oeuvre, and as a garnish for braised meat dishes e.g. *Clamart* (artichoke bottoms piped with puree of peas, brushed with melted butter and baked lightly).

Celery (*celeri*)

Celery is cooked as a hot vegetable by the braising method. The celery is tied in

MEMORY
JOGGER

If a recipe uses the term *Florentine* which vegetable will be used in the finishing of such a dish?

small bundles and set on a bed of roots having been blanched first in clean boiling salted water. The celery is placed in a suitable pan and covered with stock and cooked with a faggot of herb and some fat bacon. Served as for all braised vegetables in a *jus lié*.

Typical celery dishes are:
Céleri braisé	braised celery
Céleri a la greque	celery greek style
Céleri portugaise	Portuguese style

Celery is used for bouquet garni, soups and sauces, salads and as a braised vegetable or hors d'oeuvre.

Asparagus (*d'asperges*)

The tips of asparagus, being much more tender, cook more quickly than the stalks. The answer is to cook asparagus in an asparagus kettle (a special pan with a rack) but failing this they may be cooked tied together in bundles in a wide pan. First stand the bundles upright and cook for 10 minutes to start softening the stems, then lay flat and cook in the boiling salted water for 10–15 minutes or until tender; do not over-cook.

Typical asparagus dishes are:
Pointes d'asperges	asparagus tips
D'asperges hollandaise	with hollandaise sauce
D'asperges mayonnaise	with mayonnaise
D'asperges au beurre fondu	with melted butter
D'aperges au vinaigrette	with vinaigrette sauce

Asparagus is used in many sauces and soups and as a garnish for a wide range of dishes. e.g. canapés, salads, hors d'oeuvres, hot and cold dishes such as bouchées, vol-au-vents and fricassée.

Sea kale (*chou de mer*)

Sea kale is cooked as for cabbage recipes and can also be served cold with mayonnaise or vinaigrette.

Fennel (*fenouil*)

Cooking times for fennel vary depending on the size and quality. Fennel may be sliced and used raw in salads. Fennel top is used to flavour fish dishes and has a pronounced aniseed flavour. Cook the fennel bulb in boiling salted water for 15–20 minutes or until tender. Do not over-cook fennel, proceed as for all cauliflower recipes.

Typical fennel dishes are:
Fenouil nature	plain boiled
Fenouil au beurre	with butter
Fenouil au gratin	gratinated with cheese
Fenouil mornay	with egg and cheese sauce
Fenouil hollandaise	with hollandaise sauce

Fennel can be also braised like celery. Fennel top is a herb used in cookery for its special aniseed flavour.

Edible fungi

Cep	(Cèpe)
Chanterelle	(Egg Mushroom)

Morel	(Sponge mushroom)
Mushroom	(champignon) cup/button/field
Truffle	(White or Black)
Shiitake	(Chinese mushroom)
Boletus	(Yellow mushroom)
Wood Ears	(Chinese black fungus)
Rubber Brush	(Wood Hedgehog)
Field Mushroom	(Wild Mushroom)
Parasol Mushroom	(Umbrella mushroom)
Blewit	
Beefsteak Fungus	

MEMORY JOGGER

Why are fungi expensive to purchase in relative terms?

All fungi can be served in their own right as a vegetable or as a garnish when available. Some can be costly and need careful handling when cooking. Generally they are sautéed with butter or lightly grilled to preserve the delicate flavour. They can be purchased fresh or dried. Mushrooms are used for a wide range of dishes, soups, sauces and salads, hot and cold dishes. Fungi are expensive because they grow mainly in the wild and are not easily found.

COOKING VEGETABLE FRUITS

- Tomatoes (*tomates*)
- Ladies fingers (*okra*)
- Marrow (*courge*)
- Avocado (*avocado*)
- Egg plant (*aubergine*)
- Cucumber (*concombre*)
- Courgette (*courgette*)
- Capsicum (*pimento*)
- Sweetcorn (*mais*)

Tomatoes

Tomato are cooked in a number of ways. They form the basis of many recipes as tomato concassé (chopped tomato), or grilled, or stuffed with a number of farces. They can be grilled whole or in halves, or blanched to remove the skins. With the tops removed and the seeds scooped out, they can be filled with duxelles or rice or meat-based stuffing.

Typical tomato dishes are:

| *Tomates grillées* | grilled tomatoes |
| *Tomates farcies* | stuffed tomato |

Tomatoes are used for many salads and salad preparations.

Okra (*Gumbo, Ladies fingers*)

These are green pods of Ethiopian hibiscus plants much used in Greek, Indian and American cookery. Choose the smallest fresh looking pods. Wash, wipe dry and cook for 10–15 minutes in boiling water. Toss in melted butter. They can be sliced and used in vegetable curries. Take care not to over-cook or they will exude a slimy, sticky juice which is useful in producing a thickening agent for some dishes such as gumbo or soups.

Aubergine

Both the flesh and the skin are edible in a cooked form but remove the inedible spiny stalk before cooking. Always slice, sprinkle with salt, wash and dry to remove bitterness before cooking.

Grilling or baking: Brush 1 cm (½ in) thick prepared slices lightly with butter or vegetable oil. Bake in a medium oven 160 °C/325 °F, Gas Mark 3 for 20–30 minutes or grill for 10–15 minutes, turning once. Serve immediately.

Frying: Coat 1 cm (½ in) thick prepared slices in seasoned flour. Fry in hot butter or vegetable oil for 10–15 minutes until golden on both sides. Serve immediately.

Stuffing and baking: Cut aubergine in half lengthways. Scoop out flesh leaving 0.5 cm (¼ in) shell. Prepare in normal way with salt. A savoury filling incorporating the flesh can then be made and put back into the shells. Bake in a medium oven 160 °C/ 325 °F, Gas Mark 3 for about 20–30 mins or until shell and filling are cooked. Serve immediately.

Typical aubergine dishes are:
Aubergine frit   fried aubergine
Aubergine farcie   stuffed aubergine

Serving Suggestions: As a vegetable accompaniment to fish or meat. As a main dish combined with meat or other vegetables. Aubergines may be served cold (after cooking) and served in a yogurt and garlic based salad.

Courgette

Courgette can be prepared Provençal or Portuguese styles. Cook as for marrow

Capsicum (pepper)

Peppers are cooked sliced, diced, chopped or whole. The colour is attractive and adds to the overall presentation and flavour of any dish using pepper as an ingredient. Peppers come in red, green yellow and orange colours.

Typical pepper dishes are:
Piment grillées   grilled peppers
Piment farci   stuffed peppers

Peppers are used also to enhance salads and hors d'oeuvres, soups sauces and hot and cold dishes.

Sweetcorn

Boil baby sweetcorn whole for 5 minutes, serve with melted butter and black pepper as a side vegetable or starter. They are ideal for stir-fry, Chinese dishes or casseroles. Fully grown sweetcorn should be cooked in boiling water for 8–10 minutes. Serve with butter and freshly ground black pepper.

Broad bean (*fèves*)

Broad beans are removed from the pod and the beans cooked in boiling salted water for 5–10 mins. Refresh and peel the outer waxy skin to reveal two halves of the bean. The waxy skin can be left on when the bean is young, but as it ages this is tough to eat.

Typical broad bean dishes are:
Fèves nature   plain boiled
Fèves à la crème   with cream, yogurt or skimmed milk
Fèves persillées   with chopped parsley
Fèves au beurre   with butter

French bean (*haricot vert*)

French beans are fine beans usually cooked boiling in saltwater for a few minutes until the beans are tender, then refreshed and finished in a variety of ways.

Haricot vert au beurre	with butter
Haricot vert sauté au beurre	shallow fried in butter
Haricot vert sauté au poivre	shallow fried in butter and mill pepper.

Kenya bean (fine)

Cooked as for French beans, these fine thin beans are best lightly boiled, drained and sautéed in butter and mill pepper. They are imported from Kenya and Europe.

Runner bean

Grown throughout the UK, runner beans are best when young. Remove the stringy line down edge of bean and top and tail. Cut into diagonal thin slices and boil until tender. Serve with melted butter.

Mangetout

Thin whole young pea pods served after lightly boiling for a few minutes only have an excellent flavour. They can be eaten raw, used whole or cut as a garnish for stir-fry and vegetable compositions. They should be cooked to retain colour and crispness; it is easy to over-cook them.

Peas (*petit pois*)

Peas are used extensively on the menu as a hot vegetable dish, and as a garnish for soups and main dishes. Boil or steam for a few minutes or until tender. Serve hot with butter and/or sugar. Young peas are called *petit pois* and are small; used in salads and soups.

Typical pea dishes are:

Petits pois	young peas
Petits pois à la française	French style
Petits pois à la flamande	Flemish style
Petits pois au beurre	with butter
Petits pois au sucre	with sugar
Petits pois au menthe	with mint

QUALITY ISSUES WHEN COOKING VEGETABLES

When cooking any vegetable you should inspect each portion to ensure the food is not cooked too much or is too firm. Where vegetables are over-cooked the texture is soft and the colour poor. This detracts from the quality of the finished hot or cold vegetable dish or salad.

Food is sold by appearance, aroma and flavour, under-cooked vegetables which are difficult to eat, equally will undermine the customer perception of the establishment standard. We cook a large quantity of frozen vegetables but the use of fresh vegetables imported from all over the world has grown in recent years.

Excellent quality is now a standard for specialist vegetable foods. When cooking vegetables it is important to maintain consistency in your skills to maximise the benefit to the customer and minimise the waste by negligence. Handle vegetables carefully to avoid mechanical damage and store according to their type.

Key points to watch out for when cooking vegetables are:
● texture
● flavour

- aroma
- appearance
- consistency.

COOKING METHODS FOR VEGETABLES

Boiling vegetables

Boiling is the cooking of prepared vegetables in sufficient liquid at boiling point 100 °C / 212 °F. This can be in water, stock, milk, court bouillon or blanc.

The purpose of boiling vegetables is:
- To make foods safe to eat
- To make foods easily digestible
- To make foods palatable with a suitable texture.

Methods of boiling
There are two ways to boil vegetables: either
1 place in boiling liquid and simmer.
or
2 place in cold liquid and bring to the boil.

The main advantages of foods brought to the boil with *cold* liquids are:
- it helps to tenderise, extracts starch and some flavour
- it avoids damage to foods that might otherwise lose their shape if added to a boiling liquid.

The main advantages of foods placed into *boiling* liquids are:
- Green vegetables retain their colour and nutritive value.
- Plunge vegetables into hot water and then refresh in cold water e.g. when removing tomato skins or nut skins or parsley before it is dried. The action kills off unwanted enzymes.

Vegetables suitable for boiling:
almost all vegetables can be boiled.

Effects of boiling vegetables
The cellular structure of the vegetable is softened by the boiling process. Where vegetables are under-cooked this structure has not been softened sufficiently and where over-cooked – too much.

Time and temperature
Care should be taken to ensure that a cooking temperature is maintained at all times and that liquid replacement takes place during the cooking process to counteract evaporation. The age and size of the vegetables will effect the cooking times.

Soaking
Covering in cold water prior to boiling being carried out, is used to soften certain foods before being cooked e.g. dried vegetables and dried pulses.

Skimming
This is the removal of impurities from the boiling surface while waiting for the liquid to reach boiling point and during the boiling process.

Equipment used for boiling
- Stock pots
- Saucepans
- Sauté pans
- Colanders
- Bratt pans
- Spiders

Healthy eating

Boil vegetables as quickly as possible in a small amount of water to maintain their nutritional value.

MEMORY JOGGER

When boiling vegetables what basic rules need to be followed?

● Strainers
● Perforated spoons
● Small utensils

General rules to be followed when boiling vegetables
1 Select pans that are neither too large nor too small.
2 Remove any scum that rises to the surface.
3 Liquid should simmer and not boil vigorously, replenish with water where evaporation takes place.
4 Use only sufficient water to cover the vegetables to be cooked, using too much water wastes energy and takes longer to boil.

Shallow-frying vegetables

Equipment for shallow-frying: a sauteuse (right); a frying pan (far right)

MEMORY JOGGER

Name the four methods of shallow frying vegetables?

Shallow-frying is the cooking of food in pre-heated shallow fat, clarified butter, oil or a mixture of these.

The purpose of shallow frying is:
● to make food safe, palatable, digestible and add variety to the menu.
● to brown food giving it an interesting and attractive flavour.

Methods of shallow-frying

There are four methods of shallow-frying: shallow-frying, sauté, griddle and stir-fry.

Shallow-frying
Food is shallow-fried in a small amount of fat or oil in a frying pan or sauté pan. The food is placed presentation-side first into the pan to ensure good appearance, and then turned, until both sides are cooked. The fat is replaced as it is absorbed. This method can be applied to most vegetables.

Sauté
Sauté is a French term meaning 'to jump' or 'leap'. With sauté dishes, begin as for shallow-frying by heating the fat or oil or a mixture of oil and butter. The vegetables should be small and are raw or blanched. The small pieces are tossed rather than turned, until they are browned. They are cooked to add colour e.g. *sauté potatoes*, or re-heated prior to service e.g. *haricot vert sauté au beurre*.

Foods that are cooked sauté usually have a light golden brown colour or finish. This is only achieved if the fat, oil or butter is hot enough to colour quickly. The heat can be reduced once the food is coloured and cooked.

Techniques associated with sauté:
Proving   the heating and oiling of a pan to prevent food sticking during cooking.
Coating   used to protect certain foods when cooking.

Browning	is achieved by the careful selection of pan, fat and temperature.
Tossing and turning	is achieved by wrist and hand manipulation
Holding	is to allow food to be kept hot after being cooked.
Draining	to allow surplus fat to be absorbed by kitchen paper prior to service.

Griddle
Foods are cooked on a solid pre-heated metal plate or griddle whilst being turned regularly.

Stir-fry
Stir-frying involves fast-frying in a wok or frying pan, usually with vegetables, cut in strips.

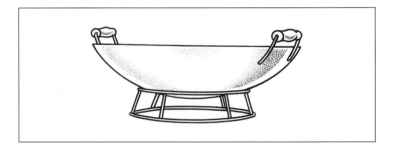

A wok

Vegetables suitable for shallow-frying
Almost all vegetables can be shallow-fried, apart from green leafy items. Some harder root vegetables will need par-boiling to soften them first.

Deep-fried vegetables

Deep-fried foods are cooked in deep pre-heated oil or fat.

The purpose of deep-frying is:
● to colour and enhance the appearance, flavour and texture of foods.

Methods of deep-frying
Deep-fried vegetables are generally coated to protect the food from the high temperature of the fat and capture the natural juices/moisture of the food.

The time needed for deep-frying is dependent upon the type of food being cooked, the volume and thickness. Practice and common sense with the aid of peer advice will develop your skills in judging when an item is cooked through and of the correct colour for service.

Vegetables suitable for deep-frying
Almost any vegetable can be deep-fried if coated in a batter, breadcrumbs or milk-and-flour coating. Many are blanched prior to cooking and have either been left whole if small, or cut into the required shape.

Popular deep-fried vegetables are: mushrooms, onions, courgette, salsify, celery, carrot, aubergine, leek, broccoli, peppers and cauliflower.

Deep-frying potatoes
If the potatoes are wet or damp when cooked the oil will bubble, which can be dangerous if the oil is very hot or the fryer is over-filled. The life of the cooking oil will also be reduced if the potatoes are damp or wet when cooked. They fry much better if dry and have had as much of the starch removed as possible by running under hot and then cold water for some time.

Healthy eating
Always drain fried foods on dish paper to reduce the amount of fat in the diet.

Healthy eating
Use polyunsaturated fat or oil for deep frying

When frying vegetable or potato dishes a 'spider' should be used regularly to remove batter or food particles from the oil; this reduces carbonisation of material and extends the life of the oil.

Always drain vegetable and potato foods that are deep-fried on dish paper.

Potato shapes for frying

Potato cuts suitable for deep-frying:
1 straw   2 matchstick   3 wafer   4 woodchip   5 cubes   6 thick matchsticks
7 pont neuf   8 French fries

English term	French term	Size
Chips	*Pommes frites*	50×10 mm ($2 \times \frac{1}{2}$ in)
Straw	*Pommes pailles*	$40 \times 4 \times 4$ mm ($1\frac{1}{2} \times \frac{1}{4} \times \frac{1}{4}$ in)
Straw (fine)	*Pommes chifonette*	$40 \times 2 \times 2$ mm ($1\frac{1}{2} \times \frac{1}{10} \times \frac{1}{10}$ in) thick
Crisps	*Pommes chip*	thin shaped slices 3 mm ($\frac{1}{10}$ in) thick
Matchstick	*Pommes allumettes*	$40 \times 3 \times 3$ mm ($1\frac{1}{2} \times \frac{1}{10} \times \frac{1}{10}$ in)
Pont neuf	*Pommes Pont Neuf*	$40 \times 20 \times 20$ mm ($1\frac{1}{2} \times 1 \times 1$ in)
Collerette	*Pommes colerette*	cylinder shaped, grooved edge
Matchstick (thick)	*Pommes mignotte*	$45 \times 5 \times 5$ mm ($2 \times \frac{1}{4} \times \frac{1}{4}$ in)
Wafer	*Pommes gaufrette*	trellis cut slices 3 mm ($\frac{1}{10}$ in) thick
Spiral	*Pommes Bénédictine*	cut spiral shape
Cubes	*Pommes bataille*	cut 15 mm ($\frac{1}{2}$ in) cubes

Grilling vegetables

Grilling is a fast method of cookery using radiant heat and is known as broiling in the USA.

The purpose of grilling is:
● to make food safe to eat, digestible and palatable
● the speed of the cooking process introduces distinctive flavour, colour, texture and eating quality
● to bring variety to the menu.

Methods of grilling
There are three methods of grilling:
1 *Over heat* (true grilling) e.g. charcoal, barbecue, gas or electrically heated grill.
2 *Under heat* – gas or electric salamander (oven-fired grill).
3 *Between heat* – Electrically-heated grill bars or plates.

The salamander can also be used for browning, gratinating and glazing certain dishes e.g. tomatoes can be marked with a hot iron before grilling and mushrooms are 'turned', cut with a small knife to indent a pattern, they are brushed with butter and grilled.

Vegetables suitable for grilling
Mushrooms, tomatoes, onions, peppers and aubergines.

Roasting vegetables

Roasting is cooking in dry heat with the aid of fat in an oven or on a spit. Using poly or mono-unsaturated fats rather than oil or dripping to roast vegetables leads to healthier eating practices.

The purpose of roasting is:
● to make the vegetables easy to digest
● to make them safe to eat
● to make them palatable
● to add variety to the menu.

Methods of roasting
True roasting is to expose food to the radiant heat of an open fire e.g. spit roasting meat or poultry. The spit constantly revolves to ensure even cooking and fat used for basting to avoid the food drying and burning. Owing to the many disadvantages of spit roasting, oven roasting has developed in its place.

Oven roasting is the application of:
● applied dry heat
or
● forced air convected heat
or
● convected heat combined with microwave energy.

Vegetables suitable for roasting:
Potatoes, parsnip, onions, sweet potato, Jerusalem artichokes and peppers .

Effects of roasting
The initial heat seals the surface adding colour and flavour. The heat is then reduced to prevent the outer surface burning. Basting has a crisping effect with potatoes but not with other vegetables. Because of the high moisture content of vegetables, when roasted they tend to soften after roasting.

Advantages of roasting
1 High quality foods are tender and succulent when roasted.
2 Foods take on a very distinctive and agreeable flavour.
3 Accurate temperature control is possible.

MEMORY JOGGER

When roasting vegetables what fat/oils can be used? How can your choice contribute to healthy eating practices?

Time and temperature control
- Shelves and temperature must be set.
- Oven must be pre-heated.
- Shape, size and quality of food will affect cooking times.
- Internal temperature of food is critical in the roasting process.

Testing for degree of cooking
When cooked the roasted vegetables or potatoes should offer little resistance when pierced with a small office or vegetable knife. The centre should be soft, not firm or woody. For most vegetables, the cooking time is not long and needs careful timing to coincide with the rest of the meal.

Equipment for roasting
- Trays should be strong, with handles in good repair.
- Trays should be thoroughly washed, dried and placed upside-down to drain after use.
- Ovens should be cleaned with hot soapy water and a mild abrasive.
- Oven trays and spits need to be thoroughly soaked before washing.
- Ovens must be inspected regularly and any fault discovered must be reported immediately.

Safety when roasting
1 Roasting trays should be of suitable size; if too small, basting becomes difficult and dangerous; if too large, fat in the tray will burn or catch fire, spoiling the flavour of the dish.
2 Handle hot roasting trays as little as possible. Always use a dry oven cloth.
3 Do not carry hot dishes any further than necessary. Make a space to set the dish down before you pick it up.

Do this

- List vegetables suitable for roasting.
- Send off for literature on types of roasting ovens.
- Which types of potatoes roast best and at which time of the year?
- Which fats and or oils are best for roasting ? How much do they cost per litre?
- Vegetables or potatoes are sometimes par boiled prior to roasting, why is this?
- Find out how large-volume operations deal with roasting for, say, over 1000 meals.

Steaming vegetables

Steaming is the cooking of prepared food by steam (moist heat). It can be done under varying degrees of pressure.

The purpose of steaming vegetables is
- to make food safe, digestible, palatable and of suitable texture
- retain as much nutrients as possible (steaming minimises nutritive loss).

Methods of steaming
1 *Low pressure* or *atmospheric*. The pressure is 0–3 lbs p.s.i. (0–17 kN/m^2).
   Food can be cooked with direct or indirect contact with the steam
   - Direct, in a steamer, or in a pan of boiling water, eg steak and kidney pudding.
   - Indirect, between 2 plates, over a pan of boiling water, ie. cabbage.
2 *High pressure* in specially designed equipment that does not allow the steam to escape, allowing it to build up pressure and increase the temperature and reduce the cooking time; 10–15 lbs p.s.i (70–105 kN/m^2).

Vegetables suitable for steaming
High-pressure steamers are suitable for almost all vegetables which retain colour

and vitamins which are not lost as in the boiling process. High-pressure steaming is used extensively today for fast cooking where prepared vegetables are processed via a high-pressure steamer, finished and served immediately.

<table>
<tr><td>

Healthy eating

Steaming vegetables retains their nutritional value better than boiling.

</td></tr>
</table>

Effect of steaming
1 The retention of natural juices and nutritional value.
2 Food is lighter and more easy to digest (ideal for invalids).
3 High pressure steam cooks and reheats food quickly.
4 Batch cooking enables small quantities of food to be cooked at regular intervals, thus retaining maximum colour, flavour and nutrition.
5 Labour saving and suitable for large scale cookery.
6 Steaming is economical on fuel in multi-tiered steamers.
7 Food does not break up.

Time and temperature control
Cooking times will vary with the size and quality of food; the type and operating pressure of equipment.

Techniques associated with steaming
Greasing This is a light coat of fat or oil applied to the mould/container.
Moulding Placing prepared food into prepared moulds.
Traying up Filling trays with containers for ease of handling.
Loading Placing trays in the steamer.
Covering A covering of greaseproof paper, foil or cling film used to cover containers to prevent moisture condensing on food.

Equipment used for steaming
There are four types of steamer:
1 Atmospheric
2 Pressure
3 High compression
4 Pressureless convection

Safety when steaming
1 Where applicable, check the water well is correctly filled and the ball valve arm moves freely.
2 Steam pressure must be reduced before opening the door.
3 Misuse of a steamer is extremely dangerous. Always take great care.

Vacuum cooking in a pouch (*sous vide*)

The food is prepared, garnished and sealed before steaming; this helps control weight loss, colour change, drying out and texture change. The method is labour saving and highly nutritious. Raw cuts of fish, chicken breasts, rice etc, are reheated in boiling water or a steamer.

Baking vegetables

Large vegetables such as potatoes and marrows can be baked whole. This method of cooking retains the nutrients and is fat free.

Potatoes are baked plain, in their skins. When cooked they can be split and served, with a variety of fillings, as 'jacket potatoes'.

New potatoes can also be baked in their skins, wrapped in foil with or without mint.

Marrows are usually de-seeded stuffed with a cooked meat or rice and vegetable farce, and wrapped in foil for baking. Do not overcook or the marrow will lose its shape.

Baked potatoes

FINISHING METHODS FOR VEGETABLES AND SALADS

Seasoning

Seasoning does not just mean adding salt and pepper but can cover a wide range of seasoning agents. Sugar, spices, herbs and oils can be used as flavouring agents to season vegetable dishes.

Mill pepper, sea salt, grain mustards, fresh herbs, nutmeg and other seasoning herbs and spices are used to flavour salads and vegetables. Coriander and thyme is used in *à la Greque* preparations, chives and mustard are used in certain salad dishes.

Seasoning is the most important aspect of food preparation and cooking. Done correctly it will bring out the flavour of individual foods: lack of seasoning will mean a dull dish lacking in flavour.

Garnishing

Vegetables themselves form the basis of garnish for many main dishes. Garnishing should only enhance the main quality of the dish and not predominate. Careful use of garnishing will provide a picture to the customer that is appealing and invites them to taste.

The shape and size of garnish is important. Parsley is used to garnish more than any other herb. It can be chopped roughly or very fine, each will present differently. Care taken to garnish dishes will mean your food appeals to the customer and demonstrates a standard of craft. Over-garnishing will have the opposite effect.

Dressing

Dressing dishes means to bring together a number of individual elements of a recipe and to construct or dress' them for presentation, hot or cold, according to the recipe instructions to create a presentation that is both individual and appetising.

Do not over-dress a vegetable dish, e.g. use too much parsley or lettuce. Dressing also refers to the addition of cold and hot sauces to the prepared dish, e.g. vinaigrette, mayonnaise, white or cheese sauce.

Tossing

Salads are tossed to combine the sauce dressing with the leaves and vegetable salad products. Normally a wooden bowl, and spoon and fork are used at the table for this purpose, but this can be done by the chef in the kitchen, especially if many portions are required for a banquet or dinner.

All ingredients should be tossed lightly to prevent mechanical damage to the vegetables. The sauce and herb dressing adds flavour and moisture to salad ingredients.

The term 'tossing' is also used for the turning over of vegetables and potatoes used in the shallow-frying method of cookery known as sauté.

Draining

Draining vegetables is carried out just prior to finishing the vegetable for service and when the vegetables are being blanched in preparation for service. Use a colander, chinois or strainer to remove all the excess water from the blanched or cooked vegetable item.

Poor draining means water will be evident in the service dish and spoil the presentation and taste of the vegetables, Spinach is a good example, being 90% water it requires good draining to remove excess moisture.

MEMORY JOGGER

When keeping vegetables chilled, hot or re-heating vegetables what is significant about the temperature range, 5 °C–65 °C?

Re-heating

When re-heating vegetables it is vital to have stored the vegetables in a safe temperature i.e. below 5 °C and to re-heat them above 65 °C.

Use hot pans of boiling salted water to re-heat blanched vegetables and to complete the cooking process. The vegetables are placed into the boiling pans, cooked, drained and finished according to the recipe instructions.

Where vegetables not required for immediate service are to be stored they should either be re-freshed in cold running water, drained and placed in the fridge or kept hot above 65 °C.

Healthy eating

When cooking and finishing vegetables for salads and hot vegetable dishes you can improve the healthy nature of prepared and cooked vegetable and salad dishes by:
- not peeling potatoes you increase significantly the fibre and vitamin content of the dish
- not removing the skin of certain vegetables such as peppers, cucumber and courgette increases the fibre content of the dish
- reducing the amount of salt used to flavour salads and dishes, sauces or dressings
- using low fat, poly or mono-unsaturated fats or oils instead of butter, dripping or saturated oils
- using cooking and finishing methods that minimise the amount of oil and fat and maximise the nutritional and vitamin content of the cooked dish e.g. methods such as steaming, boiling and grilling instead of shallow and deep frying or roasting

Essential knowledge

When cooking vegetables for hot dishes and salads you should:
- ensure all vegetables are thoroughly washed, cleaned and free from infestation or contamination by pesticides or chemicals before cooking
- cook vegetables in the minimum amount of water or by steaming to retain maximum nutritional value
- cook vegetables as close to the point of service as possible to reduce loss of nutritional value through over-cooking and ensure they are of an appetising colour and aroma
- dispose of or store unused cooked vegetables in a hygienic manner

Case study

You are required to plan a range of vegetable and salad dishes for a group of heart bypass patients who meet once a month at different local catering venues. You need to draw up a list of dishes that will meet the following criteria:
- *low fat*
- *low salt*
- *high fibre*
- *hot and cold dishes*
- *low sugar*

1   What dishes can provide high fibre intake?
2   How can you ensure no extra salt is added after the food is prepared?
3   Which methods of cookery will minimise the fat/oil levels of each dish?

What have you learned

1 What health and safety practices should be followed when cooking vegetables?
2 Why is it important to keep food preparation areas and equipment hygienic when cooking and storing vegetables?
3 What are the main contamination threats when cooking and storing vegetables?
4 What are the main categories of vegetables and which methods of cookery are applicable?
5 Which quality points should you look for with cooked vegetables?
6 When cooking vegetables why are time and temperature important ?
7 What are the main cookery methods applied to the cooking of vegetables?
8 Why should you boil or simmer vegetables gently?
9 Why should you sweat vegetables?
10 Why should vegetables be maintained at a safe temperature after cooking and when not required for immediate consumption be cooled rapidly ?
11 Which cookery methods applicable to the cooking of vegetables contribute most to minimal fat levels for healthy eating?
12 How is the reduction of salt in vegetable cookery beneficial?

Get ahead

1 Investigate unusual vegetables available from your wholesaler, supermarket or ethnic food shop.
2 Research some of the recipes used in vegetarian cookery.
3 Discuss with your peers what methods of cookery are new in vegetable cookery.
4 Draw up a list of vegetable based salads.
5 Design some creative potato dishes with a healthy bias to offer a more interesting menu option.
6 Find out what range of prepared and vacuum packed vegetable and potato products are available.

UNIT 2ND19

Prepare and cook basic vegetable protein dishes

This chapter covers:
ELEMENT 1: **Prepare basic vegetable protein dishes**
ELEMENT 2: **Cook basic vegetable protein dishes**

What you need to do

- Check that preparation, cooking areas and suitable equipment are hygienic and ready for use.
- Ensure vegetable protein and other ingredients are of the type, quality and quantity required.
- Report any problems identified with the quality of ingredients and cooked dishes promptly to the appropriate person.
- Ensure vegetable protein is correctly combined with other ingredients to meet quality requirements.
- Ensure vegetable protein dishes are prepared, cooked and finished using appropriate cooking and finishing methods to meet quality requirements.
- Ensure vegetable protein dishes not for immediate use are stored correctly.
- Check that preparation and cooking areas and equipment are cleaned correctly after use.
- Ensure all work is prioritised and carried out in an organised and efficient manner in line with appropriate organisational procedures and legal requirements.

What you need to know

- When preparing and cooking basic vegetable protein dishes what safe working practices should be followed.
- When preparing and cooking basic vegetable protein dishes why it is important to keep preparation, cooking areas and equipment hygienic.
- Why time and temperature are important when preparing and cooking basic vegetable protein dishes.
- What the main contamination threats are when preparing, cooking and storing basic vegetable protein dishes.
- What different types of vegetable protein are available and their uses in catering.
- What quality points you might look for in different types of vegetable proteins and cooked vegetable protein dishes.
- What basic preparation methods are most suitable for different types of vegetable proteins.
- Why basic vegetable protein dishes not for immediate consumption should be cooled rapidly or maintained at a safe hot temperature.
- What other alternatives are available which are suitable for vegetarians.
- What basic cooking methods are most suitable for different types of vegetable proteins, and how you would identify when different types of vegetable protein are cooked to dish requirements.
- What cooking methods and equipment can contribute to reducing the fat/oil in basic vegetable protein dishes.
- What products might be used to substitute high-fat ingredients when preparing basic vegetable protein dishes.
- Which fats and oils can contribute to

healthier catering practices.
- Why increasing the fibre content of basic vegetable protein dishes can contribute to healthy catering practices.

- Why reducing the amount of salt in basic vegetable protein dishes can contribute to healthy catering practices.

ELEMENT 1:   Prepare basic vegetable protein dishes

VEGETABLE PROTEINS

There are four types of vegetable protein available:
- reconstituted textured vegetable protein (TVP)
- tempeh
- tofu
- quorn

Reconstituted textured vegetable protein (TVP)

MEMORY JOGGER

Which type of bean is TVP produced from?

Textured Vegetable Protein (TVP) is a meat substitute made from protein obtained from soya bean, cereals, cotton-seed, wheat and oats. The soya bean is the main source of TVP because of its high protein content. TVP has a sponge-like texture and is formed into shapes during production. TVP is used mostly by manufacturing catering businesses as an alternative to meat in meat-free vegetarian dishes. Caterers can purchase TVP in bulk quantities to produce a mince suitable for use in hot and cold meat-free products.

TVP is extruded through nozzles under pressure while hot, expanding as it leaves the nozzle. TVP can be produced and purchased in flakes, granules, nuggets, strips, or small and medium-sized chunks.

Produced mainly but not exclusively in the US and the UK, TVP can be produced in a range of colours to suit the intended dish or purpose.

Tempeh

Tempeh is the result of fermenting soya cheese; this is produced by mixing soya bean and the mould *Rhizopus*. Gluten-free, tempeh, which has a chewy texture, is therefore suitable for diets that need to be gluten-free.

Tofu

Tofu is a high protein product derived from soya bean as a curd. This bean curd is produced by curdling the soya bean milk using Nigari or Epsom salts to make the milk curdle. Tofu can be purchased in soft, firm, sliced or smoked varieties. High in essential amino acids, tofu can also be bought in various shapes. Tofu can be prepared for savoury and sweet dishes.

Quorn (myco-protein)

Quorn is related to the fungi family of mushrooms and occurs as a natural product found in the earth. It is produced in sterile conditions just as commercially cultivated mushrooms are. Quorn has a low-fat base and high fibre and protein qualities. It can be purchased in ready-prepared dishes or shaped ready for preparation. Quorn is tender in texture but does have a firmness to it.

Healthy eating

Vegetable proteins are by their very nature healthy alternatives to meat and meat-based products. In recent years these types of substitute proteins have grown in popularity but are not cheap. The chef can now offer a 'chef's healthy option' on the menu to provide for a client base who are more conscious about their health.

Used with fresh vegetables, pulses and natural ingredients vegetable proteins offer the opportunity to reduce the intake of fat, bleached-flour based ingredients and higher salt, oil and fat ingredients.

INGREDIENTS USED WITH VEGETABLE PROTEINS

Fresh vegetables and fruit

Vegetable proteins are prepared with other ranges of commodities in the same way as meat or fish. Many of the vegetable protein types described often lack a determined flavour and need to be cooked with other vegetables and/or fruits, herbs and spices to impart flavour and to develop an acceptable aroma.

The combinations open to chefs for this type of cookery seem unlimited and some recipes are provided in Element 2 to demonstrate some examples of these combinations. Most vegetable types can be prepared for cooking with the range of vegetable proteins. Many formal and traditional dishes, such as lasagne, are prepared using a vegetable protein and/or myco-protein (quorn) for the 'meat content', using onions, vegetable-based stock and garlic with tomatoes to produce the lasagne.

Fresh vegetables and fruits from the range covered in Unit 2ND18 pp. 350–91 provide information on most of the fresh vegetables and fruits suitable for preparation with vegetable proteins.

Preserved vegetables and fruit

Preserved vegetables are maintained by either:
- pickling
- drying
- preserving

Pickled vegetables include onions (e.g. silverskin and sweet), beetroot (e.g. whole baby or crinkle-cut slices) and gherkins (e.g. small cocktail types or larger dill-sized pickles). Pickled vegetables are blanched and placed in malt or white distilled vinegar.

Dried vegetables and fruits such as onion and potato are dehydrated and are used by rehydrating them with hot water. Many convenience packet soups use hydrated vegetables in their composition. Dried fruits are used in many vegetable protein recipes (e.g. apricots, apples, sultanas, figs , bananas and dates). Dried mango and tropical fruits are now more widely available for use in vegetable protein preparation.

Preserved vegetables and fruits include those preserved in high-sugar or high-salt solutions. This preserving process is known as *osmosis* where a balance is maintained between strong and weak salt and sugar solutions. By osmosis, the strong preserving liquid passes across the semi-permeable membrane of vegetables, such as carrots, to mix with the weaker natural salt solution within the carrot. A balance is created and preserves the food. Prolonged preservation of vegetables by this method renders them soft. In the same way, pears and all manner of fruits are tinned in sugar syrup solutions to preserve them. The same principle of osmosis applies.

Cereals such as buckwheat, barley (pearl), oats, couscous, maize, common millet, bulgur wheat and rye are used in a range of ways for vegetable protein and vegetarian dishes. All of these cereals provide a rich source of protein.

Do this

- Design a new vegetable protein dish for each type of vegetable protein.
- Find out from nutrition books what the nutritional value is for each recipe.

Nuts are used widely in vegetarian cookery to provide protein, add flavour and texture to dishes: e.g.
- Brazil
- Cashew
- Sweet Chestnut
- Coconut
- Hazelnuts
- Almonds
- Pistachio
- Peanut
- Pine nuts
- Walnut
- Pecan

Prepared in a variety of ways nuts can be purchased in the following forms:
- whole
- split
- ground
- filets
- nibs
- kibbled
- halves
- crushed

MEMORY JOGGER

Why are nuts a useful added ingredient when used in the preparation and cooking of vegetable protein dishes?

By roasting or grilling nuts the flavour is enhanced and adds variety to vegetarian and vegetable protein dishes. However, some people have a serious allergic reaction to nuts, especially to the peanut, and in some cases people have died as a result. Any products containing nuts, in particular peanuts, need to be labelled clearly to warn customers. Nuts can be used as an ingredient cooked in with the vegetable protein dish or sprinkled on top, adding colour as a topping.

Seeds have grown in popularity in recent years, especially sesame, poppy and pumpkin. Other seed types used in vegetable protein dishes include sunflower seeds, fennel, cardamom and cumin.

PROBLEMS WHEN PREPARING AND COOKING VEGETABLE PROTEINS

You may encounter problems with vegetable proteins concerning freshness and what quantities to use. All manufacturers of vegetable protein products provide instructions on how to prepare and store their products. If staff are not used to handling these types of products, always check yourself to ensure they are fresh and stored appropriately. If you are uncertain of the freshness of any vegetable protein product do not take chances but discard the opened packet and replace it with a

MEMORY JOGGER

How much vegetable protein is used on average for a single portion?

fresh supply. TVP can be purchased in commercial quantities and once opened is best kept in a cool, dry place stored in an airtight container.

Always consult the recipe instructions for guides to quantities when using any vegetable protein product. It is usual to use 75 g (3 oz) of Quorn per person, similarly with tofu, but this does depend on the actual dish being prepared. Many products are provided with recipe suggestions and give quantities to be prepared per person or for four covers.

QUALITY POINTS TO CONSIDER WHEN PREPARING VEGETABLE PROTEINS

The main quality points to bear in mind are:
● texture
● aroma
● flavour
● appearance
● consistency

The *texture* of some vegetable proteins such as TVP, Quorn or tempeh can be firm unless cooked or prepared correctly. The presence of a liquid sauce or stock is often required to minimise the firmness of texture and make the food more acceptable to the pallet. Tofu can be produced in softer textures, lending itself to varied preparation methods.

MEMORY JOGGER

Why is appearance an important factor to consider when preparing vegetable protein dishes?

Aroma can be introduced into vegetable protein dishes from herbs, spices and commodities such as fungi, garlic and tomatoes. The *flavour* resulting from combining these types of foods will be taken up by the vegetable protein; with Quorn, for instance, many classical recipes can be produced substituting the meat or fish with Quorn pieces.

Appearance is one of the most important factors when selling food. Vegetable protein dishes should be prepared to maximise the appearance by careful preparation and production of each dish. Over time you will be able to develop these skills to provide quality vegetable protein dishes for a wider base of customers. This will lead to *consistency* of standards and should provide the organisation with customer loyalty and repeat business.

PREPARATION METHODS

The four main techniques involved in preparation are:
● soaking
● mixing
● slicing
● chopping

Soaking is a preparation method used to soften or impart flavour by marinating in stock, wine or flavoured liquid. Dried pulses, cereals and fruits are soaked to soften them prior to cooking. This preparation needs to be done in good time to allow for the food to swell or soften prior to cooking. Split peas, lentils and a variety of dried bean products are soaked prior to cooking or using in vegetable protein dishes.

Mixing applies to the combining of different ingredients to produce a blended dish or product. This might be to produce one single mixture made up from a number of individual food items, or to combine ingredients carefully so that they just cohere, prior to service or cooking.

Slicing means to cut into thin slices using a knife or mandolin. This might be done with onions, potatoes, carrots or other solid-based vegetables or vegetable protein products. Great care must be taken when slicing using sharp knives or sharp cutting tools. When using a slicing machine ensure you follow the organisational procedures for health and safety. (See Unit 2ND17 p. 93 in the Core Units book).

Chopping means to cut into cubes or very small pieces; a mirepoix is a roughly chopped selection of vegetables used in the preparation of sauces and sauce based dishes. Always use a suitable chopping board, maintain a safe work method and replace knives in their protective holders once clean. Finely chop onions and herbs, especially parsley. Some vegetable protein products do not require cooking, only heating, and they can be prepared by chopping, slicing, dicing or cutting into strip shapes prior to mixing with sauces, salads or other cooked or raw ingredients.

Essential knowledge	When preparing vegetable protein dishes you should ensure that:
	• all ingredients are of the quality and quantity required for the dishes being prepared for service and that they conform to the restrictions of the particular vegetarian diet being catered for
	• all vegetables to be included in the dishes are thoroughly washed and cleaned and are free from infestation by pests or other contamination from pesticides or cleaning chemicals
	• colour-coded chopping boards and separate equipment such as knives are used which are kept exclusively for preparing non-meat products to prevent any cross-contamination with meat products in the same kitchen
	• all ingredients requiring soaking or marinading have been prepared well in advance in accordance with recipe requirements and are stored in hygienic conditions.

What have you learned	1 When preparing basic vegetable protein dishes what safe working practices should be followed?
	2 When preparing basic vegetable protein dishes why is it important to keep preparation, cooking areas and equipment hygienic?
	3 Why are time and temperature important when preparing basic vegetable protein dishes?
	4 What are the main contamination threats when preparing basic vegetable protein dishes?
	5 What different types of vegetable protein are available and what are their uses in catering?
	6 What quality points might you look for in different types of vegetable protein?
	7 What basic preparation methods are most suitable for different types of vegetable protein?
	8 What other alternatives, apart from vegetable protein, are available which are suitable for vegetarians?
	9 What products might be used to substitute high fat ingredients when preparing basic vegetable protein dishes?
	10 Which fats and oils can contribute to healthy eating practices?
	11 How can increasing the fibre content of basic vegetable protein dishes contribute to healthy eating practices?

ELEMENT 2:   Cook basic vegetable protein dishes

KEY POINTS WHEN COOKING VEGETABLE PROTEIN DISHES

● Use only the best fresh vegetables and vegetable products for vegetable protein dishes.

MEMORY JOGGER

Why do many vegetable proteins not require cooking?

- Keep all the equipment and ingredients for this form of cookery separate from those areas using meat or meat-based products.
- Use separate pots and measuring equipment.
- Check the dates and instructions on vegetable protein products such as Quorn and tofu. Many vegetable protein products do not need to be cooked, only heated well.
- Prepare all essential ingredients first before taking vegetable protein products from their packaging or from the fridge, to ensure their freshness.
- Always use vegetable or vegetarian stocks. Do not use meat-based or fish-based pastes to produce stock.
- Use only vegetable or nut-based oils and fats; keep all suet and animal products in a different fridge to vegetable protein commodities.

Do this

1   Make a list of all the products containing trace ingredients of fish or animal products that should not be used for vegetarian cookery.
2   Make a second list of suitable alternatives to the products you have identified.

Case study

A customer orders a dish-of-the-day from the menu advertised as a dish suitable for vegan diets. The dish in question however contains myco-protein (Quorn). Upon eating the dish the customer complains.

1   What immediate action should be taken?
2   What liability might the employer and employee have in law?
3   How might this experience have been avoided?
4   Why is it important to label or advertise food and services accurately?

VEGETABLE PROTEIN COOKING METHODS

Vegetable protein can be cooked by one or more of the following methods, depending on which vegetable protein types you are using:

- grilling
- shallow-frying / stir-frying
- boiling
- braising
- stewing
- deep-frying
- roasting
- baking

The following recipes are examples of the types of dishes that can be made using vegetable protein. Each recipe suggests a range of cooking methods that are appropriate for that dish.

Tofu pâté

Tofu can be purchased in three forms:
1   Soft – medium texture
2   Silken – similar to junket texture
3   Firm – similar to firm cheese.

Ingredients

Tofu	300 g (10 oz)
Olive oil	15 ml/2 tspn (sunflower oil can also be used)
Wheatgerm	80 g (3½ oz)
Carrot	100 g (4 oz) (grated finely)
Sunflower seeds	75 g (3 oz)
Paprika	5 g (⅛ oz)
Dill weed	15 g (½ oz)

Method

1   Using a mortar and pestle grind 50% of the sunflower seeds to produce a powder.
2   Blend the tofu with the seed powder, oil and wheatgerm in a liquidiser.
3   Mix with the grated carrot and remaining ingredients, shape and serve with crisp fresh salad or cut vegetables.

Tofu quiche

Ingredients

Tofu	200 g (7 oz)
Eggs	2
Milk	150 ml (¼ pt)(skimmed)
Shallots	25 g (1 oz) (finely chopped)
Cheddar	50 g (2 oz) (vegetarian)
Mushrooms (button)	25 g (1 oz) (thinly sliced)
Pastry (wholemeal)	150 g (5 oz) (prepared and rested)
Chervil	10 g (¼ oz) (finely chopped)
Sunflower oil	10 ml/2 tspn
Seasoning to taste	

Method

1   Line a flan ring with the rested wholemeal pastry and bake blind, cool.
2   Place in finely chopped shallots that have been sweated in sunflower oil.
3   Add the raw sliced mushroom, grated cheese and chopped herbs.
4   Mix the tofu, milk, eggs and seasoning and blend well.
5   Pour into flan and bake in a moderate oven 175 °C (330 °F) for 20–25 minutes.
Cookery methods covered: shallow frying; baking.

Quorn fricassée

Ingredients

Quorn	200 g (7 oz)
Butter	25 g (1 oz)
Olive oil	25 ml (1 tbspn)
White wine (dry)	50 ml (2 tbspn)
Shallots	25 g (1 oz) (finely chopped)
Double cream	125 ml (4 fl oz)
Mixed herbs	15 g (½ oz) chervil and parsley

Method

1   Heat the oil and butter in a sauté pan.
2   Add the Quorn pieces and cook for 4–5 minutes to heat through.
3   Remove the Quorn pieces and place to one side, add the wine and shallots and cook to reduce by 50%.
4   Add the cream and Quorn pieces and cook for 5 minutes over a steady heat; make sure the Quorn pieces are thoroughly heated.
5   Add the chopped herbs and serve with brown rice or wholemeal noodles tossed in sunflower oil and freshly milled pepper.
Cookery methods covered: shallow frying; boiling.

Quorn hot pot

Ingredients

Quorn pieces	200 g (7 oz)
Butter	25 g (1 oz)
Olive oil	25 ml (1 tbspn)
Brown ale	100 ml ($\frac{1}{4}$ pt)
Shallots	25 g (1 oz) (finely chopped)
Brown vegetable stock	200 ml (7 oz)
Button onions	75 g (3 oz) (peeled)
Carrots	75 g (3 oz) (cut for baton)
Celery	75 g (3 oz) (cut for baton)
Whole beans	50 g (2 oz) (trimmed diamond shape – blanched)
Mixed herbs	15 g ($\frac{1}{2}$ oz) (tarragon and parsley – chopped finely)

Method

1 Heat the oil and butter in a sauté pan and cook the shallot, carrot and celery; sauté for 5 minutes to cook the vegetables.
2 Add the Quorn pieces and heat through.
3 Pour on the beer, stock and button onions.
4 Transfer to an oven proof dish with a tight fitting lid. Cook in the oven at 180–190 °C (350–375 °F) for 15–20 minutes.
5 Cook until the button onions are tender.
6 Strain off the liquid and thicken with fecule or cornstarch
7 Correct the seasoning and add the chopped fresh herbs.
8 Bring sauce back to the boil pour over vegetables and Quorn
9 Finish with herbs and serve with warm granary bread.

Cookery methods covered: shallow frying; braising; boiling.

Quorn tikka beignets

Ingredients

Quorn pieces	100 g (4 oz)
Cooked rice	100 g (4 oz)
Lime pickle	25 g (1 oz)
Tikka paste	10 g ($\frac{1}{4}$ oz)

Use any of these batter recipes:
Frying batter (*Pâte à frire*)

Recipe 1: Ingredients

Flour	500 g (1 lb)
Water	300 ml ($\frac{1}{2}$ pt)
Milk	325 ml (11 fl oz)
Yeast	25 g (1 oz)
Salt	15 g ($\frac{1}{2}$ oz)
Oil	25 ml (1 tbspn)

Recipe 2: Ingredients

Flour	500 g (1 lb)
Water	300 ml ($\frac{1}{2}$ pt)
Milk	300 ml ($\frac{1}{2}$ pt)
Eggs	3
Salt	10 g ($\frac{1}{4}$ oz)

Recipe 3: Ingredients

Flour	500 g (1 lb)
Water	300 ml ($\frac{1}{2}$ pt)
Milk	300 ml ($\frac{1}{2}$ pt)
Oil	25 ml (1 oz)
Egg whites	5 (stiffly whipped)

MEMORY JOGGER

Why should you advise customers that myco protein (Quorn) contains egg white protein?

Method

1 Mix the batter recipe.
2 Blend the cooked rice with the tikka paste and lime pickle.
3 Flour the Quorn pieces with seasoned flour.
4 Form a portion of the rice mixture around the Quorn piece and shape into a round ball.
5 Firm the ball well to compress the shape.
6 Flour again and dip into the prepared batter.
7 Deep-fry at 180–190 °C (350–375 °F) until golden brown.
8 Drain and serve with an appropriate sauce.

Cookery methods covered: boiling; deep-frying.

Tofu, bean and wild mushroom stew

Ingredients

Tofu	250 g ($\frac{1}{2}$ lb)
Beans	250 g ($\frac{1}{2}$ lb) (kidney, haricot and blackeyed)
Vegetable stock	750 ml ($1\frac{1}{4}$ pt)
Wild mushrooms	200 g (7 oz)
Sunflower oil	25 ml (1 tbspn)
Onions	125 g ($\frac{1}{4}$ lb)
Garlic	2 cloves
Tomato concasse	200 g (7 oz)
Seasoning of sea salt and freshly crushed black pepper	
Paprika	10 g ($\frac{1}{4}$ oz)
Parsley	20 g (chopped) ($\frac{1}{2}$ oz)

Method

1 Soak the mixed beans overnight, rinse and drain well.
2 Place the beans and stock into a pan and boil until beans are tender.
3 Fry the sliced onions in the oil until brown.
4 Add the crushed garlic and herbs with the paprika cook for a few minutes.
5 Add the remaining ingredients, tomatoes, mushrooms etc. and mix with the beans and tofu pieces.
6 Simmer gently for 20–25 minutes and serve.

Cookery methods covered: stewing; shallow frying; boiling.

QUALITY POINTS TO CONSIDER WHEN COOKING VEGETABLE PROTEINS

- texture
- appearance
- aroma
- consistency
- flavour

The *texture* can be smooth, fine or coarse. It should relate to the general structure of the dish; a balance should be achieved when the constituent parts are combined correctly.

Consistency This depends on the ingredients' holding or sticking capacity which enables them to maintain a shape or form. It is important to be able to produce similar quality each time you use similar ingredients.

Appearance The overall presentation or look of a dish when cooked and presented should be attractive and appetising

Aroma is the distinctive, pleasant smell of a dish, a subtle, pervasive quality or fragrance produced by cooking processes and the combination of ingredients.

Flavour The balanced taste of a vegetable protein dish should be not too strong nor too mild. Taste the mixtures to develop your skill in this vital area of professional cookery. Always use a clean spoon for each tasting. Never taste a mixture with a spoon already used once: this will cause cross-contamination and is very dangerous.

Healthy eating

Using vegetable protein in place of the meat ingredient in recipes is a useful way of changing from a meat based diet to a vegetarian diet, allowing time for the digestive system to adapt to the new balance of nutrients. Vegetable protein can also supply the chewy texture which some vegetarian recipes lack.

Meat eaters can use some vegetable protein as a healthy substitute for up to one half of the meat content of recipes without significantly affecting the flavour or texture. This will cut down the fat content of the dishes which are usually high in saturated fats.

Essential knowledge

- Many vegetable protein products do not require cooking and can be chopped, sliced or diced for cold and hot vegetable protein dishes.
- You should never promote a product as vegetarian if you are uncertain of the composition of any product used in its production and cooking e.g. cooking in margarine which might contain fish oil.
- Other vegetable protein products such as Wheatpro and Paneer can be used in similar ways to those described previously. Remember that Quorn contains egg whites and is not suitable for certain groups who do not eat egg or egg products.
- Know how each dish should look, smell and taste. Is it of the correct colour and consistency? Learn how to correct these quality points.

What have you learned

1 When cooking basic vegetable protein dishes what safe working practices should be followed?
2 When cooking basic vegetable protein dishes why is it important to keep preparation, cooking areas and equipment hygienic?
3 Why time and temperature are important when cooking basic vegetable protein dishes?
4 What are the main contamination threats when cooking and storing basic vegetable protein dishes?
5 What quality points might you look for in different cooked vegetable protein dishes?
6 Why should basic vegetable protein dishes not for immediate consumption be cooled rapidly and /or maintained at a safe hot temperature?
7 What basic cooking methods are most suitable for different types of vegetable proteins?
8 How would you identify when different types of vegetable protein are cooked to dish requirements?
9 What cooking methods and equipment can contribute to reducing the fat/oil in basic vegetable protein dishes?
10 How can reducing the amount of salt in basic vegetable protein dishes contribute to healthy eating practices?

Get ahead

To extend your knowledge of this emerging area of cookery look at the classification of vegetarian types ie. semi-vegetarian, ovo-lacto-vegetarian, lacto-vegetarian, ovo-vegetarian, vegan and fruitarian type diets. What is the difference between each distinct group? Make a list of food they do and do not eat.

Read about the ingredients to avoid and consider carefully before using with vegetable protein dishes.

UNIT 2ND20

Prepare and cook battered fish and chipped potatoes

This chapter covers:
ELEMENT 1:   **Prepare batter for frying**
ELEMENT 2:   **Prepare and cook battered fish**
ELEMENT 3:   **Prepare and cook chipped potatoes**

What you need to do

- Check that preparation, cooking areas and suitable equipment are hygienic and ready for use.
- Check that batter ingredients, fish and chipped potatoes are of the type, quality and quantity required.
- Report any problems identified with the quality of ingredients promptly to the appropriate person.
- Ensure batter, fish and chipped potatoes are correctly prepared using appropriate preparation and cooking methods and equipment.
- If prepared batter, fish and chipped potatoes are not for immediate use, ensure they are stored correctly.
- Ensure fish is correctly prepared for the frying process using appropriate preparation methods, and that fish is correctly combined with other ingredients ready for cooking and cooked to meet quality requirements.
- Ensure quality of the frying medium is maintained throughout the frying period.
- Ensure cooked fish is held and displayed at the correct temperature.
- Check that preparation and cooking areas and equipment are cleaned correctly after use and frying range is closed down correctly after service.
- Ensure that all work is prioritised and carried out in an organised and efficient manner in line with appropriate organisational procedures and legal requirements.

What you need to know

- When preparing and cooking batter, fish and chipped potatoes, what safe working practices should be followed.
- When preparing batter for frying, why it is important to keep preparation, cooking areas and equipment hygienic.
- What the main contamination threats are when preparing and storing batter.
- Why time and temperature are important when preparing batter for frying.
- Why time and temperature are important when preparing, cooking and storing fish.
- Why is it important to lift heavy or bulk items using approved safe methods.
- What signs to look for when oil / fat is reaching 'flashpoint'.
- What procedures should be followed when oil or fat reaches flashpoint.
- Why the temperature of the frying medium should be monitored at all times and why the frying medium should be filtered at regular intervals.
- What quality points you might look for in prepared batter, fish and chipped potatoes.
- Why it is important to test the batter consistency before frying.
- What ingredients can be used to improve the consistency of the batter.

- Why batter should be rested before frying.
- Why coatings are used when deep-frying food.
- Why it is important to keep preparation, cooking areas and equipment hygienic when preparing and cooking fish.
- What quality points you might look for in cooked battered fish and chipped potatoes.
- What the main contamination threats are when preparing, cooking and storing fish.
- How you might identify when battered fish and chipped potatoes are cooked to dish requirements.
- Why the temperature of the frying medium is important.
- Which fats /oil can contribute to healthier catering practices and why reducing the amount of salt added to chipped potatoes can contribute to healthy eating practices.

ELEMENT I: Prepare batter for frying

EQUIPMENT FOR PREPARING BATTER

The main items of equipment required for making batter are:
- automatic batter mixer
- buckets
- whisks
- measuring equipment.

Batter can be made by hand in a stainless steel bowl or bucket using a whisk to combine the ingredients or it can be prepared in an automatic mixer which blends large quantities of batter. The latter is only used in businesses specialising in fish and chips or deep-frying battered products. Mixing machines such as large hobart mixers can also be used to produce large quantities of batter.

All equipment needs to be checked for cleanliness prior to placing any ingredients in it, and if left out overnight, the bowls or buckets should be well rinsed before use to remove any dust. Batter can be made fresh or produced from pre-mixes to which water and sometimes salt is added and mixed for a specified number of minutes.

Businesses operating as fish-and-chip shops understand the importance of preparing batters that produce a crisp, light coating for their fish products. Those who 'get it right' often have a queue to buy their products; those who take less care do not.

Always keep all equipment used for the preparation of batters clean and hygienic to prevent the contamination of batters and to minimise the risk of cross-contamination with other foods, work surfaces and equipment.

Jugs and measuring equipment are important in producing batter mixes to ensure the correct measures are used in the batter preparation. Stainless steel measuring jugs are preferable to plastic ones; they are more durable and hygienic.

WHAT IS BATTER PREPARED FROM?

Batter for frying is made from either:
- fresh ingredients

or
- pre-mix powder to which water is added.

Fresh batter recipes for frying batter (*pâte à frire*)

Recipe 1

500 g (1 lb)	flour
300 ml (½ pt)	water
325 ml (11 fl oz)	milk
25 g (1 oz)	yeast
15 g (½ oz)	salt

Recipe 2

500 g (1 lb)	flour
300 ml (½ pt)	water
300 ml (½ pt)	milk
3	eggs
10 g (¼ oz)	salt

Recipe 3

500 g (1 lb)	flour
300 ml (½ pt)	water
300 ml (½ pt)	milk
25 ml (1 tbspn)	oil
5	egg whites (stiffly whipped)

These recipes produce good results for deep-fried products such as:
- fish fillets
- whole fish
- fish cakes
- sausages
- mushrooms
- burgers
- pea fritters
- pineapple / apple / apricot / banana / Mars bars in batter.

Convenience pre-mix batters

These can be purchased in commercial quantities and are produced by adding water and sometimes salt to specified quantities of powder. Each type produced will have varying instructions and mix ratios. Always follow the instructions as laid down by the manufacturer.
- When purchasing batter pre-mixes always check the use-by date on the packaging.
- Check for signs of damage to packaging when delivered.
- Check for signs of infestation and damp or dirty packaging.
- Rotate stock in order: first in, first out – last in, last out.

PREPARING BATTER MIXTURES

When preparing batter mixtures the following points need to be followed:
1 Always weigh the ingredients accurately.
2 Store opened packages, salt, flour or batter powders in airtight containers and store in a dry, cool place.
3 Measure any liquids required using a clean stainless steel or plastic measuring jug or bucket.
4 Check scales are accurately set and clean scales and measuring equipment after use.
5 If handling eggs for fresh batters, always wash your hands before handling any other ingredients or equipment to minimise the risk of cross-contamination.
6 Do not over-whisk hand-produced mixtures. This will improve the finish of the cooked batter because it does not have too many air bubbles incorporated in it.

MEMORY JOGGER

Why should powdered batter pre-mixes be stored in airtight containers once opened?

7 Mix the batter according to the recipe instructions or follow closely the manufacturer's instructions provided on the packaging.
8 Mixtures that are prepared prior to use need to be stored in clean containers, usually stainless steel or plastic buckets kept ready for use.
9 Store batters in a fridge and cover with cling film or a tight fitting lid to prevent contamination from foreign bodies or other foodstuffs.
10 When preparing batter using a mixing machine, follow the safety procedures laid down and time the mixing process correctly.

Do this

Experiment with cooking fish batters at different temperatures, writing down the results.
● Find out what the best frying temperature is.
● Does cooking fish coated in breadcrumbs affect the frying temperature?
● Why do chips sometime over-colour? What possible reasons might explain this?

Quality indicators for frying batters

The key features of a good frying batter are:
● texture
● appearance
● consistency.

The texture and appearance of a frying batter is determined not only by the recipe but its consistency and ability to coat the food to be fried. If the batter is too thin it will not stay on the food, resulting in batter particles carbonising in the frying oil. This will reduce the life of the oil and increase the cost. If the batter is too thick the food might not be cooked inside, it will also have a thick coating and not be pleasant to eat. Batter recipes if prepared correctly should be of an appetising consistency.

MEMORY JOGGER

How can you adjust the consistency of a frying batter?

If a batter is too thick, thin it with cold water; if too thin, thicken with flour. By following precisely the recipe instructions for pre-mixes, a good batter should result every time. Use a flow cup to test the flowing consistency of the batter. Test a small portion of food to check the batter cooks well and is the correct consistency.

Problems with prepared batters

The problems, in terms of freshness or quantity, that might be encountered when preparing batters are as follows:
● lumps in the mixture due to under-mixing
● too thin a consistency
● too thick a consistency
● old batter will settle in the bucket and require mixing before use
● insipid colour when fried; this results from the batter being kept too long
● batter becomes sour because of poor storage or from being stored in warm conditions.

PREPARATION METHOD

Manual methods

Batter in catering is often made by hand in stainless steel mixing bowls and left to stand before use. This is to allow the gluten content of the batter to relax prior to frying. Any batter for cooking benefits from being rested after mixing and before frying. This produces a much better batter coating than using it too fresh when the gluten has just developed; when cooked this produces a poor quality coating for fish and food items.

Mechanical methods

Mechanically made batter is produced by specialist fish-and-chip businesses. They use large quantities of frying batter and use a batter mixer to produce bulk mixes. These are set on a timer to ensure the pre-mix batter is blended for the correct amount of time.

Essential knowledge

- Store pre-mix batter powder in a sealed container in a dry store.
- Measure or weigh the correct amount of mixture required.
- Always store prepared batter mixtures in clean stainless steel containers in the fridge covered over and at least 40 cm off the floor surface.
- Always re-mix batters that have been standing for some time as the contents settle during storage. This is usually done by pouring the batter into a clean container to mix in the settled batter.
- Always test the frying batter first with a flow cup, or cook a small sample product to check the colour and consistency of the batter.
- It is important that you prevent contamination of frying batters from foreign objects, infestation by flies or other vermin and maintain the batter mixtures at a safe cool temperature to minimise the risk of contamination and food poisoning.

What have you learned

1. How is batter prepared using safe working practices?
2. Why is it important to keep preparation, cooking areas and equipment hygienic when preparing batter for frying?
3. When preparing and storing batter, what are the main contamination threats?
4. When preparing batter for frying why are time and temperature important?
5. When preparing batter, what quality points might you look for?
6. Before frying, why is it important to test the batter consistency?
7. How can you improve and correct the consistency of the batter?
8. Before frying, why should batter be rested?
9. When deep-frying food, why are coatings used.

ELEMENT 2: Prepare and cook battered fish

EQUIPMENT REQUIRED FOR BATTERED FISH PRODUCTS

Cutting boards

Cutting boards are used for fish filleting, skinning and trimming or cutting.

Food is cut on two main types of surfaces, either plastic or wood. Much debate in recent years surrounds the hygiene of both these materials in relation to bacteria and cross-contamination. Plastic blocks or chopping boards are colour-coded and have become widely used in the catering industry: but the plastic can develop mould and smell over time, whereas wood breathes and can be scrubbed easily.

Coloured boards are used to identify which board to use for each type of food:
Red   raw meat
Blue   raw fish
Yellow   cooked meats

MEMORY JOGGER

Why are cutting boards colour coded?

Green	salad / fruit
Brown	vegetables
White	dairy / bakery

The aim of colour-coding is to minimise the risk of cross-contamination between different food types e.g. fish and meat.

Fish storage containers

Fish storage containers used to be made of metal and were perforated on the base. Filled with crushed ice, the fish was kept chilled in a special fish drawer at the base of the fridge. Plastic containers are now used, made from hard-wearing, tough plastic. The fish is still kept iced or used from frozen, being defrosted in the fridge prior to cooking. Always keep these pieces of equipment cleaned daily to maintain a safe and hygienic working environment and to minimise the risk of contamination. Clearly label fish drawers with the date and types of fish in storage.

Knives

Fish knives have a flexible blade to make filleting accurate and safe. Colour-coded like cutting boards, knives are plastic-handled with a specific colour for fish.

Frying ranges

Frying ranges of the type used in fish-and-chip catering businesses are purpose-built to maintain an easy work flow for deep-frying and display. The display unit is heated and illuminated to make the food look attractive and to maintain it at a safe hot storage temperature prior to being sold.

A modern fish-and-chip frying range

The fat fryers sit underneath the display units with overhead extraction units to remove the hot steam given off during the frying process. The range also has a storage area for cooked chips and has a fold-down lid to maintain them at a safe hot temperature. These units are nearly always made from quality stainless steel and are very expensive to purchase initially when setting up the business.

Fat fryers are located underneath the display units

Fish turners/slices

These are made from stainless steel and have slatted or perforated surfaces. They are used to turn fish while cooking or to handle the fish for service in a clean and hygienic manner. *Never handle fish with your fingers: always use the fish slice or tongs provided.*

Temperature monitoring devices

When fish is cooked and stored in the display unit ready for selling it must be stored at a safe hot temperature above 65 °C (149 °F). The temperature thermometers also monitor the frying temperature and indicate the cooking temperature while fish is frying. Fish shops also use a bell timer to indicate the exact cooking time for individual fish products such as scampi or plaice fillets; these being cooked to order in most good fish-and-chip shops.

FISH AND FISH PRODUCTS FOR FRYING

Frozen fillets / portions

Fish is now as expensive to buy as meat, and in many case even more expensive. For fish-and-chip businesses cod, haddock and plaice are the most popular fish cooked and sold; plaice being the least of the sales. Fish and fish stocks are under pressure world-wide from over-fishing which drives up the price and creates shortages at certain times of the year.

Frozen fish fillets and portions are available in a wide range of fish types but cod, haddock and plaice are the most popular for deep-frying in batter. White fish is usually battered or portioned into supremes or straight fillets, in either small or large portions. Ready-to-fry portions are used alongside fresh fish when it is available. The fillets are pre-packaged according to weight and number. These are defrosted and portioned if large, or may already be pre-portioned ready to batter.

Fresh fillets / portions

Fresh fish is available daily and needs to be filleted or boned if purchased whole, then skinned, floured and battered. Pre-filleted fish must be checked for bones.

Whole fish

Whole fish are not as popular as portions or fillets. Plaice and sole are two of the popular fish cooked whole, but if battered, over-fillets are usually preferred. Two over-fillets are cut from the fish, one from above and the other below.

Problems with fish

Quantity: portion sizes

Fish used as a fish course should weigh 100 g (4 oz) off the bone and 150 g (6 oz) on the bone.

Fish used as a main course usually falls into the following weight category:

Fish fillets   150–200 g (5–7 oz)
Fish on the bone   180–220 g (6–8 oz)
Small whole fish   200–300 g (7–10 oz)
Medium whole fish   400–800 g (14 oz–1½ lb) (e.g. whole sole)
Large fish   a turbot of 3–4 kg (6–8 lb) will provide 10–12 portions

Ordering fish requires the chef to work out the number of fish fillets or whole fish required. When ordering fillets check that an equal number of white and black or dark fillets are delivered. White fillets tend to have slightly more flesh.

When catering for a banquet or dinner always order a few extra fish in case of an accident or problem.

Fresh fish not used within 24 hours of purchase should be deep-frozen having been wrapped in oiled paper and marked clearly with weight/portions and type of fish; always date each package separately.

Checking deliveries of fish

When fish is delivered it should be checked for freshness, overall quality and weighed to determine that the order and the invoice tally.

When a specific weight in fish or individual number of portions have been requested it is important to check each delivery, each day, every day.

Where problems have been identified you should inform the delivery person, and your line manager, chef or supervisor.

You can pay higher prices for fillets and prepared cuts such as supreme, tronçon or darne cuts. Check the weight trim for whole cleaned and uncleaned fish such as salmon, bass or large trout.

Work out in detail the amount of fish required on or off the bone, trimmed and untrimmed, or the specific size you want individual plaice to be. The competent chef will use more than one supplier, and will shop around on a regular basis to ensure suppliers are aware they want the best fish at the best price with the best quality of freshness – value for money.

Where persistent problems occur or where a discrepancy is noticed, always alert your chef or manager and let them deal with the problem. Do not purchase from individuals at the back door or from anyone selling fish who is not a bona-fide supplier.

> **MEMORY JOGGER**
>
> Why should all fish deliveries be checked on arrival?

PREPARATION METHODS

The main preparation stages are:
- skinning
- boning
- trimming
- filleting
- portioning
- coating

(The main methods of preparing fish are dealt with in Unit 2ND2. See pp. 73–78.)

Filleting fish

Fish is filleted using a thin flexible-bladed knife, kept sharp to maintain a clean cut when the filet is removed off the bone.

Flat fish will produce:
- 2 over-fillets; 1 white under-fillet, 1 dark over-fillet
- 4 quarter-cut fillets; 2 white under-fillets, 2 dark over-fillets.

Round fish will produce:
- 2 fillets

Filleting of flat fish
1 Make an incision with a sharp filleting knife from the head to the tail following the line of the backbone.
2 The knife should cut the flesh and skin close to the bone from the centre of the fish to the outside, lifting the fillet to keep a clear view of the knife blade.
3 With the knife blade parallel to the work surface or board, remove each fillet with the knife blade close to the bone.

Filleting of round fish
1 Remove the fish head
2 Cut along the backbone from the head to the tail to remove the first fillet.
3 Keep the knife blade close to the bone when removing the fillet.
4 Turn the fish over and cut the second fillet using the same technique but cutting this time from the tail toward the head of the fish.

Trimming

Fish is trimmed to remove fins or to shape the fish and is then cut into the appropriate shape prior to the next preparation stage or cooking process. Using a fish-filleting knife, fish scissors or cook's knife for trimming. Make sure you keep your bench clean. Work with only one knife on the bench and trim fish carefully to avoid accidents.

Cuts of fish requiring trimming:
- goujon / goujonette
- supreme
- delice
- tronçon
- darne
- filet
- paupiette
- small whole fish
- large whole fish trimmed for deep poaching.

Do this

- Find out what makes a business like *Harry Ramsden's* popular with customers.
- Explore and visit some of the fish-and-chip businesses in your area. What is different about each one?

Portioning fish

Fish is portioned to produce a particular cut and portion size, either as a:
- fish item for garnish
- fish cut for a fish course
- fish cut as a main course
- fish cut as part of a composite dish e.g. fish pie.

When cutting large fillets into smaller portions you should judge carefully the portioning of the fillet before you cut, to ensure even sized pieces result. As fish is very expensive, accurate-sized portioning is important in order to maintain cost effective controls on portion quantities.

This is a simple but vital skill to develop. Where the portion size is cut too large, then fewer portions result and more fish is required. If the portion is too small customers might complain.

Where you need to produce a certain number of portions e.g. for a fish course, weigh each large fillet and work out how many pieces must be obtained from each fillet before you start cutting.

If you get the fishmonger to portion your fish, check each piece for freshness, and then weigh the total volume of fish when delivered to confirm you have not been overcharged or delivered underweight fish – this does happen a lot in the industry, especially when chefs are too busy to check.

Coating fish

<table>
<tr><td>

MEMORY JOGGER

Name two ways fish fillets are coated for frying?

</td></tr>
</table>

Fish can be coated with batter or breadcrumbs. Usually cooked by deep or shallow-frying cookery methods, fish is coated to protect the fish from the fat or oil.

Fish can be coated with any of the following coatings:
- flour, egg and breadcrumbs
- milk and flour
- batter
- flour
- wrapped e.g. samosa, filo etc.
- seasoned flour / egg / breadcrumbs (pané à l'anglaise)
- seasoned flour and milk (pané à la française)
- batter (See batter recipes in Element 1 p. 406).

It is important to coat fish correctly prior to cooking to maintain the life of the oil or fat. The frying medium should be maintained at the correct temperature while fish and fish related products are being cooked After deep-frying always strain the oil while it is warm. Clean the fryer unit when the oil is changed.

If the frying temperature is too low the batter will not congeal and the coating will fall off the fish, resulting in a greasy product of poor quality and ruined oil.

COOKING BATTERED FISH AND FISH RELATED PRODUCTS

Essential knowledge	When the fish batters, fish and related products have been cleanly and correctly prepared and stored prior to service you will need to check the following points: ● that the frying units are filled with fresh oil or freshly strained frying oil or fat. ● that all utensils required during the service at to hand and are clean. ● extraction fans and equipment is on at the correct setting and is working correctly. ● buckets of batter are prepared and stored correctly for use during service and batter trays are clean and filled prior to frying. ● all packaging and service equipment is in place, sufficient for the volume of business, and stacked neatly. ● condiments and other products are filled and clean ready for service.

Cooking methods

Frying temperatures are maintained between 170–185 °C (325–370 °F).

Heater storage cabinets are maintained at 65–68 °C (149–155 °F) with cooked chipped potatoes being stored at approximately 150 °C (300 °F).

Healthy eating

When cooking fish or any fried food product make sure you cook at the correct temperature to minimise the absorption of fat and oil, lower cooking temperatures will result in excess fat or oil being absorbed by the product and result not only in soggy food but the consumption of high levels of fat or oil.

When the frying unit reaches frying temperature, check the oil or fat temperature and then:
● batter the fish fillets and other battered products carefully
● place battered products in the fryer, laying them away from yourself to prevent hot oil or fat splashing your hands. Always work in a clean and safe manner when working with hot oil or fat.
● when half cooked, using a fish slice or spider, turn the food over to complete the frying process.
● monitor the cooking times carefully to prevent battered fish from being over-cooked. Each fish product should cook for 3–5 minutes depending on size.
● keep the frying area clean and tidy, empty waste units regularly and wipe down fat and oil from work surfaces with a clean, hygienic cloth.
● if the floor surfaces become greasy then ensure they are cleaned or maintained to prevent accidents from occurring.

Care of frying fat and oils

To maintain the quality required for battered fish and chipped potato products you will need to monitor and maintain the frying oil or fat. Some key points to consider are set out below:
● oil or fat should be used at the correct frying temperature.
● oil or fat should be topped up as the oil level drops during the cooking process due to the absorption of some oil into the fish products.

Cooking battered fish fillets

- strain the oil at regular intervals to remove debris and carbonised waste from batter and chips.
- do not over-fill the frying unit as this reduces the useful life of the oil or fat.
- change the fat or oil when aged, if you are not certain when this should be done consult your supervisor or line manager.
- regularly remove debris waste of batter and chips by skimming with a straining tool or spider.
- try to minimise the degree to which batter drips into the fat when placing battered fish into the hot oil or fat.
- reduce the heat of frying units not being used due to slack trade.
- when not being used it is important to cover the fryers to prevent contamination and ageing of the oil from sunlight which degrades the oil over time.

Healthy eating

Well cooked fresh fish and chips can be healthy in moderation. Using the correct fat and oil will contribute to healthy catering practices: although these choices are not always the cheapest they are a good investment and marketing advantage for your business.

Safety points to consider when frying battered fish and battered products

When fat and oil ages from constant use the fryer operative needs to be aware of points which will indicate the oil needs replacing. This needs to be done to maintain the quality of cooked products and also to prevent oil or fat from reaching flashpoint.

Indications that oil or fat needs changing are:
- longer time required to cook products
- oil begins to thicken
- oil or fat is dark brown in colour
- oil or fat has an unpleasant smell or odour
- excess smoke is noticed which has a pungent unpleasant smell
- the oil or fat foams easily on the surface.

QUALITY INDICATORS WHEN FRYING BATTERED FISH

- texture
- appearance
- aroma
- flavour

Aroma Fresh fish has a clean pleasant smell or aroma; the smell should not be unpleasant but a clear fishy aroma. Any fish that has a pungent or unpleasant smell is not fresh and could well be dangerous if used.

Fresh fish has the following as indications of quality and freshness:
- gills which are bright red in colour
- the flesh of the fish should be firm not soft
- the eyes are full and bright, not sunken
- there should be no unpleasant smell or aroma
- scales should be plentiful where appropriate.

Freshness

Fresh fish is purchased daily in most catering businesses that rely on the quality of such a purchase. Some businesses purchase fresh fish every other day, but prolonged storage does affect the flavour and quality of fish. Only purchase in line with your needs. Fish used to be a cheaper alternative to meat but today fish in many cases is more expensive. Because fish is costly, due mostly to over-fishing world stocks, care in purchasing and storage should be taken.

Stored correctly on ice in a fish box, fish will keep for up to three days.
- Do not wash fresh fish but place it onto crushed ice in the fish compartment of a fridge or an a tray away from other foods, preferably at the bottom of the fridge to avoid tainting other foods.
- Where fish begins to smell or develop a pungent aroma it should be thrown away.

Never risk using fish that smells thinking the sauce will cover the flavour; it is more likely to give someone food poisoning – the risk is not worth your reputation.

In time you will develop your skills in purchasing only the best fish that is fresh and of good quality; if you pay first class prices, expect first class products.

Appearance

Fresh fish has a clean, bright appearance, the skin has a slimy film covering the fish which indicates freshness. This is true of most fish. The fish should be firm when pressed; softness might indicate a fish of lesser quality.

Detailed information about storing and purchasing fish can be found in Unit 2ND2, see pp. 70–72.

DEFROSTING FISH AND FISH FILLETS

- Defrost fish in a safe environment i.e. in the fridge, not left out in a warm room or preparation area.
- Maintain a separate area for defrosting away from the risk of contamination of cooked fish products.
- Check fish fillets are defrosted correctly
- Remove packaging safely and hygienically; remove rubbish to an appropriate area for disposal.

MEMORY JOGGER

How should fish fillets be defrosted?

- Never re-freeze fish or food that has been defrosted.
- Do not attempt to defrost fish by placing under running water or in warm water. This is dangerous and can lead to food poisoning.

Purchase fish from reputable suppliers and always return any fish that smells off or causes doubt as to its freshness and quality. Soft fish, especially in white round fish, might indicate fish that it has spawned, or is old or not fresh.

KEY POINTS TO COOKING BATTERED FISH

- Drain deep-fried battered fish well to remove excess fat or oil.
- Deep-fried fish should be crisp and dry and free from excess grease.
- The batter should be even in colour and the fish evenly coated.
- Battered fish should be served hot and seasoned according to customer's requirements.
- Check the portions ordered tally with the portions cooked, especially small and large fish fillets.
- Monitor the colour of the fish fillets.

Healthy eating

Try to suggest that reducing the level of salt on fried foods is a positive step for your customers to take but never try to force this point. The customer is always right.

What have you learned

1 How is battered fish prepared and cooked using safe working practices?
2 Why is it important to keep preparation, cooking areas and equipment hygienic when preparing battered fish for cooking?
3 When preparing, cooking and storing battered fish, what are the main contamination threats?
4 When preparing, cooking and storing fish, why are time and temperature important?
5 How do you recognise when oil or fat is reaching 'flashpoint'?
6 What action should you take when oil or fat reaches flashpoint?
7 Why should the frying medium be filtered at regular intervals and why should the temperature of the frying medium be monitored at all times?
8 When preparing battered fish, what quality points might you look for?
9 What quality points might you look for in cooked battered fish?
10 How might you identify when battered fish are cooked to dish requirements?

ELEMENT 3:   Prepare and cook chipped potatoes

Chips are probably one of the most popular dishes in the world, fish-and-chips have a world wide reputation and when they are good, business profit speaks for itself.

The majority of fish-and-chip businesses prepare their own chips from fresh potatoes and market this to attract customers. Many businesses do however use frozen or chilled fresh chips bought in from specialist suppliers. Many fruit and vegetable wholesalers produce a range of these potato products.

PREPARING CHIPPED POTATOES FOR FRYING

Machines used to peel or prepare potatoes are called potato peelers or 'rumblers'.

For small jobs a chef might use a hand peeler, but where large quantities of chips are required potato rumblers are used. A carbonised interior to the rumbler removes the skin of the potato as they revolve around, tumbling against the sides of the machine. Cold water is fed in to wash away the peelings via a filter which should be cleaned and emptied at regular intervals.

MEMORY JOGGER

What reason can you give for not over-filling a potato rumbler?

- Always turn a potato rumbler on before placing any potatoes in to minimise wear on the motor. Operate the machine according to the manufacturers' instructions.
- After rumbling, the water feed is turned off, the front flap to the machine is opened and the potatoes fall out into a sink or container.
- When empty, rinse the machine with water to remove excess peelings; often the water is left for a few minutes to rinse the system.
- A thorough clean of the machine should take place after each preparation session.
- Never put too many potatoes into the machine as this will cause problems and will reduce the life of the motor which is expensive to repair.
- Check for stones in potatoes, these can damage the machine if not removed.

Once the potatoes have been rumbled they require 'eyeing' with a turning knife or hand peeler. Place the prepared potatoes in a clean tub or container checking each individual potato for bruising, decay and green areas.

Chipping fresh potatoes

Chipping machines can be operated by hand but large businesses use electronic cutting machines to produce the chip shapes.

Buckets

MEMORY JOGGER

What safety procedures need to be followed when using potato chipping or rumbling machines?

Containers might be buckets made from plastic or stainless steel or large bins to transport and store the chips in. These should be moved safely and you should ask for help when attempting to move large loads. Lift buckets following the appropriate lifting techniques.

Eyeing tools: knives

When the tools have been used to remove the eyes from potatoes they need to be cleaned well and stored correctly to prevent loss and to minimise the risk of these small tools ending up inside machines or, worse, in food batters and mixes.

Essential knowledge

When preparing and cooking chipped potatoes:
- take care when using a chipping machine.
- do not overload the unit or force the potatoes through.
- follow the instructions for safe use and report any problems immediately.
- check a suitable container is placed to collect the chips as they emerge from the machine.
- rinse the chips well in cold water to remove excess starch
- soak in whitening agent if used by your business
- drain well to remove excess moisture before frying chips
- use whitening agents carefully and follow company procedures when soaking chips; keep whitener away from all food products to reduce the risk of contamination.

FRYING RANGES AND DISPLAY CABINETS

Chipped potatoes once prepared and drained well can be cooked in a deep fat fryer. Fish-and-chip shops use a separate frying unit for chips; this extends the life of the oil or fat and prevents the transfer of flavours between foods.

Check that the utensils required to place chips into and remove them from the range are clean and at hand prior to frying.

Check the fat temperature using the temperature monitoring device before lowering the chip baskets filled with the prepared chips into the hot fat.

COOKING CHIPPED POTATOES

A good chip is popular with customers and some travel miles just to buy chips from a business where they know how to cook them well.

Fat temperature

To impart the special flavour you need to use oil or fat at the right cooking temperature. The type of potato will also affect the finished flavour and look of the chips. Some businesses blanch their chips first to speed up the frying process, this is done at a lower temperature than for colouring.

● blanch chips at approximately 165–170 °C (310–325 °F).
● fry chips at 180–185 °C (350–365 °F).
● colour blanched chips at 185–190 °C (365–375 °F).

After removing chips from the frying oil or fat skim the oil to remove potato pieces that are small. This prevents them from carbonising and reducing the useful life of the oil. A fine-meshed sieve or spider is used to collect such debris and should be used after each batch of chips is fried.

Maintain chips once cooked and drained in a chip cabinet. These are close to the service point and are heated to maintain the chips at a safe, hot temperature. Chips should not be stored for too long prior to service or they will become soggy and cool. Finding a good balance between cooking and storing comes with practice; watch to see how a good chef knows when to cook subsequent batches.

Cook only the right quantity of chips in a batch; trying to cook too many will extend the cooking time and reduce the temperature of the oil so resulting in more fat being absorbed by the chips, which leads to unhealthy foods and overweight customers.

PORTION CONTROL WHEN SERVING CHIPPED POTATOES

Chip scoops are used to portion individual servings of hot fried chips. Chips are sold as large, standard or small portions according to the individual business.

Check that portion servers are clean and not damaged in any way: never serve undersized portions as this could affect your business.

Maintain customer satisfaction by listening carefully to the order when it is given, check if you are not sure of the portion size before it is packaged. This can save money and maintains the quality of individual products.

Never re-heat cooked chipped products, this will undermine the quality of the product and can be dangerous. Remove all cooked chips not sold and put in the rubbish bin.

Case study

For the following situations suggest what action you might take to deal with the situation.
1 *A customer complains about too much salt on their fish-and-chips.*
2 *A customer phones in an order taken correctly, but changes his mind when he arrives.*
3 *A customer returns his fish-and-chips having found a worm in the fish fillet.*
4 *A customer phones up to complain that when they got home the food was cold.*
5 *A customer is taken to hospital having swallowed a fish bone which has stuck in their throat and requires surgery.*
Discuss your answers with your manager or supervisor. Suggest how these problems might be avoided.

CLOSING DOWN PROCEDURES

When cooking has finished follow the closing down procedures set out below.

- Wipe down all surfaces and tops cleanly.
- Turn off all gas or electric controls for pilots and main gas jets.
- Switch off the main electricity feed to the frying units.
- Break down the frying unit, cabinets and equipment for cleaning.
- Wash all equipment, tools and storage bins not in use.
- Remove all waste packaging and unwanted cooked food.
- Wash away excess batter not fit for further use and wash all batter trays and bins or buckets.
- Return excess fish fillets and food products not cooked to the chiller.
- Dispose of all scraps and waste materials to the rubbish store.
- Empty bins and clean all floor and preparation surfaces hygienically.
- Check all areas and turn off extraction units; secure all store access.

What have you learned

1 How are chipped potatoes prepared and cooked using safe working practices?
2 Why is it important to keep preparation, cooking areas and equipment hygienic when preparing chipped potatoes?
3 Why is it important to use approved safe methods to lift heavy or bulk items?
4 How do you recognise when oil or fat is reaching 'flashpoint'?
5 What action should you take when oil or fat reaches flashpoint?
6 Why should the frying medium be filtered at regular intervals and why should the temperature of the frying medium be monitored at all times?
7 When preparing chipped potatoes, what quality points might you look for?
8 What quality points might you look for in chipped potatoes?
9 How might you identify when chipped potatoes are cooked to dish requirements?
10 How does reducing the amount of salt added to chipped potatoes contribute to healthy eating practices?

Get ahead

To extend your knowledge in this area of fish-and-chip cookery, investigate commercial batter powders.

- In what metric sizes are they sold, how much do they cost and what range of shelf-life do they have?
- Compare this with the cost of producing your own batters for deep-frying fish and fish related products.

Prepare, assemble and cook pizza products

This chapter covers:
ELEMENT 1: Prepare pizza products ready for cooking
ELEMENT 2: Assemble and cook pizza products

What you need to do

- Ensure preparation and cooking areas and suitable equipment are hygienic and ready for use.
- Check that ingredients are of the type, quality and quantity required.
- Report any problems identified with the quality of ingredients and pizza promptly to the appropriate person.
- Ensure ingredients and pizza are prepared, correctly combined, cooked and finished using appropriate preparation, cooking and finishing methods to meet quality requirements.
- Ensure that prepared ingredients and pizza for immediate use or consumption are finished using appropriate finishing methods to meet quality requirements.
- Ensure prepared ingredients and pizza not for immediate consumption are stored correctly.
- Ensure pizza products are correctly assembled and portioned.
- Ensure pizza and pizza products for take-away or delivery are correctly packaged.
- Ensure preparation and cooking areas and equipment are cleaned correctly after use.
- Ensure all work is prioritised and carried out in an organised and efficient manner in line with appropriate organisational procedures and legal requirements.

What you need to know

- When preparing and cooking pizza what health and safety practices should be followed.
- When preparing, cooking and finishing pizza why it is it important to keep food preparation areas and equipment hygienic.
- When preparing, cooking and storing pizza what the main contamination threats are.
- Why time and temperature are important when preparing and cooking pizza.
- Why pizza dough must be proved for the correct length of time before use.
- Which pizza menu items are suitable for vegetarians.
- What quality points to look for in pizza products and how to identify that pizza products are cooked to dish requirements.
- Which products could be used to substitute high-fat ingredients when preparing and cooking pizza products.
- Why it is important to package pizza products correctly.
- Which fats/oils can contribute to healthy eating practices.
- Why increasing the fibre content of pizza products can contribute to healthy eating practices.
- Why reducing the amount of salt added to pizza products can contribute to healthy eating practices.

ELEMENT 1:   Prepare pizza products ready for cooking

INTRODUCTION

Pizzas are a popular fast food, snack or restaurant speciality and are in great demand. Special pizza businesses have flourished in recent years providing a range of pizza and pizza related products. Pizzas can be small, medium or large, thin base or deep pan, using white or wholemeal or granary bread bases. Bread stick pizza products have developed and can be readily purchased in supermarkets and food shops.

Prepared pizza bases are available frozen or vacuum-packed as are various tomato based toppings. The pizza market is a lucrative one but there is stiff competition for business from other theme-style restaurants and food outlets.

EQUIPMENT USED IN THE PREPARATION OF PIZZA

- Proving cabinets
- Retarder units
- Food mixing machines
- Slicing and cutting equipment
- Chilled preparation tables and units
- Refrigerator cabinets
- Freezer units
- Food and storage containers

Proving cabinets

A proving cabinet provides a warm atmosphere in which the pizza bases can prove or grow in size. A heating element and moisture provide a warm environment at between 27–32 °C (81–90 °F). The prepared dough or dough pieces are placed in the cabinet and the door is shut. After the required period of time the dough is removed and 'knocked back' (to re-introduce oxygen and expel the carbon dioxide and ethanol gas) before the bases are finished and baked.

Retarder units

A retarder unit is used to hold prepared doughs at a cool temperature to prevent them from proving and to store prepared dough bases ready for proving the next day or later in the production phase. Bench retarders act as a work bench top and underneath have chilled cabinets to hold the prepared dough and dough products. The dough is held at 1–5 °C (34–41 °F). In bakeries the retarder can be programmed to change to a proving cabinet via a timer which changes the function of the unit.

Food mixing machines

Small and medium-sized mixing machines are used to mix the pizza dough which is produced with less yeast than a normal or standard bread dough recipe. A safety guard should be fitted to mixers to protect the operator from the moving parts while the dough is mixing. You should not attempt to remove any dough while the machine is in operation.

> **MEMORY JOGGER**
>
> Why should you not attempt to remove dough from a mixing machine while mixing?

Slicing and cutting equipment

Pizza ingredients are prepared using basic cooks' knives for vegetable and meat preparation. Cheese can be grated using a food processor and tins opened using a bonzer cutter. Many of the toppings will be hand cut or prepared using a food cutting machine such as a robot processor. Cooked pizzas are portioned and cut with a plain bladed wheel cutter.

When handling any sharp cutting or slicing machine or tool take care to prevent accidents to yourself or those you work with. If using a food slicer to cut thin slices of meat follow the safety guidelines laid down for their use and ensure the guard is used at all times. Employees under the age of 18 must be supervised when using such machines.

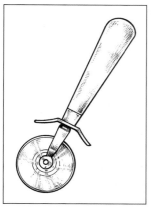

A pizza wheel cutter

MEMORY JOGGER

At what temperature should prepared food be stored and why?

Chilled preparation tables and units

These are divided into compartments that hold stainless steel containers for toppings, salads or accompanying ingredients. These can be either in the preparation area and used by staff to keep pizza ingredients cool or for customers to choose salad and other ingredients to finish their pizza themselves. Typical ingredients might be salads, sauces, cheese, dressings and cooked cold foods suitable for adding to cooked pizza such as diced ham or olives.

Refrigerator cabinets

These keep food at a safe low temperature 1–5 °C (34–41 °F). Raw and cooked food are best kept in separate cabinets to prevent contamination but if cooked and raw food must be stored in the same fridge the cooked food should be placed above the raw food. Refrigerators should be cleaned daily to maintain a clean and safe storage area for cooked and uncooked foods.

Freezer units

Frozen food products and ingredients are kept at a safe frozen temperature of −18 to −20 °C (0 to −4 °F). Frozen pizza bases for example are stored in freezer units which can be upright free-standing, walk-in or bench chest type freezers.

Food and storage containers

Fresh, unprepared, prepared, raw and cooked foods are stored or kept in containers both covered and uncovered. To prevent the risk of contamination or infestation all food containers need to be kept clean and covered as much as possible.

INGREDIENTS USED FOR PIZZA

Pizza ingredients can include fresh vegetables, salads, meat, fish and fruit or pre-prepared and convenience foods.

Pre-prepared or convenience foods include:
- tinned or jars of tomato topping
- tinned anchovies
- tins or jars of olives
- frozen dough bases or disks
- dried herbs
- pre-grated fresh, frozen or vacuum-packed cheese
- pre-sliced meats and sausage
- tinned fruit or vegetables such as sweetcorn and pineapple
- pre-diced peppers or pepperoni, salami or spiced sausage.

MEMORY JOGGER

If delivered food ingredients are found not to be of the quality required what action should you take and why?

Fresh vegetables and ingredients need to be checked on delivery for quality, fresh-ness and quantity. Where you find the vegetables or ingredients are not of the type, quality or quantity required do not accept these foods but ask for them to be returned by the delivery person and replaced with the correct items.

Check the date stamp of foods, look for mechanical damage and infestation in salads and vegetable ingredients. Rotate stock correctly use oldest stock first and fresh-est stock last.

Weigh all fresh vegetables and salad products, meat and fish ingredients delivered; keep a log of deliveries and check all delivery notes against order sheets.

Do this

Carry out a survey with your fellow employees or fellow trainees to find out which products are most popular for pizza. Ask them if they prefer white or brown bread bases, which cheese they prefer and if they like deep pan or regular pizza.

PREPARATION METHODS

Basic pizza dough recipe

Ingredients
450 g (1 lb) strong flour
25 g (1 oz) fresh or 15 g ($\frac{1}{2}$ oz) dried yeast
50 ml (2 fl oz) olive oil or sunflower oil
250 ml (9 fl oz) cold water
5 g (pinch) salt

Method
1　Sieve the flour and salt.
2　Dissolve the yeast in the water.
3　Add the water and oil to the flour and mix in a machine or by hand to produce a smooth elastic type dough.
4　Knead to develop a smooth texture to the dough before dividing into the required size pieces for pizza bases, ready for proving.

Whether you make fresh dough or use frozen or vacuum-packed products, the important processes involved in pizza preparation are :
● proving pizza dough
● chilling ingredients
● slicing ingredients

When preparing ingredients it is important to plan your time and work out a list of task priorities before you commence work.
● Start all tasks which take longest first.
● Leave quick tasks to the end.
● Leave foods which spoil easily to last e.g. salad and fruit ingredients.
● Clean as you go to maintain a clean and hygienic work area.
● Review the tasks completed against your time schedule regularly.
● Always allow time for unforeseen circumstances.
● Do not prepare too much nor too little. Over time you will be able to determine the business flow and prepare accordingly.

MEMORY JOGGER

Why should you handle raw vegetables and salads with care?

Use clean, safe and hygienic work practices to minimise the risk of contamination, accident or cross-contamination of raw and cooked foods and ingredients. Slicing equipment should be cleaned carefully each time it is used and dismantled after each service for a thorough cleaning. When preparing cooked meats use separate boards and use clean sanitised knives for fresh salad and vegetable ingredients to prevent food poisoning from bacteria transfer.

Once prepared, fresh ingredient that are raw should be stored away from cooked or processed foods. When storing food do not use aluminium or glass to keep food in, as you run the risk of the glass breaking or being chipped and cracked, or tainting the food with aluminium. Use food quality plastic or stainless steel containers to keep prepared food in.

When food has been prepared store it in a clean container with a lid on and place in the fridge until required for service or production. Do not store food in tins once opened. When opening tins always remove the lid completely and put the contents into a clean container and cover with a lid. Check tins to eliminate ones that are bulged or show signs of rust.

Proving pizza dough

Once the dough has been made it needs to be left to develop, we call this process 'proving'. This is where the yeast multiplies and produces carbon dioxide gas and at the same time ethanol gas by converting the sugar in the flour to alcohol. Once proved the dough is knocked back to expel the gases and replace the dough with oxygen, essential for successful fermentation of the dough piece.

You need to control the time the dough proves and make sure the dough is of the correct consistency to allow proving to occur. If the dough is too tight the proving process lengthens and if too slack the dough will be difficult to handle. A good recipe will produce good results each time but when making pizza dough you must take account of the weather conditions, the age of the yeast and the strength of the flour.

Chilling ingredients

All food ingredients once prepared should either be kept chilled below 8 °C (46 °F) or kept hot above 65 °C (149 °F). Chilled foods are less likely to produce harmful bacteria when prepared and stored correctly. Chiller units for presenting food to the public must be at operational cold temperatures before food is placed in them. You will be advised by your chef or supervisor when ingredients in these units need to be either topped up or replaced. Food items should not be stored for too long and should be used on a first in, first out – last in, last out basis.

Slicing ingredients

A variety of food ingredients used on pizza e.g. onions, mushrooms, meat, fruit and fish are cut into slices to provide a variety of topping ingredients and enhance the overall look of the pizza. Slices should be uniform and knives need to be used carefully. Never fool around when slicing foods. If using electric food slicers always follow laid down procedures.

QUALITY INDICATORS WHEN PREPARING PIZZA

- Fresh tomato toppings are best chilled for a few hours prior to being used.
- Keep grated cheese chilled, do not leave out in a warm environment.
- Prepare all salad ingredients away from other raw and cooked ingredients.
- Tomato bases for pizza when mixed with herbs need a period of time to infuse the flavour of other ingredients such as onions, garlic and marjoram or oregano.
- Use standard recipes to maintain consistency of flavour and appearance.

What have you learned

1 What health and safety practices should be followed when preparing pizzas and pizza ingredients?
2 Why is it important to keep food preparation areas and equipment hygienic when preparing pizzas?
3 Why are time and temperature important when preparing pizzas?
4 Why must pizza dough be proved for the correct length of time before use?
5 What benefit can be gained from using wholemeal or granary flour for pizza bases?
6 Which products could be used to substitute high-fat ingredients when preparing pizza products?

ELEMENT 2: Assemble and cook pizza products

Efficient and effective service when preparing and cooking pizza is based on organisation and being properly prepared to cope with large numbers of orders all at the same time. Practice will develop your ability to cope and maintain a high standard of production at all times. Check equipment is at hand and confirm that sufficient preparation has been done before service gets busy; to find you are running short when you are busy will often throw staff into a panic.

PIZZA EQUIPMENT

Pizza ovens

Pizza ovens can be low crown flat type ovens which operate at high temperatures or the tunnel variety where the pizza are passed through an oven tunnel on a moving conveyor. Care is needed when working with such equipment and company policies regarding operation and safety should be known by all employees to prevent accidents and maintain a safe and secure working environment.

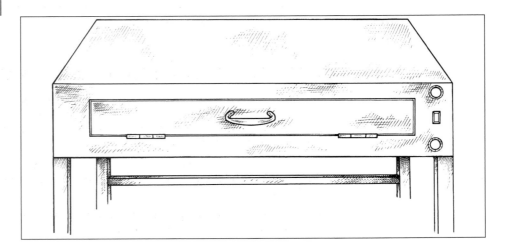

A low-crown pizza oven

- Check the ovens are switched on or the gas pilot and burner is ignited.
- Confirm that any conveyor belt mechanism is fitted correctly.
- Do not turn the equipment on too soon, this wastes energy.
- Use appropriate tongs or gloves to remove hot pizza dishes from the oven.
- Do not take short cuts by reaching inside ovens or tunnels to move goods along, you will probably cause yourself injury by doing so.
- Where a tray is hot and left to cool warn others working nearby.
- Allow ovens to cool before attempting to clean them.
- Check mains switches to oven equipment are off before cleaning begins.
- Wear eye protection when using chemicals to clean ovens.
- Store all cleaning equipment in a safe and secure cupboard especially for this purpose. These items should not be stored in the kitchen where food is being prepared.

PIZZA PRODUCTS

Assembling and portioning pizzas and pizza products

An oil pouring pot

Check that the doughs are proved and portioned into the correct weight. Form each pizza dough into the correct round shape. Some pizza operations crimp the outer edge to add to the overall presentation and keep ingredients on the base.

1 Roll out dough piece to correct shape, place into the pizza pan.
2 Add the tomato sauce and spread carefully.
3 Sprinkle on the correct weight of cheese.
4 Place on the required topping ingredients in the correct order.
5 Check the pizza is assembled correctly according to the food order.
6 Sprinkle with herbs and oil using an oil pouring pot.
7 Place into the oven or tunnel to cook.
8 Begin to assemble the next order.
9 Maintain a check on each order as it cooks.
10 Clean as you go: if quiet between order clean down and check prepared ingredients are sufficient to meet future orders.

Take care when removing a pizza from a hot pizza pan. When re-using a hot pan allow it to cool slightly before oiling it again. Lets others you work with know the pan is hot in order to prevent an accident from occurring.

Make sure you only assemble those ingredients set out on the menu descriptions for each type of pizza; when busy it is easy to make a mistake with too little or too much of one particular ingredient.

If you are learning how to assemble and produce pizza during busy periods watch an experienced member of staff working. Make notes about the routine followed and ask questions where appropriate.

BAKING OR COOKING PIZZA PRODUCTS

Small pizza will take less time to cook or bake than deep pan or large family-sized pizza. Be careful not to over or under-cook a product. You will get to know the timing with practice but times and baking temperatures will be set down for you to follow. Memorise these for each type of pizza.

Pizza tunnels take some of the pressure of the chef when cooking individual pizza. Where a pizza oven is used you will need to know how to fill and empty the oven in a safe way.

Your aim is to cook each product perfectly and as quickly as possible without compromising the quality of the product.

When removed from the oven the product is portioned with a plain wheel cutter and placed on a serving dish, taken and presented to the customer straightaway.

Other products cooked might be:
- Herb bread
- Garlic bread
- Olive bread
- Tomato bread
- Pasta items
- Bruschetta

Do this

Make a list of popular pizzas; visit your local pizza restaurant and write up the names and types of ingredients that make up each pizza. Find out what other products are sold apart from pizza.

POPULAR PIZZA DISHES

- *Hawaiian:*   tomato, pineapple, ham, chicken, mozzarella cheese.
- *Marguerita:*   tomato and mozzarella cheese, oregano, extra virgin olive oil.
- *Verdura*:   vegetable pizza with mushroom, onion, spinach, marjoram and ricotta cheese.
- *Seafood:*   mozzarella cheese, prawns, mussels, anchovies, tomato, olives and mussels.
- *Mexican:*   tomato, mozzarella cheese, pepperoni, olive oil, herbs.

Pizza of course can be made up with a selection of ingredients chosen by the customer. The list below covers a range of foods suitable for use on pizza bases.

Ham	Pineapple	Mushroom	Garlic
Banana	Onion	Peppers	Olives
Chilli	Sweetcorn	Chicken	Bacon
Tomatoes	Capers	Anchovies	Prawns
Tuna fish	Calamari	Pepperoni	Broccoli
Asparagus	Parsley	Celery	Clams
Salami	Egg	Spinach	Salmon

Bread bases can be made from:
- Plain white bread dough
- Granary dough
- Wholemeal dough
- Garlic dough or stick bases
- Hovis or stoneground dough
- Tomato or olive bread dough
- Spinach dough

Cheese used for pizza
- Mozzarella
- Parmesan
- Cheddar

Herbs used for pizza
- Marjoram
- Oregano
- Parsley
- Basil

MEMORY JOGGER

What benefit can be gained from using wholemeal or granary flour for pizza bases?

MEMORY JOGGER

Which oils contribute to healthy eating practices?

Oils used for pizza
- Extra virgin olive oil
- Virgin olive oil
- Olive oil
- Sunflower oil
- Vegetable oil

PACKAGING PIZZAS FOR TAKE-AWAY AND DELIVERY SERVICES

Before service begins you should check that take-away packaging is assembled and made up. Use the correct box for each type of pizza and cut the pizza as required

When answering the phone to take a pizza order repeat the order to the customer to confirm you have the right details, address, name and size of product required. Confirm the approximate delivery time and check that it is feasible.

It is important to use the correct size of box for each pizza to prevent them from moving during transportation and prevent the hot product from spoiling. Never cut a pizza when it if fresh from the oven; the cheese is very hot and can cause burns. Allow the pizza to stand for a minute before cutting with a rotella cutter.

Case study

You receive a telephone call for an order of pizza and garlic bread. The order is prepared and delivered in the usual way. Shortly after the driver returns a call is received to complain about the products. You listen to these complaints.
1. *How would you deal with such a problem?*
2. *Who is at fault – the customer, the supplier or the driver?*
3. *How can this be avoided in the future?*

Essential knowledge

Know what safe working practices should be followed when preparing and cooking pizza products:
1. Cutting machines should be used with care and only when you are trained to do so.
2. If you are under 18 and untrained cutting machines can only be used under supervision.
3. Do not hold food on electric slicers with your hands but use the safety guard to secure the food.
4. Never store food in glass; this can break, or chip and contaminate food.
5. Tell those you work with when pizza pans or trays are hot.
6. Wipe up spillages as soon as they occur and use wet floor notices where appropriate.
7. Take care when putting pizzas into and removing pizzas from pizza ovens and tunnel ovens.
8. Be careful when portioning a pizza as the cheese is extremely hot.
9. Use the correct cutting board for each type of food when preparing ingredients.
10. Check all salad foods and vegetables for flies, caterpillars and slugs, wash all salads well in salted water and ensure sinks are clean and hygienic.
11. Wear goggles when cleaning ovens with chemical cleaner and allow the ovens to cool before attempting to clean them.

What have you learned

1 What health and safety practices should be followed when cooking pizza?
2 Why is it important to keep food preparation areas and equipment hygienic when cooking and finishing pizza?
3 What are the main contamination threats when cooking and storing pizza?
4 Why are time and temperature important when cooking pizza?
5 How would you identify that pizza products are cooked to dish requirements?
6 Which pizza menu items are suitable for vegetarians?
7 When packaging pizza, why it is important to pack products correctly?
8 Which fats/oils can contribute to healthy eating practices?
9 How does increasing the fibre content of pizza products contribute to healthy eating practices?
10 How does reducing the amount of salt added to pizza products contribute to healthy eating practices?

Glossary

A

A la … : in the style of, for example à l'anglaise (English style), à la française (French style).

A la carte: literally 'from the card' (the card being the menu); dishes are individually priced and cooked to order.

A la crème: a term used to indicate the inclusion of cream in a dish, for example: *Escalope de veau à la crème* (Veal escalop with cream).

A la française: food coated in milk and flour and fried; mainly applied to fish but other ingredients can also be cooked this way, for example 'French fried onions'.

Albumen: white of egg.

Allumette: (matchstick) strips cut to matchstick size, commonly potato.

Anglaise: (English style) **(a)** used to define simply cooked food, fried, boiled; **(b)** (pané) a term used to describe food coated in flour, egg and breadcrumbs and deep fried.

A point: a degree of cooking steak, meaning just done.

Aspic jelly: a savoury jelly used to decorate larder work.

Au bleu: a method of cooking trout in a court bouillon.

Au gratin: to brown food under a grill, with cheese or breadcrumbs.

B

Bain-marie: (water bath) a container of hot water used for keeping food hot or slowing down the process of cookery.

Baking: a dry cookery process using an oven.

Baking beans: beans that can be specially purchased for the purpose of *baking blind*.

Baking blind: the process of part cooking a pastry case that has been lined with a circle of greaseproof paper (*cartouche*) and baking beans. This is done to avoid soggy pastry, e.g. on the base of a flan.

Barding: the covering of meat with fat bacon or pork to prevent meat drying out while roasting.

Bark: skin on meat (see *de-barking*).

Barquette: a small boat shaped piece of pastry.

Baste: to moisten with fat or cooking liquor during cooking.

Bâtons: thick short cuts of vegetables.

Battenburg: a two-coloured (pink and yellow) oblong cake, covered with marzipan.

Bavarois: a rich dessert made with egg custard (egg yolks and cream) set with gelatine.

Bean shoots: tender sprouts grown from mung beans.

Béarnaise: a rich sauce made from eggs with the addition of herbs, served with grilled meat or fish.

Béchamel: a classic white sauce made with a white roux and milk.

Beignets: fritters which may be savoury or sweet.

Betterave: French for beetroot.

Bien-cuit : well cooked.

Biscuit à la cuillière: sponge fingers, used when making Charlotte Russe.

Bitoks: similar to a freshly made beefburger, bitoks are coated in flour and shallow fried.

Blanch: **(a)** to make white or pale by scalding; **(b)** to immerse vegetables in boiling water; **(c)** the process of pre-cooking meat for a short time to remove impurities.

Blanquette: a white stew cooked in stock from which the sauce is then made.

Blast-freezing: a process of quickly freezing food at low temperatures.

Bleu: a degree of cooking steak meaning very rare.

Blinis: Russian pancakes served with caviar.

Bloom: **(a)** powdery deposit on fruit; **(b)** a green mould on the outside of naturally cured boiling hams.

Boiling: the process of cooking food in liquid.

Bouchée: a small puff pastry case.

Bouillon: a thin clear broth.

Bouquet garni: a small bundle of herbs used to flavour dishes.

Bourguignon(ne): Burgundy style; one of the most famous dishes bearing this name is *Boeuf Bourguignon*, where beef is cooked in red wine and tomatoes to which mushroom, onions and strips of bacon (*lardons*) are added.

Braising: a slow wet method of cookery, used to cook meat and vegetables that require a longer, slow cooking method.
   Brown braising: when cooking meat, meat is browned prior to braising.
   White braising: used to cook sweetbreads and vegetables, these are blanched prior to braising in white stock.

Brandy snaps: crisp rolled gingerbread wafer usually filled with cream.

Bratt pan: a piece of cooking equipment that can be used to fry, deep-fry, stew, braise or boil food.

Broth: in strict terms, a stock.

Brunoise: vegetables cut into dice.

Buttercream: a combination of nearly equal parts of butter and sugar used to decorate cakes.

C

Calamari: squid.

Canapés: small savoury mouthfuls of bread with various toppings, served hot or cold.

Caramel: literally 'burnt sugar', sugar which has been cooked until it turns brown.

Carbonised: converted into carbon, charred.

Carry-over cooking: food which continues to cook after being removed from the source of heat.

Cartouche: a greaseproof paper circle with many uses, e.g. to exclude air and prevent a skin forming on a sauce.

Cellulose: the coarse structure of fruit and vegetables that is not digested and acts as roughage.

Cereal: edible grain.

Chapati: Indian unleavened bread made from *Ata*, a fine ground wholewheat flour.

Charlotte: a pudding made of stewed fruit and layers, or a casing, of bread or cake.

Chateaubriand: a top quality steak, taken from the head of a beef fillet.

Chinois: a conical shaped strainer.

Choux paste: a pastry made from water, butter, eggs and flour, used for profiteroles and eclairs.

Ciseler: (a) to shred finely; **(b)** to score.

Coagulate: the process of liquid proteins changing to semi-solids.

Collagen: a protein found in animal connective tissue.

Combination cookery: the use of two sources of heat to cook food, for example a microwave with heating elements to brown the food already cooked; the combination speeds the cookery process.

Concasse: coarsely chopped, e.g. tomato.

Condé: a dessert consisting of creamed rice combined with fruit or jam.

Condiments: seasoning or relish with food.

Consommé: a clear soup.

Contrefilet: a whole boned sirloin.

Cook-chill: food prepared prior to use and chilled.

Coulibiac: a fish pie from Russia traditionally made using salmon and a pastry case.

Court bouillon: a cooking liquor for foods containing water, vinegar, onions, carrots, herbs and seasoning.

Couverture: confectioner's chocolate, which contains a high amount of cocoa butter.

Cromesquis: a deep-fried type of rissole covered in batter.

Croquettes: cooked food moulded into a cylinder shape, coated in flour, egg and breadcrumbs and fried.

Cross-contamination: the contamination of one food by another.

Croute: a slice of toast.

Crudités: raw, roughly prepared vegetables eaten with dips.

Crustaceans: shellfish that have outer shells.

D

Darne: a slice from a round fish, a 'steak'.

De-barking: the removal of fat or skin from meat.

Deep-frying: frying of food in deep fat.

Déglacer: to swill a pan after cooking with stock, wine etc.

Délice: a neatly trimmed and folded fillet of fish.

Demi-glace : a refined sauce made from a mixture of basic brown sauce (see *Espagnole*) and stock in equal quantities reduced by half.

Demoulding: the process of removing an item from a mould, e.g. a jelly.

Digestible: food that the body is able to absorb.

Dip: a sauce or dressing into which food is dipped before eating.

Dock (prick): to make holes through pastry when baking blind.

Dripping: fat that comes from roasting meat.

Due diligence: a term used to indicate that a person must take reasonable care in their work to avoid future problems.

Dumpling: a ball or outer casing of dough usually cooked by boiling.

Durham cutlet: a mixture of minced meat mixed with potatoes, onions and seasoning, bound with egg yolk, coated in breadcrumbs, shaped like a lamb cutlet and fried.

Duxelles: a mixture of cooked, finely chopped shallots and mushrooms.

E

Egg-wash: beaten egg used to coat foods prior to cooking, giving colour and gloss.

Elastin: a type of connective tissue.

Emulsion: the dispersion of one liquid in another, e.g. vinegar and oil in vinaigrette.

En cocotte: food cooked in a special dish called a cocotte.

En croûte: food, e.g. meat or fish, encased in pastry.

Endive: a type of plant a little like lettuce but more bitter.

Escalope: a thin slice of meat, normally associated with veal but not exclusively.

Espagnole: literally 'Spanish', most commonly used in the phrase *Sauce*

Espagnole, a basic brown sauce used in many classic dishes.

F

Farce: stuffing.

Farinaceous: derived from the French word for flour 'farin', the term is applied to pasta and gnocchi.

Fibrous: a term used to describe food that has fibres evident.

Fillet steak: a cut taken from the fillet of beef, the most tender cut.

Fish kettle: a specially shaped container for cooking (poaching) fish; specifically:
salmon – *saumonière*
trout – *truitière*
turbot – *turbotière*.

Flashpoint: oil that has reached a temperature where it may ignite.

Florida cocktail: a combination of orange and grapefruit, used as a starter.

Flouring: to coat in flour.

Fricandeau: thick slice of meat (veal) cut along the muscle of the leg.

Fricassée: a white stew where poultry and meat are cooked in a sauce.

Fritters: food which is coated in flour and batter and deep-fried.

Friture: a pan used to deep-fry food.

G

Galantine: a cold dish made from poultry or other white meat which is boned, stuffed and cooked before being decorated with a glaze.

Garam masala : the name literally means 'hot spices'. Originating in India, the mixture will vary but often includes cardamoms, cloves, peppercorns, cumin and nutmeg. It is usually added to a dish towards the end of cooking.

Gelatine: a protein that dissolves in water, it is added to food to aid setting, e.g. to make a Bavarois.

Genoese: a type of sponge which is made by whisking eggs (over water) with sugar before adding the flour.

Glaze: **(a)** to coat, as in the finish to a tart or flan to improve appearance; **(b)** to add butter and/or other ingredients to finish certain vegetables; **(c)** to colour a dish under the grill.

Gluten: the protein in flour, particularly 'strong' flour, that gives the flour its elastic properties (see *strong flour*).

Glycerine: a clear, syrupy, oily liquid.

Gnocchi: a farinaceous dish, the name means 'small dumplings'.

Goujon: a thin strip of fish coated in breadcrumbs and deep-fried.

Grenadins: a French term used to describe small slices cut across the grain.

Greying: used to describe meat that may have been poorly stored.

Griddle: a hot metal plate heated from underneath used to cook a variety of foods.

Grilling: a method of cookery using direct heat, only suitable for prime cuts of meat and other tender food items.

Gum arabic: a sticky substance which hardens when exposed to air, used in pastillage work (the technique of making models from sugar as a decoration).

H

Halal: meat which has been slaughtered according to Muslim law.

Hanging: the process of hanging meat to allow it to mature.

Holding over: warm compartment where cooked food is kept hot until service.

Hollandaise sauce: a rich sauce made from eggs and butter and served with salmon, asparagus etc.

Hors d'oeuvre: a range of dishes served before the main meal.

Hotpot: an English term for a stew or casserole dish usually made from meat topped with potatoes.

I

Insoluble: a general term applied to any substance that cannot be dissolved.

J

Jardinière: the French term for thick short strips or bâtons.

Julienne: thin strips of vegetable.

K

Kebabs: small pieces of meat, fish or vegetables placed on skewers.

Kilocalories: the measurement used to define the energy value of food.

Knock back: the action of removing trapped gases from fermented dough prior to shaping.

Kosher: food produced under conditions acceptable to people of the Jewish faith.

L

Lard: pig fat which is prepared for use in cookery.

Lardons: strips of fat bacon.

Liaison: a combination of cream and eggs, used to bind or thicken sauce.

Loin: a cut from lamb or pork indicating its position on the carcass as halfway down the spine.

M

Mandolin: a piece of equipment used to slice vegetables finely when large quantities are required.

Marbled: a term to indicate meat which has the effect of marble since it is streaked with fat; this helps to baste the meat during cooking.

Marinade: a blend of ingredients used to flavour and tenderise meat prior to cooking.

Médaillons: small round pieces of meat.

Meringue: egg whites and sugar whisked together and baked slowly.

Meunière: a term used to describe fish coated in flour and shallow fried.

Mie de pain: fresh white bread-crumbs.

Mignon: delicate or small, (*filet mignon*) tail of fillet.

Mirepoix: roughly chopped vegetables, onions and celery used as a flavouring.

Mise-en-place: basic preparation prior to service.

Molluscs: soft bodied creatures, with hard outer shell; there are three main types.

Monter au beurre: butter beaten or whisked into a sauce to enrich it.

Mornay: a béchamel based sauce, to which cheese is added.

Mortadella: a very large slicing sausage containing pork, garlic, coriander and sometimes pistachio nuts.

Mousseline: (a) a small mousse, usually served hot; **(b)** hollandaise sauce blended with cream and whisked.

Mozzarella: an unripened cheese with a rubbery texture; the classic cheese for pizza toppings.

Muesli: a cereal originally from Switzerland, made from a basic mixture of oats, dried fruit and nuts.

Muslin: a delicate woven cotton fabric which has many culinary uses.

N

Nan bread: Indian flat bread.

Navarin: a brown lamb stew.

Noisette: a French cut of meat taken from a boned out loin.

Noodles: a flat Italian pasta.

Nut brown butter: butter cooked until nut brown (beurre noisette).

Nutrients: the components of food which have chemical functions; nutrients are divided into types: carbohydrates, proteins, fats, vitamins, minerals.

O

Offal: the general classification of the edible internal organs from animals.

Onion clouté: an onion studded with a bay leaf using a clove.

P

Paillard steak: a flattened fillet steak.

Palatable : food that is both pleasant to taste and agreeable to the eye.

Palette knife: a knife used for lifting and scraping.

Pancetta: an Italian streaky bacon used to flavour dishes.

Pané: to coat with breadcrumbs; breadcrumbed.

Pasta ascuitta: best quality dried pasta.

Pasta fatta: home made pasta.

Pasteurised: subject to a process of partial sterilisation.

Pastrami: brisket of beef cured in a non-liquid mixture of sugar and spices before being smoked.

Pastry cream: (confectioner's cream, crème patissière) custard made from milk, eggs, sugar and flour, used in many different pastry dishes; on the continent it is used in dishes more than fresh cream.

Paupiette: a stuffed and rolled strip of meat or fish.

Paysanne: (peasant style) a term for evenly cut thin slices of vegetables, triangular, round or square.

Pecorino: an Italian generic term for ewes' milk cheese.

Petit four sec: very small, sweet cakes served at the end of the meal.

Pitta bread: Middle Eastern and Greek in origin. In Greece pitta is eaten with hummous and tara-masalata.

Plaque à poisson: a special poaching pan for shallow-poaching fish.

Poach: to simmer foods gently.

Polonaise: a garnish of white bread-crumbs, eggs and parley which have been chopped finely, 'Cauliflower polonaise'.

Pont neuf: the name used to describe a large chipped potato.

Porridge: an oatmeal breakfast originating in Scotland.

Proving: resting dough to allow the yeast to ferment.

Provolone: an Italian cheese, creamy white, with a slightly acid taste.

Pulses: the dried seeds of peas and beans.

Purée: finely minced food, often used to describe the pulp of vegetables.

Putrid: decomposed or rotten, poor quality, unpleasant.

Q

Quadrillage: literally 'chequer work', the process of marking flesh with a poker to give the appearance of grill bars.

Quenelle: forcemeat made from meat or fish, having a fine texture or consistency.

Quiche Lorraine: a traditional French egg and bacon flan.

R

Ratatouille: a casserole of vegetables originating in the South of France, consisting of peppers, courgettes, onions, aubergine, tomatoes and garlic.

Reduce: to reduce the liquid in a sauce.

Refresh: to cool under cold water.

Ricotta: an Italian cheese with a fairly bland flavour, used in pasta dishes as well as pastries.

Rissoles: round cakes made of meat and mashed potatoes coated in breadcrumbs.

Roasting: a dry method of cookery by convected dry heat.

Roulade: a French term meaning roll.

Roux: thickening made from fat and flour, a base for sauces.

Royal icing: a mixture of egg whites and icing sugar used to coat rich fruit cakes.

Rubber: a cloth used to remove food from the oven.

Rump steak: a cut of steak from the hind quarter of beef.

S

Sabayon: a term used to descibe the whisking of eggs with water over a bain-marie until thick.

Saffron: a spice produced from the yellow stigmas of the crocus; it has an aromatic slightly bitter flavour and is the most costly spice available.

Saignant: degree of cooking steak meaning underdone.

Salamander: a grill heated from above.

Salami: a type of dried sausage produced all over the world, made from uncooked meat, usually pork, but can be beef flavoured with garlic; some are pickled, some are dried.

Saturated fat: solid fats found mainly in meat.

Sauté: literally meaning 'to jump', to cook by tossing in hot fat.

Scum: the deposit found on the top of heated liquids containing impurities.

Seal: to set the outer surface, usually meat.

Shallow-frying: to cook in a shallow pan with heat, a dry method of cookery.

Shank: a cut from the front leg of beef, requiring a long slow cookery process.

Shin: a cut from the rear leg of beef, requiring a long slow method of cookery.

Shortening: a term given to fat used in dough, cakes and other similar products.

Silicone paper: a paper lubricated with silicone for easy release; can be used where you would use grease-proof paper.

Sinews: tough fibrous tissue that connects muscles to bones.

Skim: to remove scum from liquid.

Slack: a term applied when a mixture is too wet, e.g. dough.

Soft flour: flour with a low gluten content; can be grown in England due to the weather.

Soluble: can be disssolved in water.

Spices: a range of aromatic seasonings, usually seeds, pods, bark, berries or buds.

Steaming: a wet method of cookery, where steam surrounds the food items being cooked.

Stewing: a method of cookery by moisture in a small amount of liquid.

Stir-fry: originating from China, a quick method of cookery where food needs to be cut into small pieces before being tossed in hot oil.

Stock: a liquid produced by cooking meat or fish and vegetables with herbs and water.

Stock rotation: the process of moving old stock to the front so that it is used before new stock.

Strong flour: flour containing a large amount (10−15%) of a protein known as gluten, giving the flour an elastic character required for making bread, puff pastry etc.

Suprême: (a) the best part of a fillet of meat, poultry or fish; **(b)** a white sauce made from cream.

Sweat: to cook (under a lid) in fat without colouring the food.

Sweetbreads : a mixture of two different glands, the thyroid in the throat and the pancreas in the stomach.

Swiss roll: a sponge cake spread with jam or other ingredients and rolled up.

Syrup: a solution of sugar dissolved in water.

T

Table d'hôte: a meal at a fixed price.

Tenderise: to make food tender.

Thumbed-up: the action of using the thumb and index finger to help line tarts, flans etc.

Thymus: a gland found in the throat and included in sweetbreads.

Tikka: a name given to an Indian kebab.

Tomalley: the greenish liver found in lobsters.

Topside: a cut from the hind quarter of beef.

Torte: a name given to an open tart or rich type of cake mixture baked in a pastry case.

Tortilla: Mexican unleavened bread made from *masaharina* (a fine ground cornmeal flour ground from white maize soaked in lime water) or wholewheat flour dough.

Tournedos steak: a steak cut from the middle of the fillet.

Traying-up: the process of placing food on trays.

Tronçon: a cut taken from a slice of flat fish.

Truffle: (a) a type of fungi found underground, which is considered a delicacy and as such is very expensive; **(b)** a spherical chocolate.

Trussing: tying a bird with string, prior to cooking.

V

Velouté: a sauce made with a blond roux and stock.

Victoria sandwich: a popular cake made by the creaming method containing equal quantities of the constituent ingredients.

Vinaigrette: a salad dressing made by combining vinegar (or lemon juice), oil and mustard to form an emulsion.

Vol-au-vent: a case made of puff pastry filled with a variety of fillings.

W

Wholemeal flour: flour containing the whole of the wheat germ.

Y

Yoghurt: food made from milk to which a culture has been added.

Index

Page references in italics indicate illustrations.